CASES IN FINANCIAL ENGINEERING:

Applied Studies of Financial Innovation

CASES IN FINANCIAL ENGINEERING:

Applied Studies of Financial Innovation

Scott P. Mason
Edmund Cogswell Converse Professor of Finance and Banking

Robert C. Merton
George F. Baker Professor of Business Administration

André F. Perold
Sylvan C. Coleman Professor of Financial Management

Peter Tufano
Associate Professor of Business Administration

All of the
Graduate School of Business Administration,
Harvard University

Prentice Hall, Upper Saddle River, New Jersey 07458

Cases in financial engineering : applied studies of financial
   innovation / Scott Mason ... [et al.].
          p.   cm.
      Includes bibliographical references and index.
      ISBN 0-13-079419-8
      1. Financial engineering.   2. Securities.   3. Derivative
securities.   I. Mason, Scott P.
   HG176.7.C37   1995
   658. 15– – dc20   94-32273
                                                                                         CIP

Production Manager: Andrea G. Mulligan, Benchmark Productions
In-house Project Liaison: Alana Zdinak
Acquisitions Editor: Leah Jewell
Assistant Editor: Teresa Cohan
Editorial Assistant: Eileen Deguzman
Interior Designer: Merrill Dabcovich
Cover Designer: Tom Nery
Copy Editor: Beth A. Roberts

Cover Art: Michael Shumate/The Image Bank

Set in 10-point Minion by Benchmark Productions

© 1995 by Prentice-Hall, Inc.
A Simon & Schuster Company
Upper Saddle River, New Jersey 07458

Printed in the United States of America

10 9 8 7 6 5 4 3 2

ISBN: 0-13-079419-8

Prentice-Hall International (UK) Limited, London
Prentice-Hall of Australia Pty. Limited, Sydney
Prentice-Hall Canada Inc., Toronto
Prentice-Hall Hispanoamericana, S. A. Mexico
Prentice-Hall of India Private Limited, New Delhi
Prentice-Hall of Japan, Inc., Tokyo
Simon & Schuster Asia Pte. Ltd., Singapore
Editora Prentice-Hall do Brasil, Ltda., Rio de Janeiro

To *Linda*
    June
    Suellen
    Mary Jeanne

Contents

PART ONE—FINANCIAL ENGINEERING AND DEBT SECURITIES

ARBITRAGE FUNDAMENTALS

TAXES, REGULATION, AND ACCOUNTING: STIMULI TO INNOVATION

SECURITIZATION

PART TWO—FINANCIAL ENGINEERING AND EQUITY SECURITIES

ADDRESSING INFORMATION ASYMMETRIES

TAXES, REGULATION, AND ACCOUNTING: STIMULI TO INNOVATION

PART THREE—ENGINEERING EXPOSURES WITH DERIVATIVES

MANAGING ISSUERS' EXPOSURES

INTRODUCTION

Financial innovation is the dynamic force propelling the financial system towards its function of providing more efficient resource allocation in the economy. Innovation benefits society by lowering transaction costs, completing markets, and making prices more informative. Investors, corporations, and financial-service firms realize those benefits in the form of lowered costs of raising funds, enhanced investment returns, more precise management of risk exposures, and greater efficiency in operating under changing tax and regulatory regimes. Financial innovation, broadly defined, includes not only the creation of new types of securities, but also the development and evolution of new financial organizations. Financial engineering embodies many of the skills, techniques, and processes that produce both new securities and new financial organizations. It is the application of advances in related technologies that permit the diagnosis, analysis, design, production, pricing, and customization of solutions to problems in finance. The scope of these technologies encompasses conceptual advances in pricing and hedging that support more comprehensive derivative-securities markets and risk-management systems; improvements in computer speed and capacity that enable systems to securitize assets and monitor thousands of trading positions in real time; and developments in communications systems that facilitate the simultaneous actions needed to exploit transient arbitrage opportunities. Thus, financial engineering can be viewed as the means of implementing financial innovation. Together, financial innovation and engineering have increased the pace and complexity of change in the financial system, providing extensive opportunities for financial engineers as well as for financial managers, corporate executives, public-policy makers, and business educators.

An incorrect, but commonly held, belief is that financial engineering and financial innovation are accessible, or more importantly *relevant*, only to a small group of mathematics students or technical practitioners. The relevance of financial innovation should be measured by its impact on the effectiveness of the financial system, and not by its novelty. Similarly, the power of financial engineering should be defined not by the complexity of its models or computers but by the expanded economic or managerial flexibility it offers to its users. By these measures, financial engineering and financial innovation are relevant to a broad audience. Financial engineers can create and price an uncountable array of financing vehicles for corporations. They can structure instruments to provide risk exposures to almost any variable that an investment manager might imagine. Financial innovation and engineering give their users a myriad of new alternatives from which they must choose. Thus, financial engineering should be studied *within the context of the managerial or public-policy decisions to which it is applied*, training not only the financial engineers but also those who rely upon these engineers to solve long-standing and vexing problems of corporate finance and investment management. Training in financial engineering is also necessary for those involved in oversight, including public-policy makers whose charge is to safeguard the public interest as well as those who manage the financial-service firms that employ the engineers.

The case studies and notes in *Cases in Financial Engineering* were designed and have been used at the Harvard Business School to introduce thousands of MBA students to financial innovation and financial engineering. This material was developed to reflect the fundamental continuing changes in both the financial system and the finance profession, as well as to meet strong student demand. The case format, along with the opening chapters and notes, allows this book to be used as the primary text for an MBA course for general management students, or as a supplementary text for an advanced course designed for specialists in financial engineering. In both instances, the cases provide rich and exciting contexts for the application of financial-engineering techniques. They cover some recent innovations, as well as older products which were important milestones in the areas of swaps, securitization, interest rate derivatives, municipal bond products, and equity-linked instruments. The cases, combined with the introductory chapters that provide both a conceptual and a historical framework, were designed to highlight a number of themes: the dynamic and persistent nature of financial innovation; a functional perspective that characterizes products by the needs they satisfy; cost factors that stimulate new financial products; exploitation of apparent arbitrage opportunities; and learning and experimentation in financial markets.

Some readers will not be familiar with cases or with their use for more effective teaching. Our experience has been that the case method of instruction is very effective in teaching the concepts, as well as the managerial practicality, of financial engineering. Most cases are highly developed presentations of a business problem or issue requiring action or a decision. The cases in this book underscore to students that complex financial-engineering problems typically exist in even more complex business settings. Careful quantitative analysis is essential but not sufficient as these cases require decisions that must take into account other important business factors besides the successful application of financial modeling. In this important sense, the case method of instruction goes beyond the traditional distinction between *theoretical* and *applied*. It deals fully with the difficulty of making decisions and taking actions in a multi-faceted and changing business environment. For example, a product such as the Nikkei Put Warrants (described later in this book) offers ample opportunity to demonstrate the application of technical pricing skills. However, the case study of this product not only raises theoretical pricing issues but also forces students to consider competitive dynamics, product design and marketing considerations, and the value of innovation to an investment bank's reputation—all in an environment of incomplete information.

Case presentations and the case method of instruction make financial engineering accessible to a wide range of students. While the theoretical foundations and pure applications of methods and models are of natural interest to technically-inclined students, we have found that a broader pool of students find case studies of financial engineering stimulating, accessible, and interesting. Certainly the emphasis on managerial issues helps explain this response. It is a plain fact that many students believe that it is important to their professional careers to have a working knowledge of financial engineering. We have not sacrificed quantitative rigor to satisfy this objective but have jointly emphasized technique and managerial implications. This is precisely the role served by cases and the case method of instruction.

The sequencing of the cases and notes is not intended to define a path along which these materials should be used in a course; instead, it reflects a set of thematic groupings of the book's material consistent with the ideas developed in the introductory chapters. The two introductory chapters provide a conceptual and a historical framework for understanding financial innovation and financial engineering generally, and the cases specifically. The first chapter discusses the role of financial innovation in the financial system; the logic of considering the financial system, its institutions and products in terms of the functions they deliver, and the financial-innovation spiral, by which one innovation begets others. The second chapter attempts to place the case studies in historical context, by using the case studies in the book, along with innovations from the nineteenth and early twentieth century, to explain how cost considerations, changes in users' demands, and learning have affected the path of financial innovation.

Cases in Financial Engineering can be variously organized for use by advanced undergraduates, MBAs, or doctoral students. In general, students will benefit from a first course in derivative securities, either prior to or at the same time that they are studying these cases. It is also possible to use the case studies in a first course, interweaving technical lessons with the case discussion. The book can also be used in a more advanced course with students who already have training in derivative securities to illustrate and apply the concepts. The material fits in a number of more traditional formats, including courses in capital markets and risk management.

Plans for teaching this book can be organized along at least four dimensions: (i) by the *type of instrument* covered; (ii) the primary *end-user*; (iii) the *underlying security* on which derivatives are written, or (iv) the *rationale* for the innovation. For example, an instructor organizing a course by instrument type might group in one module the cases focusing on options and embedded options; in a second module the cases on forwards, futures, swaps; and in a third, those on securitization. The strength of this approach rests on its focus on technique, such as option-pricing technology. Its weakness is having cases span multiple instrument types, as users consider a variety of alternatives. A second design based on end-users might emphasize cases that primarily address the needs of either corporations, investment managers, or investment banks. This approach allows for focus on the needs of particular users of the financial system, but often the cases must simultaneously address the needs of two or three of these parties at once, or consider a wide range of instruments. A third alternative is to focus on the underlying securities of the derivative instruments studied: e.g., equities, fixed income, commodities. For example, all of the equity-linked products could be discussed in related sessions, allowing students to develop institutional details on particular markets. The fourth approach is to organize the material thematically, by grouping the cases broadly according to the rationale that helps explain why the innovation has been created. The organization of the book attempts to facilitate this approach by identifying a number of uses to which financial engineering has been put: exploiting arbitrage opportunities, resolving information asymmetries, optimizing with respect to the tax and regulatory environment, and managing risk. This approach is consistent with the central theme voiced in the first chapter: the most fruitful examination of complicated financial products, activities, or systems will flow from a careful consideration of the financial functions that they serve.

Acknowledgments

We would like to thank the many organizations and individuals who made these cases and this book possible. The field cases detailing industry practices could not be written without the generosity of the firms and executives who agreed to serve as case sites and willingly donated their time, expertise, and confidential data. In turning observations of these businesses into cases studies, we were assisted by outstanding research assistants, including William B. Allen, Jr., Joel Barber, Sanjay Bhatnagar, Mihir Desai, Nancy Donohue, Sally E. Durdan, Jonathan S. Headley, Barbara Kyrillos, Michael Lewittes, Martha D. N. Notaras, Jon Serbin, and Kuljot Singh. We owe a debt to our former and present colleagues at Harvard Business School who wrote or supervised some of the cases and notes in this volume, and who have graciously allowed us to reprint them in this volume: Michael E. Edleson, Nabil El-Hage, Kenneth A. Froot, William E. Fruhan, E. Philip Jones, W. Carl Kester, Joshua Lerner, Jay O. Light, David M. Meerschwam, Jeremy Stein, and Jonathan Tiemann. Our students, both in the MBA program and in numerous executive programs, endured early versions of these cases and thus helped us improve them. The President and Fellows of Harvard College, who hold the copyright on all cases appearing here, permitted their use in this book.

In bringing the cases, notes, and chapters in this book from concept to final form, we have been supported by a number of individuals. Each of our assistants—Deborah Hannon, Dee Luther, Elaine Perrine, Janice Wright—produced and proofread many versions of these materials. Andrea Mulligan, of Benchmark Productions, orchestrated the Herculean task of coordinating the production of this book. We received generous financial support from the Harvard Business School Division of Research; this work was conducted as part of the Global Financial System project at HBS, a multi-year research agenda examining the functions served by the global financial system. Finally, we acknowledge the ongoing and unfailing support of our families and friends.

Scott P. Mason
Robert C. Merton
André F. Perold
Peter Tufano

CHAPTER 1

FINANCIAL INNOVATION AND THE FINANCIAL SYSTEM

INTRODUCTION

The core function of the financial system is to facilitate the allocation and deployment of economic resources, both spatially and across time, in an uncertain environment. This system consists of the capital markets as well as the basic payment system through which virtually all transactions clear. In today's well-developed economies, capital markets include the money, fixed-income, and equity markets, as well as the new and growing markets for "derivative" securities such as futures and options. Capital market functions are also performed by financial intermediaries such as banks and insurance companies that provide more customized products and services—the kind that do not lend themselves to the standardization necessary to create a liquid market.

The capital markets make possible the basic cash-flow cycle in which household savings are channeled into capital investments by firms and then returned to households (via security repurchases, dividends, and interest payments) for consumption and recycling as new savings. The capital markets provide risk-pooling and risk-sharing opportunities for both households and business firms. These markets also serve an important function as a key source of information that helps coordinate decentralized decision-making in various sectors of the international economy.

In this chapter, financial innovation is viewed as the central mechanism pushing the financial system toward its goal of improving performance of what economists call the "real economy." The chapter begins with an assessment of the causes and consequences of the wave of recent innovations and then uses that assessment as a basis for discussing the motivations for innovation as well as its social value.

This chapter is largely a consolidation of portions of Merton (1992a; 1993), with the permission of the *Journal of Applied Corporate Finance* and the Economic Council, respectively.

The chapter continues with a focus on the core functions of the financial system. Innovations that only redistribute wealth and perhaps affect regulatory changes but do not improve the efficiency by which the financial system serves those functions will not significantly affect long-run economic efficiency. Hence, the effectiveness of financial innovation with respect to economic performance is better studied from a "functional" perspective rather than an "institutional" one.

Financial intermediation—the process of transforming financial assets from one form into another—is a central activity within all financial systems. Financial engineering is the process of tailoring financial instruments and organizational structure to improve the profitability of intermediaries' customers. This production process of intermediaries is also the principal means for implementing financial innovation into the system. In this chapter, two polar, prototypical models, "underwriting" and "synthesizing," are developed; their combinations span the range of intermediary approaches to production exemplified throughout this volume.

The institutional structure that performs the financial functions differs considerably among economies. Furthermore, the current environment of rapid technological changes and movement toward a global financial market will produce significant intertemporal shifts in the institutional structure of a given economy. However, the basic functions of a financial system are essentially the same in all economies—past and present, East and West. Therefore, as demonstrated later in this chapter, a functional approach to analyzing the dynamics of changes in the financial system may provide a more useful organizing perspective than an institutional approach. The chapter closes using functional analysis as a basis for speculating about the future of financial regulation.

FINANCIAL INNOVATION

To make the case that financial innovation over the past 20 years has led to revolutionary changes in the international financial system, one need hardly do more than mention round-the-clock-trading Tokyo-London-New York, financial futures, swaps, mortgage-backed securities, exchange-traded options, "junk" bonds, shelf registration, electronic funds transfer and security trading, automated teller machines, NOW accounts, asset-based financing, LBO, MBO, and all the other acronymic approaches to corporate restructuring. And these are but a small sampling.

Of course, financial innovation has been going on for a considerable time; many of the innovations of the last two decades, although heralded as novel, were not entirely new. Important examples are exchange-traded options, forwards, and futures contracts. The Dojima rice market in Osaka was a forward market in the seventeenth century and a fully organized futures market by the eighteenth century.[1] Organized futures exchanges were created in Frankfurt in 1867 and in London in 1877. The Chicago Board of Trade was founded in 1848 and the New York Cotton Exchange was incorporated in 1872. Options on commodity futures were traded on the Chicago Board of Trade in the 1920s. In the seventeenth century, options and contracts resembling futures accounted for the bulk of transactions on the Amsterdam stock exchange, which at the time was the financial center of the Western world. Moreover, from the accounts given by one seventeenth-century observer,[2] it appears that the regulatory concerns raised about those contracts in Amsterdam—in particular, insider trading, manipulation, excessive speculation and price volatility, and default risks—are much the same as those expressed about options and futures trading today. Some things just never change.

While options and futures may not be entirely new, the proliferation of organized trading markets in both equity and fixed-income derivative securities during the past two decades is unprecedented. Development of these standardized markets was absolutely essential for the subsequent creation of a wide range of financial products, many custom-designed to meet selected needs of investors and corporate issuers. One needs go no further than the weekly trade journal *International Financing Review* to verify the profound impact that derivative securities are having on the mainline global financing of both businesses and sovereigns. Concurrently, mainstream financial institutions and pension-fund-plan sponsors have increasingly adopted quantitative techniques, including computerized trading strategies, to help manage their investment portfolios. The composition of both their equity and fixed-income portfolios has become more global. As with issuers, such investor-side changes could not have been implemented without well-functioning derivative security markets. Those changes have been accompanied by an explosion of trading volume in just about every sector of the financial markets. All this everyone knows. The question is, what has this wave of innovation done for economic performance?

THE SOCIAL VALUE OF FINANCIAL INNOVATION

There are some in the academic, financial, and regulatory communities who see much of this alleged innovation as nothing more than a giant fad, driven by institutional investors and corporate issuers with wholly unrealistic expectations of greater expected returns with less risk, and fueled by financial-services firms and organized exchanges that see huge profits from this vast activity. From this viewpoint, pure rent-seekers develop innovations

---

1   See Schaede (1988).

2   de la Vega (1688). Bernstein (1992, Ch. 11) reports that Aristotle's anecdote about Thales in Book I of *Politics* is perhaps the first recorded mention of a financial option.

that have no function other than to differentiate their products superficially. As the story goes, beyond the direct waste of resources in this activity, the feeding of unrealistic expectations among investors and issuers can impose additional, potentially much larger, social costs in the form of ex ante distortions of investment capital allocations and ex post excessive volatility in capital market prices, as faulty expectations are not realized. Perhaps. Any virtue can readily become a vice if taken to excess, and just so with innovations. There have surely been instances of financial products and trading strategies that have not delivered ex post the performance promised ex ante. But, notwithstanding such examples, there are other, significant examples that run counter to this negative view of the relation between innovations in the recent past and economic performance. Prime among those in the United States is the development of a national mortgage market in the 1980s along with a wide array of mortgage-backed securities that transformed residential housing finance from fragmented, local-based sources to a free-flowing, international base of capital. The development of well-functioning markets for financial futures, swaps, and option contracts has made it possible for business firms to hedge efficiently against the uncertainties of currency exchange rates, interest rates, and basic commodity prices. Money-market, fixed-income, international, real-estate, and equity-indexed mutual funds and a variety of pension, life insurance, and annuity products are among the important innovations developed during the past two decades that directly benefit households around the world. Collectively, these innovations have greatly improved the opportunities for households to receive efficient risk-return tradeoffs and more effective tailoring to individual needs over the entire life cycle, including accumulation during the work years and distribution in retirement.

We could continue with a listing of past innovations and their benefits as part of an inductive process of refutation. It will perhaps instead be more interesting and instructive to examine in greater detail a single innovation that has not yet been introduced, but could be, using current technology. In keeping with our global focus, the problem that this product addresses is international diversification under capital controls.

ILLUSTRATIVE CASE: INTERNATIONAL STOCK-RETURNS SWAPS

Numerous empirical studies of stock market returns have documented the gains in diversification from investing internationally.[3] By diversifying across the world stock markets, there is significant improvement in the efficient frontier of risk versus expected return. As we know, the 1980s and early 1990s have seen widespread implementation of such international diversification among investors in the large developed countries with the major

---

3   See Grauer and Hakansson (1987) and Perold and Schulman (1988).

stock markets (e.g., the United States, United Kingdom, Germany, and Japan). However, international diversification has not yet evolved in many smaller, developed countries where indeed it may be more important.

A major barrier to foreign stock market investment by citizens of some of these countries is capital controls, imposed by their governments to prevent flight of domestic capital. A common rationale for such restrictions is that they reduce the risk that the local economy will have inadequate domestic investment to promote growth.[4] Another important barrier is that the transaction cost paid by large foreign investors when they buy shares directly in these domestic stock markets can be so large that it offsets any diversification benefits that would otherwise accrue. The cost in lost welfare from less-efficient diversification affects both large-country and small-country citizens. However, the per capita magnitude of the cost is much larger for the latter, since the potential gains from international diversification are greatest for the smallest countries with domestic economies that are by necessity less well diversified. Alternatively, part of the cost may be that domestic physical investment is driven to become more diversified than would otherwise be efficient according to the principle of comparative advantage.

Of course, one (and perhaps the best) solution is to simply eliminate capital flow restrictions and open capital markets. However, taking the capital controls as a given, the constrained solution involves separating the capital flow effects of investment from its risk-sharing aspects. Suppose that small-country domestic investors (perhaps through domestic mutual funds or financial intermediaries) who already own the domestic equity were to enter into "swap" agreements[5] with large foreign investors. In the proposed swap, the total return per dollar on the small country's domestic stock market is exchanged annually for the total return per dollar on a market-value weighted-average of the major world stock markets. This exchange of returns could be in a common currency, dollars, as described here, or adjusted to different currencies along similar lines to currency-swap agreements. The magnitudes of the dollar exchanges are determined by the "notional" or principal amount of the swap to which per dollar return differences apply. As is the usual case with swaps, there is no initial payment by either party to the other for entering the agreement.

Without pursuing too many details of implementation, we see that the swap agreement effectively transfers the risk of the small-country stock market to foreign investors and provides the domestic investors with the risk-return pattern of a well-diversified

---

4   See Tobin (1978) on using controls to avoid the hardships caused by large movements of capital in and out of a country.

5   For discussion, analysis, and references on swap contracts, see Smith, Jr., Smithson, and Wakeman (1986, 1988), Hull (1989), and Sundaresan (1990).

world portfolio.[6] Since there are no initial payments between parties, there are no initial capital flows in or out of the country. Subsequent payments, which may be either inflows or outflows, involve only the *difference* between the *returns* on the two stock market indices, and no "principal" amounts flow. For example, on a notional or principal amount of $1 billion, if, ex post, the world stock market earns 10% and the small-country market earns 12%, there is only a flow of $(.12 - .10) \times \$1$ billion or $20 million out of the country. Note further that the small-country investors make net payments out precisely when they can "best" afford it, namely, when their local market has outperformed the world markets. In those years in which the domestic market underperforms the world stock markets, the swap generates net cash flows into the country to its domestic investors. Hence, in our example, if the small-country market earns 8% and the world stock market earns 11%, then domestic investors receive $(.11 - .08) \times \$1$ billion = $30 million, a net cash inflow for the small country. Moreover, with this swap arrangement, trading and ownership of actual shares remain with domestic investors.[7]

Foreign investors also benefit from the swap by avoiding the costs of trading in individual securities in the local markets and by avoiding some tax complications (such as local dividend-withholding taxes) that often arise with cross-border investments. They also avoid the problems of corporate governance issues that arise when foreigners acquire large ownership positions in domestic companies. Unlike standard cash investments in equities, debt or real property, the default or expropriation exposure of foreign investors is limited to the difference in returns instead of the total gross return plus principal (in our example, $20 million versus $1.12 billion in exposure). The risks of default could be further reduced if the domestic party to the swap was a closed-end mutual fund with its assets invested in the domestic equity market as a hedge and its shares held entirely by local investors. The foreign counterparty to the swap could, of course, also be a closed-end fund with its assets invested in the world stock-market portfolio.

The potential exposure of foreign investors to manipulation by local investors is probably less for the swap than for direct transactions in individual stocks. It is more difficult to manipulate a broad market index than the price of a single stock. Even if settlement

---

6   Shares are assumed to be freely traded on the domestic exchange, and they are therefore priced to earn a competitive rate of return to the marginal investor. If the marginal investor is a domestic investor with no access to world stock markets, then the welfare loss is a higher cost of capital for domestic shares (and lower stock prices) than with an open economy because some of the risk perceived as systematic by constrained domestic investors would be diversifiable from a world-investor perspective. If the marginal investor is a world investor, then the welfare loss is the uncompensated excess volatility from inefficient diversification borne by domestic investors. The transfer of risk by the swap addresses both cases.

7   For incentive reasons, owners of domestic shares should have an economic interest in the firms. Hence, a significant amount but not all of the domestic risk can be swapped to nonvoting foreign investors.

intervals for swaps are standardized at six months or one year, the calendar settlement dates will differ for each swap, depending upon the date of its initiation. Hence, with some swaps being settled every day, manipulators would have to keep the prices of shares permanently low to succeed. Furthermore, with the settlement terms of swaps based on the per period rate of return, an artificially low price (and low rate of return) for settlement this year will induce an artificially high rate of return for settlement next year. Thus, gains from manipulation in the first period are given back in the second, unless the price can be kept low over the entire life of the swap. Since typical swap contract maturities might range from two to ten years (with semiannual or annual settlements), this would be difficult to achieve.

Note that this swap innovation is not designed to circumvent the stated objective of the capital-control regulation, to prevent domestic capital flight. Instead, it is designed to eliminate (or at least reduce) the unintended and undesirable "side effects" of this policy on efficient risk bearing and diversification. Although equity-return swaps based on the returns of major stock markets are common, we are not aware of their application to stock markets in countries with capital controls. However, with the current rate of innovation, it would not be surprising to see such a development soon. Whether or not this "real-time" proposed solution of using a swap turns out to be an effective real-world solution is not the central point of the exercise here. Rather, it is to demonstrate how a simple but "finely tuned" financial innovation of trivial intrinsic cost could help reduce the social cost of "blunt" policy tools that affect a number of countries around the world.

THE MOTIVES FOR FINANCIAL INNOVATION: REAL EFFICIENCIES OR ONLY REGULATORY AVOIDANCE?

Our swap example also serves to clarify another issue surrounding the relation between financial innovation and economic performance over the last two decades. A widely accepted theory is that cost reduction or otherwise lessening the constraints of regulation including taxes and accounting conventions is a driving force behind financial innovations. Indeed, Miller (1986) claims that frequent and unanticipated changes in regulatory and tax codes have been the prime motivators for financial innovation during the past quarter century. Silber's (1983) view that financial innovation arises from attempts to reduce the cost of various constraints on corporations is consistent with this view, as is Kane's theory of dynamic regulation.[8] It is a common belief among many economists that activities whose sole purpose is to circumvent regulations or avoid taxes are zero or negative-sum games of wealth transfers that can only increase the total cost of achieving the

---

8   Kane (1977, 1984, 1988). See also Folkerts-Landau and Mathieson (1988), and Finnerty (1988).

intended objectives of the regulations. From this perspective, financial innovation, as the instrument for implementing such activities, has a zero or negative social value.[9] However, as our swap example illustrates, it is possible to have an innovation entirely motivated by regulation that nevertheless reduces the social cost of achieving the intended objectives of the regulation. And this is the case, whether or not those intended objectives of the regulation are socially optimal.

In general, innovations in financial products and services can improve economic performance by (a) meeting demands for "completing the markets" with expanded opportunities for risk-sharing, risk-pooling, hedging, and intertemporal or spatial transfers of resources that are not already available; (b) lowering transactions costs or increasing liquidity; and (c) reducing "agency" costs caused by either asymmetric information between trading parties or principals' incomplete monitoring of their agents' performance. All three of these driving forces behind financial innovation are consistent with financial innovation working in the direction of improving economic efficiency.

To illustrate the point more specifically, consider the case of exchange-traded futures and options contracts on stock indexes such as the Standard & Poor's 500 or the Nikkei 225. As noted at the outset of the chapter, one of the major functions of capital markets is to provide a way of managing economic uncertainty and controlling risk.[10] The primary uses for futures and options within the financial system are in the risk management function. All risk management activities can be represented as combinations of three pure methods of managing risk. These three functional subcategories, called "the three dimensions of risk management," are:

1. *Reducing the risk by selling the source of it.* In general, adjusting a portfolio by moving from risky assets to a riskless asset to reduce risk is called *hedging*, and it can be done either in the spot cash market or in a futures or forward market. Futures, forward contracts, and swaps permit efficient implementation of this hedging dimension of the risk management function. In particular, the alternative to using derivative securities on an index is to transact simultaneously in many individual stocks (e.g., five hundred in the case of the S&P 500).

2. *Reducing the risk by diversification.* Diversification consists of simultaneously pooling and subdividing risks. While it does not eliminate risk in the aggregate, it redistributes

---

9   No credit is given to innovations that improve welfare by thwarting regulations that would otherwise impose more cost than benefit on society, because such welfare losses can, at least in principle, be eliminated more efficiently by simply changing the offending regulations.

10 Risk management is perhaps the central topic of the 1990s among managers of financial institutions and their regulators. See Freeman (1993).

it to reduce the risk faced by each individual. Broad diversification across large numbers of different securities has the drawback that adjustments in risk exposure can require a large number of relatively small-sized transactions in the various securities. Moreover, bounds on the subdivision of the units of individual securities limit the number of securities that can be held for a given level of wealth. Basket cash-market securities and futures contracts on stock- and bond-market indexes facilitate implementation of this fundamental dimension of risk management. They greatly improve transaction efficiency in both cost and speed and permit full diversification by allowing arbitrarily small ownership of the individual components of the various indexes.

3. *Reducing the risk by buying insurance against losses.* Insurance permits the owner of an asset to retain the economic benefits of ownership while eliminating the uncertainty of possible losses. Of course, this retention of the "upside" while deleting the "downside" of asset ownership is not free. The fee or premium paid for insurance substitutes a sure loss for the possibility of a larger loss. In general, the owner of any asset can eliminate the downside risk of loss and retain the upside benefit of ownership by the purchase of a put option.[11] Furthermore, the purchase of a call option is economically equivalent to owning the asset and insuring its value against loss by purchasing a put option.[12] Thus, an option, whether a put or a call, is a fundamental security that serves the central risk management function of insurance.[13] In particular, options on aggregate portfolios of securities (e.g., index options) are far more efficient for insuring an investor's asset holdings than a portfolio of options on each of the individual assets.[14]

Note that the reference to "insurance" here is to a class of contracts that serve an explicit *function*. It should be distinguished from a class of *institutions* called "insurance

---

11 During the term of the put, its owner has the right to sell the underlying asset at a fixed ("exercise") price. Thus, any losses on the asset are truncated at this level.

12 The functional and value identity is that a call option combined with a holding of the riskless asset is equivalent to holding the asset together with a put option on the asset. See Merton (1992b, 277–278) for a formal derivation of this put-call parity theorem.

13 The classic portfolio-selection theory of Harry Markowitz and James Tobin holds that the investor should control his risk exposure first by forming a well-diversified portfolio of all the risky assets and then, if necessary, to adjust the risk further by allocating his total wealth between this risky portfolio and the riskless asset. Hence, their theory covers the first two dimensions of risk management. It does not, however, explicitly take account of the opportunity structure provided by the third dimension, insurance.

14 Beyond simply the additional costs of multiple transactions, there is a fundamental difference in both the pattern of returns and the cost for an option on a portfolio of assets and a portfolio of options on those assets. See Merton, Scholes, and Gladstein (1978, 1982).

companies." The insurance function, on the one hand, is often served by a variety of institutions that are not classified as insurance companies. A prime instance is a traded-option exchange.[15] Insurance companies, on the other hand, often provide products that do not serve the insurance function. For example, insurance companies in the United States offer money-market accounts, equity mutual funds, and guaranteed investment contracts, none of which perform an insurance function.

Thus, index futures and options surely fit in the "completing the markets" category (a) of innovations that improve economic performance. However, they also fall into categories (b) and (c). As already noted, they substantially reduce transactions costs for trading in composite portfolios over the alternative of simultaneous cash-market transactions in the individual securities. Furthermore, index derivative securities belong in category (c) because they help resolve a potential asymmetric information problem: a transactor in an individual stock may be motivated to do so simply to adjust his risk exposure or to reflect his revised assessment of expected returns on the general stock market. But, the transaction may also be motivated by explicit private information, specific to the individual stock (e.g., an unannounced earnings report or a litigation decision). The prospect of the latter would rationally lead an otherwise uninformed counterparty to be reluctant to trade. This reluctance manifests itself in larger bid-ask spreads than would otherwise be the case. The increased spread is a deadweight loss to the investor who does not have information about the individual stock. The structural opportunity to trade in market aggregates provided by indexed futures and options resolves this problem because such investors can adjust their broad asset-class allocations without having to trade in individual stocks.[16]

FUNCTIONS OF THE FINANCIAL SYSTEM

As is the tradition in microeconomic theory in general, a functional perspective on the financial system treats the existence of households, their tastes, and their endowments as exogenous to the economic system. However, this tradition does not extend to other economic organizations such as business firms, markets, and financial institutions. They are regarded as existing primarily because of the functions they serve and are therefore

---

15 Thus, in the future, the prime competitor to an insurance company offering investors default insurance on municipal bonds may not be another insurance company but instead an options exchange that can create a market for put options on those bonds. The put options serve the same downside-protection function for the investors as the insurance company product. As discussed later in this chapter, this example also illustrates the difference between the institutional and functional approaches as applied to corporate competitive strategy analysis.

16 For a fuller development of this issue, see Gammill and Perold (1989).

endogenous to the system. Thus, from a functional perspective on the financial system, *institutional form follows its function.*

From the most-aggregated level of the single primary function of resource allocation, we can further distinguish six core functions performed by the financial system:

Function 1:   A financial system provides a payments system for the exchange of goods and services. To underscore the importance of this function, one need only consider those rare occasions when the payments system breaks down and transactions are reduced to ones involving bilateral barter.

Depository financial intermediaries such as banks and thrifts serve the payment system with wire transfers, checking accounts, and credit/cash cards. But, other intermediaries such as money-market mutual funds offer transaction-draft accounts; firms whose principal business is not financial, for example, AT&T, General Electric, and General Motors, offer general credit cards.

Function 2:   A financial system provides a mechanism for the pooling of funds to undertake large-scale indivisible enterprise. In modern economies, the minimum investment required to run a business is often beyond the means of an individual or even several individuals. The financial system provides a variety of mechanisms (such as security markets and financial intermediaries) through which individual households can pool (or aggregate) their wealth into larger amounts of capital for use by business firms. Looking at it from the other side, we see that the financial system provides opportunities for individual households to participate in large indivisible investments. Mutual funds that hold stocks and bonds are examples of financial intermediaries that provide nearly perfect divisibility in subdividing the individual unit size of the traded securities they hold.

Function 3:   A financial system provides a way to transfer economic resources through time and across geographic regions and industries. A well-developed, smooth-functioning financial system facilitates the efficient life-cycle allocations of household consumption and the efficient allocation of physical capital to its most-productive use in the business sector. A well-developed, smooth-functioning capital market also makes possible the efficient separation of ownership from management of the firm. This in turn makes feasible efficient specialization in production according to the principle of comparative advantage. Examples of intermediaries serving this function include banks and thrifts in financing corporate investments and housing, insurance companies and pension funds in financing corporate investments and paying retirement annuities, and mutual funds that invest in virtually all sectors.

Function 4: A financial system provides a way to manage uncertainty and control risk. A well-functioning financial system facilitates the efficient allocation of risk-bearing among households and firms. Through often elaborate financial securities and through private-sector and government intermediaries (including the system of social insurance), the financial system provides risk-pooling and risk-sharing opportunities for both households and business firms. It facilitates efficient life-cycle risk-bearing by households, and it allows for the separation of the providers of working capital for *real* investments (i.e., in personnel, plant, and equipment) from the providers of risk capital who bear the *financial* risk of those investments. In both an international and domestic context, this separation of real investment and risk-bearing permits specialization in production activities according to the principle of comparative advantage. Insurance companies are the classic example of a financial intermediary offering risk protection. They sell protection against loss in value of human capital (e.g., death and disability), physical property (e.g., fire and theft), and financial assets (e.g., municipal-bond insurance). Mutual funds help control risk by providing diversification. The three dimensions of risk management discussed in the preceding section are functional subcategories of this key function of the financial system.

Function 5: A financial system provides price information that helps coordinate decentralized decision-making in various sectors of the economy. The manifest function of financial markets is to allow individuals and businesses to trade financial assets. In addition, an important latent function of the capital market is to serve as a key source of information that helps coordinate decentralized decision-making in various sectors of the economy. Interest rates and security prices are used by households or their agents in making their consumption-saving decisions and in choosing the portfolio allocations of their wealth. These same prices provide important signals to managers of firms in their selection of investment projects and financings. While this "discovery" function of prices is characteristic of all markets in a capitalist economy, it is especially important for financial markets. Examples of intermediaries that serve this function are banks and insurance companies whose posted rates for corporate loans are used by (particularly smaller) firms to make investment decisions. In a Stiglitz-Weiss (1981) world of credit rationing, the size of the loans that those intermediaries are willing to make augments the information function served by prices.

Function 6: A financial system provides a way to deal with the asymmetric-information problems when one party to a financial transaction has information that the other party does not. A well-functioning financial system facilitates the resolution of moral-hazard and adverse-selection problems that arise from the existence of information asymmetries between transacting parties.[17] Such problems can prevent efficient separation of ownership and management of business firms (the "principal-agent" problem). They can also prevent borrowers and lenders from entering into otherwise mutually advantageous transactions. In this chapter, we refer to these collectively as "agency problems."[18] Financial intermediaries can help minimize the dead-weight efficiency losses from information asymmetries. For example, banks are specialists in making loans that are difficult to assess without detailed, and often proprietary, information about the borrower. But, for competitive reasons, borrowers are reluctant to reveal to the general public the information that would be necessary for a direct public placement of the debt. By being discreet with information provided by its borrowers and by developing a reputation for making profitable loans with its investors, banks help solve this asymmetric-information problem. As an alternative institutional form, venture-capital firms in the United States serve a similar intermediation function by providing both equity capital and information to start-up companies.

As noted in the "Introduction," for a variety of reasons—including differences in size, complexity, and available technology, as well as differences in political, cultural, and historical backgrounds—*the most efficient institutional structure for fulfilling the functions of the financial system generally changes over time and differs across geopolitical subdivisions.* Moreover, even when the corporate identities of institutions are the same, the functions they perform often differ dramatically. For example, banks in the United States in 1994 are very different from what they were in 1924 or in 1954, just as they are very different from the institutions called banks in Germany or the United Kingdom today. The financial

---

17 For instance, once an individual has purchased insurance against fire or theft, he is less likely to take precautions against them. This is the *moral-hazard* problem facing the insurer. *Adverse selection* refers to the fact that individuals who are more likely to experience losses are the ones who will tend to buy the insurance. The individual buying the insurance typically has relevant information that may not be available to the insurer. For basic definitions and a discussion of moral hazard and adverse selection in an insurance context, see Borch (1990).

18 For detailed development and a review of the literature of asymmetric information and agency theory in a financial market context, see Strong and Walker (1987). See also Barnea, Haugen, and Senbet (1985), Fama (1980), Fama and Jensen (1985), Grossman and Hart (1982), Jensen (1986), Jensen and Meckling (1976), Milgrom and Roberts (1992), Ross (1973), and Townsend (1990).

markets in New York, London, or Tokyo today are vastly different from what they were as recently as 1980—before the widespread introduction of trading in fixed-income and stock-index futures, options, and swap contracts.

In contrast, the *basic functions* of a financial system are essentially the same in all economies. And because the functions of the financial system are far more stable than the identity and structure of the institutions performing them, a functional perspective offers a more robust frame of reference than an institutional one, especially in a financial environment characterized by rapid changes. That is, when the institutional structure is changing significantly, it is difficult to use institutions as the conceptual "anchor" for analyzing the evolving financial system. Given the considerable institutional diversity across national borders, analyses using functions as their conceptual anchors are more readily adaptable to a global setting for the financial system. Indeed, with the current rate of technological advance and integration of world financial markets, a functional perspective may prove especially useful in predicting the future direction of financial innovation, changes in financial markets and intermediaries, and the places for regulatory bottlenecks.

A basic tenet of the functional perspective on predicting long-run changes in the financial system holds that the fundamental economic force of competition will tend to cause the real-world dynamic path of changes in institutional structure to evolve toward improvements in the performance of the functions of the financial system. Major technological developments over the past 20 years, especially in the areas of information processing and telecommunications, have made possible a wide range of important financial innovations. They have also helped ensure implementation of those innovations by substantially lowering the barriers to entry into financial intermediation worldwide. These same technologies have greatly increased the flexibility of financial intermediaries and markets in the choice of their geographic and regulatory locations. As a result, even national governments are increasingly acting more like competitive institutions in this domain. The functional perspective views financial innovation as the "engine" driving the financial system toward its goal of greater economic efficiency.

Theories of financial intermediation that are consistent with this view of the process tend to deal with the three broad categories of improvements in economic performance previously discussed:[19] (a) meeting investor or issuer demands to "complete the markets" with new securities or products; (b) lowering transactions costs or increasing liquidity;

19 The first is exemplified by Allen and Gale (1988, 1990), Duffie and Jackson (1989), Merton (1992b, Sections 14.3, 14.5, 14,6), and Ross (1976); for the second, see Benston and Smith (1976) and Merton (1989, 1992b, Ch. 14); for the third, see Barnea, Haugen, and Senbet (1985), Diamond (1984), Diamond and Verrecchia (1982), Fama (1980), Fama and Jensen (1985), Milgrom and Roberts (1992), Ross (1973, 1989), Strong and Walker (1987), and Townsend (1990).

and (c) reducing asymmetric information and agency costs. As forces making for financial innovation in intermediation, all three are consistent with its working to improve economic efficiency. Note, however, that this broad *anatomical* description of the role of financial innovation in the structural dynamics of the financial system does not rule out the prospect of transient *pathologies* in which specific innovations are dysfunctional and thereby reduce economic efficiency.

Financial innovation in intermediation does not, of course, proceed in a vacuum. When it happens and what specific forms it takes are significantly influenced by the surrounding institutional and regulatory environment.[20] As discussed in Merton (1993, Section 7), the adoption of a broad functional perspective on regulation in place of a narrowly defined institutional one could lead to more flexible, better-coordinated, and hence more effective oversight as well as less involvement of institutions in wasteful "regulatory arbitrage."

Application of the functional perspective is not limited to analyses at the level of the financial system. It can also be applied to the study of a *financial activity* (e.g., lending in Merton, 1990 and Merton and Bodie, 1992), a *financial institution* (e.g., thrifts and commercial banks in Merton and Bodie, 1992 and 1993, respectively), or even a *single product* (e.g., municipal-bond insurance as discussed here).

With this general background on the functional perspective, we turn now to the dynamics of institutional change.

ON THE DYNAMICS OF INSTITUTIONAL CHANGE: FINANCIAL-SPIRAL EFFECT AND THE FUTURE OF INTERMEDIARIES

As discussed, the pace of financial innovation over the past 20 years surely underscores the point that while the functions of the financial system are stable, the ways in which they are performed are not. Those two decades have seen revolutionary changes in the structure of the world's financial markets and institutions and in our understanding of how to use them to provide households and firms with new investment opportunities and ways of managing risk.[21] Those changes in the structure of the financial system came about in part because of a wide array of newly designed securities, in part because of the advances in computer and telecommunications technology that made possible the implementation of

---

20 See Kane (1977, 1984, 1988), Silber (1983), and Miller (1986, 1992) on effects of regulation on financial innovation.

21 A brief sampling is given at the outset of the section on "Financial Innovation." As Miller (1992, p. 4) describes it, "No 20-year period in financial history has witnessed an even remotely comparable burst of innovative activity."

large-volume trading strategies in these diverse set of securities, and in part because of important advances in the theory of finance.[22] Each of these has contributed to vastly reduced costs of financial transactions.

Greatly reduced trading costs would be expected to cause transaction volume in financial markets to rise substantially, which it has.[23] But, these reductions in costs more generally have contributed to an even greater expansion in markets through the process of "commodization," in which financial markets replace financial intermediaries as the institutional structure for performing certain functions. In terms of an "extended" Ross (1989) classification of financial institutions (see Figure 1.1), there appears to be a secular pattern away from opaque institutions toward transparent institutions.

Figure 1.1   Classification of Financial Institutions

Transparent				Translucent				Opaque
Govt. Bond Market	Stock Market	Futures and Options Markets	Unit Trusts	Mutual Funds	Pension Funds	Finance Companies	Insurance Companies	Commercial Banks

By way of examples, the development of liquid markets for money instruments such as commercial paper allowed the money-market mutual fund ("transparent institution") to make major inroads as a substitute institutional structure for bank and thrift ("opaque institutions") demand deposits. Financial futures on equities' indexes are an efficient alternative to market- and sector-index mutual funds. The creation of "junk-bond" and medium-term note markets made it possible for mutual funds, pension funds, and individual investors to service those corporate issuers who had historically depended on banks as their source of debt financing. Similarly, the creation of a national mortgage market

---

22   Perhaps in no other branch of economics has the implementation of theory into real-world practice been as rapid as for finance theory and the financial-services industry over this period. See Bernstein (1992) for an in-depth description of this interplay between theory and practice in bringing about some of the major innovations of the last few decades. Merton (1994) discusses this interplay in terms of feedback between advances in finance technology and the need for that technology.

23   For example, the trading volume on the New York Stock Exchange runs about 150–200 million shares a day, which is 12–15 times the volume of 20 years ago. The Exchange claims to have the technology to handle a 1-billion share day. Note: These figures overstate the increase in *transaction* capacity because the number of shares traded *per transaction* has increased significantly over this period.

allowed mutual funds and pension funds to become major funding alternatives to thrift institutions for residential mortgages. Creation of these funding markets also made entry possible by agent-type institutions (e.g., investment banks and mortgage brokers) to compete with traditional principal-type intermediaries for the origination and servicing fees on loans and mortgages.

The process of "securitization" is essentially the removal of (nontraded) assets from a financial intermediary's balance sheet by packaging them in a convenient form and selling the packaged securities in a financial market. This process of reducing the total size of assets or "footings" of intermediaries and transferring them to markets is already widespread for mortgages, auto loans, credit-card receivables, and leases on consumer and producer durables. Now established as a legitimate process, its application to other types of intermediary assets is likely to move forward even more rapidly than in the past.[24]

As a more detailed example, consider a case that has not as yet happened, but could— municipal-bond insurance. In the United States, there are specialized insurance companies that sell insurance guaranteeing interest and principal payments on municipal bonds against default by the issuer. The policies are typically sold to the issuer municipality which "attaches" them to the bonds to give them an AAA credit rating. Consider as a competing alternative that an options exchange creates a market for put options on municipal bonds. Investors could then achieve the same loss protection by buying an "uninsured" municipal bond *and* a put option on that bond.[25] Note that both structures serve the same *function* for investors—protection against loss from default. However, the *institutions* are entirely different—an options exchange is not an insurance company, and most exchanges are not even intermediaries.[26] Furthermore, the put option traded on the exchange is a different product from the insurance guarantee. Nevertheless, although the products and the institutions that provide them are quite different, the *economic function* they serve is the same.

This is hardly the place for a cost-benefit analysis of those competing ways for performing the specialized function of municipal-bond default guarantees. To make the point

---

24 See Cushman (1993) on the possibility of creating a national market for mid-market corporation bank loans. For a comprehensive discussion of the implementation of asset securitization, see Norton and Spellman (1991), Zweig (1989), and the entire Fall 1988 issue of *Journal of Applied Corporate Finance*.

25 With a standard fixed exercise price, the put would actually provide more protection because it covers losses in the value of the bond for any reason, not just issuer default. However, the coverage could effectively be "narrowed" to only default risk by making the exercise price "float" to equal the current price of an AAA bond with comparable terms to those of the covered bond.

26 For example, the New York Stock Exchange. However, options (and futures) exchanges do provide credit intermediation services because they guarantee contract performance for the life of the contract through their clearing facilities.

on interinstitutional competition, it suffices to say that the "unbundling" of the downside protection,[27] and the possibility that an options exchange with marked-to-market collateral and a clearing corporation could be a better credit risk than an insurance company, provide important potential reasons why issuers and investors might prefer the financial-market structure for guaranteeing the performance of the bonds over the intermediary one.

As these examples indicate, intermediaries and markets compete to be the provider of financial products. Improving technology and the continuing decline in transactions costs have added to the intensity of that competition. Inspection of Finnerty's (1988,1992) extensive histories of innovative financial products suggests a pattern in which products offered initially by intermediaries ultimately move to markets. This temporal pattern may seem to imply that financial intermediaries (especially opaque ones such as banks) are declining in importance and are being superseded institutionally by financial markets.[28] Perhaps. However, exclusive focus on the time path of *individual products* can lead to biased forecasts, not only with respect to the apparent secular decline in the importance of intermediation, but with respect to the general structural relations between financial markets and intermediaries.

Financial markets, as we know, tend to be efficient institutional alternatives to intermediaries when the products have standardized terms, can serve a large number of customers, and are well-enough "understood" for transactors to be comfortable in assessing their prices. As we also know, intermediaries are better suited for low-volume products. Some of these products will always have low volume either because they are highly customized or because of fundamental information asymmetries. Others, however, have low volume only because they are new. Among those, the "successes" are *expected* to migrate from intermediaries to markets. That is, once they are "seasoned," and perhaps after some information asymmetries are resolved, those products are structured to trade in a market. Just as venture-capital intermediaries that provide financing for start-up firms expect to lose their successful customers to capital-market sources of funding, so do the intermediaries that create new financial products.

Especially in periods with a high intensity of financial innovation, there is a large volume of new products created and, therefore, one expects a large number of instances of

---

27   That is, to give each individual investor the choice of whether to purchase the particular municipal bonds with or without default insurance, and to give the issuer a way to price-discriminate among investors with differing assessments of default risk.

28   This proposal is focused on the *change*, not the *level* of relative importance between intermediaries and markets. It is thus consistent with Keeley (1990), who reports that bank stocks have been losing market value for the past 20 years, and Mayer (1990), who observes that "Banks are the dominant source of external finance in all countries" (p. 313).

product migration from intermediaries to markets. Following the time path of individual products can thus lead to the belief that as technology continues to evolve, trading markets for standardized instruments such as securitized loans will ultimately replace financial intermediaries such as banks. That may indeed be the case for intermediaries that are rigidly attached to a specific product or class of products, but not for intermediation in general. Intermediaries, in addition to their manifest function of offering custom products and services, serve an important latent function of creating and testing new products as a part of the general financial-innovation process.

This dynamic product-development interaction between intermediaries and markets can be interpreted as part of a "financial-innovation spiral" pushing the financial system toward an idealized target of full efficiency.[29] That is, as products like futures, options, swaps, and securitized loans become standardized and move from intermediaries to markets, the proliferation of new trading markets in those instruments makes feasible the creation of new custom-designed financial products that improve "market completeness." To hedge their exposures on those products, the producers (typically, financial intermediaries) trade in these new markets and volume expands; increased volume reduces marginal transaction costs and thereby makes possible further implementation of more new products and trading strategies by intermediaries, which in turn leads to still more volume. Success of these trading markets and custom products encourages investment in creating additional markets and products, and so on it goes, spiraling toward the theoretically limiting case of zero marginal transactions costs and dynamically complete markets.

For an example, consider the Eurodollar futures market that provides organized trading in standardized LIBOR (London Interbank Offered Rate) deposits at various dates in the future. The opportunity to trade in this futures market provides financial intermediaries with a way to hedge more efficiently custom-contracted interest-rate swaps based on a floating rate linked to LIBOR.[30] A LIBOR rather than a U.S. Treasury rate-based swap is better suited to the needs of many intermediaries' customers because their cash-market borrowing rate is typically linked to LIBOR and not to Treasury rates. At the same time, the huge volume generated by intermediaries hedging their swaps has helped make the Eurodollar futures market a great financial success for its organizers.[31] Furthermore, swaps with relatively standardized terms have recently begun to move from being custom contracts to ones traded in markets. The trading of these so-called "pure vanilla" swaps in a market further expands the opportunity structure for intermediaries to hedge, and

---

29 See Merton (1989, 1990, 1992a, b) for further discussion.

30 See "Global Debt Monitor: Swap Players Welcome Eurodollar Gold," *International Financing Review*, Issue 934, June 20, 1992.

31 See, for example, Antilla (1992) on the Chicago Mercantile Exchange.

thereby enables them to create more customized swaps and related financial products more efficiently.

For a second example, consider the financial function of providing a well-diversified portfolio of equities for individual investors. At one time, this function was best served by buying shares on a stock exchange. However, transactions and monitoring costs as well as problems of indivisibilities significantly limited the number of companies that could be held in almost any investor's portfolio. The innovation of pooling intermediaries such as mutual funds greatly reduced those costs, provided for almost perfect divisibility, and thereby allowed individual investors to achieve vastly better diversified portfolios, such as the 500-stock, market-value weighted portfolio of the Standard and Poor's 500 Index. Subsequently, futures contracts were created on various stock indexes, both domestic and foreign. These exchange-traded contracts further reduced costs, improved domestic diversification, and provided expanded opportunities for international diversification. Moreover, these contracts gave the investor greater flexibility for selecting leverage and controlling risk. In particular, index futures made feasible the creation of exchange-traded options on diversified portfolios.[32] Recent further innovations that serve the diversification function have intermediaries using equity-return swaps to create custom contracts with individual specification of the stock index, the investment time horizon, and even the currency mix for payments.[33] Thus, the institutional providers of the stock-diversification function for households were markets; then intermediaries; then markets again; and then intermediaries again.

More generally, standardized traded-securities markets are used by financial-services firms to implement dynamic trading strategies designed to replicate the payoffs to more complex securities.[34] The synthesizing of custom financial contracts and securities is for financial services what the assembly-line production process is for the manufacturing sector. Options, futures, and other exchange-traded securities are the raw "inputs" applied in prescribed combinations over time to create portfolios that hedge the various customer liabilities of financial intermediaries which are their "outputs."

As the examples of this section suggest, following the time path of a particular financial *function* instead of a *product* leads to our identifying a very different pattern of compe-

---

32   As in the Eurodollar futures/swap example, the availability of index futures and options markets allows intermediaries to better hedge their exposures in the products they create.

33   See Perold (1992; pp. 751-764 in this volume) for a detailed case study on enhanced index equity products. As shown there, contracts are also tailored to individual tax and regulatory circumstances. Litzenberger (1992) discusses such tailoring for fixed-income products. For a more general discussion, see Scholes and Wolfson (1992).

34   See the section to follow on financial engineering.

tition between intermediaries and markets. Instead of a secular trend away from intermediaries toward markets, it is seen as more cyclical—moving back and forth between the two. Table 1.1 illustrates the generic time pattern for the institutional providers of a given financial function to households and nonfinancial firms. In this hypothetical example, households are served initially (at Time 0) by intermediaries using Product #1. In the next period, Product #1 migrates to a market and households are now served by that market. With the opportunity to trade Product #1 in a market, intermediaries can then innovate to create a new product that better performs for households and firms the function provided by Product #1. Hence, with the introduction of Product #2 at Time 2, households and nonfinancial firms are once again served by intermediaries. Following the pattern of the financial-innovation spiral, the process repeats itself with Product #2 migrating to a market, the subsequent creation of Product #3, and so on. Thus, although products tend to move secularly from intermediaries to markets, the providers of a given function tend to oscillate according to the product-migration and development cycle.

Table 1.1 Institutional Dynamics for the Providers of a Specific Financial Function to Households and Nonfinancial Firms: Intermediaries versus Markets

	TIME 0	TIME 1	TIME 2	TIME 3	TIME 4
Product #1					
Producer	INT	MKT	MKT	MKT	MKT
Customer	HH/F	HH/F	INT	INT	INT
Product #2					
Producer			INT	MKT	MKT
Customer			HH/F	HH/F	INT
Product #3					
Producer					INT
Customer					HH/F
Producers Serving HH/F	INT	MKT	INT	MKT	INT

HH/F=Households and Nonfinancial Firms
INT=Financial Intermediaries
MKT=Financial Markets

It is evident from further inspection of this dynamic interaction that intermediaries help markets grow by creating the products that form the basis for new markets and by adding to trading volume in existing ones. In turn, markets help intermediaries to innovate new, more customized products by lowering the cost of producing them. In sum, financial markets and intermediaries are surely *competing* institutions when viewed from the *static* perspective of a particular product activity. However, when viewed from the *dynamic* perspective of the evolving financial system, the two are just as surely *complementary* institutions, each reinforcing and improving the other in the performance of their functions.

FINANCIAL ENGINEERING AND THE PRODUCTION PROCESS FOR FINANCIAL INTERMEDIARIES

Financial engineering is the means for implementing financial innovation. It is a systematic approach used by financial-service firms to find better solutions to specific financial problems of their customers. The process of financial engineering for institutions can be usefully broken down into five steps:

1. *Diagnosis:* Identifying the nature and source of the problem.
2. *Analysis:* Finding the best solution to the problem in light of the current state of regulation, technology, and finance theory. The best-solution design is typically a new financial instrument (or set of instruments), but it can also be an entirely new financial intermediary.
3. *Production:* Producing the new instrument either by underwriting both sides of the transaction (agent) or by synthesizing it through a dynamic trading strategy (principal), or by a combination of both.
4. *Pricing:* Determining the cost of production and profit margin.
5. *Customization:* Further tailoring the instrument to the specific needs of each customer. In most cases, the problem addressed is relevant to more than one client. A cost-benefit tradeoff is considered in deciding whether to make detail changes to fit each individual more precisely.

The changes in finance theory and computer technology in the last decade, and the transaction-cost-reducing effect of the financial-innovation spiral, have had their greatest impact on the production part of intermediaries' financial engineering process. The increasingly more "finished" or "tailored" products that simplify financial life for customers of an intermediary somewhat paradoxically add technical and financial complexity to the operations of the intermediary. To model the production process for a generic intermediary, we consider two polar models—the "underwriting"and the "synthesizing" models—recognizing that most real-world intermediaries pursue combinations of the two. Comparison of the relative costs and benefits of these two production structures, together with an assessment of the differing skills required to implement them, provides the basis for conditional predictions of the efficient forms that will be taken by intermediaries in different environments. Instead of developing these basic approaches to production in the abstract, we present them in the context of a simple, hypothetical example.[35]

Suppose that as a result of taking the diagnosis and analysis steps in the financial engineering process, an intermediary determines that a customer's problem would be best solved if it could own the economic equivalent of 1000 shares of XYZ Corporation and have the value of the position insured so that at the end of two years, it has a minimum value of $100,000 ($100/share), which is also the current value of the stock. Thus, one "unit" of this "insured-equity" product has a contingent payoff structure equal to the maximum of the stock price or $100 per share at its maturity date in two years.[36]

Suppose further that the intermediary knows that XYZ stock will sell for either $90 or $115 per share in a year's time. If the former occurs, then the stock will either decline further to $70 per share or rebound to $110 at the end of Year 2. If instead the stock is $115 at the end of the first year, then it will sell for either $90 or $140 at the end of the second year. The intermediary also knows that XYZ will pay no dividends during this time. A tree diagram of the process is presented in Figure 1.2. The riskless interest rate is constant over time at 5% per year.

One approach to producing the product is to create a unit trust (call it "XYZ Trust") with assets of 1000 shares of XYZ and two-year U.S. Treasury (UST) bills with a face value of $100,000. The trust has two classes of liabilities: Class A and Class B. Class A is entitled to receive at the end of Year 2 either 1000 shares of XYZ or $100,000, whichever its owner prefers. During the interim period, the Class A holder receives all cash dividends paid on the XYZ shares and dictates how the shares in the trust are voted. Class B is a "residual"

---

35   A development of these production models in a more formal context with the mathematics included is presented in Merton (1989, pp. 237–242; 247–253, 1992, pp. 441–50;457–465). General overviews on financial engineering and its implementation can be found in Finnerty (1988), Smith and Smithson (1990), Eckl, Robinson, and Thomas (1990), and Marshall and Bansal (1992).

36   This product is equivalent to a "protective-put" option strategy where the investor buys the stock and a put option on the stock. Chase Manhattan Bank which issues the product based on the Standard & Poor's 500 Stock Index in the United States calls it a "market-index certificate of deposit." Swiss Bank Corporation uses the name "guarantee-return-on-investment securities" (GROIS), and Merrill Lynch calls its version "Market Index Target Term Securities" (MITTS). Leland, O'Brien, and Rubinstein offer the "SuperTrust" and "SuperShares."

security that receives whatever assets remain in the Trust, after the Class A claim has been met.[37]

Figure 1.2   Future Possible Prices of XYZ Stock

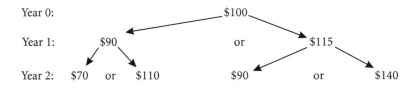

Based on the intermediary's knowledge of the price process for XYZ, the contingent payoffs to the Trust and each of its liabilities are displayed in Table 1.2. By inspection of that table, the Class A instrument has the identical payoff pattern to the insured-equity product. However, the structure of the Trust guarantees that the promised payments can be made *without making any distributional assumptions about XYZ,* because the UST bills are sufficient to meet the minimal $100,000 payment even if the XYZ shares become worthless. Thus, once the Trust is created, the intermediary can meet its customer's objective by selling it the Class A instrument, without having to convince the customer to agree with its stock-return assessments on XYZ.

The cost of funding the Trust is $190,700 (=$100,000 for 1000 shares of XYZ plus $90,700 for $100,000 face value of two-year UST bills discounted at 5% per year). Thus, to make a profit, the intermediary must receive at least $190,700 from the sale of the Class A and Class B units plus cover any other expenses of forming the Trust. The intermediary may have to commit some capital to fund the Trust while it is selling the units, but once they are sold, the intermediary has neither capital nor risk exposure to the transaction.

This approach is essentially a ("buyer-driven") underwriting activity and it emphasizes marketing or distribution skills. As with underwriting in general, the intermediary is positioned more like an agent than a principal to the transaction. In terms of product creation, it exemplifies the Ross (1989) "marketing" theory of intermediation. The unit

---

37 Although the example focuses on an equity product, this approach is widely used to produce tailored fixed-income products, often with many more than just two classes of liabilities. Indeed, the "residual" security always is called the "Class Z" security even if there are fewer than 25 other classes. Characteristics of the Class A security are designed to meet specific duration, credit-risk, regulatory, and tax clienteles. Examples are collateralized mortgage obligations (CMOs) and collateralized bond obligations (CBOs) that use mortgages, bonds, and other fixed-income assets in the trust.

trust used as the intermediation vehicle is a transparent institution. No sophisticated stock-evaluation or trading skills are needed, since operating the Trust requires only a one-time purchase of 1000 shares of XYZ and $100,000 face value of UST bills. And knowledge of the stock-price return distribution (as in Figure 1.2) is also not needed.

Table 1.2   Contingent Payoffs at Year 2

XYZ Stock Price	"Class A" Insured Equity	"Class B" Residual Claim	XYZ Trust
$ 70	$100,000	$ 70,000	$170,000
90	100,000	90,000	190,000
110	110,000	100,000	210,000
140	140,000	100,000	240,000

Because the structure of the Class A units is derived as a direct solution to a specific problem faced by an identified (class of) customer, one expects that the placement of those units is a relatively "easy" sale. However, to create the desired equity-insurance product in this fashion, it is also necessary to sell the Class B units. Because they are the residual claims, their payoff structure is not explicitly designed to fit any particular investor group's "desired habitat."[38] Thus, these units must be sold on the basis of price (i.e., as an investment "bargain") and not on the basis of convenience or performance in meeting some explicit customer objective. Therefore, to be successful, the intermediary must charge a sufficient price 'premium' (over cost) on the Class A units to offset the price "discount" on the Class B units necessary to induce "bargain-hunting" investors to buy them.

It is evident that an intermediary with a larger number of contacts with price-sensitive investors is more likely to find those who will pay a higher price for the deal.[39] Customers are always looking for "good" products, and financial product designs cannot be patented. The least-cost producer of these products is therefore likely to have an important advantage. Hence, to intermediaries that produce products by this "underwriting"

38   In a buyout or takeover with major revisions of a firm's capital structure, the residual nonequity securities issued are often called "cram-downs," reflecting the lack of a natural investor demand for their pattern of payoffs. The payoffs to the Class B units here happen to have the same structure as a two-year, zero-coupon "junk" bond (see Merton 1990, pp. 272–285).

39   Such an intermediary would also have the opportunity to "spread" the trades out with a lower quantity (and possibly higher price) per investor.

approach, a "fat" Rolodex file containing names of "bargain-investor" contacts may be more valuable than one of corresponding size filled instead with "customer" names.

An alternative to this "Rolodex" method of production through underwriting is for the intermediary to act as a principal and issue the desired insured-equity product directly to the customer as a contractual obligation of the intermediary (instead of a separate trust). In principle, the intermediary could do so by buying the same combination of XYZ stock and UST bill assets held in the Trust in the underwriting approach and financing the difference between the cost of those assets and the proceeds from sale of the insured-equity product with equity capital. This strategy would be almost equivalent to the intermediary creating the Trust and buying the Class B piece itself.[40] However, as demonstrated in the work of Grossman and Hart (1982), Jensen (1986), and others, there are potentially significant agency and tax costs associated with equity capital of firms. Those "dead-weight" costs make equity finance "expensive," and thereby limit the amount of equity that a value-maximizing intermediary would optimally issue.[41] Hence, this simple way of combining the underwriting intermediary with its bargain-hunting investors may not be efficient.

An alternative that potentially "economizes" on the amount of capital required is the "synthesizing" or "dynamic-trading" approach to production. It substitutes a strong trading facility for a strong distribution system, and it relies on the power of modern computer technology and highly skilled personnel trained in advanced methods of estimation and contingent-claims pricing.[42] With its reliance on trading, the synthesizing approach to production benefits disproportionately from the financial-innovation spiral discussed in the preceding section.

There is an enormous academic and practitioner literature on the mathematics and economics of contingent-claims pricing and dynamic replication.[43] There is no need to develop it once again here. It is enough to describe the principles and then illustrate the process for our hypothetical example.

The process of implementation is as follows. Once the specification of the terms of the customer liability to be issued is determined by the capital-markets or corporate-

40 There are some potentially important credit-risk differences between the two, depending on details of the structuring.

41 Otherwise intermediaries with liability obligations to its customers would optimally guarantee performance on those obligations by holding huge positions in liquid assets financed entirely by equity capital. See Merton (1993) for more details.

42 From the descriptions in Loomis (1992), Picker (1992), and Sanford (1993), it appears that Bankers Trust Company provides a real-world example of this approach to production.

43 See Merton (1992) for an extensive and up-to-date bibliography. Merton (1994) discusses both the historical and future influences of these mathematical models on finance practice.

finance group of the intermediary, the quantitative-analysis group uses contingent-claims analysis to design a dynamic trading strategy in securities to synthesize (replicate) the payoff structure of the customer obligation in the least-cost way.[44] In the trading operations (often called a "trading desk") of the intermediary, a "dedicated" portfolio is established with an initial investment equal to the minimum amount necessary to ensure full implementation of the strategy with no further capital infusions. The trading strategy is dynamic in the sense that it typically calls for the composition of the portfolio to be revised in response to changes in security prices and the passage of time. The trading desk is charged with implementation of the strategy.

Table 1.3 illustrates the trading process for our hypothetical example with the return dynamics of XYZ stock described in Figure 1.2.[45] This cookbook-like prescription calls for an initial investment in XYZ stock and UST bills of $106,315. If the price of XYZ rises, more shares are purchased by selling bills; if it falls, the share position is reduced and the proceeds placed in bills. At Year 2, the value of the portfolio is equal to the maximum of the value of 1000 shares of XYZ or $100,000. Hence, the portfolio exactly replicates the contractual payoffs that the intermediary has promised to its customer. Since the portfolio never requires a further infusion of capital, the initial investment of $106,315 to fund the portfolio is the production cost to the intermediary for the product.

The process of synthesizing customer financial contracts and securities is for financial intermediaries what the assembly-line production process is for the manufacturing sector. The trading-strategy rules are the "blueprints" for production. The traded securities (XYZ shares and UST bills) used in the portfolio are the raw "inputs" applied in prescribed combinations over time to create a "finished" product or "output," which is a complete set of contingent payments matched to the ones promised on the customer's contract.

---

44   There are often multiple ways to implement the strategy that are equivalent in a frictionless environment, but when transactions costs including market impact from trading, taxes, regulation, and modeling error are taken into account, they are no longer equivalent. The offset of customer exposures by netting of the intermediary's positions and hedging only the systematic components of the portfolio risks for the intermediary may also be optimal when there are costs. See Merton (1989, pp. 242–247; 1992, pp. 450–457) for further discussion of those issues.

45   The derivation of the synthesizing trading rules for the particular example here is presented in Merton (1992, pp. 337-341; 438-439).

TABLE 1.3   Production Technology and Production Cost for Insured-Equity Instrument: Dynamic Trading Rules for Replication

At Year 0

$ 70,400	Buy 704 shares XYZ @ $100/share
35,915	Short-term cash investment @ 5%
$106,315	Total investment

At Year 1

If XYZ share price is $90: Sell 454 shares @ $90/share

Value Before		**Value After**	
$ 63,360	704 shares XYZ @ $90	$ 22,500	250 shares XYZ @ $90
37,711	Cash & interest	78,571	Cash investment @ 5%
$101,071		$101,071	

If XYZ share price is $115: Buy 96 shares @ $115/share

Value Before		**Value After**	
$ 80,960	704 shares XYZ @ $115	$ 92,000	800 shares XYZ @ $115
37,711	Cash & interest	26,671	Cash investment @ 5%
$118,671		$118,671	

If share price of XYZ was $90 at Year 1 and,

At Year 2

If share price of XYZ is $70:

$ 17,500	250 shares of XYZ @ $70/share
82,500	Cash & interest
$100,000	Value of Portfolio ($100/share XYZ)

If share price of XYZ is $110:

$ 27,500	250 shares of XYZ @ $110/share
82,500	Cash & interest
$110,000	Value of Portfolio ($110/share XYZ)

If share price of XYZ was $115 at Year 1 and,

At Year 2

If share price of XYZ is $90:

$ 72,000	800 shares of XYZ @ $90/share
28,000	Cash & interest
$100,000	Value of Portfolio ($100/share XYZ)

If share price of XYZ is $140:

$112,000	800 shares of XYZ @ $140/share
28,000	Cash & interest
$140,000	Value of Portfolio ($140/share XYZ)

Compared with the underwriting approach to production, the synthesizing approach appears to have several advantages: it makes the part of the transaction seen by the customer easier for the customer because the intermediary simply issues the contract without requiring the intervening element of the trust as "another institution" involved in the transaction. The synthesizing method is considerably more efficient for an intermediary that specializes in unique or "one-off" contracts. Essentially, *any* contract with payoffs that depend on the price of XYZ stock can be produced by the same type of process described in Table 1.3.[46] Only the mixing rules for adjusting the stock-bills positions are changed. Thus, by analogy with numerically controlled machines on a physical assembly line, the intermediary need only change the "dials" (mixing rules) to have the same line produce a different output. This approach thus offers the opportunity to create custom-tailored financial products at a ("assembly-line") standard-product level of cost. Another advantage to the intermediary operating as a principal is the opportunity to "net" its transactions. Thus, an intermediary that offers a wide variety of customer contracts, each contingent in different ways on the price path of XYZ stock, can run a *single* replicating portfolio in XYZ stock and bills that hedges the *net* (aggregate of all customer exposures) contingent payouts.

All this does not imply that the synthesizing approach dominates the underwriting one. Compensation for highly skilled technical and trading employees and the high cost of the supporting technology (e.g., supercomputers) can make the cost of running the synthesizing production system greater than the underwriting system. Moreover, as principal, the intermediary (its employees and shareholders) bears the risk of errors in production. These errors range from a clerk punching in 11 million *shares* rather than *dollars* in translating the model prescriptions into orders for execution,[47] to fundamental flaws in the assumptions of the model itself (e.g., suppose at the end of Year 2, XYZ shares are selling for $50 or $170 a share, despite these being "impossible" events according to the *model* description of the process in Table 1.2).

Perhaps the most important issue surrounding the effectiveness of an intermediary acting as principal is customer perception of the intermediary as a credit risk. This topic is beyond the scope of this volume, and so, we only note here that a key factor in assessing

---

46 See Merton, op. cit., for the trading rules for a general payoff function when the dynamics for XYZ stock are as in Figure 1.2.

47 As reported in the press, this actually happened in the case of stock-index arbitrage activities at Salomon Brothers, Inc., in March 1992.

the relative costs of the synthesizing and underwriting approaches is the amount and cost of "assurance" or "risk" capital required by each to eliminate customer concern about contract performance by the intermediary.[48]

In constructing the Trust in our hypothetical example, a total of $190,700 was required to purchase the funding assets. If the $106,315 production cost by synthesis is the marginal cost of producing the Class A units for the Trust, it follows that the cost of producing the Class B units is ($190,700–106,315=) $84,385. In the presence of competition among intermediaries, it is reasonable to expect that the prices received from issuing those securities will not differ greatly from their respective marginal costs.

Since once the Trust is funded, customer holders of the Class A units can be absolutely assured of having the contractual obligations of the Trust met, the amount of capital required to provide this assurance is $84,385.[49] Hence, about 44% of the total funds to be raised by the intermediary to create the Trust must come from the "residual" piece sold to price-sensitive investors. As already discussed, placing the residual piece is the "difficult" sale, and the size of the discount required on the Class B units clearly can have a first-order impact on the profitability of the deal.

In contrast, an intermediary selecting the synthesizing approach only needs $106,315 to fund the internal production portfolio. If the insured-equity product is sold at above production cost, then the cash flow from sales to customers would seem to rule out the need for the intermediary to raise additional capital. However, this conclusion implicitly assumes (1) that customers know and agree with the intermediary's assessment for the XYZ stock-price process in Figure 1.2; (2) that customers believe the intermediary can and will undertake the dynamic strategies described in Table 1.3; and (3) that customers believe that the other activities of the intermediary will not lead to liens on the assets of the replicating portfolio by other claim holders of the intermediary. These three assumptions are not, of course, robust, especially for an opaque institution. Therefore, principal-type intermediaries will in general have to raise additional assurance capital to provide the functional equivalent of the Class B units in the agent-underwriting alternative. Which of the two (or some combination) is the more-efficient production process will depend on

---

48 See Merton (1993), Merton and Bodie (1992), and Merton and Perold (1993).

49 This measure of capital is closely related to the risk-capital measure developed more generally in Merton and Perold (1993).

the detailed structure of the transactions and the nature of asymmetric-information and agency costs.[50]

IMPLICATIONS FOR THE FUTURE EVOLUTION OF THE FINANCIAL SYSTEM

Having touched on issues surrounding financial innovation and economic performance in the past, we now turn to a prospective view on future economic performance as it relates to innovation.

The technological changes that have already dramatically reduced product-marketing and transactions costs are likely to make future changes in the institutional forms of financial-service firms even more rapid and far-reaching. Much-lower transactions and implementation costs make it profitable not only to introduce new financial products, but also to change entire institutional arrangements (including geographical and political locations) in response to much smaller shifts in customer tastes or operating costs than in the past. Those lower costs, together with the likelihood of increasing global competition in financial services, lay the foundation for a substantial increase in both the frequency and the magnitude of the changes in the institutional structure of financial firms. This forecasted reduction in the expected duration of institutional forms applies not only to financial firms, *but also to the regulatory bodies that govern them.*

The increasing flexibility and global mobility of financial institutions have far-reaching implications for regulation of those institutions in the future, both locally and at the national level. However, the influence of regulation on innovation is not considered in this section's "simulation" of the future. As Miller (1986) notes, it is *unanticipated* regulatory changes that have the major impact. Moreover, regulation both shapes and is shaped by the time path of financial innovation. Exogenous changes in regulation are surely possible in the short run; however, such changes induce responses in financial innovation, which in turn feed back into the dynamics of regulation.[51] As a result, the long-run role of regulatory change as an exogenous force for financial innovation is limited.

---

50 In the real-world versions of our insured-equity example cited in footnote 36, the banks and Merrill Lynch used the principal approach and SuperTrust of Leland, O'Brien, and Rubinstein (LOR) selected the underwriting one. In the 1980s, LOR, in creating its "portfolio-insurance" version of the insured-equity product, chose a hybrid of these two approaches in which it managed a replication portfolio, but as *agent* (not as principal) for its customers. As a concrete illustration of the complementary relation between markets and intermediaries, the existence of futures and options markets for trading the Standard & Poor's 500 Stock Index greatly facilitated the real-world production process for all these firms.

51 This feedback process is the essence of Kane's (1977) regulatory dialectic.

Consider now a small sampling of the implications for the future evolution of the system from this view of the process. In this scenario, aggregate trading volume expands secularly, and trading is increasingly dominated by institutions. As more financial institutions employ dynamic strategies to hedge their product liabilities, incentives rise for further expansion in round-the-clock trading that permits more effective implementation of these strategies. Supported by powerful trading technologies for creating financial products, financial-services firms will increasingly focus on providing individually tailored solutions to their clients' investment and financing problems. Sophisticated hedging and risk management will become an integrated part of the corporate capital budgeting and financial management process.

Retail customers ("households") will continue to move away from direct, individual financial market participation such as trading in individual stocks or bonds where they have the greatest and growing comparative disadvantage. Better diversification, lower trading costs, and less informational disadvantage will continue to move their trading and investing activities toward aggregate bundles of securities, such as mutual funds, basket-type and index securities, and custom-designed products issued by intermediaries. This secular shift, together with informational effects described in Gammill and Perold (1989), will cause liquidity to deepen in the basket/index securities while individual stocks become relatively less liquid. With ever greater institutional ownership of individual securities, there is less need for the traditional regulatory protections and other subsidies of the costs of retail investors trading in stocks and bonds. The emphasis on disclosure and regulations to protect those investors will tend to shift up the "security-aggregation chain" to the interface between investors and investment companies, asset allocators, and insurance and pension products.

Whether the financial-services industry becomes more concentrated or more diffuse in this scenario is ambiguous. The central functions of information and transactions processing would seem to favor economies of scale. Similarly, the greater opportunities for netting and diversifying risk exposures by an intermediary with a diverse set of products suggests both fewer required hedging transactions and less risk-capital per dollar of product liability as size increases. Increased demand for custom products and private contracting services would seem to forecast that more of the financial-service business will be conducted as principal instead of agent, which again favors size. On the other hand, expansion in the types of organized trading markets, reductions in transactions costs, and continued improvements in information-processing and telecommunications technologies will all make it easier for a greater variety of firms to serve the financial-service functions. These same factors also improve the prospects for expanding asset-based financing, and such expanded opportunities for "securitization" permit smaller, agent-type firms to compete with larger firms in traditionally principal-type activities. Continuing the scenario, locational and regulatory advantages currently available to some financial institutions will be reduced because more firms will be capable of offering a broader range of financial products and servicing a wider geographic area. Traditional institutional identifications with specific types of products will continue to become increasingly blurred.

As in other innovating industries, competition to create new products and services, and to find new ways to produce established ones at lower costs, could make the research-and-development activity the lifeblood of the financial-services firm. Along the hypothesized path of development, the need to distribute a larger-volume and more diverse set of products promises continued relative growth of the firm's sales activity. Controlling actual and perceived default risk for its customer-held liabilities has always been a key requirement for success of any financial intermediary. Greater customer expectations for service and greater complexity of products will intensify the attention given to this issue in the future. The finance function of financial-services firms will be significantly expanded to cover not only increased working capital needs of the firm, but also the management of its counterparty credit-risk exposure. As technology advances continue to drive down trading and custodial costs, the posting and careful monitoring of collateral is likely to be more widely adopted as the primary means for ensuring counterparty performance.[52] To implement this facility will in turn require enhanced trading skills for the firm. The trading activity is also likely to expand to meet the execution requirements for implementing more complex product technologies. As we know, many but not all of these changes have been underway and furthermore, this represents one scenario, growing out of our perspective on the innovation process. Nevertheless, it serves as a means to speculate about the future course of financial market regulation and, more specifically, public policy toward financial innovation.

FINANCIAL INNOVATION AND REGULATION

The standard mode of analysis for financial regulatory policy is still the institutional approach. In evaluating policy alternatives, this approach takes, as a *given*, the type of institutions that provide particular financial services, and then analyzes what can be done to help these institutions to perform those services more effectively. Framed in terms of *the* thrifts, *the* banks, or *the* insurance companies, policy issues are posed in terms of what

---

52   For a discussion and analysis of the importance and techniques of default-risk management, see Merton and Bodie (1992).

can be done to make these institutions safe and sound. The approach to policy evaluation taken here is different because it uses a functional perspective.

As discussed in preceding sections, a functional perspective on the financial system focuses attention on the changes in institutional structures that will perform the functions of that system more effectively in the future. From this view, government policies and regulations should facilitate the requisite changes in structure instead of attempting to protect and preserve existing ones. Its flexibility with respect to different institutional environments makes the functional perspective on regulation more readily adaptable to a global setting for financial services, which may be particularly useful if supranational regulatory bodies are to be formed.[53]

Promoting competition, ensuring market integrity including macro credit risk protections, and managing "public-good" type externalities cover the broad potential roles for regulation and other government activities in improving economic performance of the financial system. The potential costs of such activities fall into four categories: (1) direct costs to participants, such as fees for using the markets or costs of filings; (2) distortions of market prices and resource allocations; (3) transfers of wealth among private party participants in the financial markets; and (4) transfers of wealth from taxpayers to participants in the financial markets. There are five categories to classify the paths by which government affects the financial markets: (1) *as a market participant* following the same rules for action as other private-sector transactors, such as with open-market operations; (2) *as an industry competitor or benefactor of innovation*, by supporting development or directly creating new financial products or markets such as index-linked bonds or all-savers accounts; (3) *as a legislator and enforcer*, by setting and enforcing rules and restrictions on market participants, financial products, and markets such as uptick rules, margin requirements, circuit breakers, and patents on products; (4) *as a negotiator*, by representing its domestic constituents in dealings with other sovereigns that involve financial markets; and (5) *as an unwitting intervenor*, by changing general corporate regulations, taxes, and other laws or policies that frequently have significant unanticipated and unintended consequences for the financial-services industry.

The overriding theme of this chapter's scenario has financial innovation as the engine driving the financial system on its prospective journey to economic efficiency. With its focus on product and service innovations, this theme largely abstracts from the concurrent changes in financial infrastructure (institutions, regulatory practices, organization

---

53 Grundfest (1990) provides analysis and data on the globalization of world financial markets and its implications for regulation. See Merton and Bodie (1992, 1993) for a comparison of the functional and institutional approaches to regulation in the context of the savings and loan crisis in the 1980s..

of trading facilities, and the communication and information processing systems for transactions) required to support realization of this journey. But, perhaps the single most-important implication for public policy on innovation is the explicit recognition of the interdependence between product and infrastructure innovations and of the inevitable conflicts that arise between the two.

As an analogy of supreme simplicity,[54] consider the creation of a high-speed passenger train, surely a beneficial product innovation. Suppose, however, that the tracks of the current rail system are inadequate to handle such high speeds. In the absence of policy rules, the innovator, either through ignorance or a willingness to take risk, could choose to fully implement his product and run the train at high speed. If the train subsequently crashes, it is, of course, true that the innovator and his passenger-clients will pay a dear price. But, if in the process the track is also destroyed, then those, such as freight operators who use the system for a different purpose, will also be greatly damaged. Hence the need for policy to safeguard the system. A simple policy that fulfills that objective is to permanently fix a safe but low speed limit. But, of course, this narrowly focused policy has a rather unfortunate consequence that the benefits of innovation will never be realized. An obviously better, if more complex, policy solution is to facilitate the needed upgrading of the track and, at the same time, to set transient limits on speed, while there is a technological imbalance between the product and its infrastructure.

As in this hypothetical rail system, the financial system is used by many for a variety of purposes. When treated atomistically, financial innovations in products and services can be implemented unilaterally and rather quickly. Hence, these innovations take place in an entrepreneurial and opportunistic manner. In contrast, innovations in financial infrastructure must be more coordinated and, therefore, take longer to implement. As we see, for instance, with recent thrift and banking legislation in the United States, major changes, including outright elimination of obsolete institutions and their surrounding regulatory structure, take place exceedingly slowly. It is thus wholly unrealistic to expect financial innovation to proceed along a balanced path of development for all elements in the system. It is indeed possible that at times, the imbalance between product innovation and infrastructure could become large enough to jeopardize the functioning of the system; hence, the need for policy to protect against such breakdown. But, as we have seen, a single-minded policy focused exclusively on this concern could derail the engine of innovation and bring to a halt the financial system's trip to greater efficiency.

Conflicts between product innovation and the evolution of infrastructure in the financial system may be inevitable, but government actions can do much to either mitigate

---

54 This analogy is taken from Merton (1989, p. 257).

or aggravate their disruptive effects. By analogy, hurricanes are inevitable, but government policy can either reduce their devastation by encouraging early warning systems or it can aggravate the damage by encouraging the building of housing in locations that are especially vulnerable to such storms.

While government actions can significantly influence the path of development for financial services, successful public policy depends as importantly on recognizing the limitations of what government can do to control and improve the efficiency of the financial system.

A related policy issue is whether government should itself be a financial innovator. If so, should policy hold that innovative financial instruments be issued if and only if they reduce the direct cost of government financing? Are there other social benefits? Would, for example, the national mortgage market have evolved without government-guaranteed mortgages? For another example, not centered around credit enhancement, it has been suggested that there are certain types of index-linked bonds for which the government may have a comparative advantage over private-sector issuers.

The dramatic increases over the last decade in the size and complexity of transactions together with the global linking of financial markets have raised concerns about macro credit risk and the possibility of broad financial market "breakdown."[55] The 1987 crash in world stock markets still casts a shadow that heightens those concerns. The changes in practice projected by our scenario of innovation imply, *ipso facto*, further increases in the interdependence among institutions and markets in the international financial system.[56] This greater interdependence, in turn, promises renewed intensity of the policy debate on ensuring market integrity and where to draw the line on government guarantees, both explicit obligations set by contract and implicit ones set by public expectations. Our scenario on macro credit risk may thus seem to suggest an increasing role for regulation. On the other hand, continuing improvements in telecommunications, information processing, and electronic transactions technologies will make monitoring security prices and transferring securities for collateral considerably less costly. Such technologies, for example, may eventually make practical the creation within banks of segregated depository

---

55 Regulators throughout the world have expressed considerable concern about the implications of the new finance technologies, especially derivatives, for financial market stability. See, for example, Group of Thirty (1993), CFTC (1993) and GAO (1994).

56 As discussed in Merton (1989, 1990, 1993); Merton and Bodie (1992), controlling default risk for customer-held liabilities of financial intermediaries is a key element in the theory of efficient intermediation and economic performance. Furthermore, much the same point applies for the integrity of markets that trade standardized instruments, such as options, futures, and swaps. Thus, in this specific sense, the theory supports the belief that credit risk is a major macro issue for the international financial markets.

accounts, perhaps run along the lines of money-market funds, but with additional marked-to-market collateral and a federal deposit-insurance "wraparound." This less comprehensive deposit insurance, lower-cost monitoring, and lower-cost collateralization work in the direction of reducing the need for regulation.[57]

Whatever may be the change in the quantity of regulation in the future, a major change in the format of regulation from "institutional" to "functional" seems inevitable. As already noted, increasingly more sophisticated trading technologies, together with low-transaction-cost markets to implement them, tend to blur the lines among financial products and services. The existence of these technologies and markets also implies easier entry into the financial services. As a result, the lines between financial institutions are likely to become less distinct. Indeed, insurance companies now offer U.S. Treasury money-market funds with check writing, while banks use option and futures markets transactions to provide stock-and-bond-value insurance that guarantees a minimum return on customer portfolios. Credit subsidiaries of major manufacturing firms have moved from the single, specialized function of providing financing for customers of their parents to multiple-function financial institutions, with services ranging from merchant banking for takeovers and restructurings to equity-indexed mutual funds sold to retail investors. Electronics has also rendered as problematic the meaning of "the location of the vendor" of these products. In contrast, a financial product's function from the perspective of the user is relatively well defined.

Most financial regulation involves products and services for household customers, and hence the user's location is often better defined than the vendor's. Over time, functional uses of products are typically more stable than the institutional forms of their vendors. In keeping with the trend toward greater user access to international financial markets, we note further that product and service functions appear to be more uniform across national borders than are the institutions that provide them. Functional regulation also reduces the opportunities for institutions to engage in "regulatory arbitrage," which wastes real resources and can undermine the intent of the regulation. Functional regulation thus promises more consistent treatment for all providers of functionally equivalent products or services, and thereby reduces the opportunities for rent-seeking and regulatory capture. Furthermore, functional regulation can facilitate necessary changes in institutional structures by not requiring a simultaneous revision of the regulations or the

---

57   See Merton and Bodie (1992, 1993) for an analysis of the costs and benefits of government participation in deposit and loan guarantees. See also Bodie and Merton (1994) on government pension guarantees.

regulatory bodies surrounding them, as is required with an institutionally based regulatory structure.[58]

The perceived benefits from a move to functional regulation might seem to support a broader case for widespread coordination, and even standardization, of financial regulations, both domestically and across national borders. However, such extrapolation is valid *only if* the coordinated regulatory policies chosen are socially optimal. The reduction in "regulatory diversification," which by necessity occurs with more effective coordination, will accentuate the social losses if the selected common policies are suboptimal. The international issue of the tradeoff between the benefits of regulatory cooperation and the benefits of regulatory competition promises to be among the more important financial regulatory issues of the 1990s.

REFERENCES

Allen, F. and D. Gale (1988), "Optimal Security Design," *Review of Financial Studies,* 1(Fall):229–263.

———— and ———— (1990), "Incomplete Markets and Incentives to Set Up an Options Exchange," *Geneva Papers on Risk and Insurance Theory,* 15(March):17–46.

Antilla, S. (1992), "Wall Street: Boom and Bluster at the Merc," *New York Times,* September 6, 1992, Section D:15.

Barnea, A., R.A. Haugen, and L.W. Senbet (1985), *Agency Problems and Financial Contracting,* Englewood Cliffs, NJ: Prentice-Hall.

Benston, G.J. and C. Smith (1976), "A Transaction Cost Approach to the Theory of Financial Intermediation," *Journal of Finance,* 31(May):215–231.

Bernstein, P., (1992), *Capital Ideas: The Improbable Origins of Modern Wall Street,* New York: Free Press.

Black, F. and M.S. Scholes (1974), "From Theory to New Financial Product," *Journal of Finance,* 29(May):399–412.

Bodie, Z. and R.C. Merton (1994), "Pension Benefit Guarantees in the United States: A Functional Analysis," in R. Shmitt, ed., *The Future of Pensions in the United States,* Philadelphia: University of Pennsylvania Press.

Borch, K.H. (1990), *Economics of Insurance,* Amsterdam: North-Holland.

CFTC (1993), *The Report of the Commodity Futures Trading Commission: OTC Derivative Markets and Their Regulation,* Washington, D.C. (October).

---

58 See Chicago Mercantile Exchange (1993) for an example of a model for a more functionally oriented regulatory structure.

Chicago Mercantile Exchange (1993), *Model for Federal Financial Regulation*, Chicago Mercantile Exchange, Chicago.

Cushman, Jr., J.H. (1993), "Investing in Loans to Businesses," *New York Times*, March 19, 1993, Section D.

de la Vega, J. (1688), *Confusion de Confusiones*. English translation by H. Kallenbenz, No. 13, The Kress Library Series of Publications, (Harvard University, 1957).

Diamond, D.W. (1984), "Financial Intermediation and Delegated Monitoring," *Review of Economic Studies*, 51(July):393–414.

———— and R.E. Verrecchia (1982), "Optimal Managerial Contracts and Equilibrium Security Prices," *Journal of Finance*, 37(May):275–287.

Duffie, D. and M. Jackson (1989), "Optimal Innovation of Futures Contracts," *Review of Financial Studies*, 2:275–296.

Eckl, S., J.N. Robinson, and D.C. Thomas (1990), *Financial Engineering: A Handbook of Derivative Products*, Oxford: Basil Blackwell.

Fama, E. (1980), "Agency Problems and the Theory of the Firm," *Journal of Political Economy*, 88(April):288–307.

———— and M.C. Jensen (1985), "Organizational Forms and Investments Decisions," *Journal of Financial Economics*, 14(March):101–118.

Finnerty, J.D. (1988), "Financial Engineering in Corporate Finance: An Overview," *Financial Management*, 17(Winter):14–33.

———— (1992), "An Overview of Corporate Securities Innovation," *Journal of Applied Corporate Finance*, 4(Winter):23–39.

Folkerts-Landau, D. and D. Mathieson (1988), "Innovation, Institutional Changes, and Regulatory Response in International Financial Markets," in W.S. Haraf and R.M. Kushmeider, eds., *Restructuring Banking and Financial Services in America*, Washington, D.C.: American Enterprise Institute for Public Policy Reserve.

Freeman, A. (1993), "A Survey of International Banking: New Tricks to Learn," *The Economist*, April 10, 1993:1–37.

Gammill, J. and A.F. Perold (1989), "The Changing Character of Stock Market Liquidity," *Journal of Portfolio Management*, 13(Spring):13–17.

GAO (1994), *Financial Derivatives: Actions Needed to Protect the Financial System*, The General Accounting Office, Washington, D.C. (May).

Grauer, R. and N. Hakansson (1987), "Gains from International Diversification: 1968–85 Returns on Portfolios of Stocks and Bonds," *Journal of Finance*, 42 (July):721–738.

Grossman, S.J. and O.D. Hart (1982), "Corporate Financial Structure and Managerial Incentives" in J.J. McCall, ed., *The Economics of Information and Uncertainty,* Chicago: University of Chicago Press.

Group of Thirty (1993), *Derivatives: Practices and Principles,* Global Derivatives Study Group, Group of Thirty, Washington, D.C. (July).

Grundfest, J. (1990), "Internationalization of the World's Securities Markets: Economic Causes and Regulatory Consequences," *Journal of Financial Services Research,* 4(December):349–378.

Hull, J. (1989), *Options, Futures, and Other Derivative Securities,* NY: Prentice-Hall.

Jensen, M.C. (1986), "Agency Costs of Free Cash Flow, Corporate Finance, and Takeovers," *American Economic Review,* 76(May):323–329.

———— and W. Meckling (1976), "Theory of the Firm: Managerial Behavior, Agency Costs and Ownership Structure," *Journal of Financial Economics,* 3(October):305–360.

Kane, E.J. (1977), "Good Intentions and Unintended Evil: The Case Against Selective Credit Allocation," *Journal of Money, Credit and Banking,* 9(February):55–69.

———— (1984), "Technological and Regulatory Forces in the Developing Fusion of Financial-Services Competition," *Journal of Finance,* 39 (July):759–772.

———— (1988), "How Market Forces Influence the Structure of Financial Regulation," in W.S. Haraf and R.M. Kushmeider, eds., *Restructuring Banking and Financial Services in America,* Washington, D.C.: American Enterprise Institute for Public Policy Research.

Keeley, M.C. (1990), "Deposit Insurance, Risk, and Market Power in Banking," *American Economic Review,* 80(December):1183–1200.

Litzenberger, R.H. (1992), "Swaps: Plain and Fanciful," *Journal of Finance,* 47(July):831–850.

Loomis, C.J. (1992), "A Whole New Way to Run a Bank," *Fortune,* September 7, 1992:76.

Marshall, J.F. and V.K. Bansal (1992), *Financial Engineering,* Needham Heights, MA: Allyn and Bacon.

Mayer, C. (1990), "Financial Systems, Corporate Finance, and Economic Development," in R.G. Hubbard, ed., *Asymmetric Information, Corporate Finance, and Investment,* Chicago: University of Chicago Press.

Merton, R.C. (1989), "On the Application of the Continuous-Time Theory of Finance to Financial Intermediation and Insurance," *The Geneva Papers on Risk and Insurance,* 14(July):225–262.

———— (1990), "The Financial System and Economic Performance," *Journal of Financial Services Research,* 4(December):263–300.

———— (1992a), "Financial Innovation and Economic Performance," *Journal of Applied Corporate Finance*, 4(Winter):12–22.

———— (1992b), *Continuous-Time Finance,* Revised Edition, Oxford: Basil Blackwell.

———— (1993), "Operation and Regulation in Financial Intermediation: A Functional Perspective," in P. Englund, ed., *Operation and Regulation of Financial Markets,* Stockholm: The Economic Council.

———— (1994), "Influence of Mathematical Models in Finance on Practice: Past, Present and Future," *Philosophical Transactions of the Royal Society of London*, Series A, 347 (June): 451–463.

———— and Z. Bodie (1992), "On the Management of Financial Guarantees," *Financial Management*, 22(Winter):87–109.

———— and ———— (1993), "Deposit Insurance Reform: A Functional Approach" in A. Meltzer and C. Plosser, eds., *Carnegie-Rochester Conference Series on Public Policy*, Volume 38(June).

———— and A.F. Perold (1993), "Theory of Risk Capital in Financial Firms," *Journal of Applied Corporate Finance*, 6(Fall): 16–32.

————, M. Scholes, and M. Gladstein (1978), "The Returns and Risk of Alternative Call Option Portfolio Investment Strategies," *Journal of Business*, 51(April):183–242.

————, ————, and ———— (1982), "The Returns and Risks of Alternative Put Option Portfolio Investment Strategies," *Journal of Business*, 55(January):1–55.

Milgrom, P. and J. Roberts (1992), *Economics, Organization and Management*, Englewood Cliffs, NJ: Prentice-Hall.

Miller, M.H. (1986), "Financial Innovation: The Last Twenty Years and the Next," *Journal of Financial and Quantitative Analysis*, 21(December):459–471.

———— (1992), "Financial Innovation: Achievements and Prospects," *Journal of Applied Corporate Finance*, 4(Winter):4–11.

Norton, J. and P. Spellman (1991), eds., *Asset Securitization: International Financial and Legal Perspectives*, Oxford: Basil Blackwell.

Perold, A.F. (1992), "BEA Associates: Enhanced Equity Index Funds," Harvard Graduate School of Business Case #N9-293–024, Boston, MA (August).

———— and E. Schulman (1988), "The Free Lunch in Currency Hedging: Implications for Investment Policy and Performance Standards," *Financial Analysts Journal*, 44 (May/June):45–50.

Picker, I. (1992), "Banker Trust's Amazing Risk Machine," *Institutional Investor*, (August):29.

Ross, S.A. (1973), "The Economic Theory of Agency: The Principal's Problem," *American Economic Review*, 63(May):134–139.

——— (1976), "Options and Efficiency," *Quarterly Journal of Economics*, 90(February):75–89.

——— (1989), "Institutional Markets, Financial Marketing, and Financial Innovation," *Journal of Finance*, 44(July):541–556.

Sanford, Jr., C.S. (1993), "Financial Markets in 2020," Federal Reserve Bank of Kansas City Economic Symposium, (August 20).

Schaede U. (1988), "Forwards and Futures in Tokugawa-Period Japan: A New Perspective on the Dojima Rice Market," unpublished paper (May), Universitaet Marburg, Marburg, Germany.

Scholes, M.S. and M.A. Wolfson (1992), *Taxes and Business Strategy: A Planning Approach*, Englewood Cliffs, NJ: Prentice-Hall.

Silber, W. (1983), "The Process of Financial Innovation," *American Economic Review*, 73(May):89–95.

Smith, Jr., C.W. and C.W. Smithson (1990), eds., *The Handbook of Financial Engineering*, Grand Rapids, MI: Harper Business.

———, ———, and L. Wakeman (1986), "The Evolving Market for Swaps," *Midland Corporate Finance Journal*, 4(Winter):20–32.

———, ———, and ——— (1988), "The Market for Interest Rate Swaps," *Financial Management*, 17(Winter 1988):34–44.

Stiglitz, J. and A. Weiss (1981), Credit Rationing in Markets with Imperfect Information," *American Economic Review*, 71(June):393–410.

Strong, N. and M. Walker (1987), *Information and Capital Markets,* Oxford: Basil Blackwell.

Sundaresan, S. (1990), "Valuation of Swaps," in S. Khoury, ed., *Recent Advanced in International Banking and Finance*, Amsterdam: North Holland.

Tobin, J. (1978), "A Proposal for International Monetary Reform," *Eastern Economic Journal*, 4(July/August):153–159.

Townsend, R.M. (1990), *Financial Structure and Economic Organization*, Oxford: Basil Blackwell.

Zweig, P.L. (1989), ed., *The Asset Securitization Handbook*, Homewood, IL: Dow Jones-Irwin.

CHAPTER 2

SECURITIES INNOVATIONS:
A HISTORICAL AND FUNCTIONAL PERSPECTIVE

INTRODUCTION

The case studies in this book detail the invention and use of recent securities innovations, including collateralized mortgage obligations (CMOs), high-yield bonds, municipal bond swaps, exchangeable bonds, Nikkei put warrants, adjustable-rate and auction-rate preferred stocks, PERCs, SuperShares, interest-rate swaps, and natural gas derivatives. While the past two decades have produced a remarkable amount of securities innovation, creativeness has characterized the financial system for over a century. For example, in 1910, John Moody, founder of Moody's rating service, complained about the complications induced by innovation:

> Twenty-five years ago it was comparatively easy to acquire a sound knowledge of the general investment field . . . (but now) . . . the different types of securities have multiplied in number to an almost unlimited extent . . . (T)he different types of (securities) which are daily sought for investment nowadays are often so different . . . that not only must each class be judged by itself, but a great many issues of the same general class have distinct traits which go far to affect directly their position and value as investments.[1]

A Wall Street analyst trying to understand the latest products designed by financial engineers might echo Moody's sentiment.

---

1   Moody (1910, p. 545).

I would like to thank Zvi Bodie, Jon Headley, Scott Mason, Robert C. Merton, André Perold, and participants at the Virginia Tech Financial Innovation Study Committee for their comments on this work. Funding for this project was provided by the Harvard Business School Division of Research, supported by the benefactors of the Global Financial Systems Project at HBS.

Various authors have identified *institutional* factors, such as particular tax provisions or the rise of low-cost computing, as stimuli for modern securities innovations. However given the market's long history of innovation, institutionally grounded explanations can fail to capture its timelessness. For example, taxes—a pervasive force in modern innovation—cannot explain many nineteenth century securities. The *historical* perspective highlights shortcomings of purely *institutional* explanations.

The prior chapter describes a framework with which we can analyze a financial system, its institutions, and its products. This *functional* approach explains institutions or products in terms of the basic needs that they satisfy.[2] The functional approach calls attention to similarities among diverse securities by decomposing each product into the needs it satisfies. For example, portfolio insurance, a trading strategy described in a later case study that enables portfolio managers to manage risk, must be compared to other risk-management products such as exchange-traded indexed put options or explicit guarantees.[3] Voting trusts, a late nineteenth-century innovation that attempted to mediate inherent conflicts between stock-holders and bond-holders, must be compared to bond covenants and preferred stock designs with similar objectives.[4] The functional approach also recognizes that products can serve multiple functions; for example, mutual funds provide investors with risk management (through diversification), pooling (the aggregation of funds to permit economical investing), and movement of funds through time and space.[5] Various authors have used functional thinking to enlighten their understanding of specific products, and the case studies that follow can be analyzed in terms of the economic needs each product delivers.[6]

This chapter attempts to develop an understanding of the persistence of financial innovation that is consistent with the ideas underlying the functional perspective. Functional analysis holds that the financial system delivers an immutable set of functions that are the same at different points in time and in different parts of the world. If so, why do we observe so much innovation? Why does the historical record demonstrate that the financial system constantly creates new means to satisfy the same set of unchanging needs? Building upon the prior chapter's discussions of the financial innovation spiral and

---

2   As described in the prior chapter, these functions include moving funds across time and space; pooling resources to fund efficient scale enterprises; facilitating the exchange of cash, securities, and goods; creating information used in investment and consumption decisions; managing risk; and resolving the conflicts that arise from asymmetric information and agency problems.

3   See Merton and Bodie (1992).

4   For a detailed discussion, see Tufano (1992).

5   See Sirri and Tufano (1993).

6   Finnerty (1988 and 1992) analyzes recent financial innovations along a set of dimensions that resembles the six functions.

drawing upon the historical evidence, we can identify three ideas that enlighten our understanding of the historical record of securities innovation:

- First, supplying securities that satisfy the needs of society is a *costly* activity. These costs include expenses to produce and distribute securities, as well as the costs imposed by governments through taxes, judicial decrees, and regulation. Securities innovations can be explained as efforts to minimize the full costs of satisfying the needs demanded by users of the financial system.

- Second, *life cycles* of households, firms, industries, and nations as well as *exogenous shocks* affect the mix of functions the financial system is called upon to deliver. These changes in the demands, due to predictable or unpredictable changes in needs, put pressure on the financial system to develop new products, upsetting previous cost-benefit relationships.

- Finally, the history of financial innovation can be seen as a process of *experimentation*, revelation of outcomes, and learning. Financial innovation is an evolutionary process, and the inherent nature of financial contracts almost dictates that "failure" is more likely than not.

After a brief description of the history of securities innovations, the chapter examines these three ideas in detail, and concludes with predictions about the future of securities innovation.

A BRIEF REVIEW OF SECURITIES INNOVATIONS IN HISTORY

The last 20 years have witnessed extensive securities innovation.[7] There are numerous lists of recent financial innovations published by journalists, practitioners, and academics that show the wide range of innovations.[8] These lists, and the cases in this book, encompass corporate securities (e.g., zero-coupon bonds, auction-rate preferreds, PIK bonds, LYONs, SWORDs, junk bonds), securitized investments (e.g., mortgage pass-throughs, CMOs, credit card receivables), futures contracts (e.g., index futures, municipal bond futures, Eurodollar futures), municipal bond products (e.g., VRDOs), option products (e.g., Nikkei put warrants, synthetic covered equity warrants, index options, bond options), trading strategies (e.g., portfolio insurance), and swaps (e.g., interest-rate, currency, municipal bond, equity, and commodity). The case studies of securities innovations covered in this book understate the amount of financial innovation, as they do not discuss innovations in

---

7   Miller (1986 and 1992) has claimed that the period 1970-1990 is quite unique in financial history, in that "No (other) 20-year period has witnessed such a burst of innovative activity."

8   For example, see Finnerty (1988), Walmsley (1988), Coopers and Lybrand (1990).

bank lending and deposit-taking, payments technologies, computerized trading systems and exchanges, mutual funds, and a host of other developments in financial products, services, and institutions.

There are a few estimates of the degree to which the security markets of the past two decades can be considered innovative. Among publicly issued corporate securities, as much as 20% of the value of new offerings in the 1980s involved securities popularly considered to have been invented within the prior decade.[9] In 1973 open interest on exchange-traded option contracts was 250,000; by 1993 open interest had grown one-hundred-fold, to 25 million contracts.[10] In 1973 there were virtually no junk bonds issued; by the mid-1980s, total outstanding junk bonds equaled $50 billion; and by 1993 there were over $200 billion outstanding.[11] In 1980 there was no swaps market.[12] By 1993 there were an estimated $3 trillion in interest-rate swaps, as measured by the notional principal of the transactions.[13] In 1973 there were $6 billion in mortgage-backed securities outstanding, but by 1993 this total had grown 330 times, to almost $2 trillion.[14]

There can be little doubt that our generation has witnessed extraordinary innovation, but so have earlier generations. The appendix to this chapter lists major innovations in United States corporate securities from 1830 to 1930, showing the approximate date that the security was first issued in America or became popularized.[15] The chart shows the major innovations of the period, but does not communicate the enormous variety of individual contract innovations.

This diversity is well demonstrated in another appendix, this one taken from the first edition of the investing classic, Benjamin Graham and David Dodd's *Security Analysis*.[16] In the text of their 1934 book, Graham and Dodd analyzed bonds and stocks, but were stymied by the fact that many potential investments were complicated hybrid securities. In

---

9   See Tufano (1989).

10   *The Wall Street Journal*, various issues.

11   Fabozzi and Pollack (1987, p. 755) and *Investment Dealer's Digest* (January 17, 1994, pp. 16-17).

12   However, there were parallel and back-to-back loans that preceded currency swaps. For a discussion, see Beckstrom (1986).

13   Eli Remolona, "The Recent Growth of Financial Derivatives Market," *Federal Bank of New York Quarterly Review* (Winter 1992-1993) pp. 26-43.

14   Fabozzi and Pollack (1987, p. 425) and Logue (1994, pp. A1-19).

15   The securities innovations from a century ago were not only invented, but also became popular financing devices. For example, contingent charge securities (preferred stocks and income bonds), represented less than 1% of railroad capitalization in 1872, but almost 30% of the capital of the railroad industry by 1917. Total capitalization is measured as the book value of debt, contingent charge securities, and common stock. See Tufano (1992).

16   Graham and Dodd (1934). Unfortunately, this appendix was dropped from subsequent issues of the investing classic, and thus most readers will never have seen it.

the interest of full disclosure, they included an appendix entitled "A Partial List of Securities which Deviate from the Normal Patterns."

> In assembling the material presented herewith it has not been our purpose to present a complete list of all types of securities which vary from the customary contractual arrangements between the issuing corporation and the holder. Such a list would extend the size of this volume beyond reasonable limits. We have, however, attempted to give a reasonably complete example of deviations from the standard patterns.

In the following 17 pages, they described 258 securities. Put in modern language, their list included pay-in-kind bonds, step-up bonds, putable bonds, bonds with stock dividends, zero coupon bonds, inflation-indexed bonds, a variety of exotic convertible and exchangeable bonds, 23 different types of warrants, voting bonds, non-voting shares, and a host of other instruments. Graham and Dodd's appendix reads like a list of 1980s and 1990s innovations, giving credence to the adage, "There's nothing new under the sun."[17] In the following three sections, we examine how costs, changing demands, and experimentation can help us understand the innovations that Graham and Dodd categorized, as well as those which our own generation has produced.

COSTS AND SECURITIES INNOVATION

If products are no more than bundles of functions, innovation results if a lower-cost means can be found to deliver the functionality of an existing product. Costs must be broadly defined to include: (1) Marketing: costs of identifying and educating buyers and sellers; (2) Manufacturing: costs of production, including raw materials and the legal and financial engineering technologies to transform them into end-products; and (3) Taxes and regulation. This view of costs encompasses not only "frictionless" production costs, but also "transaction costs" which practitioners face (such as bid-ask spreads, taxes, and information gathering costs.)

Marketing costs are not unique to financial products, although they have received scant attention in the finance literature, with the notable exception of Ross (1989). Manufacturing costs are the expenses incurred to produce the security. These may be as straight-forward as the cost to purchase an asset and the legal fees to transfer its title to a buyer. Alternatively, for financially engineered products, production costs may include

---

17 As Miller (1992) points out, perhaps the most anomalous period in U.S. financial history was the period 1930-1960. These three decades saw relatively little innovation. Miller ascribes this lack of private sector innovation to the shrinkage of the world economy, which reduced the demand for new instruments, regulatory restrictions put in place after the Crash, crowding out of private market activities during the Second World War, and additional regulatory restrictions on international transactions.

substantial transaction costs (bid-ask spreads) involved with dynamic replication trading strategies. Taxes and regulation are costs in that they affect usable cash flows delivered to buyers. For example, the cost to deliver $1 of consumption to an investor may depend on her tax situation, and in the extreme, regulation may impose nearly infinite tolls on certain prohibited transactions.[18]

Positive costs make it infeasible to have every contract available in the market. For example, if distributing new financial products was costless, it might be sensible to sell flood insurance to residents of even very arid climates. If desert-dwellers would pay a premium of $.02 to insure against a flood, and insurers could manufacture this product (hedge themselves) for $.01, the product would be quite profitable (on a percentage basis) for insurers. However, if the marginal cost of marketing was $1.00 per policy (or if there were large fixed costs of establishing a marketing force), the insurer must charge $1.01 to break even. Distribution costs drive a wedge between the value of the contract and the price to deliver it, and no innovation takes place. However, if distribution costs fell to $.005, the new policy might be created; otherwise, homeowners might prefer to self-insure. The history of securities markets shows many examples where changes in costs have led to innovation.

IDENTIFYING AND EDUCATING BUYERS AND SELLERS

Marketing, i.e., identifying and educating potential buyers and sellers, is both a labor- and information-intensive activity. History shows that as marketing costs fall, financial innovations appear to exploit the easier access to buyers and sellers of securities. For example, during World War I, the U.S. government instituted a massive program to fund its wartime efforts through selling small-denomination bonds to individual investors. The Liberty Loan program of 1917 both identified and educated a new clientele—retail investors:

> The Treasury immediately decided to mount an intensive nationwide sales effort. Advertisements and thousands of spokesmen emphasized the security, high yield, and probable appreciation of the new Liberty bonds. Established techniques were put aside. Instead of selling substantial amounts of large denominations for holding in relatively few hands, the government issued bonds in small denominations, utilized war saving stamps widely, and permitted installment payments. All the foregoing "new" departures were designed to appeal to individuals not considered potential investors since the Civil War days of Jay Cooke.[19]

---

18 Some readers may prefer to consider taxes and regulation as "demand-side" factors, akin to the life-cycle concerns and macro-economic shocks which affect the mix of products demanded by users of the financial system.

19 Carosso (1970, p. 225).

These activities by the federal government lowered the costs for the private sector to identify and educate new potential customers. After the war, innovations in the private sector took advantage of the lowered costs of raising funds from households. These innovations, tailored to meet the needs of small savers, included "baby bonds" sold in small denominations and securities sales on installment.[20] The peacetime innovations seem to respond to the lowered marketing costs brought about by the government's wartime financing program.

More recent examples, including many of the case studies in this book, represent innovations that capitalize on reductions of marketing costs. The rise of defined-benefit pension systems created an easily identifiable, large, and concentrated pool of potential investors, whose needs were addressed by innovations of long-duration assets, including zero-coupon bonds and longer-maturity CMO tranches.[21] This easily identified clientele's needs also motivated the initial development of portfolio insurance and the subsequent creation of the SuperTrust, which are analyzed in case studies in this book. The innovators of both of these products, Leland O'Brien Rubinstein, benefited by being able to clearly identify potential users. The case study of Nikkei Put Warrants demonstrates how Goldman Sachs exploited the marketing information it gained by selling foreign currency warrants to identify latent demand for Japanese stock index puts.

Changes in the costs of marketing will continue to influence the rate of innovation. For example, in the early 1990s swap dealers sold interest-rate swaps to commercial banks that sought to mitigate interest-rate risk and create synthetic levered investments. These swaps then subjected banks to basis risk or the mismatch between LIBOR and the prime rate. Dealers with knowledge of swap users can easily identify customers for basis swaps that solve the mismatch problem.

CHANGES IN MANUFACTURING:
RAW MATERIALS AND TECHNOLOGIES

Changes in the price or availability of raw materials or production technologies lead to innovations. Smaller, cheaper semiconductors enabled manufacturers to create digital watches, palmtop computers, and smart appliances. Computer-controlled machine tools allowed firms to customize their industrial products to meet customers' precise specifications,

---

20 For a description of these innovations, see Riegel (1920).

21 For a discussion of this link, see Bodie (1990). The case studies of COUGARs and Travelers Mortgage Securities CMO detail two particular long-duration securities sought by pension funds.

creating an almost unlimited range of new products. In the financial system, too, changes in raw materials and technologies affect the innovations that are created.

Raw materials

One case study, set in the early 1980s, details the activities of Leland O'Brien Rubinstein Associates (LOR) as it began to sell a trading strategy known as portfolio insurance, which allowed institutional investors to manufacture puts on stock market indices. Initially, adoption of this innovation was slow, because early versions of the trading strategy required LOR to buy and sell common shares held by their clients. Not only was share trading costly (due to transaction costs), but also it was inconvenient to coordinate the buying and selling activities of LOR and its clients. In 1982, the Chicago Mercantile Exchange offered index futures contracts on the S&P 500. Not only were the transaction costs to buy and sell futures a third that of trading the stock basket, but also portfolio insurance executed using futures required far less coordination between LOR and its clients. LOR's business grew prior to 1987, in part due to the lower costs and increased convenience afforded by the new raw material. The BEA Associates case study provides a second example of a firm exploiting low-cost derivatives to create "synthetic equity." The LOR and BEA case studies, along with others in the book, illustrate the "financial innovation spiral," this is, how one innovation can facilitate a chain of subsequent innovations.

At the turn of the century, the sheer lack and high cost of an important raw material—credible information—affected security design. Throughout much of the nineteenth and early twentieth century, firms disclosed very little credible financial information.[22] Over time, market forces and governmental action materially increased the quantity and quality—and thus lowered the cost—of information about firms.[23] Early innovations tended to substitute for (or economize on) the use of costly information, while later innovations capitalized on its lower cost. One of the earliest innovations, the nineteenth century practice of issuing assessable stock, was designed mindful of the paucity of information. An assessable share-holder committed to supply a certain amount of money to the firm, but doled out the cash to the firm in response to regular assessments. (Dewing [1919, p. 16]). Issuers of assessable common stock were forced to return to their investors regularly and make the case for continued commitment, because investors held the option

---

22 For a description of the reporting practices of American firms, see Hawkins (1986).

23 Standards for accounting and auditing were developed (Hawkins [1986]), state and federal regulatory commissions required firms to disclose operating and financial information (Chandler [1956, p. 179]), investment bankers refined the due-diligence process as an exhaustive financial, strategic, and engineering inspection of firms (Carosso [1970, p.56]), the financial press and ratings services grew (Forsyth [1964]), and "Blue Sky" laws and the Transportation Act of 1920 brought security issuances under state, and then federal, control (Reed and Washburn [1921], Bonbright [1920, chapter 5]).

to fail to make the assessment and forfeit his interest.[24] The nineteenth century firms' almost complete reliance on secured debt for debt financing (see Ripley cited in Baskin [1988, pp. 215-216]) may also be interpreted as a costly contracting choice that substituted for more precise monitoring prevented by inadequate disclosure.

Later nineteenth century innovations took advantage of the presence of cheaper and more reliable information. Later preferred stocks conditioned their holders' voting rights on firms' failure to comply with covenant terms (Johnson ([1925], Wilson [1930], both cited in Dewing [1934, pp. 193–194]). These covenants, especially after 1900, were more likely to be tied to financial ratios (Johnson [1925], cited in Dewing [1934, p. 189]), as were bond covenants keyed to working capital tests or asset maintenance tests (Dewing [1934, pp. 313–314]). Finally, income bonds, popularized in the late nineteenth century, were completely linked to the availability of accounting information. These unsecured obligations required issuers to pay interest only if the firm earned positive accounting profits in the current period.

Technologies

At least three technologies have supported many modern securities innovations: computing technology, telecommunications, and financial engineering theory, specifically the logic of dynamic replication that underlies the Black-Scholes model and other models of derivative pricing.[25] For example, the cases of LOR's creation of portfolio insurance, Goldman Sachs' hedging of its currency exposure in Nikkei Put Warrants, and Shearson Lehman Hutton's construction of synthetic covered equity warrants show the role of up-to-date market information, pricing models, and computing capability in creating new derivative products. Mortgage-backed securities and CMOs, discussed in the Travelers Mortgage Security case study, demand computer systems to maintain timely information on thousands of individual mortgages. The case study of American Express Travel Related Services Charge-Card Receivables examines the recent phenomenon of securitizing thousands of relatively small and constantly changing credit-card balances, a feat made feasible by low-cost computing. Finally, the case study of Enron Gas Services shows how a firm combined financial engineering theory, legal innovations, and a $60-million investment in computing and communications technology to develop scores of natural gas derivatives while controlling its risk as an intermediary. These innovations would not have taken place

---

24 The initial public offering of British Telecommunications, PLC in 1984 shows a modern variant of assessable stock: the installment payment method.

25 The Note on Contingent Claims Theory details the ability of modern financial engineering (especially option pricing technology) to analyze a wide variety of security contracts.

had firms not had access to modern technologies that could produce timely and accurate information which could be confidently incorporated into pricing models.

Earlier in the century, improvements in other technologies supported the process of financial innovation. In 1866, transAtlantic cable first began to transmit information from New York to London. This technological innovation led to an important financial "innovation," the equalization of market prices for the same financial contracts between different locations. Within a few months of the introduction of the cable, the prices of U.S. government bonds sold in New York and London quickly converged.[26] However, the technological development that was probably more instrumental in explaining nineteenth century innovations was the development of new legal techniques. For example, during the late nineteenth century, the U.S. bar's skill at executing ever-more sophisticated and well-drafted security contracts improved dramatically. This technical virtuosity is exemplified by the Burlington Northern bonds issue of 1896. These bonds, described in detail by Labar (1992), had a number of unique covenants, including the requirement that proceeds from asset sales be reinvested in the railroad. Apart from the specifics of the covenants, the innovation illustrates the degree to which securities lawyers had perfected their art by the turn of the century: subsequent generations of lawyers were unable to find a loophole through which to circumvent the original drafter's intent. Just as financial engineers are indispensable to the production of modern financial innovations, the lawyers of the 1890s, such as Charles Stetson who served as J.P. Morgan's "attorney general," were indispensable to the production of the complicated corporate securities innovations a century ago.[27]

TAXES AND REGULATION

Taxes may make it expensive to deliver specific bundles of cash flow promises, and regulations may make it illegal to deliver them, or impose nearly infinite costs. Not surprisingly, these institutional features often inspire innovators. Nobel laureate Merton Miller claimed that taxes and regulation have produced the "major impulses to successful innovation over the past twenty years,"[28] and scattered empirical evidence supports this popular belief. John Finnerty (1988) lists 69 recent corporate securities innovations and identifies taxes, regulation, and legislation as primary motivations for 25 of them.

This book contains numerous examples of tax- and regulatory-induced innovations. The case studies of preferred stock innovations (ARPPS and MMP) illustrate innovations that deliver debt-like returns to investors, while enjoying the equity advantages

---

26   See Garbade and Silber (1978).

27   For a discussion of the role of Stetson, and the legal structuring he oversaw in the restructuring of American industry, see Campbell (1930) and Chernow (1990).

28   Miller (1986 and 1992).

of intercorporate dividend exclusion. The BEA case shows how withholding taxes render direct holdings of U.S. equities inferior to synthetic alternatives for foreign investors. Exchangeable debt, chosen by Dart and Kraft to monetize their holdings of 3M common stock, stemmed from the firm's desire to defer payments of taxes on capital gains. The putable structure chosen by New England Property and Casualty has, at its roots, attractive tax and accounting treatment. The purchase of COUGARs was particularly attractive to Japanese investors due to tax treatment of capital gains. In addition, numerous examples are not documented in this book. In 1988 four firms announced they would allow their common shareholders to exchange shares of common stock for a package called Unbundled Stock Units (USUs). The proposed USUs consisted of a bond that delivered the stocks' current dividend, a preferred share that enjoyed any increases in dividends, and a warrant that allowed the holder to enjoy appreciation above the level of principal delivered by the bond portion of the package. This complex package had many attractions, one of which was the effective transformation of cash dividends into tax-deductible interest. More recently, investment banks have trumpeted the creation of innovations that purport to create tax-deductible equity.[29]

A century ago, taxes were a less visible force in the U.S. economy, yet they still played some role in the process of financial innovation. In the late 1920s, a few states (Delaware, New Jersey, and New York) began to levy incorporation and transfer taxes based on the par value of firms' shares, and to assign par values of $100 to firms whose stock had zero par value. Corporations almost immediately reissued shares with small, but nonzero ($1–$5) par values (Hornberger [1933]). Equipment trust certificates, by which a railroad leased cars from a manufacturer with financing provided by the certificates secured by the equipment, were more popular in states such as Pennsylvania that subjected bonds, but not the certificates, to income taxes (Dewing [1934, p. 342]).[30]

Regulation also plays a role in the process of financial innovation. The early Eurobond market was motivated by tax and regulatory concerns. Specifically, by offering Eurodollar CDs, U.S. banks—led by Citicorp in 1966—could circumvent reserve requirements to stem the painful disintermediation they were experiencing. More recently, regulatory constraints placed upon Japanese life insurers motivated them in the late 1980s to buy the indexed-linked bonds described in the Nikkei Put Warrant case, and from which puts

---

29 See Tom Pratt, "Wall Street's Tough New-Product Puzzle," *Investment Dealer's Digest,* November 29, 1993, pp. 16-19.

30 Apart from these cases, there is little evidence suggesting that taxes and regulation were primary determinants of the timing, form, or level of historical financial innovations. One barometer of the limited role of taxation is the nearly complete absence of its discussion in early finance textbooks by Greene (1897, 1908), Meade (1910), Cleveland and Powell (1912, 1920), and Dewing (1919).

could be stripped to be resold in retail markets. The creation and restructuring of perpetual floating-rate notes, described in the Schroeders' Perpetual Floating Rate Note Exchange Offer case, was motivated by the requirement for banks to meet regulatory capital standards. Bank capital requirements also encouraged the innovation of "synthetic CMOs," or amortizing interest-rate swaps. These synthetic investments in structured mortgage securities demanded banks hold less capital than for direct CMO investments. Outside of the financial sector, deregulation of the U.S. natural gas market in the 1980s and 1990s gave rise to a business opportunity seized by Enron Gas Services, the creator of an active market in natural gas derivatives.

A century ago, judicial decisions gave rise to financial innovation. Throughout the late nineteenth century, the extreme business cycles experienced by the U.S. economy led to the massive failures of railroads and industrial firms. Security holders turned to the courts to enforce what they believed to be their legal rights, but judges set aside many "inviolable rights" to quickly reorganize the railroads. Specifically, super-senior "debtor-in-possession" financing was given priority above existing senior claimants, certain unsecured creditors were paid before secured creditors, and judges set judicial values—quite distinct from market value—for the claims of distressed firms. These legal innovations were probably not unrelated to the securities innovations of contingent charge securities and voting trusts, which supplanted traditional creditors' rights with more direct means of monitoring and control.[31]

COSTS: SUMMARY

By innovating, firms can economize on the costs of satisfying society's needs. Reductions in marketing costs, transaction costs, and taxes, or improvements in financial or legal technology render previously uneconomic innovations feasible. Some of these changes in costs can be classified as exogenous; e.g., developments in computing and telecommunications are independent of financial service sector. Changes in other costs are endogenous in that they result from activities within the financial system. For instance, low-cost futures contracts change the economics of portfolio insurance, and cross-marketing may permit information to support multiple new products. Within firms, costs of production and distribution may be characterized by learning curves, or economies of scale or of scope. Therefore, we would expect that innovators would tend to be drawn from firms enjoying scale or scope economies. Two pieces of evidence suggest that larger, presumably lower-cost, financial service firms do innovate at a disproportionate rate: the largest investment banks account for a large fraction of corporate securities innovations, and among mutual

---

31   See Tufano (1992) for a more detailed discussion of these issues.

funds, larger fund families introduce new products at a relatively higher rate than do smaller complexes.[32]

DIFFERENCES IN DEMANDS: LIFE CYCLES AND SHOCKS

Even without changing costs, securities innovation can occur as a response to changing demands that users place upon the financial system. Some innovations are tailored to address relatively predictable demands which arise from the evolution of household, firm, and industry needs. Other innovations respond to shocks in the macro-economy. In both cases, the new demands change the cost-benefit calculus that affects which new products are created. Hence, the changing demands interact with cost considerations to create new products.

LIFE CYCLES[33]

While managing risk is a universal concern, the relevant risks as viewed by a young working couple with small children, little wealth, and much human capital may differ from those of a retired couple, living on a nominal pension, with no heirs. The young couple may fear rising costs of education or disability, while their older counterparts fret about catastrophic medical problems or inflation. The financial system could create investments linked to college costs or broad consumption baskets to meet the couples' respective needs. These risk-management products could be structured as insurance policies, options, futures, mutual funds, or even bank accounts.[34]

Just as households have life cycles, so do businesses.[35] Fledgling firms, with short track records but large growth options, need infusions of cash to fund plant and equipment purchases or research and development. Mature firms, by definition the survivors, are more likely to generate predictable positive cash flow with lower risks, but have fewer

---

32 See Tufano (1989) regarding investment banking and Sirri and Tufano (1993) about mutual fund innovation. The role of large financial service firms in innovation may also reflect large fixed costs which can serve as deterrents to rival entry by small firms. For example, a financial intermediary entering the derivatives business *de novo* faces up-front fixed investments to hire and train a new staff, pay for timely valuable data, develop costly pricing and risk management systems, and establish a network of buyers and sellers. Large irreversible investments could deter potential new entrants and allow large-scale, low-cost firms to enjoy supernormal profits.

33 For a formal treatment of the household's dynamic consumption and investment decisions, see Merton (1990), chapters 4-6.

34 For example, U.S. banks have offered certificates of deposit linked to both the level of college costs and the level of the consumer price index. There have also been inflation-indexed corporate security offerings, futures, and mortgages.

35 See Jovanovic and MacDonald (1994) for a review of life-cycle considerations in industrial organization, and a specific case study of the U.S. automotive tire industry.

growth options. For young firms, there may be a large information gap between outside investors and inside managers, while for the mature firm, these differences may be modest. However, managers of mature cash-rich firms may have greater incentives to advance their own aims over their shareholders'. Securities designed to finance these two types of firms will reflect their different cash flow needs, growth options, and informational problems, just as risk-management products for young and old households differ.

Predictable differences among firms due to life cycle concerns can explain the timing and form of certain financial innovations. The earliest U.S. railroads, especially small enterprises in New England and New York, financed themselves with subscriptions of equity raised from households who lived along the road, as well as from their local governments.[36] This financing choice could be attributed to the small scale of the projects relative to the wealth of the local residents, whose proximity permitted easy monitoring. Outside New England and New York, there was insufficient capital to fund the large railroad investments, forcing railroad promoters to travel to Boston, Philadelphia, New York, and London to tap a relatively small community of wealthy investors, as well as their friends, family, and business associates. Yet, as investors grew more distant from the railroads, the primary means of raising capital also changed, from stock to bonds.[37] Using the language of functional analysis, this example demonstrates that increasing scale necessitated additional pooling, or the aggregation of small claims to fund large-scale enterprise. Given the geographic distribution of wealth, this increased demands for the financial system to move funds across larger geographic distances, which exacerbated informational asymmetries, giving rise to innovations.[38]

Later in the nineteenth century, the mortgage bond, which gave its holder a secured interest in real assets, was the predominant form of debt financing for railroads. Even as late as 1913, only 10% of railroad debt was unsecured (Ripley cited in Baskin [1988, p. 215]). This revealed preference for secured debt may have resulted from investors' desires to mitigate some of the risks of financial distress.[39] However, in the early twentieth century, the debenture—an unsecured claim—became a popular innovation, especially among industrial firms (Moody [1910, pp. 77]). At first glance, it seems odd that investors

---

36 For a discussion of the financing of the earliest railroads, see Chandler (1954). The earliest U.S. canals were also financed in this manner. For example, the first recorded use of preferred stock in the United States was the State of Maryland's investment in the Chesapeake and Ohio Canal in 1835 (Evans, 1935).

37 Chandler (1954, p. 263).

38 The case study of Arley Merchandise Corporation shows a recent innovation that attempts to address the informational asymmetry faced by a young firm.

39 See Stulz and Johnson (1985) for a theoretical discussion of the risk-reducing properties of secured debt, or Baskin (1988, pp. 215216) for a discussion of the historical role of secured debt.

would demand a secured interest in railroads, while accepting unsecured claims in what were commonly held to be much younger, riskier ventures. The popularization of industrial debentures can be understood by comparing the assets of industrial firms and railroads. Railroad trains and real estate constitute tangible assets with high resale value, as evidenced by the nineteenth century innovation of funding equipment through securitized leases in the form of equipment trust obligations (Duncan [1924]). In contrast, if a bicycle factory or other industrial firm failed—as many did in the early 20th century[40]—its specialized tools and equipment were less transferable to other users and hence might have little resale value. The most valuable assets of early industrial firms were intangibles that produced future earnings and growth options, and not tangible assets that could be secured. Thus, secured debt was less appropriate for industrial firms.

A modern analogue to the turn-of-the-century bicycle factory might be biotechnology firms, whose valuable assets are intellectual property developed through research and development, protected by patents, but not yet commercialized to produce current cash flow. One recent securities innovation that recognizes the inherent character of these assets is the sale-leaseback of patents through transactions called venture leases.[41] These financial instruments allow biotechnology firms to raise funds secured by patents, without having to surrender substantial corporate control to venture capitalists. In this book, we also see a related innovation pioneered by ALZA Corporation, in which claims on a portion of a firm's R&D portfolio were separated from the cash-flow generating portion of its existing business.

Innovations have also focused on solving the unique needs of firms under financial stress, which can occur at various points in their life cycle. Firms with extensive investment plans, and especially acquisition programs, have developed a host of securities designed to satisfy their particular needs, especially the need to avoid premature insolvency in transitional phases during which massive restructuring, such as asset sales, take place. The two case studies of RJR Nabisco, as well as the Metromedia Broadcasting case study, allow for a careful examination of these deferred-cash-flow financial innovations: pay-in-kind notes, discount debentures, step-up notes, and reset notes. In the aggregate, deferred-cash-flow instruments accounted for nearly a third of all LBO financing in the late 1980s (Tufano [1993]). Innovations have also been instrumental in funding distressed natural gas producers, in the form of "term overriding royalty interests" or "volumetric production payment" (VPP) contracts, described in the case study of Enron Gas Services. VPPs allowed natural gas producer to sell interests in their reserves using a contract that has features of

---

40   See Spitzer (1907) and Dewing (1914).
41   See the Lerner and Tufano (1994) for the case study "Aberlyn Capital Management: July 1993."

both debt and equity. Subsequently, VPPs were bundled with two swaps to engineer a structured investment resold to institutional investors seeking LIBOR-based funding.

A firm's life cycle may also be defined by its increasing geographic scope. A manufacturer that sells only in its home country may believe it has little exchange rate risk and therefore may choose to ignore its potential economic exposure. However, as the firm begins to buy and sell goods outside its home economy or to seek financing from overseas investors, it will generate increasingly obvious exchange rate exposure, and possibly decide to manage this exposure. Increasing currency exposure and cross-national investing can result in new securities, as described in the Goldman, Sachs & Co. Nikkei Put Warrant, and Walt Disney Co. Yen Financing cases.

Financial innovation seems to respond to the unique needs of firms as they move through predictable stages in their life cycles, with particular innovations directed at solving problems faced by young firms and by firms under financial stress.

VOLATILITY

Virtually every discussion of modern financial innovation holds that increased volatility in exchange rates, interest rates, and commodity prices has been a primary driver of innovation. For example, Smith, Smithson, and Wilford (1990. p. 13) document the increase in the volatility of interest rates, exchange rates, and commodity prices, and draw a link between this increase in riskiness and financial innovation:

> Uncertainty in the global financial environment has caused many economic problems and disruptions, but it has also provided the impetus for financial innovation. Through financial innovation, the financial intermediaries were soon able to offer their customers products to manage or even exploit the new risks. Through this same innovation, financial institutions became even better able to evaluate and manage their own asset and liability processes.

They list a variety of innovations spawned by increasing volatility: foreign exchange futures, swaps and options; interest-rate futures, swaps, options, and forwards; and commodity swaps, futures, and options. The cases detailing portfolio insurance and natural gas derivatives demonstrate how innovators responded to increased volatility by creating new securities.

The volatility of paper currencies or inflation rates also prompted earlier innovations. The period of World War I and its aftermath was characterized by high inflation uncertainty (Schwert [1989]). "Stabilized" (inflation-indexed) bonds, which were introduced in 1925 with an issue by Rand-Kardex, linked interest and principal payments to the wholesale price index (Masson and Stratton [1938, pp. 167–168]). This innovation, although apparently never popularized, was an explicit attempt to solve the problem of volatile prices (Fisher [1925]). The instability of currency values and exchange rates prompted innovations regarding the medium of payment for bonds (currency-choice bonds). "Legal tender" bonds gave "the *payor* ... the option of paying in any kind of legal tender (gold, silver, or currency); they give to him the benefit of the cheaper form of currency" (Cleveland [1920, p. 409]). Conversely, non-U.S. issuers, facing the problems of "disordered or unstable monetary systems...attempted to allay the fears of investors by various attempts to insure protection against depreciated currencies" (Masson and Stratton [1938, p. 173]). These innovations included indexing payments to exchange rates and permitting *investors* to choose the form of the interest payment (Masson and Stratton [1938, pp. 173–174]).[42] Stabilized and currency-choice bonds show that volatility motivated innovations in the 1830–1930 period, just as it spurs innovation today.

CHANGING DEMANDS AND INNOVATION

Predictable life-cycle factors and unpredictable shocks likely give rise to heightened demands for certain financial products. However, what is less clear is the mechanism by which they lead to innovation. Returning to the flood insurance example mentioned earlier in this chapter, a sudden desert flood may induce desert dwellers to revise their estimates of the probability and cost of future floods, and increase the amount they would pay for flood insurance. However, it is reasonable to expect that the *cost of producing* the insurance might rise as well, just as increase in the volatility of equity markets increases the demand for and the cost of manufacturing put options.[43] In order for an increase in volatility to spur innovation, the increase in the willingness of consumers to pay must exceed the new production costs plus distribution costs. Under what circumstances could this condition be met?

1. Increased volatility lowers marketing costs. Increased volatility makes potential buyers of the new product easier and cheaper to identify and educate, thus eliminating much of the wedge between production costs and consumers' willingness to pay.
2. Increased volatility increases the dispersion of beliefs and the potential for arbitrage. Intermediaries capitalize on these differences of opinion by temporarily

---

42 Rawls and Smithson (1989, p. 26) give the example of an 1863 bond issue by the Confederate States of America, which was denominated in French Francs and Pounds Sterling, and convertible into cotton.

43 The increase in volatility alone would not affect the cost of producing hedging contracts (forward, futures, and swap contracts.)

buying cheap and selling dear. In contrast, with little volatility, there may be only slight differences in valuation, so arbitrage opportunities may be scarce.[44]

3. The broadening of the potential market allows for more efficient production through economies of scale, easier diversification, lower transaction costs relative to households, or a larger base against which to justify large fixed cost investments. For example, suppose before and after the flood, the contribution (marginal revenue less marginal production cost) of each flood insurance policy is unchanged, at $.01 per policy. If entry into the flood insurance business required a $100 irreversible investment, intermediaries would not enter unless they expected to sell over 10,000 policies. After the flood, it may be possible to sell enough policies to justify the fixed investment of entry.

4. The increase in volatility is correlated with cessation of government actions that provided households with "costless" risk management. If a government stabilized its citizens' oil prices, then private efforts to sell oil-price-insurance contracts would fail, as the government's action places a zero shadow price on the private contracts. If the subsequent rise in oil price volatility results from deregulation, the zero shadow price for privately supplied risk management disappears, and the market can fill the now-unsatisfied need for risk management.

The interaction of costs and demand also can explain mechanisms by which life-cycle considerations give rise to innovation. At the simplest level, as early large-scale capital-intensive firms matured (e.g., the railroads in the early 1800s, the failed railroads in the late 1800s, and the industrial firms in the late 1800s), they put new pressures on the financial system spurring innovation. Later, as the financial system would have had experience with firms in all different stages, all of the necessary innovations may well have been created—had it not been for cost factors which prevented their initial creation. For example, suppose the investment needs of persons 100+ years old are quite unique, but historically the number of centenarians was so small that customizing products for them was infeasible due to high fixed costs. Medical advances that prolong life expectancy could swell their ranks, encouraging firms to tailor products to their needs. In a similar fashion, the aggregate demographics of firms could affect product innovation decisions as they influence the calculations of costs of delivering particular types of tailored securities.

---

44 A number of case studies deal with apparent arbitrages. For example, see the case studies RJR Nabisco Holdings Capital Corp-1991 and Arbitrage in the Government Bond Market?.

CHANGING DEMANDS: SUMMARY

While the financial system satisfies a relatively stable set of needs, the exact composition of these needs vary over time, both as households and firms progress through systematic life cycles, and as macroeconomic shocks, especially increases in volatility, suddenly increase demand for particular products and change the cost-benefit trade-off faced by the private sector.

INNOVATION, LEARNING, AND EXPERIMENTATION

One notion of innovation is that a shock occurs, and the market immediately and optimally responds with a new product. It is revealing that the word "innovation" is used by economists to mean both an exogenous shock and the response to the shock. The history of innovation confirms that this way of thinking is a useful starting point; changes in taxes, regulation, technologies, marketing costs, and volatilities have led, in relatively short order, to financial innovations. However, the long history of innovation suggests a richer and more dynamic or evolutionary story of innovation, learning, and experimentation. A shock or an unfilled need typically leads to a series of innovations, many of which prove to be unsuccessful. Three sets of examples—the evolution of income bonds, warrant contracts, and modern preferred stocks—demonstrate the point.

INCOME BONDS

In the late nineteenth century, income bonds were used to provide financing for financially distressed firms, especially railroads, and accounted for as much as 7% of all financing provided for these firms in the 1890s. Failure to pay interest due to an income bond holder was a condition of default only if the firm had sufficient accounting profits to pay the obligation. Income bonds are interesting securities in that they can enjoy tax advantages of debt without threatening financial distress. From their first use in 1848 through their near extinction in the early twentieth century, income bonds are a textbook case of how financial innovation is a process of learning and experimentation.

Virtually all of the earliest income bonds were noncumulative.[45] In any one period, the issuer was required to pay the income bondholders interest only if it had sufficient accounting earnings *in that period.* If in the next year the firm earned a great deal of money, the income bondholder could not recover the prior year's unpaid interest. In hindsight, the non-cumulative feature of income bonds allows firms to shift income to

---

45 Dewing (1934, p. 321) notes that of a sample of 27 income bonds issued prior to 1900, only two had cumulative features.

the detriment of the income bondholders.[46] Even if the income bonds had been cumulative, their holders could suffer from other accounting magic. If the income bond issuer could transform "capital investments" that were not expensed into "repairs" that were, it could harm its income bondholders. While these potential accounting abuses should have been immediately obvious to income bond buyers, it apparently took time, lawsuits, and losses to finally produce improved income bonds. For example, the Central of Georgia Railway failed to pay full interest to its income bondholders, who sued the firm in 1907 for "concealment of earnings." The court held that the railroad had concealed fully two-thirds of its earnings and ordered the firm to make full payment to its income bondholders.[47]

Ultimately, the market reworked the income bond contract to remedy obvious defects. Subsequent income bond offerings added cumulative features and carefully prescribed methods of computing earnings.[48] Recognizing shareholders' incentives to profit at their expense, later offerings included equity participation features that allowed income bondholders to recapture some of the value lost through accounting opportunism. Finally, some income bonds issued after 1925 went so far as to grant bondholders the same voting rights as common stockholders. Finally, income bonds became virtually extinct, being issued rarely in the past decades.[49] The history of income bonds seems to demonstrate how an innovation evolves—and sometimes dies—over time. The capital markets do not immediately arrive at optimal solutions, but they, like product markets, grope their way by experimenting and learning.

EARLY WARRANTS

The end of World War I brought with it renewed prosperity in the United States, a growing class of retail investors, and a general sense of optimism about the future of American business. In this environment, a number of securities were designed to sell investors the "upside" of American business, with perhaps the most interesting innovation being warrants.[50] Prior to 1925, only two U.S. firms had issued equity warrants, but by 1926, the

---

46   Suppose an issuer of a non-cumulative income bond owed income bond interest of $10 annually, and had true income of $10 annually. If it could shift its income stream to appear to alternate annually between years with $0 in income and $20 in income, it could cut its commitments to its income bondholders in half.

47   For details, see Dewing (1911).

48   See Dewing (1934).

49   See McConnell and Schlarbaum (1981) for an analysis of more "modern" income bonds.

50   Exchange-listed warrants were first sold in the United States in 1911 by American Light and Power (Dewing [1934, p. 399]). Exchange-listed stock options were first traded in the United States in 1973 by the Chicago Board Options Exchange, although commodity futures options were traded in the United States on the Chicago Board of Trade in the 1920s (Miller (1986)). Active stock options trading has been documented in seventeenth century Amsterdam by de la Vega (1688).

Magazine of Wall Street proclaimed "Bonds with Warrants—A New and Important Type of Security." The article listed 20 recent offerings with warrants and noted that in 1925, $80 million of bonds, or over 2% of all securities issued in that year, had attached warrants. These earliest warrants did not protect their holders against cash dividends, stock dividends, or stock splits. Even though the 1926 *Magazine of Wall Street* article warned investors about the dangers of firms costlessly splitting their shares and effectively making the warrants worthless, it would take further experience to teach the market this lesson.

MODERN PREFERRED STOCKS

Learning and experimentation characterize modern financial innovation as well, as shown by the case studies in this book of adjustable-rate and auction-rate preferred stock. Security designers in the early 1980s saw an opportunity to create a financing vehicle that would provide investors with a substitute for commercial paper, but which was structured as equity to enjoy intercorporate dividend exclusion. While tax rules at the time allowed corporate treasurers to pay almost no taxes on the dividends they received, cash managers would be interested in new equity cash management products only if they could be assured of virtually no potential principal losses.

The first solution was a product called adjustable-rate perpetual preferred stock (ARPPS). ARPPS paid a market rate of dividends, adjusted every 49 days (the minimum holding period to obtain favorable tax treatment for corporate investors.) In order to ensure than ARPPS had little loss of principal, their dividends were tied to fixed income indices. Unfortunately, the design neglected two problems: the credit of the issuer could deteriorate, or credit spreads in the market could widen. In either case, ARPPS could fall substantially in value. For example, in mid-1984, values of ARPPS fell well below par, and in the case of Continental Illinois, a troubled U.S. bank, fell to under 50% of par.

The failure of ARPPS to maintain stable principal values prompted the search for new solutions. Within months, Wall Street introduced convertible adjustable preferred shares, price-adjusted-rate preferred stock, auction-rate preferred stock, and remarketed preferred stock. Each attempted to solve the earlier products' flaws, occasionally introducing new wrinkles along the way. The most popular of these innovations involved setting a new dividend yield every 49 days through an auction process. However, auctions could fail—as one prominent example showed—leading to subsequent experimentation.

LEARNING AND EXPERIMENTATION: SUMMARY

Why is there so much learning and experimentation in financial innovation? At one level, new financial products are like other new products, whether software, automobiles, or children's toys. Designs may be poorly conceived, not considering every possible way in which the product could be abused or the conditions to which it could be subjected. Product designers may make conscious trade-offs (e.g., lower cost for less safety) that users may not appreciate. The raw materials may not be fully pre-tested and may fail. The implementation of a great product idea can be flawed in the manufacturing stage, with screws and bolts left on the assembly line.

One special feature of financial products can exacerbate failure. In advance, it may be optimal for two parties to contract, but after the fact, one party will likely regret its choice. What makes these regrets especially vexing is the fact that most financial innovations are incomplete contracts in the sense that the legal language cannot fully define all rights, or how those rights might ultimately be interpreted in a court of law. For example, for much of the early swap market, the legal rights of swap counterparties was quite unclear even though billions of dollars of swaps had been written. Given the incomplete nature of security contracts—especially new contracts—and the almost certainty of some regret, innovative financial contracts can produce gaming (as we saw of income bonds) or substantial redefinition sanctioned by the courts. For example, the earliest offering of PERCS, studied in two cases in this volume, stated that investors were entitled to put the instrument back to the issuer if the issuer paid dividends larger than a preset amount. The first PERCS issuer declared a dividend much larger than the one that would trigger the put feature, but made it payable seven months later, after the put feature had expired. The legal controversy surrounding this product shows the potential for firms to reinterpret key terms of incomplete contracts when it is to their benefit.

One final aspect of the financial system may affect the degree of learning and experimentation that we observe. Inventors of new drugs or technologies can protect their ideas by obtaining protection through patents. Even without patents, firms can enjoy some respite from competition if it takes rivals months or years to reverse engineer and produce competing products. In the financial system, new products receive virtually no patent protection.[51] Reverse-engineering is a rapid process and manufacturing a "knock-off" can be almost instant. It is hardly surprising that investment banking innovators are able to underwrite a median of only one deal before a competitor successfully underwrites a substitute product.[52]

In this super-charged competitive environment, competitors' innovations are quickly scrutinized by potential imitators, modified and branded to establish a new twist, and re-offered to clients. As imitators fix defects of recent offerings so as to differentiate their own

---

51 There have been a few isolated examples of firms patenting their financial innovations. See Petruzzi et al. (1988).

52 See Tufano (1989).

product, they speed up the product life cycle. The life cycle can be accelerated even further by regulatory response. New products that exploit tax or regulatory loopholes can disappear quickly as these are closed. For example, in the early 1980s, a short-lived product called Adjustable Rate Convertible Notes (ARCNs) created what looked like tax-deductible equity. After three issues, the Internal Revenue Service apparently saw through the economics of the product and disallowed new issuers from deducting interest paid on ARCNs.

SUMMARY

This chapter argues that even though the financial system delivers a stable set of functions, the historical persistence of financial innovation can be explained by (1) changing costs of producing and delivering financial products; (2) changing demands due to life cycle considerations and macro-economic shocks; and (3) the inherent character of financial innovations which produces extensive experimentation, learning, and evolution. This framework is useful if it allows us to comprehend financial innovation both today and a century ago. However, if it is to serve as more than an organizing device, it should assist us to understand future innovations, at least those not due to unpredictable exogenous forces, such as new tax, regulations, or accounting rules. It is worth noting however, that the current instability of these rules—especially with regard to derivatives—suggests more rather than less innovation may result.

While others might argue that the pace of innovation is likely to slow down relative to the 1980s,[53] cost considerations might lead the pace of innovation to quicken. Advances in pricing technologies, computing power, increased liquidity of financial markets, learning curve effects in financial engineering, and economies of scale in the production of derivatives will make it much cheaper to create a nearly infinite array of customized instruments. Furthermore, the increased use of derivatives and financial engineering has served to lower the costs of educating and identifying potential buyers and sellers.

Three forces may counteract the tendency toward increasing innovation. First, product proliferation may make it costly to sell new products. In a crowded market, it may be costly to distinguish your offering from your rivals', and rising marketing costs could inhibit some innovations.[54] Second, some recent innovations, especially futures and options on bonds, equities, and commodities, may stifle traditional innovation. As the capital markets provide issuers and investors with fundamental building-block contracts

---

53 For example, this has been Miller's prediction. See Miller (1986 and 1992).

54 Although if innovation were perceived as the method by which a firm could effectively distinguish itself, crowded markets could increase firms' desires to innovate.

that can be used to create customized solutions to problems such as risk management, there may be less demand for traditional securities innovation. For example, in the 1980s, oil-indexed notes were an innovative security that allowed investors to obtain exposure to changes in oil prices. With the development of both exchange-traded and OTC oil derivatives, future offerings of oil-linked securities may be unlikely as investors and issuers may be able to obtain more precise control over their exposures using derivatives.[55] Finally, well-publicized disasters could lead to a backlash against innovation. In 1987, portfolio insurance was made nearly extinct after being branded as having exacerbated the stock market crash. Six years later the press and regulators focused on a series of financial calamities brought about by apparently flawed derivative strategies of corporate users and investment managers. Major failures that discourage users from innovating may increase the cost of marketing and raise the cost of innovation. Failures that lead to strict regulation, but do not change fundamental demand, are more likely to force innovators underground or overseas, where they will deliver the needs demanded by their clients cloaked in forms acceptable to regulators.

---

55   The case studies of American Barrick Resources Corporation, Liability Management at General Motors, and SuperTrust show how individual firms and investment managers can use a wide range of derivative products to construct precise exposures.

APPENDIX

Appendix 1 Corporate Securities Innovations: 1830–1930

Innovation	Characteristic of Innovation	Early Use	Modern Analogue
Assessable Stock	Investor pays for stock over extended period of time. Investor has liability up to full subscription amount not yet paid.	Railroad issuers (1862?). (Dewing [1926, pp. 1020-1034]).	Partly paid Eurobonds, margin accounts
Management Stock	Certain shares, typically held by management, carry more votes than "ordinary" shares.	Goodyear (1921). (Keister [1922, p. 261]).	Supervoting shares
No-Par Stock Low-Par Stock.	The legal "par value" of common shares is zero or a small nominal amount	Popular after 1890. Popular after 1929. (Dewing [1934, pp. 93-96]).	In use today
"Emergency" Preferreds	Earliest preferred stocks. Popularized by distressed railroads. Had full voting rights, fixed dividends, exchangeable at option of issuer for common shares.	Chesapeake & Ohio Canal (1835). Popularized in 1840s. (Evans [1929]).	Mandatory convertible securities
Participating Preferred Founders Stock	In addition to fixed dividend, holder receives some portion of residual cash flow.	Chicago, Milwaukee, St. Paul Railroads, popular pre-1910. (Dewing [1934, pp. 182-193]).	Participating preferreds
Debenture Stock Interest Bearing Stock	Preferred stocks which paid holders "interest" instead of dividends. Different legal recourse for nonpayment.	Prior to 1910. (Adams [1910]).	Cf. to ARCN. (Adjustable Rate Convertible Note)
Convertible Preferred	Convertible into common stock at option of holder.	Lexington and West Cambridge Railroad (1851). (Evans [1931, p. 61]).	In use today
Guaranteed Stock Assumed Stock	In acquisition, target shareholders receive dividend paying shares, but effectively lose voting rights.	Prior to 1900. (1880s?) (Freidlander (1925) cited in Dewing [1934, pp. 138-146]).	Compare to debt for equity swaps

Appendix 1 Corporate Securities Innovations: 1830–1930 (Continued)

Innovation	Characteristic of Innovation	Early Use	Modern Analogue
Class A Common Stock	Nonvoting "stock" in which holders have no lien on corporate property and earn dividends at discretion of management.	After World War I (1919). (Dewing [1934, p. 196]).	Cf. to unbundled stock units
"Modern" Preferred	Gradual definition known today as preferred stock. Defined by: Cumulative dividends Contingent voting rights Sinking funds Call privileges Covenants No claims to residual cash	Evolved over time throughout 1850-1930. See Evans (1929, 1931) and Dewing (1934).	In use today
Forms of Secured Bonds	Early bonds were typically secured, with the form of the security determining the "type" of bond. Security included: Real estate Physical assets (railroad cars) Portfolio of securities.	Before 1830. See discussion in Cleveland (1907), Dewing (1934, Chs. 6-7).	In use today
Debentures	Unsecured debt obligations. Relatively late development.	Grew in popularity after 1900. (Robinson [1924] in Dewing [1934, p. 331]).	In use today
Assumed bonds Guaranteed bonds Joint bonds	Unsecured obligation issued in conjunction with purchases of firms. The acquirer takes responsibility for paying the indebtedness of the target.	Pre-1900. Used in railroad reorganizations. See Dewing (1934, Ch. 8).	In use today, cf. to change of control covenants.
Income Bonds Participating Bonds	Unsecured obligations with interest payable only when firm earns positive accounting earnings. Failure to pay due to zero accounting profits is not a condition of default.	Chesapeake & Ohio Canal (1848) (Dewing [1934, pp. 318-321]).	In use today, (rare).

Appendix 1 Corporate Securities Innovations: 1830–1930 (Continued)

Innovation	Characteristic of Innovation	Early Use	Modern Analogue
Very Long-Term Bonds	Bonds with maturities exceeding 40 years, typically issued by railroads and other firms involved in reorganizations.	Used in railroad reorganizations. 1850-1884. (Klingman [1925] in Dewing [1934, p. 228]).	Perpetuities: 100 year Disney Bond
Open Mortgages	Mortgage bonds that permit issuer to issue additional mortgages at the same level of seniority as open-ended instrument.	After 1901. (Dayton [1925], Richer [1930] in Dewing [1934, p. 219]; Dewing [1919, p. 26]).	In use today, "open-ended" mortgages
Fixed-Income Covenants	Restrictions on management actions. In addition to liens and security, later covenants included reporting requirements, prohibitions on asset use, and actions keyed to financial ratios, such as quick assets.	Evolved throughout period. See Rogers [1965], Dewing [1934, pp. 313-314], Draper [1930]).	In use today
Zero-Coupon Bonds	Bond that does not pay interest prior to maturity. Single payment of interest and principal at maturity.	Rio Blanco Syndicate (1911). (Hardy [1921, p. 250]).	Zero-coupon bonds
Stabilized Bonds	Interest and principal payments indexed to wholesale price index or value of a commodity bundle.	Rand-Kardex (1925). (Masson and Stratton [1938, p. 167]).	Commodity linked/indexed bonds
Currency Option Bonds	Issuer or investor chooses currency or specie for payment of interest and/or principal.	Union Pacific RR (1871). (Masson and Stratton [1938, pp.167-168]).	In use today
Baby Bonds Installment Plan	Bonds in denominations typically under $100 for sale to small investors.	Popularized in 1910s-1920s. (Riegel [1920]).	Bond mutual funds, margin accounts

Appendix 1 Corporate Securities Innovations: 1830–1930 (Continued)

Innovation	Characteristic of Innovation	Early Use	Modern Analogue
Convertible Bonds Extendable Bonds Exchangeable Bonds	Bonds convertible into common or preferred stock of the issuer. Extendable bonds are convertible into other bonds of the issuer. Exchangeable bonds are convertible into securities of a firm other than the issuer of the exchangeable bond.	Erie Railroad (1850s). (Dewing [1934, pp. 383-388]).	In use today
Warrants	Options to purchase a company's stock. Issued attached to bond but typically detachable.	American Light & Power (1911). (Dewing [1934, p. 399]).	In use today

RESOURCES

Adams, John Jr. (1910), "Stock and their Features—A Division and Classification," *Annals of the American Academy of Political and Social Sciences*, 35:525–543.

Baskin, J. B. (1988), "The Development of Corporate Financial Markets in Britain and the United States, 1600–1914: Overcoming Asymmetric Information," *Business History Review*, 62(Summer):199–237.

Beckstrom, R. (1986), "The development of the swap market" in Boris Antl, ed., *Swap Finance*, Euromoney Publications.

Black, F. and M. Scholes (1974), "From Theory to a New Financial Product," *Journal of Finance*, 29(2):399–412.

Bonbright, J. C. (1920), *Railroad Capitalization*, New York: Columbia University Studies in History, Economics and Public Law 95.

Bodie, Z. (1990), "Pension Funds and Financial Innovation," *Financial Management*, 19:11-22.

Campbell, E.G. (1938), *The Reorganization of the American Railroad System 1893-1900*, New York: Columbia University Press.

Carosso, V. (1970), *Investment Banking in America: A History*, Cambridge, MA: Harvard University Press.

Chandler, A.D. Jr. (1954), "Patterns of American Railroad Finance, 1830-1850," *Business History Review*, 28(September):248-263.

Chandler, A. D., Jr. (1956), *Henry Varnum Poor*, Cambridge, MA: Harvard University Press.

Chernow, R. (1990), *The House of Morgan*, Atlantic Monthly Press.

Cleveland, F. A. (1907), "Classification and Description of Bonds," *Annals of the American Academy of Political and Social Sciences*, 30:400–411.

Cleveland, F. A. and F. W. Powell (1912, 2nd ed.), *Railroad Finance*, New York: D. Appleton and Co.

Coopers & Lybrand (1990), *Guide to Financial Instruments*, Coopers & Lybrand.

de la Vega, J. (1688), *Confusion de Confusiones*. English translation by H. Kallenbenz, No. 13, The Kress Library Series of Publications, (Harvard University, 1957).

Dewing, A. S. (1911), "The Position of Income Bonds, as Illustrated by those of the Central and Georgia Railway," *Quarterly Journal of Economics*, 2:396–405.

———— (1914), *Corporate Promotions and Reorganizations*, Cambridge, MA: Harvard University Press.

———— (1919 [1st], 1926 [3rd], 1953 [5th]), *The Financial Policy of Corporations*, New York: Ronald Press.

——— (1934), *Study of Corporate Securities*, New York: Ronald Press. This volume references the following unpublished studies conducted at Harvard Business School:

Dayton, W. (1925), "OpenEnd Mortgages."

Donham, P. (1933), "Income Bonds."

Dow, J. K. (1926), "Class A Common Stock."

Friedlander, A. J. (1925), "Statistical Study of Industrial Bonds and Notes Between Jan. 1, 1914 and Jan. 1, 1924."

Gustaferri, J. (1930), "Class A Stock."

Hallahan, J. M. (1930), "Income Bonds."

Johnson, A. B. (1925), "The Rights and Limitations of Preferred Stockholders."

Klingman, J. C. (1925), "A Survey of Recent Refunding Operations of 50 American Railroads."

Potter, N. (1926), "Income Bonds."

Richer, J. (1930), "Analysis of Bonds 1925–1929."

Robinson, C. (1924), "Industrial Corporation Debenture Bonds."

Spaulding, P. W. (1930), "Convertible Bonds and Notes."

Summers, J. (1932, 1933), "Class A Common Stock."

Wilson, S. (1930), "Public Utility and Industrial Stocks with Preferences, 1925–1930."

Draper, C. (1930), "A Historical Introduction to the Corporate Mortgage," *Rocky Mountain Law Review*, 2:71–99.

Duncan, K. (1924), *Equipment Obligations*, New York: D. Appleton and Co.

Evans, G. H. Jr. (1929), "The Early History of Preferred Stock in the United States," *American Economic Review*, 43–58.

——— (1931), "Preferred Stock in the U. S. 1850–1878," *American Economic Review*, 56–62.

Fabozzi, F. and I. Pollack, eds. (1987), *Handbook of Fixed Income Securities*, Homewood IL: Dow Jones Irwin.

Finnerty, J. (1988), "Financial Engineering in Corporate Finance: An Overview," *Financial Management*, 17:14–33.

——— (1992), "An Overview of Corporate Securities Innovation," *Journal of Applied Corporate Finance*, (Winter):25-39.

Fisher, I. (1925), "The Stabilized Bond—A New Idea in Finance," *The Annalist*, (November 13, 1925).

Forsyth, D. (1964), *The Business Press in America: 1750–1865*, Philadelphia: Chilton Books.

Garbade, K. and W. Silber (1978), "Technology, communications and the performance of financial markets: 1840–1975," *Journal of Finance*, 33:819–832.

Graham, B. and D. Dodd (1934 [1st ed.]), *Security Analysis*, New York: Whittlesey House.

Greene, T. L. (1897, 1908 [3rd ed.]), *Corporate Finance*, New York: G. P. Putnam and Sons.

Hardy, C.O. (1921), "Some Recent Financial Devices," *Journal of Political Economy*, 29:249–251.

Hawkins, D. F. (1963), "The Development of Modern Financial Reporting Practices among American Manufacturing Corporations," in R. S. Tedlow and R. R. John, Jr. eds., *Managing Big Business*, Boston, MA: HBS Press, 1986.

Hornberger, D. J. (1933), "Accounting for No Par Stocks During the Depression," *Accounting Review*, (March).

Jovanovic, B. and G. MacDonald (1994), "The Life Cycle of a Competitive Industry," *Journal of Political Economy*, 102 (April): 322-347.

Kane, E. (1986), "Technology and the Regulation of Financial Markets," in A. Saunders and L. White, ed., *Technology and the Regulation of Financial Markets*, Lexington, MA: Lexington Books.

Keister, A. S. (1922), "Recent Tendencies in Corporation Finance," *Journal of Political Economy*, 30 (April):257–273.

Labar, G. (1922), "Bond Covenants and Foregone Opportunities: The Case of Burlington Northern Railroad Company," *Financial Management*, 21(2):71-77.

Lerner J. and P. Tufano. (1994), "Aberlyn Capital Management: July 1993," Harvard Graduate School of Business Case #N9-294-083, Boston, MA.

Logue, D., ed. (1994), *Handbook of Modern Finance*, Boston: Warren Gorham Lamont.

Masson, R. L and S.S. Stratton (1938), *Financial Instruments and Institutions: A Case Book*, New York: McGraw Hill Book Co.

McConnell, J. and G. Schlarbaum (1981), "Returns, Risks, and Pricing of Income Bonds, 1956-1976," *Journal of Business*, 54:33-63.

Meade, E.S. (1910), *Corporate Finance*, New York: D. Appleton.

Merton, R.C. (1990), *Continuous Time Finance*, Cambridge, MA: Basil Blackwell.

Merton, R.C. and Z. Bodie (1992), "On the Management of Financial Guarantees," *Financial Management*, (Winter):87-109.

Miller, M. (1986), "Financial Innovation: The Last Twenty Years and the Next," *Journal of Financial and Quantitative Analysis*, 21:459–471.

——— (1992), "Financial Innovation: Achievements and Prospects," *Journal of Applied Corporate Finance*, (Winter):4-11.

Moody, John (1910), "Preferred Stocks as Investments," *Annals of the American Academy of Political and Social Sciences*, 35 (May): 545–553.

Petruzzi, C. M. del Vale, and S. Godly (1988), "Patent and Copyright Protection for Innovations in Finance," *Financial Management*, 17:66-71.

Rawls, S. W., III, and C. W. Smithson (1989), "The Evolution of Risk Management Products," *Journal of Applied Corporate Finance*, 1(4):18-26.

Reed, R. and L. Washburn (1921), *Blue Sky Laws: Analysis and Text*, New York: Clark Boardman Co.

Riegel, R. (1920), "The Installment Plan and the Baby Bond," *Annals of the American Academy of Political and Social Sciences*, 88 (March):169–176.

Rogers, C. (1965), "The Corporate Trust Indenture Project," *The Business Lawyer*, (April):551–571.

Ross, S. (1989), "Institutional Markets, Financial Marketing and Financial Innovation," *Journal of Finance*, 44 (July):541–556.

Schwert, G. W. (1989), "Why Does Stock Market Volatility Change Over Time?" *Journal of Finance*, 44(5):1115-1154.

Sirri, E. and P. Tufano (1993), "Competition and Change in the Mutual Fund Industry," in Samuel L. Hayes, III, ed., *Financial Services: Perspectives and Challenges*, Boston, MA: Harvard Business School Press.

Smith C., C. Smithson, and D. Wilford (1990), *Managing Financial Risk*, New York: Harper Business.

Spitzer, L. (1907), "Industrial Bonds as an Investment," *Annals of the American Academy of Political and Social Sciences* 30 (September):182–191.

Stulz, R. and H. Johnson (1985), "An Analysis of Secured Debt," *Journal of Financial Economics*, 14:501–521.

Tufano, P. (1989), "Financial Innovation and First Mover Advantages," *Journal of Financial Economics* 25:213–240.

——— (1992), "Business Failure, Redefinition of Claims, and Financial Innovation: A Nineteenth Century Case Study," (unpublished manuscript).

——— (1993), "Financing Acquisitions in the Late 1980s: Sources and Form of Capital," in Margaret M. Blair, ed., *The Deal Decade*, Washington, D.C.: Brookings Institution.

Walmsley, J. (1988), *The New Financial Instruments*, New York: John Wiley & Sons.

PART ONE

FINANCIAL ENGINEERING AND DEBT
SECURITIES

ARBITRAGE FUNDAMENTALS

COUGARS

On November 17, 1983, Josephine Baker received a prospectus from A. G. Becker Paribas regarding an offering of COUGARs (Certificate on Government Receipts) (see Exhibit 1). Ms. Baker had worked for the fixed-income research department of Greenwich Mutual Funds for over a year, and while she had specialized in the U.S. government Treasury market, she had never seen this type of offering. As the U.S. government Treasury market was the largest and most vital segment of the U.S. debt markets, Ms. Baker was understandably dubious when the investment banks began touting these securities as revolutionary.

Greenwich Mutual Funds managed over $50 billion, of which $20 billion was invested in fixed-income securities. More particularly, a $3 billion fund was dedicated to investing in U.S. government securities. At this time, the U.S. Treasury had $1.4 trillion in obligations outstanding and had raised $161 billion in 1983 alone. Since her arrival at Greenwich, the mutual fund business had grown increasingly competitive, with many new entrants competing for funds, particularly in the government market. As a result of this fierce competition, every basis point ($\frac{1}{100}$th of a percent point) of yield was vital for the advertising campaigns that would attract additional funds from investors. This pressure forced managers in the government market to become more creative in their search for new instruments and tactics to garner additional yield.

In order to respond to the varied needs of their customers, a number of investment banks had created vehicles similar to the one created by A. G. Becker Paribas. In each of these vehicles, investment banks arranged for a custodian bank, in this case Manufacturers Hanover, to pass through the payments of interest and principal from an underlying U.S. Treasury bond to investors who chose the particular payments they were interested in receiving. Effectively, these investment banks were stripping the payment stream of an underlying bond and allowing investors to choose the combination of payments they were interested in. This stripping was accomplished by creating a pass-through trust where the investors in the trust were granted all the credit and tax benefits of actually owning U.S. Treasuries. In effect, these trusts exclusively held U.S. Treasuries as assets and

---

Mihir Desai wrote this case under the supervision of Scott P. Mason as the basis of class discussion.

issued liabilities that exactly corresponded to the payment stream they would receive on the U.S. Treasuries. Moreover, to avoid any reinvestment risk, the payment dates on the assets and liabilities of the trust were exactly the same.

In examining the COUGARs, Ms. Baker began her analysis by coupling the prospectus with quotes from the prior day's Treasury market trading (see Exhibit 2). She first considered the advantages and differences of these securities versus Treasuries of similar maturities. For example, she compared the COUGAR maturing on November 15, 1985, which had a yield to maturity of 10.85%, with the two Treasuries maturing on that date that had yield to maturities of approximately 10.50%. As the credit backing the COUGARs and the respective Treasuries was the same, she wondered why there was such a marked difference. She also considered how trading strategies using Treasuries in the market might duplicate the cash flows offered by the COUGARs. For example, would some combination of buying and selling existing Treasuries allow her to arrive at approximate prices for COUGARs?

Finally, Ms. Baker wondered why A. G. Becker Paribas had gone to so much trouble to structure these securities. She knew that they would be sure to extract their fees, but how? In particular, she considered the prices paid for the underlying Treasury bond assets and the sales price of the COUGARs. In addition to trying to understand Becker's motivation, Ms. Baker tried to determine which, if any, of the COUGARs might be priced attractively for her portfolio. She knew that in her search for extra yield, every basis point mattered.

Exhibit 1   Excerpts from Prospectus

$1,725,000,000 (Maximum)
Zero Coupon
Certificates on Government Receipts

Series 1
Coupon COUGARs Due Semiannually
May 15, 1984–November 15, 2003
Principal COUGARs Due November 15, 2003

Certificates on Government Receipts, Series 1 ("COUGARs") will evidence future ownership of future interest or principal payments on up to $300,000,000 United States Treasury 11⅞ Bonds due November 15, 2003 (the "Bonds") to be held by Manufacturers Hanover Trust Company, as Custodian, for the benefit of COUGAR owners.

Ownership of the interest payments due on the Bonds is being offered in the form of COUGARs with separate maturities (the Coupon COUGARs). The Coupon Cougars have 40 separate maturities, each falling on an interest payment date with respect to the Bonds, due semiannually from May 15, 1984, to November 15, 2003.

Ownership of the principal of the Bonds is being offered in the form of separate COUGARs (the principal COUGARs). The principal COUGARs mature on November 15, 2003.

The obligor with respect to the COUGARs is the United States of America.

There will not be any payments on COUGARs, and the COUGARs will not be redeemable prior to their maturities. The face amount of each COUGAR will be the payment to be received thereon.

The COUGARs are being offered at substantial discounts from their face amounts. A discussion of the U.S. tax treatment of COUGARs, including the implication of original issue discount, and a discussion of state and local taxation of COUGARs will be included in the Offering Circular under the heading "Income Tax Consequences."

Exhibit 1   Excerpts from Prospectus, Initial Offering Prices and Yields of COUGARs (Continued)

Maturities	Price as Percentage of Face Amount[a]	Yield to Maturity[b]
Coupon COUGARs		
May 15, 1984	95.866%	9.75%
Nov. 15, 1984	90.848	10.45
May 15, 1985	85.983	10.75
Nov. 15, 1985	81.447	10.85
May 15, 1986	76.279	11.40
Nov. 15, 1986	72.065	11.45
May 15, 1987	67.831	11.50
Nov. 15, 1987	64.112	11.60
May 15,1988	59.965	11.85
Nov. 15,1988	56.611	11.85
May 15,1989	53.171	11.95
Nov. 15,1989	50.173	11.95
May 15,1990	47.200	12.00
Nov. 15,1990	44.529	12.00
May 15,1991	41.861	12.05
Nov. 15,1991	39.482	12.05
May 15,1992	37.091	12.10
Nov. 15,1992	34.975	12.10
May 15,1993	32.833	12.15
Nov. 15,1993	30.952	12.15
May 15,1994	29.469	12.05
Nov. 15,1994	27.794	12.05
May 15,1995	26.356	12.00
Nov. 15,1995	24.865	12.00
May 15,1996	23.595	11.95
Nov. 15,1996	22.265	11.95
May 15,1997	21.143	11.90
Nov. 15,1997	19.956	11.90
May 15,1998	18.964	11.85
Nov. 15,1998	17.903	11.85

Exhibit 1 Excerpts from Prospectus, Initial Offering Prices and Yields of COUGARs (Continued)

Maturities	Price as Percentage of Face Amount	Yield to Maturity[a]
May 15,1999	17.025	11.80
Nov. 15,1999	16.077	11.80
May 15, 2000	15.300	11.75
Nov. 15, 2000	14.451	11.75
May 15, 2001	13.762	11.70
Nov. 15, 2001	13.001	11.70
May 15, 2002	12.283	11.70
Nov. 15, 2002	11.604	11.70
May 15, 2003	11.064	11.65
Nov. 15, 2003	10.455	11.65
Principal COUGARs		
Nov. 15, 2003	10.455%	11.65%

a. As of December 6, 1983.
b. Compounded on a semiannual basis.

Exhibit 2   Selected Treasury Quotes from Close of November 16, 1983

Maturity	Coupon	Ask Quote	Yield to Maturity
May 1984	9.25	100.01	9.18%
May 1984	13.25	101.30	9.12
May 1984	13.75	103.04	9.10
May 1984	15.75	102.08	9.33
Nov. 1984	9.88	100.02	9.80
Nov. 1984	14.38	104.13	9.61
Nov. 1984	16.00	105.29	9.62
May 1985	3.25	93.21	7.83
May 1975–1985	4.25	94.02	8.57
May 1985	9.88	99.16	10.23
May 1985	10.38	100.11	10.12
May 1985	14.13	105.11	10.17
May 1985	14.38	105.21	10.19
Nov. 1985	9.75	98.22	10.50
Nov. 1985	11.75	102.08	10.47
May 1986	7.88	94.04	10.62
May 1986	9.38	97.01	10.76
May 1986	13.75	106.12	10.77
Nov. 1986	6.13	90.30	9.69
Nov. 1986	11.00	100.07	10.91
Nov. 1986	13.88	107.11	10.93
Nov. 1986	16.13	112.31	10.93
May 1987	12.00	102.25	11.02
May 1987	14.00	108.00	11.17
Nov. 1987	7.63	89.17	10.93
Nov. 1987	12.63	104.10	11.26
May 1988	8.25	90.00	11.14
May 1988	9.88	95.06	11.27
Nov. 1988	8.75	90.25	11.21
Nov. 1988	11.75	101.15	11.35
May 1989	9.25	92.00	11.25
Nov. 1989	10.75	97.04	11.43
May 1990	8.25	86.25	11.16

Exhibit 2   Selected Treasury Quotes from Close of November 16, 1983 (Continued)

Maturity	Coupon	Ask Quote	Yield to Maturity
Nov. 1990	13.00	106.19	11.59
May 1991	14.50	113.28	11.67
Nov. 1991	14.25	113.00	11.70
May 1992	13.75	110.20	11.74
Nov. 1992	10.50	93.31	11.60
May 1993	10.13	92.00	11.53
Nov. 1993	8.63	82.28	11.56
Nov. 1993	11.75	100.13	11.68
May 1989–1994	4.13	91.18	5.18
Nov. 1994	10.13	91.12	11.53
May 1995	10.38	92.04	11.63
May 1995	12.63	105.23	11.71
Nov. 1995	11.50	99.00	11.66
May 1993-1998	7.00	69.24	11.29
Nov. 1998	3.50	91.31	4.23
May 1994-1999	8.50	77.22	11.64
May 2001	13.13	109.15	11.83
Nov. 2001	15.75	130.02	11.71
Nov. 2002	11.63	98.11	11.85
May 2003	10.75	91.25	11.83
Nov. 2003	11.88	99.28	11.89

THE U.S. GOVERNMENT DEBT MARKET AND THE STRUCTURE OF INTEREST RATES

The market for U.S. government debt is one of the largest single debt markets in the world as measured by total outstanding obligations or trading volume. In addition, U.S. government debt is considered to be of the highest credit quality, i.e., free of default risk, and as such serves as a pricing standard for many other debt instruments. For example, it is common practice for corporate bonds, Eurobonds, and mortgage-backed securities to be priced and traded in terms of the current prices and yields in the U.S. government debt market. Thus, understanding prices and yields in this debt market is a crucial first step to understanding prices and yields in a host of other debt markets.

The first objective of this note is to describe the most important types of U.S. government debt, i.e., Treasury bills, notes, and bonds, and the manner in which price and yield are expressed in these markets. The second objective is to explain how the structure of interest rates and yields in the U.S. government debt market are represented, and the practical uses of these representations by financial decision makers. Specifically, the note discusses yield curves, spot yield curves, strip yield curves, and forward rates, and how these different conventions are interrelated.

U.S. GOVERNMENT DEBT OBLIGATIONS

U.S. government debt obligations are classified as either marketable or nonmarketable, depending on the existence of a secondary market. Nonmarketable obligations include U.S. Savings Bonds, Retirement Plan Bonds, and other instruments subscribed to by foreign monetary authorities. Marketable obligations are by far the more important and include Treasury bills, Treasury notes, and Treasury bonds.

TREASURY BILLS

Treasury bills are noncoupon securities with original maturities of 13, 26, or 52 weeks. The Federal Reserve auctions the 13- and 26-week bills weekly and the 52-week bills every four

Scott P. Mason wrote this cases as the basis of class discussion.

Copyright © 1985 by the President and Fellows of Harvard College. Harvard Business School case 285-186.

weeks. Treasury bills are bought and sold on a bond discount yield basis. The price/yield calculation assumes there are 360 days in a year and relates the dollar price, P, of the bill to the maturity in days, D, and the percent discount, R, by

$$P = 100 - \frac{D}{360}\,R$$

Thus, a 68-day bill trading at an 8.7% discount yield would have a dollar price of

$$P = 100 - \frac{68}{360}\,8.70 = \$98.357$$

The true bond-equivalent yield, Y, of the bill priced at \$98.357 is

$$Y = \frac{(\text{Annualized interest})\,(100)}{\text{Price}}$$

$$= \frac{(365/68)\,(100 - 98.357)\,(100)}{98.357} = 8.97\%$$

and is always higher than the discount yield.[1] Exhibit 1 shows Treasury bill quotes as they are listed in *The Wall Street Journal*. See Appendix A for a summary of these and other common money market rate definitions.

TREASURY NOTES

Treasury notes are coupon securities with original maturities of 2–10 years. Interest payments are made semiannually. The price, P, of a note is related to its annual dollar coupon, C; the number of days to the next coupon, D; the number of days in the current coupon period, B; and annual yield, Y, by

---

1 For a bill with more than six months to maturity, the calculation of the bond-equivalent yield is a bit more involved. To be consistent with the semiannual payment pattern of bonds, the calculation assumes that the investor is paid interest at six months and that this interest compounds to maturity. In symbols, the price/bond-equivalent yield relation is

$$P + \frac{Y}{2}\,P + \frac{Y}{365}\left(D - \frac{365}{2}\right)\left(1 + \frac{Y}{2}\right)P = 1$$

Solving for Y,

$$Y = \frac{(-2D/365) + 2[(D/365)^2 - ((2D/365) - 1)(1 - 1/P)]^{1/2}}{(2D/365) - 1}$$

$$P = \frac{C/2}{(1+Y/2)^{D/B}} + \frac{C/2}{(1+Y/2)^{1+D/B}} + \cdots + \frac{C/2}{(1+Y/2)^{N-2+D/B}} + \frac{100+C/2}{(1+Y/2)^{N-1+D/B}}$$

where N is the number of remaining coupons. That is to say, price and yield are related by the convention of compounding an annual yield semiannually.[2] See Appendix B for a discussion of the sensitivity of bond price to changes in yield and the concepts of duration and convexity.

While P is the true economic value of the note, it is convention to quote the flat price, P'. The flat price is the true price, P, minus accrued interest. Accrued interest is simply the amount of interest the seller of the note has earned since the last interest payment date. The flat price is therefore related to the true price by

$$P' = P - \frac{C}{2}\left(\frac{B-D}{B}\right)$$

This correction is necessary since the new note owner will receive the entire next interest payment even though she will have held the note for less than the full coupon period.

TREASURY BONDS

Treasury bonds are coupon securities of greater than 10 years' maturity. From July 1978 to October 1980, 15-year bonds were sold at the beginning of each calendar quarter. Between January 1981 and December 1985, 20-year bonds were sold on the same schedule. Since April 1986 the Treasury has issued only 30-year bonds, typically on a quarterly basis. Those outstanding 30-year bonds that were issued before November 1984 are callable at par, plus accrued interest, in the last 5 years of their life.

The price and yield conventions for bonds are identical to those used for notes, with the exception of callable issues. It is sometimes the practice that if the price of a callable issue is above par, then the date to first call is used as the maturity date in the yield calculations. If the price is below par, then the stated maturity of the bond is used to calculate yield. Finally, there exists a class of bonds called flower bonds, which deserve special mention. These bonds, when owned by a decedent as part of his/her estate, can be redeemed at par plus accrued interest if applied to the payment of federal estate taxes. Consequently, these bonds trade at higher prices, i.e., lower yields, than other Treasury bonds. Exhibit 2

---

2   If a coupon instrument has less than six months to maturity, then the price/yield calculation is

$$P = \frac{1+C/2}{1+Y(D/2B)}$$

shows Treasury bond and note quotes as they are listed in *The Wall Street Journal*. The bonds with particularly low coupon rates and yields are flower bonds.

Since October 1984 both the coupon and principal payments associated with marketable Treasury obligations of greater than 10 years' maturity could be "stripped" and traded separately in book-entry form.[3] This is done under the STRIPS (Separate Trading of Registered Interest and Principal of Securities) program. The reconstitution of notes and bonds through the aggregation of their STRIPS components is also permitted. The price, P, of a STRIPS is related to its single promised payment, assumed here to be 100; the number of days to the next six-month period, D; the number of days in the current six-month period, B; and the annual yield, Y, by

$$P = \frac{100}{(1 + Y/2)^{N - 1 + D/B}}$$

where N is the number of six-month periods remaining in the life of the STRIPS. Exhibit 3 shows Treasury STRIPS quotes as listed in *The Wall Street Journal*.

THE STRUCTURE OF INTEREST RATES

YIELD CURVE

Financial decision makers are often interested in how the yields on U.S. government debt obligations vary with maturity. The most common representation of this relation is called the yield curve. To construct a sample yield curve, assume there are four bonds with price quotes of P_1, P_2, P_3, and P_4. Also, assume that the bonds have maturities of ½, 1, 1½, and 2 years, respectively.[4] Given each of the bonds' coupons, C_1, C_2, C_3, C_4, the price/yield on each bond is given by

$$P_1 = \frac{C_1/2 + 100}{1 + Y_1/2}$$

$$P_2 = \frac{C_2/2}{1 + Y_2/2} + \frac{C_2/2 + 100}{(1 + Y_2/2)^2}$$

---

3   Since August 1986 marketable Treasury notes and bonds have been issued in book-entry form only, that is, they exist as computer entries and not as paper securities. As of 1993, all Treasury bills and more than 90% of all Treasury notes and bonds were in book-entry form.

4   Therefore, there is no accrued interest.

$$P_3 = \frac{C_3/2}{1 + Y_3/2} + \frac{C_3/2}{(1 + Y_3/2)^2} + \frac{C_3/2 + 100}{(1 + Y_3/2)^3}$$

$$P_4 = \frac{C_4/2}{1 + Y_4/2} + \frac{C_4/2}{(1 + Y_4/2)^2} + \frac{C_4/2}{(1 + Y_4/2)^3} + \frac{C_4/2 + 100}{(1 + Y_4/2)^4}$$

To work through a specific example, consider the following data:[5]

$P_1 = 100.23$	$C_1 = 10.50$
$P_2 = 100.07a$	$C_2 = 10.00$
$P_3 = 98.10d$	$C_3 = 9.00$
$P_4 = 99.04$	$C_4 = 10.00$

Solving for the annualized yields on each bond,

$$Y_1 = 9.00\%, \quad Y_2 = 9.75\%, \quad Y_3 = 10.25\%, \quad Y_4 = 10.50\%$$

and plotting these yields against bond maturity (see Figure A), we obtain a yield curve representation of the structure of interest rates.[6]

Although yield curves are often used to represent the structure of interest rates, this is a somewhat misguided application. Recall the expression relating the price and the yield on a bond:

$$P = \frac{C/2}{(1+Y/2)^{D/B}} + \frac{C/2}{(1+Y/2)^{1+D/B}} + \cdots + \frac{C/2}{(1+Y/2)^{N-2+D/B}} + \frac{100 + C/2}{(1+Y/2)^{N-1+D/B}}$$

The yield, Y, is nothing but the internal rate of return consistent with the observed price, P, and the magnitude and timing of the payments. From this expression it is clear how, given the magnitude and timing of the payments, Y is simply another way of expressing P. The yield on a bond has little to do with any rate of interest that can actually be realized in the market. To see this, multiply both sides of the price/yield expression by

$$\left(\frac{1 + Y}{2}\right)^{N-1 + D/B}$$

---

5   An "a" or "d" indicates that 1/64 should be added to or subtracted from the stated price.
6   As an exercise, verify these yield-to-maturity calculations.

which gives

$$P\left(1+\frac{Y}{2}\right)^{N-1+D/B} = \frac{C}{2}\left(1+\frac{Y}{2}\right)^{N-1} + \frac{C}{2}\left(1+\frac{Y}{2}\right)^{N-2} + \ldots$$
$$\ldots + \frac{C}{2}\left(1+\frac{Y}{2}\right) + \left(100+\frac{C}{2}\right)$$

It then becomes clear that the only case in which an investor earns a rate of interest Y on her investment P is if all subsequent payments can be invested at the time of receipt at the rate Y for the remaining life of the bond. Therefore, it is unclear what inferences can be drawn from the yield curve concerning interest rates or investment opportunities.

Figure A   Yield Curve

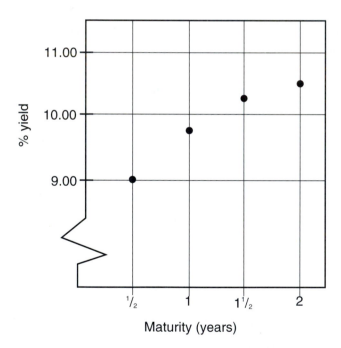

STRIP YIELD CURVE

Although they are often confounded, a yield curve is not the same as the structure of interest rates. The structure of interest rates actually corresponds to the strip yield curve, i.e., the schedule of yields associated with the STRIPS market (see Exhibit 3). The yields associated with the strip yield curve are the yields on debt obligations promising a single future payment, i.e., pure discount bonds or zero coupon bonds. Thus, an investor can actually earn a strip yield by holding a STRIPS to maturity.

Coupon bonds promise a number of different payments on a number of different future dates. In this sense, coupon bonds can be thought of as a bundle, or portfolio, of pure discount bonds. This suggests that there must be a pricing consistency between the coupon bond market and the STRIPS market. To see this, return to the earlier example and let the strip yield be designated by y. Consider the first bond, P_1, with maturity of $\frac{1}{2}$ year. Since this bond promises a single payment, 105.25, in $\frac{1}{2}$ year, it is in effect a pure discount bond. Therefore,

$$P_1 = \frac{C_1/2 + 100}{1 + y_1/2}$$

$$100.72 = \frac{5.25 + 100}{1 + y_1/2}$$

$$y_1 = \quad Y_1 = 9.00\%$$

The strip yield is the same as the standard yield. Now, consider the second bond, P_2, which promises payments in $\frac{1}{2}$ year and 1 year. This second bond can be decomposed into two discount bonds, one promising $C_2/2$ in $\frac{1}{2}$ year and the second promising $C_2/2 + 100$ in 1 year. Since the yield to be applied to the payment at $\frac{1}{2}$ year is known, y_1, it is straightforward to solve for y_2.

$$P_2 = \frac{C_2/2}{1 + y_1/2} + \frac{C_2/2 + 100}{(1 + y_2/2)^2}$$

$$100.23 = \frac{5}{1.045} + \frac{5 + 100}{(1 + y_2/2)^2}$$

$$y_2 = \quad 9.77\%$$

Continuing in the same manner with the third and fourth bonds,

$$P_3 = \frac{C_3/2}{1 + y_1/2} + \frac{C_3/2}{(1 + y_2/2)^2} + \frac{C_3/2 + 100}{(1 + y_3/2)^3}$$

$$98.30 = \frac{4.50}{1.045} + \frac{4.50}{(1.0489)^2} + \frac{4.50 + 100}{(1 + y_3/2)^3}$$

$$y_3 = 10.28\%$$

and

$$P_4 = \frac{C_4/2}{1 + y_1/2} + \frac{C_4/2}{(1 + y_2/2)^2} + \frac{C_4/2}{(1 + y_3/2)^3} + \frac{C_4/2 + 100}{(1 + y_4/2)^4}$$

$$99.125 = \frac{5}{1.045} + \frac{5}{(1.0489)^2} + \frac{5}{(1.0514)^3} + \frac{5 + 100}{(1 + y_4/2)^4}$$

$$y_4 = 10.54\%$$

In comparing yield to maturity, Y, to strip yield, y, the first thing to notice is that the difference between Y and y is small for short maturities but can increase with longer maturities:

Maturity (years)	½	1	1½	2
Y	9.00%	9.75%	10.25%	10.50%
y	9.00	9.77	10.28	10.54

Yield to maturity is actually a complex average of strip yields. Therefore, if the schedule of strip yields is rising (falling), then yield to maturity will also be rising but less than (falling but less than) the strip yield. Equivalently, the schedule of yields to maturity will have less slope (be flatter) than the schedule of strip yields.

Actually, the schedule of strip yields implied by the prices of coupon bonds, as in the preceding example, is called the *spot yield curve*. The explicit yields associated with the STRIPS market are referred to as the *strip yield curve*. In the absense of market imperfections, these two curves should be consistent. But in practice, these two representations of the structure of interest rates, i.e. the spot curve and the strip curve, may differ for a number of reasons including taxes, bid-ask spreads or non-market prices.

There are several formal theories of the term structure of interest rates, i.e., the strip yield curve. One form of the Expectations Hypothesis says that long rates are the average of today's short rate and future expected short rates. In other words this theory says that the current term structure of interest rates, i.e. the shape of the strip yield curve, is set by market participants' expectations of future short rates of interest. For example, this theory of the term structure would imply that

$$\left(1 + \frac{y_2}{2}\right)^2 = \left(1 + \frac{y_1}{2}\right)\left(1 + E\left(\frac{2y_1}{2}\right)\right)$$

$$1 + \frac{y_2}{2} = \left[\left(1 + \frac{y_1}{2}\right)\left(1 + E\left(\frac{2y_1}{2}\right)\right)\right]^{1/2}$$

where $E(\cdot)$ designates expectation and $_2y_1$ is the six-month strip yield six months from now. In other words, the Expectations Hypothesis says that the one-year strip yield, y_2, is the geometric average of the current six-month strip yield, y_1, and the expected six-month strip yield six months from now. The $1\frac{1}{2}$-year strip yield would then be

$$\left(1+\frac{y_3}{2}\right)^3 = \left(1+\frac{y_1}{2}\right)\left(1+E\left(\frac{2y_1}{2}\right)\right)\left(1+E\left(\frac{3y_1}{2}\right)\right)$$

$$1+\frac{y_3}{2} = \left[\left(1+\frac{y_1}{2}\right)\left(1+E\left(\frac{2y_1}{2}\right)\right)\left(1+E\left(\frac{3y_1}{2}\right)\right)\right]^{1/3}$$

which is the geometric average of today's six-month strip yield and the expected six-month strip yield in six months and in 1 year.

A second theory of the structure of interest rates often cited by practitioners is the Liquidity Premium Theory. This theory views investors as demanding a premium for holding longer-term bonds, i.e., long rates are higher than those suggested by the Expectations Hypothesis. The premium is necessary, according to this theory, since the principal of an investment in long bonds is viewed as being at risk should the investor liquidate prior to maturity.

FORWARD RATES

A third convention, in addition to yield curves and strip yield curves, used to represent the structure of interest rates is implicit forward rates. To understand the concept of implicit forward rates, consider investing in a 1-year discount bond. The strip yield curve gives the yield, y_2, associated with such an investment. From the earlier example, the price/yield of the discount bond would be

$$P = \frac{100}{(1 + y_2/2)^2}$$

Now consider an alternative way of investing the same moneys for 1 year: first buy a six-month bond, and six months later buy another six-month bond. What six-month yield must exist six months from now to make the two investment alternatives equivalent? The yield on the six-month bond today, y_1, is given by the strip yield curve. Therefore, the question is, for what forward, or future, six-month rate, f_2, is the following true?

$$P = \frac{100}{(1 + y_1/2)(1 + f_2/2)} = \frac{100}{(1 + y_2/2)^2}$$

This implies

$$\left(1+\frac{y_2}{2}\right)^2 = \left(1+\frac{y_1}{2}\right)\left(1+\frac{f_2}{2}\right)$$

$$\left(1+\frac{.0977}{2}\right)^2 = \left(1+\frac{.09}{2}\right)\left(1+\frac{f_2}{2}\right)$$

$$f_2 = 10.55\%$$

Therefore, if an investor were assured of a six-month rate, six months from now, of 10.55% he would be indifferent to buying a 1-year bond versus a series of six-month bonds. Said another way, when an investor buys a 1-year bond, it is as if he has "locked in" an implicit future, or forward, six-month interest rate. It is possible to calculate the forward rates further out. Given the earlier example, a 1½-year discount bond is represented as

$$P = \frac{100}{(1 + y_3/2)^3}$$

An alternative way to invest for 1½ years is to buy a 1-year bond now and buy a six-month bond 1 year from now. What future, or forward, six-month rate must exist 1 year from now to make these two alternatives equivalent?

$$P = \frac{100}{(1 + y_2/2)^2(1 + f_3/2)} = \frac{100}{(1 + y_3/2)^3}$$

$$\left(1+\frac{y_3}{2}\right)^3 = \left(1+\frac{y_2}{2}\right)^2\left(1+\frac{f_3}{2}\right)$$

$$\left(1+\frac{.1028}{2}\right)^3 = \left(1+\frac{.0977}{2}\right)^2\left(1+\frac{f_3}{2}\right)$$

$$f_3 = 11.30\%$$

Finally, the implicit six-month rate of interest 1½ years from now can be calculated as

$$P = \frac{100}{(1 + y_4/2)^4} = \frac{100}{(1 + y_3/2)^3(1 + f_4/2)}$$

$$\left(1+\frac{y_4}{2}\right)^4 = \left(1+\frac{y_3}{2}\right)^3\left(1+\frac{f_4}{2}\right)$$

$$\left(1 + \frac{.1054}{2}\right)^4 = \left(1 + \frac{.1028}{2}\right)^3 \left(1 + \frac{f_4}{2}\right)$$

$$f_4 = 11.32\%$$

Now comparing yields, strip yields, and implicit six-month forward rates, we obtain

Maturity (years)	½	1	1½	2
Y	9.00%	9.75%	10.25%	10.50%
y	9.00	9.77	10.28	10.54
f	10.55	11.30	11.32	–

It is evident that forward rates are substantially different from yields or strip yields. As can be seen from the preceding calculations, strip yields are actually geometric averages of the current short rate, y_1, and forward rates. Therefore, when forward rates are rising (falling), strip yields will also be rising (falling).

Often, implicit forward rates are referred to as expected future spot rates. This is correct if the Expectations Hypothesis is determining the strip yield curve. To demonstrate with a simple example, the Expectations Hypothesis says that the 1-year yield can be expressed as

$$\left(1 + \frac{y_2}{2}\right)^2 = \left(1 + \frac{y_1}{2}\right)\left(1 + E\left(\frac{2y_1}{2}\right)\right)$$

But comparing this to the expression for the six-month forward rate six months from now,

$$\left(1 + \frac{y_2}{2}\right)^2 = \left(1 + \frac{y_1}{2}\right)\left(1 + \frac{f_2}{2}\right)$$

demonstrates that

$$E(_2y_1) = f_2$$

However, if the Liquidity Premium Theory is a more accurate description of the strip yield curve, then the use of implicit forward rates as expectations of future spot rates is biased. Specifically, if the Liquidity Premium Theory says that long rates are higher than the geometric average of today's short rate and the expected future spot rates, then this will result in forward rates being upward-biased estimates of expected future spot rates.

APPENDIX A—MONEY MARKET RATE DEFINITIONS

(For securities with maturities of 6 months or less)

A.   For discount securities (T-bills, BAs, and commercial paper):

1. To determine the price P of a discounted security given discount rate R and a maturity in days D:

$$P = 100 - (D/360) \times R$$

2. To determine the true bond equivalent yield Y of a discount security given its price P and maturity in days D:

$$Y = \frac{(\text{Annualized Interest})}{P} \times 100$$

$$Y = \frac{(365/D) \times (100 - P)}{P} \times 100$$

3. To convert a discount rate R to a true bond equivalent yield Y for a given maturity D:

$$Y = \frac{365 \times R}{360 - \dfrac{(R \times D)}{100}}$$

4. To determine the 360-day money market yield of a discount security given its price P and maturity in days D:

$$M = \frac{(\text{Annualized interest})}{P} \times 100$$

$$M = \frac{(360/D) \times (100 - P)}{P} \times 100$$

5. To convert a discount rate R to a 360-day money market yield M for a given maturity D:

$$M = \frac{360 \times R}{360 - \dfrac{R \times D}{100}}$$

B. For securities using a 360-day money market yield accruing interest on a par price (CDs, Euronotes, and LIBOR):

1. To determine the accrued interest I for a holding period H, given a money market rate M and an original maturity in days D:

$$I = (H/D) \times M \times \text{Par}$$

2. To convert a money market yield M to a true bond equivalent yield Y:

$$Y = (365/360) \times M$$

Summary of Notation

(all rates in percent)

P = Price of discounted security

D = Days to maturity (≤ 180)

R = Discount rate expressed on 360-day basis

Y = True bond equivalent yield expressed on 365-day basis

I = Accrued interest on par priced money market securities

M = Money market yield expressed on 360-day basis

APPENDIX B—DURATION AND CONVEXITY

DURATION

With zero coupon bonds, the maturity is the "average life" of the bond, since the only cashflow occurs at the maturity of the bond. For coupon paying bonds, things are more complicated, as there is a stream of cashflows prior to maturity. The notion of *duration* extends the average life concept to coupon bonds. Suppose a bond with maturity T years consists of these semiannual cashflows through time

CF$_1$	CF$_2$........CF$_{2T}$	cashflow
½	1..........T	time in years

where CFx represents the Xth cashflow.

Then the duration of the bonds, measured in years, is defined as:

$$D = 1/P \left(\tfrac{1}{2} CF_1 / \left(1 + \frac{Y}{2} \right) + CF_2 / \left(1 + \frac{Y}{2} \right)^2 \ldots + T\, CF_{2T} / \left(1 + \frac{Y}{2} \right)^{2T} \right)$$

Or, using summation notation:

$$D = 1/P \sum_{t=1}^{2T} \frac{t}{2} CF_t / \left(1 + \frac{Y}{2} \right)^t$$

where P is the price of the bond, and Y is the bond's annual yield to maturity (i.e., its internal rate of return). Duration is just the weighted average time until receipt of cashflows, where the weights are the present values of the cashflows.

Table 1 calculates some sample values of duration, for bonds of varying maturities and coupons. All the bonds are assumed to be yielding 8%. The table makes a couple of points. First, for a given coupon rate, the duration of a bond increases with its maturity. Second, for bonds of a given maturity, those with the lower coupons have higher durations. The duration of a zero coupon is just its maturity, since all of the cashflow occurs at that time. The duration of a coupon paying bond is less than its maturity, since some of the cash is received before that date—"on average," the cash comes back prior to maturity.

This appendix based on unpublished teaching material developed by Jeremy Stein.

Table 1   Duration of Various Bonds[a]

Coupon Rate	5 years	10 years	15 years	20 years	25 years	30 years
0%	5	10	15	20	25	30
2%	4.74	8.76	11.88	14.03	15.28	15.81
4%	4.53	7.99	10.41	11.97	12.88	13.35
6%	4.36	7.45	9.55	10.92	11.79	12.32
8%	4.22	7.07	8.99	10.29	11.17	11.76
10%	4.10	6.77	8.60	9.87	10.77	11.41
12%	3.99	6.54	8.30	9.57	10.49	11.17

a. All bonds are assumed to be yielding 8%.

Duration is a useful concept because it allows us to generalize the idea that longer-lived bonds are more sensitive to rate changes than shorter-lived bonds. For a bond with initial price P, duration D, and yield to maturity Y, the following expression holds approximately for a small change in yield, ΔY:

$$\frac{\Delta P}{P} = -D \times \frac{\Delta Y}{1+Y}$$

Said another way, duration allows us to make a *linear* approximation to a bond's price-yield curve. Using duration, we can approximate bond price changes if we know yield changes, or yield changes if we know price changes. This is illustrated graphically in Figure 1, which shows a bond's price as a function of yield, as well as a duration approximation to the price about the point where yield equals 10%. The duration estimate is just the tangent to the price-yield curve at the point where yield equals 10%. This tangent has a slope of:

$$\Delta P / \Delta Y = -D \times P/(1 + Y)$$

At a yield of 10% (which corresponds to a price of 100), the bond in Figure 1 has a duration of 11 years. Hence the slope of the bond's price-yield profile $= -11 \times 100/(1.10) = (-1,000)$, i.e., if interest rates fall from 10% to 9%, the bond's price will rise by approximately $-1,000 \times (-.01) = 10$. A bond with a lesser duration will not appreciate by as much for a similar interest rate movement. For example, a bond with a duration of 5.5 that also starts out at a price of 100 and a yield of 10% will only rise to about 105 when its yield falls to 9%.

Figure 1   Price and Duration Estimate vs Yield

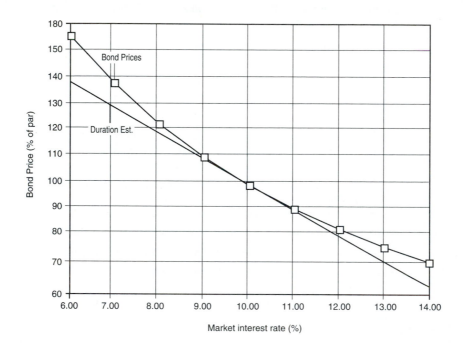

Since duration is a measure of the relative interest rate sensitivity of different bonds, it is useful in designing hedges. Suppose we have two bonds: a 30-year bond, and a 7-year bond, and we would like to hedge a long position in the 30-year by short selling the 7-year. What hedge ratio should we use? We want the hedging instrument's total dollar return, ΔP, to exactly offset that of the hedged instrument for a relatively small change in interest rates. For each 30 years, we would need to sell H 7 years, where we pick H to satisfy:

$$\Delta P_{30} = H \times \Delta P_7$$

If we make the assumption that yields on both bonds change by the same amount, $\Delta Y_{30} = \Delta Y_7$, (that is, the yield curve shifts in a parallel fashion) then the hedge ratio is simply:

$$H = \frac{P_{30}}{P_7} \times \frac{D_{30}}{D_7} \times \frac{(1 + Y_7)}{(1 + Y_{30})}$$

The above duration approach is widely used in computing hedge ratios. However, it has an obvious shortcoming—the yield curve does not always shift in parallel fashion. It is not true that ΔY_{30} always equals ΔY_7. To the extent that they differ, the hedge will not perform as desired.

It is also true that a duration-based hedge assumes that rates will only change a small amount. If rates did "jump" the curvature of the bond price-yield relationship (see Figure 1) would create problems for a duration-based hedge. This is where the concept of convexity comes in.

CONVEXITY

"Convexity" is a term that receives a lot of attention in fixed income analysis. As Figure 1 shows, duration only allows us to make a linear approximation to the price-yield profile of a given bond. In reality, the graph is somewhat curved.

If we use the duration concept to construct a hedge between two bonds, that hedge will be imperfect for large rate movements, *even* if the rates on both bonds change identically. This is because one bond may have a "curvier" price-yield profile than the other—it may be more convex.

Figure 2 illustrates a hypothetical hedge of a 10-year bond with a short position in 30 year bonds. Because the 30-year is more convex, the duration weighted 30-year position is "too large" relative to the 10-year position when rates fall, and "too small" when rates rise. Hence the hedge loses money for large rate movements in either direction. It is possible to design more sophisticated hedges that account for duration and convexity. Indeed, addressing the convexity issue is of crucial importance in dealing with bond options and other instruments that contain option features (e.g., mortgages and callable bonds), since their performance is extremely convex relative to yields. However, with non-callable bonds, convexity is not a problem of significant magnitude. Even when rates move several points, convexity considerations are quite small relative to the total price movements in the two instruments. This sort of error is likely to be dwarfed by unpredictable differentials in rate movements between the two bonds, which were assumed away in Figure 2. For example, it is possible that rates on 10-year bonds fall by 2%, while those on 30-year bonds fall by only 1.5%. This would more than offset any loss due to convexity.

Figure 2   Duration Weighted Hedge

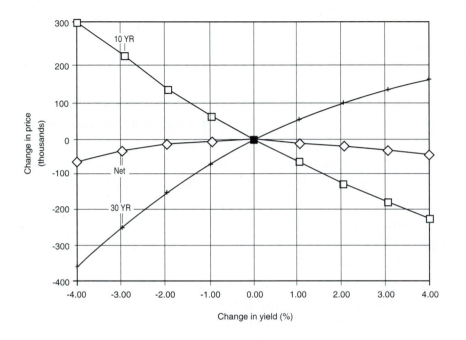

Exhibit 1   U.S. Treasury Bill Quotes, June 30, 1993

Maturity	Days to Maturity	Bid	Ask	Change	Yield
July 8, 1993	6	2.66	2.56	−.17	2.60
July 15	13	2.81	2.71	–	2.75
July 22	20	2.80	2.70	–	2.74
July 29	27	2.79	2.69	−.05	2.73
Aug. 5	34	2.84	2.80	−.04	2.85
Aug. 12	41	2.88	2.84	−.02	2.89
Aug. 19	48	2.91	2.87	−.03	2.92
Aug. 26	55	2.93	2.89	−.02	2.94
Sept. 2	62	2.98	2.96	–	3.02
Sept. 9	69	3.01	2.99	+.01	3.05
Sept. 16	76	3.02	3.00	+.01	3.06
Sept. 23	83	3.05	3.03	−.01	3.09
Sept. 30	90	3.03	3.01	–	3.07
Oct. 7	97	3.05	3.03	–	3.10
Oct. 14	104	3.06	3.04	−.01	3.11
Oct. 21	111	3.08	3.06	–	3.13
Oct. 28	118	3.05	3.03	–	3.10
Nov. 4	125	3.09	3.07	–	3.15
Nov. 12	133	3.10	3.08	−.01	3.16
Nov. 18	139	3.13	3.11	+.01	3.19
Nov. 26	147	3.13	3.11	–	3.19
Dec. 2	153	3.13	3.11	–	3.20
Dec. 9	160	3.14	3.12	–	3.21
Dec. 16	167	3.14	3.12	+.01	3.21
Dec. 23	174	3.14	3.12	−.01	3.21
Dec. 30	181	3.13	3.11	+.01	3.20
Jan. 13, 1994	195	3.16	3.14	−.02	3.24
Feb. 10	223	3.20	3.18	−.01	3.28
Mar. 10	251	3.22	3.20	−.02	3.30
Apr. 7	279	3.25	3.23	−.01	3.34
May 5	307	3.27	3.25	–	3.37
June 2	335	3.30	3.28	–	3.40
June 30	363	3.32	3.30	–	3.43

Source: *The Wall Street Journal,* July 1, 1993.
Note: The "Bid" and "Ask" prices are expressed on a discount basis. The "Change" column indicates the change in the bid price from the previous trading day. "Yield" is bond equivalent yield based on "Ask" price.

Exhibit 2   U.S. Treasury Bond and Note Quotes, June 30, 1993

Coupon Rate and Maturity	Bid	Ask	Change	Yield
7¼ July 93n	100:05	100:07	–	1.12
6⅞ July 93n	100:09	100:11	–	2.50
8 Aug. 93n	100:19	100:21	−2	2.51
8⅝ Aug. 93	100:21	100:23	−1	2.61
8¾ Aug. 93n	100:21	100:23	−1	2.73
11⅞ Aug. 93n	101:02	101:04	−1	2.48
6⅜ Aug. 93n	100:17	100:19	–	2.66
6⅛ Sept. 93n	100:23	100:25	–	2.88
8¼ Sept. 93n	101:08	101:10	–	2.82
7⅛ Oct. 93n	101:03	101:05	−1	3.01
6 Oct. 93n	100:28	100:30	–	3.09
7¾ Nov. 93n	101:20	101:22	−1	3.10
8⅝ Nov. 93	101:30	102:00	–	3.12
9 Nov. 93n	102:03	102:05	–	3.06
11¾ Nov. 93n	103:03	103:05	−1	3.07
5½ Nov. 93n	100:29	100:31	–	3.11
5 Dec. 93n	100:27	100:29	–	3.14
7⅝ Dec. 93n	102:04	102:06	–	3.13
7 Jan. 94n	101:30	102:00	–	3.21
4⅞ Jan. 94n	100:28	100:30	–	3.23
6⅞ Feb. 94n	102:04	102:06	–	3.29
8⅞ Feb. 94n	103:11	103:13	−1	3.30
9 Feb. 94	103:13	103:15	−1	3.32
5⅜ Feb. 94n	101:09	101:11	–	3.31
5¾ Mar. 94n	101:21	101:23	−1	3.40
8½ Mar. 94n	103:22	103:24	−1	3.37
7 Apr. 94n	102:23	102:25	–	3.39
5⅜ Apr. 94n	101:16	101:18	–	3.45
7 May 94n	102:30	103:00	−1	3.47
9½ May 94n	105:02	105:04	−1	3.47
13⅛ May 94n	108:08	108:10	−1	3.35
5⅛ May 94n	101:14	101:16	–	3.44
5 June 94n	101:13	101:15	–	3.48
8½ June 94n	104:26	104:28	–	3.47
8 July 94n	104:14	104:16	−1	3.54
4¼ July 94n	100:22	100:24	+1	3.54
6⅞ Aug. 94n	103:16	103:18	−2	3.61

Exhibit 2 U.S. Treasury Bond and Note Quotes, June 30, 1993 (Continued)

Coupon Rate and Maturity	Bid	Ask	Change	Yield
8⅝ Aug. 94n	105:13	105:15	−1	3.61
8¾ Aug. 94	105:18	105:22	−	3.54
12⅝ Aug. 94n	109:25	109:27	−1	3.60
4¼ Aug. 94n	100:21	100:23	−	3.61
4 Sept. 94n	100:12	100:14	−	3.64
8½ Sept. 94n	105:26	105:28	−	3.64
9½ Oct. 94n	107:05	107:07	−1	3.71
4¼ Oct. 94n	100:21	100:23	−	3.69
6 Nov. 94n	102:31	103:01	−	3.71
8¼ Nov. 94n	105:30	106:00	−	3.72
10⅛ Nov. 94	108:17	108:19	+1	3.64
11⅝ Nov. 94n	110:13	110:15	−1	3.72
4⅝ Nov. 94n	101:05	101:07	−1	3.73
4⅝ Dec. 94n	101:06	101:08	−	3.76
7⅝ Dec. 94n	105:16	105:18	−	3.76
8⅝ Jan. 95n	107:02	107:04	−	3.81
4¼ Jan. 95n	100:19	100:21	−	3.82
3 Feb. 95	99:21	100:21	−	2.58
5½ Feb. 95n	102:16	102:18	−1	3.86
7¾ Feb. 95n	106:00	106:02	−1	3.86
10½ Feb. 95	110:11	110:13	−	3.82
11¼ Feb 95n	111:16	111:18	−1	3.83
3⅞ Feb. 95n	99:31	100:01	−1	3.86
3⅞ Mar. 95n	99:30	100:00	−	3.88
8⅜ Apr. 95n	107:18	107:20	−1	3.92
3⅞ Apr. 95n	99:27	99:29	−	3.93
5⅞ May 95n	103:11	103:13	−1	3.97
8½ May 95n	108:02	108:04	−	3.95
10⅜ May 95	111:15	111:17	−	3.92
11¼ May 95n	113:02	113:04	−	3.91
12⅝ May 95	115:20	115:24	−	3.82
4⅛ May 95n	100:07	100:09	−	3.97
4⅛ June 95n	100:06	100:08	−	3.99
8⅞ July 95n	109:13	109:15	−	3.99
4⅝ Aug. 95n	101:04	101:06	+1	4.04
8½ Aug. 95n	108:29	108:31	−	4.05
10½ Aug. 95n	113:01	113:03	−1	4.00

Exhibit 2   U.S. Treasury Bond and Note Quotes, June 30, 1993 (Continued)

Coupon Rate and Maturity	Bid	Ask	Change	Yield
8⅝ Oct. 95n	109:24	109:26	–	4.09
5⅛ Nov. 95n	102:03	102:05	−1	4.16
8½ Nov. 95n	109:21	109:23	−1	4.15
9½ Nov. 95n	112:02	112:04	−1	4.08
11½ Nov. 95	116:16	116:20	−1	4.07
9¼ Jan. 96n	111:26	111:28	−3	4.26
7½ Jan. 96n	107:25	107:27	−1	4.26
4⅝ Feb. 96n	100:27	100:29	–	4.26
7⅞ Feb. 96n	108:24	108:26	−2	4.29
8⅞ Feb. 96n	111:08	111:10	−2	4.27
7½ Feb. 96n	107:29	107:31	−2	4.30
7¾ Mar. 96n	108:23	108:25	−1	4.33
9⅜ Apr. 96n	112:31	113:01	−2	4.36
7⅝ Apr. 96n	108:17	108:19	−2	4.36
4¼ May 96n	99:24	99:26	−1	4.32
7⅜ May 96n	107:29	107:31	−1	4.39
7⅝ May 96n	108:23	108:25	–	4.38
7⅞ June 96n	109:20	109:22	−1	4.39
7⅞ July 96n	109:19	109:21	−1	4.44
7⅞ July 96n	109:22	109:24	−1	4.45
7¼ Aug. 96n	108:00	108:02	−1	4.49
7 Sept. 96n	107:13	107:15	−1	4.50
8 Oct. 96n	110:13	110:15	−1	4.54
6⅞ Oct. 96n	107:02	107:04	−1	4.55
7¼ Nov. 96n	108:06	108:08	−2	4.58
6½ Nov. 96n	105:31	106:01	−1	4.57
6⅛ Dec. 96n	104:26	104:28	−2	4.60
8 Jan. 97n	110:25	110:27	−2	4.64
6¼ Jan. 97n	105:04	105:06	−2	4.66
6¾ Feb. 97n	106:27	106:29	−1	4.68
6⅞ Mar. 97n	107:11	107:13	−1	4.70
8½ Apr. 97n	112:29	112:31	−1	4.72
6⅞ Apr. 97n	107:12	107:14	−1	4.73
8½ May 97n	113:04	113:06	−1	4.73
6¾ May 97n	107:01	107:03	−2	4.74
6⅜ June 97n	105:27	105:29	−1	4.73
8½ July 97n	113:17	113:19	−1	4.76

Exhibit 2 U.S. Treasury Bond and Note Quotes, June 30, 1993 (Continued)

Coupon Rate and Maturity	Bid	Ask	Change	Yield
5½ July 97n	102:24	102:26	−1	4.73
8⅝ Aug. 97n	114:04	114:06	−1	4.79
5⅝ Aug. 97n	102:31	103:01	−2	4.81
5½ Sept. 97n	102:16	102:18	−2	4.83
8¾ Oct. 97n	114:28	114:30	−1	4.85
5¾ Oct. 97n	103:11	103:13	−3	4.87
8⅞ Nov. 97n	115:16	115:18	−2	4.88
6 Nov. 97n	104:09	104:11	−2	4.89
6 Dec. 97n	104:09	104:11	−1	4.91
7⅞ Jan. 98n	111:25	111:27	−2	4.93
5⅝ Jan. 98n	102:21	102:23	−2	4.95
8⅛ Feb. 98n	112:29	112:31	−1	4.95
5⅛ Feb. 98n	100:18	100:20	−2	4.97
5⅛ Mar 98n	100:16	100:18	−1	4.99
7⅞ Apr. 98n	112:03	112:05	−1	4.99
5⅛ Apr. 98n	100:13	100:15	−2	5.01
9 May 98n	117:02	117:04	−1	5.00
5⅜ May 98n	101:12	101:14	−1	5.04
5⅛ June 98n	100:10	100:12	−1	5.04
8¼ July 98n	113:30	114:00	−1	5.07
9¼ Aug. 98n	118:18	118:20	−1	5.08
7⅛ Oct. 98n	109:08	109:10	–	5.09
3½ Nov. 98	98:17	99:17	−2	3.60
8⅞ Nov. 98n	117:13	117:15	–	5.11
6⅜ Jan. 99n	105:22	105:24	−1	5.17
8⅞ Feb. 99n	117:24	117:26	−2	5.18
7 Apr. 99n	108:22	108:24	−2	5.23
8½ May 94-99	104:03	104:11	–	3.39
9⅛ May 99n	119:13	119:15	−3	5.23
6⅜ July 99n	105:18	105:20	−2	5.27
8 Aug. 99n	113:30	114:00	−3	5.29
6 Oct. 99n	103:15	103:17	−3	5.33
7⅞ Nov. 99n	113:19	113:21	–	5.32
6⅜ Jan. 00n	105:12	105:14	−3	5.38
7⅞ Feb. 95-00	105:20	105:24	−5	4.17
8½ Feb 00n	117:05	117:07	−4	5.38
5½ Apr. 00n	100:13	100:15	−3	5.42

Exhibit 2 U.S. Treasury Bond and Note Quotes, June 30, 1993 (Continued)

Coupon Rate and Maturity	Bid	Ask	Change	Yield
$8\frac{7}{8}$ May 00n	119:20	119:22	−2	5.41
$8\frac{3}{8}$ Aug. 95-00	108:08	108:12	+1	4.21
$8\frac{3}{4}$ Aug. 00n	119:05	119:07	−3	5.46
$8\frac{1}{2}$ Nov. 00n	117:31	118:01	−3	5.49
$7\frac{3}{4}$ Feb. 01n	113:18	113:20	−3	5.53
$11\frac{3}{4}$ Feb. 01	138:14	138:18	−1	5.49
8 May 01n	115:10	115:12	−2	5.56
$13\frac{1}{8}$ May 01	147:22	147:26	−3	5.55
$7\frac{7}{8}$ Aug. 01n	114:21	114:23	−1	5.60
8 Aug. 96-01	109:18	109:22	−4	4.63
$13\frac{3}{8}$ Aug. 01	150:09	150:13	−6	5.57
$7\frac{1}{2}$ Nov. 01n	112:07	112:09	−2	5.64
$15\frac{3}{4}$ Nov. 01	167:08	167:12	−	5.57
$14\frac{1}{4}$ Feb. 02	158:02	158:06	−1	5.64
$7\frac{1}{2}$ May 02n	112:10	112:12	−2	5.70
$6\frac{3}{8}$ Aug. 02n	104:10	104:12	−2	5.75
$11\frac{5}{8}$ Nov. 02	142:03	142:07	+1	5.74
$6\frac{1}{4}$ Feb. 03n	103:14	103:16	−2	5.77
$10\frac{3}{4}$ Feb. 03	136:08	136:12	−4	5.77
$10\frac{3}{4}$ May. 03	136:23	136:27	−3	5.80
$11\frac{1}{8}$ Aug. 03	140:01	140:05	−2	5.82
$11\frac{7}{8}$ Nov. 03	146:12	146:16	−2	5.84
$12\frac{3}{8}$ May 04	151:31	152:03	−3	5.84
$13\frac{3}{4}$ Aug. 04	164:00	164:04	−2	5.83
$11\frac{5}{8}$ Nov. 04	146:21	146:25	−2	5.92
$8\frac{1}{4}$ May 00-05	114:03	114:07	−1	5.72
12 May 05	150:27	150:31	−1	5.95
$10\frac{3}{4}$ Aug. 05	140:19	140:23	−	5.98
$9\frac{3}{8}$ Feb. 06	129:10	129:14	−3	6.01
$7\frac{5}{8}$ Feb. 02-07	110:30	111:02	−1	5.97
$7\frac{7}{8}$ Nov. 02-07	113:01	113:05	−2	6.02
$8\frac{3}{8}$ Aug. 03-08	117:10	117:14	−1	6.05
$8\frac{3}{4}$ Nov. 03-08	120:13	120:17	−3	6.06
$9\frac{1}{8}$ May 04-09	123:31	124:03	−2	6.07
$10\frac{3}{8}$ Nov. 04-09	134:26	134:30	−2	6.08
$11\frac{3}{4}$ Feb. 05-10	146:23	146:27	−2	6.07
10 May 05-10	132:24	132:28	−2	6.07

Exhibit 2 U.S. Treasury Bond and Note Quotes, June 30, 1993 (Continued)

Coupon Rate and Maturity	Bid	Ask	Change	Yield
12¾ Nov. 05-10	157:06	157:10	−4	6.09
13⅞ May 06-11	168:20	168:24	+1	6.09
14 Nov. 06-11	171:11	171:15	+2	6.10
10⅜ Nov. 07-12	138:04	138:08	−1	6.29
12 Aug. 08-13	154:28	155:00	−1	6.30
13¼ May 09-14	168:31	169:03	−1	6.30
12½ Aug. 09-14	161:19	161:23	−1	6.33
11¾ Nov. 09-14	154:08	154:12	−1	6.36
11¼ Feb. 15	153:07	153:09	−1	6.59
10⅝ Aug. 15	146:08	146:10	−2	6.61
9⅞ Nov. 15	137:16	137:18	−2	6.63
9¼ Feb. 16	130:06	130:08	−1	6.65
7¼ May 16	106:20	106:22	−1	6.68
7½ Nov. 16	109:16	109:18	−2	6.69
8¾ May 17	124:16	124:18	−1	6.68
8⅞ Aug. 17	126:01	126:03	−1	6.68
9⅛ May 18	129:09	129:11	−2	6.69
9 Nov. 18	127:30	128:00	−2	6.69
8⅞ Feb. 19	126:12	126:14	−2	6.70
8⅛ Aug. 19	117:05	117:07	−2	6.72
8½ Feb. 20	121:31	122:01	−2	6.71
8¾ May 20	125:07	125:09	−2	6.71
8¾ Aug. 20	125:08	125:10	−2	6.71
7⅞ Feb. 21	114:10	114:12	−1	6.72
8⅛ May 21	117:19	117:21	−2	6.72
8⅛ Aug. 21	117:19	117:21	−2	6.72
8 Nov. 21	116:06	116:08	−2	6.71
7¼ Aug. 22	106:06	106:30	−2	6.70
7⅝ Nov. 22	111:24	111:26	−2	6.70
7⅛ Feb. 23	105:23	105:25	−2	6.67

n = Original issue Treasury notes.
Source: The Wall Street Journal, July 1, 1993.
Note: A listing of two years (e.g., 1994–1999) in the "Maturity" column indicates a callable issue. The first year is the earliest year the bond is callable, and the second year is the maturity of the bond. The "Bid" and "Ask" prices, which are flat prices, are quoted as a percent of par, where the numbers to the right of the colons are 1/32s (e.g., a price of 98:22 is read as 98²²⁄₃₂ = 98.6875). The "Change" column shows the change in bid, expressed in 1/32s, from the previous trading day. The "Yield" column is the bond yield based on the ask price.

Exhibit 3 U.S. Treasury STRIPS Quotes, June 30, 1993

Maturity and Type		Bid	Ask	Change	Yield
Aug. 93	ci	99:19	99:20	–	3.22
Nov. 93	ci	98:26	98:26	–	3.25
Feb. 94	ci	97:31	97:31	–	3.32
May 94	ci	97:02	97:02	–	3.44
Aug. 94	ci	96:04	96:05	–	3.53
Nov. 94	ci	95:04	95:05	–	3.66
Nov. 94	np	95:02	95:03	–1	3.71
Feb. 95	ci	93:28	93:30	–	3.90
Feb. 95	np	93:31	94:00	–1	3.85
May 95	ci	93:00	93:01	–	3.90
May 95	np	92:28	92:30	–1	3.96
Aug. 95	ci	91:29	91:31	–1	3.99
Aug. 95	np	91:28	91:30	–1	4.00
Nov. 95	ci	90:21	90:23	–1	4.16
Nov. 95	np	90:25	90:27	–1	4.09
Feb. 96	ci	89:11	89:14	–1	4.31
Feb. 96	np	89:11	89:14	–1	4.31
May 96	ci	88:02	88:04	–2	4.45
May 96	np	88:03	88:05	–2	4.44
Aug. 96	ci	86:24	86:26	–2	4.58
Nov. 96	ci	85:15	85:17	–2	4.69
Nov. 96	np	85:20	85:23	–2	4.63
Feb. 97	ci	84:13	84:16	–1	4.71
May 97	ci	83:04	83:07	–1	4.81
May 97	np	83:04	83:07	–1	4.81
Aug. 97	ci	82:01	82:04	–1	4.84
Aug. 97	np	81:31	82:02	–1	4.86
Nov. 97	ci	80:20	80:24	–1	4.96
Nov. 97	np	80:21	80:25	–1	4.95
Feb. 98	ci	79:22	79:25	–	4.95
Feb. 98	np	79:11	79:15	–1	5.04
May 98	ci	78:05	78:08	–1	5.10
May 98	np	78:06	78:10	–1	5.09
Aug. 98	ci	76:26	76:30	+8	5.19
Aug. 98	np	76:24	76:27	–5	5.21
Nov. 98	ci	75:21	75:24	+8	5.24
Nov. 98	np	75:23	75:27	–1	5.22
Feb. 99	ci	74:15	74:19	–4	5.28

Exhibit 3 U.S. Treasury STRIPS Quotes, June 30, 1993 (Continued)

Maturity and Type		Bid	Ask	Change	Yield
Feb. 99	np	74:17	74:21	−1	5.27
May 99	ci	73:13	73:17	−1	5.31
May 99	np	73:10	73:14	−1	5.33
Aug. 99	ci	72:05	72:10	−1	5.37
Aug. 99	np	72:03	72:07	−1	5.39
Nov. 99	ci	70:31	71:03	−1	5.43
Nov. 99	np	71:07	71:11	−	5.37
Feb. 00	ci	69:20	69:25	−1	5.51
Feb. 00	np	69:10	69:15	−1	5.58
May 00	ci	68:11	68:15	−1	5.59
May 00	np	67:25	67:30	−1	5.71
Aug. 00	ci	67:09	67:14	−1	5.61
Aug. 00	np	66:27	66:31	−1	5.71
Nov. 00	ci	66:06	66:10	−1	5.65
Nov. 00	np	65:24	65:29	−1	5.74
Feb. 01	ci	64:29	65:02	−1	5.72
Feb. 01	np	64:22	64:26	−1	5.77
May 01	ci	63:21	63:26	−1	5.79
May 01	np	63:20	63:25	−1	5.80
Aug. 01	ci	62:13	62:18	+2	5.86
Aug. 01	np	62:19	62:24	−1	5.82
Nov. 01	ci	61:15	61:20	+2	5.87
Nov. 01	np	61:20	61:25	−1	5.84
Feb. 02	ci	59:29	60:02	−1	6.00
May 02	ci	58:25	58:30	−1	6.05
May 02	np	59:26	59:31	−1	5.85
Aug. 02	ci	57:26	57:31	−1	6.07
Aug. 02	np	58:28	59:02	−1	5.86
Nov. 02	ci	56:30	57:03	−1	6.07
Feb. 03	ci	56:01	56:06	−1	6.08
Feb. 03	np	56:28	57:01	−1	5.92
May 03	ci	54:27	55:00	−1	6.15
Aug. 03	ci	53:29	54:02	−1	6.17
Nov. 03	ci	53:00	53:05	−1	6.19
Feb. 04	ci	52:00	52:06	−	6.22
May 04	ci	51:04	51:09	−	6.24
Aug. 04	ci	50:09	50:14	−	6.25
Nov. 04	ci	49:08	49:13	−	6.30

Exhibit 3 U.S. Treasury STRIPS Quotes, June 30, 1993 (Continued)

Maturity and Type		Bid	Ask	Change	Yield
Nov. 04	bp	49:18	49:23	−1	6.24
Feb. 05	ci	48:13	48:18	−	6.31
May 05	ci	47:11	47:16	−	6.37
May 05	bp	47:27	48:00	−	6.28
Aug. 05	ci	46:14	46:19	−	6.40
Aug. 05	bp	46:28	47:01	−2	6.32
Nov. 05	ci	45:23	45:28	−	6.40
Feb. 06	ci	44:00	44:05	−1	6.58
Feb. 06	bp	45:26	46:00	−2	6.25
May 06	ci	43:03	43:08	−1	6.62
Aug. 06	ci	42:05	42:10	−1	6.66
Nov. 06	ci	41:10	41:15	−1	6.69
Feb. 07	ci	40:27	41:00	−1	6.65
May 07	ci	40:04	40:10	−1	6.66
Aug. 07	ci	39:14	39:19	−1	6.67
Nov. 07	ci	38:25	38:30	−1	6.67
Feb. 08	ci	37:11	37:16	−1	6.82
May 08	ci	36:22	36:27	−1	6.83
Aug. 08	ci	36:00	36:05	−1	6.84
Nov. 08	ci	35:11	35:16	−1	6.85
Feb. 09	ci	34:19	34:24	−1	6.88
May 09	ci	33:23	33:28	−1	6.94
Aug. 09	ci	32:30	33:03	−1	6.98
Nov. 09	ci	32:12	32:17	−1	6.98
Nov. 09	bp	32:08	32:13	−1	7.00
Feb. 10	ci	31:21	31:26	−1	7.01
May 10	ci	31:01	31:05	−1	7.03
Aug. 10	ci	30:14	30:19	−1	7.04
Nov. 10	ci	29:28	30:00	−1	7.05
Feb. 11	ci	29:19	29:24	−1	7.00
May 11	ci	29:01	29:06	−1	7.01
Aug. 11	ci	28:09	28:14	−1	7.06
Nov. 11	ci	27:21	27:26	−1	7.09
Feb. 12	ci	27:02	27:07	−1	7.11
May 12	ci	26:18	26:23	−1	7.12
Aug. 12	ci	26:03	26:08	−1	7.12
Nov. 12	ci	25:25	25:30	−1	7.09
Feb. 13	ci	25:06	25:11	−1	7.12

Exhibit 3   U.S. Treasury STRIPS Quotes, June 30, 1993 (Continued)

Maturity and Type	Bid	Ask	Change	Yield
May 13 ci	24:24	24:29	−1	7.12
Aug. 13 ci	24:09	24:13	−1	7.13
Nov. 13 ci	23:27	24:00	−1	7.13
Feb. 14 ci	23:07	23:11	−1	7.18
May 14 ci	22:20	22:24	−1	7.22
Aug. 14 ci	22:07	22:11	−1	7.22
Nov. 14 ci	21:28	22:00	−1	7.21
Feb. 15 ci	21:13	21:17	−1	7.23
Feb. 15 bp	21:18	21:23	−1	7.19
May 15 ci	21:01	21:05	−1	7.23
Aug. 15 ci	20:21	20:25	−1	7.23
Aug. 15 bp	20:22	20:26	−1	7.22
Nov. 15 ci	20:10	20:15	−1	7.22
Nov. 15 bp	20:10	20:15	−1	7.22
Feb. 16 ci	20:02	20:06	−1	7.20
Feb. 16 bp	20:00	20:04	−1	7.21
May 16 ci	19:21	19:25	−1	7.21
May 16 bp	20:02	20:06	−1	7.12
Aug. 16 ci	19:10	19:14	−1	7.21
Nov. 16 ci	19:00	19:05	−1	7.20
Nov. 16 bp	19:05	19:09	−1	7.17
Feb. 17 ci	18:18	18:22	−1	7.23
May 17 ci	18:07	18:11	−1	7.23
May 17 bp	18:07	18:11	−1	7.23
Aug. 17 ci	17:29	18:01	−1	7.23
Aug. 17 bp	17:27	17:31	−1	7.24
Nov. 17 ci	17:19	17:23	−1	7.23
Feb. 18 ci	17:11	17:15	−1	7.21
May 18 ci	17:02	17:06	−1	7.21
May 18 bp	17:00	17:04	−1	7.22
Aug. 18 ci	16:24	16:28	−1	7.21
Nov. 18 ci	16:15	16:18	−1	7.21
Nov. 18 bp	16:13	16:17	−1	7.22
Feb. 19 ci	16:06	16:10	−1	7.20
Feb. 19 bp	16:06	16:10	−1	7.20
May 19 ci	15:31	16:03	−1	7.19
Aug. 19 ci	15:23	15:27	−1	7.18
Aug. 19 bp	15:20	15:24	−1	7.20

Exhibit 3 U.S. Treasury STRIPS Quotes, June 30, 1993 (Continued)

Maturity and Type		Bid	Ask	Change	Yield
Nov. 19	ci	15:14	15:18	−1	7.18
Feb. 20	ci	15:04	15:08	−1	7.19
Feb. 20	bp	15:04	15:08	−1	7.19
May 20	ci	14:28	14:31	−1	7.19
May 20	bp	14:24	14:28	−1	7.22
Aug. 20	ci	14:19	14:23	−1	7.19
Aug. 20	bp	14:19	14:23	−1	7.19
Nov. 20	ci	14:14	14:17	−1	7.17
Feb. 21	ci	14:05	14:09	−1	7.17
Feb. 21	bp	14:08	14:12	−5	7.15
May 21	ci	13:30	14:01	−1	7.17
May 21	bp	14:01	14:05	−5	7.14
Aug. 21	ci	13:22	13:25	−1	7.17
Aug. 21	bp	13:25	13:29	−5	7.14
Nov. 21	ci	13:14	13:18	−1	7.17
Nov. 21	bp	13:22	13:26	−1	7.10
Feb. 22	ci	13:22	13:26	−1	7.04
May 22	ci	13:16	13:19	−1	7.03
Aug. 22	ci	13:09	13:13	−1	7.02
Aug. 22	bp	13:15	13:19	−5	6.97
Nov. 22	ci	13:03	13:07	−1	7.01
Nov. 22	bp	13:09	13:13	−1	6.96
Feb. 23	ci	13:23	13:27	−1	6.79
Feb. 23	bp	13:09	13:13	−1	6.90

Source: The Wall Street Journal, July 1, 1993.
Note: The "Type" column indicates the origin of the STRIPS: coupon interest (ci), note principal (np), or coupon bond principal (bp). The "Bid" and "Ask" prices are expressed as a percentage of par, where the numbers to the right of the colons are 1/32s. The "Change" column indicates the change in the bid in 1/32s from the previous trading day. The "Yield" column shows the semiannual yield computed using the ask price.

RJR NABISCO HOLDINGS CAPITAL CORPORATION — 1991

On January 15, 1991, Valerie Samuels, who analyzed and traded high-yield bonds for the firm of Mercer and Associates, noticed what she thought were discrepancies in the prices of certain bonds issued in conjunction with the leveraged buyout of RJR Nabisco in 1989. If her suspicions were correct, the prices of the bonds were out of line with one another, at least temporarily, and Mercer and its clients might be able to capitalize on these discrepancies.

Mercer and Associates was a money management firm founded in 1975 that specialized in making fixed-income (bond) investments. As of 1991, the firm managed approximately $2 billion in client assets. Mercer managed the fixed-income portions of corporations' pension plans, academic institutions' endowments, and wealthy individuals' private portfolios. Its clients typically made asset allocation decisions by which they first divided their wealth among broad classes of investments (e.g., equities, government securities, corporate bonds, international equities). Mercer then competed with other money management firms that sought to invest the portion of client portfolios earmarked for fixed-income securities.

In evaluating and compensating money managers, clients examined various measures of their historical risk-adjusted performance. Therefore, if Ms. Samuels could find a way to achieve higher returns on her clients' bond portfolios without any increase in the riskiness of their portfolios, her firm could gain and retain accounts. The RJR Nabisco bonds that had caught her attention offered an opportunity to make Mercer's clients, and indirectly Mercer and Associates, better off.

Peter Tufano wrote this case as the basis for class discussion rather than to illustrate either effective or ineffective handling of an administrative situation.

This case study describes the situation analyzed in the paper, "The Relative Pricing of High-Yield Debt: The Case of RJR Nabisco Holdings Capital Corporation," by Robert M. Dammon, Kenneth B. Dunn, and Chester S. Spatt published in the *American Economic Review*, 83 (December 1993) pp 1090-1111. We thank the authors of that paper for their permission to use the material in this case study.

BACKGROUND[1]

The firm known in 1991 as RJR Nabisco was a descendant of the tobacco firm R. J. Reynolds, founded in 1875. Through acquisitions in the 1960s, the tobacco firm entered a variety of food businesses, including beverages, prepared foods, and baking supplies. In 1979 it acquired Del Monte, a producer and marketer of canned goods and fresh fruits. In 1985 the firm acquired Nabisco Brands, which sold a variety of branded consumer food products, including Oreo and Fig Newton cookies. After its 1985 merger, the firm was renamed RJR Nabisco.

In the late 1980s the food products industry experienced massive consolidation through mergers: for example, in 1988, Grand Metropolitan PLC attempted to take over Pillsbury, and Philip Morris bid for Kraft. In this period, RJR Nabisco was also the center of a massive control contest. In 1988 two main bidders proposed to take the firm private in a leveraged buyout contest: the Management Group (RJR Nabisco president and chief executive officer, F. Ross Johnson, along with other RJR executives and the investment banking firm of Shearson Lehman Hutton) and Kohlberg, Kravis, Roberts & Co. (KKR), a firm specializing in leveraged buyouts.

At the end of a bidding war, KKR prevailed by offering shareholders $81 per share in cash plus a package of bonds valued at $28. The day before the first announcement of a possible takeover for RJR Nabisco, its stock had traded at $77.25. Thus, KKR offered common shareholders a 41% premium over the firm's pre-takeover value. To finance the buyout, KKR increased RJR's debt from $5 billion to $29 billion.

The new firm was structured as a series of holding companies, as shown in Exhibit 1. RJR Nabisco, Inc., the operating company, was owned by RJR Nabisco Holdings Capital Corporation, which itself was a subsidiary of RJR Nabisco Holdings Group, Inc., which ultimately was a subsidiary of RJR Nabisco Holdings Corporation. As Exhibit 1 shows, each of these related entities had separate obligations, issued either in conjunction with the acquisition or, in the case of RJR Nabisco, Inc, the operating company, carried over from the taken-over firm.

THREE RJR BONDS

Ms. Samuels closely followed three particular RJR Nabisco bonds. All three had been issued by RJR Nabisco Holdings Capital Corporation on May 12, 1989, in public underwritings led by Drexel Burnham Lambert and Merrill Lynch Capital Markets. The bonds

1   The material in this section is extracted from two Harvard Business School cases. See "RJR Nabisco," HBS 289-056, for background on the events leading up to the leveraged buyout (LBO) of the firm in 1988. See "RJR Nabisco—1990," in this book, for information on the firm's post-LBO refinancing activities.

were issued to raise funds to repay a portion of interim financing used to finance the 1988 acquisition. To quickly consummate large takeovers, acquirers often obtained large amounts of short-term financing with the expectation that these short-term borrowings would be eliminated within a short period of time through the issuance of longer-term borrowings or by the sale of assets. In the acquisition of RJR Nabisco, KKR obtained $5 billion in interim financing structured in the form of increasing rate notes (IRNs) placed privately with large institutions by Drexel Burnham Lambert. The increasing rate notes paid interest in cash, with the interest rate increasing each month. The longer the notes were outstanding, the higher the interest rate paid by the borrower, giving the borrower a strong incentive to quickly repay these obligations. As of May 1989 the average interest rate on RJR Nabisco's increasing rate notes was 15%, but this rate would increase each month until the notes were repaid.

The three bonds whose proceeds were used to pay off the increasing rate notes—the 13.5% subordinated debentures, the 15% payment-in-kind subordinated debentures, and the subordinated discount debentures—had many similarities. All three debentures were issued on May 15, 1989, by the same legal entity, RJR Nabisco Holdings Capital Corporation. All three matured in 12 years, on May 15, 2001. The three bonds were ranked *pari passu* relative to one another; this means that in the event of bankruptcy or default the claims have equal priority. The bonds also had similar sinking fund requirements, optional prepayment rights, and put options in the event of changes in control. At issue, the three bonds were each rated B1 by Moody's and B+ by Standard & Poor's.[2,3] Exhibit 2 lists key features common to each of the three bonds, and Exhibit 3 provides their optional prepayment schedules. While they shared many characteristics, the three bonds offered very different cash flows to investors.

---

2   Both of these represent noninvestment-grade, or junk, bonds, two full rating classes below investment-grade offerings. As of January 15, 1991, the three issues had been downgraded slightly: Moody's rated the bonds B2 (slightly less than B1), and Standard & Poor's had downgraded them from B+ to B.

3   Yields (expressed on a bond-equivalent basis) for different long-term obligations were as follows:

	5/15/89	1/15/91
Intermediate (6–9 years) Treasury bonds	9.25%	7.83%
Long-term (over 10 years) Treasury bonds	9.27	8.37
Long-term corporate bonds rated		
AAA	9.75	9.01
AA	10.10	9.47
A	10.52	9.81
BBB	10.88	10.75
BB	12.12	12.58
B	13.21	18.95

Source: Standard & Poor's Statistical Service.

The 13.5% subordinated debentures (the 13.5%s) paid interest in cash semi-annually. Thus, the holder of each $1,000 (face value) 13.5% subordinated debentures bond received $67.50 in cash interest payments every six months until the bonds were either redeemed or put back to the company as described in Exhibit 2. On the day of their issue, the subordinated debentures were offered to investors at par, or $1,000 per bond. A total of $525 million (face value) of these debentures were issued on May 12, 1989.

The 15% pay-in-kind subordinated debentures (the PIKs) had an interest rate of 15% per annum. Through May 15, 1994, the company could choose to pay the interest on the PIK bonds either in cash or in additional identical PIK subordinated debentures. For example, on November 15, 1989 (the first semi-annual interest payment date), the company owed the holder of one $1,000 (face value) PIK bond $75.00 in interest. RJR Nabisco Holdings Capital Corporation could pay this interest in cash or deliver to the holder additional bonds with face value of $75 and with terms identical to the original PIK bonds.[4] After May 15, 1994, the company was required to pay interest on the PIK bonds *in cash* at each semi-annual payment date. On May 12, 1989, at issue, the PIK bonds were offered to investors at par, or $1,000 per bond. A total of $1 billion (face value) of the PIK debentures were issued.

Unlike the 13.5% subordinated debentures and the 15% PIK subordinated debentures, the subordinated discount debentures (the Discount Debs), were offered to investors at a substantial discount. Specifically, investors paid $486.56 per bond. The bond paid no interest through May 15, 1994. However, between their issuance and May 15, 1994, the bond's principal amount would increase (or accrete) so that the bondholder's principal amount increased over time. Exhibit 4 shows the accreted value of a discount debenture prior to May 15, 1994. For federal taxes, additions to accreted value each year would be treated as taxable interest income to the holder. As of May 15, 1994, the discount debentures would have fully accreted to $1,000 per bond, and at that point the discount debentures would begin to earn and pay interest (in cash) at the rate of 15% per year, payable semi-annually. Thus, the holder of one discount debenture received semi-annual cash interest payments of $75 beginning November 15, 1994. A total of 4,110,489.97 discount debentures were sold on May 12, 1989, at $486.56 per debenture, for a total of $2 billion in gross proceeds.

---

4   Each of these "baby bonds" issued to pay the company's interest would mature in 2001, have a 15% rate of interest, rank *pari passu* with the other obligations, give the company the right to pay in cash or in kind through May 15, 1994, etc. As a practical matter, the company's agreement with its senior lenders prohibited the firm from paying interest in cash on the PIK bonds through May 15, 1994. However, this agreement could be renegotiated.

AN OPPORTUNITY: JANUARY 15, 1991

The period from late 1989 through early 1991 was a tumultuous one in the high-yield, or junk, bond market.[5] One observer described the $200 billion junk bond market as "a fragmented, inefficient market that has got to slog along for a while as the dealers rebuild."[6] The year 1989 saw 14 major companies default on $3.4 billion in junk bonds. The bankruptcies of junk-bond financed firms, including Southland, Resorts International, Braniff Inc., and Integrated Resources, appeared prominently in the news. Defaults appeared to scare off potential junk bond buyers and froze many deals in progress. During the fall of 1989, Congress acted to restrict the buying and selling of junk bonds by savings and loan institutions, which sparked fears that these depository institutions would dump their holdings and further depress the market. Perhaps most important, the investment banking firm of Drexel Burnham Lambert, which had been the major underwriter and trader in junk bonds, filed for liquidation on February 14, 1990, following the indictment of Michael Milken, who had built up the firm's high-yield business.

The problems in the junk bond market persisted into early 1991. The upset state of the market was evidenced by the scarcity of new issues of junk bonds. Exhibit 5 shows that the number of new issues of noninvestment-grade bonds dropped sharply in 1990, even though the issuance of investment-grade bonds did not. In total, only 10 issues of nonconvertible junk bonds were issued in the 13 months from January 1990 through January 1991. Earlier, that many bonds had been issued *per month* in all but the slowest months.

It was in this environment that Ms. Samuels noticed that the prices of two RJR Nabisco Holdings Capital bonds appeared to be out of line—at the very least, out of line with one another. Specifically, the difference between the discount debentures and the current pay 13.5% subordinated debentures appeared odd. By combining discount RJR bonds plus a combination of zero coupon obligations of the U.S. Treasury (STRIPs), Ms. Samuels could create "synthetic" 13.5% bonds that were superior to the current pay 13.5% RJR subordinated debentures in virtually all regards.[7] It should cost her more to create these superior synthetic 13.5% bonds than to buy the actual 13.5% RJR bonds. While this "no-arbitrage" condition was almost always satisfied, it appeared that it failed to hold on this particular day in January 1991. If her analysis was correct, she had to act quickly to capture

---

5   Bonds with the lowest credit ratings (less than BBB as rated by Standard & Poor's or Baa as rated by Moody's) were called noninvestment-grade, high-yield, or junk, bonds.

6   Leah J. Nathans, "The Junk Market's Black Hole," *Business Week*, November 27, 1989, p. 156.

7   A treasury STRIP is a zero coupon bond whose single payment is backed by the full faith and credit of the U.S. federal government. For example, a May 2001 Treasury STRIP is a security that will pay $100 in May 2001 but will make no cash payments prior to that date. As expected, Treasury STRIPs sell for considerably less than their par, or face value.

the pricing discrepancies on her clients' behalf. She began to review her clients' portfolios to determine which of her clients owned the 13.5% debentures, and she called around to various bond traders to find out if she could buy, sell, and short-sell the various bonds.[8]

Exhibit 6 gives capital markets data as of January 15, 1991.

---

8   In short-selling, a party borrows a security, sells it, and then is obligated to return the borrowed security at a later time. The party that borrows the security must promptly deliver all cash payments due to the borrowed security to the lender of the security, i.e., must pay any interest or dividends as and when they are due. Short-sellers typically pay a small fee for the privilege of being allowed to borrow the security. If the lender of the security must deliver the security to the issuer, for example, if it were redeemed, the borrower must return the security to the lender at that time.

Exhibit 1   Selected Obligations of RJR Holdings Corporation and Related Companies, December 1990

Dollar amounts given for indebtedness represent either principal amount for coupon-paying instruments or original issue price plus accrued interest for original issue discount obligations.

RJR Nabisco Holdings Corporation

Senior converting debentures, due 2009. PIK through 1993; convertible into common shares ($351 million)

Convertible preferred stock, 11.5% dividends, convertible into common shares

ESOP convertible preferred stock, convertible into common shares

Common shares (78.8% owned by KKR)

RJR Nabisco Holdings Group, Inc. (wholly owned by RJR Nabisco Holdings Corporation)

17% subordinated exchange debentures, due 2007. PIK through 1995 ($2,864 million)

RJR Nabisco Holdings Capital Corporation (wholly owned by RJR Nabisco Holdings Group, Inc.)

10.5% senior notes, due 1998 ($1,500 million)

13.5% subordinated debentures, due 2001 ($525 million)[a]

Subordinated extendible reset debentures, due 1991 ($225 million)

15% subordinated debentures, PIK through 1994, due 2001 ($1,160 million)[a]

Subordinated discount debentures, due 2001 ($2,371 million)[a]

Subordinated floating-rate obligations, due 1999 ($250 million)

Assorted bank debt ($5,464 million)

Partnership debt securities ($427 million)

RJR Nabisco, Inc. (wholly owned by RJR Nabisco Holdings Capital Corporation)

Pre-buyout debt with various maturities:

Cash-interest-paying ($4,450 million)

Zero coupon ($312 million)

PIK debentures ($3,531 million)

Source: *Moody's Industrial Manual*, 1991.
a. RJR Holdings Capital Corporation debenture that Ms. Samuels is considering.

Exhibit 2   Common Terms of the Three RJR Holdings Capital Debentures (13.5% Debentures, Discount Debentures, and 15% Pay-in-Kind Debentures)

Issuer:	RJR Holdings Capital Corporation
Issue Date:	May 15, 1989.
Maturity:	May 15, 2001.
Optional Redemption:	The bonds may be redeemed, in whole or in part, at the option of the company, at any time on or after May 15, 1994, or, in the event of a change in control, at any time after such change in control, in each case at the redemption prices set forth herein [see Exhibit 3] plus accrued and unpaid interest, if any, to the date of redemption.
Mandatory Redemption:	Equal sinking fund payments on May 15, 1999, and May 15, 2000, are calculated to retire, prior to maturity, an aggregate of 50% of the bonds issued. The company therefore will redeem at par 25% of the bonds issued on May 15, 1999, and 25% on May 15, 2000.[a]
Put Option Upon Change in Control:	If a change in control occurs, each holder shall have the right to require the company to repurchase such holder's bonds at 101% of the principal amount thereof plus accrued and unpaid interest, if any, to the date of purchase.
Ranking:	The bonds will be subordinated in right of payment to all senior indebtedness, which will include the company's obligations under the credit agreement, the working capital facility, and the first subordinated increasing rate notes. The three securities will rank *pari passu* with each other.[b]
Guarantee and Security:	The payment of principal and interest are guaranteed, jointly and severally, on a subordinated basis, by each of Holdings, Group and RJR (the operating company.) RJR's guarantee is limited to 90% of its net worth.
Covenants:	The indentures limit the ability of the company and its subsidiaries to incur indebtedness, pay dividends, transfer assets among subsidiaries, engage in transactions with stockholders and affiliates, create liens, engage in mergers and consolidations, engage in sales of assets and subsidiary stock, and make investments in unrestricted subsidiaries.
Listing:	The securities have been authorized for listing on the New York Stock Exchange. [As of January 15, 1991, all three were listed on the NYSE.]

Source: RJR Holdings Capital Corporation, prospectuses.
a. RJR can choose to satisfy the sinking fund requirement either by buying the necessary quantity of bonds on the open market or by redeeming bonds at par.
b. Securities ranked *pari passu* relative to one another have equal priorities in the event of bankruptcy.

Exhibit 3   Redemption Prices for the Three RJR Holdings Capital Debentures as a Percentage of Face
Value or Accreted Value

Year Ending May 14	13.5% Subordinated Debentures	15% PIKs and Discount Debentures
1990[a]	113.50%	115.00%
1991[a]	112.15	113.50
1992[a]	110.80	112.00
1993[a]	109.45	110.50
1994[a]	108.10	109.00
1995	106.75	107.50
1996	105.40	106.00
1997	104.05	104.50
1998	102.70	103.00
1999	101.35	101.50
5/15/99 and after	100.00	100.00

Source: RJR Holdings Capital Corporation, prospectus.
a. Until May 15, 1994, RJR Nabisco may only redeem the debentures in the event of a change in control. On or after that date, the company may redeem any or all of the debentures at the prices listed.

Exhibit 4   Schedule of Accreted Value of a Discount Debenture

	Accreted Value (per $1,000 Principal Amount)		
May 22, 1989	$ 486.56	May 15, 1992	$ 748.80
November 15, 1989	$ 521.58	November 15, 1992	$ 804.96
May 15, 1990	$ 560.70	May 15, 1993	$ 865.33
November 15, 1990	$ 602.75	November 15, 1993	$ 930.23
May 15, 1991	$ 647.96	May 15, 1994 and after	$1000.00
November 15, 1991	$ 696.56		

Source: RJR Holdings Capital Corporation, prospectus.
Note: For a discount debenture the accreted value represents the principal amount owed the debenture holder by the issuer at each point in time. For tax purposes, the addition to accreted value for any period represents interest income to the holder and interest expense to the issuer of the bond.

Exhibit 5   Number of Investment-Grade and Noninvestment-Grade Nonconvertible Corporate Bond
Offerings, 1985–1991

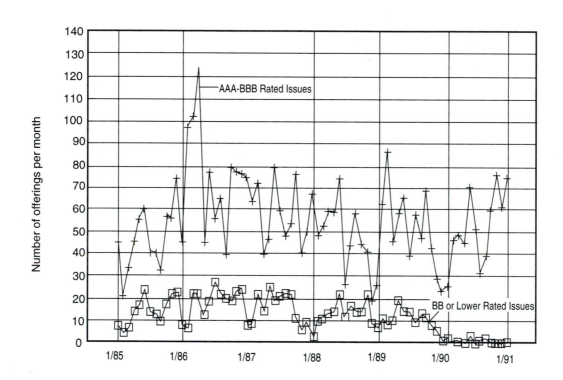

Source: Data complied from Securities Data Corporation.

Exhibit 6   Prices of the RJR Holdings Capital Debentures and Other Capital Markets Data, January 15, 1991

Treasury STRIPS Prices					
Maturity Date	Ask	Bid	Maturity Date	Ask	Bid
February 15, 1991	$99.53	$99.50	May 15,	64.50	64.16
May 15	97.94	97.91	August 15	63.22	62.88
August 15	94.81	94.72	November 15	61.59	61.22
November 15	93.06	92.94	February 15, 1997	60.28	59.91
February 15, 1992	91.50	91.38	May 15	59.00	58.63
May 15	89.81	89.63	August 15	57.81	57.44
August 15	88.28	88.09	November 15	56.38	56.00
November 15	86.31	86.13	February 15, 1998	55.13	54.75
February 15, 1993	84.69	84.44	May 15	53.94	53.56
May 15	83.03	82.78	August 15	52.91	52.50
August 15	81.81	81.56	November 15	51.59	51.19
November 15	79.72	79.47	February 15, 1999	50.50	50.13
February 15, 1994	78.13	77.88	May 15	49.44	49.03
May 15	76.56	76.28	August 15	48.28	48.00
August 15	75.19	74.88	November 15	47.31	46.91
November 15	73.34	73.03	February 15, 2000	46.34	45.91
February 15, 1995	71.91	71.56	May 15	45.41	45.00
May 15	70.44	70.09	August 15	44.72	44.28
August 15	69.28	68.94	November 15	43.38	42.97
November 15	67.31	67.00	February 15, 2001	42.44	42.03
February 15, 1996	$65.91	$65.56	May 15	41.56	41.16

Quoted Prices for RJR Nabisco Subordinated Debentures, January 15, 1991				
	Volume Traded	Ask Quote	Bid Quote	Closing Quote
Debentures 13.5%, due May 2001[b]	607	$99.00	$98.25	$98.75
Debentures 15% PIK, due May 2001	2,938	77.88	76.88	76.88
Discount debentures, due May 2001	3,274	49.13	47.88	48.38

Source: IDD Tradeline.
a. These prices reflect the current prices for U.S. government obligations that pay $100 on the date indicated, with no cash payments prior to that date. Treasury STRIPS (Separate Trading of Registered Interest and Principal of Security) are zero coupon obligations of the U.S. Treasury.
b. The 13.5% subordinated debentures are coupon-paying instruments. By bond market conventions, these quotations reflect "flat quotes," i.e., they do not include the payment by the buyer of accrued interest to the seller, reflecting the fact that the seller is compensated for the interest the instrument earned while the seller owned it. On January 15, 1991, a buyer of the 13.5% subordinated debentures would pay the quoted flat price plus accrued interest from November 15, 1990 (the last coupon payment date). This accrued interest payment would be equal to approximately $2.25 = (2 months/6 months) x (13.5%/2 x 100). Thus, a buyer of the 13.5% debentures on January 15, 1991, would pay $99.00 + $2.25 = $101.25 per $100 face value of bond for the 13.5% debentures. In contrast, quotations for the Treasury STRIPS, the PIK debentures, and the discount debentures reflect the full payment a buyer would make. Thus, on January 15, 1991, a buyer of a discount debenture would pay a total of $49.13 to purchase the discount debenture, or $491.30 per bond. All bond price quotations are expressed as a percentage of face value.

ARBITRAGE IN THE GOVERNMENT BOND MARKET?[1]

On January 7, 1991, Samantha Thompson, who analyzed and traded government bonds for the firm of Mercer and Associates, noticed what she thought were major discrepancies in the prices of a number of long-maturity U.S. Treasury bonds. These apparent discrepancies might permit Mercer and its clients to substitute superior bonds for existing holdings, and pocket a positive pricing difference as well. Her firm could also capture arbitrage profits by taking offsetting positions to the extent that they were able to establish short positions in the overpriced securities.

What made this alleged arbitrage opportunity so unusual was that it existed in the U.S. government bond market, the largest, most liquid, and closely watched fixed-income market. As of December 1990, the U.S. Treasury had almost $2.2 trillion of Treasury bills, notes, and bonds outstanding.[2] To put this market's magnitude in perspective, Treasury obligations outstanding at the end of 1990 were 1.8 times as large as total U.S. corporate bonds outstanding, 3.2 times as large as total bank loans outstanding, and 3.0 times as large as total municipal bonds outstanding.[3] Throughout the 1980s and early 1990s, raising Treasury debt through the capital markets served as the mechanism for funding the large budget deficits incurred by the federal government.

---

1 This case study describes the situation analyzed in the working paper "Negative Put and Call Prices Implicit in Callable Treasury Bonds" by Michael E. Edleson, David Fehr, and Scott P. Mason. This topic is also treated by Francis A. Longstaff in "Are Negative Option Prices Possible? The Callable U.S. Treasury Bond Puzzle," *Journal of Business* 65 (October 1992), pp. 571–592.

2 A Treasury bill has an original maturity (maturity at issue) of less than or equal to 1 year, Treasury notes have maturities of 2–10 years, and Treasury bonds have maturities of greater than 10 years. As of December 1990 there were $527 billion, $1,265 billion, and $388 billion of bills, notes, and bonds outstanding, respectively (*Economic Report of the President*, February 1992, p. 394).

3 *Federal Reserve Bulletin*, September 1991, p. A-43. Only the $3.85 trillion outstanding balance of mortgages (all classes) account for more funds than Treasury securities.

Michael E. Edleson and Peter Tufano wrote this case as the basis for class discussion rather than to illustrate either effective or ineffective handling of an administrative situation.

The Treasury market was significant not only for its size, but also for its liquidity. On an average day, approximately 5% of all government securities changed hands.[4] In comparison, turnover in the New York Stock Exchange in 1990 was 46% for the year, or approximately .2% per day.[5] The closely watched Treasury market was an unlikely place to find arbitrage opportunities. New Treasury securities were brought to market regularly, a wide group of dealers actively traded them, and prices were widely disseminated.

Of the $388 billion of Treasury bonds outstanding at the beginning of 1991, 26 issues with aggregate face value of $98 billion were callable. Callable Treasury bonds, issued during the 1973–1984 period, typically had original maturities of 30 years and coupon rates ranging from 7% to 14%.[6] What differentiated callable Treasuries from noncallable Treasury bonds was the call feature that the government retained. The Treasury retained the right, but not the obligation, to redeem the callable Treasuries at par (100) on any semiannual interest payment date within five years of maturity, provided that it gave investors four month's notice. For example, the government could redeem the 7% callable Treasury bond maturing on May 15, 1998, at face value on any of the ten semiannual interest payment dates beginning in May 15, 1993.[7] If the Treasury chose to redeem the bonds on May 15, 1993 (the first possible call date), it would need to give notice to investors no later than January 15, 1993. Exhibit 1 shows the Treasury's call policy over the past half century.

On January 7, 1991, Samantha Thompson's attention was caught by the pricing of the 8¼ May 00–05, or the 8.25% coupon Treasury bond[8] maturing May 15, 2005, first callable on May 15, 2000, whose price appeared out of line relative to other bonds in the market. By combining noncallable bonds maturing in 2005 with zero coupon Treasuries (or STRIPS)[9] maturing in 2005, Ms. Thompson could create a synthetic bond with semiannual interest payments of $4.125 per $100 face value and whose final payment of $100 at maturity exactly matched those of the callable bond—if the callable bond *was not called*. Because this synthetic bond did not surrender a redemption right to the government, it should be worth more to investors (i.e., have a higher price or a lower yield) than the callable bond of the same maturity.

4   *Joint Report on the Government Securities Markets*, January 1992, p. B-28.

5   *New York Stock Exchange Fact Book*, 1991, p. 77.

6   Longstaff, p. 573.

7   In the price listing, this callable Treasury would show up as 7 May 93–98. The first year is the call year, and the second is the final maturity if the bond is not called.

8   There is $4.2 billion (in face value) worth of this particular Treasury bond issue outstanding.

9   STRIPS (Separate Trading of Registered Interest and Principal of Securities) are effectively zero coupon bonds that are direct obligations of the federal government.

Alternatively, Ms. Thompson could construct another synthetic noncallable Treasury bond by combining noncallable bonds maturing in 2000 with STRIPS maturing in 2000; this synthetic should also be worth more than the callable 00–05. This synthetic matched the callable bond—if it *was called* at the first possible date. It too should be worth more than the callable bond. Based on the prices on January 7, 1991, these simple pricing relations seemed to be violated. Current prices for that day are given in Exhibit 2; a time series of price data for the callable bond is shown in Exhibit 3.

If Ms. Thompson's analysis was correct, it suggested a way for clients who owned the callable 00–05s to profit. Clients who paid taxes had to concern themselves with the tax ramifications of these trades (see Exhibit 4), but clients who did not pay taxes, such as pension funds, could immediately capitalize on the price discrepancy.

Investors who did not own the callable 00–05s could also profit, to the extent that they could establish short positions in the relatively overpriced security and long positions in the relatively underpriced security. "Selling short" entails borrowing a security from another party, selling it today, and promising to redeliver the security to the lender at some future time. Exhibit 5 gives additional details on short selling in the bond market and the practice of reverse repurchase agreements.

The apparent relative mispricing of the bonds had been rather persistent over the past few weeks. Ms. Thompson wondered how she could best take advantage of this pricing situation for the benefit of her various investment clients. Also, she knew that Mercer was active in the repo markets and occasionally participated in bond arbitrage on its own account. As she analyzed the numbers, she weighed the risks and rewards presented by this opportunity.

Exhibit 1 Summary of Postwar U.S. Treasury Call Policy, 1946–1991

Callable Bond		Optimal Call Date	Called	Price
3.000	June 1946–48	June 1946	Yes	101.000
3.125	June 1946–49	June 1946	Yes	101.031
2.000	Mar. 1948–50	Mar. 1948	Yes	100.343
2.000	Dec. 1948–50	Dec. 1948	Yes	100.434
2.750	Mar. 1948–51	Mar. 1948	Yes	100.688
2.000	June 1949–51	June 1949	Yes	100.313
2.000	Sept. 1949–51	Sept. 1949	Yes	100.297
2.000	Dec. 1949–51	Dec. 1949	Yes	100.434
2.000	Mar. 1950–52	Mar. 1950	Yes	100.359
2.000	Sept. 1950–52	Sept. 1950	Yes	100.359
2.500	Sept. 1950–52	Sept. 1950	Yes	100.625
4.250	Oct. 1947–52	Oct. 1947	Yes	100.281
3.125	Dec. 1949–52	Dec. 1949	Yes	100.922
2.000	Sept. 1951–53	Sept. 1951	No	100.016
2.000	Sept. 1951–53	Mar. 1952	No	100.094
2.000	Sept. 1951–53	Sept. 1952	No	100.188
2.000	Sept. 1951–53	Mar. 1953	No	100.031
2.500	Dec. 1949–53	Dec. 1949	Yes	100.688
2.250	Dec. 1951–53	Dec. 1951	Yes	100.719
2.750	June 1951–54	June 1951	Yes	100.594
2.000	Dec. 1952–54	June 1954	No	100.281
2.250	June 1952–55	June 1952	No	100.156
2.250	June 1952–53	Dec. 1952	No	100.188
2.250	June 1952–53	June 1954	Yes	100.531
3.000	Sept. 1951–55	Sept. 1951	Yes	100.063
2.000	June 1953–55	June 1953	Yes	100.188
2.000	Dec. 1951–55	Dec. 1951	No	100.031
2.000	Dec. 1951–55	June 1954	No	100.188

Exhibit 1 Summary of Postwar U.S. Treasury Call Policy, 1946–1991 (Continued)

Callable Bond		Optimal Call Date	Called	Price
2.000	Dec. 1951–55	Dec. 1954	Yes	100.656
3.750	Mar. 1946–56	Mar. 1946	Yes	101.125
2.250	June 1954–56	June 1954	Yes	100.594
2.375	Mar. 1957–59	Sept. 1958	Yes	100.406
2.250	Sept. 1956–59	Sept. 1958	Yes	100.375
2.750	Sept. 1956–59	Sept. 1956	Yes	100.406
2.875	Mar. 1955–60	Mar. 1955	Yes	100.844
2.750	June 1958–63	June 1958	Yes	100.375
2.750	Dec. 1960–65	Dec. 1960	No	100.156
2.750	Dec. 1960–65	June 1961	No	100.438
2.750	Dec. 1960–65	Dec. 1961	No	100.531
2.750	Dec. 1960–65	June 1962	No	100.625
2.750	Dec. 1960–65	Dec. 1962	Yes	100.313
7.500	Aug. 1988–93	Apr. 1991	No	100.625

Source: Francis A. Longstaff, "Are Negative Option Prices Possible? The Callable U.S. Treasury Bond Puzzle," *Journal of Business* 65 (October 1992), p. 583.
Note: This exhibit lists each of the Treasury bonds that should have been called during the 1946–1991 period. The first part of "Callable Bond" (e.g., 3.000) indicates the coupon rate (e.g., 3%). The first year is the call year, and the second is the final maturity if the bond is not called. "Optimal Call Date" indicates the month in which the Treasury had the opportunity to make a call for a bond that was trading at or above par at the beginning of the call notice month (four months prior to the actual date on which the bond could be called). "Called" indicates whether the Treasury made the call. "Price" is the bid price of the security as reported in the U.S. Treasury *Bulletin* at the beginning of the call notice month.

Exhibit 2 Capital Markets Data at January 7, 1991

	Ask	Bid
Treasury Bonds		
8¼ May 00–05	101:08	101:04
12 May 05	129:29	129:23
8⅞ May 00	104:16	104:12
Treasury STRIPS		
May 00	46:21	46:08
May 05	30:10	29:29

Note: By the conventions of the bond market, colons in bid and ask quotes represent 32ds; 101:08 means 101⁸⁄₃₂, or 101.25. For both the bonds and STRIPS, these prices reflect a purchase of $100 principal or par value of these securities.

Exhibit 3   Price of the 8¼ May 00–05 Treasury Bond

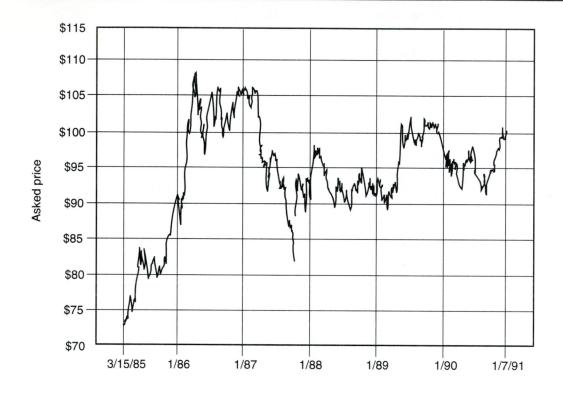

Exhibit 4   Tax Considerations in Buying and Selling U.S. Treasury Bonds and Notes

The taxation of Treasury bonds and notes reflects the fact that holders of these securities earn taxable income (and possibly losses) through three mechanisms: explicit payments of interest, implicit payments of interest, and capital gains and losses. Bond investors subject to federal taxation need to consider all these tax ramifications. The following general principles characterize the tax treatment of Treasury bonds and notes:

- Explicit interest payments are treated as ordinary income in the year in which they are made. Interest on Treasury securities is exempt from state and local taxes.
- If you pay a premium (a price over par) to buy a bond, this premium can be deducted (amortized) over time to offset a portion of taxable interest. In effect, investors are able to accelerate their recognition of these particular taxable losses and offset them against interest income.
- Changes in the price of the bond from purchase to sale are generally treated as capital gains or losses, and recognized when the bond is sold, with the exception of the following point.
- Changes in the price of a security because of implicit payments of interest (which primarily affect zero-coupon bonds or STRIPS) are taxable income each year, even though no cash interest is paid and even if the investor does not sell the bond.

The specific rules on the tax treatment of Treasury securities can be quite complex and change over time. The following examples illustrate typical applications of current tax codes:

1. Investor A buys a 7% coupon bond for $90. The semiannual interest payments of $3.50 are taxable interest in the year received. Later, the bond is worth $95. If A sells the bond at that time, she realizes a $5 capital gain[a], taxable in the year of sale. If A holds the bond to maturity, in that tax year she will recognize a $10 taxable capital gain, ($100 par value received less $90 paid).

2. Investor B pays $46.32 for a 10-year STRIP (zero coupon bond) when it is first offered. Over the coming 10 years, B receives no interest payments, and he holds the STRIP to maturity to receive $100, a gain of $53.68 over the price paid. The increase in value from $46.32 to $100 is not treated as a capital gain at maturity. Rather, this bond, selling at an original issue discount (OID), is treated as having made taxable implicit interest payments each year. Because $46.32 grows to $100 in 10 years at an 8% effective annual rate (constant yield), the bond is treated as if it pays 8% interest per year. In investor B's case, he will report OID interest in the first year of $3.71, or $46.32 × 8%. If instead of holding the STRIP to maturity, B sells it after one year for $51.32 (a $5 profit), $3.71 would be reported as interest, and the remainder, $1.29, would be taxable as a capital gain.

3. Investor C pays $116 for a seasoned 12% coupon bond that delivers eight semiannual payments of $6 and a final principal payment of $100. The $16 purchase price premium over par can be amortized over the 4 years to reduce net interest that is taxable. If the bond was issued before September 27, 1985, C would take a straight-line $4/year deduction, effectively reporting only 8% interest.[b] By taking this deduction, C would reduce the tax basis of the bond from $116 to $100 over the four years; thus there would be no capital gain or loss at maturity.

a. Complex rules affect the capital gains status on such "market discount" bonds if they were issued after July 18, 1984; in such cases, some of the gain will be reported as interest income instead of capital gain.
b. For bonds issued on or after that date, the constant yield method (IRS Publication 1212) is used.

Exhibit 5   Establishing a Short Position Through Short Selling and Reverse Repurchase Agreements in the Bond Market

An investor with a "long position" in a security *owns* the security, and this position can be set up by *purchasing* the security. Investors with long positions profit if the security's price rises. An investor with a "short position" in a security *owes* the security, and this position can be set up by *selling* the security. Investors with short positions profit if the security's price falls. It is quite common for investors to sell bonds they do not own, either through short sales or reverse repurchase agreements, thus creating a net short position.

SHORT SALES

Suppose the $8\frac{1}{4}$ May 00-05 bonds are "trading rich" (overpriced). A trader desires to sell the bond, but does not own it. To set up a short position, the trader locates an owner of the bond who is willing to lend it out. The trader borrows the bond and then sells it (a short sale). The borrowed bond will be collateralized by either cash or securities; also, a fee is paid to the lender for the borrowing privilege. The borrower must pay the lender any interest payments made while the security was borrowed. Finally, the borrower must return the borrowed bond to the lender at some time in the future, or upon the demand of the lender. At that time, having already sold that bond, the borrower must either enter into another borrowing arrangement or purchase the bond in the open market to replace the borrowed bond.

REVERSE REPURCHASE AGREEMENTS

In the Treasuries market, bond borrowing is less common than entering into reverse repurchase agreements ("reverse repo") for establishing a short position. If you own a security, you could enter into a sale-and-repurchase-agreement ("repo") by simultaneously selling the security and agreeing to repurchase it at a later date, effectively obtaining a collateralized short-term loan. Viewed from the other side of the transaction, this contract, known as a reverse repurchase agreement, commits you to buy a security now and agree to resell it at a pre-set price in the future. The reverse repo is similar to borrowing a security and providing cash collateral for a fixed term. You receive interest on the cash collateral and pay an interest fee for the privilege of borrowing the security; the resulting net interest rate is called the "repo rate." Typical time frames for repos are one day (*overnight repos*), *term* repos of a few days to a few months, or *open* repos that roll over daily automatically unless terminated by either party. For example, investor D enters into a one-week, $10 million, 5.27% reverse repo with a dealer for the $8\frac{1}{4}$ May 00-05. He has made a $10 million short-term loan[a] to the dealer; in turn he gets possession of the bond as collateral. In a week, D will get his money back (with $10,247 interest) but must return the bond.

Combining a reverse repo with a sale of the security effectively results in a short sale. In the example above, suppose D enters into the reverse repo described and receives the $8\frac{1}{4}$ May 00-05 bond as collateral. At the same time, D sells the bond in the market (receiving $10 million). In substance, D has established a short position in the bond, in that D profits if the price of the bond falls. To see this, recognize that at the outset, D paid $10 million, but simultaneously received the same amount for selling the bond. However, D is obligated to resell the bond to its counterparty in a week for $10,010,247 (the repo amount plus interest). If the bond price decreases, D purchases the bond in the market for less than $10,010,247, and delivers it at maturity of the reverse repo for a profit.[a]

---

a. Perhaps you could have received 5.87% ("market repo rate") on your money; why take 60 basis points less? If the $8\frac{1}{4}$ May 2005's are in generally high demand (e.g., to deliver against short sales), traders will pay a fee, or accept below-market rates, to gain possession of the "special" security. In rare cases, repo rates can drop to almost 0% for particular special securities.

COCA-COLA HARMLESS WARRANTS

In November 1985, Jonathan Palmer was still adjusting to his new surroundings. He had recently moved to London to take a position in the fixed-income area of Highland Associates, and if his first task was any indication, his new job's exposure to the Euromarkets would be both educational and challenging. Mr. Palmer's first assignment involved a unique offering of units from Coca-Cola that coupled a Eurodollar bond with a harmless debt warrant. While standard debt warrants were nonexistent in the U. S. market, these securities had become somewhat commonplace in the burgeoning Euromarkets. Mr. Palmer realized that his analysis of this offering, to be presented to the Highland investment committee, would be his first important assignment and an opportunity to demonstrate the relevance of his expensive U.S. business school education.

Highland Associates was a 50-person firm that managed institutional money. Mr. Palmer and three associates managed a $2 billion fixed-income portfolio in the medium- to long-term range. Their clients were mostly Continental pension funds interested in achieving enhanced market returns. The portfolio was currently 60% in corporates, 30% in governments, and 10% in cash. Mr. Palmer's new boss had handed him the Coca-Cola offering circular (see Exhibit 1) with the expectation that he would be able to offer a definitive analysis of the value in the offering. As a possible aid to his analysis, Mr. Palmer discovered in the firm's library a November 1984 Coca-Cola offering circular (see Exhibit 2) that coupled newly issued debt with standard debt warrants.

The Euromarkets had experienced tremendous growth during the early 1980s, with Eurodollar new issuance growing from $19 billion in 1980 to $79 billion in 1984 (see Exhibit 3). With such explosive growth came opportunities and pitfalls for the numerous fixed-income money managers who were focused on extracting above-average returns for their customers. While the issuance of debt warrants had become fairly standard by the middle of 1985, a new breed of so-called harmless or wedding warrants was growing increasingly popular. Unlike the standard debt warrants, such as the ones included in the 1984 Coca-Cola offering, these new warrants had different exercise terms and were coupled

Mihir Desai wrote this case under the supervision of Scott P. Mason as the basis of class discussion.

Copyright © 1994 by the President and Fellows of Harvard College. Harvard Business School case 294-107.

with callable bonds. These new warrants had grown particularly popular over the last two months, with issues launched by companies as diverse as Sumitomo Trust, Procter & Gamble, Gaz de France, and countries such as the Kingdom of Denmark and Austria. As Mr. Palmer reviewed the issurance, he wondered what motivation could have been shared by such a wide variety of issuers.

Mr. Palmer reviewed the Coca-Cola Company's recent financial statements (see Exhibit 4) in conjunction with current market information from the Euromarkets and the U.S. corporate debt market. In particular, he noted that 7-year U.S. Treasuries were trading at a 9.87% bond-equivalent yield. He also considered the differences between the two Coca-Cola issues and wondered why the company had chosen to structure its most recent offering as it did. The 1984 issue seemed quite straightforward, whereas the current issue involved considerably more complicated terms.

In considering his decision, Mr. Palmer focused on the first page of the offering circular and combined the information contained there with a few additional pieces of data. From the underwriter, he learned that the warrant attached to the $1,000 principal amount of Series A Notes was thought to be worth $6.25 and that underwriting fees for the offering were $1\frac{7}{8}$% of the stated Series A Notes principal. The underwriter also said that Coca-Cola could have issued 7-year noncallable Eurodollar debt at par with a coupon of $9\frac{3}{4}$% and underwriting fees of $1\frac{7}{8}$%. As Mr. Palmer began to untangle the offering circular, his hopes rose that his first assignment would yield significant benefits to Highland's customers and to his fledgling career.

Exhibit 1   Excerpts from November 1985 Offering Circular

$100,000,000

The Coca-Cola Company

9$\frac{7}{8}$% Series A Notes Due 1992
and 100,000 Warrants to Subscribe for
$100,000,000 9$\frac{7}{8}$% Series B Notes Due 1992

Principal and interest in respect of the 9$\frac{7}{8}$% Series A Notes Due 1992 (the "Series A Notes") and the 9$\frac{7}{8}$% Series B Notes Due 1992 (the "Series B Notes"), will be made in U.S. dollars without deduction or withholding for or on account of U.S. withholding taxes, to the extent set forth herein. Interest in respect of the Series A Notes accrues from November 26, 1985, and payable annually in arrears on November 26, commencing on November 26, 1986 . . . .

One Warrant will entitle the holder to subscribe, on the dates specified herein, for $1,000 principal amount of Series B Notes on or before November 1, 1992, at a price of 100% of the principal amount, plus accrued interest. On or prior to November 25, 1989 Warrants may be exercised only by surrender of one Series A Note, and thereafter only by payment of $1,000 plus accrued interest. The Warrants will be exercisable only upon certification as to non-U.S. beneficial ownership as described herein under "Description of the Warrants."

Interest on the Series B Notes will accrue from the November 26 next preceding the date of subscription and will be payable on the global Series B Note hereinafter referred to only upon certification that the beneficial owners thereof are not U. S. persons . . .

The Series A Notes and Series B Notes (together the "Notes") will mature on November 26, 1992, and may be redeemed at the option of The Coca-Cola Company (the "Company" or "Coca-Cola") in whole at any time at their principal amounts, plus accrued interest, in the event of certain developments with respect to United States withholding taxes, or the imposition of certain verification, information or other reporting requirements as set forth herein. The Series A Notes may be redeemed at the option of the Company in whole or in part on or after November 26, 1989, at their principal amount, plus accrued interest, as described herein. The Series B Notes may not be redeemed prior to maturity except as set forth above . . .

ISSUE PRICE FOR THE SERIES A NOTES AND WARRANTS 101$\frac{3}{8}$%

Exhibit 2   Excerpt from November 1984 Offering Circular

$100,000,000
The Coca-Cola Company
11⅜% Notes Due November 28, 1988
with Warrants to Purchase
$100,000,000 11⅜% Notes Due November 28, 1991

The issue price of the 1988 Notes with Warrants is 103.60% of the principal amount of the 1988 Notes, plus accrued interest, if any.

The 1988 Notes will be issued in bearer form in the denomination of $5,000. Interest will be payable annually in arrears on November 28, commencing November 28, 1985.

Five Warrants will entitle the holder to purchase $5,000 principal amount of 1991 Notes at any time on or before November 28, 1988, at a price of 100% of the principal amount thereof, plus accrued interest. The Warrants will be exercisable only upon certification that the beneficial owners thereof are not U.S. persons. The Warrants will expire on November 28, 1988, unless exercised on or prior thereto.

If on November 29, 1988, less than $100,000,000 principal amount of the 1991 Notes have been issued, the 1991 Notes may be redeemed at the option of Coca-Cola as a whole at 102% of their principal amount plus accrued interest. Such redemption may be made no later than January 28, 1989. Interest on the 1991 Notes will accrue from the November 28 next preceding the date of purchase (unless the date of purchase is a November 28, in which case from such date) and will be payable annually on November 28 in each year. Interest payable on the 1991 Notes prior to the exchange of the temporary global 1991 Note hereinafter referred to will be payable only upon certification that the beneficial owners thereof are not U.S. persons.

The 1988 Notes and the 1991 Notes (together the "Notes") may be redeemed in whole at any time in the event of certain developments with respect to U.S. taxes as set forth herein.

Exhibit 3   Eurodollar Market Activity, 1980–1984 (billions of dollars)

	1980	1981	1982	1983	1984
Eurobond yearly issue volume	$19	$26	$47	$47	$79
Fixed-rate	65%	64%	74%	65%	55%
Floating-rate	22%	26%	24%	32%	40%
Equity convertible and warrants	13%	10%	3%	4%	5%
US$-denominated	69%	85%	85%	79%	80%
Eurobond secondary market turnover	$192	$400	$696	$830	$1,237

Source: Philip Hubbard, "A History of Eurobonds," HBS Working Paper 1987; Euromoney, Morgan Guaranty Trust.

Exhibit 4   Financial Statements, 1982–1984 (millions of dollars except per share data)

	1982	1983	1984
Net operating revenues	$4,760	$5,056	$5,442
Cost of goods sold	2,472	2,580	2,738
Gross profit	2,288	2,476	2,704
Selling, general, and administrative expenses	1,515	1,648	1,855
Operating income	773	828	849
Net interest, equity, and other income	79	50	60
Pre-tax income	852	878	909
Taxes	379	374	360
Net income	$473	$504	$549
Net income per share	$ .66	$ .68	$ .79
Cash dividends	.41	.45	.46
Dividend payout ratio	63%	65%	58%
Cash, cash equivalents, and marketable securities	$254	$559	$768
Net property, plant, and equipment	1,233	1,247	1,284
Total assets	4,212	4,540	5,241
Long-term debt	423	428	631
Total debt	493	520	1,310
Shareholders' equity	2,779	2,912	2,751

Source: Coca Cola Company, annual reports.

TAXES, REGULATION, AND ACCOUNTING:
STIMULI TO INNOVATION

CITICORP (1985)

On June 14, 1985, Edgar Ancona, the vice president in charge of medium- and long-term funding activities for Citicorp, was undecided on the structure of a Eurodollar debt issue he planned to launch within the next few days. Although Citicorp had been very active in the capital markets over the past 18 months, continued strong growth in assets was creating a need for additional funding. Mr. Ancona was hoping to raise $200–$500 million in medium- and long-term debt in order to fund the operations of several nonbanking subsidiaries of Citicorp involved in such activities as mortgage banking, leasing, and credit card services.

In managing the medium- and long-term debt funding for Citicorp, Mr. Ancona balanced the relative proportions of fixed- and floating-rate financing and liability maturity structure with the asset mix. Citicorp had already issued a considerable amount of debt, rated Aa$_1$/AA in the past 12 months in the U.S. and Eurodollar markets. He thought that now would be a good time to launch a Eurodollar floating-rate note (FRN), although he had not ruled out another fixed-rate Eurodollar bond. He planned to review the current advantages and disadvantages of fixed- and floating-rate debt in the U.S. and Eurodollar markets. He was also aware of Citicorp's need to satisfy bank regulatory capital requirements, and he wondered if this particular issue should be designed to improve the statutory capital ratios. If so, he was unsure how this would affect his choice between fixed- and floating-rate debt. As he reviewed the recent developments in the Eurodollar debt market, he searched for a structure that would serve the purposes of Citicorp at the lowest possible cost.

BACKGROUND

Citicorp, the largest bank holding company in the United States, was the parent corporation for Citibank N.A. and other subsidiaries. Through its staff of 71,000 people in 2,600 offices in 41 states, the District of Columbia, and 91 other countries, Citicorp provided

This case was prepared by William B. Allen, Jr., under the supervision of Scott P. Mason as the basis of class discussion.

global financial services to businesses, individuals, governments, and financial institutions. Citicorp's 1984 earnings of $890 million were a record high although an increase of only 3% over 1983 earnings (see Exhibit 1). Total assets at December 31, 1984 were over $150 billion, an increase of almost 12% from the prior year (see Exhibit 2). Total assets continued to grow at about the same annual rate for the first quarter of 1985. Earnings for the first quarter of 1985 were up 24% over the first quarter of 1984, reflecting more profitable domestic corporate and individual lending opportunities and more fee business. Also, substantial profits were made in worldwide securities and foreign exchange trading.

Citicorp grouped its operations into three core business units: the Institutional Bank, the Individual Bank, and the Investment Bank. The Institutional Bank provided both traditional lending and innovative financial services, such as electronic treasury management systems, to corporations, governments, and financial institutions. Although earnings from this unit contributed two thirds of total Citicorp earnings (see Table A), the 1984 earnings represented a 3% decrease from 1983 levels. Return on average assets of .88% for 1984 remained about the same as 1983, but average assets decreased from $87 billion to $84 billion, reflecting a more selective lending program. Average assets of the Institutional Bank increased during the first quarter of 1985 only slightly, to $85 billion, while earnings increased 15% over the first quarter of 1984. Citicorp's loan portfolio, like the portfolios of other major financial institutions, was under close scrutiny by regulators, depositors, and investors because of concerns over possible losses from loans to the energy and agricultural sectors, and to developing countries. As of March 31, 1985, Citicorp reported total outstanding loans to borrowers located in countries involved in debt refinancing of $14.8 billion, of which $5.0 billion was in Brazil and $2.9 billion was in Mexico. These amounts dwarfed the allowance for possible losses on commercial loans of $604 million and were over twice the $6.5 billion in stockholders' equity at March 31, 1985.

The Individual Bank provided consumer services like checking and savings accounts, installment loans, mortgages, and credit cards. Citibank was the largest issuer of bank credit cards in the United States and also the largest marketer of student loans. This unit was active in developing and marketing new consumer savings products in the wake of new freedoms granted by the Depository Institutions Deregulation and Monetary Control Act of 1980. The acquisitions of Diners Club franchises throughout the world and of U.S. thrift institutions in Florida and Illinois as well as the expansion of banking and nonbanking branch networks in the United States and overseas contributed to the 48% increase in average assets of the Individual Bank during 1984. Earnings grew 5% in 1984 and contributed almost one fifth of Citicorp's total earnings. Return on average assets for 1984 was .49%. Average assets grew from $47 billion to $49 billion during the first quarter of 1985, and earnings for the first quarter of 1985 were over 50% greater than those for the first quarter of 1984.

Table A Citicorp Core Business Units

	Institutional Bank	Individual Bank	Investment Bank
Portion of Citicorp earnings	66%	19%	14%
Earnings change, 1984/1983	–3%	5%	25%
Earnings change, 1st Qtr 1985/1st Qtr 1984	15%	50%	8%
Return on average assets, 1984	.88%	.49%	1.25%
Average assets, 1st Qtr 1985	$85 billion	$49 billion	$17 billion
Average assets, 1984	$84 billion	$47 billion	$14 billion
Average assets, 1983	$87 billion	$32 billion	$11 billion

The Investment Bank was involved in a broad range of capital markets funds raising and consultation services, merger and acquisition services, and global securities trading. Through its merchant banking subsidiaries, Citicorp expanded its activities in Europe and the Far East. Citicorp International Banking Limited was a leader in the interest rate and currency swap markets, controlling approximately 25% of the estimated $70 billion market. The Investment Bank operated at a disadvantage in the U.S. capital markets because of the Glass-Steagall Act, which restricted the ability of commercial banks to underwrite and trade securities. Although the Investment Bank provided less than 15% of total Citicorp earnings for 1984, earnings grew 25% over 1983, and the return on average assets of 1.25% was the highest of any group in 1984. Average assets during 1984 increased 30% over 1983 levels. During the first quarter of 1985, average assets increased from $14 billion to $17 billion. Earnings for the first quarter of 1985 increased 8% over those for the first quarter of 1984.

GROWTH AND FUNDING SOURCES

With the large and sustained growth in assets over the past few years, Citicorp had been constantly searching for funding. The major banking subsidiaries, including the flagship Citibank, were able to tap relatively inexpensive funds in the short-term deposit market. Worldwide deposits totaled over $90 billion at December 31, 1984, funding the majority of the assets of the banking subsidiaries and 60% of the consolidated assets of Citicorp (see Exhibit 3). This percentage had decreased from the levels in the late 1970s. Also, the proportion of total deposits from overseas offices had declined significantly to slightly over 50% at December 31, 1984, from 75% at the end of 1979. These were almost entirely interest-bearing deposits and represented the claims of Eurodollar investors and consumer, corporate, and institutional foreign currency deposits.

Within the growing pool of domestic deposits, the relative size of interest-bearing deposits to non-interest-bearing deposits had increased from 1 to 1 in 1979 to over 4 to 1 in 1984. Most of this growth had come from the introduction of new consumer savings products that paid market rates of interest (NOW accounts). About one third of total domestic interest-bearing deposits were large-denomination, short-term time deposits and certificates of deposit (CDs) paying market rates of interest. Consumer and institutional investors shopping among diverse money market instruments seeking high rates of return provided this pool of purchase money. Citicorp viewed both the consumer and institutional liabilities as a type of medium-term floating-rate funding because investors tended to roll over their time deposits and CDs at maturity at the market rate of interest. Although not contractually committed to the bank, these funds were relatively stable over time. Other short-term borrowings (consisting primarily of federal funds purchased, securities sold under agreement to repurchase, acceptances outstanding, and other liabilities, totaling about $39 billion) funded 26% of consolidated total assets and had been relatively constant over the past few years.

The parent corporation, Citicorp, issued equity and debt in the capital markets in order to inject capital into both its banking and nonbanking subsidiaries. Since funds raised by banking subsidiaries in the deposit and capital markets could not be used to fund nonbanking subsidiaries, many of Citicorp's capital issues were designed to raise monies for entities engaged primarily in mortgage banking, credit card and consumer-related services, and leasing. Medium- and long-term debt and other sources of committed funding totaled $14.6 billion, representing about 10% of Citicorp's consolidated assets. With substantial amounts of recent debt issues, this proportion had increased over the past five years. Stockholders' equity of $6.4 billion was only 4% of consolidated total assets, representing a slight increase over the past few years. This high degree of leverage was characteristic of the U.S. banking industry. However, bank regulators had recently expressed concern about the degree of protection such small equity levels afforded depositors from write-offs in the loan portfolio, particularly as demonstrated by the July 1984 failure of Continental Illinois.

Citicorp had been quite successful in increasing both primary and total capital as defined by bank regulators over the past 18 months, largely through issues of medium- and long-term debt. (See case Appendix for a discussion of bank regulatory capital requirements.) In particular, Citicorp had issued equity contract Eurodollar FRNs as a means of increasing primary capital. Primary capital had grown to 6.03% and total capital to 8.11% of average assets for the first quarter of 1985 from 5.05% and 7.37%, respectively, at the end of 1983.

THE DECISION

FIXED-RATE ALTERNATIVES

Mr. Ancona had been mulling over various possibilities for a $200–$500 million capital markets issue for Citicorp in order to fund the growth of nonbanking operations. He quickly ruled out any sort of equity issue. Although Citicorp common stock had soared to $50, a record high, just one week before, the price had fallen back to around $47 and at that level was slightly below book value (see Exhibit 4). Citicorp had issued $200 million of auction-rate preferred stock[1] in the domestic capital markets on June 7, 1985; however, the markets for this type of preferred stock and other adjustable-rate preferred stocks were too thin to accept another large issue at that time. While fixed-rate perpetual preferred stock could be issued, the dividend rate of around 8.25% was too expensive to be considered. While debt appeared to be the best choice, Mr. Acona still faced the issues of subordination and which market to access.

Citicorp had been active in the domestic and Eurodollar debt markets over the past 12 months (see Exhibits 5 and 6). On June 3, 1985, Citicorp had launched $150 million of 10-year subordinated notes at 10.5% in the domestic debt market. Mr. Ancona suspected that the domestic markets would not be receptive to another fixed-rate issue at that time. Citicorp had not offered a fixed-rate Eurodollar bond since May 10, 1985. Investment bankers believed Citicorp could issue a 10-year fixed-rate subordinated Eurodollar bond at par with an annual coupon of $10\frac{7}{8}$% and front-end fees of 2.0%. With the most actively traded, "on-the-run," 10-year Treasuries yielding 10.1%, Mr. Ancona wondered if the resulting spread over Treasuries from this issue would be within his target of 70–80 basis points (bp).[2] At the same time, a comparable 10-year U.S. domestic fixed-rate bond could be issued at par with a semiannual coupon of $10\frac{7}{8}$% and front-end fees of .75%.

---

1   "Auction-rate preferred stock" was similar to money market preferred stock and used a Dutch-auction technique for periodically resetting the dividend rate. In a Dutch auction, market participants are asked to bid for an amount of stock and the dividend rate they would accept.

2   Investment bankers typically quoted the all-in cost of fixed-rate bonds to an issuer as a spread over the yield of similar-maturity Treasury securities. In the Eurodollar markets, bankers determined the annual coupon rate that investors would accept and, after subtracting front-end fees, calculate the internal rate of return for the cash flows. This was the annual all-in cost. This rate was then converted to a semiannual bond-equivalent yield in order determine the spread over Treasuries.

FLOATING-RATE ALTERNATIVES

If a floating-rate debt issue were chosen, Mr. Ancona believed, Citicorp could obtain better terms in the Eurodollar market than in the domestic market. Citicorp could easily issue a Eurodollar FRN with a coupon of $\frac{1}{16}$% over three-month LIBOR. With three-month LIBOR then around 7.80%, the current coupon on a Eurodollar FRN would be about 7.86%. Although Citicorp had never issued a domestic LIBOR-based FRN, Mr. Ancona believed that the coupon would probably be $\frac{1}{8}$% over three-month LIBOR. Over the past few years, Citicorp had frequently used domestic FRNs with coupon formulas based on three-month T-bills. Since three-month T-bills had historically averaged 10–150 bp below three-month LIBOR (see Exhibit 7), Citicorp's domestic FRNs paying a coupon equal to T-bills plus 60–70 bp were substantially less costly than either domestic or Eurodollar LIBOR-based FRNs. Recently, however, two factors had made domestic T-bill-based FRNs less attractive: the T-bill-LIBOR spread had narrowed to less than 100 bp, and domestic investors had begun to demand higher margins over the T-bill benchmark. Mr. Ancona thought that Citicorp would now have to pay 100 bp or more over three-month T-bills on a domestic FRN.

He also recognized that the smaller average size and shorter maturities for domestic FRNs made them less attractive than Eurodollar FRNs. Averaging $100 million to $150 million, domestic FRNs were much smaller than in the Eurodollar market, where issues from $200 million to $500 million were popular because the large size improved secondary trading and liquidity. Furthermore, domestic FRN investors typically demanded shorter maturities than those in the Eurodollar markets. For example, U.S. thrift institutions, major purchasers of domestic FRNs, were encouraged by regulations to hold securities with final maturities of 3 years or less.

Mr. Ancona reviewed an analysis of Citicorp's debt structure as of the previous day (see Exhibit 8). He wanted to add debt with a maturity of 10–15 years in order to lengthen the average maturity of Citicorp's debt. Also, he thought Citicorp would inevitably have to add more floating-rate debt in order to provide a better match with the growing volume of floating-rate assets and thereby lessen the sensitivity of overall corporate earnings to changes in the level of interest rates. Although overnight and short-term liabilities would provide floating-rate repricing, medium- and long-term debt would generate increased liquidity. The decision between a fixed-rate Eurodollar bond and a Eurodollar FRN needed to be carefully evaluated. Given the current term structure of interest rates in the Eurodollar market (see Exhibit 9), he wondered if a fixed-rate issue made sense. Although the current coupon on a Eurodollar FRN would certainly be well below the all-in cost on a Eurodollar fixed-rate bond, he wasn't sure how to make a direct comparison between the relative costs of fixed- versus floating-rate debt. In addition, he knew that the size of the issue and the maturity would influence the choice between fixed- and floating-rate.

SUBORDINATION

Mr. Ancona also wondered whether to subordinate this debt and how this would affect the choice between fixed- and floating- rate debt. Recent regulations seemed to favor increases in capital ratios through specially qualifying debt as a means not only of increasing "market discipline" of banks but also of providing additional protection to depositors. The expected growth of assets through 1985 would decrease the primary capital ratio to a level uncomfortably close to the regulations. As of June 1985, Citicorp exceeded the 20% maximum limitation on capital notes included as primary capital; however, Mr. Ancona forecasted that 1985 earnings would increase equity, allowing Citicorp to issue more capital notes qualifying as primary capital. Investors had typically demanded a 10–12 bp premium for subordinated fixed-rate Eurodollar bonds qualifying as secondary capital over senior fixed-rate Eurodollar bonds. Mr. Ancona, however, believed that the differential for Citicorp, if any, would be less. In contrast, the Eurodollar FRN markets had not required any premium for either subordinated secondary capital or primary capital FRNs, including both equity commitment notes and equity contract notes.

Although the fixed-rate Eurodollar bond market at that time preferred traditionally structured issues generally not exceeding $200 million to $300 million in size with 7–10 years maturity, the Eurodollar FRN market was more receptive to larger issues with longer maturities and innovative structures. Citicorp could choose among various coupon formulas and other features for the structure of a Eurodollar FRN. Mr. Ancona reviewed a list of representative recent bank Eurodollar FRNs (see Exhibits 11 and 12) in order to get a better idea how he could design an appropriate FRN for Citicorp. He noted that standard major international bank Eurodollar FRNs typically had maturities ranging from 10 to 15 years with coupons calculated as three-month LIBOR plus $\frac{1}{16}$%. Front-end commissions and fees usually ranged from .30% to .50%. However, Citicorp had always been considered one of the most innovative and aggressive issuers in the Eurodollar markets (see Exhibit 10), and Mr. Ancona preferred to price Eurodollar FRNs based on LIBID rather than gamble on the LIBID-LIBOR spread remaining constant in the future. He thought Citicorp could issue a standard Eurodollar FRN at a spread of $\frac{3}{16}$% over three-month LIBID.

RECENT INNOVATIONS

Citicorp could try for even finer terms by issuing a Eurodollar FRN with an innovative structure (see Exhibit 12). By and large, these variations created distinct coupon and maturity structures tailored for issuer or investor demands. One of the most popular innovative structures was the mismatch formula, such as the Eurodollar FRN issued by Manufacturers Hanover on March 18, 1985. In this structure, the coupon was based on six-month LIBID but was recalculated monthly. The cumulative interest amount for each one-month period was then paid at the end of the six-month coupon period. This structure allowed FRN investors to match assets that paid a six-month interest rate with funding from one-month liabilities.

Another popular structure, issued primarily by the large British commercial banks, was the perpetual Eurodollar FRN. Bank regulators in certain foreign countries, notably the Bank of England, counted perpetual debt as statutory capital. Two recent issues by Lloyds Bank and Midland Bank in the spring of 1985 had been well received by investors because of the healthy ¼% spread over six-month LIBOR. Another issue, by National Westminster Bank, had been more tightly priced, at ¼% over six-month LIMEAN,[3] and had not sold as well. Even though both the nominal coupons and the front-end fees were considerably higher on these perpetuals, Mr. Ancona realized that the all-in costs, after annualizing the front-end fees and spreading them over a much longer period, were probably only slightly greater than those of standard 12-year Eurodollar FRNs. However, he believed the IRS might not classify these instruments as debt and thus not allow interest deductions on the perpetual debt coupons. Accordingly, he had not pursued the idea.

He also remembered several minimax Eurodollar FRNs, such as the Commerzbank issue in February 1985. This issue carried a coupon of ¼% over six-month LIBOR with a minimum coupon of 10% and a maximum coupon of 11⅞%. At that time, six-month LIBOR was between 9.00% and 9.50%; with the then-current coupon less than the floor, the investors would receive the minimum of 10%. Market observers thought that the coupon on a fixed-rate issue of comparable maturity for Commerzbank would have been at least 12%.

Another innovative structure, the partly paid tap Eurodollar FRN, had been introduced in June by Banque Nationale de Paris (BNP). BNP launched an issue of up to $600 million, but only $100 million was initially paid in. As with the popular Note Issuance Facilities (NIFs),[4] BNP could demand any amount of the remaining unpaid balance from investors over the next 10 years. (This was called "turning on the tap.") However, unlike the NIF case, BNP did not have the flexibility to continually draw down and repay debt in a revolving manner. The coupon was .05% over six-month LIBOR, which accrued only on

---

3   LIMEAN denotes the average of LIBID and LIBOR. Historically, the LIBOR-LIBID was ⅛%; hence, LIMEAN was ¹/₁₆% over LIBID.

4   Note Issuance Facilities (NIFs) were Eurodollar market arrangements giving the borrower the ability to continually issue short-term notes, in varying amounts not to exceed the total facility amount, over the life of the facility at a rate that would not exceed a specified maximum spread over a floating-rate benchmark.

the amount paid in. When the front-end fees of .275% were annualized over the 10-year life, BNP had obtained a very inexpensive backstop facility. Because Citicorp was looking for complete funding rather than backstop facilities, Mr. Ancona rejected this alternative but thought some of the other features and flexibilities of the NIFs might possibly be incorporated into standard Eurodollar FRNs.

In fact, one of Citicorp's investment bankers had recently suggested a Eurodollar FRN structure whereby Citicorp would have the right to vary the length of the coupon period and the benchmark rate. In this proposal, Citicorp would choose, at the beginning of each coupon period, a one-, three-, or six-month period and the coupon rate would be based on the specified spread over the benchmark rate corresponding to the period chosen. Mr. Ancona suspected that the market would not demand a premium for this structure, and he believed he could get Citicorp's normal FRN terms of $^3/_{16}$% over LIBID with front-end fees between .30% and .50%.

Just a few days earlier, on June 12, 1985, Banque Indosuez had issued a Eurodollar FRN with an unusually rich coupon of $^3/_8$% over three-month LIMEAN but with a maximum interest rate (a cap) of $13^1/_{16}$%. Rumors were that Lehman Brothers International, the lead manager, had bought the cap away from Banque Indosuez with an up-front payment which, when annualized over the 12-year life, brought the effective all-in cost below that of standard Eurodollar FRNs. With the cap sold, Mr. Ancona was not sure exactly what payments Banque Indosuez would make to the holders of FRN and the owners of the cap if rates ever exceeded the cap level. Also, he wondered why investors would buy capped FRNs, what Lehman would do with the cap, how much the cap was really worth, and whether it made sense for Citicorp to try this structure.

With only a few days left before he had promised to award a mandate to his investment and merchant bankers, Mr. Ancona was still undecided whether to issue subordinated debt and, if so, whether it should be in the form of secondary capital or primary capital (either equity commitment or equity contract notes). He knew that this decision, along with the size and maturity of the issue, would affect his choice between fixed- and floating-rate debt. He thought a good starting point would be to summarize the current advantages and disadvantages of Eurodollar fixed- versus floating-rate debt and compare the costs of each. Based on this analysis, if he were to choose floating-rate debt, he would then have to recommend an appropriate coupon formula and other features that would give Citicorp some degree of flexibility at the lowest possible cost.

APPENDIX

Bank Regulatory Capital Requirements

Bank regulators defined and monitored two levels of statutory capital for bank holding companies: primary capital and secondary capital. Primary capital included total common stockholders' equity, perpetual and preferred stock, qualifying subordinated capital notes, loan loss reserves, and minority interests in consolidated subsidiaries. Secondary capital included redeemable preferred stock, other qualifying unsecured senior and subordinated debt with maturities of 7 or more years not included in primary capital, and qualifying, convertible notes. In July 1984, soon after the failure of Continental Illinois Bank, the Federal Deposit Insurance Corporation, the Comptroller of Currency, and the Federal Reserve Board proposed minimum capital requirements for all bank holding companies that would mandate a minimum 5.5% primary-capital-to-total-assets ratio and a minimum 6.0% total-capital (primary and secondary)-to-total-assets ratio. These guidelines were officially adopted in March 1985. Many of the major banks fell below these new ratios, particularly in primary capital (see Table A1). The Comptroller of Currency announced shortly after these guidelines were proposed that the new rules would force over 500 U.S. banks to raise more than $5.7 billion in new capital.

Following the capital ratio announcements, most banks began voluntarily implementing strategies to meet the new requirements. Some banks decided to curtail growth and reduce assets by selling loans. A few banks sold their headquarters premises in order to book large gains, which increased retained earnings. Other banks searched for inexpensive ways to raise primary capital in the markets in order to meet asset growth objectives. Equity issues were historically the most expensive source of capital. For the past few years, bank stocks had been depressed by concerns over the stability of the international financial system, threats of debt repudiation by developing countries, and domestic loan problems in energy and agriculture. Preferred stock, with a lower nominal cost to the issuer because corporate investors were able to exclude 85% of dividends from taxation, had to be perpetual and meet other tests in order to qualify as primary capital. However, the cost of preferred stock was often substantially above the after-tax cost of debt for banks with high marginal tax rates. There was also considerable uncertainty whether this tax advantage would be changed in a new tax proposal being prepared by the U.S. Treasury. Larger loan loss reserves increased primary capital directly, but the resulting decrease in after-tax earnings reduced retained earnings, a component of stockholders' equity, and partially offset the increase in primary capital. Changes in loan loss reserves had to pass the scrutiny of the bank's auditors, and because of special tax regulations affecting banks, increases in loan loss reserves might not have been fully tax-deductible.

Table A1   Capital Ratios of Major Bank Holding Companies (Primary Capital as a Percentage of Assets), for Years Ending December 31, 1983 and 1984

	1983	1984
Bank America Corp.	5.06%	5.86%
Bankers Trust Corp.	5.64	6.28
Chase Manhattan Corp	5.48	6.42
Chemical New York Corp.	5.52	6.32
Citicorp	5.05	6.03
Continental Illinois Corp.	5.20	6.90
Crocker National	6.21	6.33
First City Bancorp of Texas	6.35	7.48
Manufacturers Hanover Trust Co.	5.01	5.77
Marine Midland Bank	5.75	6.91
J. P. Morgan	6.97	7.08
Republic Bank Corp.	5.80	6.10
Wells Fargo & Co.	5.68	6.65

Source: The Bankers Magazine, September-October, 1985.

The other alternative for raising primary capital was qualifying subordinated capital notes. In order to qualify as primary capital, these subordinated capital notes had to be mandatorily convertible into some type of equity that would be acceptable to the regulators. Since 1982 two types of capital notes qualified as part of bank holding companies primary capital:

1. Equity commitment notes. Banks committed to redeem the notes from the proceeds of the sale of equity. The debt could have a maximum maturity of 12 years with no stipulated minimum maturity. However, one third of the notes had to be converted (that is, equity had to be issued) within the first one third of the life of the notes, and two thirds of the notes had to be converted within two thirds of the life of the notes. Up to 10% of primary capital (excluding these notes) could be in the form of equity commitment notes.

2. Equity contract notes. The purchasers of the notes agreed to accept equity at maturity of the notes if the bank was unable to sell equity in the market. These notes could also have a maturity of up to 12 years with no stipulated minimum maturity. Unlike the equity commitment notes, there was no requirement for any conversion

before the final maturity date. Up to 20% of primary capital (excluding these notes) could be in the form of equity contract notes.

The total amount of primary capital notes, both equity commitment and equity contract notes, included as part of primary capital could not exceed 20% of primary capital (excluding the capital notes).

Most of these primary capital notes were issued in periods of steep yield curves and were structured as FRNs, although there were no regulations prohibiting the use of fixed-rate debt. (Subordinated debt qualifying as secondary capital was often fixed-rate.) Since capital notes were, for all practical purposes, noncallable, issuers preferred to use FRNs rather than take the chance of getting stuck with high-coupon, fixed-rate, noncallable debt. In addition, banks suspected that individual investors, insurance companies, and trust and pension funds, the primary purchasers of fixed-rate bonds, would not react favorably to fixed-rate primary capital notes. These investors generally preferred fixed-rate bonds, which could be tucked away until maturity, and both the credit of issuers over the long term and the degree of subordination of the debt were paramount concerns. Furthermore, most individual and institutional bond investors were not interested in the equity issuance provisions at maturity. On the other hand, the traditional FRN investors, banks and other financial institutions, were less concerned about the credit problems or the settlement arrangements at maturity and bought most of the primary capital notes.

Exhibit 1 Consolidated Income Statements, Citicorp and Subsidiaries, for Years Ending December 31, 1979–1984, and First Quarters 1984 and 1985 (millions of dollars except per share data)

	1979	1980	1981	1982	1983	1984	1st Qtr 1984	1st Qtr 1985
Revenues from interest and fees on loans and leases	$7,640	$9,958	$12,779	$12,957	$12,376	$14,459	$3,344	$3,766
Other interest revenues	2,458	3,082	3,879	3,216	2,821	3,735	857	960
	10,098	13,040	16,658	16,173	15,197	18,194	4,201	4,726
Interest expense on deposits	5,551	7,401	9,591	8,505	6,894	8,631	1,942	2,218
Interest expense on other borrowed money	1,839	2,846	4,235	2,908	2,885	3,582	872	838
Interest on bonds and notes	199	248	353	1,234	1,375	1,662	399	436
	7,589	10,495	14,179	12,647	11,154	13,875	3,213	3,492
Net interest revenues	2,509	2,545	2,479	3,526	4,043	4,319	988	1,234
Loan loss expense	234	298	305	473	520	619	81	223
	2,275	2,247	2,174	3,053	3,523	3,700	907	1,011
Fees, commissions, and other revenues	802	1,157	1,574	1,595	1,840	2,300	526	695
	3,077	3,404	3,748	4,648	5,363	6,000	1,433	1,706
Other operating expenses	2,211	2,574	2,936	3,398	3,757	4,456	1,004	1,191
Profit before taxes	866	830	812	1,250	1,606	1,544	429	515
Income taxes	325	331	281	527	746	654	206	238
Net income	541	499	531	723	860	890	$ 223	$ 277
Earnings per share	$4.34	$4.02	$4.20	$5.60	$6.48	$6.45	$1.64	$2.02

Source: Citicorp annual reports.

Exhibit 2   Consolidated Balance Sheets, Citicorp and Subsidiaries, At December 31, 1979–1984, and First Quarter 1985 (millions of dollars except per share data)

	1979	1980	1981	1982	1983	1984	1st Qtr 1985
Assets							
Cash and short-term deposits	$23,486	$19,342	$15,588	$16,195	$15,434	$14,285	$15,982
Investment and trading account securities	7,759	9,627	8,767	6,942	9,624	11,667	11,955
Federal funds sold and securities purchased under resale agreements	1,813	3,242	2,852	3,292	3,596	5,141	6,154
	33,058	32,211	27,207	26,429	28,654	31,093	34,091
Net commercial loans and lease financing	50,738	56,099	60,667	64,677	61,514	60,366	59,272
Net consumer loans and lease financing	13,348	15,664	18,355	23,015	28,769	42,341	44,286
	64,086	71,763	79,022	87,692	90,283	102,707	103,558
Other assets	9,227	10,856	13,003	15,876	15,718	16,786	16,954
Total Assets	106,371	114,830	119,232	129,997	134,655	150,586	154,603
Liabilities							
Non-interest-bearing deposits in domestic offices	$8,812	$10,075	$7,560	$7,193	$7,836	$8,111	$7,225
Interest-bearing deposits in domestic offices	8,704	10,038	12,467	18,397	21,091	34,535	35,546
Deposits in overseas offices	52,775	51,658	52,098	50,958	50,867	47,703	51,267
Total deposits	70,291	71,771	72,125	76,538	79,794	90,349	94,038
Purchased funds and other borrowings	18,438	22,529	22,366	22,857	22,299	24,390	23,527
Acceptances outstanding	3,808	5,370	6,592	9,414	8,816	7,970	8,320
Accrued expenses and other liabilities	5,735	5,307	5,406	5,807	5,754	6,769	7,452
Medium- and long-term debt	4,144	5,567	8,072	10,176	11,832	12,981	12,911
Convertible notes	357	355	350	350	349	12	11
Subordinated capital notes	—	—	—	—	—	1,649	1,649
Redeemable preferred stock	40	40	40	40	40	40	40
Total Liabilities	102,773	110,939	114,951	125,182	128,884	144,160	147,948

Exhibit 2 Consolidated Balance Sheets, Citicorp and Subsidiaries, At December 31, 1979–1984, and First Quarter 1985 (millions of dollars except per share data) (Continued)

	1979	1980	1981	1982	1983	1984	1st Qtr 1985
Stockholder's Equity							
Preferred stock	—	—	—	—	$540	$640	$640
Common stock and surplus	$1,285	$1,294	$1,363	$1,417	1,460	1,514	1,556
Retained earnings	2,435	2,760	3,093	3,579	4,129	4,637	4,825
Treasury stock (at cost)	−122	−163	−175	−181	−358	−365	−366
Stockholders' equity	3,598	3,891	4,281	4,815	5,771	6,426	6,655
Total liabilities and Stockholders' equity	$106,371	$114,830	$119,232	$129,997	$134,655	$150,586	$154,603

Source: Citicorp, annual reports.

Exhibit 3   Ratios of Sources of Citicorp Funding to Consolidated Total Assets, for Years Ending December 31, 1979–1984, and First Quarter 1985

	1979	1980	1981	1982	1983	1984	1st Qtr 1985
Non-interest-bearing deposits in domestic offices	8.3%	8.8%	6.3%	5.5%	5.8%	5.4%	4.7%
Interest-bearing deposits in domestic offices	8.2	8.7	10.5	14.2	15.7	22.9%	23.0
Deposits in overseas offices	49.6	45.0	43.7	39.2	37.8	31.7	33.2
Total deposits	66.1	62.5	60.5	58.9	59.3	60.0	60.9
Purchased funds and other borrowings	17.3	19.6	18.8	17.6	16.6	16.2	15.2
Acceptances outstanding	3.6	4.7	5.5	7.2	6.5	5.3	5.4
Accrued expenses and other liabilities	5.4	4.7	4.5	4.5	4.3	4.5	4.8
Medium- and long-term debt	3.9	4.8	6.8	7.8	8.8	8.6	8.4
Convertible notes	.3	.3	.3	.3	.3	0	0
Subordinated capital notes	0	0	0	0	0	1.1	1.1
Redeemable preferred stock	0	0	0	0	0	0	0
Total liabilities	96.6	96.6	96.4	96.3	95.7	95.7	95.8
Preferred stock	0	0	0	0	.4	.4	.4
Common stock and surplus	1.2	1.1	1.1	1.1	1.1	1.0	1.0
Retained earnings	2.3	2.4	2.6	2.8	3.1	3.1	3.1
Treasury stock (at cost)	−.1	−.1	−.1	−.1	−.3	−.2	−.2
Stockholders' equity	3.4	3.4	3.6	3.7	4.3	4.3	4.3
Total liabilities and Stockholders' equity	100.0%	100.0%	100.0%	100.0%	100.0%	100.0%	100.0%

Source: Citicorp, annual reports.

Exhibit 4   Summary of Citicorp Common Stock Values, 1979–1985

	Book Value per Share	Market Value per Share		
		High	Low	Close
1979				
Qtr. I	26.67	26.63	22.13	22.75
Qtr. II	27.35	25.50	22.38	25.13
Qtr. III	28.15	26.25	22.13	24.00
Qtr. IV	29.04	24.63	20.25	23.75
1980				
Qtr. I	29.41	24.75	17.00	18.38
Qtr. II	30.45	23.13	18.00	22.13
Qtr. III	31.32	23.88	19.63	20.38
Qtr. IV	31.73	24.38	18.88	24.25
1981				
Qtr. I	32.03	25.00	20.88	23.50
Qtr. II	32.44	30.38	21.50	27.00
Qtr. III	33.10	27.13	21.88	24.00
Qtr. IV	34.17	27.88	23.50	25.25
1982				
Qtr. I	35.05	27.63	23.38	25.88
Qtr. II	35.64	29.63	24.25	25.13
Qtr. III	36.73	27.88	21.50	27.50
Qtr. IV	37.85	40.00	27.38	32.50
1983				
Qtr. I	38.87	42.50	32.50	41.25
Qtr. II	39.82	46.13	37.88	39.50
Qtr. III	40.97	40.50	34.63	35.88
Qtr. IV	41.99	37.50	30.50	37.13
1984				
Qtr. I	43.06	39.13	33.13	34.00
Qtr. II	43.79	34.88	27.38	30.63
Qtr. III	44.69	39.00	27.50	36.75
Qtr. IV	45.82	40.50	33.25	38.75
1985				
Qtr. I	47.16	47.13	36.88	43.25
4/1/85-6/13/85	48.00 (est.)	50.00	36.88	47.13

Source: Citicorp, annual reports; 10-Qs; *The Wall Street Journal.*

Exhibit 5   Summary of Citicorp and Subsidiaries Domestic Debt Issues, June 1, 1984–June 3, 1985 (millions of dollars)

Offer Date	Issuer	Amount	Maturity	Coupon/Spread	Description
June 1, 1984	Citicorp	150	1987/1996	13.75%	3-yr extendible reset notes. Coupon resets every 2 years at 101% of benchmark Treasury rate.
July 14, 1984	Citicorp	250	1986/1999	13.6%	2-yr extendible reset notes. Coupon resets every 2 years at 101% of benchmark Treasury rate.
July 18, 1984	Citicorp	250	1989	14.125%	5-yr notes
July 19, 1984	Citicorp	200	1986/1996	13.625%	2-yr extendible reset notes. Coupon resets every 2 years at 101% of benchmark Treasury rate.
Sept. 20, 1984	Citicorp Homeowners Mortgage	500	Various to 2008	Various	Collateralized mortgage obligations
Oct. 15, 1984	Citicorp	250	1989	12.875%	5-yr notes
Oct. 19, 1984	Citicorp	250	1986/1996	11.875%	2-yr extendible reset notes. Coupon resets every 2 yrs at 101% of benchmark Treasury rate.
Dec. 18, 1984	Citicorp	300	1986/1994	10.25%	2-yr extendible reset notes. Coupon resets every 2 yrs at 101% of benchmark Treasury rate.
Jan. 15, 1985	Citicorp	250	1989	11.6%	4-yr notes
Jan. 23, 1985	Citicorp	150	1995	11.875%	10-yr subordinated capital note[a]
Mar. 13, 1985	Citicorp	100	1988	3-mo. T-bill + 75 bp	3-yr FRN
Apr. 4, 1985	Citicorp	150	1988/2000	3-mo. T-bill + 65 bp	3-yr extendible FRN
Apr. 9, 1985	Citicorp	160	2000	12.5%	15-yr mortgage pass-through certificate
Apr. 17, 1985	Citicorp	250	1990	11.5%	5-yr notes
May 15, 1985	Citicorp	100	2015	12.5%	30-yr mortgage pass-through certificate
May 24, 1985	Citicorp	50	2000	11.5%	15-yr mortgage pass-through certificate
June 3, 1985	Citicorp	150	1995	10.5%	10-yr subordinated capital notes[a]

Source: Citicorp, annual reports.
a. Qualified as secondary capital under U.S. banking regulations.

Exhibit 6 Summary of Recent Citicorp and Subsidiaries Eurodollar Debt Issues, July 4, 1985–May 10, 1985 (millions of dollars)

Offer Date	Issuer	Amount	Maturity	Coupon/Spread	Description
July 4, 1984	Citicorp Overseas Finance Corp NV[a]	100	1994	14.0%	10-yr notes (put in 1986/88/90/92)
Aug. 2, 1984	Citicorp Overseas Finance Corp NV[a]	250	1996	3-mo. LIMEAN flat	12-yr subordinated capital FRN[b]
Sept. 4, 1984	Citicorp Overseas Finance Corp NV[a]	250	1996	3-mo. LIMEAN + 12.5 bp	12-yr subordinated capital FRN[b]
Oct. 2, 1984	Citicorp Overseas Finance Corp NV[a]	150	1986/1996	12.375%	12-yr retractable notes
Oct. 5, 1984	Citicorp Overseas Finance Corp NV[a]	400	1996	3-mo. LIMEAN + 12.5 bp	12-yr subordinated capital FRN[b]
Jan. 7, 1985	Citicorp person-to-person	250	1997	3-mo. LIBID + 25 bp	12-yr subordinated capital FRN[b]
Jan. 7, 1985	Citicorp	100	1992	11.75%	7-yr subordinated capital notes[c]
Jan. 28, 1985	Citicorp	200	1997	11.75%	12-yr subordinated capital notes[c]
May 10, 1985	Citicorp	$150	1995	11.5%	10-yr subordinated capital notes[c]

Source: International Financing Review.
a. Citicorp Overseas Finance Corp NV was the Netherlands Antilles Finance subsidiary, which issued Eurodollar bonds for Citicorp in order to avoid U.S. withholding tax on interest payments to nonresident investors. This law was repealed in 1984, and Citicorp issued Eurodollar debt directly in 1985.
b. Qualified as primary capital under U.S. banking regulations.
c. Qualified as secondary capital under U.S. banking regulations.

Exhibit 7   Reference Rates in the Floating-Rate Note Market

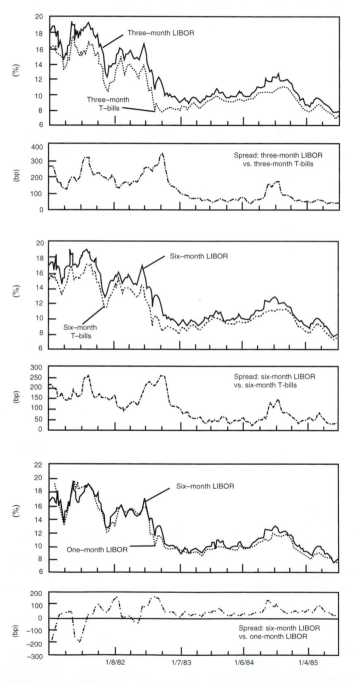

Source: Floating Rate Quarterly, Salomon Brothers.

Exhibit 8 Analysis of Citicorp Debt Structure at June 13, 1985 (millions of dollars)

Maturity	Fixed	Floating	Per Year Amount	Per Year Percent	Cumulative Amount	Cumulative Percent
1985	$ 0	$ 0	$ 0	0%	$ 0	0%
1986	410	138	548	4.6	548	4.6
1987	445	150	595	5.0	1,143	9.7
1988	443	100	543	4.6	1,686	14.3
1989	1,072	185	1,257	10.7	2,943	25.0
1990	758	0	758	6.4	3,701	31.4
1991	0	100	100	.8	3,801	32.3
1992	100	957	1,057	9.0	4,858	41.2
1993	310	0	310	2.6	5,168	43.8
1994	0	500	500	4.2	5,668	48.1
1995	300	600	900	7.6	6,568	55.7
1996	350	1,850	2,200	18.7	8,768	74.4
1997	200	294	494	4.2	9,262	78.6
1998	0	455	455	3.9	9,717	82.4
1999	0	350	350	3.0	10,067	85.4
2000 and beyond	938	781	1,719	14.6	11,786	100.0
Totals	$5,326	$6,460	$11,786	100.%		

Source: Citicorp, annual reports.

Exhibit 9 Eurodollar Term Structure of Interest Rates, June 14, 1985

Overnight	$7\frac{7}{16}\%$
One-week	$7\frac{11}{16}\%$
One-month	$7\frac{3}{4}\%$
Three-month	$7\frac{13}{16}\%$
Six-month	8%
1-year	$8\frac{7}{16}\%$
3-year	$9\frac{1}{2}\%$
4-year	$9\frac{3}{4}\%$
5-year	10%
7-year	$10\frac{1}{4}\%$
10-year	$10\frac{3}{8}\%$
12-year	$10\frac{1}{2}\%$

Source: Morgan Guaranty Ltd.; and *Financial Times*, London.

Exhibit 10 Notable Achievements by Citicorp in International Financial Markets

First negotiable CD in U.S. domestic markets, 1962

First negotiable Eurodollar CD, issued by Citibank, London, 1966

First Note Issuance Facility, for New Zealand shipping corporation, 1978

First Eurodollar FRN to use three-month LIBOR as benchmark, March 1979

First Eurodollar FRN to use three-month LIMEAN as benchmark, August 1979

First Eurodollar FRN to use rolling-rate concept, a forerunner to the mismatch formula, November 1979

First Eurodollar FRN to use LIBOR flat coupon pricing in November, 1979

First Eurodollar FRN to use LIBID as benchmark, March 1980

First perpetual FRN, called an undated putable, March 1980

Source: *Floating Rate Notes*; *Euromoney*, 1981.

Exhibit 11 Issues by Bank Holding Companies of Standard Eurodollar Floating-Rate Notes, January–April 1985 (millions of dollars)

Issuer	Rating on Senior Long-Term Debt (Moody's/S&P)	Offer Date	Amount	Maturity	Coupon Formula	Fee	Description
First Chicago Corp.	A1/A	Jan. 16, 1985	$200	1997	3-mo. LIBOR + $\frac{3}{16}$%	.60%	12-yr subordinated FRN[b]
Wells Fargo & Co.	Aa2/AA–	Jan. 16, 1985	250	1997	3-mo. LIBOR + $\frac{1}{8}$%	.45	12-yr subordinated FRN[a]
Chemical New York Corp.	Aa2/AA	Jan. 25, 1985	300	1997	3-mo. LIBOR + $\frac{1}{16}$%	.24	12-yr subordinated FRN[b]
Bankers Trust Corp.	Aa2/AA+	Feb. 6, 1985	300	2000	3-mo. LIBOR + $\frac{1}{16}$%	.32	15-yr subordinated FRN[a]
Chase Manhattan Corp.	Aa2/AA	Apr. 11, 1985	250	2000	3-mo. LIBOR + $\frac{1}{16}$%	.38	15-yr subordinated FRN[a]
First Chicago Corp.	A1/A	Apr. 17, 1985	200	1992	3-mo. LIBOR + 10 BP	.375	7-yr subordinated FRN[a]

Source: International Financing Review.
a. Qualified as secondary capital under U.S. banking regulations.
b. Qualified as primary capital under U.S. banking regulations.

Exhibit 12   Issues by Bank Holding Companies of Innovative Eurodollar Floating-Rate Notes, January–June 1985 (millions of U.S. dollars)

Issuer	Rating on Senior Long-Term Debt (Moody's/S&P)	Offer Date	Amount	Maturity	Coupon Formula	Fee	Description
Security Pacific Group	Aaa/AA+	Jan. 29, 1985	$250	1997	3-mo. LIBOR + $\frac{1}{16}$% (reset and paid monthly)	.4%	12-yr subordinated FRN with mismatch structure and quarterly payment[a]
Bank America Corp.	Aa/A+	Feb. 12, 1985	$400	1997	3-mo. LIBOR + $\frac{1}{16}$% (reset quarterly)	.32	12-yr subordinated FRN with mismatch structure and semiannual payment[a]
Christiana Bank (Norway)	NR/NR	Feb. 19, 1985	≤ $100	1995	6-mo. LIBOR + $\frac{1}{8}$% (interest: min 10$\frac{1}{2}$%; max 11$\frac{1}{2}$%)	.49	10-yr senior FRN with minimax structure—$75 million paid initially with tap for additional $25 million
Commerzbank (Germany)	NR/NR	Feb. 20, 1985	$100	1995	6-mo. LIBOR + $\frac{1}{4}$% (interest: min. 10%; max. 11$\frac{1}{8}$%)	.75	10-yr subordinated FRN with minimax structure
Wells Fargo & Co.	Aa2/AA–	Mar. 12, 1985	$200	2000	1-mo. LIBOR + $\frac{1}{8}$% (reset and paid monthly)	.43	15-yr subordinated FRN with monthly payment[b]
Manufacturers Hanover Trust Co.	Aa3/AA–	Mar. 18, 1985	$200	1997	6-mo. LIBID flat (reset monthly)	.3	12-yr subordinated FRN with mismatch structure and semiannual payment [a]
Lloyds Bank (U.K.)	NR/NR	Apr. 30, 1985	$750	N/A	6-mo. LIBOR + $\frac{1}{4}$%	.95	Perpetual junior subordinated FRN
Midland Bank (U.K.)	Aa3/A	May 7, 1985	$750	N/A	6-mo. LIBOR + $\frac{1}{4}$%	.65	Perpetual junior subordinated FRN
National Westminster Plc (U.K.)	Aaa/AA+	May 13, 1985	$1,000	N/A	6-mo. LIMEAN + $\frac{1}{4}$%	.765	Perpetual junior subordinated FRN
Banque Nationale de Paris (France)	Aaa/AA+	June 12, 1985	≤ $600	1995	6-mo. LIBOR + 5 bp (on amount paid in)	.275	Partly paid structure, up to $600 million of unsubordinated FRNs with $100 million initially paid in
Banque Indosuez (France)	NR/NR	June 12, 1985	$200	1997	3-mo. LIMEAN + $\frac{3}{8}$% max. interest 13$\frac{1}{6}$%	.50	12-yr unsubordinated FRN with interest -rate cap

NR = Not rated.
Source: International Financing Review.
a. Qualified as primary capital under U.S. banking regulations.
b. Qualified as secondary capital under U.S. banking regulations.

NEW ENGLAND PROPERTY AND CASUALTY

On April 4, 1985, Katherine Oster, a bond portfolio manager for New England Property and Casualty, reviewed the terms of a tax-exempt portfolio divestiture program proposed to New England by the investment bank of Mathers and Knight. Mathers and Knight had developed the proposed structure, called Tender Option Put Securities (TOPS), early in 1983. Under the TOPS program, large institutional investors offered seasoned municipal bonds held in their tax-exempt portfolios to the secondary market with one or more puts[1] attached. Terms of the put options varied among offerings, but usually provided for exercise at par within 1–5 years of issuance.

The accounting treatment for municipal put bonds made the TOPS structure extremely attractive to institutions, like New England Property and Casualty, whose tax liabilities had declined significantly subsequent to their purchase of tax-exempt securities. Put bond issuance was viewed as an asset sale for tax purposes, thereby preserving the tax exemption of coupon income to the purchasers of the bonds. At the same time, such transactions qualified as financings for regulatory and accounting purposes. As a result, the TOPS structure enabled commercial banks, savings institutions, and property/casualty insurers holding discounted municipal bonds to trade out of tax-exempts and into higher-yielding taxable securities without recognizing capital losses on their investment portfolios.

THE PROPERTY AND CASUALTY INSURANCE INDUSTRY

Property and casualty insurance companies (PCs) had historically been significant investors in tax exempt municipal securities, holding over 22% of all municipal bonds outstanding in 1980. (See Exhibit 1.) PCs provided individuals and corporations with coverage

---

[1] Each put provided the holder with the right to sell (tender) the bond to which it was attached to the issuer at a prespecified price (the strike price) on a specific date (the exercise date).

This case was prepared by Salley E. Durdan, under the supervision of Scott P. Mason as the basis of class discussion.

against a variety of risks, including property damage, third-party liability, and theft. The principal categories of coverage provided by PCs are shown in Table A.

Table A   Types of PC Coverage and Relative Revenue

Line	Percent of 1984 Industry Premium Revenue
Automobile	
Liability	28.6%
Physical damage	21.0
Workers compensation	14.5
Homeowners multiple peril	13.4
Commercial multiple peril	7.7
Fire	2.6
Medical malpractice	1.7

Property and casualty insurers generally wrote policies of short duration, collecting cash premiums in exchange for the assumption of uncertain future liabilities. Although premiums were prepaid in full at the time a policy was written, premium revenues ("earned premiums") were recognized only gradually over the life of a policy. In order to match expenses with revenues, insurers expensed the estimated value of claims related to insured events occurring each reporting period. The portion of the total loss estimate that remained unpaid at the end of each period was added to a loss reserve account.

Property and casualty underwriting profitability was measured in terms of two simple operating ratios. The expense ratio (marketing and administrative expenses as a percentage of premiums written) measured the efficiency of a PC's underwriting operations, while the loss ratio (claims expense as a percentage of premiums earned) measured its skill at risk selection. The sum of these ratios, known as the combined ratio, represented the total cost of underwriting as a percentage of premium revenues. (See Exhibit 1.)

State regulatory agencies monitored the financial viability of property and casualty insurers, and, in some states, were authorized to establish prices for various lines of insurance. Regulatory oversight focused on the adequacy of an insurer's statutory surplus, or net worth[2], in meeting uncertain future policy claims. As a general rule, regulators recom-

---

2   Because statutory accounting rules differed from GAAP, statutory surplus was generally somewhat lower than the net worth reported in an insurer's GAAP accounting statements.

mended that the ratio of an insurer's annual written premium volume to statutory surplus not exceed a level of 3-to-1.

Historically, PC underwriting profitability had varied over a cycle of approximately six years, known as the "underwriting cycle." Highly profitable years were usually followed by periods of intense price competition and/or regulatory pressure to restrain price increases. As claims began to exceed premiums earned, underwriting losses mounted and combined ratios rose above 100%. In the remainder of the cycle, competitive and regulatory pricing pressures eased and PC profitability recovered.

In addition to these cyclical earnings effects, PC insurers were exposed to uncertainty as to the size, frequency, and duration of policy claims. Unlike life insurance claims, which were fixed nominally under the terms of life policies, PC claims varied with the value of insured properties and the size of court-awarded damages. As a result, PC insurers' liabilities were sensitive to both economic inflation and "social inflation," or increases in the size of damages awarded in litigated liability cases. In addition, the timing of some PC claims, such as catastrophic losses from natural disasters and long-tailed[3] liabilities, could not be predicted accurately from actuarial data. As a result of these systematic distortions in the size and frequency of property and casualty claims, PCs' earnings tended to be more volatile than those of life insurance companies.

The substantial time lag between the receipt of premium payments and the payment of claims enabled property and casualty insurers to accumulate large cash reserves which they invested in a variety of financial assets. In structuring investment portfolios, PCs balanced the conflicting objectives of preserving principal, maximizing investment returns, hedging against inflation, and maintaining liquidity. PCs shifted in and out of tax-advantaged investments as their taxable income, which was taxed at the full corporate rate (46%), varied over the underwriting cycle.

Accounting standards in the industry required that common and nonredeemable preferred stocks be valued at market, with unrealized capital gains and losses netted against stockholders' equity each reporting period. Bonds and redeemable preferred stocks were valued at cost less amortized bond discount or premium. Realized capital gains and losses on the sale of stocks and bonds flowed through the income statement. Because fluctuations in the market value of equities could severely erode a property/casualty company's statutory surplus, most PCs held rather modest proportions of equity securities in their portfolios.

---

3   The term "long-tailed" liability referred to a liability which was not paid until long after an insured event occurred, such as claims paid to asbestos workers forty years after their exposure to asbestos fibers.

From 1978 to 1985 the property and casualty insurance industry suffered the longest and most severe down cycle in its history. The industry's problems developed when real interest rates soared in the late 1970s, prompting PCs to underprice policies in an effort to attract investable assets. Because investment earnings had proved insufficient to recover underwriting losses on these policies, the industry was expected to record a net loss for the seventh consecutive year in 1985.

MUNICIPAL SECURITIES

Municipal securities were the fixed-income obligations of state and local governments. Some 50,000 of the 80,000 governmental entities authorized to issue municipal debt had tapped the municipal securities market by 1985. The federal government exempted coupon income on such securities from federal income tax, providing states and municipalities with a subsidy in the form of reduced borrowing costs.[4] Although municipal bond income was subject to state and local taxes, most states provided for double- or triple-tax exemption on in-state municipal bond issues.

TYPES OF MUNICIPAL SECURITIES

There were two basic types of municipal instruments: general obligation bonds (GOs) and revenue bonds. General obligation debt was secured by the full faith and credit (i.e., the unlimited taxing power) of a governmental issuer. Most state constitutions restricted the issuance of GO debt, imposing limits on total GO borrowings, restricting the use of GO funds raised, and, in some states, requiring prior voter approval of GO issues.

In contrast, revenue bonds were secured solely by the cash flows of a specific revenue-generating project, enterprise, loan program, or tax. Normally, municipalities established single-purpose authorities, public corporations, or commissions to issue revenue bonds. Because the issuing municipality was not obligated to repay revenue debt from its general funds if the revenues pledged to fund the bonds proved inadequate, revenue bond issuance did not draw upon the credit capacity of the issuing government. By 1985, revenue bonds had been issued to finance the construction of bridges, roads, airports, water and sewer treatment facilities, health care facilities, state and local housing projects, college dormitories, qualifying industrial developments, and pollution control facilities, and to fund student loan and subsidized mortgage lending programs. (See Appendix 1.) While GO financing had historically dominated the municipals market, representing two-thirds of the municipal debt issued in 1970, by 1985 revenue financings had grown to represent over 70% of municipal debt issues. (See Exhibit 2.)

---

4   Capital gains realized on municipal bond investments were not exempt from federal tax.

RATING AGENCIES

Monitoring the credit of the numerous municipal bond issues outstanding was difficult because municipal issuers did not adhere to standardized financial reporting procedures and were exempt from SEC disclosure regulations. Moody's Investors Service and Standard & Poor's Corporation provided investors with assessments of the current credit quality of municipal bonds using a rating scale identical to that used in the corporate bond market. (See Appendix 2) The criteria used to rate municipal bonds included economic factors, such as per capita income levels, population and employment growth trends, and the diversity of the economic base of the issuing municipality. The rating agencies also examined a variety of debt factors, including an issuer's debt history, the magnitude of its current debt obligations relative to budgeted resources, and estimates of its future capital requirements. Several debt ratios were used to measure a municipality's debt capacity: net GO debt per capita, net GO debt to total real estate valuation, and net GO debt to total personal income. Finally, the professionalism of a municipality's administration and the quality of its control systems were considered in assigning ratings.

In the case of revenue bonds, the terms of the bond indenture and the level and stability of projected debt service coverage were key rating criteria. For example, the obligations of municipal power, water, and sewer utilities operating as legislated monopolies were supported by stable and predictable cash flows. As a result, such issues received higher ratings than the debt of hospitals or industrial developments operating in competitive markets. High-quality revenue bonds usually carried rate covenants obligating the issuing authority to charge rates, tolls, fees, or taxes sufficient to pay all cash expenses, including debt service. However, the lack of full faith and credit backing on revenue issues was reflected in revenue bond yields, which usually equaled those on GO bonds rated one-half rating category lower, e.g., AAA revenue yields generally approximated AA/AA+ GO yields.

THE MARKET FOR MUNICIPAL SECURITIES

Long-term municipal bonds were usually offered in serial maturities, enabling issuers to spread debt service over a period of several years. Short-term municipal instruments, such as tax, revenue, grant, and bond anticipation notes and tax-exempt commercial paper, were used to fund temporary cash shortfalls caused by the uneven flow of income into state and local treasuries. As a result, a broad menu of maturities was available to investors in the tax-exempt market.

Although the obligations of large, prime-credit municipalities were distributed nationally, the market for the debt of smaller, less-active, and lower-quality governmental issuers was essentially regional. Secondary market trading in municipal bonds was conducted over-the-counter by a network of approximately 1000 municipal bond dealers. Under the provisions of the Glass-Steagall Act, commercial banks, as well as securities dealers, were allowed to underwrite and trade general obligation municipal debt. Municipal bonds were issued in $5,000 denominations and were usually traded in lots of five bonds or more. Although the total volume of municipal bonds traded in the secondary market was substantial, trading in many individual issues was infrequent due to the large number of municipal issues outstanding and the small average issue size.

The principal investors in the municipal market were institutions and individuals subject to high marginal tax rates. (See Exhibits 3 and 4.) Commercial banks and property/casualty companies had traditionally dominated the municipals market, adjusting the mix of taxable and tax-exempt securities in their investment portfolios in response to changes in their expected net income. Given the short duration of their liabilities and regulatory restrictions on the quality of securities in which they could invest, commercial banks generally purchased short- to intermediate-term, general obligation municipal bonds. Property and casualty companies were active at the long end of the municipal market, exhibiting a preference for higher-yielding revenue bonds.

In the early 1980s, the declining profitability of commercial banks and property and casualty insurers reduced institutional demand for tax-exempt bonds, transforming the municipal market from an institutional to a primarily retail market. Unfortunately, changes in the municipal environment made this transition a difficult one. During this period, the credit quality of many municipalities deteriorated as taxpayer revolts like Proposition 13 and cutbacks in federal aid reduced state and municipal revenues. In 1983, the default by the Washington Public Power Supply System on a $2.25-billion revenue obligation shattered market confidence in the credit quality of municipal issuers. The WPPSS default, coupled with the retail investor's relative lack of sophistication in analyzing municipal credits, prompted issuers of lower-rated or complex securities to use credit enhancements to reduce their financing costs and enhance the marketability of their bonds.

CREDIT ENHANCEMENT

In 1985, letters of credit secured approximately 12% of all new municipal issues. Commercial bank letters of credit provided for accelerated payment of principal and accrued interest in the event of a default on a municipal bond. Annual fees of 0.5–1.5% of the total credit facility were typically charged for such guarantees. However, the use of letters of credit to enhance municipal credits was limited because banks were generally unwilling to write guarantees extending beyond ten years. In addition, few domestic banks had the long-term AAA rating necessary to participate in the municipal bond guarantee market.

More common than the letter of credit was municipal bond insurance, which guaranteed the timely payment of principal and interest on insured securities through maturity. Upfront premiums totaling 0.5 1.5% of the insured debt service (the nominal sum of all coupon and principal payments) were paid by the issuer for these irrevocable guarantees, which were most commonly applied to BBB- or A-rated revenue bond issues. Issuers elected to purchase insurance only if the resultant reduction in financing costs exceeded the insurance premium.

The municipal bond insurance market was dominated by four mono-line insurers, each rated AAA by Standard & Poor's: The Municipal Bond Insurance Association (MBIA), AMBAC Indemnity Corporation, Bond Investors Guaranty Insurance Company (BIGI), and Financial Guaranty Insurance Company (FGIC). These bond insurers were owned by consortiums of commercial banks, investment banks, and insurance companies. They typically insured only investment-grade issues and tried to diversify their policy mix by region, bond type, and issue size.

Although the methodologies employed to price bond insurance varied among market participants, each insurer performed independent analyses of municipal credits. In addition, bond insurers estimated claims experience on an insured portfolio by simulating the performance of insured credits under varying economic conditions, including periods of growth, recession, and depression. Depression scenarios, or "stress tests," incorporated statistics on actual default experience during the Great Depression of the 1930s, when cumulative municipal defaults peaked at 16% of total debt service. The model assumed that most of the interest and principal on this defaulted debt would eventually be repaid by municipalities anxious to regain access to the public, tax-exempt market, as was the experience following the Depression.

Based on these models of the timing and magnitude of expected claims, bond insurance premiums were fixed at levels sufficient to recover losses and provide a return to the insurer's shareholders. Because insurers were at risk for each insured issue through maturity, premium schedules were not adjusted in response to short-term fluctuations in municipal credit spreads. Premiums were quoted as a percentage of total nominal debt service and varied according to the risk classification of an issue.

Considerable controversy existed over the viability of the booming market for financial guarantees, including municipal bond insurance. Some insurers believed that the industry would experience few, if any, losses against the $650 million in bond insurance premium income generated in 1985. Robert Meyer, president of BIGI, had stated that "the value-added [in insuring municipal bonds] is not risk assumption but credit enhancement. We expect no losses." In contrast, another market observer insisted that "if people are willing to pay premiums for insurance, there must be a risk. To assert differently is to say that all investors are dumb."[5] Historically the municipal bond insurance industry had experienced only minimal default claims, aggregating $40 million since the first bond insurance policy was written in 1971.

Experience with insured municipals indicated that insuring a complex revenue bond issue or an offering from an infrequent municipal borrower could improve market access and reduce financing costs. Bonds insured by an AAA-rated insurer traded at AA/AA+ yields, typically saving A/BBB issuers 25 to 75 basis points over the cost of the insurance. AMBAC and FGIC had also begun to insure portfolios of seasoned municipal issues, creating a national secondary market for issues which had previously traded only regionally.

MUNICIPAL PUT BONDS

While concern over the credit quality of municipal debt was growing, the increasing volatility of municipal rates weakened investor interest in long-term municipal securities. Even when the Treasury yield curve inverted in the early 1980s, the municipal curve retained a steep positive slope, with yield differentials between prime 1-year notes and 30-year municipal bonds at times widening to 500 basis points. In response to retail resistance to long-term, fixed-rate municipal instruments, issuers relied increasingly on short-term and variable-rate financings. In 1984, variable-rate issues represented 28% of total tax-exempt volume, versus 7% in 1983. At the same time, investment bankers began to attach put options to long-term bonds to provide investors with downside protection against interest rate volatility. (See Exhibit 5.)

Although put bonds were first introduced in the primary municipals market, the put bond structure was also used in the secondary market by institutions interested in liquidating portfolios of seasoned municipal bonds. By the early 1980s, many financial institutions holding tax-exempt portfolios had accumulated substantial tax loss carryforwards, rendering the tax-exemption feature of municipal bond income valueless. At the same time, sale of their municipal bonds into the long-term market would have forced recognition of capital losses on their investment portfolios, reducing regulatory capital to unacceptable levels.

Early in 1983, Mathers and Knight developed an alternative to the outright sale of discounted municipal securities, called Tender Option Put Securities (TOPS). TOPS were long-term municipal bonds sold with one or more put options attached. The put options were usually secured by some form of liquidity support, such as an irrevocable letter of credit from a commercial bank. The accounting treatment for municipal put bonds made

---

5   Jonathan R. Laing, "Accident Waiting to Happen?" *Barron's*, December 16, 1985, p. 9.

the TOPS structure extremely attractive to institutions. Put bond issuance was viewed as an asset sale for tax purposes, preserving the tax exemption of coupon income to the purchase of the bonds. At the same time, such transactions qualified as financings for regulatory and accounting purposes. As a result, the TOPS structure enabled commercial banks, savings institutions, and property/casualty insurers holding discounted municipal bonds to trade out of tax-exempts without recognizing capital losses on their investment portfolios.

In order to qualify for this favorable tax treatment, substantial incidence of ownership of the bonds had to pass from the issuer to the TOPS buyer. To ensure that the buyer would be fully exposed to market risk over the initial put period, TOPS could not be called before the first put date. In order to pass the credit risk of the issue to the buyer, the obligation of the issuer under each put agreement was to terminate in the event of a default on the bond to which it was attached. As a result, early TOPS issues consisted primarily of high-grade municipal bonds.

THE MATHERS AND KNIGHT PROPOSAL

As Katherine Oster reviewed her notes from a conversation with Michael Kennedy, a vice president of Mathers and Knight, she confirmed that the TOPS structure was ideally suited to New England Property and Casualty's needs. Over the previous five years, New England had experienced severe underwriting losses in its commercial property and casualty insurance lines. As its taxable income declined, New England had begun to liquidate its tax-exempt portfolio, often at large losses, to facilitate a shift in its investment mix from tax-exempt to taxable securities. However, in 1984, payment of unanticipated claims on toxic waste and hazardous substance policies had forced New England to record a net operating loss of $224.5 million, reducing its statutory surplus to $746.3 million from $1,036.0 million in 1983. As a result, New England was unwilling to further erode its surplus by recognizing losses on the sale of tax-exempt securities in 1985. (See Exhibits 6 and 7.)

Ms. Oster had asked Mr. Kennedy to evaluate alternatives for liquidating a $60,000,000 (face value) portfolio of tax-exempt bonds. (See Exhibit 8.) Although the market value of these bonds was estimated at only $42,265,620, or 70.4% of par, on April 4, Mr. Kennedy had estimated that sale of the portfolio with three-year puts attached would yield proceeds of $58,593,203, or 97.66% of par. (See Exhibits 9 and 10.) Underwriting fees were to total 1.80% of the proceeds, or $1,054,678. In addition, Mathers and Knight was to charge a fee of 1.51% of the face value of the portfolio, or $906,000, for structuring the put options and securing a letter of credit from the Marine Midland Bank to provide liquidity support for the put.

Because the municipal bonds to be sold were not of prime quality, Mr. Kennedy had suggested that New England consider purchasing bond insurance for the proposed TOPS offering. Early in 1985, Mathers and Knight, in coordination with AMBAC Indemnity Corporation, had developed a municipal bond insurance program suitable for TOPS. This program, called PIMS (Portfolio Insurance for Municipal Securities), required prepayment of insurance premiums by the issuer through the put exercise date, but was renewable annually thereafter at the option of the bondholder.[6] The policy was noncancellable by AMBAC, and the annual premium to be paid per bond was fixed at the time the policy was written. Kennedy had indicated that the present value of the annual premiums under this structure was generally lower than the prepaid premiums required on traditional bond insurance. He had estimated that the initial insurance premium (prepaid through the 1988 put date) for the New England offering would cost $9.90 per $1000 par value of bonds, or $594,000, but would reduce New England's financing costs from an average rate of 7.78% to 7.28%. Assuming credit spreads between A and insured AAA bonds remained at this level through the offering date, New England could increase its proceeds, net of PIMS premiums, by $186,437 by purchasing the AMBAC policy. (See Exhibit 11.)

Mathers and Knight had urged New England to move quickly on the TOPS proposal. The enactment of tax reform legislation was expected to dramatically alter the municipal bond market in 1986. The reform bill under consideration would reduce maximum marginal individual and corporate tax rates to 38% and 36%, respectively. Additionally, the bill would place limits on the volume of "nongovernmental" tax-exempt bonds (such as industrial, hospital, housing, and university revenue bonds) issuable per year, eliminate many popular tax shelters, disallow commercial banks from deducting the interest cost of carrying tax-exempt bonds purchased after December 31, 1985,[7] and impose an indirect tax on property and casualty insurers' income from municipal bonds purchased after November 15, 1985. Such changes were expected to sharply reduce the volume of tax-exempt issuance and to result in a significant flattening of the municipal yield curve.

---

6   Note that the attachment of PIMS insurance to a tender option bond did *not* protect an investor from termination of her put option in the event of a default on the underlying bond. Although New England could, at its sole discretion, elect to purchase insured bonds that were technically in default on the TOPS tender date, it was not legally obligated to do so.

7   In general, the IRS disallowed the interest deduction on funds borrowed to purchase or carry tax-exempt obligations. This rule prevented taxpayers from receiving both an exemption and a deduction from taxes on a single transaction. However, through 1985 a series of revenue rulings had allowed banks and certain other financial institutions to deduct up to 85% of municipal bond carrying costs from their taxable income.

As Ms. Oster studied the Mathers and Knight proposal, several issues concerned her. First, she was puzzled that the market value of her bond portfolio remained 30% below par despite the recent declines in interest rates on taxable securities. Why were her municipals still deeply under water when long-term Treasury rates were approaching the levels prevailing in 1979, when a number of the bonds in the New England portfolio had been purchased?

Although the proposed AMBAC insurance program would increase net proceeds from the TOPS offering, Ms. Oster knew that New England management would question her extensively regarding the purchase of bond insurance. Why was there a positive spread between New England's interest cost savings and the cost of the AMBAC insurance? How did the PIMS structure differ from traditional bond insurance?

Ms. Oster knew that put bonds had been issued recently with exercise dates ranging from 1 to 5 years. Why had Mathers and Knight recommended a 3-year put? What factors influenced the choice of put maturity?

Finally, Ms. Oster did not understand why the market was willing to pay 250 basis points for 3-year put options on New England's municipal bonds. What were the risks to New England of writing these puts? How would the enactment of tax reform legislation affect the decision to issue put bonds? Ms. Oster resolved to pose these questions to Mr. Kennedy when she visited Mathers and Knight in New York the following week.

Exhibit 1 Composition of Property and Liability Companies' Investment Portfolios, 1980–1985 (billions of dollars)

Instrument	Total Holdings 1980		1985		Annual Net Increase in Holdings 1980	1981	1982	1983	1984	1985
U.S. governments	$12.0	6.4%[a]	$25.4	9.7%	$1.6	$1.4	$0.6	$3.3	$4.9	$3.2
Federal agencies	6.2	3.3	16.5	6.3	.2	.8	1.5	2.2	3.2	2.6
Corporate and foreign bonds	23.5	12.5	26.4	10.1	0	2.8	-.5	-4.2	2.6	2.2
State and local securities	79.9	42.3	86.1	32.8	7.7	4.0	3.0	-.3	-1.9	1.4
Total credit	121.6	64.4	154.4	58.8	9.5	9.0	4.7	1.0	8.8	9.3
Stocks	50.0[b]	26.5	53.8[b]	20.5	3.1	2.0	2.7	2.1	-3.3	.3
Checkables, currency, and miscellaneous	17.1	9.1	54.2	20.7	2.4	3.2	6.4	12.0	9.3	6.2
Total assets	$188.7	100.0	$262.4	100.0%	$15.0	$14.2	$13.8	$15.0	$14.8	$15.8
Combined Ratio					103	106	110	112	118	117

Source: Salomon Brothers Inc.
Note: 1985 figures are projected.
a. Percent of portfolio.
b. At market.
c. Industry average.

Exhibit 2   State and Local Securities, Annual Issuance, Retirements, and Net Increases in Amounts Outstanding, 1980–1985 (billions of dollars)

Net increases	1980	1981	1982	1983	1984	1985	Amount Outstanding 1985
Revenue Bonds							
Corporate purpose	$4.4	$6.9	$10.1	$7.4	$13.8	$11.7	—
Hospitals, education, etc.	8.3	9.5	16.3	15.6	15.0	26.9	—
Housing	14.3	6.8	15.7	16.8	18.6	24.0	—
Utility and public facilities	9.5	8.5	15.1	18.2	27.2	28.9	—
General obligation and other	10.7	11.9	20.0	21.0	24.7	46.2	—
New bond issues[a]	47.1	43.6	77.2	79.1	99.4	137.7	—
Less: Refundings[b]	2.4	2.1	1.3	3.5	3.7	12.1	—
Less: Maturities	16.1	18.4	20.7	22.0	23.0	25.1	—
Less: Sinking fund purchases	15.0	10.0	11.5	13.0	15.0	17.3	—
Net increase in bonds	13.6	13.1	43.7	40.6	57.7	83.1	606.2
New note issues[c]	26.5	34.4	43.4	35.7	31.1	20.5	—
Less: Maturities	24.7	33.3	37.7	36.2	34.0	24.1	—
Net increase in notes	1.7	1.1	5.7	-0.5	-3.0	-3.6	8.2
Total net increase	15.4	14.2	49.4	40.1	54.7	79.5	614.4
Outstanding municipal debt as percent of GNP	14.3%	13.2%	14.3%	14.5%	14.6%	15.8%	

Source: Salomon Brothers Inc.
Note: 1985 figures are projected.
P = projected.
a. Maturities greater than 1 year, including both fixed- and variable-rate issues.
b. Refunding issues are used to defease outstanding municipal debt. Proceeds are typically used to purchase T-bonds sufficient to fund the debt service on the original bond issue, which are placed in an escrow fund. Refundings are undertaken to reduce interest costs following a decline in interest rates, remove restrictive covenants, or alter debt maturity schedules.
c. Maturities of 12 months or less.

Exhibit 3   Ownership of Municipal Securities by Category of Investor, 1980-1985 (billions of dollars)

Ownership	Total Holdings				Annual Net Increase in Municipal Holdings					
	1980		1985		1980	1981	1982	1983	1984	1985
Thrifts	$3.5	.9%[a]	$2.9	.5%[a]	$-.5	$0	$-.3	$-.2	$-.3	$.2
Life insurance companies	6.8	1.8	10.3	1.7	.3	.4	1.9	.9	-.2	.5
Property liability companies	79.9	21.2	86.1	14.0	7.7	4.0	3.0	-.3	-1.9	1.4
State and local retirement funds	4.0	1.1	1.9	.3	.1	-.2	-.7	-1.1	-.4	.3
Municipal bond funds	26.6	7.1	159.4	25.9	-1.7	7.5	29.1	23.1	25.8	47.3
Security brokers and dealers	1.0	.3	4.2	.7	0	.2	-.2	.4	.6	.2
Total nonbank finance	121.9	32.4	264.8	43.1	5.9	11.9	32.8	22.7	23.5	51.9
Commercial banks	149.2	39.6	188.5	30.7	13.6	5.0	4.7	3.8	12.5	13.5
Nonfinancial corporations	3.4	.9	4.6	.7	-.2	0	.1	.7	-.1	.5
Residual: Households direct	102.0	27.1	156.5	25.5	-4.0	-2.7	11.8	12.9	18.9	13.6
Total ownership	$376.5	100.0%	$614.4	100.0%	$15.4	$14.2	$49.4	$40.1	$54.7	$79.5

Source: Salomon Brothers Inc.
Note: 1985 figures are projected.
a. Percent of outstanding.

Exhibit 4   Distribution of Household Income and Tax Rates, 1984

1984 Taxable Income	Marginal Tax Rate	Percent of Households in Bracket
Under $10,000	14%	14%
$10,000–$20,000	18	22
$20,000–$35,000	28	30
$35,000–$50,000	38	18
Over $50,000	50	16

Source: IRS tax tables.

Exhibit 5   Municipal Bond Yields versus Treasuries, 1965–1984

Yield Profile: Long-Term Exempt and Taxable Yield Levels

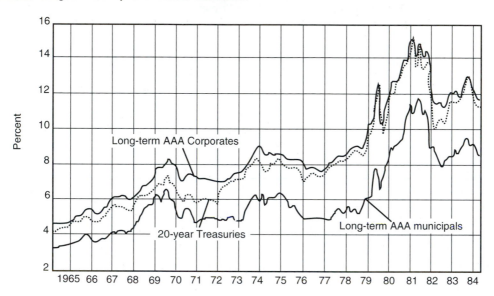

Yield Profile: Short-Term Exempt and Taxable Yield Levels

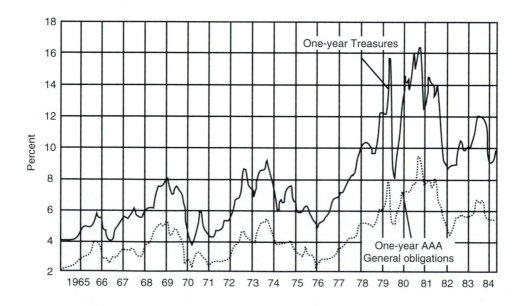

Exhibit 5   Municipal Bond Yields versus Treasuries, 1965–1984 (Continued)

Municipal Yields as a Percentage of Taxable Yields (12-Month Moving Average)

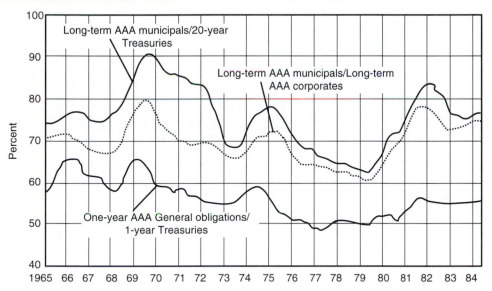

Municipal Yields as a Percentage of Taxable Yields, April 1985

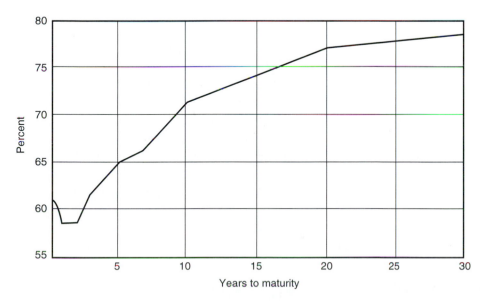

Source: Salomon Brothers Inc.

Exhibit 6 Consolidated Statements of Income and Retained Earnings of New England Property and Casualty for Years Ending December 31, 1979–1984 (millions of dollars)

	1979	1980	1981	1982	1983	1984
Written premiums	$2,681.6	$2,921.6	$3,101.4	$3,326.4	$3,186.3	$3,611.6
Increase (decrease) in unearned premiums	50.1	(81.8)	78.6	165.5	58.4	179.7
Earned premiums	2,631.5	3,003.4	3,022.8	3,160.9	3,127.9	3,431.9
Investment income[a]	335.6	365.2	412.9	434.9	514.9	559.4
Total revenues	2,967.1	3,368.6	3,435.7	3,595.8	3,642.8	3,991.3
Losses	1,674.7	2,057.6	2,129.4	2,269.9	2,104.1	2,537.0
Loss adjustment expenses	244.1	294.9	277.6	274.2	310.1	398.5
Amortization of deferred acquisition costs	352.5	380.8	394.4	425.4	449.7	483.1
Investment expenses	11.6	10.9	18.3	19.1	50.0	77.3
General and administrative expenses	402.8	423.8	487.8	543.3	573.6	645.6
Dividends to policyholders	48.1	44.2	44.4	73.1	74.7	74.3
Total losses and expenses	2,733.8	3,212.2	3,351.9	3,605.0	3,562.2	4,215.8
Operating income (loss) before federal income taxes	233.3	156.4	83.8	(9.2)	80.6	(224.5)
Current taxes	42.6	8.6	(58.4)	(32.5)	(32.7)	(116.8)
Deferred taxes	(3.0)	(19.8)	(.3)	(69.5)	(18.2)	(9.4)
Total federal income taxes	39.6	(11.2)	(58.7)	(102.0)	(50.9)	(126.2)
Operating income (loss)	193.7	167.6	142.5	92.8	131.5	(98.3)
Realized investment gains (losses), net of taxes	1.8	(18.8)	(5.7)	(11.2)	(17.0)	(3.0)
Net income (loss)	195.5	148.8	136.8	81.6	114.5	(101.3)
Retained earnings, beginning of year	1,039.7	1,202.3	1,317.3	1,377.8	1,404.1	1,427.1
Dividends to shareholders	(91.0)	(105.4)	(122.4)	(138.3)	(150.7)	(161.4)
Other	58.1	71.6	46.1	83.0	59.2	61.8
Retained earnings, end of year	$1,202.3	$1,317.3	$1,377.8	$1,404.1	$1,427.1	$1,226.2
Combined ratio						
Commercial lines	103%	111%	111%	112%	121%	132%
Personal lines	101	103	106	111	102	103
Gross investments in fixed maturities						
Taxable	$0	$0	$174	$376	$1,769	$1,007
Tax-exempt	433	415	171	200	78	0

a. Includes both taxable and tax-exempt investment income.

Exhibit 7   Consolidated Balance Sheets of New England Property and Casualty at December 31, 1979–1984 (millions of dollars)

	1979	1980	1981	1982	1983	1984
Bonds	$3,987.3	$4,066.2	$4,059.1	$4,201.5	$4,548.8	$4,449.9
Redeemable preferred stocks	75.0	124.7	164.1	153.9	159.3	156.0
Equity securities[a]						
Common stocks	235.1	472.0	463.1	405.8	271.2	304.6
Nonredeemable preferred stocks	39.1	37.2	28.3	34.4	30.6	32.1
Mortgage loans	170.5	162.7	192.5	191.9	219.5	210.2
Investment real estate	2.2	33.8	41.8	42.1	1.8	2.0
Other investments	.6	2.5	8.4	21.6	12.6	15.3
Total long-term investments	4,509.8	4,899.1	4,957.3	5,051.2	5,243.8	5,170.1
Cash and short-term securities	278.1	179.7	217.3	387.4	845.3	901.2
Total cash and invested assets	4,787.9	5,078.8	5,174.6	5,438.6	6,089.1	6,071.3
Loans to subsidiaries	92.7	76.1	63.6	83.6	62.5	71.3
Investment income accrued	92.4	96.0	106.5	123.4	150.9	162.8
Premium balances receivable	735.6	984.7	1,270.6	1,478.5	1,603.6	1,733.6
Deferred acquisition costs	153.5	163.3	170.4	181.4	195.9	222.0
Other assets	210.2	240.5	275.7	435.4	460.1	471.0
Total assets	$6,072.3	$6,639.4	$7,061.4	$7,740.9	$8,562.1	$8,732.0
Loss reserves	$3,051.3	$3,437.8	$3,781.3	$4,084.8	$4,284.5	$4,507.0
Loss adjustment expenses	493.1	551.9	596.2	620.2	636.5	721.5
Unearned premiums	810.6	728.8	807.4	972.9	1,031.3	1,083.5
Commercial paper	5.1	8.9	5.5	111.8	633.4	601.5
Other policyholder funds	33.4	50.8	57.0	65.3	82.2	85.3
Debentures due in 1995	70.8	70.1	67.0	64.0	64.0	64.0
Accrued expenses	91.5	96.9	100.4	118.8	121.5	124.9
Other liabilities	277.1	293.2	240.4	271.1	327.3	342.1
Total liabilities	4,832.9	5,238.4	5,655.2	6,308.9	7,180.7	7,529.8
Preferred stock	1.9	.5	.3	—	—	—
Common stock	113.7	113.8	113.9	114.0	114.1	114.2
Additional paid-in capital	5.3	6.2	7.2	8.7	9.8	10.1
Unrealized investment gains (losses)	27.2	79.1	19.7	42.5	(24.2)	5.6
Retained earnings	1,202.3	1,317.3	1,377.8	1,404.1	1,427.1	1,226.2
Treasury stock, at cost	(111.0)	(115.9)	(112.7)	(137.3)	(145.4)	(153.9)
Equity	1,239.4	1,401.0	1,406.2	1,432.0	1,381.4	1,202.2
Total liabilities and equity	$6,072.3	$6,639.4	$7,061.4	$7,740.9	$8,562.1	8,732.0

a. At market value.

Exhibit 8 Proposed Offering of Various Maturities of Separate Issues of Tender Option Bonds (Tops)—Description of Municipal Portfolio

Item No.	Issuer and Title of Bonds	Face Amount (000)	Interest Rate (% per annum)	Maturity (mo/day/yr)	Interest Payable (mo/day)	Sinking Fund Redemptions (mo/day/yr)[a]	Optional Redemptions (mo/day/yr)[a]	Ratings (Moody's/S&P)	Tender Date (mo/day/yr)	Strike Price (% of par)[b]	Yield to Tender Date[c]	Reoffering Price (% of Par)
ARIZONA												
1	Salt River Project Agricultural Improvement Power District, Salt River Project Electric System Revenued Bonds, 1976 Series D, dated 11/1/76, CUSIP 795747KG8	3,000	6.40	1/1/16	1/1-7/1	1/1/07	1/1/87 @ 103%	Aa/AA	4/15/88	100	7.70	96.58
ARKANSA												
2	City of Rogers, Arkansas, Residential Housing Facilities Board, Single Family Mortgage Revenue Bonds (Privately Insured or Federally Insured or Guaranteed Mortgage Loans) 1979 Series, dated 9/1/79, CUSIP 77507AU4	2,460	7.25	9/1/11	3/1-9/1	9/1/99	9/1/89 @ 103%	NR/AA	4/15/88	100	7.60	99.08
CALIFORNIA												
3	Industry Urban—Development Agency, Civic—Recreational—Industrial Redevelopment Project No. 1, Tax Allocation Refunding Bonds, 1975, dated 5/1/75, CUSIP 456567CD6	1,000	7.75	11/1/00	5/1-11/1	—	11/1/85 @ 102%	NR/A	4/15/88	100	7.75	100.00
COLORADO												
4	City of Colorado Springs, Utilities System Revenue Refunding Bonds, Series 1975, dated 8/15/75, CUSIP 19663OLL9	150	7.35	11/15/98	11/15-5/15	—	11/15/95 @ 100%	Aa/AA	4/15/88	100	7.35	100.00

Exhibit 8 Proposed Offering of Various Maturities of Separate Issues of Tender Option Bonds (Tops)—Description of Municipal Portfolio (Continued)

Item No.	Issuer and Title of Bonds	Face Amount (000)	Interest Rate (% per annum)	Maturity (mo/day/yr)	Interest Payable (mo/day)	Sinking Fund Redemptions (mo/day/yr)[a]	Optional Redemptions (mo/day/yr)[a]	Ratings (Moody's/S&P)	Tender Date (mo/day/yr)	Strike Price (% of par)[b]	Yield to Tender Date[c]	Reoffering Price (% of Par)
CONNECTICUT												
5	State of Connecticut Health and Educational Facilities Authority, Revenue Bonds, St. Francis Hospital Issue, Series A, dated 7/1/71, CUSIP 207741LW7	400	6.875	7/1/03	1/1-7/1	7/1/89	7/1/85 @ 104%	NR/A	4/15/88	100	7.90	97.31
6	Connecticut Housing Finance Authority, Housing Mortgage Finance Program Bonds, 1976 Series B, dated 11/15/76, CUSIP 207745GZ7	3,000	6.40	11/15/19	5/15-11/15	11/15/96	11/15/86 @ 103%	Aa/AA	4/15/88	100	7.60	96.83
FLORIDA												
7	Greater Orlando Aviation Authority, Airport Facilities Revenue Bonds, 1978 Series of City of Orlando, Florida, dated 9/1/78, CUSIP 39227 4AR7	2,400	7.00	10/1/08	10/1-4/1	10/1/96	10/1/88 @ 102.5%	A/A-	4/15/88	100	7.90	97.64
8	State of Florida. Division of Bond Finance of the Department of General Services, Department of Transportation. Turnpike Revenue Bonds, Series of 1970, dated 11/1/70, CUSIP 343136AB3	500	7.10	11/1/10	5/1-11/1	—	5/1/85 @ 103%	A/BBB	4/15/88	100	7.90	97.50

Exhibit 8 Proposed Offering of Various Maturities of Separate Issues of Tender Option Bonds (Tops)—Description of Municipal Portfolio (Continued)

Item No.	Issuer and Title of Bonds	Face Amount (000)	Interest Rate (% per annum)	Maturity (mo/day/yr)	Interest Payable (mo/day)	Sinking Fund Redemptions (mo/day/yr)[a]	Optional Redemptions (mo/day/yr)[a]	Ratings (Moody's/S&P)	Tender Date (mo/day/yr)	Strike Price (% of par)[b]	Yield to Tender Date[c]	Reoffering Price (% of Par)
GEORGIA												
9.	City of Atlanta, Airport Extension and Improvement Revenue Bonds, Series 1975, dated 1/1/75, CUSIP 047789YA4	1,790	6.50	1/1/04	1/1-7/1	—	1/1/86 @ 103%	A/A	4/15/88	100	8.20	95.56
ILLINOIS												
10.	The Board of Trustees of the University of Illinois, University of Illinios Auxiliary Facilities System Revenue Bonds, Series M, dated 6/1/78, CUSIP 914352Y60	2,000	6.75	10/1/08	4/1-10/1	10/1/07	non-callable	Aa/AAA	4/15/88	100	7.40	98.28
IOWA												
11.	City of Council Bluffs, Hospital Facility Revunue Bonds, Series 1976 (Jennie Edmundson Memorial Hospital Project), dated 7/1/76, CUSIP 222150AP9	100	7.40	7/1/01	1/1-7/1	7/1/92	7/1/86 @ 103%	A1/A+	4/15/88	100	7.60	99.47
MAINE												
12.	Town of Skowhegan, Pollution Control Revenue Bonds (Scott Paper Company Project), Series A of 1975, dated 7/1/75, CUSIP 830802AA2	2,500	7.625	7/1/00	1/1-7/1	7/1/91	7/1/85 @ 104%	A2/A–	4/15/88	100	7.70	99.80

Exhibit 8 Proposed Offering of Various Maturities of Separate Issues of Tender Option Bonds (Tops)—Description of Municipal Portfolio (Continued)

Item No. Issuer and Title of Bonds	Face Amount (000)	Interest Rate (% per annum)	Maturity (mo/day/yr)	Interest Payable (mo/day)	Sinking Fund Redemptions (mo/day/yr)[a]	Optional Redemptions (mo/day/yr)[a]	Ratings (Moody's/S&P)	Tender Date (mo/day/yr)	Strike Price (% of par)[b]	Yield to Tender Date[c]	Reoffering Price (% of Par)
MICHIGAN											
13 Michigan State Housing Development Authority, Housing Development Bonds, 1971 Series A, dated 7/1/71, CUSIP 594649CM5	600	6.50	7/1/03	1/1-7/1	—	7/1/85 @ 103%	A1/A+	4/15/88	100	8.00	96.07
MISSOURI											
14 Missouri Housing Development Commision, Housing Development Bonds (Federally insured Mortgage Loans) Series July 15, 1978, dated 7/15/78, CUSIP 606353KN9	2,000	6.60	7/15/21	7/15-1/15	7/15/04	7/15/89 @ 103%	Aa/AA	4/15/88	100	7.80	96.84
NEW HAMPSHIRE											
15 New Hampshire Housing Finance Agency, Single Family Mortgage Purchase Bonds, 1979 Series A, dated 5/1/79, CUSIP 644685DG1	2,000	7.10	1/1/11	1/1-7/1	1/1/00	1/1/90 @ 103%	A1/A+	4/15/88	100	7.75	98.29
NEW JERSEY											
16 The Bergen County Utilities Authority, Revenue Refunding Bonds (Series 1978), dated 8/15/78, CUSIP 083786AV5	3,800	6.40	12/15/09	6/15-12/15	12/15/01	12/15/87 @ 102%	Aa/A+	4/15/88	100	7.75	96.45
17 The Montville Township Municipal Utilities Authority, Revenue Bonds, Series A, dated 6/1/71, CUSIP 615305BZ1	200	7.00	12/1/03	6/1-12/1	—	6/1/85 @ 104%	A/NR	4/15/88	100	7.90	97.64

Exhibit 8 Proposed Offering of Various Maturities of Separate Issues of Tender Option Bonds (Tops)—Description of Municipal Portfolio (Continued)

Item No. Issuer and Title of Bonds	Face Amount (000)	Interest Rate (% per annum)	Maturity (mo/day/yr)	Interest Payable (mo/fday)	Sinking Fund Redemptions (mo/day/yr)[a]	Optional Redemptions (mo/day/yr)[a]	Ratings (Moody's/S&P)	Tender Date (mo/day/yr)	Strike Price (% of par)[b]	Yield to Tender Date[c]	Reoffering Price (% of Par)
18 The Montville Township Municipal Utilities Authority, Revenue Bonds, Series A, dated 6/1/71, CUSIP 615305CA5	210	7.00	12/1/04	6/1-12/1	—	6/1/85 @ 104%	A/NR	4/15/88	100	7.90	97.64
19 The Montville Township Municipal Utilities Authority, Revenue Bonds, Series A, dated 6/1/71, CUSIP 615305CB3	225	7.00	12/1/05	6/1-12/1	—	6/1/85 @ 104%	A/NR	4/15/88	100	7.90	97.64
20 The Montville Township Municipal Utilities Authority, Revenue Bonds, Series A, dated 6/1/71, CUSIP 615305CC1	240	7.00	12/1/06	6/1-12/1	—	6/1/85 @ 104%	A/NR	4/15/88	100	7.90	97.64
21 The Montville Township Municipal Utilities Authority, Revenue Bonds, Series A, dated 6/1/71, CUSIP 615305CD9	125	7.00	12/1/07	6/1-12/1	—	6/1/85 @ 104%	A/NR	4/15/88	100	7.90	97.64
22 North Jersey District Water Supply Commission, Water System Bonds (Series A), dated 5/1/77, CUSIP 660160AW2	3,000	6.70	11/1/17	5/1-11/1	11/1/08	11/1/87 @ 103%	NR/A	4/15/88	100	8.00	96.59
23 The Western Monmouth Utilities Authority, Sewer Revenue Bonds, Series of 1978, dated 1/15/78, CUSIP 958700BT2	2,000	6.80	2/1/14	2/1-8/1	2/1/96	non-callable	Baa1/BBB	4/15/88	100	8.40	95.83

Exhibit 8 Proposed Offering of Various Maturities of Separate Issues of Tender Option Bonds (Tops)—Description of Municipal Portfolio (Continued)

Item No. Issuer and Title of Bonds	Face Amount (000)	Interest Rate (% per annum)	Maturity (mo/day/yr)	Interest Payable (mo/day)	Sinking Fund Redemptions (mo/day/yr)[a]	Optional Redemptions (mo/day/yr)[a]	Ratings (Moody's/S&P)	Tender Date (mo/day/yr)	Strike Price (% of par)[b]	Yield to Tender Date[c]	Reoffering Price (% of Par)
24 New Jersey Economic Development Authority Economic Development First Mortgage Revenue Bonds, Series A 1979 (Lodi), K mart Corporation—Tenant and Guarantor, dated 4/1/79, CUSIP 645775BG1	2,500	7.00	4/1/05	4/1-10/1	4/1/90	4/1/89 @ 103%	A1/NR	4/15/88	100	8.00	97.38
NEW YORK											
25 New York State Energy Research and Development Authority, Pollution Control Revenue Bonds (New York State Electrical & Gas Corporation Projects), Series A, dated 12/1/76, CUSIP 649845AA2	2,500	6.875	12/1/06	6/1-12/1	12/1/92	12/1/86 @ 103%	Baa2/BBB+	4/15/88	100	8.25	96.41
26 Dormitory Authority of the State of New York, Revenue Bonds, Cornell University Issue, Series G, dated 7/1/77, CUSIP 649831AS3	3,000	6.50	7/1/02	1/1-7/1	7/1/93	7/1/87 @ 103%	Aa/AA	4/15/88	100	7.50	97.36
27 Power Authority of the State of New York, General Purpose Bonds, Series F, Due January 1, 2010, dated 2/1/77, CUSIP 649892LF1	2,000	6.625	1/1/10	7/1-1/1	1/1/93	2/1/87 @ 104%	A1/A+	4/15/88	100	7.60	97.43
28 Power Authority of the State of New York, General Purpose Bonds, Series A, Due January 1, 2010, dated 2/1/75, CUSIP 649892JL1	1,600	7.875	1/1/10	1/1-7/1	1/1/87	7/1/85 @ 104%	A1/A+	4/15/88	100	7.50	100.99

Exhibit 8   Proposed Offering of Various Maturities of Separate Issues of Tender Option Bonds (Tops)—Description of Municipal Portfolio (Continued)

Item No. Issuer and Title of Bonds	Face Amount (000)	Interest Rate (% per annum)	Maturity (mo/day/yr)	Interest Payable (mo/day)	Sinking Fund Redemptions (mo/day/yr)[a]	Optional Redemptions (mo/day/yr)[a]	Ratings (Moody's/S&P)	Tender Date (mo/day/yr)	Strike Price (% of par)[b]	Yield to Tender Date[c]	Reoffering Price (% of Par)
OKLAHOMA											
29 Grand River Ddm Authority Revenue Bonds, 1978 Series, dated 8/1/78, CUSIP 386442EV5	1,000	7.40	6/1/08	6/1-12/1	6/1/99	6/1/88 @ 103%	A/A–	4/15/88	100	7.50	99.74
OREGON											
30 State of Oregon, Housing Finance Revenue Bonds (Single-Family Mortgage Programs), 1978 Series A, dated 6/1/78, CUSIP 686077BY3	500	6.70	7/1/09	1/1-7/1	7/1/99	7/1/88 @ 103%	A1/A+	4/15/88	100	8.20	96.08
PENNSYLVANIA											
31 Bensalem Township Authority, Bucks County, Pennsylvania, Water and Sewer Revenue Refunding Bonds, 1978 Series, dated 5/1/78, CUSIP 082365EZ6	335	6.75	12/1/14	6/1-12/1	12/1/99	12/1/88 @ 103%	A/A+	4/15/88	100	8.00	96.72
32 City of Philadelphia, Water and Sewer Revenue Bonds, First Series, dated 5/1/74, CUSIP 717890BJ5	3,000	7.00	4/1/09	10/1-4/1	4/1/00	10/1/85 @ 102.5%	A/A	4/15/88	100	8.00	97.38
PUERTO RICO											
33 Puerto Rico Housing Finance Corporation, Mortgage Revenue Bonds, Series 1978E (Alturas del Senorial Section 8 Assisted Project/FHA Insured Mortgage), dated 10/1/78, CUSIP 745270AX6	1,000	7.25	7/1/20	1/1-7/1	7/1/85	7/1/88 @ 103%	NR/AA	4/15/88	100	100	100.00

Exhibit 8 Proposed Offering of Various Maturities of Separate Issues of Tender Option Bonds (Tops)—Description of Municipal Portfolio (Continued)

Item No. Issuer and Title of Bonds	Face Amount (000)	Interest Rate (% per annum)	Maturity (mo/day/yr)	Interest Payable (mo/day)	Sinking Fund Redemptions (mo/day/yr)[a]	Optional Redemptions (mo/day/yr)[a]	Ratings (Moody's/S&P)	Tender Date (mo/day/yr)	Strike Price (% of par)[b]	Yield to Tender Date[c]	Reoffering Price (% of Par)
34 Puerto Rico Housing Finance Corporation, Mortgage Revenue Bonds, Series 1979B, Lagos Del Norte project (FHA Insured Mortgage Loan-Section 8 Assisted Project), dated 4/1/79, CUSIP 745270BB3	1740	7.40	11/1/11	5/1-11/1	5/1/85	5/1/94 @ 103%	NR/AA	4/15/88	100	7.30	100.27
35 Puerto Rico Highway Authority, Highway Revenue Bonds (Series B), dated 1/1/70, CUSIP 745194BS8 ...	1,000	7.00	7/1/98	1/1-7/1	7/1/91	7/1/85 @ 102.5%	Baa1/A	4/15/88	100	7.90	97.64
36 Puerto Rico Highway Authority, Highway Revenue Bonds (Series D), dated 1/1/71, CUSIP 745194DN7	1,000	6.75	7/1/01	1/1-7/1	7/1/93	7/1/85 @ 102%	Baa1/A	4/15/88	100	8.00	96.73
37 Puerto Rico Water Resources Authority, Electric Revenue Bonds (Series 1971), dated 1/1/71, CUSIP 745264LD1) ..	1,000	6.75	1/1/01	1/1-7/1	—	7/1/85 @ 102%	Baa1/A	4/15/88	100	8.00	96.73
SOUTH CAROLINA											
38 Berkeley County, Pollution Control Facilities Revenue Bonds, Series 1979 (Alumax Project), dated 6/1/79, CUSIP 084193AE1	125	7.00	12/1/08	6/1-12/1	12/1/00	6/1/89 @ 103%	A2/A	4/15/88	100	7.90	97.64

Exhibit 8 Proposed Offering of Various Maturities of Separate Issues of Tender Option Bonds (Tops)—Description of Municipal Portfolio (Continued)

Item No. Issuer and Title of Bonds	Face Amount (000)	Interest Rate (% per annum)	Maturity (mo/day/yr)	Interest Payable (mo/day)	Sinking Fund Redemptions (mo/day/yr)[a]	Optional Redemptions (mo/day/yr)[a]	Ratings (Moody's/S&P)	Tender Date (mo/day/yr)	Strike Price % of par[b]	Yield to Tender Date[c]	Reoffering Price (% of Par)
TEXAS											
39 City of Houston, Texas, Water System Revenue Bonds, Series 1969, dated 9/1/69, CUSIP 44243BDG9	250	6.50	12/1/02	12/1-6/1	—	non-callable	Aaa/AAA	4/15/88	100	7.30	97.88
40 Lower Colorado River Authority Revenue Bonds, Series 1975, dated 7/1/75, CUSIP 548100HJ8	250	6.50	5/1/00	5/1-11/1	—	non-callable	Aaa/AAA	4/15/88	100	7.30	97.88
WEST VIRGINIA											
41 West Virginia Housing Development Fund, Single-Family Mortgage Program Bonds, 1979 Series A, dated 4/1/79, CUSIP 956626JW6	3,500	7.125	7/1/10	1/1-7/1	7/1/00	7/1/89 @ 102.5%	Aaa/AA−	4/15/88	100	7.60	98.75

a. Redemptions next occur commencing on the date specified. Sinking fund redemptions generally redeem only part of an issue at the par value of the Bonds selected for redemption in accordance with the specific provisions thereof. Optional redemptions may be exercised in whole or part initially at the price specified and thereafter at prices often declining to par in accordance with the provisions of the Bonds. Certain Bonds may be redeemable at par in whole or in part prior to the sinking fund or optional redemption dates, or at any time thereafter, as a result of extraordinary or special mandatory redemptions. Purchasers of the Bonds are advised to inform themselves of the specific redemption provisions applicable thereto. As described under "THE OPTION AGREEMENT—Termination of Obligation to Purchase" and "THE LETTER OF CREDIT" in the Secondary Reoffering Circular, the obligations of New England PC to purchase the bonds under the Option Agreement and of the Tender Agent to draw under the Letter of Credit terminate in the event of an early redemption of the Bonds.

b. Plus accrued interest on the Bond at the rate stated therein to the Tender Date.

c. Plus accrued interest on the Bond to the date of delivery.

Exhibit 8 Proposed Offering of Various Maturities of Separate Issues of Tender Option Bonds (Tops)—Description of Municipal Portfolio (Continued)

Portfolio Summary

(April 4, 1985)

Total Face Value:	$60,000,000	
Weighted Average Coupon:	6.89%	
Weighted Average Maturity:	24 years, 1.5 months	
Weighted Average Rating:	Strong A	

	$	% of Par	Yield
Estimated Reoffering Proceeds (TOPS):	58,593,203	97.66	7.78%[a]
Estimated Market Value of Straight Bonds:	42,265,620	70.44	10.21%[b]

a. Yield to maturity.
b. Yield to tender date (put exercise date).

Exhibit 9 Municipal Bond Yields, April 3, 1985

Municipal Bonds

NEW ISSUE SCALES

Yields	Chg (bp) 3 Apr85	Wk	Past 12 Mos High	Low
Prime-Grade GO				
1-Yr	5.25%	-25	6.75%	4.50%
3-Yr	6.75	-5	8.00	6.20
5-Yr	7.25	-5	8.40	6.80
10-Yr	8.40	-10	9.60	7.80
15-Yr	9.10	-5	10.40	8.60
20-Yr	9.25	-10	10.70	8.75
30-Yr	9.30	-10	10.75	8.85
Med-Grade GO				
30-Yr	9.95	-5	11.25	9.50
Revenue (Long)				
3-Yr Put AA	7.50	-25	8.75	7.25
Elec AA	10.13	-12	11.25	9.60
Elec A	10.38	-12	11.75	9.75
Wtr-Sew AA	10.00	-13	11.38	9.38
State HFA A	10.25	-13	12.00	9.63
Hosp A	10.25	-13	11.88	9.75
Util P.C A	10.50	0	11.88	9.75

Yield Spreads (bp)	3Apr 85	Chg (bp) Wk	4 Wks	Past 12 Mos Max	Avg	Min
INTRAMARKET						
6 Mo NYS vs Mig 1 Note	-25	0	—	—	—	—
New Lg-Med vs Prime GO	65	5	0	70	54	30
A Rev vs Med GO	43	-7	-7	98	44	8
A Rev vs AA Elec Rev	25	0	-12	50	25	12
Prime Yld Curve						
1-Yr vs 6-Mo Mig 1 Nt.	25	-50	—	—	—	—
10-Yr vs 1-Yr	315	15	5	330	269	190
20-Yr vs 10-Yr	85	0	5	130	96	75
30-Yr vs 20-Yr	5	0	0	15	8	5
30-Yr vs 1-Yr	405	15	10	435	374	300
INTERMARKET						
Prime GO as % Govt (Pretax)						
5-Yr	64	-1	1	69	63	59
10-Yr	72	-1	0	76	71	66
30-Yr	79	-1	1	87	79	73
Lg AA Elec Rev as % U.S.	86	-1	1	94	85	78
Prime as % AAA Util	73	01	1	82	73	67
New A Util PC vs Corp	-250	13	50	-163	-313	-400

Exhibit 9 Municipal Bond Yields, April 3, 1985 (Continued)

Municipal Bonds

	Yield (3 Apr 85)
Seasoned Issues	
AAA-Rated State GOs	9.42%
A-Rated Revenue Bonds:	
State Multifamily Housing	10.30
State Single-family Housing	10.30
Electric Revenue	10.30
Pollution Control/Utility	10.30
Pollution Control/Industrial	10.17
Turnpike Revenue	10.17
Hospital Revenue	10.30
Water and Sewer Revenue	10.05
Airport Revenue	10.30

Source: Salomon Brothers Inc.

Exhibit 10 Yields on Selected Fixed Income Instruments, April 3, 1985

Maturity	Instrument	Yield
One-Year	Treasury	9.51%
	AA Financials	10.00
Three-Year	Treasury	10.85
	AA Financials	11.25
Five-Year	Treasury	11.29
	Agency	11.60
Ten-Year	Treasury	11.68
	Agency	11.95
	AAA Industrial	12.00
	A Industrial	12.50
	GNMA (12 1/2%)	12.94
Twenty-Year	Treasury	11.88
Thirty-Year	Treasury	11.76
	AAA Industrial	12.38
	A Industrial	12.75

Exhibit 11 AMBAC Portfolio Insurance for Municipal Securities (PIMS) 1985 Premium Schedule

Classification		Interest Rate of Bonds										
		Less than 5%			5% to less than 6%			6% to less than 7%			7% to less than 8%		
	S&P Bond Rating	Regular Annual Premium ($)	Initial Servicing Fee	Total Annual Cost ($)	Regular Annual Premium ($)	Initial Servicing Fee	Total Annual Cost ($)	Regular Annual Premium ($)	Initial Servicing Fee	Total Annual Cost ($)	Regular Annual Premium ($)	Initial Servicing Fee	Total Annual Cost ($)
CLASS 1													
General Obligation & Utilities	AAA	.95	1.05	2.00	1.00	1.05	2.05	1.05	1.05	2.10	1.10	1.05	2.15
	AA	1.10	1.05	2.15	1.20	1.00	2.20	1.30	1.00	2.30	1.40	1.00	2.40
Revenue Bonds	A	1.40	1.00	2.40	1.55	.95	2.50	1.70	.90	2.60	1.85	.90	2.75
	BBB	1.80	.90	2.70	2.00	.85	2.85	2.20	.80	3.00	2.40	.80	3.20
CLASS 2													
Revenue Bonds	AAA	1.43	.97	2.40	1.50	.95	2.45	1.58	.97	2.55	1.65	.95	2.60
Other Than	AA	1.65	.95	2.60	1.80	.90	2.70	1.95	.85	2.80	2.10	.85	2.95
Utilities	A	2.10	.85	2.95	2.33	.82	3.15	2.55	.75	3.30	2.78	.72	3.50
Revenue Bonds	BBB	2.70	.70	3.40	3.00	.65	3.65	3.30	.60	3.90	3.60	.55	4.15
CLASS 3													
Unsecured	AAA	1.90	.90	2.80	2.00	.85	2.85	2.10	.85	2.95	2.20	.80	3.00
Pollution Control	AA	2.20	.80	3.00	2.40	.80	3.20	2.60	.75	3.35	2.80	.70	3.50
Revenue Bonds	A	2.80	.70	3.50	3.10	.65	3.75	3.40	.60	4.00	3.70	.50	4.20
	BBB	3.60	.55	4.15	4.00	.45	4.45	4.40	.40	4.80	4.80	.30	5.10

Exhibit 11   AMBAC Portfolio Insurance for Municipal Securities (PIMS) 1985 Premium Schedule (Continued)

Classification			Interest Rate of Bonds											
			8% to less than 9%			9% to less than 10			10% to less than 11%			11% to less than 12%		
		S&P Bond Rating	Regular Annual Premium ($)	Initial Servicing Fee	Total Annual Cost ($)	Regular Annual Premium ($)	Initial Servicing Fee	Total Annual Cost ($)	Regular Annual Premium ($)	Initial Servicing Fee	Total Annual Cost ($)	Regular Annual Premium ($)	Initial Servicing Fee	Total Annual Cost($)
CLASS 1														
General Obligation &Utilities		AAA	1.15	1.05	2.20	1.20	1.05	2.25	1.25	1.05	2.30	1.30	1.00	2.30
		AA	1.50	.95	2.45	1.60	.95	2.55	1.70	.90	2.60	1.80	.90	2.70
Revenue Bonds		A	2.00	.85	2.85	2.15	.80	2.95	2.30	.80	3.10	2.45	.80	3.25
		BBB	2.60	.75	3.35	2.80	.70	3.50	3.00	.65	3.65	3.20	.60	3.80
CLASS 2														
Revenue Bonds		AAA	1.73	.92	2.65	1.80	.90	2.70	1.88	.87	2.75	1.95	.90	2.85
Other Than		AA	2.25	.80	3.05	2.40	.70	3.20	2.55	.75	3.30	2.70	.70	3.40
Utilities		A	3.00	.65	3.65	3.23	.62	3.85	3.45	.55	4.00	3.68	.52	4.20
Revenue Bonds		BBB	3.90	.50	4.40	4.20	.40	4.60	4.50	.35	4.85	4.80	.30	5.10
CLASS 3														
Unsecured		AAA	2.30	.80	3.10	2.40	.80	3.20	2.50	.75	3.25	2.60	.75	3.35
Pollution Control		AA	3.00	.65	3.65	3.20	.60	3.40	3.40	.55	3.95	3.60	.55	4.15
Revenue Bonds		A	4.00	.45	4.45	4.30	.40	4.60	4.60	.35	4.95	4.90	.30	5.20
		BBB	5.20	.25	5.45	5.60	.25	6.00	6.00	.25	6.25	6.40	.25	6.65

Exhibit 11   AMBAC Portfolio Insurance for Municipal Securities (PIMS) 1985 Premium Schedule (Continued)

Classification		Interest Rate of Bonds												
		12% to less than 13%			13% to less than 14%			14% to less than 15%			16% to less than 17%		
	S&P Bond Rating	Regular Annual Premium ($)	Initial Servicing Fee	Total Annual Cost ($)	Regular Annual Premium ($)	Initial Servicing Fee	Total Annual Cost ($)	Regular Annual Premium ($)	Initial Servicing Fee	Total Annual Cost ($)	Regular Annual Premium ($)	Initial Servicing Fee	Total Annual Cost ($)
General Obligation & Utilities	AAA	1.35	1.00	2.35	1.40	1.00	2.40	1.45	1.00	2.45	1.50	1.00	2.50
	AA	1.90	.90	2.80	2.00	.85	2.85	2.10	.85	2.95	2.20	.80	3.00
Revenue Bonds	A	2.60	.75	3.35	2.75	.70	3.45	2.90	.70	3.60	3.05	.65	3.70
	BBB	3.40	.55	3.95	3.60	.55	4.15	3.80	.50	4.70	4.00	.45	4.45
CLASS 2													
Revenue Bonds	AAA	2.03	.87	2.90	2.10	.85	2.95	2.18	.82	3.00	2.25	.80	3.05
Other Than	AA	2.85	.70	3.55	3.00	.65	3.65	3.15	.65	3.80	3.30	.60	3.90
Utilities	A	3.90	.50	4.40	4.13	.47	4.60	4.35	.40	4.75	4.58	.37	4.95
Revenue Bonds	BBB	5.10	.25	5.35	5.40	.25	5.65	5.70	.25	5.95	6.00	.25	6.25
CLASS 3													
Unsecured	AAA	2.70	.70	3.40	2.80	.70	3.50	2.90	.70	3.60	3.00	.65	3.65
Pollution Control	AA	3.80	.50	4.30	4.00	.45	4.45	4.20	.40	4.60	4.40	.40	4.80
Revenue Bonds	A	5.20	.25	5.45	5.50	.25	5.75	5.80	.25	6.05	6.10	.25	6.35
	BBB	6.80	.25	7.05	7.20	.25	7.45	7.60	.25	7.85	8.00	.25	8.25

Note: Initial Servicing fee schedule assumes minimum Bond denominations of $5,000 per Statement of Insurance. Such fees mat be higher than those indicated for lesser denominations.

APPENDIX 1

DESCRIPTION OF TYPICAL MUNICIPAL REVENUE BOND STRUCTURES

Airport Revenue Bonds

Secured by traffic-generated revenues, such as landing fees, concession fees, or airline fueling fees, or lease revenues for the use of specific facilities like terminals and hangars. The credit quality of the lessee is a key determinant of the rating of lease-based revenue bonds.

College and University Revenue Bonds

Secured by dormitory-room rental fees, tuition payments, and in some cases, the general assets of the issuing institution.

Hospital Revenue Bonds

Secured by the operating income of hospitals, which usually depends on federal and state reimbursement programs like Medicaid and Medicare, third-party commercial payers like Blue Cross, and individual patient payments.

Single-Family Mortgage Revenue Bonds

Secured by mortgage loan repayments on single-family home mortgages. Mortgages usually carry FHA, VA, or private mortgage insurance.

Multifamily Revenue Bonds

Issued to fund construction of multifamily housing projects for senior citizens and low-income families. Some are secured by federally insured mortgages, others by federal government operating subsidies.

Industrial Development and Pollution Control Revenue Bonds

Issued on behalf of corporate borrowers to fund a variety of industrial and commercial activities, including construction of manufacturing plants and shopping centers. Secured by lease payments from the corporation operating the facility.

Public Power Revenue Bonds

Secured by revenues generated by electric power plants. Some are used to fund a single issuer, who constructs and operates power plants and sells the electricity generated. Others are issued by groups of public and private investor-owned utilities for the joint financing of one or more power plants. The output from these plants is then distributed by the several issuers.

Resource Recovery Revenue Bonds

A resource recovery facility converts refuse (solid waste) into commercially salable energy, recoverable products, and residue to be land-filled. Revenues from such a facility consist of "tipping fees" per ton paid by those who deliver garbage to the facility for disposal; revenues from the steam, electricity, or refuse-derived fuel produced by the facility and sold to an electric power company or other energy user; and revenues from the sale of recoverable materials.

Seaport Revenue Bonds

Secured by specific lease agreements or pledged marine terminal and cargo tonnage fees.

Sewer Revenue Bonds

Secured by hookup fees and user charges. In most cases, substantial portions of sewer construction budgets are financed with federal grants.

Sports Complex and Convention Center Revenue Bonds

Secured by revenues from sporting or convention events held at the facilities and, in some instances, from related tax revenues, such as local motel and hotel room taxes.

Student Loan Revenue Bonds

Secured by repayments on student loans guaranteed by the federal government or by a state guaranty agency.

Toll-Road and Gas Tax Revenue Bonds

There are two types of highway revenue bonds. The bond proceeds of the first type are used to build such specific revenue-producing facilities as toll roads, bridges, and tunnels, and are secured by prospective toll collections. The second type of highway bond is secured by designated revenues other than toll collections, such as gasoline taxes, automobile registration payments, and driver's license fees.

Water Revenue Bonds

Water revenue bonds are issued to finance the construction of water treatment plants, pumping stations, collection facilities, and distribution systems, and are secured by connection fees and charges paid by the users of the water systems.

Source: Frank J. Fabozzi and Irving M. Pollack, eds. *The Handbook of Fixed-Income Securities* (Homewood, Ill.: Dow Jones Irwin, 1983).

APPENDIX 2

MUNICIPAL S&P DEBT RATING DEFINITIONS

A Standard & Poor's municipal debt rating is a current assessment of the credit worthiness of an obligor with respect to a specific obligation. This assessment can take into consideration obligors such as guarantors, insurers, or lessees.

The debt rating is not a recommendation to purchase, sell, or hold a security, inasmuch as it does not comment as to market price or suitability for a particular investor.

The ratings are based on current information furnished by the issuer or obtained by S&P from other sources it considers reliable. S&P does not perform an audit in connection with any rating and, on occasion, relies on unaudited financial information. The ratings could be changed, suspended, or withdrawn as a result of changes in, or unavailability of, such information, or for other reasons.

The ratings are based, in varying degrees, on the following considerations:

1. Likelihood of default—the capacity and willingness of the obligor as to the timely payment of interest and repayment of principal in accordance with the terms of the obligation
2. Nature and provisions of the obligation
3. Protection afforded by, and relative position of, the obligation in the event of bankruptcy, reorganization, or other arrangement under the laws of bankruptcy and other laws affecting creditors' rights

The following are the S&P ratings:

AAA—The highest rating assigned by Standard & Poor's. Capacity to pay interest and repay principal is extremely strong.

AA—Indicates a very strong capacity to pay interest and repay principal and differs from the highest-rated issues only in small degree.

A—indicates a strong capacity to pay interest and repay principal, although the debt was somewhat more susceptible to the adverse effects of changes in circumstances and economic conditions than debt in higher-rated categories.

BBB—Debt rated 'BBB' was regarded as having an adequate capacity to pay interest and repay principal. Whereas it normally exhibited adequate protection parameters, adverse economic conditions or changing circumstances were more likely to lead to a weakened capacity to pay interest and repay principal for debt in this category than in higher rated categories.

BB, B, CCC, CC—This debt is regarded, on balance, as predominantly speculative with respect to capacity to pay interest and repay principal in accordance with the terms of the obligation. BB indicates the lowest degree of speculation, and CC the highest degree. While such debt would likely have some quality and protective characteristics, these are outweighed by large uncertainties or major risk exposures to adverse conditions.

C—This rating is reserved for income bonds on which no interest is paid.

D—Indicates debt is in default, and payment of interest or repayment of principal is in arrears.

Plus (+) or Minus (−)—The ratings from AA to B can be modified by the addition of a plus or minus sign to show relative standing within the major rating categories.

NR—Indicates that no rating has been requested, that there is insufficient information on which to base a rating, or that S&P did not rate a particular type of obligation as a matter of policy.

Debt obligations of issuers outside the United States and its territories are rated on the same basis as domestic municipal issues. The ratings measure the credit worthiness of the obligor but do not take into account currency exchange and related uncertainties.

Under commercial bank regulations issued by the Comptroller of the Currency, bonds rated in the top four categories (AAA, AA, A, BBB, commonly known as investment grade ratings) are generally regarded as eligible for bank investment. In addition, the laws of various states governing legal investments impose certain rating or other standards for obligations eligible for investment by savings banks, trust companies, insurance companies and fiduciaries generally.

Source: Standard & Poor's Credit Overview: Municipal Ratings (New York: Standard & Poor's Corporation, 1983).

Schroders' Perpetual Floating-Rate Note Exchange Offer

On July 22, 1987, Yoshiharu Yamamoto, director and general manager of the Maruzen Bank and Trust Company,[1] looked at the telex his assistant had just handed him, which stated that the British merchant bank J. Henry Schroder Wagg & Co. Limited was offering an exchange (see Exhibit 1). Selected perpetual-floating rate notes plus specified amounts of cash could be exchanged for floating-rate notes due in 2015, plus nonvoting shares in a new company to be formed for the purpose of issuing the new floating-rate notes and the non-voting shares.

For Mr. Yamamoto the offer provided an opportunity to exchange Maruzen Bank's holdings of perpetual floating-rate notes (perps). The bank held $1 million face value of perps of the Bank of Ireland. These perps had coupons of three-month LIBOR plus 25 basis points (bp), and were trading at 78% of face value in July 1987. Maruzen also held $1 million face value of six-month LIMEAN plus 25 bp Barclays perps, trading at 91.25%. Maruzen had invested in the perps when they were trading close to face value. For the exchange, Maruzen would have to add cash of $217,600 to the Bank of Ireland perps and $144,700 to the Barclays perps (see Exhibit 2).

Mr. Yamamoto had been concerned about Maruzen Bank's perp holdings for some time. The discount on the perps seemed heavy and had not improved since the market turmoil that had started at the end of 1986. Furthermore, he was worried about the bank's capital position. There were persistent rumors in the financial district of Tokyo that the Japanese Ministry of Finance, like the Bank of England and the Federal Reserve, would shortly require Japanese banks to write down primary bank capital on a one-for-one basis due to the losses on their perp holdings.

When AAA floating-rate collateralized mortgage obligations (CMOs) first appeared in October 1986 at rates significantly above the rates on perps (LIBOR plus 40 bp versus

---

1   Maruzen Bank and Trust is a disguised Japanese bank.

This case was prepared by David M. Meerschwam as the basis of class discussion.

Copyright © 1987 by the President and Fellows of Harvard College. Harvard Business School case 288-057.

LIBOR plus 25 bp), Maruzen Bank had considered selling the perps and investing in the CMOs but decided to observe this new market for a period of time. Now it was unclear whether Mr. Yamamoto could still make this swap, because liquidity had dried up for some perps. Perhaps Schroders' offer presented a good opportunity, but he wondered how to evaluate the offer.

THE FLOATING-RATE NOTE MARKET

By the mid-1970s, the floating-rate note (FRN) market had grown to become a major part of the Euro securities markets. In response to increased interest-rate volatility and the floating-rate syndicated loan market, a new market developed for dated securities whose interest rates were linked to widely available reference rates (such as LIBOR, LIMEAN, U.S. Treasuries). While the first FRNs were issued in 1970, the instrument gained popularity in the early 1980s. In 1985, FRN issuance totaled $55.4 billion, representing about half of all new issues in the international capital market. Perps were floating-rate notes of infinite maturity. In 1985, they made up 29% of the total FRN market, and in 1986, with the overall floating-rate market shrinking (issue volume $48 billion), perps represented 46% of the FRN market.

Most of the perps issued were callable and linked most often to three-month or six-month LIBOR. LIBOR was the London Interbank Offer Rate, charged to the most creditworthy banks for borrowings. LIBID and LIMEAN were also used, to a lesser extent, as base rates for perps. LIBID was the London Interbank Bid Rate, i.e., the rate banks pay to attract Eurodollar deposits from their best customers. LIMEAN was the mean of LIBOR and LIBID. The coupon on floating-rate note instruments could be reset at different frequencies, but typically the base rate period was used (i.e., once every six months for six-month LIBOR).

Perps were issued by financial institutions, including U.S. thrifts, British building societies, and commercial banks. For many commercial banks, the perps could function as primary capital. Soon after the first perp issue in April 1984 by National Westminster Finance B.V. (Nat West Finance), the bank of England became the first monetary authority to include perps in the calculation of bank primary capital, in November 1984. And soon after the Federal Reserve Bank ruled on November 3, 1986, that perps could be included in the capital base of banks, given their infinite maturity, Citicorp entered the market on November 6 for $500 million, at three-month LIBID plus 37.5 bp.

Interest paid on the perps was deductible from profit before taxes in the United Kingdom and most other countries. In the United States, the Internal Revenue Service would not allow tax deductibility for an instrument of infinite maturity. To overcome this objection, the Citicorp perp carried a 30-year put provision, thereby satisfying the IRS.

Recognition of perps as primary bank capital in both the United States and the United Kingdom was important for the regulators, given their attempts to harmonize bank capital requirements across the three primary capital markets: Tokyo, New York, and London. Banks in the United Kingdom and in the United States that invested in perps were required to write their capital down (on a one-for-one basis). Also, many perps had a provision that under certain circumstances the interest would not be paid, in which case the dividends on preferred and common stock were omitted.

BRITISH COMMERCIAL BANK ISSUES

The four large British clearing banks used the perp market actively (see Table A). The first issuer in this market was National Westminster Bank (NatWest), which through a finance subsidiary, NatWest Finance, issued $500 million at six-month LIBOR plus 37.5 bp (500 6MLIBOR .375) in April 1984. By October 1984, Barclays had followed with an issue of $600 million at six-month LIBOR plus 25 bp (600 6MLIBOR .250). Lloyds entered the market in May 1985 with an issue of $750 million at six-month LIBOR plus 25 bp, and Midland had an identical issue that month. Maruzen Bank had invested in the Barclays 1 issue.

Table A   British Clearing Bank Perp Issues

Bank	Date	Issue
NatWest Finance	Apr. 1984	500 6MLIBOR .375
NatWest A	May 1985	500 6MLIMEAN .250
NatWest B	May 1985	500 6MLIMEAN .250
NatWest C	Nov. 1985	500 3MLibid .250
Barclays Overseas	Oct. 1984	600 6MLIBOR .250
Barclays 1	June 1985	600 6MLIMEAN .250
Barclays 2	Jan. 1986	750 6MLIBID .250
Midland 1	May 1985	750 6MLIBOR .250
Midland 2	Aug. 1985	500 6MLIBOR .250
Midland 3	Nov. 1986	300 6MLIBOR .100
Lloyds 1	May 1985	750 6MLIBOR .250
Lloyds 2	Oct. 1985	500 6MLIBOR .188
Lloyds 3	July 1986	600 6MLIBOR .100

THE PERP CRISIS

It is difficult to point to a precise date or cause for the decline in the market for perps. What is clear is that until December 1986 perps typically traded within half a point of their face value; then several perps started to trade around the mid-90s, and by January a number of perps were trading in the mid-80s (see Exhibit 3). While no one knew exactly what had caused this price dislocation, it was suspected that the behavior of Japanese investors was an important factor.

Market participants estimated that apart from significant dealer inventories that were rumored to exist, Japanese investors, notably banks, had accounted for 80% of all perp purchases. Also it was rumored that a November 27, 1986, issue for Standard Charter, a highly rated U.K. bank, at 6MLIBOR .150 had put significant pressure on the market, and that the manager of the issue, CSFB, had not fully supported the issue. Nonetheless, many issues had been priced even more aggressively than the Standard issue, some as low as 6MLIBOR .100.

In addition to the uncertainty about the causes of the collapse of the perp market, with many issues losing up to 25% of their face value, there was uncertainty about the appropriateness of the pricing method used in the market. A number of observers noted that it was difficult to price floating-rate note instruments and that perps were even harder to value. By the summer of 1987 perp prices had not recovered, liquidity in the market was highly uncertain, and regulators began to display concern. Several solutions to the perp problem were offered, including Schroders' exchange offer.

THE EXCHANGE OFFER

THE EXCHANGE

The offer proposed to exchange specified perps and specified amounts of cash for 28-year dated floating-rate notes (at LIBOR plus 30 bp) and shares in a special-purpose company. Units of $1 million face value of perps with the appropriate amounts of cash (see Exhibit 2) would be exchanged for $930,000 face value of FRNs and 50 B shares. A new special-purpose company, Security Investment Holdings Limited, was formed for this purpose.

ELIGIBILITY

Only specified series of perps were eligible for exchange. The company would determine which perps it would be willing to accept and what cash amounts were required.

INSURANCE

The FRNs that would be issued would be fully insured by Financial Security Assurance and were expected to be rated AAA. Part of the cash proceeds associated with the exchange would be used to purchase the insurance.

COMPANY INVESTMENTS

The company would use the remaining cash proceeds of the offering to purchase 28-year zero coupon bonds (from the highest-rated issuers like the U.S. Treasury and the World Bank) to defease the principal of the 28-year FRNs.

BANK OF ENGLAND

The Bank of England made it clear that for banks under its supervision it would not consider holdings of the FRNs to be issued by the company as holdings of other bank capital.

THE B SHARES

During years 1–28, the owners of the B shares would have the right to all income of the company after paying the interest on the FRNs and service costs of the company. After redemption in year 28 of the FRNs, the shares would be entitled to 90% of the assets and income (after service costs) of the company.

SERVICE COSTS

During the first 28 years service costs charged by the company would be $1,000 per year per $930,000 of new FRNs. After maturity of the FRNs, $100 per year per 50 B shares would be charged.

AUTHORIZED SHARE CAPITAL

Some 300,000 B class shares would be authorized. Also, 100 A class shares would be issued at par ($1) to an indirect, wholly owned subsidiary of the parent company of Schroder's. As such, the A class shares would be entitled to the remaining 10% of the assets and income after year 28.

THE DECISION

As Mr. Yamamoto considered the exchange offer, he noted that LIBOR was 8% and 30-year U.S. Treasuries were yielding 8.6%. Schroders informed him that the average coupon on all the perps listed as eligible for exchange was LIBOR plus 18.7 bp and that the average trading price was 88% (see Exhibit 4). Mr. Yamamoto was also told that FRNs like the new ones to be issued were trading at LIBOR plus 50 bp.

With these facts, Mr. Yamamoto began to review the balance sheet of this new company and the source of value to Schroders, Financial Security Assurance, and Maruzen Bank. He also tried to decide if either the Bank of Ireland or Barclays perps should be exchanged by considering the value of the B shares and the new FRNs. Finally, he took into account the regulatory environment regarding the treatment of perps and the new FRNs.

Exhibit 1   Schroders' Exchange Offer Circular

INFORMATION MEMORANDUM

EXCHANGE OFFER
by
SECURITY INVESTMENT HOLDINGS LIMITED
(Incorporated with limited liability in the Cayman Islands)
OF UP TO
U.S. $1,000,000,000
Guaranteed Secured Floating Rate Notes Due 2015
Comprising up to 29 Series
and
UP TO
53,763
Class B Non-voting Shares
The Notes will be Unconditionally and Irrevocably Guarenteed as to
Payment of Principal and Interest Pursuant to
a Surety Bond Issued by Financial Security Assurance Inc.

This Information Memorandum relates to an offer by Security Investment Holdings Limited (the "Company") to exchange selected Perpetual Notes and specified Dollar Amounts (each as defined herein) for Guaranteed Secured Floating Rate Notes Due 2015 (the "Notes") and Class B Non-voting Shares (the "B Shares") at a rate of $930,000 of Notes and 50 B Shares for every $1,000,000 of Perpetual Notes tendered upon the terms and are subject to the conditions set forth herein. The amount of the Notes and the number of the B Shares to be issued are subject to increase as described under "Terms and Conditions of the Exchange Offer."

The Notes will be issued in up to 29 series (each a "Series"), secured as described herein and unconditionally and irrevocably guaranteed as to payment of principal and interest pursuant to a surety bond (the "Surety Bond") issued by Financial Security Assurances Inc. ("Financial Security"). The notes will initially be in bearer form but will be subject to mandatory conversion into Notes in registered form in the circumstances described in "Conditions of the Notes" and in "Registration."

Interest on each Series of the Notes is payable in arrears on Interest Payment Dates (as defined herein) falling 4 business days after the interest payment dates for the corresponding exchanged issue or issues of Perpetual Notes, at a rate of 0.30 of 1 percent per annum above London interbank offered rates determined as provided herein.

The Notes will mature at par on 20th November, 2015. The Notes of any Series may be redeemed prior to maturity in whole or in part at par on any Interest Payment Date by the Company at the direction of Financial Security. In addition, Notes of any Series will, in certain circumstances, be redeemed mandatorily at par prior to maturity on any Interest Payment Date."

The B Shares will be in bearer form and will be issued subject to the Memorandum and Articles of Association of the Company—see "Description of the Shares."

Exhibit 1   Schroders' Exchange Offer Circular (Continued)

Application will be made to list the Notes and the B Shares on the Luxembourg Stock Exchange. If granted, the listing for the B Shares will not become effective until 120 days after completion of the distribution of all the B Shares, as determined by J. Henry Schroder Wagg & Co. Limited ("Schroders").

The Notes are expected, on issue, to be assigned as AAA rating by Standard & Poor's Corporation and Nippon Investors Service Inc., and an Aaa rating by Moody's Investors Service, Inc. A credit rating is not a recommendation to buy, sell or hold securities and may be subject to revision or withdrawal at any time by the assigning rating organization.

The Notes of each Series will be represented initially by a temporary Global Note to be deposited with a common depositary for Morgan Guaranty Trust Company of New York, as operator of the Euro-clear System ("Euro-clear") and CEDEL S.A. ("Cedel") on or about 13th August, 1987. Each temporary Global Note will be exchangeable for definitive Notes, in bearer form, with detachable coupons and talons, not earlier than 90 days after the completion of the distribution of all the Notes, as determined by Schroders, upon certification that the beneficial owners thereof are not U.S. persons (as defined herein). The B Shares will be represented initially by a single bearer certificate which will be deposited with the common depositary in like manner. Such share certificate will be exchangeable for definitive bearer share certificates (in units of 5 B Shares or an integral multiple thereof), with coupons for dividends and other rights attached, not earlier than 120 days after completion of the distribution of all of the B Shares, as determined by Schroders, upon certification as aforesaid.

J. Henry Schroder Wagg & Co. Limited

Salomon Brothers International   Nomura International
        Limited   Limited

Dated 22nd July, 1987

Source: Financial Security Assurance.

Exhibit 2 Cash Amounts Required for Each $1 Million Face Value of Eligible Perpetual Floating-Rate Notes until July 24, 1987, at 4 p.m.

Eligible Perps	Additional Cash Required from Perp Holder for Exchange
Bank of Ireland	$217,600
Bank of Scotland	174,800
Banque Nationale de Paris	164,700
Banque Paribas	164,400
Banque Paribas	167,900
Barclays Overseas Investment Co. BV	139,900
Barclays Bank Plc (Series 1)	144,700
Barclays Bank Plc (Series 2)	144,100
Bergen Bank A/S	177,600
Canadian Imperial Bank of Commerce	174,900
Christiania Bank of Kreditkasse	174,300
Citicorp	142,500
Commissioners of the State Bank of Victoria	142,800
Den Danske Bank of 1871 A/S	174,900
Den Norske Creditbank	174,600
Genossenschaftliche Zentralbank A/S	175,200
Hong Kong and Shanghai Banking Corp. (Series 1)	187,700
Hong Kong and Shanghai Banking Corp. (Series 2)	192,200
Hong Kong and Shanghai Banking Corp. (Series 3)	197,300
Hydro-Quebec	142,400
Lloyds Bank Plc (Series 1)	152,600
Lloyds Bank Plc (Series 2)	154,400
Lloyds Bank Plc (Series 3)	157,900
Midland Bank Plc (Series 1)	172,500
Midland Bank Plc (Series 2)	172,500
Midland Bank Plc (Series 3)	177,100
National Westminster Finance BV	139,900
National Westminster Bank Plc (Series A)	143,900
National Westminster Bank Plc (Series B)	143,900
National Westminster Bank Plc (Series C)	143,900
Republic New York Corp.	157,400

Exhibit 2   Cash Amounts Required for Each $1 Million Face Value of Eligible Perpetual Floating-Rate Notes Until July 24, 1987, at 4 p.m. (Continued)

Eligible Perps	Additional Cash Required from Perp Holder for Exchange
Royal Bank of Canada	172,400
Royal Bank of Scotland Group Plc	174,700
Royal Trust Co. Ltd.	217,300
Société Générale	167,400
Standard Chartered Plc (Series 3)	197,400
Standard Chartered Plc (Series 4)	197,400

Source: International Financing Review, July 1987.

Exhibit 3   Price Profile, National Westminster Bank Perpetual Floating-Rate Notes versus Dated Floating-Rate Notes, Daily Data, January 2, 1986–June 5, 1987

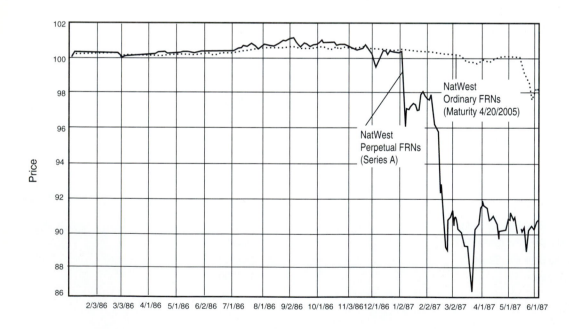

Source: Salomon Brothers Inc.

Exhibit 4 Selected Details of the Eligible Perpetual Note Issues

Issuer	Issue Amount ($ millions)	Coupon
Bank of Ireland	$150	3M LIBOR+25 bp
Bank of Scotland	250	6M LIMEAN+25 bp
Banque Nationale de Paris	500	6M LIBOR+7.5 bp
Banque Paribas	200	3M LIMEAN+37.5 bp
Banque Paribas	400	3M LIBOR+12.5 bp
Barclays Overseas Investment Company BV	600	6M LIBOR+25 bp
Barclays Bank Plc (Series 1)	600	6M LIMEAN+25 bp
Barclays Plc (Series 2)	750	6m LIBID+25 bp
Bergen Bank A/S	200	6M LIBOR+12.5 bp
Canadian Imperial Bank Commerce	300	6M LIBOR+25 bp
Christinina Bank of Kreditkasse	200	6M LIBOR+18.75 bp
Citicorp	500	3M LIBID+37.5 bp
The Commisioners of the State Bank of Victoria	125	6M LIBOR+6.25 bp
Den Danske Bank of 1817 A/S	100	6M LIBOR+25 bp
Den Norske Creditbank	150	3M LIBOR+25 bp
Genossenschaftliche Zentralbank AG	100	6M LIBOR+25 bp
HongKong & Shanghai Banking Corp (Series 1)	400	6M LIBOR+25 bp
HongKong & Shanghai Banking Corp (Series 2)	400	3M LIMEAN+25 bp
HongKong & Shanghai Banking Corp (Series 3)	400	3M LIMEAN+18.75 bp
Hydro Quebec	400	6M LIBOR+6.25 bp
Lloyds Bank Plc (Series 1)	750	6M LIBOR+25 bp
Lloyds Bank Plc (Series 2)	500	3M LIBOR+18.75 bp
Lloyds Bank Plc (Series 3)	600	6M LIBOR+10 bp
Midland Bank Plc (Series 1)	750	6M LIBOR+25 bp
Midland Bank Plc (Series 2)	500	6M LIBOR+25 bp
Midland Bank Plc (Series 3)	300	6M LIBOR+10 bp
National Westminster Finance BV	500	6M LIBOR+12.5 bp
National Westminster Bank Plc (Series A)	500	6M LIMEAN+25 bp
National Westminster Bank Plc (Series B)	500	6M LIMEAN+25 bp
National Westminster Bank Plc (Series C)	500	3M LIBID+25 bp
Republic New York Corp	150	6M LIBOR+25 bp
Royal Bank of Canada	300	3M LIMEAN+25 bp
Royal Bank of Scotland Group Plc	350	6M LIMEAN+25 bp
Royal Trust Co. Ltd.	150	6M LIBOR+15 bp
Societe Generale	300	6M LIBOR+7.5 bp
Standard Chartered Plc (Series 3)	400	6M LIBOR+27.5 bp
Standard Chartered Plc (Series 4)	300	6M LIBOR+15 bp

Source: Information Memorandum, Financial Security Assistance.

Metromedia Broadcasting Corporation

"Good luck, Tom—you're going to need it!"

As Mr. Tom Forsyth put down his phone he began to question his plans to recommend a significant expansion in high-yield, or junk, bond investments to the board of directors of Anchor Savings and Loan. Mr. Forsyth had called David Willis, chairman and chief executive officer of Anchor, to request that his high-yield investment proposal be added to the agenda of the board's November 24th meeting. Upon hearing the subject of Mr. Forsyth's presentation, the chairman had warned him to expect a lively debate of the prudence of Anchor's investing in high-yield securities.

Anchor first purchased high-yield bonds in 1982, following the passage of legislation empowering federally insured thrifts to make commercial loans in amounts equal to 10% of their assets.[1] Like many thrifts, Anchor had suffered substantial losses on its portfolio of fixed-rate mortgages in the early 1980s. When its lending powers were broadened in 1982, Anchor aggressively sought high-yield investments to rebuild its diminished capital base. High-yield corporate bonds, which were debt issues rated below investment grade by the bond-rating agencies (Ba1 or lower by Moody's Investor Services, BB+ or lower by Standard & Poor's, or unrated), had seemed a particularly attractive diversification opportunity for Anchor. Publicly issued high-yield bonds offered investors liquidity as well as rich yields, which ranged 250-550 basis points over comparable maturity Treasuries over the period 1980-1984 (see Exhibit 1). Mr. Forsyth, who was responsible for Anchor's investment activities, had initiated the thrift's move into high-yield corporate bonds.

Early in November 1984, Mr. Forsyth had become concerned that Anchor's $9 million portfolio of 14 high-yield issues was inadequately diversified. In conversations with

---

1   Although there was no formal ruling on the matter from the Federal Home Loan Bank Board (FHLBB), federally insured thrifts were generally allowed to classify investments in high-yield securities as commercial loans.

This case was prepared by Sally E. Durdan under the supervision of Scott P. Mason as the basis of class discussion. Copyright © 1985 by the President and Fellows of Harvard College. Harvard Business School case 286-044.

analysts at Drexel Burnham Lambert Inc., an investment bank active in the high-yield market, he had learned that 20–30 issues were required to properly diversify a portfolio of high-yield bonds. Because significant liquidity existed only in large blocks (positions of $1 million or more), he planned to recommend that Anchor increase its investment in high-yield securities to $25–$30 million. As a first step, he planned to recommend the purchase of one or several pieces of a forthcoming issue of Metromedia Broadcasting Corporation debt securities.

Unfortunately, David Willis had indicated, the board was unlikely to be receptive to Mr. Forsyth's investment proposal. Although Anchor's high-yield portfolio had performed well the previous year, several board members were alarmed by thrift regulators' recent criticisms of thrift's investments in high-yield securities. Eric I. Hemel, director of the Federal Home Loan Bank Board's (FHLBB) office of policy and economic research, had warned member thrifts that "the rapidly growing high-yield market opened a relatively new, high-risk investment strategy to savings institutions." The FHLBB, which regulated federally insured thrifts, and the Federal Savings and Loan Insurance Corporation (FSLIC), which insured thrift deposits of up to $100,000, were considering imposing stringent diversification requirements on thrift's investments in low-grade corporate securities. In addition, members of both houses of Congress had introduced legislation prohibiting federally insured thrifts from holding any securities rated below investment grade.

SAVINGS AND LOAN INDUSTRY

Savings and loan (S&L) associations, along with mutual savings banks, made up the thrift industry. Historically, thrifts had been in the business of accepting savings deposits from individuals and lending these funds to homebuyers. During the Great Depression over 1,700 thrifts failed. Legislation in the 1930s then bolstered the industry, creating the Federal Home Loan Bank system, which could lend to thrifts requiring extra funds; establishing federally chartered S&Ls through the FHLBB; and establishing the FSLIC to provide deposit insurance to thrifts.

The traditional thrift business resulted in a balance sheet characterized by long-term, fixed-rate assets and short-term, floating-rate liabilities (see Exhibit 2). With higher interest rates in the late 1970s, this mismatched balance sheet became highly problematic. While the cost of deposit funds rose, the revenue from the fixed-rate, long-term mortgages remained flat. Furthermore, as interest rates went still higher in the early 1980s, depositors began withdrawing their funds from thrifts as well as from commercial banks to invest elsewhere because depository institutions were legally restricted as to the maximum rate they could pay on accounts. This disintermediation was particularly troublesome for thrifts because it was caused by the same thing, i.e., higher interest rates, that caused the value of fixed-rate mortgages to fall. Thus thrifts had to sell mortgages at a loss in order to fund the withdrawals of depositors.

By the early 1980s the S&L industry was in a crisis. Many S&Ls failed or merged out of existence, with the total number of S&Ls decreasing from 6,300 in 1960 to about 4,600 in 1980. A commonly held view at the time was that a relaxation of government regulations was needed to ensure the viability of the industry. The Depository Institutions Deregulation and Monetary Control Act (DIDMCA) of 1980 and the Garn-St. Germain Depository Institutions Act of 1982 were designed to alleviate the plight of the ailing thrifts. The legislation permitted S&Ls to hold up to 30% of their assets in credit cards and consumer loans, up to 40% in commercial real estate loans, and up to 11% in commercial and industrial loans. Thrifts could even participate in corporate equity ventures if they did so through a service corporation subsidiary that comprised less than 3% of total assets. The new legislation also addressed the net worth requirements for thrifts. Prior to 1980 regulatory requirements mandated a net worth level of 5% of liabilities. However, the DIDMCA of 1980 allowed the FHLBB to set the net worth requirements at between 3% and 6%. In 1982 the standard was set to 3% by the FHLBB.

By year-end 1984, S&L holdings of mortgage loans, insured mortgages, and mortgage-backed securities, as a percentage of total assets, were down to 72.3%, from 84.2% in 1980. Those thrifts that grew significantly tended to decrease their holdings of residential mortgages in favor of investments in nontraditional thrift assets (see Exhibit 3). At the same time, regulatory examinations or audits of thrifts actually declined. Although the FHLBB justified the decrease in examinations by the decrease in the number of thrifts, the examinations per thrift nonetheless declined somewhat, and the examinations per billion dollars of assets in fact declined precipitously (see Exhibit 4).

HIGH-YIELD SECURITIES MARKET

Moody's Investors Service and Standard & Poor's Corporation provided investors with estimates of the default risk of corporate bonds. Moody's used a set of nine rating symbols to represent groups of bonds with broadly similar credit characteristics. The first four categories (Aaa, Aa, A, and Baa) were investment-grade ratings, with Aaa representing the highest investment quality and Baa medium investment quality. The remaining five categories (Ba, B, Caa, Ca, and C) covered more speculative issues, including securities that were near or in default. Standard & Poor's issued similar ratings using the symbols AAA, AA, A, and BBB to denote investment-grade securities and BB, B, CCC, CC, C, and D to denote more speculative bonds.

In rating corporate bonds, Moody's and Standard & Poor's relied heavily on measures of historical financial performance, including ratios of book debt to total capitalization, cash flow to debt, and before-tax fixed-charge coverage ratios. Exhibit 5 shows suggested values for these and other ratios of industrial bond issuers of varying credit quality. Bond ratings appeared to be related to company size in that only *Fortune 500* firms were awarded AAA and AA ratings. Although rating agencies considered such qualitative factors as a company's industry, market share, relative cost position, accounting policies, and quality of management in assigning credit ratings, financial measures tended to dominate their analyses. It was estimated that 85% of all U.S. public corporations would be rated below investment grade.

Historically, investor interest in low-rated debt had been weak because of legal or self-imposed quality restrictions on institutional investors' purchases of corporate bonds. Most state and local government pension funds were prohibited by law from investing in bonds rated below single A. Trust funds and corporate pension funds were generally subject to "prudent investor" tests, which authorized fiduciaries to "invest in such securities as would be acquired by prudent men of discretion and intelligence in such matters who are seeking a reasonable income and preservation of their capital." The vague wording of such tests prompted most fiduciaries to adopt conservative investment policies.

Because many institutions were unable or unwilling to buy securities rated below investment grade, the public corporate debt market was dominated by investment-grade issuers through 1977. The $25 billion high-yield bond market consisted primarily of the outstanding debt of large, troubled companies whose credit quality had fallen from investment grade. Reflecting the lack of investor interest in the high-yield sector, yield spreads between high-grade and low-grade corporate securities were inefficiently wide, providing investors with yield premiums in excess of those required to offset losses from default (see Exhibit 6).

In the mid-1970s, Drexel Burnham Lambert developed techniques for analyzing the credit quality of low-grade issuers. Focusing on market-adjusted leverage ratios, projected cash flows, business fundamentals, and management quality rather than on historical financial data, Drexel identified mature, downgraded issuers likely to achieve rating upgrades. In addition, Drexel noted that many small- and medium-sized "emerging growth" companies possessed sound financial prospects, although they would likely be rated below investment grade in view of their small size and brief credit histories. In 1977, Drexel pioneered the underwriting of high-yield securities for these unseasoned or highly leveraged companies, which had traditionally relied on commercial bank lending, private placements of debt, or equity issues for capital to finance their growth.

The issuance of public debt offered low-rated issuers several advantages over their traditional sources of funding:

1. Access to permanent, fixed-rate capital without the restrictive covenants imposed by institutional purchasers of private placements;
2. Call features, enabling issuers to refund debt in the event of a decline in interest rates;
3. Visibility in the public markets, which occasionally enhanced investor interest in a high-yield issuer's equity as well as debt securities; and
4. An alternative to equity issuance, enabling companies to increase financial leverage above historic levels.

Over the period 1977–1984, the high-yield debt market tripled in size as over 350 low-rated companies issued $36.1 billion of original-issue high-yield debt (see Exhibits 8). The volume of high-yield securities outstanding (including bonds of utilities and municipalities, preferred stocks, high-premium convertible bonds, and private placements of debt with registration rights) was expected to total $100 billion by year-end 1984. The largest public components of the high-yield bond market, straight industrial and finance issues ($48 billion face value) and straight utility issues ($11 billion face value), had grown to represent 14% of all public, straight corporate debt outstanding in 1984.

Some $14 billion of public high-yield debt was placed in 1984, representing 35% of all public, straight corporate debt issued in that year. Growth in the high-yield market was expected to continue at a rapid pace as new issuers entered the market (see Exhibit 7). At year-end 1984, investment bankers had identified 2,000 potential high-yield issuers who had yet to tap the public debt markets. In addition, high-yield debt was being used with increasing frequency to finance merger and acquisition transactions, including leveraged buyouts and highly publicized hostile tender offers by corporate "raiders," such as Boone Pickens and Carl Icahn. Some observers believed the development of the original-issue, high yield debt market had increased the level of acquisition activity by providing small acquirers with the capital necessary to acquire large corporations. Approximately 12% of the public high-yield debt issued in 1984 was used to finance leveraged buy-outs or acquisitions.

By educating the investment community about the exceptional returns realized historically on high-yield investments and maintaining a secondary market in high-yield issues, Drexel Burnham Lambert and other underwriters (see Exhibit 9) persuaded a broad range of institutions to invest in the high-yield sector. By 1984 high-yield mutual funds, insurance companies, bank trust departments, 200 of the *Fortune 500* pension funds, commercial banks, and thrifts were active in the high-yield market. However, yield spreads between low-grade and investment-grade corporate bonds remained high. Market observers attributed the persistence of excessive yield on low-grade securities to a surge in new-issue volume in the second half of 1984. Among the largest issues brought to market during this period was a $1.3 billion offering of senior and subordinated debt securities by the Metromedia Broadcasting Corporation (MBC).

MBC OFFERING

In 1984 the principal business of Metromedia, Inc. (Metromedia) was the ownership and operation of seven television and nine radio stations. The company's television stations included six independents and one network affiliate located in seven of the country's ten largest media markets. The television group, whose size was limited to a maximum of seven stations under Federal Communications Commissions. (FCC) licensing rules, reached approximately 24% of all U.S. television homes, representing the largest audience coverage of any commonly owned television station group. Metromedia also produced television programming and was active in telecommunications, outdoor advertising, and other entertainment businesses.

On June 21, 1984, Metromedia was taken private by its management in a leveraged buyout transaction. John W. Kluge, chairman of the company and owner of 26% of Metromedia's equity prior to the leveraged buyout, joined three Metromedia managers in offering shareholders a package of cash, debentures, and debenture-purchase warrants valued at $41.50 per share in exchange for their stock. The offer represented an 85% premium over Metromedia's April 1984 stock price of $22 per share. The buyout was financed with $1.2 billion in bank debt, $125 million of preferred stock purchased by the Prudential Insurance Company, and $10 million of nonvoting common stock purchased by venture investors. The proceeds of this financing were used to make cash payments to Metromedia shareholders and to provide working capital for operations. The buyout increased John Kluge's ownership interest in Metromedia to 75.5% of total equity and raised Metromedia's total debt from 75% to over 90% of total capital.

The bank debt used to finance Metromedia's buyout carried an 8-year maturity and interest pegged to the prime rate. Upon entering into this credit agreement Metromedia paid lenders origination fees equal to 1% of its total borrowings. The terms of the agreement, which included a $100 million minimum net worth requirement, would have required Metromedia to sell a significant broadcasting asset by June 1985 in order to make a mandatory principal prepayment of $200 million.

In September 1984, Metromedia's management investigated a variety of alternatives for avoiding the asset sale required under the terms of its bank facility. Management was anxious to avoid the significant tax liability that would have resulted from such a sale, and, more importantly, it believed that a reduction in the television group's audience coverage would adversely affect its competitive position. In October, Metromedia announced that it planned to refinance its bank indebtedness by raising approximately $1.3 billion in a public offering of senior and subordinated debt securities. The debt securities were to be issued by MBC, a wholly owned subsidiary of Metromedia, to which substantially all of Metromedia's broadcasting assets were to be transferred.

The MBC offering consisted of a series of four securities designed by Drexel Burnham Lambert (see Exhibit 10). All of the securities had been approved for listing on the American Stock Exchange and were to be underwritten by Drexel Burnham Lambert and Bear, Stearns.

All but $50 million of the net proceeds of the offering were to be advanced to Metromedia to repay the senior bank indebtedness it had incurred in connection with its June 1984 leveraged buyout. The remaining $50 million were to be added to MBC's working capital and, if certain financial ratios were met during a period of two years, were to be advanced to Metromedia (see Exhibit 11). Metromedia was not an obligor on the debt securities and had no responsibility to provide financial support to MBC.

In anticipation of the refinancing, Metromedia entered into a management agreement with MBC, pursuant to which Metromedia was to provide MBC with legal, accounting, cash management, and strategic and major financial planning services. In compensation, MBC was to pay Metromedia's out-of-pocket expenses and a monthly fee equal to 1.5% of MBC's gross revenues. This management fee was to be deferred until the end of the first 12-month period during which MBC achieved a ratio of operating cash flow (before deduction of the management fee) to cash interest expense of 1.25 to 1. Upon achieving this ratio, MBC could pay Metromedia up to one year's deferred management fees.

The serial zero coupon notes consisted of six series of discount notes priced at the following yields:

Series	Maturity	Yield to Maturity[a]
1	Dec. 1, 1988	13¾%
2	Dec. 1, 1989	14
3	Dec. 1, 1990	14⅜
4	Dec. 1, 1991	14¾
5	Dec. 1, 1992	15
6	Dec. 1, 1993	15¼

a. Assumes semiannual compounding of interest.

The notes were to rank equally in right of payment with other senior indebtedness of MBC, including the senior exchangeable variable-rate debentures due 1996, and were to be senior to the $15\frac{5}{8}$% senior subordinated debentures due 1999 and adjustable-rate participating subordinated debentures due 2002. The notes were redeemable at the option of the company at any time at par.

Interest on the senior exchangeable variable-rate debentures was to be paid quarterly at a rate equal to the greatest of (1) the three-month Treasury rate plus 375 basis points, (2) LIBOR plus 250 basis points, or (3) 107% of the ten-year Treasury rate, in each case adjusted quarterly, except that until June 1, 1985, a minimum rate of 15% per year was to be paid. The variable-rate debentures were redeemable at the option of the company at any time after December 1, 1987, in whole or in part, at the following prices (percent of par) together with accrued interest:

12 months beginning	
Dec. 1, 1987	105%
Dec. 1, 1988	103

On any quarterly interest payment date on or after December 1, 1985, and before December 1, 1989, the company could exchange all, or a portion equal to $50 million or any multiple thereof, of the variable-rate debentures for fixed-rate debentures maturing December 1, 1996. Any variable-rate debentures outstanding on December 1, 1989, were to be automatically exchanged. The fixed-rate debentures were to pay interest quarterly at a rate equal to 131% of the ten-year Treasury rate determined as of the exchange date. They were subject to redemption at the company's option at any time on or after the third anniversary of the final exchange of the variable-rate debentures at the following prices (percent of par) together with accrued interest:

12-month period from date of final exchange	
Fourth	105%
Fifth	103
Sixth	101
Seventh	100

The fixed-rate debentures carried sinking fund provisions requiring the retirement of debentures in the aggregate principal amount of $110 million on December 1, 1994, and December 1, 1995.[2]

The 15⅝% senior-subordinated debentures were to rank senior in right of payment to the adjustable-rate participating subordinated debentures but junior to MBC's senior indebtedness. The debentures were to bear interest at an annual rate of 15⅝%, payable semiannually, and were to mature on December 1, 1999. They were redeemable in whole or in part at the company's option at any time after December 1, 1987, at 111.025% of par plus accrued interest on or after December 1, 1994. No redemption was to be made prior to December 1, 1989, using funds borrowed at an effective cost of less than 15¾%. A sinking fund requiring annual payments of $56,250,000 beginning December 1, 1996, was to retire 75% of the debentures prior to maturity.

The adjustable-rate participating subordinated debentures were to bear interest at annual rates of 13⅛% prior to December 1, 1989, and 17% thereafter, in each case payable semiannually. Commencing in 1988, holders of the debentures were to be entitled to additional interest based on increases in the company's participating operating cash flow, which was defined as net income before taxes and interest income, plus depreciation, amortization, and interest expense.

Average Percent Increase in Participating Operating Cash Flow Over 3 Previous Fiscal Years	Additional Interest (as Percent of Principal)
0-10%	0%
10-14	1.5
14-17	2.5
17 +	4.0

The debentures were to be subordinate to $1,520 million principal amount of senior and senior subordinated debt. The debentures were not to be redeemable by the company unless separate certificates representing the right to receive payments of additional interest had been distributed to the debenture-holders. Once such a distribution had been made, the debentures were to be redeemable at the company's option in whole or in part at any time after December 1, 1987, except that no redemption was to be made prior to

---

2   Under the terms of the several bond indentures, MBC could fulfill its sinking fund obligations either by redeeming the specified principal amount of fixed-rate debentures or senior-subordinated debentures at par or by purchasing an equivalent principal amount of the securities in the open market.

December 1, 1994, using funds borrowed at an effective cost of less than 17%. The debentures were to be redeemable at the following prices (percent of par) together with accrued interest:

12 months beginning

Dec. 1, 1987	104%
Dec. 1, 1988	103
Dec. 1, 1989	102
Dec. 1, 1990	101
Dec. 1, 1991 and thereafter	100

A sinking fund requiring annual payments of $66 million beginning December 1, 1997 was to retire 83% of the debentures prior to maturity.[3]

The covenants of the debt securities prohibited MBC from incurring additional senior debt and limited its ability to make payments to affiliated companies. The covenants also prohibited MBC from entering into mergers outside the broadcasting industry or liquidating substantial portions of its assets unless the proceeds of such transactions were used to repay the principal of the notes, the senior variable-rate debentures, or the senior-subordinated debentures (except that no more than 50% of such proceeds could be used to repay the senior-subordinated debentures). All of the senior and senior subordinated securities carried defeasance clauses enabling the company to discharge substantially all its obligations under the bond indentures by depositing in trust for the bondholders funds or U.S. government obligations sufficient to provide for all payments of the notes and debentures.

The prospectus for the offering clearly outlined Metromedia's reasons for refinancing its bank debt. First, Metromedia's cash interest expense over the succeeding 4 years was to equal 10.3% of the net proceeds of the offering, a reduction from the 14.9% rate paid on its bank debt. At the same time, tax-deductible interest expense was to increase from a rate of 14.9% to an average 15.4% of borrowings. The refinancing would defer all principal repayments, which would have totaled $290 million through 1988 under the terms of the bank debt, until the first series of senior notes matured in 1988 (see Exhibit 12). Under the refinancing Metromedia would be released from numerous affirmative and negative covenants, including those necessitating the sale of a broadcasting asset in 1985. Because the

---

3   Under the terms of the bond indenture, MBC could fulfill its sinking fund obligations either by redeeming the specified principal amount of adjustable-rate participating subordinated debentures at par or by purchasing an equivalent principal amount of the securities in the open market.

broadcasting assets were to be segregated from Metromedia's other operations, Metromedia would be free to borrow additional funds for use in its telecommunications and other activities.

Pro forma financial statements for MBC (see Exhibit 13) indicated that interest coverage subsequent to the refinancing would be less than 1:1 and a deficit of $53 million would be recorded in MBC's stockholders' equity account. Due principally to large goodwill amortization charges, MBC was expected to continue to report substantial accounting losses following the offering. The MBC prospectus described the risks to investors in the debt securities as follows:

> Based on current levels of operation (assuming no growth in revenue), the company's cash flow would be insufficient to make interest payments on the debt securities (other than the serial senior notes) and it would have to use other funds, to the extent available, to make such interest payments. However, the company has historically experienced significant rates of growth in broadcast revenues and cash flow . . . and expects continued growth which, if attained, would generate sufficient cash flow to enable it to make interest payments on the debt securities. Such payments would consume all or substantially all of such cash flow . . .
>
> Based on current levels of operations and anticipated growth, the company does not expect to be able to generate sufficient cash flow to make all of the principal payments due on the serial senior notes, which commence on December 1, 1988, without taking action to refinance a portion of its indebtedness. No assurance can be given that such refinancing can be successfully accomplished.

Standard & Poor's rated the debt securities "highly speculative," noting that "this is an enormous amount of debt, even for (Metromedia's) good cash-generating properties" to support. However, Tom Forsyth had learned in a road show presentation preceding the offering that cash flow coverage of current interest expense would exceed 1:1, assuming cash flow growth of only 8% per year, a conservative estimate compared to Metromedia's historic growth rates of 15%-20%. In addition, he had learned that industry experts considered Metromedia's broadcasting assets to be highly marketable, estimating their market value at the time of the offering at $1.8 billion.

INVESTMENT CHARACTERISTICS OF HIGH-YIELD BONDS

As he prepared his presentation on high-yield bond investments for Anchor's board of directors, Mr. Forsyth reviewed several recent academic studies documenting the performance of high-yield securities since the mid-1970s. He was searching for statistics on default rates, return volatility, and secondary market liquidity of low-rated debt to help him respond to the board's questions concerning the riskiness of high-yield investments.

A study of default rates on low-rated debt published by Professor Edward Altman of New York University provided overwhelming evidence that yields on low-rated bonds had historically been sufficient to compensate investors for losses from defaults. Altman found that an average of 1.6% of the par value of low-rated debt outstanding defaulted annually over the years 1974–1984, a period that included two recessions (see Exhibit 14). Because securities in default continued to trade at an average of 41% of par, actual losses from default were only 100 to 106 basis points per year. Although these defaults rates were substantially higher than those for the total straight corporate debt market, which averaged 8 basis points per year over the same period, Professor Altman noted that yields on low-rated debt had provided investors with adequate compensation for the increased risk of default. He estimated that returns on low-rated debt (net of losses from default) had averaged 490 to 580 basis points above the long-term government bond index over the period 1978–1983. Exhibit 15 gives selected bonds yields for November 1984.

Professors Marshall Blume and Donald Keim of the Wharton School compared the volatility of returns (as measured by the standard deviation of monthly returns) on an index of lower-quality bonds with those of corporate bonds rated A and AAA and the S&P 500 from January 1982 through May 1984. The Blume-Keim study confirmed Altman's findings, estimating average annual returns on low-grade bonds, net of losses from default, at 20.3% per year versus 16.6% for A-rated bonds and 15% for AAA-rated bonds. The study also indicated that a diversified portfolio of lower-quality bonds experienced less volatility, or risk, than higher-grade corporates or equities over the period studied (see Exhibit 16). The authors of the study noted that "this result was somewhat surprising," and suggested that much of the risk in low-grade corporate securities may be firm-specific, and thus diversifiable.

Although few statistics on the secondary market for low-rated debt were publicly available, Mr. Forsyth was aware that Drexel Burnham Lambert, with a trading inventory of over $1 billion, handled approximately two-thirds of all trading volume in high-yield securities (see Exhibit 17). Drexel estimated average daily trading volumes in high-yield bonds at 10% of the NYSE volume, or $300 million per day. However, many high-yield issues were lightly traded, and trading spreads ranged as high as 100 basis points.

While Mr. Forsyth was relieved that academic research had confirmed his belief that high-yield bond investments had historically provided superior returns to investors, he remained uncertain of his recommendation to Anchor's board. He was troubled by speculation in the press that future performance in the high-yield market might not mirror the outstanding results of the previous ten years:

> About $24 billion, or 80%, of outstanding "new issue" junk was floated in the past three years and was buoyed by an expanding economy and generally declining interest rates. Many of these companies are so laden with debt that even a modest shortfall in cash flow could have dire consequences. "The next time we have a recession, there's going to be a fallout," predicts

Warren Greene, president of American Investors Income Fund, a 10-year old junk mutual fund. "You've got to be careful you don't end up with three or four old maids at the end of the game."[4]

Mr. Forsyth realized that the task of convincing the board to triple its investment in the high-yield market would be a difficult one, particularly since the risk-return performance of high-yield investments was not readily explainable. Why was the volatility of returns on high-yield bonds lower than that of investment-grade corporates? Why hadn't lower-grade spreads been arbitraged away as the high-yield market developed? How much liquidity could a small investor like Anchor expect in the secondary market? Given Anchor's weak capital position (see Exhibit 18), was the risk of default on high-yield securities, including the Metromedia issue, too great for Anchor to bear?

---

4   "The Growing Respectability of the Junk Heap," *Business Week*, April 22, 1985.

Exhibit 1   DBL 100 Yield Versus Treasuries, 1980–1985

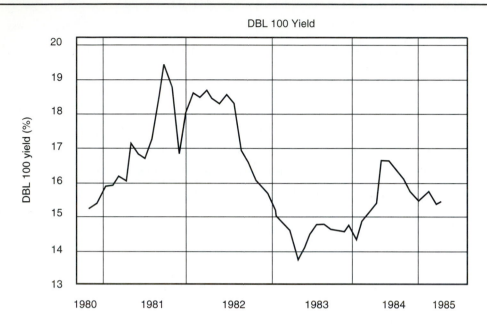

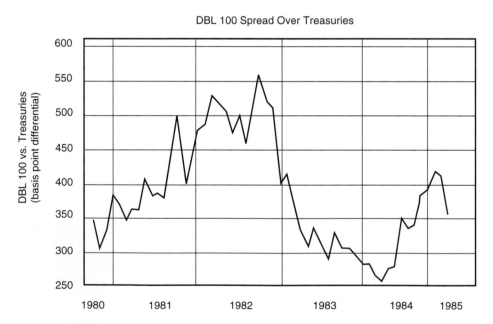

Source: Drexel Burnham Lambert.
Note: The DBL 100 indexed the 100 largest fixed coupon, nonutility, high-yield issues outstanding over the period 1980–1985. In November 1984, the average coupon of the index was 13.2%, the average maturity November 2000, and the average quality slightly higher than single B.

Exhibit 2   Assets and Liabilities of All Savings and Loan Associations, at Year-End, 1980 and 1984
(billions of dollars)

	1980		1984	
Mortgage loans outstanding	$502.8	79.8%	$599.0	61.2%
Insured mortgages and mortgage-backed securities	27.5	4.4	108.2	11.1
Mobile home loans	2.8	.4	5.3	.5
Home improvement loans	5.6	.9	5.6	.6
Loans on savings accounts	7.1	1.1	3.9	.4
Education loans	1.3	.2	3.8	.4
Miscellaneous consumer loans	na	na	18.4	1.9
Cash and investments eligible for liquidity	49.6	7.9	99.9	10.2
Investments in service corporations	3.1	.5	17.0	1.7
All other assets	30.0	4.8	117.5	12.0
Total assets	$629.8	100.0%	$978.5	100.0%
Savings deposits	$511.0	81.1%	$784.7	79.9%
FHLB advances	47.0	7.5	71.7	7.3
Other liabilities	38.5	6.1	84.1	8.6
Net worth	33.3	5.3	37.9	3.9
Total liabilities and net worth	$629.8	100.0%	$978.5	100.0%

Source: United States League of Savings Associations, *1981 Savings and Loan Source book* and *1985 Savings Institutions Source book* (Chicago, 1981; 1985).
na = not available

Exhibit 3   Asset Growth and the Asset/Liability Composition of FSLIC-Insured Thrifts at June 1984

	Asset Growth			
	<15%	15%–25%	25%–50%	>50%
Composition of Assets:				
Residential mortgages and mortgage-backed securities[a]	68.1%	67.1%	63.4%	53.0%
Commercial mortgages	6.6	8.3	8.2	10.8
Land loans	1.2	1.8	2.5	5.8
Nonmortgage loans	3.7	3.6	4.6	5.0
Real estate investments	.2	.6	.7	1.2
Other assets	20.2	18.6	20.6	24.2
Total assets	100.0%	100.0%	100.0%	100.0%
Composition of Liabilities:				
Retail deposits	80.9%	72.4%	64.7%	59.0%
Large-denomination deposits[b]	7.3	11.6	14.5	18.1
Repurchase agreements	2.4	4.0	6.8	10.4
FHLB advances	6.7	8.1	9.6	7.3
Other liabilities	2.7	3.9	4.4	5.2
Total liabilities	100.0%	100.0%	100.0%	100.0%

Source: Mahoney and White (1985).
Note: Annual rate of growth extrapolated from growth in the first half of 1984.
a. Includes the category "other mortgage-related assets."
b. Above $100,000.

Exhibit 4 FSLIC-Insured Thrift Examinations, 1980–1984

	Examinations	Number of FSLIC-Insured Thrifts	Thrift Industry Assets ($billions)	Examinations per Thrift	Examinations per Billion Dollars of Assets
1980	3,210	3,993	$593.8	.80	5.41
1981	3,171	3,731	639.8	.85	4.96
1982	2,800	3,287	686.2	.85	4.08
1983	2,131	3,146	813.8	.68	2.22
1984[a]	2,347	3,136	976.9	.75	2.40

Source: FHLBB data; Barth, Bartholomew, and Bradley (1989).
a. Includes special, limited-scope examinations.

Exhibit 5 Median Financial Ratios for Standard & Poor's Rated Industrial Issuers, 1982-84

	Standard & Poor's Rating					
	AAA	AA	A	BBB	BB	B
Fixed charge coverage[a]	7.90	3.96	2.85	2.25	1.77	1.34
Funds from operations/Long-term debt (%)	308.72%	111.02%	68.89%	43.31%	22.78%	14.19%
Funds from operations/Total debt (%)	161.48	77.16	58.39	38.07	21.23	12.35
Long-term debt/Capitalization (%)	8.50	19.67	25.08	31.31	48.36	59.78
Total debt/Capitalization including short-term debt (%)	15.25	24.80	28.94	34.81	50.33	63.38
Total liability/Tangible shareholders' equity and minority interest	69.56	99.34	112.37	127.26	197.78	294.65

Source: "Key Industrial Financial Ratios," *Standard & Poor's Creditweek,* August 19, 1985, p. 12.
a. A fixed-charge coverage ratio is the ratio of pre-tax income to interest and rental expenses.

238 Cases in Financial Engineering

Exhibit 6   Low-Rated Bond Returns Versus Treasuries, 1977–1984

Initial S&P Rating	Annual Rate of Return Versus Comparable Maturity Treasuries[a] (in percentage points)
BBB	+3.02
BB	+4.43
B	+3.87
CCC	+5.49

Source: Drexel Burnham Lambert.
a. Return comparisons are based on a study of the 391 original issue high-yield bonds underwritten over the period 1977–1984. Returns represent compound average annual returns from equal dollar investments in high-yield bonds and comparable maturity U.S. Treasury securities, assuming coupons are reinvested in each high-yield or Treasury issue. Results are time-weighted, such that issues outstanding four years are given twice the weight of issues outstanding two years, etc.

Exhibit 7   Recent Issuers of High-Yield Securities

Beverly Enterprises	Lifemark (AMI)
Caesars World	Lorimar
Charter Medical Corporation	MCI Communications
Circus Circus	MGM Grand Hotels
Coastal Corporation	National Medical Enterprises
Comdisco	Occidental Petroleum
Eastern Airlines	People Express Airlines
Fairfield Communities	Resorts International
Golden Nugget	Southmark Corporation
Humana Inc.	Sunshine Mining
Integrated Resources	Texas International
Kinder-Care	Universal Health

Exhibit 8 High Yield Bond Issuance: 1977–1984 ($ billions)

	1977	1978	1979	1980	1981	1982	1983	1984	Total
New Issues	$.55	$1.45	$1.30	$1.27	$1.38	$2.51	$7.52	$14.21	$30.19
Exchange Offers	.50	.68	.30	.68	.32	.53	.49	.70	4.20
Utilities	.01	.00	.09	.11	.04	.14	.48	.87	1.74
Total	$1.06	$2.13	$1.69	$2.06	$1.74	$3.18	$8.49	$15.78	$36.13

Source: *The Case for High-Yield Bonds*, Drexel Burnham Lambert, March 1985, p. 3.
Note: These figures include public, straight industrial, finance, transportation and utility new issues of $10 million or more. Bonds issued below 70% are counted at issue price. All others are included at face value.

Exhibit 9 Leading Underwriters of High-Yield Debt Offerings (Full credit to book manager)

	1984			1983			1982		
	Rank	Amount	%	No. of Issues	Rank	Amount	%	No. of Issues	Rank	Amount	%	No. of Issues
Drexel Burnham Lambert	1	$9,555.2	67.6	68	1	$4,380.9	58.1	8	1	$1,380.8	55.3	25
Prudential-Bache	2	979.6	6.9	15	5	251.6	3.3	6	8	37.0	1.5	1
Salomon Brothers	3	850.7	6.0	9	3	443.4	5.9	5	—	—	—	—
Merrill Lynch Capital Markets	4	709.4	5.0	6	2	688.7	9.1	8	2	597.2	23.9	7
Shearson Lehman Brothers	5	484.5	3.4	7	6	202.4	2.7	1	10	21.2	.8	1
First Boston	6	368.6	2.6	5	9	149.1	2.0	2	—	—	—	—
Bear Stearns	7	345.1	2.4	4	4	354.8	4.7	5	9	31.2	1.3	1
Morgan Stanley	8	306.3	2.2	5	13	80.0	1.1	1	—	—	—	—
E.F. Hutton	9	143.4	1.0	3	8	190.0	2.5	2	4	72.0	2.9	2
Goldman, Sachs	10	98.8	.7	1	11	112.8	1.5	1	—	—	—	—
Paine Webber	11	73.4	.5	2	7	196.3	2.6	2	3	177.0	7.1	4
L.F. Rothschild, Unterberg, Towbin	12	54.5	.4	2	12	96.5	1.3	2	—	—	—	—
Donaldson, Lufkin & Jenrette	13	47.9	.3	1	—	—	—	—	—	—	—	—
Kidder, Peabody	14	40.0	.3	1	10	134.6	1.8	2	—	—	—	—
Rooney, Pace	15	24.7	.2	1	—	—	—	—	—	—	—	—
Dean Witter Reynolds	16	15.0	.1	1	—	—	—	—	—	—	—	—
Advest	17	12.0	.1	1	—	—	—	—	—	—	—	—
Werbel-Roth Securities	18	2.3	.0	1	—	—	—	—	—	—	—	—
Total other banks				—		253.3	3.7	13		182.6	7.3	15
Total		$14,111.4		133		$7,534.4		98		$2,499.0		56

Source: IDD Information Services.
Note: High-yield nonconvertible debt offerings only. Debt at offering price.

Exhibit 10 Description of Securities Issued by MBC (November 29, 1984)

Security	Principal Amount ($ millions)	Maturity	Price to Public (%)	Aggregate Price	Underwriting Commissions	Proceeds to Company
Zero Coupon Senior Notes[a]						
Series 1	$ 160	12/1/88	58.834%	$ 94,134,400	$ 2,353,360	$ 91,781,040
2	160	12/1/89	50.911	81,457,600	2,036,440	79,421,160
3	160	12/1/90	43.545	69,672,000	1,741,800	67,930,200
4	160	12/1/91	36.986	59,177,600	1,479,440	57,698,160
5	160	12/1/92	31.489	50,382,400	1,259,560	49,122,840
6	160	12/1/93	26.685	42,696,000	1,067,400	41,628,600
				$397,520,000	$ 9,938,000	$ 387,582,000
Senior Exchangeable Variable Rate Debentures[a]	335	12/1/96	99.000	331,650,000	7,463,800	324,186,200
15⅝% Senior Subordinated Debentures[b]	225	12/1/99	99.250	223,312,500	5,861,250	217,451,250
Adjustable Rate Participating Subordinated Debentures[b]	400	12/1/02	87.299	349,196,000	9,888,000	339,308,000
Total	$1,920			$1,301,678,500	$33,151,050 (2.55%)	$1,268,527,450

a. The senior debt securities were rated B+ by Standard & Poor's, B1 by Moody's.
b. The subordinated debt securities were rated B- by Standard & Poor's, B3 by Moody's.

Exhibit 11 Pro Forma Consolidated Condensed Balance Sheet for Metromedia, Inc. and Subsidiary at September 30, 1984 (thousands of dollars)

	Historical September 30, 1984[a]	Adjustments Increase/Decrease BondTransaction	Pro Forma
Cash and marketable securities at cost, which approximates market	$ 11,093	$ 50,000 [b]	$ 61,093
Accounts receivable, less provisions for doubtful accounts of $943	129,132	—	129,132
Film rights	87,872	—	87,872
Refundable income taxes	39,794	—	39,794
Other current assets	32,488	—	32,488
Current assets	300,379	50,000	350,379
Property, plant, equipment, at cost	284,485	—	284,485
Less: accumulated depreciation	7,776	—	7,776
Film rights—noncurrent	136,081	—	136,081
Investment in tax leases	8,181	—	8,181
Intangible assets	1,277,736	—	1,277,736
Other noncurrent assets	139,081	35,740 [b]	174,821
Total assets	$2,138,167	$ 85,740	$2,223,907
Current portion of long-term debt	$ 191,385	$ (95,973)[b]	$ 95,412
Film rights payable	87,592	—	87,592
Accounts payable	80,739	—	80,739
Accrued interest	68,558	(66,966)[b]	1,592
Other current liabilities	39,774	—	39,774
Current liabilities	468,048	(162,939)	305,109
Long-term debt	1,165,248	(1,053,000)[b]	112,248
Serial zero coupon senior notes, net of estimated discount of $562,480	—	397,520[b]	397,520
Senior Exchangeable Variable Rate Debentures, net of estimated discount of $3,350	—	331,650[b]	331,650
15⅝% senior subordinated debentures, net of estimated discount of $1,687	—	223,313[b]	223,313
Adjustable rate participating subordinated debentures, net of estimated discount of $50,804	—	349,196[b]	349,196
Discount debentures, net of discount	196,605	—	196,605
Film rights payable, noncurrent	86,750	—	86,750
Deferred income taxes	25,357	—	25,357
Other noncurrent liabilities	42,172	—	42,172

Exhibit 11 Pro Forma Consolidated Condensed Sheet for Metromedia, Inc. and Subsidiary at September 30, 1984 (thousands of dollars) (Continued)

	Historical September 30, 1984[a]	Adjustments Increase/Decrease BondTransaction	Pro Forma
Deferred credit, warrants	9,325	—	9,325
Total liabilities	1,993,505	85,740	2,079,245
Redeemable preferred stock	128,125	—	128,125
Class A nonvoting common stock	10,000	—	10,000
Common stock, authorized 6,300,000 shares,			
$.01 par value, issued 4,858,000	49	—	49
Paid-in capital	50,304	—	50,304
Accumulated deficit	(37,216)	—	(37,216)
Less: Notes receivable, management group	6,600	—	6,600
Voting common stockholders' equity	6,537	—	6,537
Total liabilities and net worth	$2,138,167	$ 85,740	$2,223,907

Source: Metromedia Broadcasting Corporation prospectus dated November 29, 1984.
a. Historical consolidated condensed balance sheet of Metromedia, Inc. at September 30, 1984.
b. Adjustments related to the issuance by MBC of the debt securities and the use of all but $50 million of the net aggregate proceeds of the offerings to repay senior bank indebtedness and accrued interest related to such debt. Net proceeds from the issuance of the debt securities total is $1,265,939 as follows: (thousands of dollars)

Serial Zero Coupon Senior Notes—net of estimated discount of $562,480	$ 397,520
Senior Exchangeable Variable Rate Debentures—net of estimated discount of $3,350	331,650
15 5/8% Senior Subordinated Debentures—net of estimated discount of $1,687	223,313
Adjustable Rate Participating Subordinated Debentures— net of estimated discount of $50,804	349,196
	1,301,679
Less: Debt expenses	35,740
Net proceeds	$1,265,939

MBC will transfer all but $50 million of the aggregate net proceeds of the offerings of the debt securities to Metromedia, including a $1,141 million dividend, and a $75 million advance in the form of a note receivable. It is contemplated that if at the end of 1985, or at the end of any consecutive twelve-month period thereafter, MBC has achieved a ratio of operating cash flow (before deduction of the proposed Management Fee payable to Metromedia) to cash interest expense of 1.10 to 1, $25 million may be advanced to Metromedia and the note referred to above shall be increased by such amount. If, at the end of 1986 (or at the end of any consecutive twelve-month period thereafter), MBC has achieved a ratio of operating cash flow to cash interest expense (as determined above) of 1.25 to 1, an additional $25 million may be advanced to Metromedia and the note referred to above shall be further increased by such amount.

Metromedia will use the $1,141 million dividend and the $75 million advance to repay senior bank indebtedness of $1,149 million and accrued interest of $67 million.

Exhibit 12 Schedule of Principal Payments on the Debt Securities (millions of dollars)

	Serial Senior Notes	Senior Variable Rate Debentures	Senior Subordinated Debentures	Participating Subordinated Debentures	Total
1988	$160	—	—	—	$160
1989	160	—	—	—	160
1990	160	—	—	—	160
1991	160	—	—	—	160
1992	160	—	—	—	160
1993	160	—	—	—	160
1994	—	$110	—	—	110
1995	—	110	—	—	110
1996	—	115	$56	—	171
1997	—	—	56	$66	122
1998	—	—	56	66	122
1999	—	—	57	66	123
2000	—	—	—	66	66
2001	—	—	—	66	66
2002	—	—	—	70	70

Source: Metromedia Broadcasting Corporation Prospectus dated November 29, 1984.

Exhibit 13 Selected Historical and Pro Forma Consolidated Financial Statements for MBC, 1979–1984 (thousands of dollars)

	Historical Financial Data[a] Predecessor Operations[b]								
	Fiscal Year[c]					Jan.2– July 3, 1983	Jan. 1–June 20, 1984	June 21–Aug. 5, 1984	Aug. 6–Sept. 30, 1984
	1979	1980	1981	1982	1983				
Net revenues	$138,816	$172,468	$207,323	$270,799	$343,742	$154,351	$175,429	$38,476	$58,748
Depreciation and amortization	3,947	4,282	5,119	9,365	14,970	6,526	8,877	3,676	4,771
Operating income[d]	51,354	54,101	68,490	88,839	97,467	40,202	46,864	6,183	12,087
Allocated interest expense[e]	7,093	7,057	7,580	24,238	28,172	11,930	14,382	17,043	20,544
Net income (loss)	22,155	23,683	30,048	30,771	30,625	12,493	14,684	(10,860)	(8,457)
Ratio of earnings to fixed charges[f,g]									

Pro Forma Financial Data—Metromedia Broadcasting Corporation and Subsidiaries[h]

	Fiscal Year 1983	Jan. 2–Oct. 2, 1983	Jan. 1–Sept. 30, 1984
Income Statement Data			
Net revenues	$354,998	$251,842	$272,653
Depreciation and amortization	32,232	24,020	25,132
Operating income	81,676	51,806	55,713
Interest expense (excluding amortization of debt discount and expenses)	133,719	100,289	100,289
Amortization of debt discount and expenses	70,341	52,756	52,756
Net loss	(122,384)	(101,239)	(97,332)
Ratio of earnings to fixed charges[f,i]			

Exhibit 13 Selected Historical and Pro Forma Consolidated Financial Statements for MBC, 1979–1984 (thousands of dollars) (Continued)

	Pro Forma Financial Data—Metromedia Broadcasting Corporation and Subsidiaries[h]
	At Sept. 30, 1984
Balance Sheet Data	
Working capital[j,k]	$ 97,022
Total assets[j,k]	1,452,736
Intangible assets, net of amortization	997,686
Serial zero coupon senior notes	397,520
Senior exchangeable variable rate debentures	331,650
15⅝% senior subordinated debentures	223,313
Adjustable-rate participating subordinated debentures	349,196
Stockholder's equity (deficiency)[j,k]	(52,900)

Source: Metromedia Broadcasting Corporation Prospectus dated November 29, 1984.
a. Prior to management's leveraged buyout of Metromedia.
b. WCVB-TV (Boston) was acquired in May 1982; WFLD-TV (Chicago) was acquired in April 1983; KRLD-TV (Dallas) was acquired in December 1983. The historical financial statements include the results of operations of such stations since their respective dates of acquisition.
c. The company's fiscal year approximates a calender year.
d. A restatement of the historical financial statements gives effect to the management agreement, pursuant to which Metromedia will provide certain administrative, tax, legal, cash management, and financial advisory services for a fee.
e. The historical financial statements include an allocation of interest expense from Metromedia based on (1) specific borrowings identifiable with the acquisition of the broadcasting properties and (2) a general allocation based on the ratio of total assets of the broadcasting properties to total consolidated Metromedia assets (exclusive of specific borrowings identifiable with assets other than the broadcasting properties).
f. Earnings used in computing the historical and pro forma ratios of earnings before fixed charges consist of earnings before fixed charges and taxes based on income. Historical fixed charges consist of allocated interest [See Note (e)] and one third of rental expense, which is deemed to be representative of the interest factor of rental payments. Pro forma fixed charges consist of interest expense, amortization of debt discount and expenses, and one third of rental expense.

Exhibit 13 Selected Historical and Pro Forma Consolidated Financial Statements for MBC, 1979–1984 (thousands of dollars) (Continued)

g. The amount of earnings coverage deficiency for the period June 21, 1984 to August 5, 1984, and August 6, 1984, to September 30, 1984, were $10,860,000 and $8,457,000, respectively. In view of significant changes in capital structure, the ratio of earnings to fixed charges for predecessor operations has not been included.

h. The pro forma financial data is based on the historical financial statements of the Company, giving effect to the acquisitions of WFLD-TV (Chicago) and KRLD-TV (Dallas) consummated during 1983, the effect of a real estate sale-leaseback transaction completed in November 1983, the merger on June 21, 1984, pursuant to which Metromedia became a privately held company, the contribution by Metromedia to the Company of the stock of two of its subsidiaries which own the broadcasting properties; the issuance of the debt securities; and the dividend or advance of all but $50 million of the net proceeds of the offerings of the Debt Securities. The pro forma income data for the periods January 2, 1983, to October 2, 1983, and January 1, 1984, to September 30, 1984, and for the fiscal year ended December 31, 1983, assume that the issuance of the Debt Securities and the other transactions described above took place at the beginning of each of such fiscal periods. The pro forma balance sheet data assume that Metromedia contributed the stock of its two subsidiaries which own the broadcasting properties to the company on September 30, 1984, and that the issuance of the debt securities and the dividend or advance of all but $50 million of the net proceeds of the offerings of the debt securities took place on September 30, 1984. [see note (k)].

i. The amount of earnings coverage deficiency on a pro forma basis for the fiscal year ended December 31, 1983, was $122,384,000. The amounts of earnings coverage deficiency on a pro forma basis for the periods from January 1, 1984, to September 30, 1984, and January 2, 1983, to October 2, 1983, were $97,332,000 and $101,239,000, respectively.

j. All but $125 million of the aggregate net proceeds of the offerings of the debt securities will be dividended to to Metromedia. Of such $125 million, $75 million will be advanced to Metromedia and $50 million will be added to the company's working capital. [see note (k)].

k. It is contemplated that, if at the end of 1985 (or at the end of any consecutive twelve-month period thereafter) MBC has achieved a ratio of operating cash flow (before deduction of the management fee) to cash interest expense of 1.15 to 1, $25 million may be advanced to Metromedia. If, at the end of 1986 (or at the end of any consecutive twelve-month period thereafter), the Company has achieved a ratio of operating cash flow (as determined above) to cash interest expense of 1.30 to 1, an additional $25 million may be advanced to Metromedia. If the $50 million referred to above was advanced to Metromedia simultaneously with the $75 million advance, pro forma total assets would be approximately $1,403 million, working capital would be approximately $47 million and stockholder's deficiency would be approximately $103 million as of September 30, 1984.

Exhibit 14 Public Straight Debt Default Rate as a Percentage of High-Yield Debt Outstanding, 1974–1984

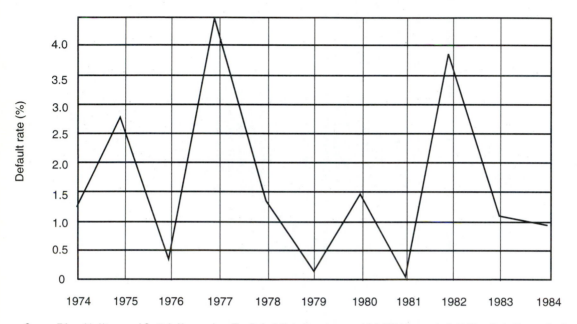

Source: Edward I. Altman and Scott A. Nammacher, *The Default Rate Experience on High Yield Corporate Debt* (New York: Morgan Stanley, 1985), p. 15.

Exhibit 14 Public Straight Debt Default Rate as a Percentage of High-Yield Debt Outstanding, 1974–1984 (Continued)

Yield on 20-Year U.S. Treasuries, 1974–1984

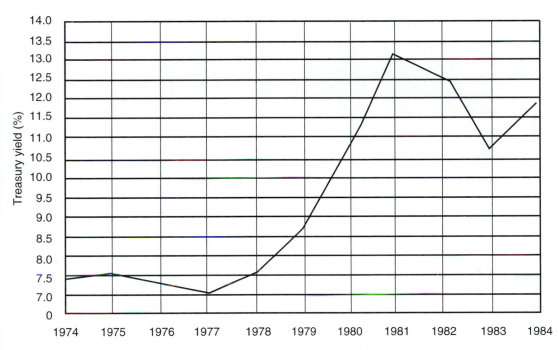

Source: Salomon Brothers, Inc.

Exhibit 15   Selected Bond Yields, November 23, 1984

Maturity	Instrument	Yield to Maturity
1-Year	Treasury bills	8.65%
3-Year	Government bonds	10.63
	Zero coupon government bonds	10.90
5-Year	Government bonds	10.99
7-Year	Government bonds	11.21
	Zero coupon government bonds	11.53
10-Year	Government bonds	11.27
	New Industrials (Aaa)	11.50
	New Industrials (A)	11.75
15-Year	Government bonds	11.36
25-Year	Government bonds	11.43
	New Industrials (Aaa)	11.88
	New Industrials (A)	12.25

Exhibit 16   Summary Statistics of Monthly Returns on Low-Quality Bonds versus Other Securities (January 1982 to May 1984)

Profile of Indices at Jan. 1, 1984					
			Average Returns		Standard Deviation
Index	Average Coupon (%)	Average Maturity (years)	Monthly (%)	Annualized (%)	of Monthly Returns[a] (%)
Low-Quality Bonds	12.72	17	1.55	20.3	2.74
Corporate Bonds					
A Rating	9.58	22	1.29	16.6	3.49
AAA Rating	9.09	24	1.17	15.0	3.59
Salomon Long Government Bond Index	10.67	23	1.02	13.0	3.55
S&P 500	na	na	1.12	14.3	4.15

Source: Marshall E. Blume and Donald B. Keim, *Risk and Return Characteristics of Lower-Grade Bonds* (Rodney L. White Center for Financial Research, University of Pennsylvania, The Wharton School) December 1984, Appendix Table 1.
na = not available.

a. Standard deviation is a statistical measure of the dispersion of actual returns around their average, or expected, value. In general, the probability is 67% that the actual return on a portfolio will lie within one standard deviation of its expected value and 95% that the return will lie within two standard deviations of the expected value.

Exhibit 17 News Profile, *Inc. Magazine*, November 1983

MAKING THE MARKET

No man is a market. But in the highly specialized world of low-rated debt, Drexel Burnham Lambert Inc.'s Michael Milken comes awfully close. In the late 1960s, Milken, now a 37-year-old senior vice-president, demonstrated in his MBA thesis for the University of Pennsylvania's Wharton School that companies with debt rated B or less were far less prone to bankruptcy than most people had assumed. Upon joining Drexel in 1968, the enterprising analyst/salesman began introducing his new employer to an unexploited corner of the corporate underwriting market—one that has become the envy of Wall Street.

Drexel's strong franchise in low-rated debt didn't materialize overnight. In the early days, Milken worked long and hard out of Philadelphia and, later, New York, as a bond analyst, researching more than 2,000 issues—many of them the downgraded bonds of ailing conglomerates. But, as he and the firm's credit analysts began learning more about the high-yield, or "junk," bond universe than anyone else on Wall Street, Milken proposed—and got approval—to take the next step. "We started making markets in these securities," he says.

Once Drexel's knowledge of buyers and sellers took hold, the firm's investment bankers, headed by Fredrick Joseph, began underwriting new debt issues in 1977 for younger and smaller companies. In doing so, however, they have drawn heavily on Milken's talents for both structuring deals and selling them. Says one investor: "It's no exaggeration to say he knows nearly all the buyers and what they want. He's the one who's sold them on junk bonds."

Five years ago, in recognition of Milken's unique market grasp, Drexel management signed off on his unusual request to move the entire high-yield and convertible-bond department from Wall Street to Los Angeles. The three-hour difference in time zones enables Milken, a workaholic of legendary proportions, to stay in touch with buyers and sellers on both coasts. On a typical day, he commutes 20 minutes from his San Fernando Valley home (once the residence of Clark Gable) to be in Drexel's Beverly Hills trading room by 5 a.m. For the next 14 hours or so, he quarterbacks a team of more than 50 analysts, traders, and salespeople from the center of a large, X-shaped trading desk. Competitors estimate that Drexel's Los Angeles operation accounts for 60% to 70% of the trading volume of a booming over-the-counter market that, Milken claims, never closes. "If a guy called me at home and wanted to sell, I'd buy on a Sunday morning," he says. At a price, he notes, "there's always a market."

Even with some of Wall Street's biggest guns angling to become more influential in low-rated bond trading and underwriting, Milken claims he doesn't feel pressure. "We've worked hard for many years and brought in lots of capable people." With confidence, he shrugs and says, "Others have always been interested in the market. But time is the greatest competitor. You have only so much time in a day."

Exhibit 18 Anchor Savings and Loan Consolidated Balance Sheet at June 30, 1984 (millions of dollars)

Cash	$ 52	Deposits	$ 870
Loans receivables	735	Accounts payable and accruals	21
Investments		Notes payable	49
Government and agency securities	105	Federal Home Loan Bank advances	52
Corporate bonds (investment-grade)	96	Other liabilities	10
		Total liabilities	$1,002
Commercial loans	9	Stockholders' equity	45
Federal Home Loan Bank stock	21	Total liabilities and stockholders' equity	$1,047
Real estate held for sale or investment	16		
Other assets	13		
Total assets	$1,047		

Note: Anchor Savings and Loan was a federally chartered thrift insured by the Federal Savings and Loan Insurance Corporation.

SECURITIZATION

TRAVELERS MORTGAGE SECURITIES CMO

On February 17, 1984, Maureen Golden, a portfolio manager for the life insurance division of Pacific Life and Casualty Insurance, Inc., was reviewing a preliminary prospectus for a series of collateralized mortgage obligations (CMOs) to be issued by a wholly owned finance subsidiary of the Travelers Corporation. As Ms. Golden reviewed the terms of the offering, she realized that this deal warranted special attention. While CMOs had been introduced some eight months earlier, in June 1983, Pacific Life and Casualty had yet to include CMOs in its portfolio of mortgage-related securities. Given the positive reception afforded CMOs by a wide range of fixed-income investors since their introduction, She was determined to understand the CMO structure and to prepare a recommendation on CMO investments for Pacific Life and Casualty's Investment Policy Committee.

In addition, Ms. Golden was intrigued that this CMO series was to be issued by a subsidiary of a large, diversified insurance company. Most CMOs to date had been issued by the Federal Home Loan Mortgage Corporation (FHLMC, or Freddie Mac) or by investment banks. She wondered why Travelers, an insurance company active in both the life and property/casualty markets, had chosen to issue this security. Recognizing the similarities between Travelers' asset management objectives and her own, Ms. Golden was anxious to understand the value of collateralized mortgage obligations to issuers as well as investors.

INSURANCE INDUSTRY BACKGROUND

Life insurance companies have long been major investors in fixed-income instruments, including corporate bonds and mortgages. Before 1980, the principal business of life insurers was to sell and administer whole-life insurance policies. Whole-life policies combined insurance against an early death with a savings provision. As annual payments, or

This case was prepared by Salley E. Durdan under the supervision of Scott P. Mason as the basis of class discussion.

"premiums," were received, the insurer accumulated a pool of savings, called the policy's cash surrender value, on behalf of the policyholder. Simultaneously, various reserves were accrued on the liability side of the insurer's balance sheet to provide for the future liabilities of the policies, including death benefits and payment of cash surrender values in the event of policy termination. Because these liabilities were long-term and, in the aggregate, had a fairly predictable nominal value, most of an insurer's funds were invested in long-term financial assets yielding relatively certain nominal returns. Accordingly, many of a typical insurer's funds were invested in illiquid assets such as private placements, real estate, and commercial mortgages.

Asset-liability management for life insurers was complicated by the inclusion of "policy loan" options in many life insurance policies. Policyholders were given an option to borrow against the cash surrender value of their policies at predetermined fixed rates. In periods of high interest rates, policyholders capitalized on these advantageous rates and insurers experienced disintermediation as policy loans expanded sharply.

The problem of disintermediation was particularly threatening to insurers in the high-inflation, high-interest environment of 1979–1982. During this period, increasingly sophisticated consumers became dissatisfied with the terms of whole-life policies. Inflation had severely eroded the value of whole-life death benefits, and the meager 3.5–4.0% (tax-free) earnings paid on the savings portions of the policies were uncompetitive with rates offered on money market instruments. As individuals terminated whole-life policies and withdrew accumulated cash balances at unprecedented rates, insurers were faced with the prospect of liquidating long-term, fixed-rate assets at substantial losses.

As the whole-life business deteriorated, insurers introduced new interest-sensitive insurance products, such as universal life, which combined low-cost insurance coverage with savings pegged to short-term interest rates. At the same time, they expanded their involvement in a number of other financial service businesses. By 1984, life insurance companies were selling a wide range of annuity contracts, which provided a continuous income stream to the purchaser in exchange for a lump-sum payment. As an example, a pension plan sponsor could purchase an insured pension fund agreement to provide a continuous stream of specified benefits to its employees. Similarly, insurers sold various financial contracts, often to pension funds or other large investment pools, guaranteeing a certain future sum in return for a current lump-sum payment or stream of payments. Many of these were known as Guaranteed Investment Contacts (GICs). In most states, life insurance companies were also allowed to manage investment accounts for pension funds, separate from or without respect to the regulatory restraints imposed on their other businesses.

In response to their experience with depressed profitability and disintermediation, insurers began to adopt more sophisticated asset-liability management techniques in the early 1980s. Increasingly, insurers looked for liquidity in prospective investments. The accurate matching of asset and liability durations and the introduction of new, shorter-duration insurance products resulted in a shortening of the maturities of many insurers' asset portfolios.

MORTGAGE-BACKED SECURITIES

Among the instruments to which insurers directed their investment in the early 1980s were mortgage-backed securities. Insurers and other institutional investors had historically been relatively inactive in the residential mortgage market, holding only 13% of the residential mortgage debt outstanding in 1970. Although they had purchased some government-insured Federal Housing Authority and government-guaranteed Veterans Administration (FHA/VA) mortgages, investors had been reluctant to purchase "whole loans" because of the cumbersome documentation required to transfer title to individual loans and the relative illiquidity of the whole-loan market. Instead, residential mortgage capital had been provided by thrift institutions and commercial banks who originated, serviced, and funded fixed-rate mortgages by keeping them on their balance sheets. However, as mortgage-related securities offering homogeneous terms and an active secondary market were introduced during the 1970s, a broad range of investors, including insurance companies, expanded their involvement in the residential mortgage market.

Government agencies and quasi-agencies, such as the Government National Mortgage Association (GNMA, or Ginnie Mae), the Federal National Mortgage Association (FNMA, or Fannie Mae), and the Federal Home Loan Mortgage Corporation (FHLMC or Freddie Mac), were charged with providing broader and more stable sources of capital to the residential mortgage market. These agencies pioneered the securitization of mortgage assets by purchasing home mortgage loans from local lenders and guaranteeing securities backed by pools of residential mortgages. As a result, these agencies expanded the volume of funds available for housing and helped to redistribute mortgage funds from capital-surplus to capital-deficit regions.

Although a variety of mortgage-backed security structures had been introduced by 1984, *pass-through securities* had dominated the mortgage securities market since its inception. An issuer created a pass-through security by placing a pool of mortgages, comprising one to several thousand individual mortgage loans of similar term, interest rate, and quality, in trust with a bank. In return, the issuer received pass-through certificates representing pro rata ownership interests in the pooled mortgages. The pass-through certificates were then sold to investors either directly by the issuer or, more commonly, by a securities dealer.

The trustee holding title to the pooled mortgages oversaw the orderly distribution of principal and interest flows from the underlying mortgages, less servicing and guarantee fees, to investors. Although the issuance of pass-through securities represented a sale of the underlying mortgage assets, thus removing the pooled mortgages from the issuer's balance sheet, the loan originator continued to administer the mortgages and therefore continued to receive servicing fees over the life of the securities (see Exhibit 1).

In most cases, the loans underlying pass-through securities were fixed-rate mortgages on one- to four-family homes carrying maturities of approximately 30 years. The cash flows from these traditional mortgages differed from those of standard fixed-income instruments in several respects. While a simple bond investment provided an investor with a fixed, semiannual flow of coupon payments and a single repayment of principal at maturity, traditional mortgages were repaid in level monthly installments of principal and interest. Payments made early in the life of the mortgage consisted primarily of interest on the outstanding principal balance. However, the principal portion increased over time until, at maturity, the payment was almost entirely principal (see Exhibit 2). In addition, traditional mortgages offered generous prepayment provisions to the mortgagor (the homeowner). A mortgagor had the right at any time to make a payment in excess of the amount currently due. These "prepayments" were applied to the outstanding mortgage balance, thus reducing the amount of the loan. Prepayments usually resulted from a sale of the mortgaged property,[1] destruction of the property (in which case the mortgage was repaid from the insurance proceeds), or a decline in interest rates, which prompted the homeowner to refinance his mortgage at more attractive current rates.

Given the unique cash flow characteristics of mortgages, mortgage-backed securities embodied several classes of risk. In addition to cash flow uncertainty, or "prepayment risk," mortgage securities were subject to the interest rate, liquidity, reinvestment, and default risks typical of any fixed-income instrument. The credit quality of a mortgage pass-through was determined by the characteristics of the mortgages in the pass-through pool, including the terms of the pooled mortgages, the creditworthiness of the pool's mortgagors, the number of mortgages in the pool, and the geographic diversity of the mortgage portfolio.

---

1   Many conventional residential mortgages contained "due-on-sale clauses" which required that a mortgage be repaid in full in the event of a sale or transfer of the mortgaged property. In contrast, FHA/VA loans were assumable by the purchaser of a mortgaged property.

Mortgages have historically been considered secure instruments because of home-owners' reluctance to risk foreclosure on their homes by defaulting on mortgage payments. In addition, private mortgage insurance was often used by lenders to reduce default risk on mortgages with high loan-to-value (i.e., leverage) ratios. Such policies provided coverage against default up to some percentage of the initial mortgage balance. Nevertheless, it was difficult for investors in pass-through securities to adequately evaluate the credit risks of the many small mortgages in a pool. As a result, issuers used guarantees and/or pool insurance to elevate the credit of pass-throughs above that of whole loans.

PASS-THROUGH ISSUERS

The activities of GNMA, FNMA, and FHLMC differed in the types of underlying mortgages, the issuing structure, and the nature of the guarantuees. The creator and, through 1984, the largest guarantor of pass-through securities, was a wholly owned U.S. Government Corporation within the Department of Housing and Urban Development (HUD). GNMA pass-throughs were issued by private mortgage institutions (principally mortgage bankers) and were backed by pools of newly issued FHA/VA single-family mortgages. GNMA guaranteed the timely payment of scheduled monthly principal and interest on GNMA pass-throughs. Such guarantees represented full faith and credit obligations of the U.S. Government.

The FHLMC, a corporate instrumentality of the United States, purchased primarily uninsured or privately insured conventional loans and loan participations (50–95% ownership interests in loans) from thrifts and banks. The FNMA, a private corporation, purchased both FHA/VA loans and conventional loans from mortgage banks, thrifts, and commercial banks. In some cases FHLMC and FNMA compensated mortgage originators with cash, holding purchased loans in portfolio or pooling them for issuance as pass-throughs. Under their guarantor programs, FNMA and FHLMC "swapped" mortgages for pass-through securities, which originators held in portfolio or reissued publicly.

FHLMC and FNMA pass-through securities, called FHLMC Participation Certificates (PCs) and FNMA Mortgage Pass-through Certificates (FNMAs), differed from GNMA securities in several respects. First, FHLMC PCs and FNMAs were issued directly by the FHLMC and FNMA, not the loan originator. In addition, FHLMC and FNMA issued securities backed by seasoned discount mortgages as well as newly originated mortgage product. Although FHLMC and FNMA guaranteed payment of principal and interest on their pass-through securities, such guarantees did not represent direct obligations of the U.S. Government. As a result, FHLMC PCs and FNMAs traded at yields at least 10–15 basis points over yields on comparable GNMA securities. (See Exhibit 3 for a comparison of issuers.)

Since 1977 a variety of private issuers (commercial banks, savings and loans, and mortgage banks) had issued pass-throughs backed by conventional loans. Private "pool insurance" covering homeowner defaults up to approximately five percent of the initial principal amount of a mortgage pool was typically used to guarantee private pass-throughs.

INNOVATIONS IN THE MORTGAGE SECURITIES MARKET

By February 1984, approximately $300 billion of the $1.2 trillion of residential mortgage debt outstanding had been securitized. Secondary market trading volumes in mortgage securities had grown rapidly, although turnover ratios remained far lower than those of Treasury securities (see Exhibit 4). This growth in the issuance and trading of mortgage securities was accompanied by a number of changes in the structure of mortgages and mortgage securities.

In 1981 regulators authorized mortgage lenders to issue adjustable-rate mortgages (ARMs). Although an inverted yield curve made ARMs unattractive to borrowers in 1981–1982, ARM volume grew to 38% of total residential mortgage originations when the yield curve assumed a positive slope in early 1983. Unlike fixed rate mortgages, ARMs had not yet been successfully securitized. Because they were designed as portfolio investments for the savings institutions originating them, ARMs lacked the standardization of terms required for securitization. In addition, most ARMs featured complex terms, including rate caps and low initial "teaser" rates, that complicated their valuation. In February 1984 it was estimated that ARMs would represent two-thirds of 1984 mortgage originations. The dominance of ARMs was expected to hinder GNMA pass-through issuance, which was reliant on originations of fixed-rate mortgages, and spur the development of an ARM security.

By 1984, a variety of debt securities collateralized by fixed-rate mortgages or pass-through securities had been introduced. These new securities differed from pass-throughs primarily in the nature and allocation of key risk components. *Mortgage-backed bonds*, which were debt obligations collateralized by mortgage loans, assigned prepayment risk to the issuer, who retained ownership of the collateral portfolio. These bonds usually had a stated maturity of 5 to 12 years and paid interest semiannually. The credit quality of a mortgage-backed bond was determined by the credit of the issuer, the quality of the collateral used, and a required collateralization level.

Collateralization levels, expressed as a percentage of the par value of a mortgage-backed bond, were designed to ensure that, in the event of a default, proceeds from the liquidation of the collateral would be sufficient to redeem the mortgage-backed bond at par plus accrued interest. Although collateral values were reevaluated at pre-specified dates, usually once per quarter, over-collateralization levels as high as 150–200% were deemed necessary by rating agencies to protect investors against declines in collateral market values between evaluation dates. Such declines could result from increases in market interest rates, defaults, or declines in the outstanding balance of the mortgage collateral. Thus, while bond issuance enabled mortgage portfolio investors, such as thrifts, to raise long-term funds at attractive fixed rates, it was a relatively inefficient use of mortgage collateral.

Pay-through bonds were hybrids of the mortgage-backed bond and pass-through structures. Like mortgage-backed bonds, pay-throughs were debt obligations collateralized by pass-through securities or whole-loan portfolios. However, unlike mortgage-backed bonds, all collateral principal flows, including prepayments, flowed through to investors as received. As a result, pay-through issuance enabled mortgage investors, such as banks or thrifts, to liquify "under-the-water" portfolios while avoiding the extensive over-collateralization required in structuring mortgage-backed bonds. Thus, pay-through bonds shifted prepayment risk to the investors and a more efficient disposal of mortgages for the issuers.

In the early 1980s issuers sought to expand the market for mortgage securities by designing an instrument that offered improved call protection and a broader menu of maturities to mortgage investors. In June 1983, Freddie Mac, with the help of its investment banker, First Boston, accomplished these objectives with the successful introduction of the first *collateralized mortgage obligation (CMO)*. A CMO was a pay-through bond collateralized by pass-through securities or whole-loan portfolios segmented into a series of two or more maturity classes. Collateral principal payments flowed through to investors in order of maturity, such that no principal payments were made on the second class until the first had been fully retired, etc. Most CMO series included a discount zero-bond, or "Z-bond," as the longest maturity class. Interest on Z-bonds was accrued, but not paid, until all previous maturity classes had been fully retired. Interest accrued in this manner was applied to principal payments on the shortest maturity class outstanding.

A CMO was usually issued by a limited purpose finance subsidiary to ensure that the issue would be rated solely on the basis of its collateralization, without regard for the credit of its parent. The parent was required, for tax purposes, to invest equity in the issuing subsidiary equal to 2% of the subsidiary's total assets. IRS regulations also required that CMOs be structured so as to differentiate the bonds being issued from the collateral underlying them. As a result, CMOs paid interest quarterly or semiannually while collateral interest accumulated monthly. (See Exhibit 5 for CMO issuance activity.)

INNOVATIONS IN MORTGAGE SECURITIES PRICING

Estimating mortgage prepayment experience was the central issue in valuing mortgage securities, as this would allow one to project cash flows to the investor. Early in the evolution of the mortgage securities market, dealers adopted the convention of quoting mortgage yields to a 12-year fully prepaid life. This convention simplistically assumed that 100% prepayment would occur in a lump-sum payment at the end of 12 years, the average life of a typical 30-year mortgage. As the mortgage securities market developed, more sophisticated prepayment models were developed using actual prepayment experience statistics compiled by HUD as actuarial data for the FHA's insurance activities.

A prepayment rate was defined as the percentage of outstanding mortgages in a pool that terminated in a given year of mortgage life. Because the terms of most mortgage securities provided for immediate repayment of principal in the event of a mortgagor default, prepayment rates reflected mortgage defaults as well as voluntary prepayments. "FHA experience" tables of prepayment rate estimates were developed using statistics on FHA-insured and VA-guaranteed mortgages endorsed between 1957 and 1981. For each year of a mortgage's life, HUD tabulated the percentage of loans that terminated at that age during the period 1957–1981, regardless of when the experience took place. As a result, statistics for each later year of mortgage life incorporated data from one less calendar year. Since the actual data did not cover the entire 30-year life of the mortgages, prepayment rates for the later years were projected by HUD (see Exhibit 6a).

In 1984 recently issued, i.e., current coupon, pass-through securities, whose yields were relatively insensitive to prepayment assumptions, continued to trade at prices reflecting quoted yields to a 12-year life. However, mortgage securities dealers had begun to price seasoned pass-throughs and CMOs on the basis of cash flow yields. Seasoned pass-throughs were generally assumed to prepay at constant annual rates, such as 2%, 4%, or 6% of outstanding principal per year. In contrast, CMOs were priced at prepayment assumptions expressed as a percentage of FHA experience statistics, which modeled changes in prepayment rates over the life of a mortgage pool. Recognition that prepayment rates were usually slowest early in the life of a mortgage pool was critical to providing buyers of the shortest maturity class in a CMO series with an adequate return. In pricing a new CMO issue, a prepayment assumption (i.e., 75% or 100% FHA) was chosen on the basis of actual prepayment experience on the securities collateralizing the CMO over the 12 months preceding the issue date (see Exhibit 6b).

Prices of seasoned pass-throughs and CMOs were computed by discounting estimated cash flows at a yield equal to a spread over a comparable maturity Treasury security. Although there was no greater credit risk in a GNMA pass-through than in a comparable maturity government security, large spreads had historically been demanded as compensation for the prepayment uncertainty inherent in mortgage investments (see Exhibit 7). Furthermore, 60% of all fixed-income investors were inactive in the mortgage securities market in 1984.

THE TRAVELERS MORTGAGE SECURITIES CORPORATION CMO

The Travelers Mortgage Securities Corporation GNMA/FNMA-Collateralized Obligations offered in February 1984 consisted of four classes of securities aggregating $1,250,000,000 in principal:

Class	Original Principal Amount ($)	Interest Rate (%)	First Mandatory Principal Payment Date[a]	Stated Maturity[a]	Price to Public[b,c] (%)
A	270,000,000	10.625	September 1, 1984	March 1, 1987	99.9375
Z-1	455,000,000	12.000	September 1, 1987	September 1, 1997	100.0000
C	375,000,000	12.000	March 1, 1998	September 1, 2000	96.4062
Z-2	150,000,000	12.000	March 1, 2001	March 1, 2014	84.5000

a. The "stated maturity" of each bond class was the date by which the entire principal amount was to be fully paid, assuming no prepayments on the GNMA and FNMA certificates and reinvestment at the assumed reinvestment rate (defined below).
b. Plus accrued interest, if any, from March 1, 1984.
c. The underwriting discount was to vary by class, totaling $4,653,750, or .384% of the aggregate price to the public. Aggregate proceeds to the issuer, before deducting expenses of $770,000, were to total $1,208,450,938.

The bonds were to be issued in fully registered form in minimum denominations of $1000. The sole underwriter of the bonds was to be Salomon Brothers, Inc. The issuer, Travelers Mortgage Securities Corporation, was a wholly owned limited-purpose finance subsidiary of the Travelers Corporation. Neither the Travelers Corporation nor any other affiliate of the issuer had guaranteed or was otherwise obligated with respect to the bonds. The issuer was to apply the net proceeds of the sale of the bonds toward the purchase of the GNMA and FNMA Certificates pledged as collateral. The prospectus indicated that all the Class Z-1 Bonds were to be purchased by The Travelers Insurance Company, an affiliate of the issuer.

Interest on the Class A and Class C Bonds was to be paid semiannually on each March 1 and September 1, beginning September 1, 1984. The Class Z-1 and Z-2 Bonds were compound-interest bonds. Interest on the Class Z-1 Bonds was to accrue but not be paid until the Class A Bonds had been fully retired. Accrued interest was to be added to the principal of the Class Z-1 Bonds on each semiannual payment date. Interest on the Class Z-2 Bonds was to accrue in a similar fashion until the Class A, Class Z-1, and Class C Bonds had been paid in full.

Principal payments on the bonds were to be made on each semiannual payment date in an amount equal to the sum of (1) interest accrued but not paid on the Class Z-1 and Z-2 bonds over the previous six months, and (2) the applicable "bondholders' percent-ages" of all distributions of principal on the GNMA/FNMA collateral received since the last payment date. Principal payments were to be applied to the classes of bonds in order of maturity, such that no payment was to be made on a class until all earlier classes had been fully retired.

The term "bondholders' percentage" referred to the ratio of the aggregate principal of the bonds issued to the aggregate principal of the collateral securities (see Exhibit 8a). The bonds were to be secured by excess collateral in order to meet the collateralization guide-lines required for AAA rating of the issue. Rating agency standards required that an issuer demonstrate that scheduled monthly distributions on the GNMA and FNMA Certificates securing the bonds, together with earnings on the reinvestment of such distributions accrued during the six-month periods between bond payment dates, would be sufficient to make timely payments of interest on the bonds, begin payment of principal of each class of bonds not later than its First Mandatory Principal Payment date, and retire each class not later than its Stated Maturity. Such demonstrations of collateral adequacy were calculated assuming no prepayment of principal and intraperiod reinvestment at very conservative rates: 5% the first year, 4% the second year, and 3% each year thereafter.

The Travelers issue was to be subject to special redemption, in whole or in part, on the first day of any month, at 100% of the unpaid principal amount of the bonds redeemed plus accrued interest, if, as a result of substantial payments of principal of the underlying mortgages and low reinvestment yields, it was determined that insufficient cash would be available on the next payment date to make required payments on the bonds. A special redemption of the bonds would not shorten the maturity of any class of bonds by more than five months. In addition, the Class Z-2 Bonds were callable at 100% of the unpaid principal amount plus accrued interest on any payment date on or after March 1, 2009, or on any earlier payment date on or after March 1, 2004 if the principal amount of the bonds outstanding was less than $250 million.[2]

---

2   Although the initial principal of the Class Z-2 bonds totaled only $150,000,000, the Z-2 principal was to grow to $408,500,000 by 1996 (assuming prepayment at 75% FHA) as a result of the accrual of interest at a rate of 12.0%.

The bonds were to be secured by GNMA and FNMA Certificates having aggregate principal balances of $1,295,681,394, a weighted average pass-through rate of approximately 11.66%, and a weighted average remaining term to maturity of approximately 28.5 years. (Some of the conventional loans underlying the FNMA Certificates, and all of the FHA/VA loans underlying certain of the FNMA Certificates and all of the GNMA Certificates, did not contain "due-on-sale clauses" and, accordingly, were not subject to acceleration upon a transfer of the mortgaged property.)

All distributions on the GNMA and FNMA Certificates were to be remitted directly to a collection account administered by Texas Commerce Bank, N.A. As trustee, Texas Commerce was to be empowered to invest the collection account funds in any of a variety of high-grade investments maturing no later than the day before the next semiannual payment date, including Treasury bills, AAA-rated commercial paper, certificates of deposit, and guaranteed investment contracts. Unless an event of default had occurred and was continuing, amounts remaining in the collection account after a semiannual payment date would be paid to the issuer and, upon such payment, would be free from the lien of the bond indenture. Such residual cash flows were referred to as the issuer's "spread."

Holders of the compound interest bonds (Classes Z-1 and Z-2) and any other bond classes issued with an original issue discount were to be subject to tax on the amortization of original issue discount over the life of the bonds. Although it was unclear at the time of the issue, it was possible that bondholders would be required to periodically recompute the original issue discount in recognition of prepayments of principal of earlier classes of bonds. (See Appendix A for a brief outline of collateralization process associated with CMOs.)

MAUREEN GOLDEN'S ANALYSIS AND DECISION

As Maureen Golden studied the Travelers CMO prospectus, she compared the investment characteristics of CMOs with those of standard pass-through securities. She also evaluated the pricing of the Travelers offering by analyzing current levels of interest rates and assessing the credit quality and cash flow uncertainty of the four securities offered (see Exhibits 8B, 9, 10, and 11).

In the course of investigating the Travelers Mortgage Securities offering, Ms. Golden learned that Travelers had an interest beyond the purchase of the Class Z-1 Bonds. Travelers had owned the $500 million of GNMA 11.5s included in the CMO collateral pool at the time the deal was structured. She believed the GNMAs, which were yielding 12.89% (assuming prepayment at 75% FHA) in February 1984, had been held in a portfolio backing five-year GICs. These contracts obligated Travelers to pay pension clients a fixed sum in five years' time. Maureen also reviewed Travelers financials (see Exhibit 12) and noted the growth of "pension deposit funds" on their balance sheet and surmised that these were related to the GLCs.

The FNMA securities to be used as collateral were to be purchased on the open market. Ms. Golden was unsure how the inclusion of FNMA collateral would influence the credit quality of this issue. To date, most CMO issues brought to market had been collateralized exclusively by GNMAs (see Exhibits 5, 8a, and 12).

As Ms. Golden began to analyze Travelers' motivations in issuing this CMO, several questions ran through her mind. Why did Travelers choose to liquidate its GNMA portfolio? Given the decision to liquidate, why hadn't Travelers merely sold the GNMAs and reinvested in another five-year maturity rather than issuing an instrument as complex as the CMO? Maureen suspected that CMO issuance provided Travelers with something more than a convenient vehicle for liquidating its pass-through portfolio.

Exhibit 1   The Pass-Through Process for GNMA Securities

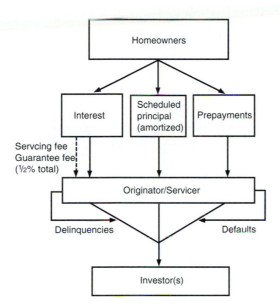

Source: Frank J. Fabozzi and Irving M. Pollack, editors. *The Handbook of Fixed Income Securities*, Dow Jones-Irwin, Homewood, Illinois, 1983.

Exhibit 2   Monthly Mortgage Payments-Interest/Principal (30-year, 10 % conventional loan)

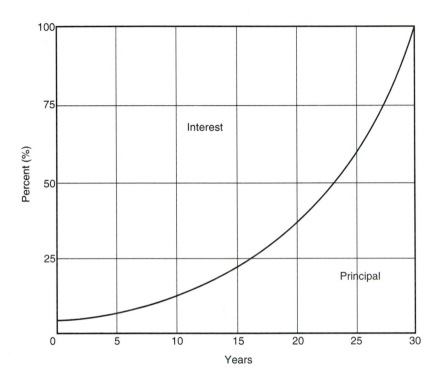

Exhibit 3 Issuers of Pass-Through Securities

	Component Mortgages	Guarantees[a]	Pool Insurance	Programs	Minimum Pool Size	Geographic Distribution
GNMA (Pass-Throughs)	Newly-issued FHA/VA single family	Fully modified pass-through	No	GNMA I	$1 Million	Narrow (Single issuer)
				GNMA II	Jumbo Pools (size varies)	Broad (Multiple issuers)
FHLMC (Participation Certificates)	Conventional, fixed-payment mortgages on 1–4 family homes (95% less than one- year old)	Modified pass-through (Guarantees payment of principal within one year of due date)	No	Guarantor	$1 Million	Narrow
				Portfolio	$50 Million	Broad (National)
FNMA (Mortgage Pass-Through Certificates)	Conventional, fixed payment mortgages on 1–4 family homes (seasoned as well as newly issued)	Fully modified pass-through	No	Swap	$2 Million	Narrow
				Portfolio	$100 Million	Variable (Multistate)
Private Issuers (Pass-Throughs)	Conventional mortgages	None	Yes		Varies	Variable

Source: Frank J. Fabozzi and Irving M. Pollack, editors. *The Handbook of Fixed Income Securities,* Dow of Fixed-Income Securities, Dow Jones-Irwin, Homewood, Illinois, 1983.
a. Fully Modified—Guarantee of timely payment of interest and scheduled principal amortization,
Modified—Guarantee of timely payment of interest.

Exhibit 3   Issuers of Pass-Throufg Securities (Continued)

Issuance of GNMAs, FNMAs, and FHLMC PCs, 1970–1984

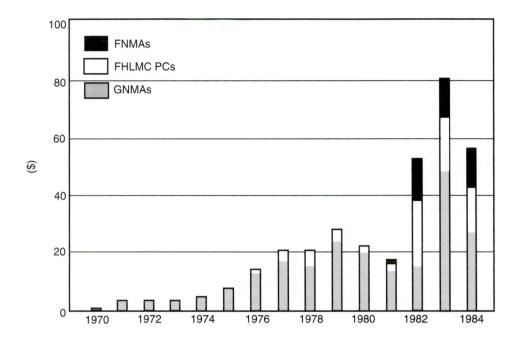

Source: GNMS, FNMA, and FHLMC.

Exhibit 4   Liquidity of Mortgage Pass-Throughs vs. Treasuries: Secondary Market Activity (Trades in Billions of Dollars)

	Whole Mortgage Loans		Mortgage Pass-Throughs		Treasury Securities	
	Trades	Turnover Ratio[a]	Trades	Turnover Ratio[a]	Trades	Turnover Ratio[a]
1981	49	.05	131	.95	6,224	8.02
1982	100	.09	230	1.37	8,140	9.34
1983	163	.15	506	2.14	10,609	9.70
1984[b]	146	.13	734	2.62	12,600	10.27

Source: HUD, Federal Reserve Bank of New York.
a. Dollar volume of trades divided by dollar volume of outstanding issues.
b. Estimated.

Exhibit 5 Publicly Offered CMOs by Issuer, Collateral and Maturity Class, June 1983[a]-February 1984
(Dollars in Billions)

Parent of Issuer	June–Dec. 1983	Jan.–Feb. 1984	Total	Jan. 1983-Feb. 1984 Percent of Total
FHLMC	1.69	.53	2.22	29.7
Investment Bankers	1.50	.50	2.00	26.8
Home Builders	.95	.75	1.70	22.8
Mortgage Bankers	.44	1.10	1.54	20.7
Insurance Companies	—	—	—	—
Commercial Banks	—	—	—	—
S&Ls	—	—	—	—
Collateral				
GNMAs	2.90	1.92	4.82	64.7
Conv. Mortgage Loans	1.68	.88	2.56	34.3
FNMAs/FHLMC PCs	—	.08	.08	—
Maturity Classes				
Three	1.79	—	1.79	24.0
Four	1.79	2.88	4.67	62.6
Five	.50	—	.50	6.7
Six or More	.50	—	.50	6.7
Collateral Coupon Rate				
10% or Less	.01	.53	.54	7.2
10.1%–12%	1.66	1.70	3.36	45.0
12.1%–14%	1.35	.65	2.00	26.9
14.1% or More	1.56	—	1.56	20.9

Source: Salomon Brothers, Inc.
a. Inception of CMO issuance.

Exhibit 6a FHA Experience Prepayment Rates (30-Year Term FHA-Insured Home Mortgages)

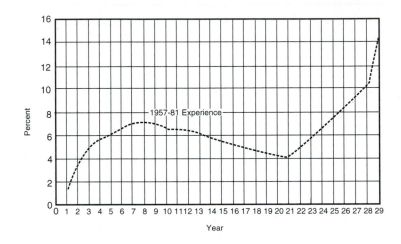

FHA Experience Prepayment Rates (30-Year Term) 1957–1981

Year	Rate (%)	Year	Rate (%)
1	1.13	16	5.34
2	3.77	17	5.10
3	5.17	18	4.88
4	5.73	19	4.65
5	6.21	20	4.39
6	6.80	21	4.12
7	7.12	22	4.97
8	7.23	23	5.82
9	7.00	24	6.72
10	6.68	25	7.65
11	6.59	26	8.57
12	6.42	27	9.49
13	6.11	28	10.39
14	5.86	29	14.47
15	5.60		

Source: Salomon Brothers, Inc.

Exhibit 6b Sensitivity of Pass-Through Duration to Changes in Principal Prepayment Rates
11% GNMA/FNMA Certificates (30-year term)

Prepayment Rate as a % of FHA Experience	Average Life (yrs.)	Duration[a] (yrs.)
0	22.3	8.2
50	16.3	6.9
75	14.2	6.4
100	12.4	6.0
125	11.0	5.6
150	9.8	5.3
200	8.1	4.7

Source: Salomon Brothers, Inc.
a. At par.

Exhibit 7 Yield Profile GNMA 12s Versus 10 Yr Treasuries, Weekly Data—10/15/82 to 3/30/84

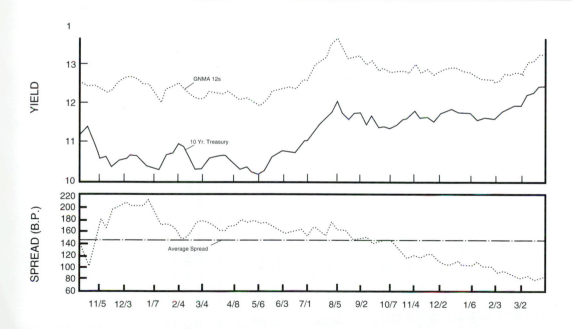

Source: Salomon Brothers Inc.

Exhibit 8a Description of GNMA/FNMA Collateral Securities Backing Travelers Mortgage Securities CMO

GNMA/FNMA Coupon Group[a]	Approximate Outstanding Principal Amount[b]	Approximate Weighted Average Remaining Term to Stated Maturity	Approximate Attributable Bond Value	Bondholders' Percentage
GNMA 11.50%	$ 505,519,907	29.3	$ 485,042,490	95.9492362%
FNMA 12.75	28,000,000	30.0	28,000,000	100.0000000
FNMA 12.50	170,367,264	29.4	170,367,264	100.0000000
FNMA 12.25	12,000,000	29.5	12,000,000	100.0000000
FNMA 12.00	124,799,798	29.3	124,799,798	100.0000000
FNMA 11.75	5,626,382	29.5	5,511,101	97.9510784
FNMA 11.50	291,317,858	26.8	279,391,795	95.9061679
FNMA 11.00	145,768,625	27.1	133,858,860	91.8296788
FNMA 10.75	12,281,559	30.0	11,028,695	89.7987970
Totals	1,295,681,393		1,250,000,000	

a. Each coupon group contained GNMA or FNMA certificates bearing the same pass-through coupon.
b. Approximately one-half of the mortgages underlying the FNMA collateral securities were FHA/VA mortgages. The remaining mortgages were conventional.

Exhibit 8b GNMA/FNMA—Collateralized Obligations, Series 1984-1, Yield Table at Indicated Prepayment Rates

Prepayment Rate as a % of FHA Experience	Class A			Class Z-1			Class C			Class Z-2		
	Yield (%)	A/L (yrs.)	Duration (yrs.)	Yield (%)	A/L (yrs.)	Duration (yrs.)	Yield (%)	A/L (yrs.)	Duration (yrs.)	Yield (%)	A/L (yrs.)	Duration (yrs.)
0%	10.66%	1.83	1.68	12.00%	9.48	7.43	12.54%	15.18	7.19	12.84%	24.26	21.21
50	10.67	1.49	1.40	12.00	6.62	5.58	12.59	11.91	6.52	12.97	22.14	18.41
75	10.68	1.37	1.30	12.00	5.72	4.98	12.62	10.68	6.19	13.04	21.04	17.13
100	10.68	1.27	1.21	12.00	5.08	4.51	12.66	9.66	5.87	13.12	19.83	15.96
125	10.68	1.21	1.15	12.00	4.64	4.13	12.69	8.82	5.59	13.20	18.52	14.90
150	10.69	1.14	1.09	12.00	4.21	3.82	12.73	8.13	5.33	13.28	17.32	13.95
200	10.69	1.02	0.99	12.00	3.61	3.35	12.79	7.05	4.88	13.44	15.11	12.33
Initial Purchase Price	99.9375%			100.0000%			96.4062%			84.5000%		

Source: Salomon Brothers Inc.
Example: The cash flow yield, initial average life, and initial duration on Class A bonds purchased at 99.9375% on March 1, 1984, assuming a 75% FHA experience prepayment rate, are 10.68%, 1.37 years, and 1.30 years, respectively.

Exhibit 9 Selected FNMA Financial Data

The following selected financial data for the years 1978 through 1982 have been summarized or derived from FNMA's audited financial statements. The financial data for the nine months ended September 30, 1982 and 1983 are unaudited and include, in the opinion of FNMA's management, all adjustments (consisting only of normal recurring accruals) necessary for a fair presentation.

Condensed Statements of Operations[a] (dollars in millions, except per share amounts) December 31

	For the Year Ended December 31					Nine Months Ended September 30	
	1978	1979	1980	1981[b]	1982	1982	1983
Interest margin	369	322	(21)	(463)	(506)	(429)	(60)
Commitment, guaranty, and other fees	106	60	68	125	301	231	190
Gain (loss) on sales of mortgages	—	(2)	—	—	44	26	77
Other expenses	(75)	(81)	(63)	(22)	(96)	(65)	(92)
Income (loss) before federal income taxes and extraordinary item	400	299	26	(360)	(257)	(237)	115
Provision for federal income taxes	191	137	12	(170)	(123)	(109)	53
Income (loss) before extraordinary item	209	162	14	(190)	(134)	(128)	62
Extraordinary item: gain on early retirement of debt[c]	—	—	—	—	29	29	—
Net income (loss)	209	162	14	(190)	(105)	(99)	62
Earnings (loss) per share:							
Before extraordinary item:							
Primary	3.81	2.81	.24	(3.22)	(2.20)	(2.16)	.94
Fully diluted	3.47	2.68	.23	(3.22)	(2.20)	(2.16)	.93
Net:							
Primary	3.81	2.81	.24	(3.22)	(1.72)	(1.67)	.94
Fully diluted	3.47	2.68	.23	(3.22)	(1.72)	(1.67)	.93
Cash dividends per share	1.15	1.28	1.12	.40	.16	.12	.12

Exhibit 9 Selected FNMA Financial Data (Continued)

Condensed Balance Sheet[a] (dollars in millions)

	1978	1979	At December 31 1980	1981[b]	1982	At September 30 1982	1983
Assets							
Mortgage portfolio, net	42,010	49,655	55,742	59,846	69,714	66,987	72,789
Other assets	1,355	1,424	2,426	2,052	3,753	4,491	2,821
Total assets	43,365	51,079	58,168	61,898	73,467	71,478	75,610
Liabilities							
Bonds, notes and debentures:							
Due within one year	9,018	13,087	15,542	17,365	25,781	25,604	23,841
Due after one year	31,826	35,116	39,338	41,186	43,833	42,234	47,417
Other liabilities	1,159	1,375	1,831	2,104	2,650	2,429	3,089
Total liabilities	42,003	49,578	56,711	60,655	72,264	70,267	74,347
Stockholder's equity	1,362	1,501	1,457	1,243	1,203	1,211	1,263
Total liabilities and stock-holders' equity	43,365	51,079	58,168	61,898	73,467	71,478	75,610

Condensed Statements of Changes in Financial Position (dollars in millions)

	Nine Months Ended September 30 1982	1983
Funds Provided		
Operations	(270)	54
Extraordinary gain[c]	—	—
Proceeds from issuance of debentures and bonds	15,314	14,947

Exhibit 9   Selected FNMA Financial Data (Continued)

	Nine Months Ended September 30	
	1982	1983
Mortgage repayments, less discount amortized	930	5,057
Sales of mortgages, excluding gains and losses	542	3,869
Net increase in stockholders' equity resulting from debt exchange and debenture conversion	103	5
Other items	329	215
Total funds provided	16,948	24,147
Funds Applied		
Debentures and bonds retired	8,727	10,672
Mortgage purchases including refinancings, less discount	9,064	12,163
Mortgage refinancings	(482)	(108)
Decrease (increase) in short-term notes	(2,687)	2,646
Dividends paid	7	8
Total funds applied	14,629	25,381
Increase (decrease) in cash and marketable securities	2,319	(1,234)
Beginning balance, cash and marketable securities	1,066	2,453
Ending balance, cash and marketable securities	3,385	1,219

a. Data for years 1978 through 1981 have been reclassified to achieve comparability.
b. Results for the year ended December 31, 1981 include a $42.0 million reduction in the allowance for loan losses effected in the second quarter. There was also a decrease in the rate of providing for losses on conventional loans that resulted in a reduction in the loss provision of $8.3 million during the last three quarters of 1981. Exclusive of these reductions, the 1981 loss would have been $217.0 million or $3.67 per share.
c. In September 1982, FNMA entered into a nontaxable transaction that resulted in the issuance of 6.3 million shares of its common stock in exchange for $101 million of its long-term debentures, which were retired. This transaction had no funds effect.

Exhibit 10 Selected Short-, Intermediate-, and Long-Term Yields, 2/17/84

Maturity	Instrument	Yield (%)
1-Year	T-Bill	10.190
2-Year	Governments	10.854
4-Year	CATS	11.810
5-Year	Governments	11.601
	Federal Agency Securities	11.800
	New Industrials (Aa)	12.550
	New Financials (Aa)	12.250
6-Year	CATS	11.980
7-Year	Governments	11.808
	Federal Agency Securities	12.050
8-Year	CATS	12.130
10-Year	Governments	11.902
15-Year	Governments	11.820
17-Year	CATS	12.000
19-Year	CATS	11.920
20-Year	Governments	12.044
25-Year	Governments	12.015

Source: Salomon Brothers, Inc.

Exhibit 11   CMO Spreads over Comparable Maturity Treasuries (February 1984)

1. Current-Coupon CMOs (GNMA Collateral)

Approximate CMO Weighted Average Life[a] (years)	Spread over Comparable Maturity Treasuries (basis points)
2	40
5	55
10	70
20	105

2. Current-Coupon CMOs (FNMA, FHLMC, and Conventional Mortgage Collateral)

Approximate CMO Weighted Average Life[a] (years)	Spread over Comparable Maturity Treasuries (basis points)
2	52
5	75
10	88
20	124

Source: Salomon Brothers, Inc.
a. Weighted average life assuming prepayment at 75–100% FHA.

Exhibit 12 The Travelers Corporation and Subsidiaries—Life Business Combined Balance Sheet (at December 31, in millions)

	1979	1980	1981	1982	1983
Assets					
Fixed maturities					
Bonds	4,902.7	5,511.2	6,490.3	8,518.3	9,940.4
Redeemable preferred stocks	45.1	49.5	53.0	52.7	51.5
Equity securities					
Common stocks	41.9	46.7	43.4	56.0	33.8
Nonredeemable preferred stocks	21.1	21.7	16.7	19.0	18.6
Mortgage loans	5,524.3	6,069.2	6,417.2	6,717.6	8,425.2
Investment real estate	87.2	84.1	128.0	210.3	334.2
Other investments	104.2	149.5	191.3	236.3	319.8
Total long-term investments	10,726.5	11,931.9	13,339.9	15,810.2	19,123.5
Cash and short-term securities	111.9	322.7	359.9	583.8	492.2
Policy loans	337.6	401.4	470.0	496.9	489.2
Total cash and invested assets	11,176.0	12,656.0	14,169.8	16,890.9	20,104.9
Investment income accrued	224.3	267.4	308.1	397.5	521.6
Premium balances receivable	459.9	436.5	547.0	590.6	680.1
Deferred acquisition cost	194.8	205.6	228.6	252.6	253.3
Company-occupied real estate	106.9	107.1	96.1	102.3	107.0
Separate and variable account assets	798.6	1,134.5	1,324.8	1,705.5	2,102.6
Other assets	89.2	128.6	166.4	194.8	411.8
Total assets	13,049.7	14,935.7	16,840.8	20,134.2	24,181.3
Liabilities					
Future policy benefits					
Life insurance	2,181.6	2,221.6	2,288.8	2,540.6	2,735.4
Annuities	5,562.5	6,320.7	6,710.5	7,250.0	8,032.9
Accident and health	36.1	31.8	31.3	35.6	71.3
Policy and contract claims	1,079.3	1,064.4	992.9	1,057.6	944.0
Commercial paper	—	—	—	16.9	150.8
Provision for experience rating refunds	740.8	708.8	801.0	820.3	1,189.1
Pension deposit funds	790.7	1,465.7	2,460.0	4,254.7	5,980.4
Other policyholder funds	363.0	376.4	357.8	355.3	399.0
Accrued expenses	127.9	124.4	134.3	137.4	140.3
Separate and variable account liabilities	798.3	1,134.2	1,324.7	1,704.7	2,102.2
Other liabilities	337.3	335.5	431.4	550.5	918.6
Total liabilities	12,017.5	13,783.5	15,532.7	18,723.6	22,664.0

Exhibit 12 The Travelers Corporation and Subsidiaries—Life Business Combined Balance Sheet (at December 31, in millions) (Continued)

	1979	1980	1981	1982	1983
Equity					
Common stock	107.6	106.6	106.6	106.6	104.1
Additional paid-in capital	25.4	25.5	25.6	25.6	79.8
Unrealized investment gains (losses)	(16.7)	(21.6)	(24.1)	(18.9)	(23.9)
Retained earnings	915.9	1,041.7	1,200.0	1,297.3	1,357.3
Total equity	1,032.2	1,152.2	1,308.1	1,410.6	1,517.3
	13,049.7	14,935.7	16,840.8	20,134.2	24,181.3

Combined Statement of Sources and Uses of Cash—Life Business (for the year ended December 31, in millions)

	1979	1980	1981	1982	1983
Sources of Cash					
Net income	190.8	199.8	213.6	201.3	175.9
Change in noncash items					
Insurance reserves and accrued expenses	1,279.2	1,431.0	1,506.3	2,745.3	3,107.3
Deferred acquisition costs	(6.4)	(10.8)	(23.0)	(24.0)	1.2
Investment income accrued	(34.1)	(43.1)	(40.7)	(89.4)	(124.9)
Premium balances receivable	(14.7)	23.4	(110.5)	(43.6)	(94.3)
Other	47.4	(2.9)	23.1	11.4	179.1
Cash provided by operations	$1,462.2	$1,597.4	$1,568.8	$2,801.0	$3,244.3
Investment repayments					
Fixed maturities	189.8	243.5	331.4	316.4	956.9
Mortgage loans	246.9	289.7	237.7	292.9	283.0
Cash provided by operations and investment repayments	$1,898.9	$2,130.6	$2,137.9	$3,410.3	$4,484.2
Carrying value of investments sold					
Fixed maturities	8.0	11.7	36.1	55.9	1,682.8
Equity securities	39.3	55.7	91.9	104.6	113.8
Mortgage loans	—	—	—	—	127.4
Investment real estate	21.9	18.9	1.7	5.6	6.9
Issuance of commercial paper, net	—	—	—	16.9	133.9
Other, net	25.5	(47.2)	41.6	34.5	(32.5)
Total cash provided	$1,993.6	$2,169.7	$2,309.2	$3,627.8	$6,516.5

Exhibit 12 The Travelers Corporation and Subsidiaries—Life Business Combined Balance Sheet (at December 31, in millions) (Continued)

	1979	1980	1981	1982	1983
Uses of Cash					
Dividends to parent company	$97.0	$58.0	$64.5	$124.0	$80.0
Investments in:					
Fixed maturities	778.4	871.6	1,365.8	2,399.9	4,059.0
Equity securities	42.3	64.6	87.9	111.6	96.1
Mortgage loans	1,102.7	842.6	606.5	574.2	2,135.1
Investment real estate	17.9	11.3	33.6	105.7	126.3
Policy loans, net	40.0	63.8	68.6	26.9	(4.4)
Other	21.8	47.0	45.1	61.6	116.0
Total cash used	$2,100.1	$1,958.9	$2,272.0	$3,403.9	$6,608.1
Net Change in Cash and					
Short-term Securities	$(106.5)	$210.8	$37.2	$223.9	$(91.6)

APPENDIX A

TRAVELERS MORTGAGE SECURITIES CMO,
DESCRIPTION OF COLLATERALIZATION PROCESS

CMOs were collateralized by:

1. segmenting the collateral securities into groups of pass-throughs with similar coupons.

2. computing the "bond value" of each coupon group by discounting the scheduled collateral principal and interest flows, plus reinvestment earnings at the assumed rate (5/4/3), at the highest coupon rate offered on any of the CMO classes. This process ensured that debt service on the CMOs would be fully funded by scheduled collateral distributions even after lower-coupon CMO classes had been retired.

3. limiting these bond values (per coupon group) to a maximum value of par. Bond values were subject to a "par cap" to ensure that the CMO principal could be fully repaid even if the collateral securities prepaid in full immediately upon issuance of the CMO.

The maximum amount of CMO principal issuable against a collection of collateral was then determined by summing the bond values of the collateral coupon groups.

The bond value of a collateral security would be less than its market value (resulting in "over-collateralization") if:

1. intraperiod reinvestment rates (5/4/3) were lower than the market yields-to-maturity on the collateral.

2. premium collateral were used.

3. coupons on the CMO classes were not uniform, or

4. discount collateral were used and the market assumed prepayment at a rate greater than 0%. If discount coupon pass-throughs were used to collateralize current coupon CMOs, the collateral principal amount would exceed the CMO principal, and some portion of the collateral principal flows would fund CMO interest payments.

Once collateralization requirements were determined using the "bond value" method described above, the issuer capitalized the issuing finance subsidiary at a rate of 2% of assets to meet IRS regulations (and preserve the tax-deductibility of CMO interest). If the net proceeds of the issue were less than the cost of the CMO collateral, the issuing subsidiary's balance sheet would appear as follows:

Assets		Liabilities	
Collateral securities (at cost, or current MV)	$100	Collateralized Mortgage Obligations	$98
		Net worth	
		Shareholder's equity	$2

The issuer would have contributed $2 to the vehicle to fund the purchase of the collateral securities. In the event that the CMO proceeds exceeded the cost of the collateral, the issuer would merely contribute cash, securities, or a demand note to the finance subsidiary to meet the IRS's net worth requirement.

AMERICAN EXPRESS TRS CHARGE-CARD RECEIVABLES

Early in February 1992, Jay Stevelman, treasurer, and Art Berman, vice president for funding and financial analysis, of the American Express Travel Related Services Company, Inc. (TRS), were considering a proposal to finance accounts receivable that were generated by TRS's charge card business. Before them was a proposal from Lehman Brothers to create the first-ever securitization of charge-card receivables. The proposal offered TRS an opportunity to diversify its sources of funding and the potential to achieve a lower cost of funds. Mr. Stevelman and Mr. Berman wondered whether the proposal made sense, and if this was an opportune time to adopt such a program.

AMERICAN EXPRESS COMPANY

American Express Company was a globally diversified travel and financial services firm. In addition to TRS, at the end of 1991, American Express owned, in part or whole, the IDS Financial Corporation, First Data Corporation, American Express Bank, and Shearson Lehman Brothers Holdings, Inc. See Exhibit 1 for selected financial information on American Express and its subsidiaries.

TRS provided a wide range of financial and travel services to individuals and businesses. It was a premier provider of financial services in the charge-card and consumer-lending businesses through the American Express® Card (i.e., the Green card), the American Express® Gold Card, the Platinum Card®, the Corporate Card, and the Optima^{SM} Card. Another well-known product was the American Express® Travelers Cheque, which was used by travelers as a safe and convenient alternative to carrying currency. At the end of 1991, TRS offered travel services through a network of 1878 offices and independent agencies situated in over 120 countries. The services included retail, wholesale, and custom travel activities such as trip planning, reservations, and ticketing.

TRS's other businesses included the American Express Publishing Corporation, whose portfolio of magazines included *Travel and Leisure*®, *Food and Wine*®, *L.A. Style*®, *Atlanta*®, *American Express*® *Card Connections*, *Departures*™, *D Magazine*®, and *Your Company*™. TRS also provided direct-mail merchandising services, database marketing and management, and insurance services. These services were often offered in conjunction with the American Express cards. For example, AMEX Life Assurance Company and the AMEX Assurance Company, wholly owned subsidiaries of TRS, provided life and property-casualty insurance, respectively, to American Express cardholders and other customers. See Exhibit 2 for selected financial information on TRS.

Of American Express's other businesses, IDS Financial Corporation provided financial planning and asset management products and services to individuals, institutions, and businesses; First Data Corporation provided information processing and related services to a variety of industries, notably the credit- and debit-card industry, the consumer funds transfer industry, the telemarketing and teleservices industry, the mutual fund industry, and the health care industry;[1] and Shearson Lehman Brothers, Inc., was a leading full-line securities firm that served institutions, governments, and individual investors in the United States and throughout the world. The American Express Bank provided financial services to wealthy individuals and select financial institutions. The bank did not do any business in the United States except as an incident to activities conducted in other countries.

TRS'S CARD BUSINESS

At the end of 1991, there were 36.6 million American Express cards in force worldwide. In 1991 the total billed business on the cards was $111 billion, of which $76.6 billion was billed to cardholders domiciled in the United States. At the end of 1991, American Express cards were accepted at over 3.5 million establishments around the world (see Exhibit 2).

One component of TRS's strategy was to provide cardholders with a high level of service. It promoted its cardholders as being "cardmembers." All cards except Optima were charge cards that were designed as a convenient method of payment rather than as a means of financing purchases. Except in the case of Optima and extended-payment plans (see the example of an extended-payment plan on the next page), cardmembers had to pay for purchases in full when billed by TRS. There was no pre-set spending limit on the charge cards. Further, virtually every purchase was cleared in "real time." Charges were approved automatically if the purchase was supported by the cardmember's past spending and payment patterns and personal resources. Purchases that did not meet standard criteria

---

1   FDC was a leading third-party processor of MasterCard® and VISA® transactions. However, it was not responsible for processing transactions related to the American Express cards.

were resolved at the point of purchase through a brief telephone conversation between a TRS representative and the cardmember.

The Optima Card was a revolving credit card that was issued by the American Express Centurion Bank, a wholly owned subsidiary of TRS. Purchases made with the Optima Card could be paid over time, and generally accrued interest at a variable rate tied to the prime rate.

In addition to the ability to charge purchases at participating establishments, TRS offered all cardmembers a variety of services, including extended-payment plans like the Sign & Travel® account, which offered participating cardmembers the option to pay for travel expenses over time. Other services, like an annual summary of charges and a line of credit established with a participating financial institution (like Centurion Bank), were available primarily to Gold cardmembers and Platinum cardmembers.

TRS charged cardmembers an annual fee that depended on the type of card, the number of cards for each account, the country of residence of the cardmember, and the currency in which the card was denominated. Card fees were an important component of TRS's revenue, totaling $1.8 billion in 1991 (see Exhibit 2).

In a typical charge- or credit-card transaction, TRS paid the merchant within a set period after the cardmember's purchase. The amount paid was the face value of the purchase less a discount which depended on the type of merchant, the volume of charges, the timing and method of payment to the establishment, and the method of submission of charges. In 1991, TRS's revenues from these discounts were $3.5 billion on total charges of $111 billion (see Exhibit 2). The cardmember, however, was required to pay only when billed; in full if charged on a charge card, and over time with interest if charged on the Optima Card. Because there was a lag between the time TRS paid the merchant and the time the cardmember paid TRS, each purchase made by a cardmember generated receivables that had to be financed. The cost of financing receivables was a major expense for TRS's card operations. TRS financed U.S. charge-card receivables through its wholly owned subsidiary, American Express Credit Corporation (Credco), and financed Optima and extended-payment-plan receivables partly through Credco but primarily through Centurion Bank.

CREDCO

Credco was incorporated in 1962 as a finance company based in Delaware. It was acquired by American Express in 1965 and became a wholly owned subsidiary of TRS in 1983. Its purpose, which was primarily to finance TRS's charge-card receivables, was similar to that of other finance companies like the General Motors Acceptance Corporation, which financed automobile loan receivables, and the Sears Roebuck Acceptance Corporation, which financed retail sales. Its assets were primarily American Express charge-card receivables and to a lesser extent Optima and extended-payment-plan receivables. Its liabilities consisted principally of debt which was used to finance the receivables. See Exhibit 4 for selected financial information on Credco.

Credco purchased charge-card receivables from TRS at a discount[2] from face value because no interest was charged on these receivables. In contrast, Credco purchased interest-bearing receivables like those of Optima at face value. All receivables purchased by Credco were billed, collected, and serviced by the card issuers (TRS for charge cards, and Centurion Bank for the Optima Card) at their own expense. Charge-card receivables were purchased continuously as generated and their average life was fairly constant at 43 days (see Exhibit 4).

All receivables were purchased by Credco without recourse to TRS. However, receivables arising from unauthorized or fraudulent charges (for example, charges made with a lost or stolen card) were repurchased by TRS. Thus, Credco bore the risk of cardmember defaults.

At the end of 1991, Credco had outstanding $7.9 billion of short-term debt (of which $7.5 billion was in commercial paper) and $3.9 billion of medium-term and long-term debt. All of Credco's debt was unsecured. See Exhibit 4 for details on Credco's debt.

Credco's debt was not guaranteed by TRS or American Express. Credco was implicitly supported by TRS, however, through a policy that related the discount at which Credco purchased the charge-card receivables to its expenses. The discount rate was chosen so that the ratio of Credco's earnings before interest and taxes (but after deducting losses due to cardmember defaults) to its interest expense was at least 125% on an annual basis.[3] Between 1987 and 1991 this coverage ratio had been fairly steady at 128% and the annual average discount rate had varied between 1.55% and 1.78%.

At the end of 1991, Credco's commercial paper was rated A–1+/P1 by the Standard & Poor's and Moody's credit-rating agencies, respectively. Credco's strong commercial paper rating was contingent in part on the firm maintaining an unused committed line of credit of at least 50% of its outstanding commercial paper. This line of credit totaled $3.9 billion at the end of 1991. In late 1991, Credco's long-term debt had been downgraded by Moody's from Aa2 to Aa3 along with American Express's long-term debt, which had been

---

2　This discount was not related to the discount charged to the merchants.

3　This policy and the terms at which the receivables were sold to Credco were articulated in a "receivables purchase agreement" between Credco and TRS. This agreement required TRS and Credco to adjust the discount rate in order to maintain the ratio at 125% or greater. It also allowed TRS and Credco to change the ratio in certain circumstances, for instance, in response to significant changes in money-market rates.

downgraded from Aa2 to A1. The rating agencies had cited asset quality problems at Shearson Lehman Brothers, credit losses at Optima, and uncertainty about TRS's earning power as reasons for making these downgrades.

Credco varied the maturity of its debt offerings in order to manage its interest expense and its exposure to interest rate movements. Credco also issued foreign currency denominated debt in order to hedge foreign receivables against exchange rate variability. Jay Stevelman, Art Berman, and the treasury group at TRS decided the proportions of different maturities (for example, 60% short-term and 40% long-term) based on factors like the trend and seasonality in the receivables (for example, the receivables portfolio tended to be larger during the Christmas holiday season) and current and future anticipated interest rates. Generally, short-term debt tended to be cheaper because of an upward sloping yield curve. However, this cost advantage had to be traded off against the interest rate certainty and the liquidity protection provided by long-term, fixed-rate financing.

Actual pricing and placement decisions for short-term debt were made by Credco staff, who monitored market conditions and offered commercial paper over a broad spectrum of maturities ranging from 1 to 270 days. Orders for commercial paper were taken both directly from institutional investors and indirectly through financial intermediaries by a staff of nine telephone operators (out of a total employee strength of 26) who were dedicated to this task.

In 1991, Credco had established "shelf" registration facilities with the Securities and Exchange Commission for its medium-term and long-term debt. These registrations allowed Credco to issue the notes at short notice. At the end of 1991, there remained $865 million of medium-term and long-term debt available for issuance under these facilities.

To date, Jay Stevelman and Art Berman had relied almost exclusively on Credco to finance the charge-card receivables. However, over the past few years, they had been approached by a number of investment banks that offered securitization as a way to finance receivables. Following the securitization of mortgages, securitization of assets (also known as "structured finance") had become a major source of financing for a variety of issuers. See Exhibit 6 for selected information on the asset-backed securities market. Observers attributed the growth of securitization to the deteriorating credit risk of unsecured corporate borrowing and the increased sophistication of institutional investors who could value and price the securities. See Exhibit 7 for a typical investor breakdown in new-issue, credit-card receivables-backed securities. Securitization was also seen as a cost-effective and efficient source of funding for certain types of receivables, for example, consumer-credit receivables. See Exhibit 8 for the growth in consumer credit.

In 1991, excluding mortgage-backed securities, new asset-backed issues totaled $49.9 billion, of which $20.8 billion was in securitized credit-card receivables. The first credit-card receivables securitization was a $200-million offering in January 1987 by the RepublicBank Delaware, a subsidiary of RepublicBank of Texas. At the end of 1991, the major credit-card issuers had outstanding receivables of about $102 billion, of which 40% had been securitized. See Exhibit 3 for the proportion of receivables securitized by major credit-card issuers.

In contrast, charge-card receivables *per se* had yet to be securitized. Given the ready acceptance of asset-backed securities, Jay Stevelman and Art Berman felt that they should give serious consideration to the Lehman proposal. If implemented, it would represent an important innovation in asset-backed financing.

THE LEHMAN BROTHERS PROPOSAL

The Lehman Brothers proposal involved securitizing a portion of American Express's consumer (Green, Gold, and Platinum) charge-card receivables' portfolio. As with other securitizations, this proposal involved the issuance of debt securities explicitly collateralized by the receivables. The receivables would be segregated from TRS's portfolio in order to protect them from TRS's and Credco's claimants and creditors. This would be done by transferring them to a specially designated trust that would be the entity to issue the debt securities.

The trust would be given title to all current and future receivables generated by *designated* charge-card accounts. The accounts would be designated at the outset, and would be chosen randomly from eligible[4] accounts within TRS's portfolio. Because the accounts would be fixed in advance, the trust's outstanding balance of receivables would fluctuate with the purchasing and payment patterns of the particular cardmembers.

The trust would be a "master trust" designed to give TRS the flexibility to issue multiple types of debt, to issue debt at different times, and even to add or remove accounts from the trust at later dates.[5] The use of a master trust and designated accounts were typical features of credit-card receivables securitizations.

A novel feature of the Lehman proposal related to the treatment of interest. In the case of credit cards, receivables were composed of finance and principal charges, where

---

4   Among other eligibility requirements, an account had to be a Green, Gold, or Platinum card account, had to be payable in U.S. dollars, and should have been created under credit standards that were no less stringent than generally applied by TRS.

5   As in other securitizations, TRS would only be able to add or remove those accounts from the master trust that met certain "eligibility" criteria and were legally assignable to the trust. Further, such changes would require notification to the credit rating agencies.

finance charges were the sum of interest on balances, annual fees, and discount fees, and principal charges were the face value of purchases made with the credit card. Typically, interest on the trust's debt was paid out of finance-charge collections, and until required for repayment of debt principal, principal collections were reinvested in the trust by purchasing new receivables. Finance charges in excess of the interest owed to debtholders were used to cover losses due to defaults and other trust expenses. Because credit-card receivables were purchased at par, the trust's profitability depended on the amount by which the finance charges exceeded the trust's expenses.

To illustrate, consider the case of Citicorp's credit card portfolio which, in 1991, yielded 19.9% in finance charges (see Exhibit 10). Losses due to cardholder defaults were 6.5% and servicing and collection charges were 2.0%, so that the portfolio's yield after these expenses was 11.4%. This net yield would be available for interest payments to debtholders, and the residual after these expenses would provide protection to debtholders against increases in cardholder defaults or a decline in portfolio yield. See Exhibit 11 for the loss, payment, and yield experience of select credit-card receivables portfolios.

Because American Express charge cardmembers paid no interest on purchases, Lehman had to devise a way to create income for the trust to absorb losses due to defaults, pay trust expenses, and pay interest on the trust's debt. As a solution, they proposed to have TRS sell receivables to the trust at a discount from the face amount, and hence treat part of the receivables as interest and the rest as principal. The interest part was referred to as the "yield" component and would initially be set at 3%.[6] Therefore, the trust would purchase the receivables at 100% minus the yield (here, 97%). To mirror the sale, every $100 of receivables collected would be divided into $3 of yield and $97 of principal. The yield component of receivables collected would be used for interest payments on the debt, and other expenses such as servicing fees[7] and losses due to cardmember defaults. As with credit card securitization, the principal component of receivables collected would be reinvested in new receivables until required to make principal repayments on the trust's debt.

Lehman's proposal was to initially sell about $1 billion of "class A" debt securities. Depending on the success of this offering and TRS's future needs, the trust could later issue additional debt. In order to provide this flexibility, TRS would initially transfer about $2.5 billion in receivables to the trust. As in other recent securitizations, Lehman suggested creating a "class B" subordinated debt security in order to ensure a AAA credit-rating for

---

6   This percentage could be increased to a maximum of 5% at TRS's option. It could not be decreased below 3%, however.

7   Servicing charges were estimated to be about 2% (of the outstanding receivables in the trust) per annum.

the class A debt. They also suggested that unlike the class A debt, the class B debt be sold privately.

As was typical of other receivables securitizations, the debt would have claim on only a pro-rata share of the receivables in the trust because only a portion of the $2.5 billion in receivables was being funded by it. This share, referred to as the "investor's interest," would equal the ratio of class A debt principal plus class B debt principal to total trust receivables (initially 41.4%, i.e., $1.035 billion/$2.5 billion; see paragraph below for the amount of class B debt). The remaining share, the "seller's interest," would be held by TRS and could be used as collateral for future debt issues.[8] Lehman suggested that until such additional debt was issued against the trust, the seller's interest be purchased by Credco. The seller's interest and the investor's interest would have *pari passu* claims on the assets of the trust, meaning that their claims would be of equal seniority in proportion to their interests. See Exhibit 9 for a schematic representation of the claims on the proposed master trust.

Lehman thought that the proportion of class B debt to class A debt did not have to be very large for the class A debt to be rated AAA. While in a typical credit card structure, the extra protection provided by this form of credit enhancement was in the range of 10% to 15%, they thought that here it could be as low as 3.5% (i.e., $35 million on the $1 billion of class A debt). They felt that this would be acceptable to the credit-rating agencies because of the charge cards' high and consistent yield and payment rate, and the "real time" clearing of every cardmember purchase.

With this structure, if the designated accounts in the trust generated and paid off receivables according to historical patterns (see Exhibit 12 for statistics on TRS's consumer charge-card portfolio), the cash flow allocable to the investor's interest would be sufficient to make all the required payments on both classes (A and B) of debt, and the portion of the cash flow allocable to investor's interest that was not paid out to debtholders could revert to TRS. On the other hand, if the trust suffered large losses due to cardmember defaults, or if large numbers of cardmembers stopped or reduced the use of their American Express cards, the trust may not have sufficient funds to make interest payments on both classes of debt. This situation could trigger an "early amortization event" in which the investor's interest share of collections would be used first to repay the accrued interest and principal amount of the class A debt and then interest and principal on the class B debt.

The use of subordination for credit enhancement, that is, overcollateralization with a subordinated debt claim, was most typical of recent asset-backed deals. Early securitizations

---

8   As in other securitizations, TRS would be required to maintain a minimum seller's interest, which in this case would be about 3%.

had primarily used third-party letters of credit to ensure the desired credit rating for the trust's debt. In the past few years, letters of credit had been used less frequently because issuers of such letters (usually banks) were themselves experiencing credit deterioration. See Exhibit 13 for recent trends in the form of credit enhancement in the asset-backed market.

HOW SECURITIZATION WOULD AFFECT CREDCO'S BALANCE SHEET

Prior to securitization, Credco's balance sheet as of the end of 1991 could be represented as (see Exhibits 4 and 5):

Assets	$ Billions	Liabilities	$ Billions
Accounts receivable	12.2	Short-term debt	8.7
		Long-term debt	3.1
Other	1.9	Equity	2.3
Total	14.1	Total	14.1

Securitization would involve selling $2.5 billion of Credco's consumer charge-card receivables to the master trust. Simultaneously, the master trust would sell to investors the class A and B certificates (investor's interest) and Credco would buy the remaining interest (seller's interest). If the net sale proceeds (about $1 billion) were then used by Credco to reduce its short-term debt, its approximate balance sheet after securitization could be represented as:

Assets	$ Billions	Liabilities	$ Billions
Accounts receivable	9.7	Short-term debt	7.7
Seller's interest	1.5	Long-term debt	3.1
Other	1.9	Equity	2.3
Total	13.1	Total	13.1

This meant that the ratio of Credco's debt to equity (i.e., its leverage ratio) would be reduced from 5.1 to 4.7.

IMPLICATIONS FOR ACCOUNT SELECTION, DISCLOSURE, AND REPORTING

The rules governing selection, addition, and removal of accounts from the master trust would have to be formulated in consultation with the credit-rating agencies and the Securities and Exchange Commission. In order to satisfy these entities, an independent auditor would have to certify that these rules had been correctly implemented. For example, the auditor would have to certify that the designated accounts were chosen randomly from TRS's portfolio.

In a typical credit-card securitization, the card issuer was required to disclose business as well as asset-specific information in the securities' sale prospectus. This information would include not only general details on the credit-card business, but also the historical performance of the card issuer's portfolio. The card issuer would also provide aggregate statistics like the age and geographic dispersion of the designated accounts and their purchase, payment, delinquency, and loss history. However, the issuer was not required to disclose individual account information.

To provide this information, TRS would have to modify and adapt its existing information, servicing, and collection systems. These changes would have to address the needs to identify and segregate the receivables generated by the designated accounts from TRS's portfolio, and to provide trust performance information on a monthly basis. The performance information would include changes in the trust's outstanding receivables balance and the monthly collection, purchase, loss, recovery, and delinquency experience on the designated accounts. These changes would have to be implemented with the cooperation of different groups within TRS. Also, an independent auditor would have to certify these abilities in order to satisfy the credit-rating agencies and the Securities and Exchange Commission.

Jay Stevelman and Art Berman were concerned that TRS might have to disclose strategically sensitive business information because of the disclosure requirements. Unlike financing through Credco, securitization would require detailed information on the historical performance of the consumer charge-card portfolio.

THE DECISION

Mr. Stevelman and Mr. Berman were trying to weigh the merits of the securitization proposal as an alternative source of funding for TRS. Primarily, they hoped to diversify TRS's funding sources by attracting investor groups that traditionally had not invested in Credco's commercial-paper and long-term debt. They thought that the receivable-backed securities' AAA rating and securitization structure would be attractive to these nontraditional investors. Securitization, however, posed a number of questions:

- Did this proposal represent a cost advantage over long-term debt financing through Credco? Historically, AAA-rated, credit-card receivable-backed securities had been issued at yields higher than AAA-rated finance company debt and at yields comparable to AA-rated finance company debt. They wondered whether investors would find this first securitization of charge-card receivables more appealing than existing securitizations of credit-card receivables, or if they would be confused by the novel structure in which noninterest-bearing receivables were being securitized, thus resulting in a higher issuing cost. (See Exhibit 14 for current interest rates and interest-rate spreads for various securities.)

- How, in general, would investors in the fixed-income market react to the securitization? Would they consider it a sign of financial strength, or one of weakness? Also, given the recent downgrade of Credco's and American Express's debt and the perceived financial weakness of credit-card, receivable-backed issuers (mostly banks), how would investors have to be educated if TRS decided to go ahead?

- How would the securitization affect the strength of Credco's balance sheet? Since Credco would now have a lower debt-to-equity ratio, would Credco's debt now get a higher rating? Also, should the relative amounts of short-term versus long-term, fixed-rate debt be changed?

Jay Stevelman and Art Berman wondered if TRS should establish a long-term presence in the asset-backed market and if this was the right time to do so.

Exhibit 1   Selected Financial Information on American Express

Consolidated Financial Data[a]	1987	1988	1989	1990	1991
Operating Data ($ millions)					
Revenues	15,962	20,895	25,047	24,332	25,763
Expenses					
Interest	4,884	7,422	9,879	8,492	8,252
Provision for losses					
Annuities	424	537	700	847	1,039
Life insurance	355	339	442	485	539
Investment certificates	99	135	206	269	264
Banking, credit and other	1,818	1,045	1,472	1,913	2,606
Other (marketing, human resources, etc.)	7,808	10,086	10,821	11,601	12,304
Total expenses	15,388	19,564	23,520	23,607	25,004
Income tax provision (benefit)	154	343	370	387	(30)
Net income	420	988	1,157	338	789
Balance Sheet Data ($ millions)					
Cash and time deposits	6,549	9,299	6,539	5,605	4,876
Investments (U.S. gov't bonds, munis, preferred stock, etc.)	42,067	50,410	45,441	51,452	55,828
Securities purchased under agreements to resell	19,160	23,489	13,191	13,189	15,686
Accounts receivable and accrued interest, net of loss reserves	25,338	28,749	30,393	29,257	29,882
Loans and discounts, net	12,583	17,031	19,405	20,915	20,648
Other	10,808	13,775	15,886	17,264	19,521

Exhibit 1 Selected Financial Information on American Express (Continued)

Consolidated Financial Data

Balance Sheet Data ($ millions)	1987	1988	1989	1990	1991
Total assets	116,505	142,753	130,855	137,682	146,441
Customers' deposits and credit balances	26,374	34,656	31,191	27,843	24,778
Travelers cheques outstanding	3,602	3,820	3,834	4,225	4,375
Securities sold under agreements to repurchase	21,485	26,611	17,207	24,139	23,229
Insurance and annuity reserves	7,917	10,022	12,207	14,789	17,741
Short-term debt	17,289	20,685	17,457	19,609	22,398
Long-term debt	10,186	12,744	13,495	12,521	13,292
Shareholders' equity	4,529	5,023	5,691	6,635	7,465
Other	25,123	29,192	29,773	27,921	33,163
Total liabilities and shareholders' equity	116,505	142,753	130,855	137,682	146,441

Source: American Express Company Annual Reports, 1989, 1990, and 1991.
a. All data includes Credco.

Industry Segment Financials[a]

	Travel Related Services[b]	IDS Financial Services	First Data Corporation	American Express Bank	Shearson Lehman Brothers	Corporate and Other	Adjustments and Eliminations	Consolidated
1989								
Revenues	8,357	1,934	660	2,100	12,501	193	(698)	25,047
Pretax income (loss) before general corporate expenses	1,187	229	118	10	104	77	(10)	1,715

Exhibit 1   Selected Financial Information on American Express (Continued)

| | Industry Segment Financials[a] | | | | | | | |
	Travel Related Services[b]	IDS Financial Services	First Data Corporation	American Express Bank	Shearson Lehman Brothers	Corporate and Other	Adjustments and Eliminations	Consolidated
1989								
General corporate expenses						(188)		(188)
Pretax income (loss)	1,187	229	118	10	104	(111)	(10)	1,527
Net income (loss)	830	175	83	122	58	(101)	(10)	1,157
Assets	32,725	19,531	2,035	17,163	63,548	1,102	(5,429)	130,855
1990								
Revenues	9,698	2,200	827	1,814	10,177	173	(557)	24,332
Pretax income (loss) before general corporate expenses	1,332	256	140	146	(875)	35	(15)	1,019
General corporate expenses						(294)		(294)
Pretax income (loss)	1,332	256	140	146	(875)	(259)	(15)	725
Net income (loss)	956	207	103	111	(832)	(192)	(15)	338
Assets	36,838	23,230	2,376	14,855	64,781	1,352	(5,750)	137,682
1991								
Revenues	9,905	2,554	995	1,503	11,177	144	(515)	25,763
Pretax income (loss) before general corporate expenses	415	314	159	38	114	9	(9)	1,040
General corporate expenses						(281)		(281)
Pretax income (loss)	415	314	159	38	114	(272)	(9)	759
Net income (loss)	396	248	118	60	159	(184)	(8)	789
Assets	37,912	27,660	3,172	14,367	67,387	2,814	(6,871)	146,441

Source: American Express Company Annual Report, 1991.
a. All figures are in $ millions.
b. Travel Related Services' figures include Credco.

Exhibit 2   Selected Financial Information on TRS

	1989	1990	1991
Operating Data ($ billions)			
Revenues			
Card discount	3.3	3.6	3.5
Card fees	1.5	1.8	1.8
Interest and dividends	1.8	2.3	2.5
Other	1.8	2.0	2.1
Total revenues	8.4	9.7	9.9
Expenses			
Interest expense			
Credco	0.9	1.0	0.9
Other	0.8	0.9	0.8
Total interest	1.7	1.9	1.7
Provision for credit losses			
Charge card	0.8	1.0	1.1
Lending (Optima etc.)	0.4	0.5	1.1
Other	0.1	0.1	0.1
Total provision for losses	1.2	1.6	2.3
Human resources	1.3	1.7	1.8
Marketing and promo	1.0	1.0	1.0
Other	2.0	2.2	2.7
Total expenses	7.2	8.4	9.5
Net income before tax	1.2	1.3	0.4
Net income after tax	0.8	1.0	0.4
Balance Sheet Data ($ billions)			
(Year ended December 31)			
Accounts receivable	13.4	15.4	14.8
Loans and discounts		8.3	9.5
Other	19.3	13.1	13.6
Total assets	32.7	36.8	37.9
Total debt	12.5	16.3	17.0
Travelers cheques outstanding	3.8	4.2	4.4
Shareholders' equity and other	16.4	16.3	16.5
Total liabilities and shareholders' equity	32.7	36.8	37.9

Exhibit 2   Selected Financial Information on TRS (Continued)

	1989	1990	1991
Other Statistics			
Card billed business ($ billions)			
Domestic (U.S.)	71.6	77.6	76.6
International	28.3	33.9	34.9
Total	99.9	111.5	111.5
Cards in force (millions)			
Domestic (U.S.)	24.3	25.9	25.8
International	9.8	10.6	10.8
Total	34.1	36.5	36.6
Service establishments accepting the card (millions)	3.0	3.3	3.5

Source: American Express Company Annual Reports, 1990 and 1991.

Exhibit 3   Securitization Levels of Major Credit-Card Issuers

Issuer	Receivables Portfolio ($ billions)	Proportion securitized (%)
American Express Centurion Bank	6.9	0
AT&T Universal Card	3.8	0
Bank of America	6.2	0
Bank of New York	3.9	35
Chase Manhattan Bank	10.3	29
Chemical Bank	5.9	6
Citibank	34.2	64
Discover	11.6	46
First Chicago	7.0	53
Household Finance	3.8	57
MBNA	8.2	32
Total receivables/Weighted average proportion	101.8	40

Source: Lehman Brothers.

Exhibit 4   Selected Financial Information on Credco

	1987	1988	1989	1990	1991
Operating Data ($ millions)					
Receivables purchased [a]	72,589	82,481	90,584	103,440	99,778
Revenues [b]	1,279	1,459	1,731	2,131	2,070
Interest expense	638	745	898	1,022	946
Provision for doubtful accounts, net of recoveries	452	506	565	811	855
Income tax provision	59	56	71	99	87
Net income	122	147	190	191	174
Balance Sheet Data ($ millions)					
(Year ended December 31)					
Accounts receivable	9,323	10,525	10,733	13,068	12,220
Reserve for doubtful accounts	484	524	550	719	731
Other	(467)	581	1,327	435	1,176
Total assets	9,340	11,630	12,610	14,222	14,127
Short-term debt	4,159	4,930	5,506	7,450	7,918
Current portion of long-term debt	354	270	771	823	768
Long-term debt	3,502	4,322	3,795	3,403	3,136
Shareholders' equity	1,085	1,232	1,422	1,610	1,784
Other (e.g., loans to foreign subsidiaries)	240	876	1,116	936	521
Total liabilities and shareholders' equity	9,340	11,630	12,610	14,222	14,127
Key Statistics					
Ratio of earnings to fixed charges	1.28	1.27	1.29	1.28	1.28
Average life of cardmember receivables (days)	43	42	43	43	43
Loss ratio, net of recoveries [c]	0.62%	0.55%	0.57%	0.70%	0.18%
Ratio of total debt to equity	7.15	7.5	6.67	7.2	6.44
Weighted average interest rate on total debt	8.3%	8.6%	9.4%	8.9%	7.7%

Source: American Express Credit Corporation Annual Report, 1991.
a. Receivables purchased by Credco ($99.8 billion) do not equal TRS's total billed business ($111 billion) because Credco did not purchase all receivables generated by foreign subsidiaries of TRS and did not purchase all Optima and extended-payment-plan receivables.
b. Revenue includes finance charge income on interest bearing receivables and discount revenue from purchases of charge-card receivables. A portion (equal to the provision for doubtful accounts) of this discount revenue is recognized at the time of purchase while the rest is deferred and recognized ratably over the period the receivables are outstanding.
c. The loss ratio is the ratio of write-offs net of recoveries for the year to the receivables purchased in that year.

Exhibit 5   Credco's Debt

Short-term debt ($ millions)	Year	Balance at end-of-period	Year-end wtd. avg. interest	Maximum monthly balance
Commercial paper	1989	5,197	8.3%	5,197
	1990	7,253	7.6%	7,592
	1991	7,504	5.2%	9,181
Borrowings from affiliates	1989	28	8.3%	950
	1990	17	6.8%	1,112
	1991	173	5.2%	1,215
Borrowings under lines of credit	1989	160	14.5%	535
	1990	65	12.5%	524
	1991	153	8.7%	220
Other	1989	121	8.3%	179
	1990	115	7.2%	189
	1991	88	4.1%	150

Long-term debt ($ millions) except current portion	1990	1991
U.S. dollar Senior notes, 7.375% to 13.125% due through 2013	2,448	2,165
Japanese Yen senior bonds, notes, and loans, 4.9% to 8% due through 1996	361	362
Pound Sterling notes, 9.625% to 11.375% due through 1994	227	170
Canadian Dollar notes, 9% to 11.75% due through 1994	140	139
Japanese Yen bonds, 6.9% due through 1995	66	62
Subordinated notes and debentures, 7.8% to 9% due through 1998	26	16
Borrowing agreements with bank trust departments	114	10
Other senior notes	10	27
Medium-term notes		195
Other long-term debt	19	
Net unamortized bond discount	(8)	(10)
Total long-term debt	3,403	3,136
Total current portion of long-term debt	823	768

Source: American Express Credit Corporation Annual and 10-K Reports, 1991

Exhibit 6 The Asset-Backed Securities Market (Public Transactions Only)

Market Size — Amount issued ($ billions)

Collateral Type	1985	1986	1987	1988	1989	1990	1991	Total
Credit-card receivables			2.4	7.4	11.4	22.5	20.8	64.5
Auto loans	0.9	9.9	6.5	6.1	7.7	12.1	16.7	59.9
Home equity loans					2.7	5.6	10.3	18.6
Other[a]	0.3	0.4	1.2	2.7	3.2	1.9	2.1	11.8
Total issuance	1.2	10.3	10.1	16.2	25.0	42.1	49.9	154.8

Percent of total issuance

Originator Type	1985	1986	1987	1988	1989	1990	1991	Total
Bank	12.9	5.6	38.2	62.2	48.3	52.1	42.1	45.0
Finance company	69.8	88.7	46.6	13.1	35.1	37.7	47.8	42.2
Retailer				13.2	10.7	8.4	5.4	7.1
Thrift	17.3	5.7	11.2	11.2	4.4	1.5	4.4	5.0
Other			4.0	0.4	1.5	0.3	0.2	0.7

Exhibit 6   The Asset-Backed Securities Market (Public Transactions Only) (Continued)

Market Chronology

Collateral type	Date of first issue	Amount issued through 12/31/91 ($ billions)
Computer lease	March 1985	1.3
Automobile loans	May 1985	60.0
Credit-card receivables	January 1987	64.6
Trade receivables	September 1987	0.3
Consumer loans	November 1987	1.1
Truck loans	May 1988	0.6
Boat loans	September 1988	1.0
Manufactured-housing loans	September 1988	5.2
Aircraft leases	September 1988	0.2
Equipment leases	October 1988	0.6
RV loans	December 1988	1.4
Home equity loans	January 1989	18.5
Timeshare receivables	August 1989	0.1
Total		154.8

Source: Lehman Brothers
a. This category includes the following collateral types: Manufactured-housing loans, Wholesale auto loans, RV loans, Computer Equipment leases, Boat loans, etc.

Exhibit 7 Typical Investor Breakdown in New-Issue, Credit-Card Receivables Backed Securities

Investor type	Percent of amount issued
Money managers	25
Pension funds	15
Corporations	5
Bank portfolios	10
Bank-trust departments	10
Insurance companies	25
Government entities (e.g., federally sponsored agencies)	10
	100

Source: Lehman Brothers

Exhibit 8 The Consumer Credit Market

	Consumer Credit Outstanding ($ billions)						
Type	1985	1986	1987	1988	1989	1990	1991
Automobile loans	211	245	267	284	291	285	268
Revolving credit	123	135	159	184	210	232	248
Home equity loans	108	131	179	220	238	264	296
Total	442	511	605	688	739	781	812

Source: Lehman Brothers.

Exhibit 9 The Master Trust

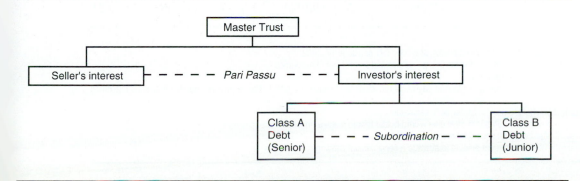

Exhibit 10 Statistics on the Credit-Card Portfolio of Citibank (South Dakota) and Citibank (Nevada)

	Years Ended December 31		
	1989	1990	1991
Receivables			
1. Average receivables outstanding ($,000)	20,409,498	25,796,848	29,112,792
Loss Experience			
2. Net loss ($,000)[a]	949,487	1,305,598	1,899,902
3. Net loss as a percentage of 1	4.7%	5.1%	6.5%
4. Net loss as a percentage of gross loss[b]	85.3%	86.4%	88.6%
Yield			
5. Finance charges and fees billed ($,000)	4,138,851	5,197,971	5,803,520
6. Average revenue yield (5/1)	20.3%	20.1%	19.9%
Payment Rate [c]			
7. Monthly average	13.4%	12.8%	12.6%
8. Highest month	15.3%	14.0%	13.7%
9. Lowest month	12.3%	11.6%	11.3%
Expenses			
10. Servicing and collection expenses as a percentage of 1[d]	2.0%	2.0%	2.0%

Delinquency Experience

	Average of Twelve Months Ended December 31					
	1989		1990		1991	
Number of days delinquent[e]	Delinquent Amount	Percentage[f]	Delinquent Amount	Percentage[f]	Delinquent Amount	Percentage[f]
35 to 64 days	716,322	3.5	964,077	3.7	1,130,161	3.9
65 to 94 days	285,197	1.4	402,132	1.6	510,995	1.8
95 days or more	430,146	2.1	603,792	2.3	855,187	2.9
Total	1,431,665	7.0	1,970,001	7.6	2,496,343	8.6

Source: Standard Credit Card Master Trust Prospectus, May 14, 1991 and June 17, 1992.
a. Losses include write-offs of principal and finance-charge receivables and are net of recoveries.
b. Gross losses are losses before recoveries.
c. The proposal rate is the ratio of monthly cardholder payments (principal and finance charges) to the receivables outstanding at the beginning of the month.
d. Servicing and collection charges are the casewriter's estimates.
e. Delinquency is measured as the number of days after a card holder fails to make a "minimum due" payment.
Charges are written off after being delinquent for more than 185 days.
f. Percentage is the ratio of the delinquent amount to average receivables outstanding.

Exhibit 11   The Loss, Payment, and Yield Experience of Select Credit-Card Receivables Portfolios

Issuer	Loss Ratio (%)[a]			
	1988	1989	1990	1991
Citibank	4.5	4.7	5.1	6.5
Sears	2.1	2.0	2.5	3.1
First Chicago	3.6	3.7	4.2	5.2
MBNA	1.2	1.4	1.8	2.7
Discover	2.7	2.5	3.1	3.5
Chase	3.4	3.0	3.4	4.7

Issuer	Payment Rate (%)[b]			
	1988	1989	1990	1991
Citibank	13.3	13.4	12.8	12.6
Sears	9.3	7.9	7.3	7.0
First Chicago	13.3	13.9	14.5	14.3
MBNA	15.2	14.9	14.5	13.7
Discover	13.2	12.8	13.4	14.2
Chase	12.1	12.9	12.3	11.7

Issuer	Yield (%)[c]			
	1988	1989	1990	1991
Citibank	20.6	20.3	20.1	19.9
First Chicago	19.3	19.7	19.7	19.3
MBNA	16.6	17.2	18.1	18.8
Chase	19.3	20.8	21.1	20.6

Source: Lehman Brothers.

a. Loss ratio is the ratio of the amount written off (net of recoveries) during the year to the average receivables outstanding during that year. The recoveries for First Chicago, MBNA, and Discover were assumed by the casewriter to equal those of Citibank (i.e., about 80 basis points per year).

b. Payment rate is the average of monthly payment rates, where the monthly payment rate is the ratio of monthly payments to the receivables outstanding at the beginning of the month.

c. Yield is the ratio of the finance charges and fees to the average receivables outstanding during the year.

Exhibit 12   Statistics on TRS's Domestic Consumer (Green, Gold, and Platinum) Charge-Card Business

	Years Ended December 31,		
	1989	1990	1991
Receivables			
1. Charge volume and fees ($,000)	47,351,438	48,920,154	46,864,766
2. Average receivables outstanding ($,000)	6,144,729	6,479,805	6,109,547
3. Receivables turnover rate (1/2)	7.7	7.6	7.7
Payment Rate [a]			
4. Monthly average	70.2%	68.4%	71.5%
5. Highest Month	76.5%	75.5%	74.8%
6. Lowest Month	64.9%	62.5%	61.8%
Loss Experience			
7. Gross loss ($,000)[b]	462,623	577,587	615,605
8. Gross loss as a percentage of 1	1.0%	1.2%	1.3%
9. Recoveries ($,000)	105,467	107,804	133,231
10. Recoveries as a percentage of 1	0.2%	0.2%	0.3%
11. Net loss	357,156	469,784	482,374
12. Net loss as a percentage of 1	0.8%	1.0%	1.0%

Delinquency Experience

	Average of Twelve Months Ended December 31,					
	1989		1990		1991	
Number of days delinquent[c]	Delinquent Amount ($)	Percentage[d]	Delinquent Amount ($)	Percentage[d]	Delinquent Amount ($)	Percentage[d]
30 to 59 days	162,574	2.9	181,413	3.1	165,027	3.0
60 to 89 days	70,493	1.3	80,076	1.4	76,024	1.4
90 to 119 days	60,025	1.1	65,140	1.1	62,709	1.1
120 or more days	203,501	3.7	236,515	4.0	227,768	4.1
Total	496,594	9.0	563,144	9.6	531,528	9.6

Source: Prospectus, July 24, 1992.
a. The payment rate is the ratio of collections made during the month to the opening balance of receivables for that month.
b. Gross Losses in any period are the charges written-off during that period.
c. Delinquency is measured as the number of days after a charge is first included with an unpaid "previous balance" on a cardmember's statement. Charges are written-off after being delinquent for 360 days.
d. Percentage is the ratio of delinquent amounts to the average billed receivables during the period.

Exhibit 13 Credit Enhancement of Credit-Card, Receivables-Backed Securities

	Percentage of total issuance[a]				
Credit enhancement type	1987	1988	1989	1990	1991
Subordination[b]		14	24	56	60
Letter of credit[c]	100	73	76	43	4
Cash collateral[d]				1	35
Other[e]		13			1
Total	100	100	100	100	100

Source: Lehman Brothers.
a. Percentage is the ratio of the asset-backed amount issued with the particular credit-enhancement type to the total issuance in that year.
b. The investor's interest is divided into two classes of debt: A small "B" class and a larger "A" class such that class A payments are senior to class B payments.
c. A bank or insurance company provides a letter of credit that protects the investor's interest from losses up to a fixed maximum amount.
d. The provider of this type of enhancement (typically a bank) makes a loan to the trust at the time of debt issuance. This loan and generally an additional cash contribution from the asset originator provide loss protection to the investor's interest.
e. Includes company guarantees, reserve funds, surety bonds, and overcollateralization (other than subordination).

Exhibit 14 Interest Rates and Interest-Rate Spreads as of January 31, 1992

Interest rates on Treasury securities

3-year notes	5.7%
5-year notes	6.4%
7-year notes	7.0%

Yield spreads (basis points)
on 5-year, non-callable notes over 5-year Treasuries

AAA credit-card receivables backed	50–55
AAA finance company	35–40
Credco	60

LEHMAN BROTHERS AND THE SECURITIZATION OF AMERICAN EXPRESS CHARGE-CARD RECEIVABLES

It was late in the evening of July 22, 1992 and the asset-backed securities (ABS) banking group at Lehman Brothers was discussing the imminent pricing of American Express charge-card receivables-backed certificates. The group had just returned after an extensive three-day-long "road show" during which they and representatives from American Express Travel Related Services Company, Inc. (TRS), had presented investors with the merits of these new securities. At 10 a.m. the next morning, Lehman would announce the price range, and investors would then place their orders. The pricing had to be done carefully so that it reflected the value of the securities relative to other asset-backed issues and relative to American Express Credit Corporation's unsecured debt.

LEHMAN BROTHERS

Lehman Brothers was the investment banking and capital markets division of Shearson Lehman Brothers, Inc., a subsidiary of the American Express Company. It was one of the oldest investment banks in the United States and had served the financial needs of institutional, corporate, and governmental clients for almost 150 years. It had grown to be a leading global financial institution with operations that spanned domestic as well as international financial markets.

Lehman Brothers was comprised of five major operating business divisions: Investment and Merchant Banking; Fixed Income; Equities; Swap and Financial Products; and Foreign Exchange, Futures, and Commodities. A sixth group, Trading Services, provided trading technology systems and transaction processing support to the firm.

The asset-backed securities banking group was a part of the Fixed Income division. This division was responsible for the origination, sales, and trading of fixed income instruments

Kuljot Singh prepared this case under the supervision of André F. Perold as the basis for class discussion rather than to illustrate either effective or ineffective handling of an administrative situation.
Copyright © 1993 by the President and Fellows of Harvard College. Harvard Business School case 293-121

such as government and government agency bonds, mortgage and asset-backed securities, corporate debt, municipal debt, and commercial paper. Lehman was one of the leading dealers in asset-backed securities and had built its secondary market strength by actively making markets in these securities. (See Exhibit 1 for the market share of lead underwriters of asset-backed securities.) In addition, the firm had recently strengthened its origination capabilities significantly by increasing the size of the ABS group and focusing senior management's attention on this growing market. Lehman saw the American Express charge-card deal as an important demonstration of its structuring abilities and as a means by which it could further establish itself as an innovative and leading underwriter of asset-backed securities.

As was typical of other asset-backed new-issues, the American Express charge-card securitization project was staffed by a cross section of professionals from different groups within Lehman's Fixed Income division. The ABS banking group had overall responsibility for structuring the transaction, negotiating with the rating agencies and advising TRS on systems, accounting, and legal issues. The ABS trading group was responsible for maintaining a secondary market in the new issue. The Fixed Income Research group was responsible for designing a strategy to educate investors on the relative value of the new securities. The Fixed Income Syndicate group was responsible for pricing the issue and coordinating the underwriting and selling syndicates. The Financing Coverage group, which advised TRS on all its capital raising strategies, was the primary investment banking liaison between Lehman and TRS.

THE AMERICAN EXPRESS DEAL

In February 1992, TRS had decided to proceed with Lehman's proposal to securitize a portion of the receivables generated by the American Express consumer charge cards. This involved approximately $2.4 billion of receivables generated by the American Express® Card (i.e., the Green card), the American Express® Gold Card, and the Platinum Card®. Initially, only two $500-million series of debt with maturities of five and seven years would be sold to investors. The remainder would be retained by TRS, and depending on the success of the initial offerings and TRS's future needs, could be used to issue additional debt. (See *"American Express TRS Charge-Card Receivables,"* HBS No. 293-120, for details on TRS's charge-card business and securitization structure.)

The securitization involved important modifications to TRS's information systems for both reporting and operational purposes. The modifications would isolate the designated accounts and enable TRS to provide trust performance statistics on a monthly basis. Representatives from TRS and the ABS banking group had made multiple visits to TRS's

Western Regional Operation Center (WROC) to coordinate these changes. WROC was located in Phoenix, Arizona, and was responsible for servicing, collecting, and maintaining information systems for the charge-card portfolio. By early June, the computer programs had been completed and used in trial runs and had been validated by an independent auditor.

In May, 6,995,152 accounts were chosen randomly from eligible accounts[1] within TRS's consumer (Green, Gold, and Platinum) charge-card portfolio. These were the designated accounts whose receivables were to be securitized. On June 30, the outstanding receivables on these accounts totaled $2,433,528,576. The accounts were geographically dispersed across the United States, with 15.0% of the receivables in California, 15.0% in New York, 9.3% in Texas, 6.5% in New Jersey, and the remainder in the remaining 45 states with none of the states representing more than 4.3%. See Exhibit 2 for the breakdown of designated accounts by account balance, payment status, and length of membership.

GAINING RATING AGENCY APPROVAL

For a broad group of investors to be attracted to the receivables-backed securities, a AAA credit rating would be essential. Thus, the rating agencies had to be extremely confident that investors would receive their principal and promised yield. As in other asset-backed deals, the rating agencies would investigate the issuer's business, the mechanics and legal structure of the securitization, the economics of the securitized assets, and the level and type of credit enhancement before assigning a rating.

Lehman had informed the rating agencies of the impending securitization soon after obtaining TRS's approval in February 1992. In early June, analysts from the agencies' "structured finance" groups were given a presentation on TRS's servicing and collection abilities and details on the charge-card business. The structured finance analysts were accompanied by the analysts who rated the debt obligations of American Express and TRS's finance subsidiary, Credco. These analysts typically belonged to a distinct "financial institutions" group within a rating agency. Although their role was to help the structured finance analysts understand the charge-card business, they also benefited from the greater detail TRS was providing. Looking back, Murray Weiss, a vice president at Lehman's ABS banking group, remarked:

> As a first step, we had given the agencies a detailed tour of TRS's facilities in Phoenix and had presented them with TRS's cardmember and service establishment strategies. We felt that it

---

1   Among other eligibility requirements, an account had to be a Green, Gold, or Platinum card account, had to be payable in U.S. dollars, and should have been created under credit standards that were no less stringent than generally applied by TRS.

was absolutely necessary that they should be convinced of the health and soundness of TRS's business and management objectives.

Second, we presented them with the legal structure of the trust and the receivables' purchasing and servicing agreements. In order to focus the rating agency analysis on the charge-card receivables, the legal structure was designed so that the trust was assigned a "first-perfected security interest" in the receivables.[2]

Third, in our negotiations with the rating agencies, we emphasized the differences between TRS's charge-card business and the credit-card business. We did this because ours was the first-ever securitization of charge-card receivables, and we felt that certain characteristics of the charge-card receivables had helped create a security that was superior to those backed by credit-card receivables. Our challenge was to demonstrate to the agencies that we had a unique asset and a securitization structure that required minimal levels of credit support relative to typical AAA credit-card deals.

There were three major aspects of a securitization that the credit rating agencies were typically concerned about. First, the yield on the securitized assets should be sufficiently large to pay interest on the asset-backed securities, cover losses and servicing and collection fees, and provide a residual "excess yield" cushion. This excess yield, often around 4% to 6% for credit-card securitizations, typically ranged from 75% to 150% of the annual cardholder default rate. The larger the cushion, the more protection the investor would have from credit losses or from a decline in portfolio yield.

Second, a highly rated receivables-backed security must be able to withstand significant credit deterioration so that the return of investor principal and payment of interest were not jeopardized. In imposing a credit enhancement level, the rating agencies would assess the credit quality of the portfolio. Portfolio characteristics that lowered the required credit enhancement level included low losses, high yield, high payment rate, and high seasoning (length of time since cardholder opened his or her account).

Third, if either the credit losses were to increase or if the portfolio yield was to decline beyond a certain level, the ABS should prepay rather than allow losses to accumulate. To ensure that this would happen, safeguards would be designed in the form of "early amortization events," which, if triggered, would cause prepayment. Typical early amortization events would include insolvency of the servicer, insufficient yield to cover expenses, and the level of credit enhancement falling below a critical level. Structures that facilitated early detection of credit problems and limited loss accumulation through prepayment were considered superior.

---

2   The rating agencies would typically be concerned that in the unlikely event of an American Express or TRS bankruptcy, the receivables owned by the trust could become part of TRS's or American Express's bankruptcy estate. To minimize the probability of this occurrence, the trust's structure and its relationship with TRS had to be such that the receivables transferred to it would be considered sold in a "true sale" or having resulted in the trust gaining a "first perfected security interest" in the receivables. A claim was considered "perfected" if it had been properly registered under the Uniform Commercial Code to protect the investors' "interest," and "first" indicated the priority of that claim. Thus obtaining a "true sale" or "first perfected lien" secured the investors' claim to the receivables.

As in other securitizations, legal opinions from national law firms would be provided to the rating agencies to characterize the transfer of receivables to the trust. The purchasing agreement, which was the legal document that detailed the terms and conditions under which the trust would purchase receivables from TRS, and the servicing agreement, which detailed the terms and conditions under which TRS would service the designated accounts, could reinforce the "true-sale" opinion by showing that the relationship between TRS and the trust was at arms-length.

Our negotiations with the rating agencies had addressed these concerns by highlighting the very favorable characteristics of American Express's charge-card receivables:

Because cardmembers did not have the option to revolve charge-card balances, the American Express charge-card receivables portfolio had a historically high and consistent turnover rate. The turnover rate, which had ranged from 7.5 to 7.7 times per year during the 1989 – 1991 period, was a measure of how often the portfolio completed a full charge/repayment cycle each year. Thus, with a yield factor of 3% and an assumed 7.5 turnover rate, the portfolio would generate a gross annual yield of 22.5%. This ability to generate a high and predictable yield, which was further enhanced by TRS's option to increase the yield factor, was superior to a credit-card portfolio's ability to sustain yield because credit-card interest rates were susceptible to competitive and legislative pressures.[3]

We also emphasized TRS's abilities to stem credit losses. Unlike credit cards, there was no pre-set spending limit on the charge cards. Thus, all purchases made by cardmembers had to be underwritten by TRS at the point of purchase. The ability to clear every purchase in "real time" helped reduce the incidence of fraud. Cardmembers also had to pay their accounts in full when billed, which meant that bad accounts could not accumulate charges unnoticed and would be identified earlier than credit-card account holders who could revolve balances by simply paying the minimum principal amount and finance charge until their spending on the card reached their credit limit.

The charge-card receivables' low loss ratio and high payment rate were also important factors in the analysis. Based on historical performance, approximately $1 would be eventually written off for every $100 of charge-card volume. Even if the securities were to "early amortize," it would be extremely unlikely that the class A investors would suffer any principal or interest loss because of the high payment rate.

Other factors emphasized by us were the high average seasoning (length of membership) and geographical diversity of the accounts.

The key objective of the negotiation process was to minimize the credit enhancement level that the agencies would require for a AAA rating. In addition to the review of the deal structure, legal documentation and opinions, and TRS's servicing capabilities and management expertise, the rating agencies would test the proposed securitization under various hypothetical scenarios. The three primary portfolio characteristics of yield, loss rate, and payment rate were subjected to severe "stress tests" to ensure that even in highly unfavorable scenarios, the class A investors would not suffer any principal or interest loss.

The typical stress test for credit-card receivables would reduce the portfolio yield by 50%, reduce payment rate by 50%, and increase losses by 300%. Such analysis generally resulted in credit enhancement levels of 10% for high-quality portfolios and 15% for low-quality portfolios.[4] We felt that although these tests were applicable to credit-card receivables portfolios, they were less relevant to a charge-card receivables portfolio because its yield was not affected by credit-card interest rates (i.e., competitive pressures), and its payment rate was unlikely to change very much because charge-card members had to pay their balance in full each month.

---

3   In 1991, Congress considered limiting the maximum interest that could be charged on credit-card purchases. At that time, the threat of this legislation had resulted in a temporary collapse in the price of credit-card receivables-backed securities.

4   Here, the credit enhancement level refers to the subordinated debt (class B) principal as a proportion of senior debt (class A) principal.

Given the quality of the charge-card receivables, we thought that the subordination level should range from 3.5% to 5% which would imply 3.5 to 5 times loss coverage per receivables turn.[5] The credit enhancement on typical credit-card deals would cover approximately 3 to 3.5 times losses per receivables turn. However, the rating agencies determined that because TRS wrote off delinquent charges after one year (as opposed to six months for most credit cards), the loss coverage should be somewhat higher.[6]

After negotiations, the class A certificates were given a AAA rating with 5.5% subordination. Because the AAA rating was based on a multiple of loss per turn, it was also dependent on TRS's ability to generate and transfer new receivables to the trust and the financial condition of American Express and TRS.

THE ROAD SHOW

Lehman suggested worldwide distribution for the class A certificates in order to fully capitalize on American Express's name recognition and to more completely diversify TRS's funding sources. An underwriting syndicate, which included foreign as well as minority-owned firms, had been chosen to ensure worldwide liquidity for the new issue in the secondary market. The Lehman team believed that success depended on communicating the unique aspects of the deal both to investors and the underwriting group, therefore, an extensive "road show" was undertaken by senior management representatives of Lehman Brothers and TRS. A series of meetings were held with prospective investors in major financial centers in the United States, Europe, and Japan. Basil Williams, lead investment banker on the transaction, commented:

> Our objective was that this issue be perceived by investors as superior to a traditional credit-card securitization and therefore, that it justified premier pricing.

A typical presentation would begin with an overview of American Express, TRS, and the charge-card business. Topics addressed included TRS's business outlook and strategies for maintaining and developing its cardmember base and service establishment relationships, TRS's ability to maintain credit standards in the existing cardmember base, and specific measures that were being taken to ensure the quality of future cardmembers and widespread acceptance of the American Express cards. Statistics on TRS's U.S. consumer charge-card portfolio were also presented.

---

5   Historically, the charge-card receivables had averaged around a 1% loss on every turn (see Exhibit 13 of "*American Express TRS Charge-Card Receivables,*" HBS No. 293-120), therefore, subordination of 3.5% meant that it was 3.5 times the loss per turn.

6   Losses were recorded only after a charge was written off. Therefore, a loss of 1% per turn did not imply that cash payments per turn were 99%. Instead, some of the receivables would become delinquent every turn and either pay off or be written off over the course of time.

TRS's business overview would be followed by the presentation of the deal structure and transaction details, including the terms and conditions of the class A certificates, characteristics and statistics on the designated accounts to be securitized, the benefits of the master trust structure, relevant charge-card characteristics, yield and trust expense computation, and the method of credit-enhancement. Differences between charge-card receivables and credit-card receivables would be highlighted.

Finally, a valuation analysis of the class A certificates would be presented. AAA- and AA-rated corporate debt and AAA-rated asset-backed securities would be compared with the class A certificates. Emphasis was placed on the declining supply of high-quality (AAA/AA) corporate debt (see Exhibit 3). American Express's international name recognition and the global demand for its securities would also be heavily emphasized.

Beth Starr, a vice president in Lehman's Fixed Income research group, remarked:

> We emphasized our belief that the American Express charge-card receivables-backed class A certificates had less event risk in the form of potential credit-rating downgrades than AAA-rated corporate debt. Since January of 1990, there had been a total of 27 downgrades of AAA corporate debt issuers, while no downgrades had occurred among AAA-rated ABS that used subordination as the means of credit enhancement.

PRICING AND AUCTION STRUCTURE

As is the case with the initial offering of most fixed income instruments, asset-backed securities were priced through a negotiation involving the issuer and the underwriter. The pricing negotiation process would start with the underwriter announcing a price range for the security to be sold. Investors would then place their orders contingent on the issue pricing within the announced range. While these orders did not constitute an investor's "firm commitment," they were expected to be honored in all but highly unforeseeable circumstances.

If the quantity ordered was significantly more than the securities for sale, that is, the issue was highly oversubscribed, the lead manager would close the deal and no more orders would be accepted.[7] At that point, the lead manager could elect to lower the indicated spread and retake investor orders. If undersubscribed, a new price range would be announced (a higher spread over the comparable Treasury), orders would be taken, and the process repeated.

After being closed, the price would be finalized in discussions with the issuer. The main price determinant would be the level of demand. If the issue was oversubscribed, the securities would be priced at the tighter end of the announced range (the lower end of the

---

7   Normally, the lead underwriter would close the deal when the orders exceeded 1.3 to 1.5 times the securities for sale.

spread), whereas if it was only fully subscribed, it would be priced at the middle or higher end of the spread. Once the issue was priced, the underwriting group would allocate securities to the investors and confirm their orders.[8] The transaction would be settled one week after being priced, at which time the investors would make full payment and take delivery of the security.

In the case of the American Express charge-card receivables, the Lehman team thought that the certificates would be priced at lower yields than similarly rated credit-card securities and somewhat higher yields than similarly rated corporate debt. In fact, on the road show, Lehman had indicated its belief that the certificates should be priced between noncallable corporate AAA debt and credit-card receivables-backed AAA securities. Lisa James, senior vice president and the head ABS trader at Lehman Brothers, remarked:

> We believed that TRS's charge-card receivables were a more desirable asset type than credit-card receivables. It was important to persuade investors that this security had less credit risk, less event risk, and less prepayment risk than credit-card receivable-backed securities. The spread on new five-year, AAA-rated credit-card receivables-backed securities issued in early 1992 had been 55 and 60 basis points over Treasuries. And in June 1992, AAA-rated credit-card deals were trading at 50 and 55 basis points above Treasuries for five-year and seven-year maturities, respectively. (See Exhibit 4 for secondary market spreads. The current yield on five-year Treasuries was 5.64% and on seven-year Treasuries was 6.17%.)
>
> On the other hand, noncallable AAA corporate debt had almost no prepayment risk. Consequently, equivalently rated corporate debt traded at tighter spreads to Treasuries. Also, within the corporate debt market, debt issued by industrial companies traded at tighter spreads in comparison to similarly rated debt issued by finance companies. In the case of the American Express deal, we considered the key comparable in the corporate sector to be debt issued by finance companies, which at that time had been trading at a 35/45 (AAA/AA) basis point spread over Treasuries for the five-year maturity and 40/50 basis point spread for the seven-year maturity. (See Exhibit 4.)
>
> While we expected a spread over the corporate AAA yield because of slight prepayment risk versus noncallable corporate bonds, we did not think the spread would be large, in part because the certificates represented the first-ever securitization of charge-card receivables and thus had "scarcity value," and in part because of the superior structural and economic characteristics of this deal.

---

8 Allocation would normally be done on a pro-rata basis, however, the underwriters were not required to do so.

RISKS TO LEHMAN

Although Lehman had discussed the pricing strategy with TRS and other syndicate members, as the lead underwriter it was the primary entity responsible for successfully pricing the deal. Further, because TRS was the flagship firm of Lehman's parent, the American Express Company, senior managers at Lehman Brothers and at American Express were paying close attention.

Tim O'Neill, a senior vice president in Lehman's Fixed Income Syndicate group, remarked:

> We needed to strike a price that would neither be so high (i.e., low yield) that it could create unsold inventory for us and the underwriting syndicate, nor so low (i.e., high yield) that it could cause TRS's cost of funds to be unduly high.

Exhibit 1   Lead Underwriters in the Asset-backed Securities Market

| | Amount issued | | | | | | | |
	1985	1986	1987	1988	1989	1990	1991	Total
Total Issuance ($ billions)	1.2	10.3	10.1	16.2	25.0	42.1	49.9	154.8

| | Percent of total issuance | | | | | | | |
Lead Underwriter	1985	1986	1987	1988	1989	1990	1991	Total
First Boston	77.9	88.1	51.2	26.5	39.9	23.5	27.7	34.3
Merrill Lynch	–	–	1.8	11.8	19.3	24.8	23.7	18.9
Salomon Brothers	13.2	10.1	28.3	17.1	3.4	10.9	16.3	13.2
Goldman, Sachs	–	–	9.7	8.5	19.9	11.7	3.5	9.0
Dean Witter	–	–	–	6.3	7.9	11.3	8.7	7.8
Chemical Securities	–	–	–	12.2	4.2	3.7	.4	3.1
Chase Securities	–	–	–	–	–	1.2	6.6	2.5
Morgan Stanley	–	–	.9	2.6	.5	4.5	1.2	2.0
Lehman Brothers	–	–	2.1	1.4	1.3	1.2	2.4	1.6
Drexel	8.9	1.9	4.4	8.2	.7	–	–	1.5
Citicorp	–	–	–	4.7	–	3.3	–	1.4
J.P. Morgan	–	–	–	–	–	1.5	2.5	1.2
UBS Securities	–	–	–	–	–	–	2.8	.9
Bear Stearns	–	–	–	–	.4	0.9	1.8	.9
Prudential Securities	–	–	–	–	2.0	.7	.7	.7
Donaldson Lufkin	–	–	–	–	–	.7	1.5	.7
Kidder Peabody	–	–	1.5	.7	.5	–	–	.3
Daiwa Securities	–	–	–	–	–	–	.2	.1
BT Securities	–	–	–	–	–	.2	–	.1
Total	100	100	100	100	100	100	100	100

Source: Lehman Brothers.
Note: The lead underwriter was given full credit for each transaction.

Exhibit 2 The Designated Accounts as of June 30, 1992

Composition of Designated Accounts by Account Balance

Account Balance Range	Number of Accounts	Percentage	Receivables Outstanding ($)	Percentage
Credit balance	104,205	1.5	(18,686,293)	−.8
No Balance	2,866,817	41.0	0	0
$1 – $500	2,752,599	39.4	477,882,124	19.6
$501 – $1,000	638,296	9.1	452,486,052	18.6
$1,001 – $2,000	390,361	5.6	541,925,529	22.3
$2,001 – $3,000	120,662	1.7	292,425,977	12.0
$3,001 – $5,000	77,176	1.1	291,480,810	12.0
Greater than $5,000	45,036	.6	396,014,377	16.3
Total	6,995,152	100.0	2,433,528,576	100.0

Composition of Designated Accounts by Payment Status

Payment Status[a,b]	Number of Accounts	Percentage	Billed Receivables Outstanding ($)[c]	Percentage
Current and less than 30 days delinquent	6,667,509	95.3	2,145,439,187	91.5
30 to 59 days delinquent	152,639	2.2	53,785,080	2.3
60 to 89 days delinquent	48,350	.7	25,797,668	1.1
90 to 119 days delinquent	32,129	.5	22,091,997	.9
120 or more days delinquent	94,525	1.4	98,037,853	4.2
Total	6,995,152	100.0	2,345,151,785	100.0

Exhibit 2   The Designated Accounts as of June 30, 1992 (Continued)

Composition of Designated Accounts by Lengths of Membership

Length of membership[d]	Number of Accounts	Percentage	Receivables Outstanding ($)	Percentage
Less than 12 months	505,771	7.2	149,119,946	6.1
12 to 23 months	670,891	9.6	182,949,097	7.5
24 to 35 months	727,828	10.4	198,569,544	8.2
36 to 47 months	710,921	10.2	204,289,911	8.4
48 to 59 months	593,644	8.5	181,047,914	7.4
Greater than 60 months	3,786,097	54.1	1,517,552,164	62.4
Total	6,995,152	100.0	2,433,528,576	100.0

Source: *American Express Master Trust Prospectus*, July 24, 1992.
a. Delinquency is measured as the number of days after a charge is first included in an unpaid "previous balance."
b. The payment status of each designated account is based on the oldest balance in that account.
c. Unbilled receivables were $88,376,791. Therefore total receivables in the second panel are not the same as in the other two panels.
d. Determined from date of initial cardmembership.

Exhibit 3   Market Value of AAA and AA Bonds in the Lehman Brothers Corporate Bond Index
(as a % of total)

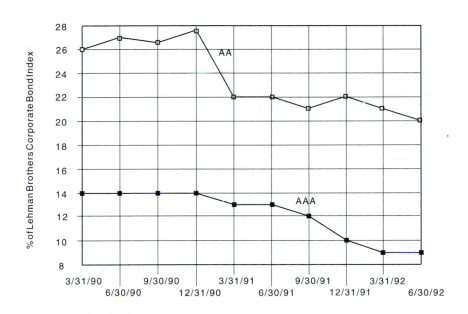

Source: Lehman Brothers.

Exhibit 4   Secondary Market Spreads in the Credit-card Receivables-backed Market and the Corporate Debt Market.

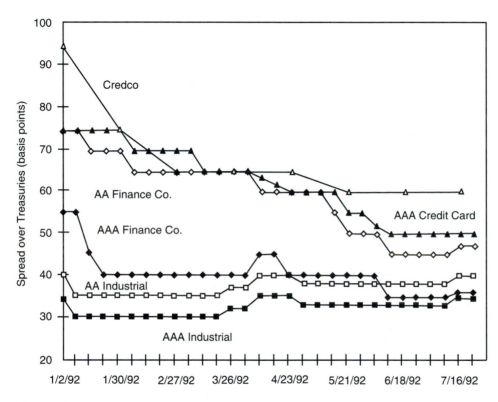

Source: Lehman Brothers.
Note: All securities are noncallable and have a five-year maturity.

PART TWO

FINANCIAL ENGINEERING AND EQUITY SECURITIES

ADDRESSING INFORMATION ASYMMETRIES

ARLEY MERCHANDISE CORPORATION

In the fall of 1984, the Arley Merchandise Corporation was considering how to raise $5 million to repay debt and position itself for future growth. The company was a leading privately owned manufacturer of curtains, draperies, and bedcoverings. It had enjoyed 32 years of continuous profitability. Present management of Arley had increased their ownership of the company's common stock following a December 31, 1981, leveraged buyout of shares owned by a founder of the company for almost $8 million in cash and notes. Arley's three senior officers currently owned 54.4% of the outstanding shares in approximately equal proportions. The investment firm that participated in the leveraged buyout owned 19.3% of the stock. The balance of the shares (26.3%) were owned in smaller blocks of less than 5%.

Arley's decision to raise new financing followed a 2-year period of sharply increasing earnings. For the fiscal year ending June of 1982, Arley had earned $.15 per share. In the two subsequent years, earnings per share had surged to $.41 and $1.03, respectively (Exhibit 1).

While the company desired to raise capital through an initial public offering of shares, it was not anxious to do so while earnings per share were rising at a rate in excess of 150% per year. Instead, Arley's owners hoped to fully demonstrate the earning power of the company *before* bringing it public in order to achieve a more attractive selling price for the firm's shares. Unfortunately, just as the company's income statements began to reflect its full earning power, investor enthusiasm for new issues of common stock of small firms was rapidly receding (Exhibit 2).

The dollar volume of new issues of common stock of small firms during the first ten months of 1984 fell to 30% of the level it had reached in the prior year. While this volume was still significant by historical standards, there was little reason to believe that the downward spiral was any more likely to flatten out or reverse than continue in its present direction. The mid-1970s era demonstrated just how fickle the new equity issue market could

This case was prepared by William E. Fruhan as the basis of class discussion rather than to illustrate either effective or ineffective handling of an administrative situation.

become for small firms. During the interval from 1973 through 1979 the market for new equity issues of small firms effectively disappeared (Exhibit 3).

Arley and its investment bankers had been discussing some innovative financing alternatives that would allow the company to sell its stock at a price high enough to be acceptable to the current owners of the business but not so high as to make it unmarketable for the underwriters. Exhibit 4 indicates that the common stocks of large established firms in the home furnishings industry were trading at prices equal to 8 or 9 times annual earnings. A new public offering of the common stock of a small firm in this industry (such as Arley) would presumably be priced on a pro forma basis (assuming the new capital structure for Arley) at a price/earnings ratio below the level of more seasoned firms.

Arley's current owners felt that any price less than $8 per share was unacceptable, while Arley's investment bankers did not feel that a price above $6.50 per share would represent an acceptable underwriting risk given existing conditions in the financial markets.

The price gap that had to be bridged was about $1.50 per share. Several alternatives for bridging the gap were considered, each of which included some form of money-back guarantee to an investor purchasing a newly issued Arley share. The money-back guarantee might take several forms. It could be $8 per share in cash, $8 per share in Arley notes, or $8 per share in market value of Arley common or preferred stock as of the date the guarantee was utilized. The point in time at which the money-back guarantee might be exercised was also an issue under consideration. It might take effect, for example, at the end of 1 year, at the end of 2 years, at the end of 5 years, or at the end of 10 years. Alternatively, the guarantee could be exercisable continuously over some time period rather than on a specific date. While the potential variations in the design of the proposed security seemed unlimited, Arley's investment banker recommended the following terms for the offering:

> 750,000 *units* consisting of
> 750,000 *shares* of common stock

and

> 750,000 *rights* to sell common stock

Each unit would consist of one share of common stock and one right to sell common stock, each right entitling the holder to sell to the company one share of common stock at $8, subject to adjustment, during a 15 business day period beginning 2 years from the date of issuance. The company may pay for the common stock in cash or an equivalent amount of the company's senior subordinated notes due 10 years from the date of issuance, as the company may specify by notice to the holders of the rights no later than 60 days prior to the commencement of the rights period. In the event notes were offered as payment in whole or in part for shares of common stock, cash would nevertheless be paid if the aggregate value of the common stock to be repurchased by the company were not more than $1 million. The common stock and rights included in the units were separately transferable immediately upon issuance at the option of the holder.

The notes, if issued, would bear interest payable quarterly at 128% of the ten-year Treasury rate determined as of the date of the notice. The notes may be redeemed at the option of the Company, in whole or in part, at any time after 2 years from the date of issuance at redemption prices declining from 106% of par at the end of 2 years to 100% of par at the end of 5 years. The notes would be subject to a mandatory sinking fund commencing 4 years from the date of issuance, calculated to retire 75% of the notes prior to maturity. The notes would be subordinated to all senior indebtedness (as defined) of the company ($14,310,000 at September 21, 1984).

The sale of the units at $8 per unit would raise a total of $5,054, 000 net of underwriting discounts and expenses associated with the offering. The proceeds of the offering would be utilized to repay bank debt currently borrowed at the prime rate (12.5%).

Around the date of the proposed Arley offering, low-rated straight debt was trading in a yield range of 14%–16% (Exhibit 5). Convertible subordinated debentures were trading at interest rates equal to about 70% of the rate appropriate for straight debt of equivalent bond ratings. Convertible debt also carried a conversion premium of about 20% (Exhibit 5). Baa-rated debt of industrial firms was yielding about 115% of 10-year Treasury debt, a figure somewhat below the average ratio for the past 2 or 3 years (Exhibit 6). Ninety-day Treasury bills were yielding approximately 10%.

Exhibit 1 Historical Financial Data, 1980–1984 (thousands of dollars except per share data)

	Fiscal Year Ending					1st Qtr. Ending	
	June 30, 1980	June 30, 1981	June 30, 1982	June 24, 1983	June 22, 1984	Sept. 23 1983	Sept. 21, 1984
Income Statement Data							
Net sales	$36,658	$40,015	$46,830	$49,968	$67,571	$14,101	$17,348
Cost of goods sold	28,078	29,453	35,652	36,070	46,861	9,689	11,670
Gross profit	8,580	10,562	11,178	13,898	20,710	4,412	5,678
Selling, shipping, and administrative expenses	6,195	6,785	8,351	8,819	10,478	2,426	3,056
Interest expense	268	301	1,011	1,911	1,841	358	580
Income before taxes	2,117	3,476	1,816	3,168	8,391	1,628	2,042
Net income	$ 902	$ 1,742	$ 945	$ 1,667	$ 4,167	$ 814	$ 1,021
Weighted average shares outstanding	8,945	8,945	6,500	4,055	4,055	4,055	4,094
Earnings per share	$ .10	$ .19	$ .15	$ .41	$ 1.03	$ .20	$ .25
Dividends per share[a]	0	0	0	0	0	0	0
Balance Sheet Data							
Working capital	$8,690	$9,847	$ 9,774	$10,131	$11,039	—	$10,607
Total assets	15,424	18,672	20,684	22,944	29,173	—	39,977
Total long-term debt (less current maturities)	2,334	1,892	10,673	9,520	6,761	—	9,248
Redeemed stock	—	—	(7,796)	—	—	—	—
Stockholders' investment	7,805	9,737	2,888	4,553	8,720	—	10,290

a. Arley had paid no dividends in the past and did not anticipate paying any dividends in the foreseeable future.

Exhibit 2 Underwritten Initial Public Equity Offering of Small U.S. Firms 1983–1984 (millions of dollars)

	Number of Issues Underwritten	Index of Offerings for 1983 Dollars Underwritten	Number of Issues Underwritten	Index of Offerings for 1984 Dollars Underwritten
January	19	$ 163	43	$ 353
February	26	345	24	147
March	42	432	27	141
April	29	268	19	89
May	42	349	23	135
June	68	932	16	96
July	75	772	20	109
August	64	678	22	188
September	56	396	16	110
October	53	467	16	79
Total 10 mos.	$474	$4,802	226	$1,447

Source: Venture Capital Journal.
Note: Small firms are defined as having less than $10 million of net worth prior to their initial public equity offerings.

Exhibit 3   Historical Underwritten Initial Public Equity Offerings of Small U. S. Firms, 1968–1983 (millions of dollars)

	Number of Issues Underwritten	Total Size of Offerings	S&P 500 Average
1968	358	$ 745	106.5
1969	698	1,367	91.1
1970	198	375	90.1
1971	248	551	99.2
1972	409	896	117.5
1973	69	160	94.8
1974	9	16	67.1
1975	4	16	88.7
1976	29	145	104.7
1977	22	75	93.8
1978	21	129	96.1
1979	46	183	107.9
1980	185	1,307	135.8
1981	390	2,646	122.6
1982	153	1,131	140.6
1983	611	5,740	164.9
1983 10 mos.	474	4,802	163.6
1984 10 mos.	226	1,447	166.1

Sources: *Venture Capital Journal*; Standard & Poor's Statistical Service, "Security Price Index Record."
Note: Small firms are defined as those with less than $5 million of net worth prior to their initial public offerings through 1975. In 1976, the cutoff point was raised to include all firms with less than $10 million of net worth prior to their initial public offerings.

Exhibit 4 Return on Equity, Price/Earnings Ratio, and Market Value/Book Value Ratio Data for the Common Stocks of Selected Home Furnishing Manufacturers, November 1984

Firm	ROE	P/E Ratio	Market Value/Book Value
Armstrong World	.141	8.0	1.1
Bassett Furniture	.138	8.7	1.2
Flexsteel Industries	.167	7.7	1.3
Hendredon Furniture	.145	10.8	1.5
Lane Co.	.159	8.1	1.3
La-Z-Boy Chair	.165	7.1	1.2
Leggett & Platt	.180	8.2	1.4
Mohasco Corp.	.070	9.4	.7
Thomas Industries	.159	9.6	1.5
Nine company average	.147	8.6	1.2

Source: Value Line Investment Survey.

Exhibit 5 Corporate Offerings of Straight Debt and Convertible Debt, October—November 1984 (millions of dollars)

Offering Date	Amount Sold	Issuer	Maturity	Bond Rating	Yield	Conversion Premium
Straight Debt						
10/23/84	$1,200	Occidental Petroleum	10-year	Ba2	14.5%	
10/23/84	50	Horn & Hardart	7-year	B1	14.5	
10/23/84	30	MacLeod-Stedman	7-year	B3	15.5	
10/23/84	58	Showboat, Inc.	20-year	B3	15.8	
10/25/84	70	Cannon Group	10-year	B2	15.4	
10/30/84	200	Chrysler Financial	15-year	Ba2	13.0	
11/2/84	115	Elsinore Finance	15-year	B2	15.5	
11/8/84	180	Lear Petroleum	10-year	B1	14.5	
Convertible Debt						
10/5/84	$ 100	Lorimar	20-year	B2	8.9%	20%
10/5/84	175	Texas Eastern	25-year	Baa3	12.0	28
10/5/84	60	SCM	25-year	Ba1	10.0	16
10/5/84	30	Mobile Comm. Corp. of America	20-year	B1	11.0	26
10/11/84	55	Wetterau	20-year	Baa3	9.3	20
10/15/84	25	Richardson Electric	20-year	B2	9.9	17
10/24/84	75	First Boston	25-year	A3	9.3	20
11/1/84	50	Communications Industries	25-year	Ba2	9.0	19
11/2/84	35	Insilco Corp.	26-year	Baa3	9.0	25

Source: Moody's Bond Survey; Investment Dealers' Digest.

Exhibit 6   Yields on Long Term Baa Industrial Bonds Versus 10-Year Treasury Bonds, January 1982—October 1984

| | Yield to Maturity | | |
	Long Term Baa	10-year Treasury	Baa/Treasury
1/82	16.75%	13.93%	1.20%
2/82	17.00	14.19	1.20
3/82	17.00	13.99	1.22
4/82	17.25	14.17	1.22
5/82	16.75	13.81	1.21
6/82	16.75	13.69	1.22
7/82	17.00	14.32	1.19
8/82	16.63	13.63	1.22
9/82	15.25	12.77	1.19
10/82	14.75	11.93	1.24
11/82	13.38	11.05	1.21
12/82	13.50	10.69	1.26
1/83	13.13	10.31	1.27
2/83	13.13	10.75	1.22
3/83	12.75	10.24	1.25
4/83	12.75	10.59	1.20
5/83	11.88	10.18	1.17
6/83	12.50	10.79	1.16
7/83	12.75	10.89	1.17
8/83	13.75	11.67	1.18
9/83	13.88	11.92	1.16
10/83	13.25	11.39	1.16
11/83	13.50	11.71	1.15
12/83	13.38	11.58	1.16
1/84	13.38	11.76	1.14
2/84	13.25	11.59	1.14
3/84	13.88	12.04	1.15
4/84	14.00	12.43	1.13
5/84	14.75	12.78	1.15
6/84	16.00	13.78	1.16
7/84	15.50	13.75	1.13
8/84	14.75	12.85	1.15
9/84	14.63	12.76	1.15
10/84	14.38	12.40	1.16

AVON PRODUCTS, INC.

On June 1, 1988, Hicks B. Waldron, chairman and chief executive officer of Avon Products, Inc., was reviewing a package of proposals that he and his financial advisors were to present to the Avon board of directors for final approval the following day. These proposals included (1) a public announcement that Avon would explore plans to divest two of its businesses, probably at a considerable book loss; (2) a reduction of the dividend on Avon's common stock; and (3) an exchange offer under which Avon would issue an unusual preferred stock in exchange for up to 25% of its common shares.

BACKGROUND

Avon Products, Inc., founded in 1886, was one of the world's largest manufacturers and marketers of beauty products. The company was famous for its direct selling beauty business, in which a sales force of independent contractors purchased products from Avon and then resold them door-to-door, largely to their friends and neighbors. In addition, by the mid-1980s, the company was an important national provider of sub-acute health care services.

Avon's Beauty Group produced and sold cosmetics, fragrances, toiletries, and fashion jewelry and accessories; it also sold gift and decorative products. While it sold several fragrances through retail establishments, most of the Beauty Group's revenues were from its direct sales operations. In 1988 Avon had 1.4 million active sales representatives worldwide, including 400,000 in the United States. Avon's other principal business group was its Health Care Group, which comprised Foster Medical Corporation, the Mediplex Group, and Retirement Inns of America. They provided home health care, operated retirement living facilities, and provided certain sub-acute health care services. Exhibit 1 gives a 10-year review of Avon's financial performance, and Exhibit 2 gives data by lines of business for the period 1982-1987. Exhibit 3 shows balance sheets for 1986 and 1987, and Exhibit 4 gives an historical perspective on Avon's stock price.

This case was prepared by Jonathan Tiemann as the basis of class discussion.
Copyright © 1989 by the President and Fellows of Harvard College. Harvard Business School case 289-049.

RECENT COMPANY HISTORY

As a result of its strong cash flow, Avon was able to increase its dividend regularly in the late 1970s while aggressively seeking acquisitions. By 1981 Avon had raised the dividend on its common stock to $3.00, up from $2.55 in 1978. But more important, in the early 1980s, Avon made the major strategic decision to diversify its business by entering the health care field. Its first acquisition in that field was in January 1982, when Avon acquired Mallinckrodt, Inc., a specialty chemical company whose sales were largely to the health care industry.

However, during this same period, an important demographic shift was beginning to threaten Avon's Beauty Group. The majority of Avon's sales representatives and their customers had traditionally been women who spent much of the day at home. But increasingly these women were entering occupations that required them to be away from home during the day. Therefore Avon was losing both its sales force and its customers. From 1979 to 1981, Avon's margins on beauty product sales declined as the company broadened its direct-sales product line and offered increasingly generous sales incentives, and by 1982 beauty product sales began to decline as well.

By mid-1982, Avon suddenly found itself in a weakening cash flow position as a result of the declining beauty business and the $710 million Mallinckrodt acquisition. Strapped for cash, the company reduced its dividend in August 1982 from $3.00 to $2.00 per share per year. Avon's stock price hardly moved when the company made the dividend announcement, but the *Wall Street Journal* reported at the time that observers had expected the dividend reduction. In any event, Avon's stock price had dropped from $30 per share at the end of 1981 to $20.375 per share immediately before the dividend announcement.

In 1984, having just become Avon's CEO, Mr. Waldron began to reshape the company's beauty operations. Instead of remaining primarily a direct sales company, he decided, Avon would broaden its approach to the beauty business by developing additional distribution channels. The company also continued to look for acquisitions in the health care area, so that Avon could remain viable in the event the changes it was making to its beauty business failed.

In May 1984, Avon acquired Foster Medical Company in a share exchange. Foster Medical seemed a particularly attractive acquisition because of the possibility that public health care policy would change to encourage a shift from expensive, hospital-based care to the less expensive home care, which was a major part of Foster's business. Avon also acquired Retirement Inns of America in November 1985 and the Mediplex Group in April 1986. Mediplex operated sub-acute health care facilities such as alcohol and drug abuse treatment centers, nursing homes, and psychiatric hospitals. Mediplex and Retirement

Inns both managed retirement living centers of various types. Consistent with this increasing focus on the provision of health care, Avon sold Mallinckrodt in 1986 for $675 million.

Although Mediplex and Retirement Inns served patients who paid for care themselves or through private insurers, Foster Medical's revenues came primarily from Medicare, the largest public health insurance program in the United States. A change in Medicare in 1986 effectively cut Foster Medical's charges for Medicare patients by 18%. Foster Medical was not able to respond successfully to this change, and in 1987, Avon's management recommended to the board that it review Avon's commitment to the health care industry. The board concluded that Foster Medical, Mediplex, and Retirement Inns could no longer grow at an attractive rate and still show acceptable profits. In addition, by 1987 the performance of the Beauty Group had begun to improve markedly. The board decided that the Beauty Group's strength permitted Avon to shed the Health Care Group companies. It started by selling Foster Medical Supply, a distribution company, in November 1987. Early in 1988, Avon also began the process of selling the entire Foster Medical Corporation. Avon anticipated an after-tax loss of $125 million on the sale.

Also in 1987, Avon acquired Giorgio, Inc. for $165 million in cash and Parfums Stern, Inc. for $160 million. These acquisitions not only added prestige fragrances, sold through retail stores, to Avon's beauty line but also continued Avon's transition away from the direct sales approach to the beauty business.

THE EXCHANGE OFFER

Mr. Waldron felt that at the same time that Avon was reorganizing its business, it should also reconsider its financial policies, including its dividend policy. The company was about to begin the last phase of its exit from the health care business with the sale of Mediplex and Retirement Inns. In addition, Mr. Waldron and the board agreed that Avon should redouble its commitment to its core beauty products business, whose recent results were encouraging. Among other things, this implied that Avon would continue to invest significant additional capital in that business.

In December 1987, Avon raised additional capital by selling 40% of the common stock of its wholly-owned Japanese subsidiary, Avon Products Company Limited, in a public offering in Japan that raised $218 million. The price was over six times book value and around 50 times earnings. Avon booked an after-tax gain of $121.1 million, or $1.72 per share, on the sale.

The board also felt that Avon should conserve cash flow by reducing its dividend from $2.00 to $1.00 per share, but Mr. Waldron worried about the consequences of simply cutting Avon's dividend. Avon had maintained its dividend at $2.00 per share per year since the dividend cut in August 1982. Although that reduction had not resulted in any sudden drop in Avon's stock price, Avon's stock had been falling for some time in advance of the cut. This time might be different. Avon's 1987 annual report had stated that the firm expected to maintain the current annual $2.00 dividend, and Avon's stock price had remained fairly steady during 1988.

Exhibit 5 lists the 25 largest institutional holders of Avon stock. Many of those investors might sell their Avon shares quickly if Avon simply reduced its dividend. As Mr. Waldron put it, "For five years I had been telling them that we weren't going to cut the dividend, and for five years they had been telling me they didn't believe me." Some investors had stated that they held Avon stock because it paid a high dividend. Avon's board asked its financial advisor, Morgan Stanley and Co., what steps the company could take to avoid having the dividend reduction drive down the stock price. The exchange offer was one element of the solution.

Morgan Stanley proposed that Avon offer to exchange one share of a new $2.00 preferred equity-redemption cumulative stock (PERCS) for each of up to 18 million of Avon's 71.7 million outstanding common shares. The new preferred would pay, on the same dividend dates as its common stock, cumulative quarterly dividends of 50 cents ($2.00 a year) accrued from September 1, 1988 to September 1, 1991.[1] Although the company would be able to redeem the preferred shares at any time before September 1, 1991, according to a declining schedule,[2] the important provisions concerned mandatory redemption of the PERCS shares on September 1, 1991.

On that date the PERCS shares would expire. Their holders would receive one common share for every PERCS share if the price of the common stock was less than or equal to $31.50, or $31.50 worth of common stock per PERCS share if the common stock was above that price.

As was usual with preferred stock, Avon would not be able to pay its common dividend at any time its preferred dividend was in arrears. In addition, this preferred stock included a restriction providing that Avon could never pay a common dividend of $1.50 or more per share per year unless it first redeemed the preferred.

Mr. Waldron felt confident that the financial markets would understand the new security. Third-party issuers had successfully marketed at least one product similar to the

---

1   Short-term U.S. Treasury notes were paying about 8.2% per year at that time.

2   The redemption price would be $34.75 per share, plus accrued dividends, for the quarter starting June 1, 1988. It would decline by 25 cents per share for each quarter thereafter through the quarter beginning March 1, 1991. The redemption price would fall to $31.75 per share on June 1, 1991, and then to $31.50 per share on June 1, 1991. The company would have the option of redeeming the preferred for either cash or common shares.

PERCS, Americus Trust PRIME units. An Americus Trust was a corporation whose sole asset was common stock of a particular company. The basic idea was that shareholders of that company placed their shares in the trust, which issued two units, called a PRIME and a SCORE, against each share. The PRIME units received all the dividends the stock earned; the SCORE units received no dividends. At a predetermined terminal date, the trust would liquidate the shares it held. The PRIME holders would receive the value of the shares up to a certain predetermined level, and the SCORE holders would receive any excess. The PERCS might appeal to investors who would buy PRIMEs.

Mr. Waldron realized that he would need to convince his colleagues on the board that the terms of the offer would be fair to all the company's shareholders and also appealing to those who especially desired high dividends. Avon's stock closed at $24.125 per share on June 1, 1988. Exhibit 6 gives the June 1 closing prices of options on Avon's stock which were listed on the Chicago Board Options Exchange.

Exhibit 1   Ten-Year Financial Summary, 1978–1987 (million of dollars except per share data)

	1978	1979	1980	1981	1982	1983	1984	1985	1986	1987
Net sales	$2,014.7	$2,377.5	$2,569.1	$2,613.8	$3,000.8	$3,000.1	$3,141.3	$2,470.1	$2,883.1	$2,762.5
Cost of sales	721.0	899.7	959.9	1,018.1	1,278.7	1,290.1	1,330.4	959.5	1,034.0	980.3
Marketing, distribution, administrative expenses	859.5	1,034.8	1,169.4	1,199.2	1,306.8	1,368.7	1,435.0	1,256.3	1,530.4	1,495.3
Interest expense, net	(24.5)	(33.4)	(39.8)	(49.3)	(7.2)	4.3	19.3	16.9	38.6	46.2
Other (income) expense, net	2.7	(3.8)	7.3	.1	30.5	26.8	20.4	13.1	6.5	(143.8)
Total expenses	1,558.7	1,897.3	2,096.8	2,168.1	2,608.8	2,689.9	2,805.1	2,245.8	2,609.5	2,378.0
Pre-tax earnings from continuing operations	456.0	480.2	472.3	445.7	392.0	310.2	336.2	224.3	273.6	384.5
Income taxes	228.1	229.5	231.0	225.8	195.4	145.8	154.5	96.1	114.9	146.3
Net earnings from continuing operations	227.9	250.7	241.3	219.9	196.6	164.4	181.7	128.2	158.7	238.2
Discontinued operations										
Net earnings (loss)	—	—	—	—	—	—	—	34.9	–	(55.4)
(Loss) on sale, net	—	—	—	—	—	—	—	(223.0)	–	(23.7)
Net earnings (loss)	$227.9	$250.7	$241.3	$219.9	$196.6	$164.4	$181.7	$(59.9)	$158.7	$159.1
No. of common share (millions)	58.16	60.14	60.15	60.15	71.46	74.49	83.84	79.35	71.65	71.65
Net earnings per share	3.92	4.17	4.01	3.66	2.75	2.21	2.16	(.76)	2.23	2.26
Cash dividend per share	2.55	2.75	2.95	3.00	2.50	2.00	2.00	2.00	2.00	2.00
Cash, short-term investments	$339.6	$307.0	$308.4	257.8	$161.2	$183.7	$124.5	$86.1	$80.2	$73.8
Net property and equipment	285.7	382.2	465.8	518.3	729.6	760.4	807.7	666.4	743.2	637.5
Capital expenditures	74.8	116.3	117.7	114.2	128.9	128.3	140.5	91.2	120.5	90.8
Total assets	1,226.1	1,406.0	1,571.4	1,567.8	2,233.2	2,285.5	2,437.7	2,289.0	2,296.3	2,559.2
Long-term debt	3.1	4.1	2.6	4.8	297.3	318.4	440.5	617.8	709.2	816.4
Shareholders' equity	738.4	857.2	921.2	933.0	1,219.4	1,204.2	1,157.1	926.4	681.3	758.6
Return on equity	30.9%	29.2%	26.2%	23.6%	16.1%	13.7%	15.7%	–	23.3%	21.0%

Exhibit 2   Line-of-Business Data, 1982–1987 (millions of dollars)

1982

	Net Sales	Pre-tax Earnings	Identifiable Assets
Cosmetics, fragrances, toiletries	$1,998.0	$279.8	$969.1
Fashion jewelry, accessories	338.3	61.9	185.J
Health care	340.6	52.7	713.3
Direct response	124.3	17.1	32.4
Fine jewelry, tableware	114.6	6.7	111.2
Other	86.9	7.5	87.3
Corporate, eliminations	(1.9)	(10.4)	134.1
Consolidated	$3,000.8	$415.3	$2,233.2

1983

	Net Sales	Pre-Tax Earnings	Identifiable Assets
Cosmetics, fragrances, toiletries	$1,884.3	$219.8	$945.7
Fashion jewelry, accessories	330.2	43.5	166.7
Health care	402.2	63.6	747.6
Direct response	144.0	11.7	55.7
Fine jewelry, tableware	124.6	8.1	127.8
Other	119.7	14.2	87.8
Corporate, eliminations	(4.9)	(19.6)	154.5
Consolidated	$3,001.1	$341.3	$2,285.8

1984

	Net Sales	Pre-tax Earnings	Identifiable Assets
Cosmetics, fragrances, toiletries	$1,832.3	$237.2	$932.9
Fashion jewelry, accessories	350.9	55.0	201.3
Health care	542.9	91.7	961.3
Direct response	186.0	2.9	100.2
Other	234.3	11.7	142.5
Corporate, eliminations	(5.1)	(22.6)	99.5
Consolidated	$3,141.3	$375.9	$2,437.7

1985

	Net Sales	Pre-Tax Earnings	Identifiable Assets
Cosmetics, fragrances, toiletries	$1,609.6	$192.3	$963.2
Fashion jewelry, accessories	394.2	42.3	244.2
Health care	260.3	51.2	315.6
Direct response	205.2	8.8	128.8
Discontinued operations	–	–	524.9
Corporate, eliminations	.8	(40.3)	112.3
Consolidated	$2,470.1	$254.3	$2,289.0

1986

	Net Sales	Pre-tax Earnings	Identifiable Assets
Cosmetics, fragrances, toiletries	$1,923.8	$236.8	$1,089.1
Fashion jewelry, accessories	310.0	45.0	204.1
Health care	431.8	65.0	731.9
Direct response	216.2	11.6	139.7
Other	1.3	–	.7
Corporate, eliminations	–	(39.7)	130.8
Consolidated	$2,883.1	$318.7	$2,296.3

1987

	Net Sales	Pre-Tax Earnings	Identifiable Assets
Cosmetics, fragrances, toiletries	$1,807.9	$251.3	$1,385.5
Gift and decorative	412.3	54.6	157.0
Fashion jewelry, accessories	375.2	45.7	237.3
Health care	167.1	10.1	396.5
Discontinued operations	–	–	253.4
Corporate, eliminations	–	22.8	129.5
Consolidated	$2,762.5	$384.5	$2,559.2

Exhibit 3   Balance Sheets, 1986 and 1987 (millions of dollars)

	1986	1987
Cash and equivalents	$80.2	$73.8
Accounts receivable (less allowance)	371.6	310.5
Inventories	410.1	398.6
Prepaid expense and other current	184.8	144.1
Current assets	1,046.7	927.0
Total property and equipment	1,132.4	1,046.4
Less, accumulated depreciation	389.2	408.9
Net property and equipment	743.2	637.5
Net assets of discounted operation	–	253.4
Other assets	506.4	741.3
Total assets	$2,296.3	$2,559.2
Short-term debt	$110.2	$62.4
Accounts payable	169.0	196.1
Accruals	211.0	277.7
Taxes payable	182.7	222.6
Current liabilities	672.9	758.8
Long-term debt	709.2	816.4
Other liabilities	66.2	117.3
Deferred income taxes	166.7	108.1
Net worth	681.3	758.6
Total liabilities and net worth	$2,296.3	$2,559.2

Exhibit 4   Stock Price Performance, 1978–1988

	Price			Average Weekly Volume (000 shares)	S & P 500
	High	Low	Closing		
1978	$63	$43⅞	$50¾	373.5	96.11
1979	56	37¼	39⅜	420.5	107.94
1980	40¾	31⅛	34⅛	570.0	136.76
1981	42⅜	29⅛	30	491.4	122.55
1982	30½	19⅜	26¾	992.7	140.64
1983	36⅞	21¼	25⅛	1,277.2	164.93
1984	26	19¼	21⅞	1,229.2	167.24
1985	29	17⅞	27⅝	1,572.4	211.28
1986					
First Quarter	34	25¾	33½	1,319.6	238.90
Second	36⅜	30¾	35¾	1,217.6	250.84
Third	36⅛	31¼	32⅞	1,026.2	231.22
Fourth	34⅝	27	27	1,296.7	242.17
1987					
First	32½	26¼	31⅛	1,769.3	291.70
Second	35	28¾	33¾	1,577.2	304.00
Third	35⅝	32⅞	35⅛	1,503.6	321.83
Fourth	35	19¼	25¾	1,345.8	247.08
1988					
First	28⅜	22⅝	24⅛	1,369.1	258.89
Second (through 6/1)	26¼	22⅝	24⅛	1,310.9	266.69

Note: As of June 1, 1988, the historical volatility of Avon stock was 31.3% per year over the previous six months and 35.5% per year over the previous three months.

Exhibit 5 Twenty-Five Largest Institutional Shareholders

	Shares Purchased or Sold Jan. 1–Mar. 31, 1988	Shares Held Mar. 31, 1988	Percent of Total Avon Shares Outstanding	Primary Investment Objectives of Owner
Delaware Management Co.	-1,489,400	4,467,900	6.3%	Yield
United Banks of Colorado	0	3,603,425	5.1	Turnaround
Lazard Freres & Co.	0	3,515,800	4.9	Yield
Barrow Hanley Mewhinney	1,665,500	3,487,300	4.9	Yield
PNC Financial Corp.	0	1,618,037	2.3	Mixed
Wells Fargo Bank N.A.	0	1,479,546	2.1	Index
Scudder, Stevens & Clark	0	1,443,733	2.0	Mixed
New York St. Common Ref.	0	1,202,200	1.7	Index
Irving Trust Company	0	1,136,781	1.6	Mixed
Lord Abbett & Company	0	1,090,200	1.5	Yield
Bankers Trust NY Corp.	211,025	934,856	1.3	Index
Dreyfus Corporation	0	884,700	1.2	Mixed
Capital Research & Mgmt.	0	800,000	1.1	Mixed
Center Bancorporation	0	770,783	1.1	Mixed
Amsouth Bancorporation	0	764,343	1.1	Mixed
College Retire. Equities	−165,700	712,000	1.0	Index
Dean Witter Reynolds Int.	0	700,090	1.0	Mixed
Mellon Bank Corporation	0	699,693	1.0	Index
Eaton Vance Management	0	650,000	.9	Mixed
E. I. du Pont de Nemours	382,600	598,760	.8	Mixed
General Electric Master Ret.	0	596,800	.8	Mixed
Hagler Mastrovita & Hewitt	−175,600	520,300	.7	Mixed
California Public Empl. Ref.	0	499,000	.7	Index
American National B&T	0	494,275	.7	Index
Chase Manhattan Corp.	12,400	489,695	.7	Mixed
Total	+440,825	33,160,217	46.5%	
		Yield	17.6%	
		Turnaround	5.1	
		Mixed	15.3	
		Index	8.5	
			46.5%	

Source: 13-F filings with the Securities and Exchange Commission.

Exhibit 6   Chicago Board Option Exchange, Listed Options Trading, Closing Prices, June 1, 1988

Strike Price	Calls			Strike Price	Puts		
	June	July	October		June	July	October
$22½	$2	r	$3⅛	$22½	$3/16	r	$1 1/16
$25	$7/16	$⅞	$1 13/16	$25	r	$1⅞	$2½
$30	r	$¼	$9/16	$30	r	r	r

r = not traded that day.

The closing price for Avon Products common stock on June 1, 1988, was $24 ⅛.

Note: An option is a contract giving the holder the right, but not the obligation, to buy or sell a given asset at a specified price (the *exercise price* or *strike price*) on or before a given date (the *exercise date* or *expiration date*). A *call* option gives the holder the right to buy, while a *put* option gives the holder the right to sell. The right is valuable, and options on many stocks are traded on organized exchanges. Exchange-listed options like these expire on the Saturday after the third Friday of the month indicated. A contract represents an option on 100 shares. The entries in the table give the prices (sometimes called option *premia*) of the options themselves, per share of Avon stock. Thus, one June 25 call option contract gives the holder the right to buy 100 shares of Avon stock for $25 per share on or before Saturday, June 18, 1988. Such a contract traded on June 1 for $43.75, which is $7/16 × 100. Tables like this one for most exchange-listed options appear daily in financial publications, including *The Wall Street Journal* and the business section of the *New York Times*.

CONTINGENT CLAIMS ANALYSIS

Contingent Claims Analysis (CCA) is a technique for determining the price of a security whose payoffs depend upon the prices of one or more other securities.[1] It can, for example, be used to determine the value of a convertible bond in terms of the price of the underlying stock into which the bond can be converted. It can also be used to estimate the value of the flexibility associated with a multipurpose production facility. As suggested by these brief examples, the technique is wide ranging in that it can fruitfully be applied to a number of tactical and strategic corporate financial decision problems.

The origins of CCA are found in the theory of option pricing. While formal approaches to the evaluation of call and put options can be traced back to at least the turn of the century, the major breakthrough came in a 1973 paper by Fisher Black and Myron Scholes. The Black and Scholes analysis contains a qualitative insight which may prove to be of even greater practical significance than their famous quantitative formula: Namely, *corporate liabilities, in general, can be viewed as combinations of simple option contracts.* This insight provides a unified framework in which to view the structure of corporate liabilities and implies that option pricing models can be used to price corporate securities. Such generalized option pricing models are the quantitative foundation for Contingent Claims Analysis.

This note presents an overview of CCA and its application to a variety of corporate financial problems. The focus is on providing a functional understanding of the technique. The balance of this introduction, together with the following section, "Corporate Liabilities as Options," develops the basic concepts and presents in greater detail the historical development of CCA. The balance of the note is devoted to applications of CCA broken down roughly along temporal lines: The section entitled "The Black and Scholes Option Pricing Model" represents the "past" in the sense of applications that are firmly

---

1   Portions of this note are excerpted from "The Role of Contingent Claims Analysis in Corporate Finance" by Scott P. Mason and Robert C. Merton, which appears in *Recent Advances in Corporate Finance*, edited by Edward Altman and Marti Subrahmanyam, Richard D. Irwin, 1985.

---

established in financial practice. "Contingent Claim Analysis and the Pricing of Corporate Liabilities" is the "present" in terms of those applications which are state-of-the-art in financial practice. Finally, "The Role of CCA in Capital Budgeting Decisions" discusses those applications which are by and large still in the development stage within academic research but which hold forth the promise of becoming a part of financial practice in the future.

There are two basic types of options: the call option, which gives its owner the right to buy a specified asset at a specified price on or before a specified date, and the put option, which gives its owner the right to sell a specified asset at a specified price on or before a specified date.[2] Recently, with Intel stock trading at $62¾ per share on the NASDAQ National Market, the Chicago Board Options Exchange (CBOE) was trading both calls and puts written on 100 shares of Intel stock with an exercise price of $70 per share and a maturity of five months. The calls were trading for $325 and the puts for $988. These options have value because they are "rights," not obligations, to transact in the Intel stock. The owner of the Intel call options will only exercise his or her right to purchase Intel stock in five months if the price then exceeds $70. The Intel put options owner will only exercise his or her right to sell Intel stock in five months if the price is then below $70. The value of the options is contingent upon the value of Intel stock, i.e., the options are contingent claims.

To understand how the concept of contingent claims is related to corporate liabilities, imagine a firm's "economic" balance sheet. The left-hand side of the balance sheet represents the economic value of the firm, while the right-hand side lists the economic value of all of the firm's liabilities. For example, consider the particularly simple firm that has only two classes of liabilities: equity and a zero-coupon bond that matures in one year with a promised principal of $10 million. One year from now, if the value of the firm exceeds $10 million, then the firm will retire the debt and the equity will be worth the difference between the value of the firm and $10 million. However, if the value of the firm is less than $10 million, the firm will then default. In such an event, the equity will be worth zero and the debt will be worth the value of the firm. Thus, the value of both the equity and debt is contingent upon the value of the firm; i.e., equity and debt are also contingent claims.

Black and Scholes demonstrate that corporate liabilities can be viewed as combinations of simple options contracts. "Corporate Liabilities as Options" demonstrates the generality of this insight and the important fact that this correspondence is not dependent on any particular option pricing model. Black and Scholes are able to derive their option

---

2   Options can be of either American or European type. An American-type option allows exercise on or before the expiration date, while a European-type option allows exercise only on the expiration date.

pricing model because of the additional important observation that it is possible to replicate options using the underlying stock and the risk-free asset.

"The Black and Scholes Option Pricing Model" describes the replication argument. By combining the results of this section and "Corporate Liabilities as Options," it is possible to quantify the characterization of corporate liabilities as combinations of simple option contracts. The section following describes CCA as a generalization of the Black and Scholes insights and discusses the pricing of several simple corporate securities. The final section of this case describes the potential role of CCA in capital budgeting decisions and the characterization of a project's strategic value as a series of "operating options."

CORPORATE LIABILITIES AS OPTIONS: THE BASIC CONCEPTS

To see the correspondence between corporate liabilities and options, it is first necessary to understand the most fundamental options: calls and puts. An American call option, whose price is denoted by C, gives its owner the right to purchase one share of stock, with current price S, at an exercise price X, on or before an expiration date that is T time periods from now. The call option owner will only exercise his or her right to buy if it is to his or her advantage. Figure 1 depicts the value of the call option as it depends on the stock price on the expiration date. Should the stock price on the expiration date be less than the exercise price, then the call option owner will not exercise his or her right to purchase the stock and the option will expire worthless, i.e., $C = 0$. If, however, the stock price is greater than the exercise price, then the call option will be worth $S - X$, the difference between the stock price and the exercise price. Thus, at the expiration date, the value of the call option is

$$C = \max(S - X, 0) \tag{1}$$

Expression (1) says that the value of the call option at expiration is the maximum of $(S - X)$ and 0. Expression (1) is also true for European call options, which only allow for exercise on the expiration date, $C = \max(S - X, 0)$, since at expiration an American and European option are identical.

An American put option, P, gives its owner the right to sell one share of stock S, at an exercise price X, on or before its expiration date T periods from now. Again, the put option owner will only exercise his or her right to sell if it is to his or her advantage. Figure 2 depicts the value of the put option on its expiration date.

Figure 1   Structure of Payoff to Call Option

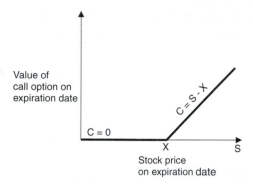

Value of call option on expiration date

C = 0

C = S - X

X

S

Stock price on expiration date

Figure 2   Structure of Payoff to Put Option

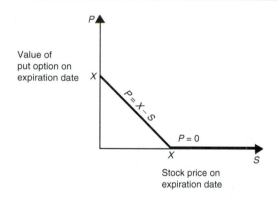

Value of put option on expiration date

P

X

P = X - S

P = 0

X

S

Stock price on expiration date

If the stock price on the expiration date is greater than the exercise price, the put option owner will not exercise his or her right to sell the stock and the put option will expire worthless, $P = 0$. However, should the stock price be less than the exercise price, the put option owner will then exercise his or her right to sell the stock, and the put option will be worth $X - S$, the difference between the exercise price and the stock price. Thus, at the expiration date, the value of the put option is

$$P = \max(X - S, 0) \tag{2}$$

Expression (2) says that the value of the put option at expiration is the maximum of ($X - S$) and 0. Figure 2 makes it clear why puts are often characterized as insurance since they pay off when "things go badly," i.e., when the stock price is low. Expression (2) is also true for European puts, $p = \max(X - S, 0)$, because American and European options have identical values at expiration.

An important relationship between European call and put prices can be derived from Figures 1 and 2. Consider an investment position, I_1, which has purchased a European call and sold a European put on the same stock, with the same exercise price and expiration date. Therefore,

$$I_1 = c - p \tag{3}$$

The value of this investment position at expiration of the options is depicted in Figure 3.

Figure 3   Structure of Payoff to Call-Put Position

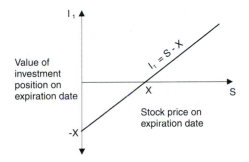

The value of the investment position on the expiration date is $S - X$, the difference between the stock price and the exercise price. The investment can have negative value if the stock price is below the exercise price because the call will expire worthless and the put will be exercised against its seller. However, there is another investment position, I_2, involving no options that can replicate the payoff depicted in Figure 3. Consider buying one share of stock, S, and borrowing on a discount basis X dollars for T time periods at rate r, i.e., the proceeds from the loan will be $X/(1 + r)^T$ allowing for discounting. Therefore

$$I_2 = S - \frac{X}{(1 + r)^T} \tag{4}$$

In T periods, the value of this position will be $I_2 = S - X$, since the position owns one share of stock and owes X dollars. But, if I_1 and I_2 have precisely the same value at some future date, then it must be true that the initial net investment necessary to establish the positions be the same.

$$c - p = S - \frac{X}{(1+r)^T} \tag{5}$$

Expression (5) is known as "put-call parity." The equation simply says that prices in the call, put, stock, and lending markets must be such that (5) is always true. If this was not the case, traders would simply buy the lower-priced alternative and sell the higher priced alternative, and earn an immediate riskless return on zero net investment.[3]

With these fundamental options properties as background, the correspondence between options and corporate liabilities can now be established. Consider Figure 4, the economic balance sheet of a simple firm that has only two liabilities, equity E and a single issue of zero coupon debt D where the equity receives no dividends and the firm will issue no new securities while the debt is outstanding.

Figure 4   Firm's Economic Balance Sheet

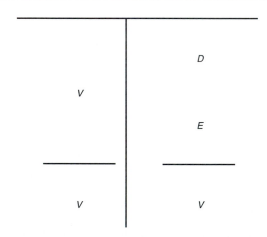

The left-hand side of the balance sheet represents the economic value, V, of the firm. The right-hand side lists the economic value of all the liabilities of the firm.

Figures 5 and 6 depict the value of equity and risky debt as they depend on the value of the firm on the maturity date of the debt. If, on the debt's maturity date, the value of the firm is greater than the promised principal, $V > B$, then the debt will be paid off, $D = B$,

---

3   Expression (5) is true only for European options written on a stock paying no dividends.

and the equity will be worth $V - B$. However, if the value of the firm is less than the promised principal, $V < B$, then the equity will be worthless, $E = 0$, since it is preferable to surrender the firm to the debtholders, $D = V$, than to repay the debt.

Figure 5   Structure of Payoff to Equity

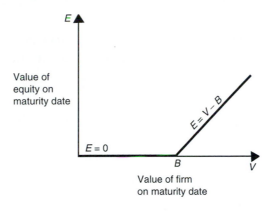

Figure 6   Structure of Payoff to Debt

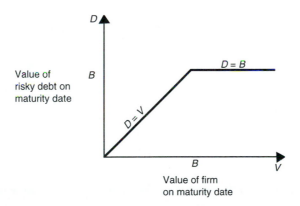

Thus, on the maturity date of the debt, the value of equity can be represented as

$$E = \max(V - B, 0) \qquad (6)$$

Expression (6) says that the value of equity on the debt's maturity date is the maximum of the difference between the value of the firm and the promised principal payment and zero. The value of the risky debt D on its maturity date can be represented as

$$D = \min(V,B) \tag{7}$$

Expression (7) says that the value of the risky debt on its maturity date is the minimum of V and B. Both equity and risky debt are contingent claim securities whose value is contingent on the value of the firm.

It follows immediately from the comparison of (1) and (6) or by inspection of Figures 1 and 5 that equity in the presence of zero coupon risky debt is directly analogous to a European call option written on the firm value V with an exercise price B equal to the debt's promised principal, and an expiration date equal to the maturity date of the debt.

$$E = c \tag{8}$$

In other words, equity can be viewed as a call option with the right to buy the firm for B dollars T time periods from now.

Now, return to the put-call parity result, (5), for options demonstrated earlier. In the characterization of corporate liabilities as options, the value of the firm V is the underlying asset on which the options are written, the debt's promised principal B is the exercise price, and the debt's maturity date is the option's expiration date. With this correspondence in mind, (5) can be rearranged and restated as

$$V = c + \frac{B}{(1 + r)^T} - p \tag{9}$$

But, since the value of the firm is the sum of the value of the equity and the value of the debt,

$$V = E + D \tag{10}$$

and since the value of the equity is given by (8), then it follows that

$$D = \frac{B}{(1+r)^T} - p \tag{11}$$

The value of risky debt is equal to the price of a risk-free bond with the same terms minus the price of a put written on the value of the firm.

Expression (11) has an intuitive interpretation. It is commonly understood that risky debt plus a loan guarantee has the same value as risk-free debt. The loan guarantee is like insurance, i.e., it will pay any shortfall in the value of the firm necessary to fully repay the debt. Figure 7 depicts the value of a loan guarantee G on the maturity date of the risky debt:

Figure 7 Structure of Payoff to Loan Guarantee

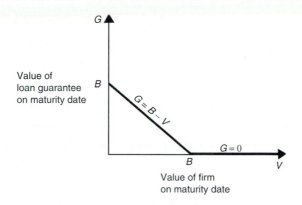

If on the maturity date of the debt the value of the firm is greater than the debt's promised principal, i.e., $V > B$, then the guarantee will pay nothing since the firm is sufficiently valuable to retire the debt. However, if the value of the firm is less than the promised principal, $V < B$, then the guarantor must pay the difference between the promised principal and the value of the firm, $B - V$, in order that the debt be fully repaid. Thus, on the maturity date of the debt, the value of the loan guarantee can be represented as

$$G = \max(B - V, 0) \tag{12}$$

Now compare either (2) and (12) or Figures 2 and 7. It is evident that a loan guarantee is analogous to a European put option written on the value of the firm, i.e., $G = p$, and, therefore, (11) is simply the statement that risky debt plus a loan guarantee is equal to a risk-free bond.

To demonstrate that the characterization of corporate liabilities as options goes much deeper than the simple corporate securities studied so far, assume that the debt receives coupon payments, $\bar{c}$. Equity here can then be thought of as analogous to a European call option on a dividend paying stock where $\bar{c}$ is the "dividend." Now assume the coupon bond is callable under a schedule of prices K. The equity is now analogous to an American call option on a dividend paying stock where the exercise price changes according to the schedule K. Furthermore, the value of the call provision can be characterized as the difference between the value of an American and European call option where the exercise price changes according to K. The value of call protection against redemption for the first $T_1 < T$ time periods can be viewed as the difference between the values of two American call options on a dividend paying stock, where the first call can be exercised at any time according to K and the second call can only be exercised in the last $T - T_1$ time periods. As is evident from these examples, the correspondence between corporate liabilities and options extends to a wide variety of securities and covenants.

As shown, equity, zero-coupon debt, and loan guarantees can be represented as combinations of simple option contracts. The correspondence is, moreover, sufficiently robust that it is possible to characterize many of the complex securities and covenants encountered in practice by similar analogies to basic options. Note that this correspondence is not dependent upon any particular option pricing model, but instead is a fundamental relationship that must hold independently of how options and corporate securities are assumed to be priced. Therefore, given any option pricing model with all its direct implications for pricing stock options, that same model has corresponding direct implications for the pricing of corporate liabilities. Black and Scholes have developed a particularly attractive option pricing model that provides the means for quantifying this qualitative characterization of corporate liabilities as options. The Black and Scholes option pricing model is described below, and the section following it makes explicit the implications of the Black and Scholes option pricing model for the pricing of corporate liabilities.

THE BLACK-SCHOLES OPTION PRICING MODEL[4]

Historically, option pricing models have fallen into two categories, ad hoc models and equilibrium models. Ad hoc models generally rely only upon empirical observation or curve fitting and, therefore, need not reflect any of the price restrictions imposed by economic equilibrium. Equilibrium models deduce option prices as the result of maximizing behavior on the part of market participants. This latter approach to option pricing dates back to the work of Bachelier (1900)[5]. While the economics and mathematics of Bachelier's work are flawed, his research served to point the way for a number of attempts to describe an equilibrium theory of option pricing. All of these early models essentially equate the value of an option to the discounted expected payoff to the option. The expected payoff to the option clearly depends on the assumed probability distribution of future stock prices. In addition, the proper rate to discount the expected payoff to the present must also be specified. Thus, in order to complete these models it is necessary to make specific and typically quite restrictive assumptions about individual risk preferences and/or the pricing structure in market equilibrium. These assumptions limit the generality (and practicality) of these early results.

---

4   See "Option Pricing," HBS Case Services 286-112, for a more complete treatment of the Black and Scholes model.

5   Bachelier, L., "Theory of Speculation" (1900) (translation), reprinted in *Cootner* (1967).

Black-Scholes (1973)[6] derive an equilibrium model of option pricing that avoids restrictive assumptions regarding individual risk preferences and market equilibrium price formation. Black and Scholes demonstrate that it is possible to construct a portfolio involving positions in the stock and the risk-free asset where the return to the portfolio over a short time interval exactly replicates the return to the option. In addition, Black and Scholes show precisely how the composition of the portfolio must continually change in response to movements in the stock price and the passage of time, such that the replication of the return to the option is maintained.

The Black-Scholes insight of replication can be demonstrated with a simple example. Assume that prices move each period in a simple two-state fashion. If the current stock price is S, then the end of the period price must be either S^+ or S^-.

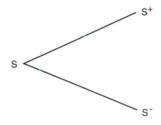

The price of a one-period call option written on this stock with an exercise price X will move in a similar, two-state fashion

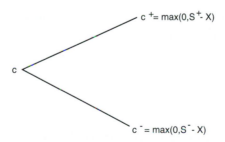

where c^+ is the value of the call option if the end of period stock price is S^+, and c^- is the value of the call option if the end of period stock price is S^-.

Black and Scholes ask, what appropriately levered position in the stock will *perfectly replicate* the payoff to the call option at the end of the period? To find the appropriate stock-borrowing position, consider buying N shares of the stock and partially financing

---

6   Black, F., and M. Scholes, "The Pricing of Options and Corporate Liabilities," *Journal of Political Economy*, 81 (1973), 637–659.

this purchase through borrowings of b dollars at an interest rate of r. The cost today of such a position is $NS - b$. At the end of one period of time, this position will be worth either of two amounts depending on the end of period stock price. The possible outcomes are

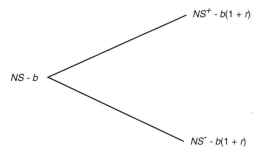

In order to perfectly replicate the call option, N and b must be chosen in such a way that no matter what the end of period stock price is, the payoff to the levered position will exactly match the payoff to the call option. In other words, for what N and b is it true that

$$NS^+ - (1 + r)b = c^+$$
$$NS^- - (1 + r)b = c^-$$

Solving the equations for N and b

$$N = \frac{c^+ - c^-}{S^+ - S^-} \qquad b = \frac{S^- c^+ - S^+ c^-}{(S^+ - S^-)(1 + r)}$$

Therefore, a position of N shares of the stock partially financed by borrowings of b will exactly replicate the payoff to the call option. If this is true then, in order to preclude risk-free arbitrage opportunities, the call option and the levered position in the stock must have the same initial value,

$$c = NS - b$$

To demonstrate, consider the following example. Assume that the current stock price is $S = \$80$ and end-of-period stock prices can be represented as

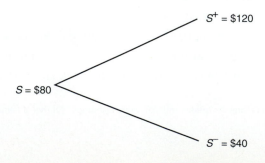

What would be the value of a one-period call option written on one share of the stock with an exercise price of $60 when the one-period interest rate is 20%? The price of the call option will move in a similar two-state fashion.

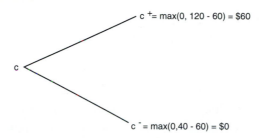

$c^+ = \max(0, 120 - 60) = \$60$

c

$c^- = \max(0, 40 - 60) = \$0$

What levered position in the asset will exactly replicate the payoff to this option? Substituting into the expressions for N and b,

$$N = \frac{c^+ - c^-}{S^+ - S^-} = \frac{60 - 0}{120 - 40} = .75$$

$$b = \frac{S^- c^+ - S^+ c^-}{(S^+ - S^-)(1 + r)} = \frac{40(60) - 120(0)}{(120 - 40)(1.2)} = \$25$$

Thus, if you buy .75 shares of the stock and partially finance the purchase by borrowing $25, then you have established that levered position in the stock that will exactly replicate the end of period payoff to the call option.

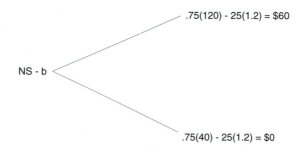

$.75(120) - 25(1.2) = \$60$

NS - b

$.75(40) - 25(1.2) = \$0$

Since prices today must be set to preclude risk-free arbitrage, the value of the call must be equal to the value of the levered position in the stock

$$c = NS - b$$
$$= .75(80) - 25$$
$$= \$35$$

While the actual mathematics underlying the Black and Scholes model are more complex than this simple model, the economics of the Black and Scholes model is essentially the replication or arbitrage argument presented here.

CONTINGENT CLAIM ANALYSIS AND THE PRICING OF CORPORATE LIABILITIES

The traditional approach to the pricing of corporate liabilities is exemplified by the organizational structure of a typical, vintage corporate finance textbook: a chapter on the pricing of equity; a chapter on long-term debt; a chapter on preferred stock; a chapter on warrants and convertible securities; etc. Each chapter employs a different valuation technique and rarely, if ever, are any attempts made to integrate the various components of the firm's capital structure as even a check on the internal consistency of these diverse valuation methodologies. In contrast, the contemporary CCA approach to the pricing of corporate liabilities begins with the firm's total capital structure and uses a single evaluation technique to simultaneously price each of the individual components of that structure. Thus, the CCA methodology takes into account the interactive effects of each of the securities on the prices of all the others and ensures a consistent evaluation procedure for the entire capital structure. In short, the pricing of corporate liabilities becomes a single chapter (albeit, a long one).

The development of the CCA approach began when it was first recognized that the payoff structures of risky discount debt and levered equity are identical to the structure of simple call and put option strategies. These basic corporate liabilities can, therefore, be priced using the call and put option formulas derived by Black and Scholes. With this insight, further demonstrations followed rather rapidly, showing that the same valuation procedure can be used to price multiple issues of coupon bonds as well as convertible securities and warrants. The procedure can, moreover, accommodate further refinements such as call provisions, sinking fund requirements, and other covenants frequently required in the indentures of corporate securities.

Merton (1977)[7] showed that the return to any corporate liability can be replicated using an investment strategy similar to the one demonstrated previously for options. Again, a simple binomial example will demonstrate the point. Assume that a firm is totally capitalized with equity and zero coupon debt. The equity receives no dividends and the debt is due its principal B at the end of one time period. Lastly, assume that the value V of the firm moves in a simple two-state fashion.

---

7   Merton, R. C. "On the Pricing of Contingent Claims and the Modigliani Miller Theorem," *Journal of Financial Economics*, 15, No. 2 (1977b), 241–250.

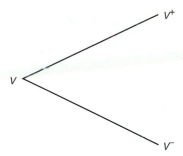

Given the payoff structure to the equity and debt, (6) and (7), their values will both move in a similar two-state fashion

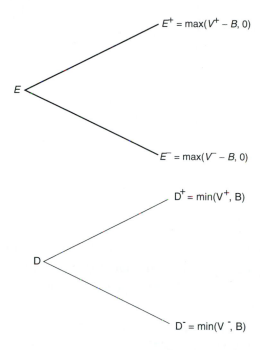

where E^+ (D^+) is the value of the equity (debt) if the end-of-period firm value is V^+, and E^-(D^-) is the value of the equity (debt) if the end-of-period firm value is V^-.

Merton shows that for *any* corporate security there is a portfolio comprised of a position in the entire firm V and borrowings that will replicate the security's payoff. For example, what levered position in the firm will exactly replicate the payoff to risky debt? The levered position of N amount of the firm and borrowings of b at a rate of r will be worth either of two amounts at the end of one time period.

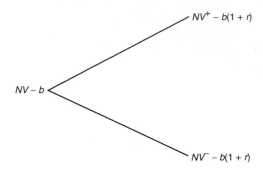

In order to replicate the payoff to the risky debt, N and b must be chosen such that

$$NV^+ - (1+r)b = D^+$$
$$NV^- - (1+r)b = D^-$$

Solving for N and b

$$N = \frac{D^+ - D^-}{V^+ - V^-} \qquad b = \frac{V^- D^+ - V^+ D^-}{(V^+ - V^-)(1+r)}$$

Therefore, a portfolio of N amount of the firm and borrowings of b will replicate the payoff to risky debt. If this is true, then to avoid arbitrage,

$$D = NV - b$$

the cost of establishing either position must be the same.

To demonstrate with an example, assume that the debt has a principal amount of $100 and the risk-free rate of interest over the time period is $r = 10\%$. Let the current value of the firm V be $100, and the possible end-of-period values be

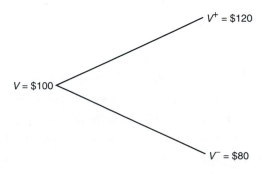

Then the risky debt will move in the following fashion

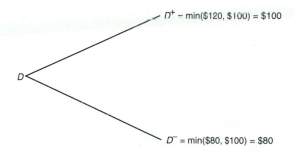

What portfolio will replicate this payoff? Substituting into the expressions for N and b

$$N = \frac{D^+ - D^-}{V^+ - V^-} = \frac{100 - 80}{120 - 80} = .5$$

$$b = \frac{V^- D^+ - V^+ D^-}{(V^+ - V^-)(1 + r)} = \frac{80(100) - 120(80)}{(120-80)(1.1)} = -\$36.36$$

Therefore, a portfolio comprised of one-half of the firm and *lending* $36.36 will replicate the payoff to the risky debt. To check this

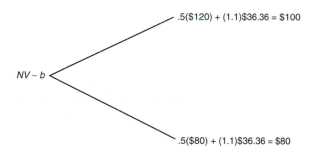

Since the payoff to this portfolio is the same as the payoff to the risky debt, the initial cost of either alternative must be the same:

$$\begin{aligned} D &= NV-b \\ &= .5(100) + 36.36 \\ &= \$86.36 \end{aligned}$$

As an exercise, work through the portfolio argument for the equity and confirm its value must be

$$\begin{aligned} E &= V - D \\ &= 100 - 86.36 \\ &= \$13.64 \end{aligned}$$

What portfolio of equity and riskless lending will replicate the payoff to risky discount debt?

While the evaluation of levered equity and risky debt for the simple firm considered above is instructive, the more practical interest in CCA evolves from its ability to handle many of the complexities encountered with more realistic securities and capital structures. For example, Merton (1974)[8] describes the valuation of callable coupon debt in the presence of equity that is receiving a dividend. Another interesting application of CCA to complex securities is the evaluation of callable convertible debt. The CCA formulation of this problem is due to Ingersoll (1976)[9] and Brennan and Schwartz (1977).[10] Other examples of CCA research include the work of Galai and Masulis (1976)[11] on the effects of mergers, acquisitions, scale expansions, and spin-offs on the relative values of levered equity and risky debt; Black and Cox (1976)[12] on the evaluation of specific bond indentures such as safety covenants, subordination agreements, and restrictions on the financing of payouts; and Jones, Mason, and Rosenfeld (1984)[13] on the theory and empirical testing of the CCA valuation of capital structures comprised of multiple callable coupon bonds with sinking funds.

The CCA model captures in a quantitative fashion what practitioners have long known to be the major determinants of value for corporate liabilities: (1) business risk, (2) financial risk, (3) level of interest rates, and (4) covenants. The notion of business risk is captured directly by the volatility of the rate of return to the firm. Clearly the value, and riskiness, of a firm's liabilities is in part driven by the riskiness of its assets. CCA captures financial risk through knowledge of the value of the firm V and the amount and timing of mandatory payouts. Two firms may have the same value and business risk, but the more levered firm's debt will be worth less. The model is given a direct indication of the level of interest rates through the specification of r, the riskless rate of interest. Lastly, a security's covenants, e.g., callability, convertibility, etc., are also fully recognized.

---

8   Merton, R. C., "On the Pricing of Corporate Debt: The Risk Structure of Interest Rates," *Journal of Finance*, 19, No. 2 (1974), 449–470.

9   Ingersoll, J. E., "A Contingent Claims Valuation of Convertible Securities," *Journal of Financial Economics*, 4, No. 3 (1977), 269–322.

10 Brennan, M. J., and E. S. Schwartz, "Convertible Bonds: Valuation and Optimal Strategies for Call and Conversion," *Journal of Finance*, 32, No. 5 (1977a), 1699–1715.

11 Galai, D., and R. W. Masulis, "The Option Pricing Model and the Risk Factor of Stock," *Journal of Financial Economics*, 3, (1976), 53–81.

12 Black, F., and J. C. Cox, "Valuing Corporate Securities: Some Effects of Bond Indenture Provisions," *Journal of Finance*, 17, No. 2 (1976), 351–367.

13 Jones E. P., S. P. Mason, and E. Rosenfeld, "Contingent Claims Analysis of Corporate Capital Structures: An Empirical Investigation," Journal of Finance, 3, (1984).

CCA, in its more general application, also provides many of the same advantages of the original Black-Scholes option pricing model in that many of the inputs required in the evaluation formula are directly observable. Mandatory payouts, maturities, and covenants are easily determined from indenture provisions. The risk-free rate r is also observable. The volatility of the return to the firm can be estimated from a time series of firm values. Again, as with the Black-Scholes model, the CCA model does not depend on the expected rate of return on the firm, nor are any assumptions concerning individual risk preferences or market equilibrium necessary.

As is evident from our examples, much research work has been done with CCA in the area of pricing corporate liabilities. There is, however, still much development work to do before its full practical potential can be realized. To date, applications in the financial community have been focused on the pricing of convertible and other equity-type securities, and on pricing the call option component of essentially default-free debt. Empirical testing of the model's accuracy in pricing complex capital structures is just beginning. With these developments, CCA will become an increasingly more useful tool for analyzing corporate liability strategy and planning. The capability to simulate a virtually unlimited range of financial packages presents the opportunity to determine the firm's most efficient capital structure. The cost in terms of reduced flexibility caused by the terms and covenants of financial instruments can be explicitly evaluated. The trade-offs between tax shields, financial distress, and the corporate need for additional funds under various contingencies can also be analyzed. Indeed, perhaps the most important application of CCA will turn out to be in the strategy and planning activities surrounding the combined capital budgeting and financing decision problem.

THE ROLE OF CCA IN CAPITAL BUDGETING DECISIONS

For more than a generation, finance academics have taught the net present value method as the correct procedure to use in making capital budgeting decisions. If recent survey statistics are accurate, then this view is also widely shared in practice where apparently the majority of corporations now use some version of discounted cash flow analysis to evaluate their projects. Nevertheless, these capital budgeting techniques have their critics, with some of the sharpest criticisms coming from those in business policy and strategy. As an example, Hayes and Garvin (1982)[14] assert that discounted cash flow methods cause a systematic undervaluation of projects because, among other reasons, the strategic value of projects is ignored. As an alternate and more direct remedy of this claimed undervaluation

---

14   Hayes, R. H., and D. A. Garvin, "Managing as If Tomorrow Mattered," *Harvard Business Review*, 50, No. 3 (1982), 70–79.

bias, Hayes and Garvin suggest that major investment decisions simply be made on the basis of judgment and strategic considerations alone, without subjecting them to the "distortions" of quantitative methods at all.

One does not have to embrace the suggested solution of Hayes and Garvin to accept as a valid concern that current capital budgeting practices fail to properly account for all the important sources of value associated with a specific project. Such failures, when they occur, reflect the shortcomings of the particular evaluation technique used and not the quantitative approach itself. In this final section of the note, the potential of CCA is explored to correct some of these shortcoming, and CCA is shown to be especially well-suited to the task of evaluating what strategists call the "flexibility" of a project.

Although not a precisely defined technical term, the flexibility of a project is nothing more (or less) than a description of the options made available to management as part of the project. Baldwin, Mason, and Ruback (1983)[15] call such options "operating options." As an example, the management of an electric utility faces a choice between building a power plant that burns only oil and one that can burn either oil or coal. Although the latter costs more to build, it also provides greater flexibility because management has the option to select which fuel to use and can switch back and forth, depending upon energy market conditions. In making its choice, management must, therefore, weigh the value of this operating option against its cost.

Operating facilities (such as oil refineries and chemical plants) that can use different mixes of inputs to produce the same output or the same inputs to produce various arrays of outputs are general examples of this type of flexibility. That such options have value has, of course, long been recognized. As a practical matter, however, these option values are rarely incorporated into the capital budgeting process except, perhaps, in a qualitative fashion. With its proven record in valuing financial options, CCA shows great promise for providing the quantitative methods necessary to include explicitly the value of such options as part of the project evaluation procedure. To provide a sense of the range of application, a brief catalog of examples is presented of various operating options that could be evaluated by CCA.

Traditional capital budgeting procedures typically assume that a project will operate in each year of its anticipated lifetime. However, especially for projects involving production facilities, it may not be optimal to operate a plant in a given year because project revenue is not expected to cover variable cost. Explicit recognition of this type of management

---

15 Baldwin, C. Y., S. P. Mason, and R. S. Ruback, "Evaluation of Government Subsidies to Large-Scale Energy Projects: A Contingent Claims Approach," Harvard Business School Working Paper, 83–66 (1983).

flexibility is particularly important when choosing among alternative production technologies with different ratios of variable-to-fixed costs.

Another closely related type of flexibility is the option to expand or contract the scale of the project. Changes in the total output of the project can be achieved by changing the output rate per unit time or by changing the total length of time of the production run. Management may choose, for example, to build production capacity in excess of the expected level of output so that it can produce at a higher rate if the product is more successful than was originally anticipated. Management can also choose to build a facility whose physical life exceeds the expected duration of its use, and thereby provide the firm with the option to produce more output over the life of the project by extending the production period. By choosing a plant with high maintenance costs relative to original construction costs, management gains the flexibility to reduce the life of the plant and contract the scale of the project by reducing expenditures on maintenance.

In addition to the option to temporarily shut down the project, management also has the option to terminate it. The value of this option can be substantial for large capital-intensive projects like nuclear power plants which have long construction periods. It is also important in the evaluation of projects involving new products where their acceptance in the market is uncertain.

Just as the option to abandon can be an important source of flexibility in a project, the option to choose when to initiate a project can be valuable. For example, the purchaser of an offshore oil lease can choose when, if at all, during the lease period to develop the property. An analysis by Paddock, Siegel, and Smith (1982)[16] suggests that this option can represent a significant part of the value of such leases. Their analysis implies, for example, that if the U.S. government was to require immediate development as a condition for granting such leases, then the prices paid for the leases would be considerably less than under current conditions, including, in some cases, no purchases at all.

Much the same analysis would apply to the evaluation of exploration activities. If natural resource companies were somehow committed to produce all resources discovered, then they would never explore in areas where the estimated development and extraction costs exceed the expected future price at which the resource could be sold. However, because they can choose when to initiate such development, it may pay to explore in high production cost areas in order to gain the option to produce if the price of the resource at some later date is higher than was expected.

---

16 Paddock, J. L., D. Siegel, and J. L. Smith, "Valuation of Corporate Bids for Hydrocarbon Leases," Working Paper, Alfred P. Sloan School of Management, MIT, Cambridge, MA (1982).

As discussed in Kester (1984)[17], an important strategic issue is the sequencing of investments in projects, and this, too, can be analyzed in an options-evaluation framework. Examples would be projects involving the production of basic consumer products like soap and light bulbs. In the successful marketing of such products, a brand name plays an important role, not only because of consumer recognition, but also because a brand-name product is more likely to obtain "shelf space" from distributors such as supermarkets. For a firm evaluating projects to produce a number of consumer products, it may be advantageous to implement these projects sequentially instead of simultaneously undertaking them in parallel. By pursuing the development of a single product first, the firm can resolve at least some of the uncertainty surrounding its ability to establish a brand name and can determine the likelihood of obtaining the necessary shelf space for subsequent products. This resolved, management then has the option to proceed or not with the development of these other products. If, instead, these projects were undertaken in parallel, then management would already have spent the resources, and the value of the option not to spend them is lost.

Unlike the previous examples of intraproject options, the sequencing of projects involves the creation of options on one or more projects as the direct result of undertaking another project. Because the standard capital budgeting procedure is to evaluate a project on a "standalone" basis, the value of such interproject options can easily be missed. While neglecting such linkages may cause small errors in the evaluation of some projects, it can cause a significant undervaluation for others. Such a polar case would be research and development projects whose only source of value is the options they create to undertake other projects. More generally, interproject options are created whenever management makes an investment that places the firm in a position to use new technology or to enter a different industry.

As discussed in Myers (1977)[18], option analysis is important to the proper evaluation of a firm's "growth opportunities." As is well known in financial analysis, the value of a firm can exceed the market value of its projects currently in place, because the firm may have the opportunity to earn a return in excess of the competitive rate on some of its future projects. The standard methodology for evaluating such projects is to discount back to the current time their net present values as of the anticipated implementation dates. It, therefore, implicitly assumes that the firm is committed to undertake the projects although, in fact, management need not make such a commitment before the implemen-

---

17 Kester, C., "Growth Options and Investment: Reducing the Guesswork in Strategic Capital Budgeting," *Harvard Business Review* (March/April 1984).

18 Myers, S. C., "Determinants of Corporate Borrowing," *Journal of Financial Economics*, 5, No. 2 (1977), 147–175.

tation date. The standard method, therefore, neglects the value of the option not to go forward if conditions change before the implementation date.

Throughout this sampler of operating options examples, the failure of traditional capital budgeting techniques to properly take into account the value of these options has been noted. Although ignoring any single operating option may not introduce an important error in a project's evaluation, the cumulative error of ignoring all the operating options embedded in that project can cause a significant underestimation of its value. This is not, however, to say that standard techniques systematically and significantly undervalue *all* types of projects. Many classes of projects provide few, if any, operating options, and for others, the cumulative value of all such options will be small. Indeed, by neglecting the option components, these techniques may overestimate the values of some projects by failing to recognize the losses in flexibility to the firm caused by their implementation.

While rejecting the universal condemnation of current capital budgeting procedures expressed by some corporate strategists, we tend to agree with the more selective criticisms expressed by others in that community. As discussed in Myers (1984)[19], the focus of these criticisms is on the evaluation of long-horizon and broadly defined projects whose future profitabilities can only be estimated with great imprecision. It is under just such conditions that taking account of the associated operating options is most important. Hence, for projects of this sort, an evaluation technique that neglects these options can produce significant undervaluations. Moreover, as Myers (1977) has demonstrated, the choice of capital structure for the firm can also significantly affect the value of such projects. Although current capital budgeting procedures typically do make some provision for the tax deductibility of interest paid by the firm, they do not take into account the flexibility of its capital structure. Like operating flexibility, financial flexibility can be measured by the value of the financial options made available to the firm by its choice of capital structure. The interactive effects between financial and operating flexibility can be quite strong for major long-term investment projects involving considerable uncertainty. CCA would, therefore, appear to be a particularly useful tool to the corporate strategist because it provides an integrated analysis of both the operating and financial options associated with the combined investment and financing decision.

---

19   Myers, S. C., "Finance Theory and Financial Strategy," *Interfaces* (January/February, 1984).

ALZA AND BIO-ELECTRO SYSTEMS (A)
TECHNOLOGICAL AND FINANCIAL
INNOVATION

In September 1988, Martin Gerstel, co-chairman and chief executive officer of ALZA Corporation, reread the draft prospectus for the rights offering that would create Bio-Electro Systems, Inc. (BES). This new organizational entity and the drug delivery technologies it would develop would play a key role in the future of ALZA. This very uncertain and risky venture resembled ALZA in its early days, when Gerstel joined the firm in 1968 as its chief financial officer with a newly minted MBA degree from Stanford University. In 1968, ALZA had just been founded, had no products, and was years from earning profits. Two decades later, ALZA was a recognized leader in drug delivery technologies. A few of the products it had developed were among the most successful in the industry, with others under development. ALZA held 342 U.S. patents, generated positive profits and operating cash flow, and was regarded by Wall Street analysts as a relatively low-risk yet high-profit player in the growing pharmaceutical segment.

Mr. Gerstel realized that ALZA's success had spurred its rivals to accelerate their drug delivery development efforts, and that new technologies could significantly affect the company's future. ALZA's continued growth, profitability, technical preeminence, and ability to attract and retain its unique staff depended upon advancing these new drug delivery technologies. Mr. Gerstel and the board of directors of ALZA accepted this imperative but still had to address how to organize and pay for a $40 million new development effort. Months of discussions between him and David Hoffmann, ALZA's vice president and treasurer, had led to the complicated proposal to create BES as a new type of R&D offshoot of ALZA.

The proposal was unique. (Selected excerpts from its 53-page prospectus are given in Exhibit 1.) ALZA would sell common shares in an entity, Bio-Electro Systems, Inc., which would have virtually no employees. BES would contract with ALZA to research and

Joshua Lerner and Peter Tufano prepared this case as the basis for class discussion rather than to illustrate either effective or ineffective handling of an administrative situation.

develop the new technologies. ALZA retained the right to license any products developed, and it held the option to buy out the BES shareholders at a preset schedule of prices. In addition, purchasers of BES shares would receive a warrant allowing them to purchase shares of ALZA common stock for $30 in the next 5 years.

Mr. Gerstel had to determine whether this proposal was the best for ALZA or whether another plan might work better. Should he commit ALZA to an untested financing strategy, or would it be better to fund the initiative from internal resources? Would ALZA shareholders understand this proposal? What was a fair price for the BES share plus warrant package?

THE ROOTS OF ALZA: SYNTEX

ALZA's early history was closely linked with the Syntex Corporation, from which the firm drew its founder and much of its initial credibility.[1] In the 1930s, Dr. Russell Marker, a chemistry professor at Pennsylvania State University and a leading researcher in the synthesis of human hormones, discovered a family of Mexican plants that could easily and cheaply produce human hormones. At the time, steroids and hormones were distilled from animal carcasses and body fluids through a time-consuming and costly process. Dr. Marker's discovery held the promise of making the therapeutic use of human hormones less restricted and costly.

While Dr. Marker was an adept researcher, with over 75 patents and over 160 published articles, he was a less able businessman. Unable to interest any pharmaceutical firm in funding his work, he began his own enterprise in 1943. Within two years, he resigned his university position, moved to Mexico, single-handedly produced a supply of the human hormone progesterone equal to the world's annual production, formed a Mexico City–based company with two European refugees, fought with those partners, and resigned. Rather than buy the rights back from his partners, he set up a competing firm, which soon failed.

Dr. Marker's former partners continued the product development effort by recruiting George Rosenkranz, a Hungarian chemist who had fled to Cuba from Nazi Germany. Mr. Rosenkranz assembled a team of European refugees, Mexican scientists trained in the United States and Mexico, and (increasingly in the 1950s) U.S. academic scientists. From its Mexico City base, Syntex emerged as a center of research in the production of human

---

1   This discussion of Syntex's history is drawn from "Mexican Hormones," *Fortune,* May 1951, pp. 86–90, 161–68; "Syntex Doesn't Want to Rely on the Pill," *Business Week,* May 20, 1972; Syntex Corporation, *A Corporation and a Molecule: The Story of Research at Syntex,* Palo Alto, Syntex, 1966; and discussions with ALZA management.

hormones from plants. In the years after World War II, Syntex produced human hormones at a fraction of the price of animal-derived products.

Syntex's laboratories blossomed, but its business operations were less healthy. During the 1950s the firm derived almost all its revenues from bulk sales of hormones to the major pharmaceutical manufacturers, which then resold them for many times the price they paid Syntex. The conflict between the innovative research and conservative marketing strategy led to a rift between Mr. Rosenkranz and the firm's owners. The conflict was resolved in 1956 when New York investor Charles Allen bought out the firm and installed Mr. Rosenkranz as Syntex's president.

Mr. Allen, founder of the investment bank Allen and Company, had a reputation as one of the most savvy investors in emerging companies. In 1958 he distributed Syntex shares to his investors, thereby turning the firm into a public company. The company sold $2.2 million of additional shares to the public in 1960, and with the capital began building its own marketing force. The firm renegotiated its contracts with the major pharmaceutical houses so that the prices for raw materials were tied to eventual product revenues, in a royalty-like arrangement. By 1963 the firm was profitable and seemed poised for boundless growth as a major supplier of hormones for birth-control pills. Syntex's valuation soared: In late November 1963 the firm commanded a market capitalization of $855 million, even though annual sales and assets were only $16 million each.

Syntex emerged as the first major pharmaceutical firm to be established after World War II. Sales grew steadily, not only of hormones for birth-control pills but also of steroid-based products for treating inflammation and of animal growth hormones. Investors also paid attention to Syntex's creative research organization, which had the capacity for producing a wide variety of products. While its pharmaceutical competitors turned inward, Syntex built relationships with the academic research community by constructing a major research center near Stanford University, encouraging its researchers to publish in scientific journals, and aggressively recruiting recent Ph.D. graduates. Much of the credit was given to Dr. Alejandro Zaffaroni, a Uruguay-born biochemist who joined Syntex in 1951. After receiving medical training in Uruguay, Dr. Zaffaroni specialized in steroidal chemistry while obtaining his Ph.D. degree at the University of Rochester. He served as Syntex's executive vice president and directed the firm's research from 1956 to 1968. During the 1960s, Dr. Zaffaroni focused on structuring innovative collaborative research and marketing deals for new products.

THE POTENTIAL OF DRUG DELIVERY SYSTEMS

In the 1960s, Dr. Zaffaroni became fascinated by the medical and economic potential of new drug delivery systems. Until the 1930s pharmaceutical companies manufactured the active ingredients in drugs, while pharmacists converted these into final products, using traditional drug delivery systems of pills, ointments, or liquids. Over the succeeding decades, drug manufacturers vertically integrated, manufacturing the drug delivery vehicles. Dr. Zaffaroni felt that drug companies had neglected research into the mechanisms through which active ingredients were directed into the body in favor of the more glamorous discovery research. He was fond of pointing out that the most common drug delivery mechanism, the pill, had changed little since its invention by the ancient Egyptians in the fifteenth century B.C.

Pills have several medical disadvantages. First, they are rapidly absorbed into the blood stream through the stomach. Thus, a pill administers its dose in a single jolt—an initial overdosage followed by a period of underdosage—when a continuous series of small doses usually is preferable. Consequently, many drugs that work effectively within a narrow dosage range would be rejected in clinical trials. Improved drug delivery systems could release drugs into the body in a slow and controlled manner.

Second, pills commonly deliver many times the needed dosage because only a small portion of the therapeutic agent reaches the desired part of the body. The remainder of the agent goes elsewhere in the body, causing unfortunate side effects in other body organs. Improved delivery systems could limit the probability of side effects by ensuring that the drug was absorbed mainly by the part of the body where it was needed.

Improved delivery systems promised both economic and medical advantages. Firms developing new drugs applied for patent protection, which typically enabled them to market the product for 10 – 15 years without competition. Once the patent expired, generic competitors frequently entered the market. Existing products about to go "off-patent" could be repackaged with advanced drug delivery systems to improve their safety, efficacy, or convenience. The "new and improved" version of the drug might allow a firm to maintain attractive sales, even in the face of generic competitors to the drug in its original form.

Dr. Zaffaroni tried to persuade Syntex to make a major development push into drug delivery systems. The firm resisted the suggestion, arguing it would be too great a distraction from its efforts to develop new chemical entities, which was the primary focus for all major pharmaceutical companies and seen as the only important way to create new pharmaceutical products. Moreover, it argued that it was unclear how great the reward from drug delivery systems would be. Advanced drug delivery systems might be expensive to develop and to manufacture, while pills and other traditional delivery systems were already available at a negligible cost. Doctors and patients might not see the benefits of these novel delivery systems as justifying any added expense. Finally, the scientific understanding of drug delivery was still rudimentary. Unpleasant surprises might await: for instance, patients might develop a tolerance to a drug more quickly when it was continuously delivered in small doses.

THE BIRTH AND CRISIS OF ALZA

Failing to persuade Syntex to invest in drug delivery technologies, Alejandro Zaffaroni left Syntex in 1968 to begin his own firm.[2] He named the new firm ALZA (after the first two letters of his first and last names). ALZA was capitalized with $3 million of Dr. Zaffaroni's own money. Its only other assets were Syntex's patents and research personnel in the area of drug delivery. As part of the disengagement agreements between Dr. Zaffaroni and Syntex, Syntex acquired 25% of ALZA's equity at a nominal cost. Syntex distributed its ALZA shares to its shareholders in 1970, transforming ALZA into a publicly traded start-up just as Syntex had been.

Despite ALZA's weak capitalization and the anticipated long delays and large capital demands until the firm reached profitability, there was a tremendous interest in the financial community about the future potential of the company. Within a few days of the distribution to Syntex's shareholders, ALZA (trading on the Pacific Stock Exchange) had a market capitalization exceeding $100 million. In 1969 and 1970, ALZA raised funds through private placements from successful entrepreneurs, including the presidents of Marion Laboratories and Memorex. Priced at between $10 and $15 per share (the higher priced offerings also included a warrant), the private placements raised nearly $19 million. In 1971, ALZA also raised $12 million in a rights offering to existing shareholders managed by Allen and Company, in which a share and a warrant were sold for $15.

One of Dr. Zaffaroni's first priorities was to build a blue-chip panel of scientific advisors and a board of directors, including Nobel laureates, noted academics, and business leaders. Dr. Zaffaroni had known many of the scientists while at Syntex; others were attracted by his reputation as a leading researcher-turned-entrepreneur. Based on his experience at Syntex, he took care to develop a research-oriented culture at ALZA. After recruiting a former M.I.T. professor specializing in membrane technology to lead the

---

2 This discussion of ALZA's history is drawn from Gene Bylinsky, "Visionary on a Golden Shoestring," *Fortune*, June 1973, pp. 150–53, 226–30; Ignatius Chithelen, "Drug Extender," *Forbes*, July 10, 1989, pp. 95–96; Yves Doz, "Technology Partnerships Between Larger and Smaller Firms: Some Critical Issues," *International Studies of Management and Organization*, 17, 1988, pp. 31–57; David A. Loehwing, "ALZA to Zoecon," *Barron's*, October 14, 1974, pp. 3, 8, 13, 18; analysts' reports; and discussions with ALZA management.

research effort, Dr. Zaffaroni focused on recruiting researchers in their twenties and thirties. Researchers were drawn from many disciplines rarely seen in pharmaceutical firms, including physicists, polymer chemists, and mechanical engineers. He cultivated an informal atmosphere with few administrative structures. Scientific project leaders often bypassed the firm's formal organizational structure and spoke directly to Dr. Zaffaroni on key issues. As he noted in one interview, "There isn't a company outside the Metropolitan Opera that functions this way."[3] Neither base pay nor bonuses were high, but stock options were made widely available. The Palo Alto facility was located next to that of another Syntex spin-off, Zoecon, and informal contact between the researchers was encouraged.

ALZA's initial development focus was on two products: the Ocusert and Progestasert. Glaucoma, a chronic condition in which excessive pressure builds up in the eyeball, could cause blindness unless treated by the drug pilocarpine. The traditional drug delivery method, eye-drops applied four times a day, resulted in blurred vision for up to an hour after each administration. ALZA developed a tiny polymer Ocusert pouch, to be inserted under the eyelid. Each pouch, which lasted for a week, slowly released pilocarpine into the eye. With the steady doses of the drug from the Ocusert, the debilitating vision-blurring did not occur. ALZA's second product, the Progestasert, provided birth control for an entire year without replacement. An intrauterine device that released small amounts of the same hormone used in birth-control pills, it prevented conception while eliminating the potentially serious side effects of the pills.

ALZA also pursued long-range development projects in a variety of other areas. These projects advanced basic science and worked to perfect therapeutic systems, or alternative technologies to deliver drugs to the body. The two most promising therapeutic systems were membrane-coated capsules that released drugs only very slowly, which the firm dubbed the oral osmotic (OROS) system, and transdermal patches placed like adhesive bandages on the skin that allowed drugs to be very gradually absorbed into the body. Once the therapeutic systems were developed, they could be combined with a wide variety of different drugs to produce an almost endless number of different products.

By 1974, ALZA had filed for marketing approval for its first two products. In anticipation of commercialization, the firm had established a substantial manufacturing facility and had begun building up a sales force. This significantly increased the expenditures of ALZA. The firm met its financing needs by selling 1.25 million common shares at $12.50 per share and arranging a $20 million line of credit from a group of banks led by Chase Manhattan. The financial planning was based on the expectation that sales of the first two

---

3   Bylinsky, p.219.

products would reach at least $20–30 million within the first few years of marketing and that at this sales level ALZA could achieve profitability.

By 1976 the Food and Drug Administration (FDA) had approved ALZA's first two products, and they had been introduced into the marketplace. Unfortunately, sales in fiscal year 1976 were a little over $2 million; in 1977, only $7 million. More ominously, by mid-1977 it was apparent that these products would not reach the necessary volumes for ALZA to report positive profits. Both products encountered market resistance, exacerbated by unfortunate external events. Elderly glaucoma patients, reluctant to insert Ocusert pouches under their eye-lids, chose to remain with eyedrops, which had the added benefit of costing about $1 a day less than ALZA's new product. At about the same time, Merck introduced an improved eye-drop medication for glaucoma, which sharply reduced the blurring of vision. Meanwhile, patients resisted trying the new Progestasert device. One reason was that the initial expenditure was much higher than either birth-control pills or competing intrauterine devices. In addition, another company's intratuerine device, the Dalkon Shield sold by A.H. Robbins, was at this time the focus of intense negative publicity and litigation. Doctors were reluctant to recommend the new Progestasert, or any other intrauterine device, because of concerns about product safety and litigation.

As monthly sales fell in early 1977, ALZA faced a major financial crisis. Marketing and R&D operations each consumed $2 million a month. The firm had little more than $1 million in cash on hand, its bank line of credit was rapidly being drawn down, and it was in violation of several bank covenants. Apart from its dwindling sales, its only other source of revenues was a small amount of contract research it did for major pharmaceutical houses. As ALZA's share price fell, the firm was criticized in the financial community for its inflated promises. Dr. Zaffaroni realized that in this environment another public equity issue would be impossible. Instead, he sought an equity investment by a major U.S. pharmaceutical or, less satisfactorily, chemical firm. Failing to interest U.S. firms, he looked overseas.

ALZA AND CIBA-GEIGY

In 1977 and 1978, Dr. Zaffaroni convinced Ciba-Geigy, a multinational chemical and pharmaceutical firm based in Basel, Switzerland, with 75,000 employees and sales of $1.2 billion, to invest in ALZA. Ciba-Geigy laboratories had been relatively active in exploring pharmaceutical delivery systems, recently developing a slow-release capsule. ALZA began negotiating with Ciba-Geigy in April 1977, and the two firms continued to negotiate for most of the year. In January 1978, Ciba-Geigy's U.S. subsidiary purchased $30 million of a new class of convertible preferred stock in ALZA, and Ciba-Geigy agreed to commission at least $15 million of contract research from ALZA over a 5-year period, thus allowing ALZA to continue its corporate life.

In return, Ciba-Geigy gained control over ALZA's corporate affairs. Ciba-Geigy was granted 80% of the voting rights and eight of eleven ALZA board seats.[4] ALZA's research projects (with the exception of a small amount of discretionary research) needed to be approved by a joint review board of ALZA and Ciba-Geigy representatives. In view of its 80% voting rights, Ciba-Geigy could consolidate ALZA's financial statements with its own for tax purposes. Hence the Swiss firm could enjoy the accumulated tax losses of ALZA, which included not only an operating loss carryforward of $30.4 million but also $32.2 million of deferred research costs and $2.9 million of deferred patent costs to be amortized over future periods.[5] Ciba-Geigy had the exclusive right to license virtually all of ALZA's existing and future technology for at least a decade, by paying ALZA royalties of 5% of sales for most products and 10% for a few products already under development by ALZA and nearing commercialization. ALZA was allowed to license its technologies to third parties, but only with the approval of Ciba-Geigy. Ciba-Geigy was allowed to treat the $15 million payments for contract research as the first $20 million in paid-in royalties. Thus, ALZA would not receive any royalties until Ciba-Geigy had sold between $200 and $400 million of ALZA- derived products. Finally, Ciba-Geigy was granted the right to take over the manufacture of any product being produced by ALZA, if it felt significant cost savings could be achieved.

From January 1977 to the end of 1978, ALZA's staff fell from 700 to just under 400 as marketing and production were dramatically cut back. The R&D effort was left untouched. The implementation of this agreement encountered difficulties. ALZA's managers perceived Ciba-Geigy's research personnel as lacking interest in ALZA technologies and its sales force as indifferent to the promotion of ALZA products. Delays in processing ALZA's requests to undertake collaborations with third parties were another source of frustration. Meanwhile, Ciba-Geigy management was frustrated by ALZA's increasing losses and its constant requests to develop products with other pharmaceutical companies. The reported financial losses resulted from the sluggish sales of ALZA's two existing products. At the time the agreement was signed, these had been projected to be $43 million in the years 1978–1980, but actual sales in this period totaled $8 million. Additional tensions

---

4   Ciba-Geigy purchased a new class of preferred stock. If it converted the preferred shares into common stock, it would hold 53% of the equity in ALZA.

5   ALZA Corporation, *Proxy Statement*, December 23, 1977, p. 25. These two benefits were expected to yield savings to Ciba-Geigy of at least $27 million over a 5-year period ["Advanced Drug Delivery Systems: ALZA and Ciba-Geigy (B)," unpublished INSEAD case, 1988].

were introduced by the conflict between the highly informal, nonhierarchical approach of ALZA and Ciba-Geigy's more restrained corporate culture.

Rather than renew the agreement in 1981, Ciba-Geigy determined to give up control of ALZA through a series of complex agreements. Ciba-Geigy's licenses to ALZA technologies were converted into nonexclusive licenses, giving ALZA the freedom to offer these technologies to others. In view of the fact that ALZA was losing money in 1981 and had no obvious sources of capital, Ciba-Geigy provided ALZA with $10 million. Ciba-Geigy exchanged its preferred shares for non-voting class B common shares, representing approximately 40% of the equity of ALZA.[6] In addition, Ciba-Geigy obtained nonvoting "series 1982" convertible preferred shares that ALZA would redeem and thereby repay Ciba-Geigy $10 million plus interest. Ciba-Geigy surrendered its board seats, and the marketing and production agreements were canceled. In turn, ALZA gave up all claims to royalties from Ciba-Geigy on its existing technologies, with the exception of two skin patches expected to reach the market in 1983 for which Ciba-Geigy was to pay a 5% royalty (reduced from 10% in the original agreement).

ALZA was once again an independent entity, but it was thinly capitalized and faced a skeptical capital market. The total market value of the firm's equity was under $20 million. The company was not profitable and still owed approximately $10 million to the banking syndicate that had provided the loans to commercialize its first products.

THE REBIRTH OF ALZA

Several favorable events in 1983 helped boost ALZA's chances for survival as an independent company. First, Ciba-Geigy's first skin patch (developed by ALZA and for which ALZA received a royalty of 5%), which delivered nitroglycerine to angina sufferers, proved an unqualified success. While nitroglycerine drugs had previously been applied in ointments, the skin patch was easier and more effective. Ciba-Geigy's sales of the skin patch soon exceeded the cumulative sales of all other nitroglycerine-based drugs. Another patch product introduced at about the same time that dispensed the drug scopolamine (which prevents motion sickness) also proved successful.

ALZA discovered that the drug industry's interest in alternative delivery systems had increased dramatically since 1977, in part because of the publicity associated with the firm's ties with Ciba-Geigy and the success of the first two transdermal products. Freed from the oversight of Ciba-Geigy, ALZA quickly signed licensing agreements with other firms, including Eli Lilly, Glaxo, Pfizer, and Schering-Plough. ALZA confined its efforts to

---

6   Common stock held by other entities was renamed class A common. At the same time, a substantial employee stock ownership plan was established for all ALZA employees, using class C common shares.

R&D in delivery systems, leaving the discovery of new drug entities and the marketing of the resulting pharmaceutical products to other firms. It would profit by allowing pharmaceutical firms to license its technology, in return for which they would pay ALZA royalties.

Soon ALZA was able to approach the capital markets again. In 1983 it raised money three times. First, ALZA issued a $17 million public offering for an R&D limited partnership to develop products based on its transdermal technologies, placed by Merrill Lynch White Weld. Second, it sold $25 million of convertible subordinated debentures, again managed by Merrill Lynch White Weld, which was used to buy back Ciba-Geigy's preferred shares. Finally, ALZA undertook a $31 million private placement for an R&D limited partnership to develop products based on its OROS technologies.

The firm's strategy proved increasingly successful as the 1980s progressed. Not only did the firm's market capitalization climb steadily, but new offerings were well received. In 1985, ALZA raised $93 million through the sale of 3 million shares of class A common stock, underwritten by Merrill Lynch Capital Markets. With the proceeds, it repurchased half the class B shares held by Ciba-Geigy for $43 million (these were convertible into 2.9 million class A shares). In 1986 its rising stock price allowed it to call its convertible debt issue. A year later ALZA raised $75 million, through the sale of convertible Eurobonds, co-managed by Merrill Lynch Capital Markets, Credit Suisse First Boston, and Smith Barney.

By 1988 ALZA had signed contracts with over a dozen major pharmaceutical firms and had over 40 products in development that delivered existing drugs through its delivery systems, nine of which were awaiting final marketing approval by the FDA. In these agreements, ALZA's partner incurred all costs of developing the product, and ALZA would receive a revenue stream in the form of royalties on net sales if it succeeded.[7] Both the skin-patch technology and the controlled-release OROS system proved highly successful, able to accommodate the release of a wide variety of drugs. ALZA owned 342 U.S. patents and had another 104 U.S. patents pending. Although by the late 1980s a number of other companies were attempting to develop drug-delivery technology, ALZA continued to be recognized as the worldwide leader in its field. ALZA's product pipeline in 1988 is shown in Exhibit 2, and its financial history is summarized in Exhibit 3.

Based on its successes to date in developing and licensing its drug delivery technologies to established pharmaceutical firms, ALZA had created an enviable royalty stream.

---

7 Among the companies funding R&D at ALZA in 1987 were American Home Products, Baxter, Boehringer-Ingelhiem, Bristol-Myers, Ciba-Geigy, Cyanimid, Du Pont, Glaxo, Hoffman-LaRoche, Johnson and Johnson, Merck, Merrell-Dow, Monsanto, Pfizer, Recordati, Sandoz, and Schering-Plough. ALZA also continued to sell its own drugs, but its sale of the three products—the Ocusert, the Progestasert, and the Alzet, a slow release tablet for animal studies—totaled only $7 million.

Many Wall Street analysts, projecting ALZA's future revenues (see Exhibit 4), were optimistic about the company:

> The translation of ALZA's technology base to practicable systems defined the high-risk phase both for the company and for investors. That has passed. At this stage, applying ALZA's systems to product development provides leverage that is inherently lower risk and lower cost than traditional pharmaceutical developments. Indeed, multiple product marketing opportunities emerge, limited only by the imagination of ALZA and its pharmaceutical company clients.[8]

Another analyst dubbed ALZA "the ultimate royalty trust"[9] in that its shareholders were the residual claimants to the large stream of royalties the firm enjoyed from licensing its drug delivery technologies to other firms. As of mid-1988, nearly half of ALZA's common stock was held by institutions (mutual funds, pension plan advisors, bank trust departments, and insurance firms); Mr. Gerstel sensed that a material proportion of these investors held ALZA because it allowed them to participate in a high-growth product segment via a relatively low-risk firm with lower fixed costs and more stable cash flows than many of its rivals.

OPPORTUNITIES AND CHALLENGES OF INNOVATION

Just as new technologies had led to ALZA's current success, they posed challenges and opportunities for ALZA's future. As the firm's success had been increasingly recognized, several competitors accelerated their drug delivery development efforts. These included both established pharmaceutical firms and venture capital–financed startup firms. Several of the new firms explicitly noted their intention to become "the next ALZA" in their promotional material. Recent advances in materials science and biotechnology suggested that the fundamental technologies of drug delivery were likely to change dramatically in the years to come.

Advances in materials, electronics, and the understanding of the human body had made possible an array of new delivery mechanisms. ALZA management considered two technologies to be especially critical to their long-run success. The first was bioerodible polymer technologies. ALZA was experimenting with a variety of advanced materials, which released drugs slowly and then degraded. These "Alzamer" materials combined

---

8 A.M. Haley et al., "ALZA Corp.—Company Report," analyst's report, Alex. Brown & Sons, October 17, 1988.

9 Royalty trusts were first pioneered in the mid-1980s by Mesa Petroleum to spin off oil and gas reserves to a trust, thereby avoiding corporate taxation of the earnings on these revenue streams. ALZA's structure was not a royalty trust in the same fashion, in that as a corporation its revenues were subject to corporate taxation.

features of fabric and plastics. Such advanced polymer technologies had been important to ALZA since its initial formation, but the extent to which the rate and duration of drug delivery could be controlled had increased vastly. Their potential was enormous. For instance, pouches of drugs could be surgically implanted into the human body and remain active for up to six months, accelerating the healing of broken bones or damaged tissues. After the drug was delivered, the packet containing the drug would erode. Similarly, chemical implants could be placed next to cancerous tumors, avoiding most of the debilitating side effects of chemotherapy.

A second emerging technology for drug delivery was electrotransport. ALZA's skin patches had been based on passive diffusion: the drug crossed the skin barrier on its own accord and entered the blood stream. By running a low electric current through the drug reservoir, the rate of transport and the types of drugs that could be transmitted both increased. For instance, complex molecules like proteins, which would not move through the skin on their own accord, could be delivered through electrotransport. This technology also permitted much more control over the drug delivery process. For instance, a patient facing chronic pain might adjust the flow of a drug as needed. In other cases, electronic monitors could assess the patient's condition and adjust the drug delivery rate.

Individual products incorporating these therapeutic systems were not likely to reach the marketplace until at least the mid-1990s. The two technologies had the potential, however, to open up the field of drug delivery to many applications that would not be possible with the company's OROS and transdermal drug delivery technologies. Mr. Gerstel was aware that several competitors had targeted these technologies as well and had launched their own R&D programs. Wall Street observers felt that many of these competing products might infringe on ALZA's patents, but it would take protracted litigation to resolve this issue. Exhibit 5 summarizes some of these competitors and their key products in 1988.

The strategic future of the firm demanded investments in polymer and electrotransport drug delivery. From an operational and organizational perspective, the research to bring these technologies to fruition would best be done by ALZA scientists in ALZA laboratories. The research team and the informal open environment that Dr. Zaffaroni had put in place and that Mr. Gerstel and Dr. Jane Shaw (ALZA's president and chief operating officer) had cultivated were ideally suited for work on these two newest technologies. In addition, ALZA's two decades of experience negotiating with large pharmaceutical firms gave its executives the skills and contacts to profitably license any products the technologies might produce without surrendering these benefits to their much larger partners. Stripping the necessary people from ALZA to staff a stand-alone entity would damage the base business, and trying to reconstruct the research environment using outsiders would be costly and risky. Therefore, the technologies would need to be developed in ALZA laboratories and commercialized by ALZA executives dealing with ALZA customers.

FINANCING ALTERNATIVES

Funding the new technologies would not be inexpensive, as shown in Exhibit 6. Bringing the therapeutic systems to the point where they could incorporate products and their continued development could be underwritten by potential licensees would cost more than $40 million over the coming 5 years. Mr. Gerstel could identify at least three broad alternatives for financing the new technologies: (1) using ALZA's money, whether internally generated funds or new securities issued by the firm, and organizing the new venture inside ALZA, (2) establishing a joint venture with a major pharmaceutical company, or (3) setting up a partly ALZA-owned R&D organization funded by ALZA and equity investors in the subsidiary.

While the first choice was feasible, it had unattractive financial implications. Even though the $40 million was arguably a long-term investment in the future like an investment in property or plant, FASB rules insisted that these R&D costs be expensed each year. Thus, a current direct investment in these technologies, if funded either through internally generated funds or by external funds raised directly by the firm, would substantially depress ALZA's reported earnings. Mr. Gerstel worried about the effect this might have on ALZA's stock price.

Most important, funding these newer, riskier products through ALZA would subject its clientele of shareholders to much higher risk than present in its traditional product development and licensing business. Mr. Gerstel publicly stated his concerns about existing shareholders:

> ALZA is an extremely low-risk pharmaceutical company . . . (but) in addition to just developing products for today, we want to continue to be a world leader in new technology. This involves much higher risk. ALZA shareholders have waited a long time for us to be as successful as we are today. If we're going to develop higher-risk technology, we want to give our shareholders a choice in whether they want to participate.[10]

ALZA's second alternative was to enter into a joint venture agreement with a cash-rich large pharmaceutical firm. This arrangement could be structured to have much less effect on ALZA's reported earnings, but to the degree that ALZA had an ownership interest, it would need to report losses. A large pharmaceutical partner might be able to contribute

---

10 Comments by Martin Gerstel, reported in Stuart Weiss, "Beating SWORDs into Stock Shares" *CFO Magazine*, August 1990, p. 46.

skills and expertise to the projects, but ALZA's experience with Ciba-Geigy demonstrated the potential problems of managing these relationships. Furthermore, negotiating with a pharmaceutical firm from the outset meant that ALZA's shareholders would surrender much of the upside of the new technologies. In exchange for providing the financing, ALZA's potential corporate partner almost surely would demand unrestricted rights to use the technology and perhaps even the right to sublicense it to others. Mr. Gerstel guessed that bringing in a large pharmaceutical partner would reduce ALZA's potential profits from the technologies by 50% or more.

A third alternative to fund the new technologies was for ALZA to sell equity in an off balance sheet R&D subsidiary to several investors. If the Tax Reform Act of 1986 had not been enacted, Mr. Gerstel could have funded the work on polymers and electrotransport using a vehicle called an R&D limited partnership (RDLP). This financing structure is diagrammed in Exhibit 7, using as an example one of ALZA's RDLPs. ALZA had funded the development of products incorporating its two main delivery technologies, the transdermal and OROS delivery systems, through off balance sheet RDLPs in 1983.

In an RDLP the sponsoring corporation sets up the partnership, licenses the rights to a technology to the partnership for specific uses, and obtains a general partner's interest in the partnership. As general partner, the sponsoring corporation acts as manager of the partnership, making operating decisions for the partnership. Limited partners, who do not manage the day-to-day operations of the venture, invest money in the project, but their personal liability is limited to the amount of their capital contributions. In a standard RDLP the sponsoring corporation retained the right to buy out the limited partners and obtain exclusive right to use or license the technology through purchase or license options.

One clear appeal of RDLPs in the early 1980s was their tax advantages. The R&D ventures funded typically produced large losses in their early years, given that moneys spent on R&D were expensed and not capitalized. These losses were passed through to the limited partners, who were then able to use them to reduce their personal income taxes. Therefore, RDLP investors were typically individuals with high marginal tax rates. In contrast, sponsoring corporations generally faced lower marginal tax rates, and with net operating loss carry forwards, would have had to effectively defer the use of these taxable losses for many years. Many of the investors in ALZA's RDLPs were thought to be highly taxed individuals also holding ALZA common stock.

A second appeal of RDLPs was their accounting treatment from the sponsoring firm's perspective. The partnership contracted with the sponsoring corporation to conduct the actual R&D and paid development fees to the sponsoring corporation. Thus, the sponsoring corporation could effectively convert its R&D activities from expenses to revenues.

Mr. Gerstel was reluctant to use an RDLP to fund the polymer and electrotransport drug delivery research. The Tax Reform Act (TRA) of 1986 significantly diminished the attractiveness of RDLPs. Not only did the TRA lower the top marginal tax rate on households from 50% to 28% and raise the tax on capital gains relative to ordinary income, it also severely limited the deductions individuals could take from investments like RDLPs, which were termed passive activities. As a result, the RDLPs were out-of-fashion and hard to sell.

The proposal on Mr. Gerstel's desk to form Bio-Electro Systems, Inc. had many similarities to the earlier RDLPs. As in an RDLP, ALZA would contribute certain technologies to the new firm, would contract to conduct BES's R&D, and would retain the right to obtain exclusive licenses to the technology and ultimately to purchase the common stock of BES along a predetermined schedule. Yet the proposal to create BES had some striking differences from a typical RDLP. First, it would be funding therapeutics systems research much further from commercialization than the product development in a typical RDLP. Second, it would create an exchange-listed investment vehicle, as compared with illiquid, nontradable limited partnership interests. Unlike RDLPs sold to high net worth individuals, the investment would likely be targeted to the normal buyers of initial public offerings, i.e., institutional investors like mutual funds, pension plans, and individual shareholders. Finally, it would give BES shareholders a warrant to buy ALZA shares.

If the BES proposal was sensible, Mr. Gerstel still had to worry about its execution. His initial reaction, reflected in the offering document, was to distribute the BES units through a nonunderwritten rights offering. In a rights offering, existing shareholders are given an opportunity (or right) to purchase a new security by paying a subscription price. Shareholders who do not wish to subscribe can either let their right expire or sell the right to others who choose to exercise it, pay the subscription price, and receive the new security. In contrast to a rights offering, a public offering would have been made to all interested parties regardless of whether they currently held shares. While rights offerings were typically less costly than public offerings, they were uncommon because of their greater complexity. Whether a security is offered narrowly through a rights offering or broadly through a public offering, the issuer must decide whether to have the offering underwritten. If an offering is underwritten, an investment bank commits to purchase the unsold or unsubscribed portion of the deal at an agreed-upon price. While virtually all public offerings by major firms were underwritten, not all rights offerings were.

If he went forward with a nonunderwritten rights offering, Mr. Gerstel would have to price the units to be attractive to ALZA shareholders, so that they could sell their rights if they chose not to subscribe. Setting the price of the novel BES units was a challenge. There were few publicly-traded companies to compare to BES. Several startups were specializing in advanced drug delivery systems but remained privately held; other, more established firms were developing such systems as part of a range of R&D activities. None of these utilized the financial innovation embodied in the BES proposal. Data that Mr. Gerstel and his team would use to set the price of the offering are included in Exhibits 8 and 9.

By structuring the offering as a pure rights offering, Mr. Gerstel would not have an investment bank's sales force to sell the novel deal to his shareholders. To the extent practical and allowed by the Securities and Exchange Commission, Mr. Gerstel would meet with groups of ALZA investors to explain the plan. In addition, ALZA retained Merrill Lynch to serve as financial advisor, for which it would be paid 3.2% of the gross proceeds raised. Merrill Lynch had helped prepare the financing plan and would assist in presenting the deal to ALZA shareholders and in pricing the BES units.

While Mr. Gerstel was confident that ALZA needed to move forward on the polymer and electrotransport research, how it would be financed was not a trivial decision. ALZA's future dictated that the firm find $40 million to fund new high-risk businesses that would be advanced inside the firm. Yet for accounting reasons and based on his reading of his shareholders, Mr. Gerstel would prefer that these new research efforts reside outside the firm or off its balance sheet. As he reviewed the proposed plan, he wondered whether it made sense, how he would sell it to his shareholders, and what price he should charge them for the right to participate in BES.

Exhibit 1   Excerpts from BES Offering Statement

$45,416,943

BIO-ELECTRO SYSTEMS, INC.
ALZA CORPORATION

4,128,813 Units
Each Unit Consisting of One Share of Class A Common Stock of
Bio-Electro Systems, Inc. and
One Warrant to Purchase One Share of Class A Common Stock of
ALZA Corporation

**THESE SECURITIES ARE SPECULATIVE AND INVOLVE A
HIGH DEGREE OF RISK. SEE "RISK FACTORS."**

Transferable rights ("Rights") to subscribe for units ("Units") consisting of one share of callable Class A Common Stock of Bio-Electro Systems, Inc. ("BES") and one Warrant ("Warrant") to purchase one share of Class A Common Stock of ALZA Corporation ("ALZA") are being distributed (the "Subscription Offering") to the holders of ALZA Class A Common Stock and ALZA Class B Common Stock of record on November 18, 1988 (the "Record Date"). Eight Rights are required to subscribe for one Unit, and the subscription price of each Unit (the "Subscription Price") is $11, subject to possible reduction as described under "The Offering—Subscription Offering—Subscription Price Reduction." Each ALZA stockholder of record on the Record Date will receive one Right for each share of ALZA Class A Common Stock held, and one Right for each share of ALZA Class A Common Stock into which each share of ALZA Class B Common Stock held is convertible. Persons exercising Rights are also entitled to subscribe for any additional Units ("Additional Units") which may be available as a result of Rights expiring without exercise. Ciba-Geigy Corporation, the sole holder of ALZA's Class B Common Stock, Dr. Alejandro Zaffaroni, the founder and Co-chairman of the Board of ALZA, and ALZA's Employee Stock Ownership Plan have indicated their intention to exercise all their Rights (to subscribe for approximately 699,000 Units in the aggregate) and have agreed not to subscribe for Additional Units.

The Units have been approved for listing on the American Stock Exchange upon official notice of issuance. The callable BES Class A Common Stock and the Warrants comprising the Units will be traded only as units until two years after the closing of the offering or such earlier day on which ALZA's Purchase Option (as defined below) is exercised (the "Separation Date"). After the Separation Date, it is expected that the Warrants will be listed on the American Stock Exchange but that the callable BES Class A Common Stock will not be eligible for listing on the American Stock Exchange or any other national securities exchange or for quotation on the NASDAQ National Market System. The Warrants may not be exercised before December 13, 1990 and expire five years after the closing of this offering. The exercise price of the Warrants is $30 per share. See "The Warrants."

The Rights are evidenced by divisible, transferable certificates and expire at 5:00 p.m., Eastern Standard Time, on December 12, 1988, if not exercised at or before that time. The Rights will trade on the American Stock Exchange under the symbol AZA.RT until 4:00 p.m., Eastern Standard Time, on December 9, 1988.

Beginning on the earlier of (i) February 1, 1991 and (ii) the day BES provides ALZA with quarterly financial statements of BES showing stockholders' equity of less than $4 million, and ending on the earlier of (i) January 31, 1995 and (ii) the 90th day after BES provides ALZA with quarterly financial statements of BES showing stockholders' equity of less than $4 million, ALZA will have an option (the "Purchase Option") to purchase all (but not less than all) of the shares of callable BES Class A Common Stock at a substantial premium over the Subscription Price. See "The Agreements and the Purchase Option—Purchase Option."

If the aggregate proceeds of all Units subscribed for in the Subscription Offering are less than $30 million, BES and ALZA will either (i) withdraw the Subscription Offering or (ii) attempt to raise additional proceeds through an underwritten offering of Units (the "Underwritten Offering"); if, however, such Underwritten Offering is undertaken and the aggregate proceeds of the Subscription Offering and the Underwritten Offering are less than $30 million, BES and ALZA will withdraw the Subscription Offering by December 31, 1988. In the event of any such withdrawal, all subscription payments will be refunded (together with interest earned thereon), and an additional $.25 per Unit (excluding Additional Units) subscribed for will be paid to subscribers. In the event of such withdrawal, purchasers of Rights in the market or through the subscription agent for the offering will not recover the consideration paid for such Rights. See "The Offering."

**THESE SECURITIES HAVE NOT BEEN APPROVED OR DISAPPROVED BY THE
SECURITIES AND EXCHANGE COMMISSION NOR HAS THE COMMISSION
PASSED UPON THE ACCURACY OR ADEQUACY OF THIS PROSPECTUS.
ANY REPRESENTATION TO THE CONTRARY IS A CRIMINAL OFFENSE.**

	Subscription Price(1)	Financial Advisory Fee(2)	Proceeds to BES(2)(3)
Per Unit	$11.00	$.352	$10.648
Total Offering	Minimum $30,000,000 Maximum $45,416,943	Minimum $960,000 Maximum $1,453,342	Minimum $29,040,000 Maximum $43,963,601

(See footnotes on following page)

The date of this Prospectus is November 21, 1988.

Exhibit 1   Excerpts from BES Offering Statement (Continued)

(Footnotes from preceding page)

(1) The Subscription Price is subject to reduction if there is an Underwritten Offering of Units at a lower price to the public. See "The Offering—Subscription Price Reduction."

(2) Assumes that the Units are sold in the Subscription Offering. To the extent that any Units are sold in the Underwritten Offering, the proceeds to BES will be lower. See "The Offering—Potential Underwritten Offering of Unsubscribed Units."

(3) Before deducting expenses, estimated at $1.0 million, payable by BES. ALZA will not receive any of the proceeds of this offering.

AVAILABLE INFORMATION

ALZA is subject to the information requirements of the Securities Exchange Act of 1934, as amended (the "Exchange Act") and, in accordance therewith, files reports, proxy statements and other information with the Securities and Exchange Commission (the "Commission"). Such reports, proxy statements and other information can be inspected and copied at the public reference facilities maintained by the Commission at 450 Fifth Street, N.W., Judiciary Plaza, Washington, D.C. 20549, and at the regional offices of the Commission, Everett McKinley Dirksen Building, 219 South Dearborn Street, Room 1204, Chicago, Illinois 60604, 26 Federal Plaza, Room 1028, New York, New York 10278, and 5757 Wilshire Boulevard, Suite 500 East, Los Angeles, California 90036. Copies of such material can also be obtained at prescribed rates from the Public Reference Section of the Commission, 450 Fifth Street, N.W., Washington, D.C. 20549. ALZA Class A Common Stock is traded on the American Stock Exchange and copies of all reports and proxy materials filed with the Commission and other information concerning ALZA can be inspected at such Exchange.

BES will be required to file reports and other information with the Commission pursuant to the Exchange Act. Holders of BES Class A Common Stock will receive annual reports containing financial information including the report of certified public accountants as to the financial statements of BES.

ALZA and BES have filed with the Commission a Registration Statement under the Securities Act of 1933, as amended (the "Act"), with respect to the securities offered by this Prospectus. This Prospectus does not contain all of the information set forth or incorporated by reference in the Registration Statement and the exhibits thereto. For further information with respect to ALZA, BES and the securities offered hereby, reference is hereby made to such Registration Statement and exhibits, which may be obtained from the Public Reference Section of the Commission, 450 Fifth Street, N.W., Washington, D.C. 20549, upon payment of the fees prescribed by the Commission.

DOCUMENTS INCORPORATED BY REFERENCE

ALZA hereby incorporates by reference in this Prospectus the following documents filed by ALZA with the Commission:

(a) ALZA's Annual Report on Form 10-K for the fiscal year ended December 31, 1987 filed pursuant to the Exchange Act, which report incorporates, by reference to ALZA's 1987 Annual Report, ALZA's consolidated financial statements for such fiscal year.

(b) ALZA's Quarterly Reports on Form 10-Q for the quarters ended March 31, June 30 and September 30, 1988.

(c) All other reports filed by ALZA pursuant to Sections 13 or 15(d) of the Exchange Act since December 31, 1987.

(d) ALZA's definitive proxy statement (the "Proxy Statement") filed pursuant to Section 14 of the Exchange Act in connection with ALZA's 1988 annual meeting of stockholders.

All documents subsequently filed by ALZA pursuant to Sections 13, 14, or 15(d) of the Exchange Act prior to the termination of the offering made hereby will be deemed to be incorporated by reference in this Prospectus and to be a part hereof from the date of filing of such documents.

Any statement contained in a document incorporated by reference herein shall be deemed to be modified or superseded for purposes of this Prospectus to the extent that a statement contained herein or therein or in any other subsequently filed document which also is incorporated by reference herein modifies or supersedes such statement. Any such statement so modified or superseded shall not be deemed, except as so modified or superseded, to constitute a part of this Prospectus.

Upon written or oral request directed to Corporate Public Relations, ALZA Corporation, 950 Page Mill Road, P.O. Box 10950, Palo Alto, California 94303-0802 (telephone: (415) 494-5222), ALZA will provide, without charge, to any person to whom this Prospectus is delivered, a copy of any document incorporated by reference in this Prospectus (not including exhibits to any such document except to the extent any such exhibits are specifically incorporated by reference in the information incorporated in this Prospectus).

Exhibit 1 Excerpts from BES Offering Statement (Continued)

PROSPECTUS SUMMARY

The information set forth below should be read in conjunction with, and is qualified in its entirety by, the information appearing elsewhere in this Prospectus and incorporated herein by reference, including "Risk Factors."

The Subscription Offering:

In the Subscription Offering, transferable Rights to subscribe for Units are being distributed to the holders of ALZA Class A Common Stock, $.01 par value ("ALZA Class A Common Stock"), and ALZA Class B Common Stock, $.01 par value ("ALZA Class B Common Stock"), of record at the close of business on November 18, 1988 (the "Record Date"). Each Unit consists of one share of BES Class A Common Stock, $.01 par value ("BES Callable Class A Common Stock"), and one Warrant to purchase one share of ALZA Class A Common Stock. Eight Rights are required to subscribe for one Unit at a Subscription Price of $11 per Unit, subject to possible reduction as described under "The Offering—Subscription Offering—Subscription Price Reduction." Each ALZA stockholder of record on the Record Date will receive one Right for each share of ALZA Class A Common Stock held, and one Right for each share of ALZA Class A Common Stock into which each share of ALZA Class B Common Stock held is convertible. Rights also entitle holders to subscribe for Additional Units. Subscriptions for Units (including Additional Units) must be accompanied by payment of the total Subscription Price therefor. See "The Offering." The Chase Manhattan Bank, N.A. is acting as the Subscription Agent (the "Subscription Agent") for the Subscription Offering.

Ciba-Geigy Corporation, the sole holder of ALZA's Class B Common Stock, Dr. Alejandro Zaffaroni, the founder and Co-chairman of the Board of ALZA, and ALZA's Employee Stock Ownership Plan (the "ESOP") have indicated their intention to exercise all their Rights (to subscribe for approximately 699,000 Units in the aggregate) and have agreed not to subscribe for Additional Units. Ciba-Geigy Corporation, Dr. Zaffaroni and the ESOP have agreed not to sell Units until at least 90 days after the closing of this offering.

If the aggregate proceeds of all Units subscribed for in the Subscription Offering are less than $30 million, BES and ALZA will either (i) withdraw the Subscription Offering or (ii) attempt to raise additional proceeds through an Underwritten Offering; if, however, such Underwritten Offering is undertaken and the aggregate proceeds of the Subscription Offering and the Underwritten Offering are less than $30 million, BES and ALZA will withdraw the Subscription Offering by December 31 1988. In the event of any such withdrawal, all subscription payments will be refunded (together with interest earned thereon), and an additional $.25 per Unit (excluding Additional Units) subscribed for will be paid to subscribers. In the event of such withdrawal, purchasers of Rights in the market or through the Subscription Agent will not recover the consideration paid for such Rights. See "The Offering."

Potential Underwritten Offering:

If fewer than all of the Units are subscribed for in the Subscription Offering, BES and ALZA may attempt to arrange for an Underwritten Offering of all or some portion of the unsubscribed Units through Merrill Lynch Capital Markets ("Merrill Lynch"), which has acted as financial advisor to BES and ALZA in respect of the Subscription Offering. The ability of BES and ALZA to arrange for such an Underwritten Offering will depend, among other things, upon market conditions, the aggregate number of Units subscribed for in the Subscription Offering, and the ability of BES and ALZA to reach agreement with Merrill Lynch as to pricing and other terms of the Underwritten Offering.

If an Underwritten Offering were to occur, the closing of the Subscription Offering and the Underwritten Offering would be simultaneous and the

Exhibit 1   Excerpts from BES Offering Statement (Continued)

	price paid by subscribers in the Subscription Offering and by purchasers in the Underwritten Offering would be the same. There can be no assurance that the Underwritten Offering will occur. See "The Offering—Potential Underwritten Offering of Unsubscribed Units."
American Stock Exchange Information:	The Rights will trade on the American Stock Exchange under the symbol AZA.RT until 4:00 p.m. Eastern Standard Time, on December 9, 1988. The Units have been approved for listing on the American Stock Exchange upon official notice of issuance, to trade under the symbol AZA.U. The BES Callable Class A Common Stock and the Warrants will trade only as units until the Separation Date. After the Separation Date, it is expected that the Warrants will be listed on the American Stock Exchange, but that the BES Callable Class A Common Stock will not be eligible for listing on the American Stock Exchange or any other national securities exchange or for quotation on the NASDAQ National Market System.
ALZA:	ALZA is the recognized leader in the development of advanced pharmaceutical products incorporating drugs in therapeutic systems that control not only the quantity, but also the rate and duration, of drug release. ALZA's therapeutic systems are designed to improve the medical value of drugs by reducing many of their harmful or undesirable side effects while preserving or enhancing their beneficial action. In addition, these therapeutic systems are designed to simplify therapy and make it more convenient by reducing the number of times medication needs to be administered. The majority of ALZA's research and development activities are, and for the past five years have been, directed toward development of products incorporating specific drug compounds into various ALZA delivery systems. These systems include oral, rectal and implantable systems based on osmotic technology, diffusional systems for transdermal and site specific delivery and elastomeric intravenous infusors. Research and development activities are undertaken through joint arrangements with client companies, including two research and development partnerships, which arrangements generally provide for the client companies to reimburse ALZA for its fully burdened costs. In 1987, worldwide sales by ALZA and its client companies of ALZA-developed products were estimated to be $350 million. ALZA currently has approximately 40 products in various stages of development, including nine products currently awaiting United States Food and Drug Administration ("FDA") marketing approval.
Bio-Electro Systems:	BES was formed in October 1988 to develop drug delivery systems incorporating ALZA's proprietary ALZAMER® Bioerodible Polymer ("ALZAMER Polymers") and electrotransport ("Electrotransport") drug delivery technologies (together, the "Technologies") and to commercialize, most likely through licensing, products utilizing such systems for use in the prevention, treatment or cure of human illness, disease or other medical condition (the "Field"). BES has conducted no business to date. Building upon and expanding ALZA's research, BES intends to develop various systems utilizing the Technologies, which systems could provide the basis for commercial products. BES anticipates that it also will commence product development of selected products and that, if the maximum net proceeds are realized, up to three ALZAMER Polymer products and up to three Electrotransport products will enter final product development. It is also anticipated that additional funds will be required from third parties to complete the development of products, including those on which development work is performed by ALZA for BES, and to develop other products. See "Bio-Electro Systems—ALZAMER Bioerodible Polymers—Development Budget" and "Bio-Electro Systems—Electrotransport—Development Budget."

Exhibit 1   Excerpts from BES Offering Statement (Continued)

Reasons for BES and Benefits to ALZA:	While a significant amount of basic research on the Technologies has been done by ALZA, the Technologies are at an earlier stage of development than certain of ALZA's other technologies, which have been or are soon expected to be incorporated in commercial products. The development of new delivery systems and products based on the Technologies will involve significantly increased risks compared to ALZA's development activities based on its currently available systems. Funding of BES as contemplated in this Prospectus allows ALZA stockholders to choose whether or not they wish to participate in these higher risk development projects and, if such projects are successful, to obtain the potential rewards associated with them. The licensing of the Technologies to BES, and the subsequent funding by BES of systems development of the Technologies, will allow ALZA to more effectively utilize its funds in product development and commercialization activities on its other technologies. If the systems development work on the Technologies is successful, ALZA could exercise the Purchase Option and thus regain the exclusive right to use the Technologies.
The Technologies:	*ALZAMER® Bioerodible Polymers.* The ALZAMER Polymers comprise a family of polyorthoester bioerodible polymers patented by ALZA which can be used for the controlled delivery of many compounds. In the presence of moisture, an ALZAMER Polymer will erode, thereby permitting a drug compound formulated within the ALZAMER Polymer matrix to be released at a controlled rate over an extended period of time. The erosion rate of the ALZAMER Polymers, and therefore the rate of drug release, can be carefully controlled. In addition, since the ALZAMER Polymers can be processed to have physical properties ranging from free-flowing or slow-flowing viscous liquids to glassy or elastic solids, they offer many potential product opportunities. Possible uses of the ALZAMER Polymers include wound care products, topical dosage forms, injectables, tissue repair products, periodontal products and surgical "leave behind" products. Under agreements with third parties, two potential ALZAMER Polymer products are in the early stages of product development. *Electrotransport.* ALZA's Electrotransport involves the delivery of drug compounds across the skin, nails or mucosal membranes under the influence of an extremely low electric current. Electrotransport systems can be used to deliver drug compounds that cannot be delivered through the skin from passive transdermal systems. For example, polypeptides from the biotechnology field are candidates for Electrotransport because these molecules are too large to transport across skin by the process of passive diffusion. Electrotransport systems also can be used to deliver compounds in precise patterns or on an as-needed basis by the patient. BES expects initially to develop three basic Electrotransport systems—a zero order system (delivering a continuous steady amount of drug), a patterned delivery system (for example, providing periodic high doses with intervening small doses) and a patient controlled system. ALZA is evaluating various forms of these systems, and has fabricated and is testing in pilot clinical studies a prototype of a zero order system.
Development Contract:	BES has entered into a development contract with ALZA (the "Development Contract") under which ALZA will use diligent efforts to conduct systems research and development and to commence product development. ALZA has the right, subject to certain dollar limitations, to designate drugs for screening and has the right to designate one ALZAMER Polymer product and one Electrotransport product to be under development. Payment to ALZA under the Development Contract will be the full amount of all Development Costs (as defined in the Development Contract) incurred by ALZA beginning on January 1, 1988 in performing these activities

Exhibit 1   Excerpts from BES Offering Statement (Continued)

<table>
<tr><td></td><td>(approximately $2.6 million through September 30, 1988). Development Costs will be charged on the same basis as ALZA generally charges its client companies. ALZA will provide appropriate scientific and technical personnel, necessary laboratories and equipment, and administration of research and development operations. BES is required to pay to ALZA under the Development Contract substantially all of the proceeds of this offering, any interest earned thereon, and any revenues received by BES under any agreements with ALZA. It is anticipated that such amounts will be expended under the Development Contract by the end of 1993. The Development Contract terminates at the earlier of January 31, 1995 or expenditure of all available funds thereunder. See "The Agreements and the Purchase Option—Development Contract."</td></tr>
<tr><td>License Option:</td><td>BES has granted ALZA an option to acquire a license to use the Technologies on a product by product basis (the "License Option"). The License Option is exercisable with respect to any product at any time after a screening evaluation has been completed for that product and remains exercisable until 90 days after approval to market the product has been received from the FDA, but in no event after the earlier of January 31, 1995 or 60 days after termination of the Development Contract. If the License Option is exercised as to any product, ALZA will acquire a worldwide license, with the right to sublicense, to make, have made, use and sell the product. ALZA's license for each product will be exclusive until seven years after FDA marketing approval of the product and nonexclusive thereafter. ALZA will make the following payments to BES with respect to each licensed product:

(a) if the product is sold by ALZA or an ALZA affiliate, base royalties of 3% of net sales of the product and additional royalties of up to 3% of such net sales, the exact amount of additional royalties to be determined based upon the portion of the total research and development costs with respect to such product paid by BES;

(b) if the product is sold by a third party, base sublicensing fees of 25% of (i) any royalties or percentage of sales payments received by ALZA or an ALZA affiliate, and (ii) any "front-end" distribution fees, prepaid royalties or similar one-time, infrequent or special payments received by ALZA or an ALZA affiliate, and additional sublicensing fees of up to 25% of such payments, the exact amount of such additional sublicensing fees to be determined based upon the portion of the total research and development costs with respect to such product paid by BES; and

(c) 10% of certain amounts paid by any third party to ALZA or an ALZA affiliate, before January 1, 1999 for research and development activities relating to products utilizing the Technologies in the Field.

The payments under (a) and (b) above will continue on a country by country basis until the expiration in such country of the last to expire of any patents covering the licensed product or, if there never are any patents in such country, until December 31, 2007. If the License Option is not exercised with respect to any product developed under the Development Contract, the rights to such product will remain in BES and BES will need to find other methods of commercially exploiting the product.

ALZA has the right to develop products utilizing the Technologies in the Field for its own account and for third parties in addition to the activities funded by BES under the Development Contract. In such cases (i) no BES funds will be used for product development, (ii) BES will have an exclusive license to the technology developed (other than technology relating to a third party's proprietary compound) and any products will be subject to ALZA's License Option, (iii) if the License Option is exercised for any</td></tr>
</table>

Exhibit 1   Excerpts from BES Offering Statement (Continued)

	product, BES will receive royalties and sublicensing fees as described above and (iv) BES will receive the payments described in (c) above, whether or not the License Option is exercised. See "The Agreements and the Purchase Option—License Option."
Purchase Option:	ALZA has the right to purchase all of the BES Callable Class A Common Stock (the "Purchase Option"). The Purchase Option will be exercisable by notice given at any time beginning on the earlier of (i) February 1, 1991 and (ii) the day BES provides ALZA with quarterly financial statements of BES showing stockholders' equity of less than $4 million, and ending on the earlier of (i) January 31, 1995 and (ii) the 90th day after BES provides ALZA with quarterly financial statements of BES showing stockholders' equity of less than $4 million. If the Purchase Option is exercised, the purchase price calculated on a per share basis (the "Purchase Option Exercise Price") will be as follows:

If the Purchase Option Is Exercised	Purchase Option Exercise Price(1)
At any time before February 1, 1991(2)	$23
On or after February 1, 1991 and on or before January 31, 1992.....	$23
On or after February 1, 1992 and on or before January 31, 1993.....	$31
On or after February 1, 1993 and on or before January 31, 1994.....	$42
On or after February 1, 1994 and on or before January 31, 1995.....	$57

(1) If the Subscription Price is reduced as a result of the sale of Units to the public in the Underwritten Offering at a lower price (see "The Offering—Subscription Offering—Subscription Price Reduction"), the Purchase Option Exercise Price will be reduced by the same percentage.

(2) The Purchase Option may be exercised before February 1, 1991 only if, prior to that date, BES provides ALZA with quarterly financial statements of BES showing stockholders' equity of less than $4 million. It is not expected that this will occur before that date, even if the minimum proceeds are realized. See "Use of Proceeds."

The Purchase Option Exercise Price may be paid in cash, in ALZA Class A Common Stock or in any combination of cash and ALZA Class A Common Stock, at ALZA's sole discretion. See "Federal Income Tax Consequences."

Under its Restated Certificate of Incorporation, BES will be prohibited from taking or permitting any action inconsistent with ALZA's rights under the Purchase Option. In addition, until the expiration of the Purchase Option, BES will not be able, without the consent of ALZA, as the holder of the BES Class B Common Stock, to issue additional capital stock, merge, liquidate, sell all or substantially all of its assets, or amend its Restated Certificate of Incorporation to alter the Purchase Option or the rights of the Class B Common Stock. See "BES Capital Stock."

Services Agreement:	BES has entered into a services agreement (the "Services Agreement") with ALZA pursuant to which ALZA has agreed to provide management and administrative services to BES on a fully burdened cost reimbursement basis. The Services Agreement has a one-year term and may be renewed for successive one-year terms during the term of the Development Contract at the option of BES. In addition, BES may terminate the Services Agreement at any time upon 60 days' notice. Under the Services Agreement, ALZA will be reimbursed for its expenses associated with this offering.
The Warrants:	Each Unit includes a Warrant to purchase one share of ALZA Class A Common Stock. The Warrants will be exercisable from December 13, 1990 until the date that is five years after the closing of the offering (the "Warrant Expiration Date") at $30 per share (the "Exercise Price"). The

Exhibit 1   Excerpts from BES Offering Statement (Continued)

Warrants will trade separately from the BES Callable Class A Common Stock beginning on the Separation Date. See "The Warrants."

Federal Income Tax Consequences:

Material federal income tax consequences applicable to the receipt of Rights, the purchase of Units in the Subscription Offering or in the Underwritten Offering and the sale of Rights, Warrants and BES Callable Class A Common Stock by purchasers in such offerings are discussed under "Federal Income Tax Consequences."

Use of Proceeds:

The estimated net proceeds of this offering will be at least $28 million and at most $43 million. BES will receive all of the net proceeds of the offering. BES expects to use substantially all of such proceeds to undertake systems research and development, screening evaluations and, to the extent funds are available, product development under the Development Contract. BES expects that during the term of the Development Contract it will be engaged solely in research and development of the Technologies and will have very limited sources of revenue other than the net proceeds of this offering, plus interest earned thereon. See "Use of Proceeds."

ALZA Summary Financial Data (in thousands, except per share data)

	Years Ended December 31,					Nine Months Ended September 30,	
	1983	1984	1985	1986	1987	1987	1988
						(unaudited)	
Statement of Income Data:							
Total Revenue	$22,454	$30,484	$45,547	$57,799	$70,812	$51,544	$62,052
Income Before Extraordinary Item(1)	732	2,968	5,055	9,005	13,984	9,947	12,623
Net Income	1,320	5,938	9,707	16,753	13,984	9,947	12,623
Income Before Extraordinary Item Per Share(1)	.03	.12	.19	.28	.42	.30	.38
Net Income Per Share	.05	.24	.36	.52	.42	.30	.38
Balance Sheet Data:							
Working Capital	$16,909	$19,713	$ 81,797	$ 84,610	$148,614	$152,848	$146,109
Total Assets	39,572	44,871	160,444	137,306	243,479	229,116	248,105
Convertible Debentures	25,000	25,000	22,575	—	75,000	75,000	75,000
Other Long Term Liabilities	3,067	3,095	2,894	2,686	6,090	5,599	7,780
Stockholders' Equity	3,415	10,007	79,042	121,219	138,985	133,434	153,169

(1) The extraordinary item for 1983 to 1986 relates primarily to the use of United States federal income tax net operating loss carryforwards.

Exhibit 2   ALZA Project Portfolio, January 1988

		Sold Under License		
Name	Sold By	Disease/Use	Royalties on Net Sales	1987 Gross Sales ($ mil.)
Transdermal Systems				
Transderm-Nitro	Ciba-Geigy	Angina	5%	234
Transderm-Scop	Ciba-Geigy	Motion sickness	5	17
Estraderm	Ciba-Geigy	Female hormone	1[a]	20
Catapres-TTS	Boehringer	Hypertension	7.5	30
Oral Osmotic and Related Technologies				
Acutrim	Ciba-Geigy	Appetite suppression	0%	--
Acusystem C	American Health	Vitamin C	5–10	1
Volmax	Glaxo	Asthma	5–10	3
Travenol-Infuser	Baxter	Cancer patients	5–10	16

	Selected New Drug Applications Filed by ALZA or Its Licensees		
Name	Sponsor	Use	New Drug Application Filed
Transdermal Systems			
TTS-testosterone	ALZA TTS	Male hormone	Sept. 1987
TTS-fentanyl	ALZA TTS	Analgesic	Dec. 1987
Oral Osmotic Systems			
Procardia-GITS (nifedipine)	Pfizer	Angina/hypertension	Jan. 1987
Minipress-GITS (prazosin)	Pfizer	Hypertension	Sept. 1987
OROS-albuterol (Volmax)	Glaxo	Asthma	June 1986
Pseudoephedrine/ brompheniramine	ALZA OROS	Decongestant/antihistamine	Dec. 1986
Chlorpheniramine	ALZA OROS	Allergy remedy	Sept. 1987
Potassium chloride	ALZA OROS	Hypertension	Sept. 1987
Veterinary Osmotic System			
RUTS-selenium[b]	Schering-Plough	Cattle supplement	Sept. 1987

ALZA OROS = ALZA OROS Products Limited Partnership; ALZA TTS = ALZA TTS Research Partners Ltd.
Source: Compiled from analyst reports.
a. Estraderm was royalty-free under Ciba-Geigy's termination agreement, but Ciba-Geigy subsequently provided a 1% royalty to ALZA in exchange for its cooperation in completing product development.
b. Food Additive Petition pending.

Exhibit 3   ALZA Corporation Financial Statements, 1970–1987 (millions of dollars)

	Fiscal Year Ending June 30								Fiscal Year Ending December 31										
	1970[a]	1971	1972	1973	1974	1975	1976	1977	1977	1978	1979	1980	1981	1982	1983	1984	1985	1986	1987
Income Statement Data																			
Revenues																			
Own sales [b]	$0	$0	$0	$0	$0	$0	$2.4	$6.7	$4.5	$3.7	$2.6	$2.8	$4.6	$4.8	$4.8	$5.8	$15.1	$15.8	$19.4
Research revenues	0	0	0	0	0	0	.4	1.1	1.7	5.0	7.9	7.6	6.6	9.1	12.5	15.6	19.1	22.8	25.9
Other noninterest revenues [c]	0	0	0	0	0	0	0	0	0	0	.6	1.1	.8	1.8	5.2	9.1	11.3	19.4	25.5
Expenses																			
Research and development	1.9	2.4	4.2	6.7	8.1	9.0	8.4	8.1	7.6	8.0	8.4	8.2	8.4	10.1	10.0	11.8	14.5	19.4	23.0
Cost of goods sold	0	0	0	0	.8	.7	2.2	3.7	4.0	3.8	3.4	3.0	4.6	4.0	4.5	4.8	12.5	11.7	13.8
General and administrative	.7	1.1	1.3	1.7	3.7	7.1	8.4	9.1	8.1	3.7	3.4	3.0	3.3	4.3	4.8	4.6	5.8	7.7	8.6
Depreciation	.1	.1	.3	.2	.6	.9	.9	.9	1.0	1.0	.8	.4	1.0	.5	1.2	1.1	1.6	1.8	3.4
Income taxes	0	0	0	0	0	0	0	0	0	0	0	0	0	.1	0	.1	1.0	1.5	9.4
Net income	(2.0)	(3.5)	(4.4)	(7.0)	(10.3)	(15.0)	(16.3)	(16.2)	(17.5)	(9.0)	(7.1)	(2.9)[d]	(6.6)	9.7[e]	1.3	6.1	9.7	16.8	14.0
Assets																			
Cash and short-term investments	$4.1	$25.8	$21.0	$19.8	$18.9	$10.1	$4.5	$1.6	$.9	$4.2	$3.4	$5.1	$1.1	$6.7	$17.5	$15.8	$77.8	$81.2	$142.8
Other current assets minus current liabilities [f]	(.2)	(.3)	(.1)	(.2)	(.8)	3.3	1.8	(9.6)	(17.0)	2.4	1.6	1.1	2.8	4.2	(.4)	4.1	4.2	3.6	6.0
Gross plant, property, and equipment	3.5	3.9	6.0	7.6	11.9	16.3	18.2	18.9	19.0	19.0	20.6	17.4[d]	19.1	19.8	21.3	26.6	32.9	50.7	83.2
Total assets	9.6	30.6	27.0	22.4	32.0	30.6	23.5	23.3	21.3	23.1	22.2	21.0	18.5	26.7	39.6	44.9	160.4	137.3	243.5

Exhibit 3   ALZA Corporation Financial Statements, 1970–1987 (millions of dollars)   (Continued)

	Fiscal Year Ending June 30								Fiscal Year Ending December 31											
	1970[a]	1971	1972	1973	1974	1975	1976	1977	1977	1978	1979	1980	1981	1982	1983	1984	1985	1986	1987
Capital structure																			
Long-term debt	$.4	$5.0	$0	$0	$0	$6.1	$2.8	$1.7	$1.7	$21.7	$22.5	$16.8	$14.4	$10.2	$3.1	$3.1	$2.9	$2.7	$6.0
5½% convertible debt	–	–	–	–	–	–	–	–	–	–	–	–	–	–	–	–	–	–	75.0
8% convertible debt	–	–	–	–	–	–	–	–	–	–	–	–	–	–	25.0	25.0	22.6	–	–
Series 1982 preferred stock	–	–	–	–	–	–	–	–	–	–	–	–	–	11.4	–	–	–	–	–
6% preferred stock	–	–	–	–	–	–	–	–	–	10.5	16.1	21.7	29.0	–	–	–	–	–	–
Class A common[g]	–	–	–	–	–	–	–	–	–	–	–	–	–	81.9	82.1	86.6	152.3	177.7	0.30[h]
Class B common[g]	–	–	–	–	–	–	–	–	–	–	–	–	–	18.7	18.7	18.7	9.3	9.3	0.01[h]
Class C common[g]	–	–	–	–	–	–	–	–	–	–	–	–	–	.9	.9	–	–	–	–
Common stock[g]	3.0	5.0	5.0	5.1	6.1	6.2	7.6	7.8	7.8	7.8	7.8	7.8	7.8	–	–	–	–	–	–
Paid-in capital	5.6	30.8	34.6	37.3	50.8	55.6	71.8	73.9	73.7	73.7	73.7	73.7	73.7	–	–	–	–	–	–
Deficit	2.0	5.5	10.0	16.9	27.2	42.3	58.6	74.8	83.6	92.5	99.7	102.6	109.2	99.4	98.2	92.2	82.5	65.8	51.8
Market value of equity at fiscal year end	99[i]	74[i]	138[i]	99[i]	121[i]	161	128	55	42	48	55	67	69	230	200	235	446	601	837

Source: Corporate documents, Compustat, and Daily Stock Price Guide.

a. 1970 income statement includes period from inception (June 1968 through June 30, 1970).
b. Own sales include sales of manufactured products to other pharmaceutical firms, which then resell them under license.
c. Other revenues are primarily royalties and fees.
d. 1980 net income includes $4.3 million from the sale of a major ALZA facility.
e. 1982 net income includes a one-time payment of $10 million from Ciba-Geigy.
f. Defined as all current assets except cash and short-term investments minus current liabilities (excluding current portion of long-term debt).
g. ALZA common stock had never paid a dividend.
h. ALZA reincorporated in 1987 in Delaware, leading to a change in the accounting treatment of equity.
i. These calculations are based on the mid-point of the share price range in the second quarter of the calendar year.

Exhibit 4 ALZA Corporation Financial Statements, December 31, 1987, and Analysts' Estimates, October 1988–1992 (millions of dollars except per share data)

	Actual 1987	Estimates[a]				
		1988	1989	1990	1991	1992
Income Statement Data						
Royalties and fees	$17.1	$20.5	$46.5	$80.0	$138.5	$205.0
Net sales	19.4	24.5	37.0	60.0	100.0	170.0
Research revenues[b]	25.9	29.0	32.6	37.5	42.0	48.0
Other, primarily interest income	8.4	9.1	8.5	8.0	10.5	13.5
	70.8	83.1	124.6	185.5	291.0	436.5
Cost of goods shipped	13.8	15.0	25.2	40.2	66.0	108.8
R&D	23.0	28.5	36.0	46.5	60.0	75.0
General, administrative, and marketing	8.6	10.9	13.0	16.0	20.5	25.0
Interest expense	2.0	3.4	3.8	2.0	.5	.5
	47.4	57.8	78.0	104.7	147.0	209.3
Net income before taxes and extraordinary items	23.4	25.3	46.6	80.8	144.0	227.2
Taxes	9.4	8.0	16.8	29.1	51.8	81.8
Net income	$14.0	$17.2	$29.9	$51.7	$92.2	$145.4
Shares outstanding (millions)[c]	33.6	33.6	33.6	34.5	35.4	35.5
Earnings per share	$ .42	$ .51	$ .89	$1.5	$2.6	$4.1
Statement of Cash Flows						
Cash flow from operating activities						
Net income	$14.0	$17.2	$29.9	$51.7	$92.2	$145.4
Depreciation	3.6	3.7	4.9	6.0	7.2	.5
Change in working capital and deferred taxes	(1.2)	(1.3)	(5.5)	(7.8)	(12.9)	(17.3)
	$16.4	$19.6	$29.3	$49.9	$86.5	$136.6
Cash flow from investment activities						
Capital expenditures[d]	(32.5)	(25.0)	(22.5)	(25.0)	(27.5)	(24.0)
Purchase of OROS[e]	–	(5.0)	(2.0)	(3.0)	(3.0)	(3.0)
Other	(8.9)	–	–	–	–	–
	$(41.4)	$(30.0)	$(27.5)	$(28.0)	$(30.5)	$(27.0)
Planned cash flows from financing activities[f]						
Sale of 5.5% convertible subordinate debentures	$72.8	–	–	–	–	–
Principal payments on debt	(.2)	(.2)	(.1)	(.1)	(.1)	(.1)
Issuance of stock[c]	3.8	1.5	1.8	2.5	2.5	2.5
	$76.4	$1.3	$1.7	$2.4	$2.4	$2.4

Exhibit 4   ALZA Corporation Financial Statements, December 31, 1987, (millions of dollars except per share data) (Continued)

Balance Sheet 12/31/87

Cash and investments	$142.8
Receivables	19.6
Inventories	6.0
Other current assets	3.6
Current assets	172.0
Net property plant and equipment	67.3
Other assets	4.2
Total assets	$243.5
Current liabilities[g]	$23.4
5.5% convertible subordinated debentures	75.0
Other liabilities	6.1
Total liabilities	104.5
Class A common stock[h]	.3
Class B common stock[i]	.01
Additional paid-in capital	190.5
Accumulated deficit	(51.8)
Stockholders' equity	139.0
Total liabilities and stockholders' equity	$243.5

Source: ALZA 1987 annual report for actual numbers. Estimates from analysts' reports published July–October 1988.

a. Analysts' estimates, October 1988. These numbers do not reflect the impact of BES on ALZA's financial statements.

b. In 1987, ALZA received $5.9 million in research revenues from its two R&D limited partnerships.

c. Analyst has included additional shares due to projected exercise of stock options.

d. For facilities expansion, additional R&D campus, and new commercial manufacturing facilities.

e. Represents payments to holders of OROS R&D Limited Partnership.

f. ALZA paid no cash dividends at any point through 1988.

g. Includes $.2 million of current portion of long-term debt.

h. 29.7 million shares outstanding; pays no dividends.

i. 1.45 million class B shares outstanding granted to Ciba-Geigy in conjunction with 1982 restructuring agreement. These shares are nonvoting and are not listed. Otherwise these shares are equivalent to class A shares. Convertible at Ciba-Geigy's option into two shares of ALZA class A shares. These shares pay no dividends.

Exhibit 5   Key Competitors of ALZA Corporation, 1988

Company	Product	Status	Type of Firm
Transdermal Delivery			
Key Pharmaceuticals	Nitroglycerine patches	Manufacturing product	Subsidiary of U.S. firm traded on New York Stock Exchange
G.D. Searle	Nitroglycerine patches	Manufacturing product	Subsidiary of U.S. firm traded on New York Stock Exchange
Health-Chem	Nitroglycerine patches	Manufacturing product	U.S. firm traded on American Stock Exchange
Health-Chem	Other patch products	Product trials	U.S. firm traded on American Stock Exchange
Elan Corporation	Nicotine patch	Early stage research	Irish firm, publicly traded
Forest Laboratories	Nitroglycerine patches	Early stage research	U.S. firm traded on American Stock Exchange
Moleculon	Several patch products	Early stage research	U.S. firm traded on NASDAQ
Cygnus Research	Several patch products	Product trials	U.S. firm, privately held and venture-financed
Several Japanese firms	Nitroglycerine patches	Product trials	Japanese firms, publicly traded
Oral Drug Delivery			
PennWalt	Ion-exchange mechanisms	Product trials	U.S. firm traded on New York Stock Exchange
KV Pharmaceutical	Various technologies	Product trials	U.S. firm traded on American Stock Exchange
Elan Corporation	Liquid suspensions	Product trials	Irish firm, publicly traded
Elan Corporation	Slow-release tablets	Product trials	Irish firm, publicly traded
Forest Laboratories	Controlled release tablets	Manufacturing product	U.S. firm traded on American Stock Exchange
Gacell Laboratories	Slow-release tablets	Manufacturing product	Subsidiary of major Swedish firm
Astra	Slow-release tablets	Product trials	Major Swedish firm
Drug Delivery to Eye			
Merck	Eye injections	Early stage research	U.S. firm traded on New York Stock Exchange
Diversified Tech, Inc.	Eye pouch insert	Early stage research	U.S. firm traded on NASDAQ
Bausch and Lomb	Corneal shield	Early stage research	U.S. firm traded on New York Stock Exchange
Intrauterine Devices			
Gynopharm	Various technologies	Early stage research	U.S. firm, privately held

Exhibit 5   Key Competitors of ALZA Corporation, 1988 (Continued)

Company	Product(s)	Status	Type of Firm
Electrotransport			
Motion Control	Anaesthesia delivery in surgery	Product being marketed	U.S. firm, privately held
Medtronic	Hypertension drug delivery	Early stage research	U.S. firm traded on New York Stock Exchange
Drug Delivery Systems	Polypeptide drug delivery	Early stage research	U.S. firm, privately held
MacroChem	Polypeptide drug delivery	Early stage research	U.S. firm traded on NASDAQ
Lectec	Antibiotic delivery	Early stage research	U.S. firm, privately held and venture-financed
Cygnus Research	Delivery of various drugs	Early stage research	U.S. firm, privately held and venture-financed
Advanced Polymers			
INTERx	Delivery of various drugs	Early stage research	Subsidiary of U.S. firm traded on New York Stock Exchange
Nova Pharmaceutical	Delivery of cancer drugs	Early stage research	U.S. firm traded on NASDAQ
Eli Lilly	Delivery of insulin	Early stage research	U.S. firm traded on New York or American Stock Exchange
Enzytech	Delivery of various drugs	Early stage research	U.S. firm, privately held and venture-financed

Sources: Analysts' reports, Corporate Technology Directory, Moody's Industrial Directory, Moody's OTC Directory, BioScan, and other directories.

Exhibit 6 Bio-Electro Systems Projected Financial Statements, 1988–1993 (millions of dollars)

	1988	1989	1990	1991	1992	1993	Total
Cash Flow Assuming Maximum Net Proceeds Raised from Offering							
Beginning cash balance	–	$39.7	$35.2	$27.9	$19.5	$9.8	–
Net offering proceeds	43.0	–	–	–	–	–	43.0
Interest income[a]	.3	2.4	2.0	1.5	.9	.3	7.4
Total	43.3	42.1	37.2	29.4	20.4	10.1	50.4
Development contract payments[b]							
"Alzamer" polymers	1.8	2.7	4.5	5.1	5.8	5.2	25.1
Electrotransport	1.7	3.7	4.2	4.2	4.2	4.3	22.3
General and administrative expenses[c]	.1	.5	.6	.6	.6	.6	3.0
Total	3.6	6.9	9.3	9.9	10.6	10.1	50.4
Ending cash balance[d,e]	$39.7	$35.2	$27.9	$19.5	$9.8	–	–
Cash Flow Assuming Minimum Net Proceeds Raised from Offering							
Beginning cash balance	–	$24.5	$19.2	$12.7	$6.9	$3.3	–
Net offering proceeds	$28.0	–	–	–	–	–	$28.0
Interest income[a]	.1	1.4	1.0	.6	.2	.1	3.4
Total	28.1	25.9	20.2	13.3	7.1	3.4	31.4
Development contract payments[b]							
"Alzamer" polymers	1.8	2.5	3.0	2.5	.9	.6	11.3
Electrotransport	1.7	3.7	3.9	3.3	2.3	2.2	17.1
General and administrative expenses[c]	.1	.5	.6	.6	.6	.6	3.0
Total	3.6	6.7	7.5	6.4	3.8	3.4	31.4
Ending cash balance[d,e]	24.5	19.2	12.7	6.9	3.3	–	–

Source: BES prospectus.

a. BES was not projected to earn any revenues other than interest income over this period. The ultimate revenue potential of products incorporating BES's therapeutic systems was thought to be in the "hundreds of millions of dollars," although it was impossible to estimate a more exact value.

b. These payments will be made from BES to ALZA and recognized as revenue by ALZA.

c. These charges include virtually no noncash charges like depreciation or amortization.

d. BES's stockholders' equity in each year would be calculated as its capital raised from the offering less cumulative *pre-tax* losses.

e. While BES's cumulative losses would generate substantial net operating losses for financial reporting purposes, they would not generate large net operating losses for tax purposes.

Exhibit 7   Example of an R&D Limited Partnership: ALZA TTS Research Partners, Ltd.

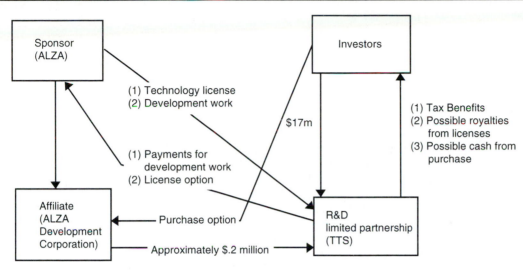

In February 1983, an R&D limited partnership, ALZA TTS Research Partners, Ltd., was set up to develop three to six products in certain specified therapeutic categories. ALZA gave TTS a nonexclusive, royalty-free license to use ALZA's TTS technology for the specific products identified. ALZA's wholly owned subsidiary, ALZA Development Corporation, as the general partner of ALZA TTS, contributed 1% of the cash capital to the partnership. TTS entered into a development contract with ALZA by which ALZA would use its best efforts to complete development of the products.

An offer of 3,200 units of Class A limited partnership interests was made to investors for $5,000 per unit, raising about $17 million. (Class B partnership units were also privately placed.) Effectively, 99% of the tax losses generated by TTS were passed along to the Class A limited partners, while ALZA Development Corporation received 1% of the tax losses.

While TTS owned the products it developed, as part of the agreement setting up the RDLP, it granted ALZA Development Corporation certain rights. ALZA Development Corporation retained the right, but not the obligation, to acquire the interests of the limited partners by paying a lump sum equal to $60 million, $90 million, or $120 million if it bought them out the limited partners' interests in 1987, 1988, or 1989 and beyond, respectively. ALZA also retained the right to continue development of products once TTS ran out of funds, and to licence individual products, paying predetermined royalty fees.

TTS ran out of funds in 1987, and as of November 1988, ALZA Development Corporation had not exercised its purchase option. However, in 1987, ALZA exercised its option to continue product development for two of the partnerships products and entered into a marketing agreement with a partner for one of these products.

Exhibit 8 Capital Markets Data, November 18, 1988

ALZA class A common	$23 ⅛

Interest Rates[a]

Treasury securities

1-Month	6.86%
6-Month	8.36
1-Year	8.57
3-Year	8.83
5-Year	8.91
10-Year	9.03

Long-term corporate bonds by credit rating [b]

AAA	9.70%
AA	10.08
A	10.53
BBB	10.86
BB	11.78
B	12.25

Source: Interactive Data Corporation (IDC).
a. Expressed on a bond-equivalent yield basis.
b. ALZA senior debt was rated Ba or BB at this time.

Exhibit 9   ALZA Corporation Common Stock Price Data

ALZA Class A Common Stock Price, 1983–November 18, 1988[a]

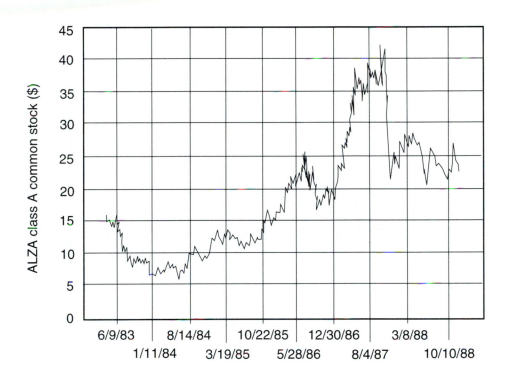

Exhibit 9   ALZA Corporation Common Stock Price Data (Continued)

Annualized Volatility of ALZA Class A Common Stock, 1983–November 18, 1988[b]

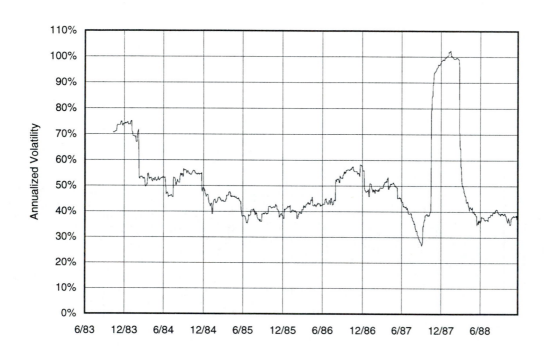

Source: IDC (stock price data), case writers' analysis (volatility), Value Line (beta estimate).
a. Corrected for July 1986 two-for-one common stock split.
b. Calculated on the basis of past three months' data. ALZA's common stock beta was 2.0 (calculated on basis of prior 60 months' data).

R JR NABISCO—1990

In the spring of 1990 the firm of Kohlberg Kravis Roberts & Co. (KKR) was in negotiation with lenders regarding the refinancing of a $1.2-billion bridge loan due to be repaid in full by February 1991. The bridge loan was part of the $24-billion financing of KKR's leveraged buyout of RJR Nabisco in early 1989. Originally, KKR had planned to retire the loan with the proceeds of a $1.25-billion public offering of senior debt. However, in December 1989, Moody's failed to give the issue an investment-grade rating. Moody's also downgraded RJR's other debt, a move that triggered substantial declines in the market prices of RJR's securities. Faced with an unreceptive public market, KKR withdrew the debt offering and began discussions with RJR's lending banks.

For the banks, a major concern was the uncertainty surrounding the upcoming interest rate reset on $7 billion of RJR's pay-in-kind (PIK) bonds. Indentures required that on or before April 28, 1991, RJR reset the rate so that the bonds would trade at par (see Exhibit 1). In the spring of 1990, the bonds were selling at steep discounts to par (see Exhibit 3). The market obviously saw substantial risk that the reset would fail, which would put RJR in violation of its bond covenants.

The reset bonds came into being as the "cram-down" securities in the RJR buyout. The distinctive feature of these bonds was the reset provision, which at the time of the buyout was a key factor in KKR's victory over a management group led by then RJR Nabisco's CEO, F. Ross Johnson.[1] Weeks of escalating bidding, which had begun with a $75 per share all-cash bid by the management group, ended with the RJR board of directors having to choose between two final bids: KKR's offer of $81 per share in cash plus PIK reset bonds it valued at $28 per share, versus the management group's offer of $84 per share in cash plus PIK bonds it valued at $28 per share. The latter PIK bonds did not have a reset feature, however. The board's financial advisors, Dillon Read and Lazard Freres,

---

1   Burrough, Bryan, and Helyar, John, *Barbarians at the Gate*, Harper & Row, New York, c. 1990, pp. 441–442, p. 485, p. 493, p. 497–498.

Joel Barber and André F. Perold perpared this case as the basis for class discussion rather than to illustrate either effective or ineffective handling of an administrative situation.

concluded that the two offers were "substantially equivalent," in effect valuing the management group's PIK bonds at only $25 per share.[2] They reasoned that the KKR bonds were effectively "guaranteed." If the market didn't judge the securities to be worth $28, the interest rate would be reset to make them worth $28. KKR had "put its money where its mouth was," something the management group had been unwilling to do. With a "substantially equivalent" opinion from its financial advisors, the board felt free to evaluate the offers based on other considerations. The board declared KKR the winner on the basis of the firm's pledge not to effect large layoffs after the deal was consummated, and the fact that KKR offered stockholders the option to acquire up to 25% of the new company at a point in the future, whereas the management group offered them an option for only 15%.[3]

As a consequence of the buyout, RJR's total debt ballooned to $29 billion. KKR's strategy for servicing this debt rested on asset sales and improved internal cash flow. Except for the stumbling block created by Moody's downgrade, the plan had proceeded as forecast: through March 31, 1990, asset sales (Exhibit 2) and cash flow met or exceeded targets and all required debt payments were made.

There was considerable speculation as to how KKR might try to deal with the reset problem, the resolution of which had now become intertwined with the bridge loan refinancing. With respect to the latter, covenants effectively prevented any course of action other than the raising of external funds to retire the loan. With respect to the reset provision, however, KKR faced a richer array of alternatives, although just about any financial restructuring would require the consent of the banks in view of the tight restrictions imposed by the Credit Agreement (discussed below).

First, the firm could try to raise external funds and repurchase all or a portion of the PIK reset bonds. In recent times, many companies had been repurchasing their "junk" securities: $2.5 billion alone in the first quarter of 1990, versus $5.5 billion in 1987, 1988, and 1989 combined.[4] Potentially, the funds for a bond buyback could come from additional bank borrowings and/or the sale of equity, preferred stock, or other securities. An often-mentioned source of money was KKR's LBO fund, which still had several billion dollars available for investments (described more fully below). How many of the reset bonds would have to be repurchased was not obvious. Conceivably, with an external funds

---

2   Burrough, Bryan, and Helyar, John, "How Underdog KKR Won RJR Nabisco Without Highest Bid," *The Wall Street Journal*, December 2, 1988.

3   Ibid.

4   Mitchell, Constance, "Junk Market Could Stay in Disarray but Buy-Backs Are Ray of Hope," *The Wall Street Journal*, February 20, 1990.

infusion, it might not even be necessary to repurchase any of the bonds, since a strengthened balance sheet might give sufficient boost to their values.

A second alternative was to raise internal funds for a bond buyback through the sale of additional assets—the most marketable of which were believed to be RJR's U.S. food businesses, estimated to be worth over $12 billion (see Exhibit 3). However, this was one of KKR's least-attractive alternatives, since its strategy was to develop, rather than liquidate, RJR's major food businesses. Moreover, asset sales would generate substantial capital gains taxes, estimated to be around 20% of gross proceeds for the food businesses, and 30% for the tobacco businesses.

As a third possibility, KKR could try to renegotiate the terms of the reset bonds or give holders the opportunity to exchange their bonds for equity and other securities.

Any of the aforementioned approaches would have the effect of reducing or eliminating the number of reset bonds outstanding. Many argued that a reduction in the supply of these bonds would create value in and of itself, since they accounted for over 60% of the high-yield PIK bond market. In other words, conditions of oversupply, and not necessarily poor fundamentals, could have been causing the depressed prices of the reset bonds.[5] Some bolstered this view that the company was basically healthy by pointing out that the equity warrants were trading above their initial book value of $5 per share.[6]

Finally, KKR could simply wait and hope that the prices of the reset bonds would recover by early 1991. If they did not recover, and the reset proved infeasible, KKR could then try to negotiate with the bondholders and banks, or seek Chapter 11 protection, or both.

KOHLBERG KRAVIS ROBERTS & CO.

Kohlberg Kravis Roberts & Co. was started in 1976 by Jerome Kohlberg Jr., Henry R. Kravis, and George R. Roberts, then 50, 32, and 33 years old, respectively. All three had left Bear Stearns where they had been doing "bootstrap" (as in "pull yourself up by your bootstraps") financings, the name given to leveraged buyouts back then. Kohlberg had done his first LBO in 1965.

---

5   The junk bond market collapsed in mid-1989 and remained extremely weak through the first quarter of 1990. As causes, various observers cited the troubles and ultimate bankruptcy of Drexel Burnham Lambert, the savings and loan crisis, the financial distress of Campeau Corporation, and fears that economic recession would trigger numerous junk bond defaults.

6   The warrants were transferable beginning May 22, 1990; prior to that, Salomon Brothers made a market in options on the warrants. These options, with a strike price of a penny per share, began trading in May 1989 at $7, and at one point reached a high of $11 before falling to a low of $4 in February 1990. On June 11, 1990 the warrants began trading directly on the New York Stock Exchange and closed the day at $7.

From its modest beginnings, KKR came to control companies with annual revenues of almost $50 billion, putting the firm in the same league as industrial giants like General Electric and IBM. And KKR accomplished this with a professional staff of fewer than two dozen.

KKR first attracted serious notice in 1979 when it took Houdaille Industries, the firm's first major New York Stock Exchange-listed company, private in a leveraged buyout. In 1984, KKR did the first billion-dollar buyout (Wometco Enterprises), and in the same year did the first large buyout through a public tender offer (Malone & Hyde). In 1986, KKR set a size record with its $8.2-billion buyout of Beatrice, a record that stood until the RJR Nabisco buyout three years later.

In the 13 years prior to the RJR buyout, KKR completed over 30 leveraged buyouts with a total purchase price exceeding $30 billion. Equity investments made during this period by KKR partnerships totaled $2.2 billion, on which KKR achieved a compounded annual return of 60% for its investors, or 49% after KKR took its share of the profits. While KKR did not promise such returns in the future, investors clearly hoped such would be the case.

KKR raised its first LBO equity investment fund in 1978, receiving commitments from institutional investors for $30 million, to which the KKR partners added $3 million of their own money. In subsequent years, KKR obtained ever greater commitments from its growing stable of investors. The fund reached $75 million in 1980, was up to $316 million in 1982, $1 billion in 1984, and $1.8 billion in 1986.

Dwarfing its predecessors, the 1987 fund attracted particular media attention: it had $1.3 billion in unused commitments from the 1986 fund plus $4.3 billion of new commitments, bringing total funds available in 1987 to $5.6 billion. KKR invested $56 million of its own money in the fund, or 1% of the total. The second-largest LBO fund at the time was that of Forstmann Little at $3 billion.

Many participants in the 1987 fund had invested money with KKR since the beginning of the decade. Among them were the Oregon Public Employees Retirement System, which had $600 million committed to the 1987 fund, and First Chicago Venture Capital, which had $300 million committed. Other investors who had contributed to earlier KKR funds and were believed to have committed to the 1987 fund included the Washington State Investment Board, the Minnesota State Board of Investment, the New York State Retirement Fund, the endowments of Harvard University and the Massachusetts Institute of Technology, and a number of corporate pension funds.[7]

---

7   Anders, George, "KKR's Backers Wary of Any Hostile Bid for RJR;," *The Wall Street Journal*, October 28, 1988.

The principal transaction to date of the 1987 fund was the RJR deal. The fund invested $1.5 billion in equity and $500 million in bridge financing (the "Partnership Debt Securities"). In the spring of 1990 the fund was believed to have $3 billion in unused commitments. KKR had more or less free reign over how the funds could be invested.

Through its investments in the funds, KKR participated as a principal in the transactions it concluded. And in the RJR Nabisco deal, KKR partners invested another $80 million directly.[8] However, a significant portion of its earnings came from various fees it charged its investors, including commitment fees, a carrying charge, and investment banking fees.

Commitment fee: To participants in its funds, KKR charged 1.5% per annum of the amount committed but uninvested. Payments of such fees began soon after the fund closed and were intended to continue on uninvested funds for a six-year commitment period.

Carrying fee: KKR received 20% of the profit on individual deals, i.e., 20% of the amount that realized equity returns exceeded the initial equity investment. Thus far, KKR had liquidated many of its earlier investments within three to seven years of making them.

Investment banking fees: On its deals, KKR typically charged 1% of the total size of the transaction as its fee for arranging and completing the buyout, but this percentage could vary. On the RJR Nabisco deal, KKR charged $75 million, or 0.3% of the transaction size. Fees charged on other large deals (as a percentage of the total transaction in parentheses) were: Owens-Illinois, $60 million (1.5%); Safeway, $60 million (1.3%); Beatrice, $45 million (0.7%); Jim Walter, $35 million (1.4%); and Stop & Shop, $28 million (2.3%). In addition, KKR charged continuing fees for such services as arranging divestitures, asset sales, and refinancings.

KKR'S EXPERIENCE WITH A PREVIOUS RESET

Hillsborough Holdings Corporation, a KKR limited partnership, purchased Jim Walter Corporation in a 1987 leveraged buyout valued at $2.4 billion. At the time, the company was embroiled in numerous asbestos-related product liability lawsuits stemming from the manufacture of asbestos building materials by the company's Celotex Corporation subsidiary.

Reportedly, KKR did not think the plaintiffs would prevail. KKR also believed it could insulate the company and itself from legal liability by selling the Jim Walter holding company, and thereby rid itself of the problematic Celotex subsidiary, while retaining the operating assets under the newly organized Hillsborough Holdings Corp.[9] However, in the summer of 1988 the plaintiffs successfully added Hillsborough Holdings and KKR to the list of defendants in the case. The state district court judge in Texas agreed with plaintiffs'

---

8   *The New York Times*, "Corrections," September 18, 1989.

9   Hilder, David B., and Smith, Randall, "Kohlberg Kravis Sails Into Rough Waters With Hillsborough Unit Chapter 11 Filing," *The Wall Street Journal*, December 29, 1989.

contention that the LBO was a fraudulent scheme designed to shield the company from asbestos litigation.[10]

Prices of Hillsborough's $624-million, high-yield buyout debt plummeted. These bonds carried a provision which stipulated that the interest coupon would be reset in December 1989 so that the bonds would trade at slightly above par. Failing such a reset, the bonds would become due and payable almost immediately.

In November 1989 it became apparent that the reset rate would have to be in excess of 20%. Hillsborough could not support such a burden, and KKR attempted to restructure the debt through an exchange offer that included new bonds with higher interest rates, some cash, and a 10% equity stake in the company.

Agreement by holders of 80% of the bonds was required to effect the exchange. Large holders included Fidelity Investments ($30 million), First Executive Corporation ($91 million), Columbia Savings and Loan Association ($25 million), Kemper Life Insurance Company ($40 million), General Electric pension fund ($19 million), and various accounts of Drexel Burnham Lambert ($73 million). While many went along with the proposal, there were a number of holdouts, including Fidelity Investments, who turned a deaf ear to the personal pleas of Henry Kravis.[11] Faced with the bonds coming due shortly and asset sales precluded by the asbestos litigation, KKR filed for Chapter 11 protection for Hillsborough.

THE RJR CAPITAL STRUCTURE

Post buyout, RJR was structured in terms of a hierarchy of holding companies. The operating company, RJR Nabisco, Inc., was held by RJR Holdings Capital Corporation ("Capital"), which in turn was held by RJR Holdings Group, Inc. ("Group"), which in turn was held by RJR Holdings Corporation ("Holdings").

Exhibit 1 summarizes this structure and describes the various securities issued by each of these entities. After the equity of Holdings, the most junior securities were the Senior Converting Debentures followed by the Exchange Debentures. These were the PIK reset bonds. Next in seniority were the Partnership Debt Securities (the KKR bridge loan alluded to earlier), followed by the so-called Permanent Debt Securities (all such Subordinated Debentures ranking *pari passu* with one another), followed by the Increasing Rate Notes (bridge loans privately placed by Drexel Burnham Lambert and Merrill Lynch). Most senior was the bank debt and the existing debt (the debt of RJR Nabisco, Inc., prior

---

10   Stertz, Bradley A., and Harlan, Christi, "Legal Beat," *The Wall Street Journal*, September 29, 1989.

11   Ibid.

to the buyout). The majority of the existing debt was secured "equally and ratably" with the bank debt, while some existing debt was actually junior to the banks' claims.

The two PIK reset issues differed in essentially two ways: the Exchange Debentures were more senior, while the Converting Debentures gave holders the right to convert into 25% of the equity of Holdings on a *fully diluted* (i.e., antidilutive) basis. The reset provisions of the two bonds were essentially identical, and prior to reset, the two bonds would pay the same interest rate.

RESTRICTIONS ON ADDITIONAL INDEBTEDNESS AND THE MOVEMENT OF CASH

RJR's ability to incur additional indebtedness and to move cash from Capital to Group and Holdings was tightly constrained by the agreement between RJR and its lending banks (the "Bank Credit Agreement" or "Credit Agreement") and by the indentures of the Subordinated Debentures and Increasing Rate Notes. The Credit Agreement most limited RJR's freedom of action. Thus, the restrictive covenants of the bond and note indentures only assumed relevance upon expiration of the Credit Agreement (which remained in effect as long as there was bank debt outstanding).

The raison d'etre of the Bank Credit Agreement was primarily to ensure that the banks were paid off ahead of anybody else; exceptions to this principle were few. Importantly, the banks' reach extended upward to Group and Holdings. For example, without the banks' permission, funds raised through an equity issue by Holdings could not be used to buy back junior debt. And, as already noted, RJR was not permitted to repay the $1.2-billion bridge loan due in February 1991 with internally generated funds.

Other stipulations in the Credit Agreement restricted RJR's ability to make investments and limited capital expenditures to $900 million in 1989, $800 million in 1990, and $500 million per annum thereafter.

Finally, the Credit Agreement required RJR to maintain certain specified levels of net worth and ratios regarding fixed charge coverage, cash interest coverage, and leverage. In the spring of 1990 RJR was in compliance with all such covenants and no violation of same appeared imminent.

The indentures of the Increasing Rate Notes and the Subordinated Debentures allowed considerably more leeway regarding the issuance of additional debt and the uses of cash. In particular, Capital or its subsidiaries could borrow as much as $2.5 billion additional senior debt without limitation as to its use. Capital could also issue $1.5 billion of subordinated debt provided that Capital's consolidated fixed charge ratio exceeded 1:1 after giving effect to the additional subordinated borrowings. Analysts thought RJR would be within this 1:1 ratio, although barely so, if it issued the full $4 billion of debt as per the above. The indentures made separate allowance for the refinancing of the $1.2-billion bank bridge loan and the $500-million KKR bridge loan.

With respect to the movement of cash generated by the operating company, up to $2 billion of funds could be made available to Group or Holdings for the purpose of buying back the Exchange or Converting Debentures, provided that if the funds made available for such purpose exceeded $1 billion, Capital's consolidated fixed charge ratio would be 1.19:1 or better. Capital could also make funds available for the repurchase of Exchange and Converting Debentures, with no specified limit, provided that for every $6.00 par amount of Exchange or Converting Debentures repurchased, $5.00 par amount of Increasing Rate Notes and Subordinated Debentures were repurchased.

RJR NABISCO THROUGH MARCH 31, 1990

Exhibit 4 shows the transformation of the RJR Nabisco balance sheet starting with the historical statement of RJR Nabisco, Inc. on December 31, 1988 and proceeding to the pro forma balance sheet of the same date showing the expected changes following the LBO. The balance sheets on December 31, 1989 and March 31, 1990 are those of the consolidated entity.

Exhibit 1 details the composition of long-term debt, including initial amounts issued (with respect to buyout-related debt) and amounts outstanding on March 31, 1990.

OPERATING PROJECTIONS

Historically, RJR Nabisco's tobacco operations provided just over half of the company's sales, and about three-fourths of its profits. In the latter half of the 1980s, domestic tobacco operating margins consistently exceeded 30% and in 1989, they were 38%. International tobacco operations, which contributed about a quarter of total RJR tobacco sales, exhibited lower operating margins—18% in 1986, declining to 14% in 1988, and rebounding to 16% in 1989. During this period, operating margins for the retained food operations were in the range of 12%–14%.

Exhibit 5 gives projections of RJR Nabisco's operating results for the years 1990–1993. These projections are in the midrange of those of Wall Street analysts who were closely following the RJR situation. Food sales were forecast to grow at 8.6% per annum, and food business operating margins of 15% were thought to be achievable.

Tobacco revenue was projected to grow at 8.7% annually. Domestic unit sales were forecasted to fall 5% each year, while international unit sales were expected to rise 6% annually. Domestically, price increases averaging 10% a year were seen as more than offsetting the decline in units sold. Internationally, price increases of 4% a year were expected. As a result of cost-cutting efforts, operating margins in the domestic tobacco segment were estimated to reach 40% in 1990 and were forecasted to remain flat thereafter. In the first five months of 1990, RJR in fact realized margins of 42% in the domestic tobacco business.[12] Internationally, operating margins were estimated at 16% in 1990 and were projected to remain at that level.

Exhibit 5 also gives a cash flow analysis based on the above projected operating results. As shown there, RJR was forecasted to have $1.4 billion of cash flow available in 1990 after required debt repayments. This would allow the company to make over $1 billion of optional debt repayments in 1990 and still have enough to service the required 1991 payments, on the assumption that external financing was obtained for the $1.2-billion bridge loan. The projections show there being ample cash available to make required debt repayments in 1992 and 1993.

The relatively optimistic outlook for RJR's tobacco businesses was not without considerable uncertainty. As noted above, cigarette shipments in the U.S. market had been falling in recent years due to changes in attitudes toward smoking, a drop-off that could accelerate if societal pressures turned even more sharply against smoking. Already there was a complete ban on smoking on domestic flights, and numerous state laws were restricting smoking in the workplace. Under pressure from their constituencies, university endowments and public pension funds were beginning to divest themselves of tobacco securities.[13] In Canada, demand for cigarettes was down over 10% following a complete ban on cigarette advertising since January 1989.[14] Finally, federal tobacco excise taxes, currently at $0.16 per pack of cigarettes, would likely be raised soon.

TOBACCO-RELATED LITIGATION

During the 1980s, investors were concerned that the tobacco companies would be hit with large product liability damage awards. Thus far, RJR and other tobacco companies had been quite successful in defending themselves in such lawsuits. While there had been court decisions against the tobacco companies, none of any significance stood on appeal.

Plaintiffs' arguments, by and large, fell into two general camps: "design defects" and "failure to warn." Design defect arguments usually took one of three forms: "consumer expectation" (contending that smoking was more dangerous than consumers

---

12 Wallace, Anise C., "Capital Spending Cut by RJR," *The New York Times*, July 2, 1990.

13 Myerson, Allen R., "Dumping Tobacco Stocks," *The New York Times*, May 27, 1990.

14 Lipman, Joanne, "Decline of Tobacco Sales in Canada Fuels Ad Debate," *The Wall Street Journal*, June 12, 1990.

ever contemplated); "risk/utility" (maintaining that product risks outweigh product utility); and "negligence" (alleging that tobacco companies failed to take reasonable steps to design a safe product). Failure-to-warn cases focused on the years prior to 1966 when federal law began to require that consumer warnings be printed on cigarette packaging. As the pre-1966 smoking population aged, the number of failure-to-warn cases declined over time.

In March 1990 there were 31 product liability cases pending against RJR; compared to 97, 69, and 48 such cases at the end of 1986, 1987, and 1988, respectively. On April 12, 1990, RJR discontinued its practice of buying tobacco liability insurance, becoming self-insured for all tobacco-related product liability risks.

BONDHOLDER LITIGATION

When news broke of F. Ross Johnson's bid for RJR, the company's then outstanding bonds fell 15% in value. Metropolitan Life and Jefferson-Pilot, holding $250 million and $10 million, respectively, of these bonds, filed suit against RJR Nabisco, seeking to be repaid at par. Were the plaintiffs to prevail, other holders of RJR Nabisco bonds likely would be able to "piggyback" on the decision and effectively force RJR to refinance the entire $5 billion of debt outstanding prior to the LBO.

The case, still undecided as of March 1990, rested on certain "negative pledge" covenants in the bond indentures that required the bonds be secured "equally and ratably" with other lenders, including the banks. The plaintiffs maintained they were defrauded when RJR Nabisco used the proceeds of asset sales to pay down bank debt.

Exhibit 1 Corporate Structure and Description of Securities (in millions of dollars)

Company and Security	3/31/90 Amounts[a]	Initial Amounts[b]	Current Rating[c]
RJR Holdings Corporation			
Senior Converting PIK Debentures	$2,115	$1,806	B3/B+
Common Stock[d]	1,024	1,952	
(308 MM shares held by: KKR, 95.7%; ML, 1.7%; and Management, 2.6%)			
Common Stock Warrants[e]	208	190	
(45.5 MM warrants)			
RJR Holdings Group, Inc.			
Exchange PIK Debentures	4,765	4,067	B3/B+
RJR Holdings Capital Corporation			
Bank Debt	4,942	12,175	
Increasing Rate Notes[f]	1,000	5,000	
Permanent Debt Securities:			
13.5% Subordinated Debentures	525	525	B2/B+
Sub. Extendible Reset Debentures	225	225	B2/B+
15% PIK Subordinated Debentures	1,132	1,000	B2/B+
Subordinated Discount Debentures[g]	2,264	2,000	B2/B+
Subordinated Floating Rate Notes	250	250	B2/B+
Partnership Debt Securities	582	500	
RJR Nabisco, Inc.			
Pre-buyout Debt[h]	5,053	5,312	Ba3/BB

Exhibit 1   Corporate Structure and Description of Securities (Continued)

SENIOR CONVERTING PIK DEBENTURES DUE 2009

Interest

14.7% for the period 2/9/89 to 10/31/89. Thereafter, the rate is adjusted semi-annually, based on the highest of the 3 month, 10-year and 30-year treasury bill/note/bond rates, plus 550 basis points. The rate must be in the range of 12.625% and 16.625%. On 11/1/89 the rate was adjusted to 13.71%, and on 5/1/90 to 14.07%.

The debentures must at some point be reset to a fixed rate to maturity. The reset provision was described as follows in the KKR/RJR proxy statement to stockholders:

> "[On or prior to April 28, 1991], the Board of Directors of Holdings shall elect, upon not less than 48-hours notice to Dillon, Read & Co., Inc. ("Dillon"), and Lazard Freres & Co. ("Lazard") to cause the interest rate to cease to be floating and to be set permanently at a fixed rate (the "Fixed Rate"). The Fixed Rate will be equal to a rate determined by Holdings' financial advisors on the one hand, and Dillon and Lazard on the other hand, designed to result in the Debentures trading at par on a fully distributed basis, without giving effect to the conversion feature of the Debentures. If Holdings' financial advisors on the one hand, and Dillon and Lazard on the other hand, are unable to agree on the Fixed Rate within three business days, Holdings' financial advisors on the one hand, and Dillon and Lazard on the other hand, shall appoint an independent nationally recognized investment bank to determine the Fixed Rate and such determination by such bank shall be final."

Calls

Callable at par any time after 5/1/93. The Bank Credit Agreement and Subordinated Debt imposed tight limitations on the call provision.

Conversion

On 5/1/93 convertible into RJR Holdings Corporations common stock which would represent a 25% equity interest in the company on a fully diluted basis. If the conversion occurs, the bondholders forego the right to the interest accrued on the debentures.

Market

Listed on the New York Stock Exchange.

EXCHANGE PIK DEBENTURES DUE 2007

Interest

Same interest rate provisions as on the Senior Converting Debentures described above.

On or prior to April 28, 1991, RJR must set a fixed rate to maturity on the debentures. The reset provision is substantially identical to that of the Senior Converting Debentures described above.

Calls:

Callable at par at any time. The Bank Credit Agreement and the Subordinate Debt imposed strict limitations on the call feature.

Exhibit 1 Corporate Structure and Description of Securities (Continued)

Sinking Fund

Equal payments due on 5/15/2005 and 5/15/2006 that together retire 50% of the Debentures.

Market

Listed on the New York Stock Exchange.

Increasing Rate Notes due 1997

Cash interest. Interest rate reset monthly at a short-term floating rate benchmark, plus a fixed spread, plus an additional spread that increases over time; interest over 18% payable in kind. Callable at par at any time. Registered, but not listed on an exchange.

PERMANENT DEBT SECURITIES

13.5% Subordinated Debentures due 2001

Cash interest. Callable in 1994 at 106.75, declining to par by 1999. Listed on the NYSE.

Subordinated Extendible Reset Debentures due 2001

Cash interest. First maturity in 1991, but can be extended each year for one year up to final maturity in 2001. Upon election to extended maturity, interest rate must be reset to obtain a bid value of 101, but must be in the range of 13.125% to 15.625%. Pays 101 at maturity. Listed on the NYSE.

15% PIK Subordinated Debentures due 2001

PIK interest to 5/15/94, cash thereafter. Callable in 1994 at 107.50, declining to par in 1999. Sinking fund: 25% of initial principal outstanding due in each of 1999 and 2000. Listed on the NYSE.

Subordinated Discount Debentures due 2001

Interest accrues at 15% to 5/15/94, cash thereafter. Callable in 1994 at 107.50, declining to par in 1999. Sinking fund: 25% of initial principal outstanding due in each of 1999 and 2000. Listed on the NYSE.

Subordinated Floating Rate Notes during 1999

Cash interest payable quarterly. LIBOR plus 385 basis points. Callable at a small premium to par on any interest payment date. Publicly traded.

Partnership Debt Securities due 1997

PIK interest through 2/9/94, cash thereafter. Interest rate variable at the greater of 50 basis points over the IRN rate (see above) or an increasing spread (over time) over the rate on the seven-year Treasury note.

Exhibit 1 Corporate Structure and Description of Securities (Continued)

BANK DEBT

Asset Sale Bridge Facility

Initial amount $6,000 million, paid down to $263 million by 3/31/90.

Refinancing Bridge Facility

Initial amount $1,500 million, paid down to $1,179 million by 3/31/90. Balance due 2/9/91.

Revolving Credit Facility

$1,750 million, all of which was available on 3/31/90. Could be used for day-to-day operating needs and/or to refinance the remaining ($1,000 million) IRNs, but not for repayment of the Refinancing Bridge Facility.

Term Loan Facility

$3,500 million outstanding on 3/31/90. Due in 16 quarterly installment payments beginning in May 1991.

Working Capital Facility

$750 million of which $187 million was undrawn on 3/31/90.

Exhibit 1   Corporate Structure and Description of Securities (Continued)

PRE-BUYOUT DEBT

Amount[i]

Price	Coupon	Euro/Dom	Maturity	Call Date	Call
$125.0	8⅝%	Euro	09/20/91	NCL[j]	N/A
400.0	Zero	Euro	02/19/92	02/08/82	100.00
250.0	10¾	Dom	08/01/93	08/01/91	100.00
125.0	7⅜	Euro	01/21/94	01/21/91	101.50
30.0	7⅞	Dom	09/01/94	09/01/88	100.38
24.8	7⅜	Dom	02/01/01	02/01/88	102.24
122.0	8	Dom	01/15/07	01/15/89	104.16
250.0	9⅜	Dom	04/01/16	04/01/88	108.44
487.0	8⅜	Dom	02/01/17	02/01/88	107.96
300.0	8⅛	Dom	04/15/91	NCL	N/A
100.0	8¾	Dom	06/01/92	NCL	N/A
300.0	8⅞	Dom	11/15/92	NCL	N/A
100.0	8¾	Euro[k]	06/30/94	NCL	N/A
100.0	8⅞	Dom	01/15/95	NCL	N/A
300.0	9¼	Dom	05/01/95	NCL	N/A
100.0	8⅝	Dom	02/15/96	02/15/93	100.00
200.0	8⅞	Dom	03/01/98	03/01/95	100.00
491.0	8⅝	Dom	03/15/17	03/15/88	108.19
22.5	7¾	Dom	05/01/01	05/01/88	102.48
24.4	7¾	Dom	11/01/03	11/01/88	102.90
19.6	6¾	Dom	06/01/93	06/01/88	100.00
8.7	7¾	Dom	05/01/01	05/01/88	102.48
31.6	9½	Dom	12/15/04	12/15/88	104.07

Source: Salomon Brothers

a. Outstanding amounts on March 31, 1990 including all pay in kind and zero coupon interest accrued through such date.

b. Original amounts at time of issue (in the case of Pre-buyout Debt, amount outstanding on 12/31/88). Amounts shown were not necessarily outstanding simultaneously. *See Note f.*

c. As of July 2, 1990.

d. Book values. Initial amount consisted of $1,500 million cash contributed by KKR, Merrill Lynch, and Drexel Burnham Lambert (which shares were subsequently bought back by KKR), plus $452 million attributed to the equity conversion feature of the Senior Converting Debentures.

e. Sold for $.01 each to holders of Increasing Rate Notes who agreed to purchase the Subordinated 15% PIK and Discount Debentures. Exercisable at $.07 per share during the one-year period following the effective date of SEC registration of the common stock, or 5/22/98, whichever was earlier.

f. $4,000 million of the Increasing Rate Notes were refinanced with proceeds of Permanent Debt Securities issued in May 1989.

g. Initial amount shown was gross proceeds at time of issue. Par value was $4,110 million.

h. Outstanding long-term debt of RJR Nabisco, Inc., including current maturities.

i. Dollars in millions.

j. Non call life.

k. Puttable June 30, 1991.

Exhibit 2   Summary of Completed and Planned Divestitures of RJR Nabisco Operating Units

	Gross proceeds[a]	Closing date
Completed sales		
Food businesses:		
Nabisco International-European Food	$2,500	6/06/89
Chun King	52	6/21/89
Associated Biscuits Ltd.	44	7/07/89
Oxford Biscuit/Nabisco Brands Norge	20	7/28/89
Nabisco International-Spain & Portugal	78	12/04/89
Del Monte Tropical Fruit	875	12/05/89
Del Monte Processed Food	1,475	1/10/90
Curtiss Confections	370	2/23/90
Nabisco International-NZ/Malay/HK	180	4/02/90
Total, food	$5,594	
Tobacco businesses:		
Brazil operations	$50	4/09/90
Total completed sales	$5,644	4/30/90
Planned sales[b]		
Food business:		
Nabisco International-Latin American	$250	
Milk Bone Dog Biscuits	350	
Possible sales[b]		
Food business:		
A-1 Steak Sauce/Grey Poupon Mustard	$400	
Chewing gum	225	
Nonoperating assets:		
20% equity ownership in ESPN	200	
Total planned and possible sales	$1,425	

Exhibit 2   Summary of Completed and Planned Divestitures of RJR Nabisco Operating Units
(Continued)

	Gross proceeds[a]	Closing date
Estimated value of remaining assets[b]		
Food businesses:		
Nabisco-Canada	670	
Nabisco U.S.A.	5,900	
Remaining Grocery operations	4,025	
Planters/LifeSavers	2,100	
Total, food	12,695	
Tobacco businesses:		
Domestic and International	18,000	
Remaining liquidation value	$30,695[c]	

a. Dollars in millions. Figures do not take into account capital gains taxes.
b. Estimates by Salomon Brothers, May 16, 1990.
c. Approximately an 8 × multiple of projected 1990 EBITDA.

Exhibit 3 RJR Nabisco—1990

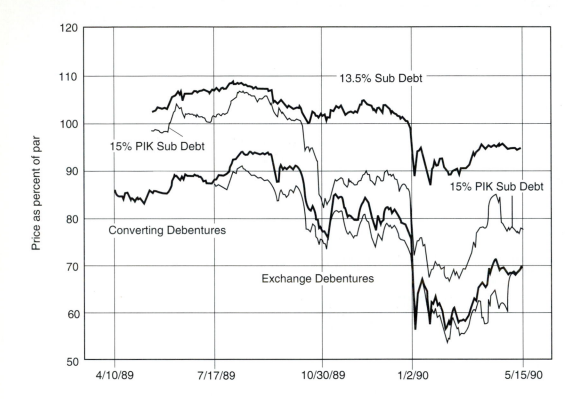

Exhibit 4 Consolidated Balance Sheets, RJR Holdings Corporation (dollars in millions)

	12/31/88[a]	Pro forma 12/31/88[b]	12/31/89	3/31/90
Assets				
Current assets:				
Cash and cash equivalents	$1,425	$958	$142	$21
Accounts and notes receivable	1,920	1,920	998	662
Inventories[c]	2,571	4,021	2,876	2,882
Prepaid expenses and excise taxes	265	265	358	380
Net assets available for sale[d]			2,300	625
Total current assets	6,181	7,164	6,674	4,570
Property, plant, and equipment, net	6,149	6,149	5,019	4,952
Trademarks and Goodwill, net	4,555	21,716	23,736	23,585
Other assets and deferred charges	866	1,570	983	815
	$17,751	$36,599	$36,412	$33,922
Liabilities and Stockholders' Equity				
Current liabilities:				
Notes payable	$423	$423	$181	713
Accounts payable and accrued accounts	3,220	3,181	3,265	2,838
Income taxes accrued	300	260	490	291
Total current liabilities[e]	3,943	3,864	3,936	3,842
Long-term debt[e]	5,312	28,671	24,951	22,645
Other noncurrent liabilities[c,f]	1,617	1,012	2,502	2,556
Deferred income taxes[c]	1,060	1,060	3,786	3,855
Total liabilities	11,932	34,607	35,175	32,898
Redeemable preferred stock	125			
Common stockholders' equity	5,694	1,992	1,237	1,024
	$17,751	$36,599	$36,412	$33,922

a. Balance sheet of RJR Nabisco, Inc., on December 31, 1988.
b. The December 31, 1988 balance sheet revised in the April 5, 1989 KKR proxy statement to stockholders to show the projected results of the leveraged buyout.
c. The acquisition was to be accounted for under the purchase method; accordingly, the purchase cost of RJR Nabisco's assets and liabilities was allocated to reflect fair market value.
d. The Nabisco International and Del Monte operations, including both segments already sold and those planned to be sold, are presented on December 31, 1989 and March 31, 1990 as discontinued operations. Assets that are planned to be sold are included at estimated fair market value under "Net assets available for sale."
e. Current portion of long-term debt is included in "Long-term debt." Current portion of long-term debt was $337, $5,337, $2,632, and $1,705 million on 12/31/88, Pro forma 12/31/88, 12/31/89, and 3/31/90, respectively.
f. Accrued interest on PIK and zero coupon debt through the balance sheet date is included in "Long-term debt."

Exhibit 5   Consolidated Operating, Cash Flow and Balance Sheet Projections, 1990–1993
(dollars in millions)

	1987A	1988A	1989A	1990E	1991P	1992P	1993P
A: Projected Operating Results							
Tobacco revenue	6,346	7,068	6,981	7,721	8,206	8,824	9,618
Food revenue[a]	5,419	5,567	5,783	6,067	6,533	7,200	7,833
Total revenue	11,765	12,635	12,764	13,788	14,739	16,024	17,451
Operating margin[b]	20.8%	21.0%	21.6%	25.5%	25.5%	25.5%	25.5%
Tobacco EBITA	1,822	1,924	2,016	2,625	2,790	3,000	3,270
Food EBITA	624	730	742	910	980	1,080	1,175
Total EBITA	2,446	2,654	2,758	3,535	3,770	4,080	4,445
Corporate expense	189	166	138	125	125	130	135
Amortization[c]	117	121	567	610	610	610	610
Cash interest	413	506	1,731	1,415	1,131	892	663
Noncash interest	41	43	1,653	1,589	1,980	2,402	2,820
Total interest[d]	454	549	3,384	3,004	3,111	3,294	3,483
Pre-tax income	1,686	1,818	(1,331)	(204)	(76)	46	217
Taxes[e]	591	654	(222)	0	132	223	281
Net income[f]	1,179	1,378	(1,153)	(204)	(207)	(177)	(64)
B: Validation							
EBITDA	2,607	2,868	3,069	3,885	4,120	4,425	4,785
multiples of EBTIDA							
5×				19,425	20,600	22,125	23,925
6×				23,310	24,720	26,550	28,710
7×				27,195	28,840	30,975	33,496
8×				31,080	32,960	35,400	38,280
C: Cash Flow							
Net income	1,179	1,378	(1,153)	(204)	(207)	(177)	(64)
Add back:							
Amortization	117	121	567	610	610	610	610

Exhibit 5   Consolidated Operating, Cash Flow and Balance Sheet Projections, 1990–1993
(Dollars in Millions) (Continued)

	1987A	1988A	1989A	1990E	1991P	1992P	1993P
C: Cash Flow (Continued)							
Depreciation	350	380	449	475	475	475	475
Noncash interest	41	43	1,653	1,589	1,980	2,402	2,820
Less:							
Capitol expenditures	733	837	522	512	525	538	551
Increase in working capitol[g]	124	264	(203)	(275)	200	225	250
Plus:							
Net proceeds f/ sale of assets	1,595	115	3,545	1,805			
Cash available for debt repayment	2,425	936	4,742	4,038	2,133	2,547	3,040
Required debt repayments:							
Pre-buyout Debt				370	726	816	405
Bank Debt				2,262	1,742	938	613
Optional debt repayments:							
Bank Debt				1,071	0	793	173
IRNs							1,000
Remaining cash (accumlated)				335	0	0	849
D: Projected LTD and Net Worth							
Pre-buyout Debt				4,776	4,084	3,302	2,931
Bank Debt				4,268	2,527	815	0
Increasing Rate Notes				1,000	1,000	1,000	0
Permanent Debt Securities				4,786	5,375	6,056	6,843
Partnership Debt[h]				655	775	921	1,099
PIK Exchange Debentures[h]				5,276	6,156	7,247	8,531
PIK Converting Debentures[h]				2,344	2,735	3,219	3,790
Total Long-term Debt				23,105	22,652	22,560	23,194
Net Worth				1,033	826	649	585

a. Stated to reflect Nabisco International and Del Monte as discontinued operations.
b. Assumed tobacco margins of 34% and food margins of 15% from 1990 through 1993.
c. Assumed straight-line amortization of trademarks and goodwill over a 35-year period.
d. Assumed the following interest rates: Pre-buyout Debt, 9%; Bank Debt, 13%; IRNs, 16% (and increasing according to terms); Extendible Debentures, 13.125%; Floating Rate Notes, 13.85%; Partnership Debt, 16.5% (and increasing according to terms); PIK Converting and Exchange Debentures, 14.07% until fixed permanently at 17% in April 1991.
e. Assumed tax rate of 34%.
f. Included is nonrecurring net income of $84, $214, and ($44) million in 1987, 1988, and 1989, respectively.
g. Included are other sources of cash equal to $153 million in 1989. Assumes that $475 million of accounts receivable are sold in 1990.
h. Assumed interest rates are consistent with the operating projections. *See note d.*

SALLY JAMESON: VALUING STOCK OPTIONS IN A COMPENSATION PACKAGE[1]

Sally Jameson, a second-year MBA student at Harvard Business School, was thrilled but confused. It was late May 1992, graduation was approaching, and she had finally landed the job of her choice. She had just finished an early morning telephone conversation with Bob Marks, the MBA recruiting coordinator at Telstar Communications, a large, publicly held multinational company. Mr. Marks had offered Ms. Jameson a unique position in operations at Telstar, and from the description, it sounded exactly like the job that she wanted. Since her first interview with Telstar, she had been very impressed with the company and its people. While Ms. Jameson was certain that she would accept the job, there was still one unsettled, yet crucial, matter—her compensation.

During the conversation with Mr. Marks, Ms. Jameson had asked what her compensation package would be.

Marks: "Well, Sally, we are all very impressed with you and would like to offer you a starting salary of $50,000. In addition, you will also receive a signing bonus."

Jameson: "The base salary is a little below what I had expected. Is that negotiable?"

Marks: "I'm afraid not. That's the same starting package all MBAs get. However, you will receive a bonus upon accepting our offer. You can receive $5,000 in cash, or choose stock options instead."

Jameson: "I'm not too familiar with stock options. Could you explain to me what they are?"

Marks: "Sure. Executives at Telstar have been eligible to receive stock options for years. The goal was to tie management's compensation more closely to increases in shareholder value. Although our stock has performed erratically over the last ten years, the board continues to

---

1   This case, though patterned after an actual event, is fictitious.

Michael Lewittes wrote this case under the supervision of Peter Tufano as the basis for class discussion rather than to illustrate either effective or ineffective handling of an administrative situation.

believe that stock options are the best form of incentive compensation. Because the options represent the right to buy Telstar stock at a set price, after a set period of time, management has an incentive to take actions to move the stock price upward. Several months ago, we had a consulting firm examine our compensation structure. They recommended that we extend eligibility for stock options to all employees as part of our new incentive-based compensation plans. Thus, the two MBAs that we hope to hire this year will be the first employees who will be offered stock options. Given that this is an experiment, we decided to give MBAs a choice between cash or options."

Jameson: "How much are these options worth?"

Marks: "To tell you the truth, I'm not really sure. All I know are the details: each of the 3,000 options you'll be granted allows you to buy one share of Telstar stock at $35.00 per share at the time of your fifth anniversary with the firm.[2] Yesterday, our stock, which pays no dividend and is not expected to pay one in the foreseeable future, closed at $18.75. Should you leave at any point before your fifth year, you lose the options. You can't take them with you.

"I have been told by our legal staff that these incentive stock options meet the IRS code for special treatment—that means you won't pay any taxes on the options until you actually exercise them and then sell the shares. At that point, your gains on the shares (equal to the difference between their fair market value at that time and $35.00) will be taxed at either ordinary tax rates or at capital gains rates, depending on whether you've held the stock for less than or more than one year after exercising the option. If you choose the cash signing bonus, it is taxed at ordinary tax rates.[3] It's your choice, Sally, but just between you and me, I'd take the cash bonus. Telstar stock is only at $18.75; it doesn't seem to me that these options are worth the paper that they're printed on. I think it's just another example of consultants trying to justify their fees. You do what you think is best; either way, though, I need to know by tomorrow if you accept the offer and, if you do, which compensation package you'd prefer."

While Bob Marks seemed to prefer the cash bonus, Sally Jameson was less sure. Taking out her *Wall Street Journal*, she noticed that both short-term and long-term Telstar options were traded (see Exhibit 1). From an online financial database, she got a graph of Telstar's common stock price and a plot of the historical volatility of the stock price as measured by the annualized standard deviation of the stock's returns (See Exhibits 2 and 3). She also found data on government bill, note, and bond yields that would be useful in her analysis (see Exhibit 4).

As she thought about the problem, she decided to approach it in two steps: first, she would attempt to determine what the options were worth, assuming she stayed at Telstar for at least five years. Then, she would consider other issues, including the likelihood that she might not stay at Telstar that long.

---

2 *Casewriters' note:* Stock options of this sort would more typically be written with a strike price equal to or just slightly above the current price.

3 In May 1992, Ms. Jameson's marginal tax rate would be 28%. The maximum marginal tax rate was 31%. The capital gains rate was 28%.

Exhibit 1   Listed Telstar Options Quotations as of Close of Market—May 27, 1992

Strike Price	Calls					Puts		
	Expiration Date (1992)					Expiration Date (1992)		
	June 20	July 18	Oct 17	Jan 22, 1994		June 20	July 18	Oct 17
$12.50	r	r	r	$7¾		r	r	r
$17.50	1⁷⁄₁₆	1⅞	2½	4⅝		³⁄₁₆	r	1¹⁄₁₆
$20.00	³⁄₁₆	½	1⁵⁄₁₆	3¾		1⅜	r	r
$22.50	r	⅛	⁹⁄₁₆	r		r	3½	r

r = not traded

Source: Wall Street Journal, May 28, 1992.

Exhibit 2   Stock Price of Telstar Common Stock 1/4/82 through 5/27/92

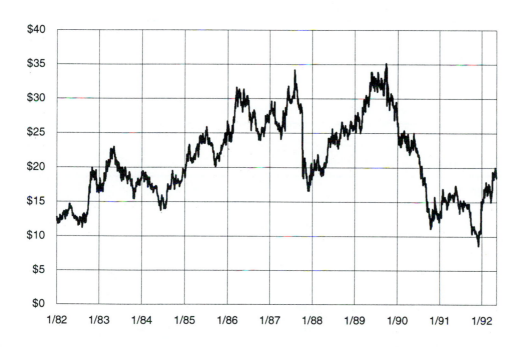

Note: Stock price has been adjusted for stock splits and stock dividends. On May 27, 1992, Telstar stock closed at $18.75 per common share.

Exhibit 3   Volatility of Telstar Common Stock, 1982 through May 27, 1992

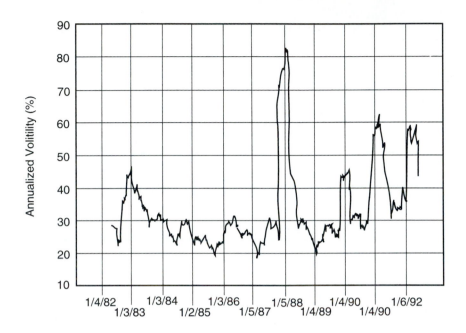

Note: Volatility measured by the annualized standard deviation of daily stock returns measured over the prior 90 days.

Exhibit 4   Treasury Security Yields as of May 27, 1992

Annualized Treasury Bill and Bond Yields

1-month	3.70%
2-month	3.72%
3-month	3.69%
6-month	3.81%
1-year	4.02%
2 -year	5.25%
5-year	6.02%
7-year	7.08%
10-year	7.41%
30-year	7.89%

Note: Rates all quoted on a bond equivalent yield basis.

TAXES, REGULATION, AND ACCOUNTING: STIMULI TO INNOVATION

Arpps: Adjustable Rate Perpetual Preferred Stock

On February 23, 1983, Susan Blanchon, an assistant treasurer at one of the largest U.S. computer firms, was considering the purchase of some shares of a new issue, the adjustable rate perpetual preferred stock (ARPPS) of J. P. Morgan. Among her duties in the treasurer's office were the management of cash and of the firm's marketable securities portfolio. The $190 million marketable securities portfolio was used as a secondary source of corporate liquidity; it was currently invested in large CDs of major banks, commercial paper, and some very short-term tax-exempt municipal notes. The current returns on these instruments, and other capital market rates, are shown in Exhibit 1. Ms. Blanchon's objective was to generate as high a return as possible from this portfolio, subject to the constraint of maintaining high liquidity and minimal risk. The CDs, commercial paper, and tax-exempt notes were all of the highest credit quality and represented, in her view, minimal credit risk.

DEVELOPMENT OF ARPPS

The ARPPS security was first conceived and developed in mid-1982 as one of a variety of different methods of raising capital for large commercial banks. Each of the ARPPS preferred stocks issued since then had the same general characteristics. Each carried a floating-rate dividend that was to be reset at the beginning of each quarter at some spread (the reset rate) above or below a benchmark U.S. Treasury rate. The benchmark Treasury rate was always equal to the highest of three Treasury rates that were reported weekly by the Federal Reserve: the three-month Treasury bill rate, a representative 10-year Treasury bond rate, and a representative 20-year Treasury bond rate. In addition, each ARPPS specified a minimum "floor" and a maximum "ceiling" rate as limits for the dividend rate regardless of market interest rates. Exhibit 2 shows the particular terms for the J. P. Morgan ARPPS that Ms. Blanchon was currently considering.

Jay O. Light perpared this case as the basis for class discussion rather than to illustrate either effective or ineffective handling of an administrative situation.

The first ARPPS was issued by Chemical Bank in May 1982 and was based upon a reset formula for the adjustable dividend of 50 basis points above the highest of the three Treasury rates. Because 85% of their dividends can be excluded from taxable income by any incorporated investor (as can 85% of any dividend income, whether from common or preferred stock), these securities were attractive to corporate cash managers. The prices of the first several ARPPS issues rose substantially in the secondary market, producing both impressive capital gains and tax-exempt income. Since May 1982 almost $4 billion of ARPPS had been issued by 29 issuers at terms that had become gradually more generous to the issuers, mirroring the increasing popularity of this innovative new type of security. Exhibit 3 shows a history of selected ARPPS issues.

In the week ending February 23, there had been eight separate new issues of ARPPS, with an aggregate value of just over $1 billion, which had been successfully underwritten and sold. These included the last four new issues in Exhibit 3. While the market had some temporary difficulty digesting this volume, it soon stabilized and rallied. Indeed, like their predecessors, these most recent new issues of ARPPS were trading at a premium by February 23.

SUPPLY AND DEMAND FOR ARPPS

The most common issuers of ARPPS had thus far been the parent holding companies of very large commercial banks. During this period, many of these large banks had been under pressure from banking regulators to increase their capital-asset ratios, because the banks' prior growth had eroded capital-asset ratios to levels that seemed low relative to the risks that might arise in their loan portfolios. The new ARPPS securities seemed particularly well suited to the needs of these large one-bank holding companies, who could augment their banks' capital base by transferring the proceeds of the preferred stock offerings to their subsidiary banks.

In addition, however, a number of nonbank firms had just begun to issue ARPPS, including some large utilities and steel companies. Ms. Blanchon suspected that shifting corporate marginal tax rates might be affecting and be affected by the ARPPS market. As part of the 1981 tax cuts, depreciation allowances and corporate investment tax credits had been greatly expanded. Because of these tax law changes and the recession, a surprising number of companies were currently paying minimal or no federal income taxes and had substantial tax credit carryforwards (see Exhibit 4, for example).

As more new issues had come to market, the demand for the ARPPS securities had continued to grow. More and more executives in large corporations were deciding that this "85% tax-exempt money market" was an attractive alternative. An active and surprisingly liquid secondary market developed to complement the active new issue market. In the past several weeks, a number of ARPPS mutual funds had been formed by prominent mutual fund management companies specifically for the purpose of allowing smaller companies to invest in a commingled pool of these securities. It appeared that the demand for ARPPS from small companies might grow considerably as a result of these new funds.

THE DECISION

Ms. Blanchon had initially been intrigued by but cautious toward this new market. Because her firm's marginal tax rate was the normal 46% corporate rate, the after-tax ARPPS yields looked attractive. On the other hand, liquidity was one of her most important considerations, and she had earlier been concerned about the liquidity of the secondary market that might develop. The trading volume for these securities in the most recent week appeared to have exceeded 1 billion dollars, though; if these trading volumes could be maintained, liquidity would not be a problem.

In addition, the new AAA-rated J. P. Morgan ARPPS seemed particularly attractive. While some serious concerns were beginning to develop about the loan portfolios of all money center banks, the paper of J. P. Morgan was generally considered to be the safest and of the highest credit quality. Indeed, the Morgan bank's CDs and J. P. Morgan holding company's commercial paper were already significant holdings in the portfolio. Ms. Blanchon thought that the Morgan bank might be an appropriate name with which to begin her participation in this market. It certainly wouldn't hurt in the process of selling this idea to her boss, and in allaying any fears that might arise from investing in a new type of security for the first time. The underwriter of the J. P. Morgan ARPPS was waiting for Ms. Blanchon's decision. This new issue promised to be quickly sold out.

Exhibit 1   Interest Rates on Short-term Securities and Other Capital Market Rates, February 23, 1983

Average yields on short-term (3–6 months) securities in portfolio

CDs of high-quality banks	8.45
Commercial paper (highest grade)	8.35
Short-term tax-exempt notes (AAA)	4.40

Other capital market rates

Three-month Treasury bills	8.08
10-year Treasuries [a]	10.60
20-year Treasuries[a]	10.90
10-year AAA noncallable notes	11.10
30-year callable debentures	
AAA-rated bonds	11.95
AA-rated bonds	12.50
A-rated bonds	13.50

---

a. These 10- year and 20-year Treasurys are the basis of the Federal Reserve Board's "constant maturity rate" series, published weekly. These average yields, along with the three-month T-bill rate, determine the applicable rate (the benchmark rate) in the ARPPS securities that have been issued.

Exhibit 2   Terms for J. P. Morgan ARPPS

Prospectus

2,500,000 Shares

J. P. Morgan & Co. Incorporated

Adjustable Rate Cumulative Preferred Stock, Series A
(Stated Value $100 Per Share)

Dividends on the Adjustable Rate Cumulative Preferred Stock. Series A (the "Series A Preferred Stock") are cumulative from the date of issue and are payable quarterly on March 31, June 30, September 30 and December 31 of each year, except that the initial dividend period will be from the date of issue through June 30, 1983. The dividend rate on the Series A Preferred Stock for the initial dividend period ending June 30, 1983 will be 9.25% per annum. Thereafter, dividends will be at the "Applicable Rate" in effect from time to time. The "Applicable Rate" for any quarterly dividend period will be (a) 4.875% less than (b) the highest of the "Treasury Bill Rate", the "Ten Year Constant Maturity Rate" and the "Twenty Year Constant Maturity Rate" determined in advance of such dividend period. However, the Applicable Rate for any dividend period will in no event be less than 5.00% per annum or greater than 11.50% per annum. See "Description of Series A Preferred Stock—Adjustable Rate Dividends."

The Series A Preferred Stock will not be redeemable prior to March 1, 1986. The Series A Preferred Stock will be redeemable at the option of the Company, in whole or in part, on or after March 1, 1984 through February 29, 1988 at a redemption price equal to $103.00 per share, and thereafter at $100.00 per share in each case plus accrued and unpaid dividends.

Application will be made to list the Series A Preferred Stock on the New York Stock Exchange.

THESE SECURITIES HAVE NOT BEEN APPROVED OR DISAPPROVED BY THE SECURITIES AND EXCHANGE COMMISSION NOR HAS THE COMMISSION PASSED UPON THE ACCURACY OR ADEQUACY OF THIS PROSPECTUS. ANY REPRESENTATION TO THE CONTRARY IS A CRIMINAL OFFENSE.

	Price to Public [a]	Underwriting Discounts and Commission	Proceeds to Company [b]
Per Share	$100,000	$1.625	$98, 375
Total	$250,000,000	$4,062,500	$245, 937, 500

a. Plus accrued dividends, if any, from date of issue.
b. Before deduction of expenses payable by the company, estimated at $270, 050

The Series A Preferred Stock is offered by the Underwriter for delivery when, as and if issued to and accepted by the Underwriter and subject to its right to reject orders in whole or in part. It is expected that the Series A Preferred Stock so offered by the Underwriter will be delivered on or about March 2, 1983.

Merrill Lynch White Weld Capital Markets Group
Merrill Lynch, Pierce, Fenner & Smith Incorporated

The date of this Prospectus is February 23, 1983

Exhibit 3   History of Selected ARPPS Issues, May 1982–February 1983

| Issuer[a] | Issue Date | Size of Offering ($ millions) | Initial Rate | Adjustable Rate Formula[b] | | | Credit Rating |
				Reset	Floor	Ceiling	
Chemical New York	5/11/82	$200	14.20%	+.50	7.50	16.25	Aa2
Chase Manhattan	5/25/82	250	14.10	+.50	7.50	16.25	Aa1/AA
Manufacturers Hanover	5/27/82	200	14.05	+.50	7.50	15.75	Aa2/AA–
Manufacturers Hanover	7/22/82	200	13.25	–.60	7.50	15.50	Aa2/AA–
Aetna Life & Casualty	7/28/82	200	13.20	–.90	7.50	15.25	Aaa/AAA
Chemical New York	8/12/83	100	13.36	–.65	7.50	15.25	Aa2
U.S. Steel	8/25/83	200	13.50	+.35	7.50	15.75	A3/A
First Chicago	10/15/83	125	11.00	–1.00	7.00	15.00	Aa3/A+
BankAmerica	10/22/83	300	10.25	–2.00	6.50	14.50	Aa2/AA
Irving Bank	11/19/83	75	10.00	–2.25	6.50	14.00	Aa3/AA–
Puget Sound Power & Light	12/14/83	40	10.00	–1.00	7.00	14.50	Baa3/BBB
Norstart Bancorp	2/03/83	75	9.50	–3.00	6.00	13.00	Aa3/A+
BankAmerica	2/11/83	400	9.25	–4.00	6.00	12.00	Aa2/AA-
Bank of New York	2/15/83	100	9.40	–3.50	6.00	12.00	A2
Northern Indiana Publ. Service	2/17/83	50	9.25	–2.75	6.00	12.50	A3/BBB
First Chicago	2/17/83	125	9.40	–3.75	6.00	12.00	Aa3/A+
Citicorp	2/18/83	400	9.75	–4.125	6.00	12.00	Aa1/AA

a. All these ARPPSs could be called at 103% of par (their new issue price) after 5 years.
b. In all these ARPPS issues, the adjustable rate was pegged at some spread (reset) over/under a Treasury benchmark rate, which was the highest of the three-month Treasury bill rate, a 10-year Treasury rate, and a 20-year Treasury rate.

Exhibit 4   Article on Taxes, *The Wall Street Journal*, November 15, 1983

TAX BURDEN INCREASES FOR PEOPLE AND EASES ON FIRMS, STUDY FINDS
WIDELY DISPARATE RATE FOUND FOR DIFFERENT INDUSTRIES BY CONGRESSIONAL SURVEY

By Jeffrey H. Birnbaum
Staff Reporter of *The Wall Street Journal*

Washington—Corporations' share of the U.S. tax burden has been falling while levies on personal income has made up an even-larger portion of federal tax receipts, a congressional study found.

The study also found some startling differences in the effective tax rate paid by different industries. Of the 29 industries examined, the effective tax rate on U.S. income in the fiscal year Sept. 30, 1982 varied from 39% in the rubber industry to minus 17.7% in chemicals.

The report was made by the Joint Taxation Commitee, with the assistance of the General Accounting Office, Congress's investigative arm. It was released by two members of the tax-writing Ways and Means Committee, Reps. Don Pease (D., Ohio) and Byron Dorgan (D., N.D.). The two lawmakers used the report to buttress their claims that the tax code is inequitable and that changes are needed, such as imposing a minimum corporate income tax.

In fiscal 1982, the study said, corporate income taxes as a percentage of the total federal tax receipts fell to 8.1% from 11.5% the year before and from 28.3% in 1950. In contrast, the personal income tax share of total federal taxes rose in fiscal 1982 to 49% from 47.5% in fiscal 1981 and from 39.2% in 1950.

Mr. Pease said that corporate payments declined precipitously in recent years partly because of the recession, which trimmed business profits. He added, though, that personal income taxes continued to increase their proportion of the total, despite personal-tax cuts.

The minus 17.7% effective tax rate for the chemical industry isn't entirely representative. Rep. Pease noted that over three years, the industry's effective tax rate was a positive 4.3%.

Four of the 29 industries reviewed had negative rates in 1982, which means, Rep. Pease explained, that they were either paid or owed money by the federal government. In addition to chemicals, the industries were insurance, minus 6.3%; commercial banking, minus 3.8%, and aerospace, minus 0.6%. Three others had positive rates of less than 10%; telecommunications, 1.6%; railroads, 4.1%; and broadcasting, 8.9%.

In contrast, five industries had effective tax rates higher than 35%: rubber, 39%; trucking, 36.9%; tobacco, 36.3%; wholesalers, 36.1%; and paper and wood, which usually is a very low tax-rate industry, 36.1%.

The study also found wide differences between the tax rates on corporate income from the inside, and outside the U.S. U.S. corporations paid an average 16.1% effective tax rate on U.S. income, 55% on foreign-earned income and 29.6% on world-wide income, the report said.

Rep. Dorgan placed the blame for relatively low corporate tax rates on the Reagan administration's 1981 business tax cut which, he said, "virtually wiped out the income-tax obligation for a number of industries, even though they earn substantial profits. Many of them are no longer paying income taxes to the federal government."

The study was based on a survey of the financial reports of 213 large corporations.

Exhibt 5 Money Market Rates and Long-Term Interest Rates, 1978–1983

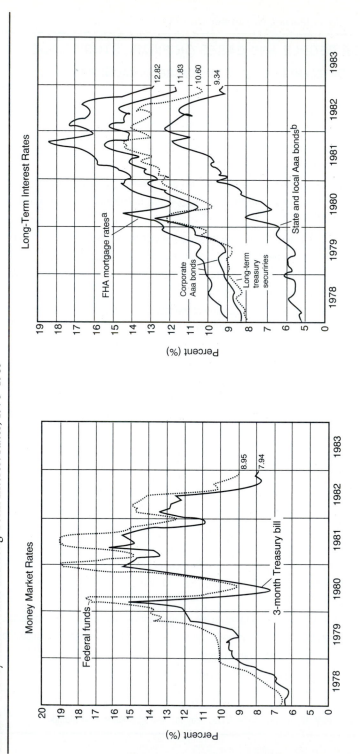

Source: Federal Reserve Bank of St. Louis.
a. FHA 30-year mortgages. Dashed lines indicate data not available.
b. Monthly averages of Thursday figures.
c. Average of yields on coupon issues due or callable in 10 years or more excluding issues with federal estate tax privileges.

MMP™: MONEY MARKET PREFERRED STOCK

On October 15, 1984, William Tennant, a financial officer of a large data-processing firm, was trying to decide whether to place a bid for a few shares of American Express Company Money Market Preferred Stock™, and how to price his bid. The MMP stock had been invented two months earlier by Lehman Brothers, an American Express subsidiary, and was the first public security that would be priced periodically through the Dutch Auction mechanism.

In deciding whether to invest some of his company's cash in the MMP security, Mr. Tennant was particularly concerned about its future liquidity; he also wanted to maximize the return on the investment. With the security rated Aa3 by Moody's and AA- by Standard & Poor's, he was not too concerned about its credit risk.

FLOATING-RATE PERPETUAL PREFERRED STOCKS

The Money Market Preferred Stock was the latest in a family of floating-rate preferred (FRP) stocks that had first appeared in mid-1982. Most FRPs had been issued by large commercial banks as a means of increasing their capital base. Because FRPs were perpetual stocks (there was no mandatory redemption), they were treated as primary capital by bank regulators and hence were viewed by the banks as an alternative to issuing common equity. More recently, a number of nonbank companies had also issued floating-rate preferred stocks. Depending on the particular circumstance, the issuer of an FRP could look at it as an alternative to debt or to equity. Companies whose common stocks were trading below book value (e.g., U. S. Steel or the large banks) probably viewed FRPs as a cheaper, non-dilutive source of equity. Others probably viewed FRPs as a cheaper alternative to debt. Although dividend payments on preferred stock were not deductible for tax purposes, the forgone tax shield meant little or nothing to a company with a low marginal tax rate. For example, a utility making large capital investments had a very low marginal rate, since the

Nabil El-Hage prepared this case as the basis for class discussion rather than to illustrate either effective or ineffective handling of an administrative situation.

advent of ACRS in 1981 had increased the generosity of accelerated depreciation and substantially reduced the effective tax rate of such companies.

From the corporate investors' point of view, FRPs were in many respects an attractive investment alternative to either debt or equity. As was the case with any dividend income, 85% of the FRP dividend income was exempt from taxation for corporate holders. Hence, for a tax-paying corporate investor, after-tax returns on FRP holdings could equal or exceed the rate of return on many other securities despite a lower pre-tax dividend rate. Similarly, the return on FRPs was perceived as more stable than that on investments in common equity because most FRPs had been designed to protect the principal value.

ADJUSTABLE RATE PERPETUAL PREFERRED STOCK (ARPPS)

The ARPPS security had been the first of the floating-rate preferred stocks and had met with considerable success in the marketplace. Most ARPPS had been designed fairly uniformly. It carried a dividend that would be reset quarterly based on a benchmark Treasury rate. Generally, the benchmark rate was the highest of a three-month Treasury bill rate, a 10-year Treasury bond rate, and a 20-year Treasury bond rate. The actual dividend was to equal the benchmark rate plus or minus a certain predetermined spread. This spread varied between issues, depending on market supply and demand factors, as well as other factors specific to the issuing companies. Additionally, the ARPPS dividend was only allowed to fluctuate within a specified fixed range, such as, for example, 6%–12%. Exhibit 1 describes a J. P. Morgan ARPPS that Mr. Tennant currently held in his firm's portfolio, and Exhibit 2 lists the terms of selected ARPPS issues. By summer 1984, over $10 billion of ARPPS had been issued, and there was a considerable and liquid secondary market.

Unfortunately, ARPPS prices had been less than completely stable. Exhibit 3 shows the price histories of several of these securities.

CONVERTIBLE ADJUSTABLE PREFERRED STOCK (CAPS)

Although most Wall Street observers agreed that ARPPS had been a reasonably successful innovation, its price volatility was troubling to many corporate cash managers. Consequently, the investment banking community continued to innovate in its search for a security with a more stable price.

For a while, CAPS was hailed as an answer to that search. CAPS was a floating-rate preferred stock that was convertible into the issuing company's common stock at the option of the holder. Each share of CAPS could at any time be converted into as many common shares as it took to obtain a market value equal to the CAPS par. At the option of the company, a CAPS holder submitting shares for conversion might receive cash instead of common stock.

Although there were some limitations on the number of common shares that CAPS could be converted into, these were not significant. For example, Consolidated Foods Corporation, which issued the first CAPS in September 1983, made each $50-par CAPS share convertible into a maximum of two common shares. At the time, its common stock was trading at $45¾ per share. Exhibit 4 gives a detailed description of the Consolidated Foods CAPS.

This conversion mechanism was expected to prevent any drop in the CAPS value and thus allow CAPS issuers to pay a lower dividend rate than on the more volatile ARPPS. The CAP dividend-setting formula was similar to that for the ARPPS, with one noteworthy difference. As in the ARPPS case, the CAPS dividend was equal to the benchmark rate plus or minus a certain spread (-4.00 initially in the Consolidated Foods issue). This spread, however, could at any time be altered at the sole discretion of the issuer. See Exhibit 5 for CAPS securities terms and price histories.

PRICE-ADJUSTED RATE PREFERRED STOCK (PARP)

Despite the relative success of ARPPS and CAPS in the marketplace, the search for an FRP that would always trade at par continued, with PARP being the next to make it to market. The PARP security was similar to ARRPS, although it had additional features meant to ensure greater price stability. As its name indicates, the dividend on the PARP stock was inversely proportional to the observed trading price of the security itself in a specified two-week period. That is, if for any reason, the price of PARP stock began to slip, the subsequent quarterly dividend would automatically rise. This anticipated increase in the dividend, it was said on Wall Street, would always bring the price of PARP stock back up to par. Exhibit 6 describes the Citicorp PARP and its pricing mechanism.

The PARP formula appeared to have inspired so much confidence at First Boston, the PARP inventor, that there seemed to be no need to limit the range within which the dividend would be allowed to fluctuate. Despite all the original confidence, only one $100 million PARP issue ever made it to market (in February 1984), and the secondary market for the security was not known to be very liquid.

MONEY MARKET PREFERRED STOCK (MMP)

The MMP security was introduced in August 1984 by Lehman Brothers as yet another potential successor to ARPPS. Although issuance of MMP aimed to achieve many of the same goals of the original ARPPS and its subsequent hybrids, the MMP pricing mechanism was somewhat simpler, at least conceptually. Every 49 days, the yield on the MMP security would be reset through a Dutch Auction. The 49-day period was chosen because an investor had to hold stocks for at least 46 days to qualify for the 85% tax exclusion

In the Dutch Auction buyers would in effect set the yield on the MMP so as to guarantee it would trade at par. Every 49 days investors would submit a bid to the issuer's agent to buy, hold, or sell MMP shares. A bid specified the annualized dividend rate at which the bidder would be willing to buy a certain number of shares. The agent then "accepted" as many bids (starting with the lowest rate) as it took to place all the outstanding MMP shares. All "winners" of MMP shares would then receive the same dividend rate in the future 49-day period, equal to the highest bid that cleared the market (the "winning bid"). All former holders who had placed sell orders, or who had placed buy (contingent hold) orders but were not among the winners, were taken out at par. Because the dividend rate in the subsequent 49-day period would be set precisely to lead to a "par price," any MMP holders who wished to sell their shares were said to be almost certain to be able to do so at par.

The dividend yield on MMP stock (the "winning bid") was allowed to fluctuate but not to exceed 110% of the 60-day AA composite commercial paper rate. If an insufficient number of buy or hold bids were submitted to place all outstanding MMP shares, then the dividend rate would be set at the maximum allowable rate (110% of the 60-day AA composite commercial paper rate) and certain existing MMP holders would have to continue to hold the security, in effect against their wishes. Exhibit 7 describes the American Express MMP issue.

Lehman Brothers had issued the American Express MMP in August at a 9% dividend yield for the first 49 days. The first auction was to be held on October 16, 1984, and it was for this auction that Mr. Tennant was preparing.

MR. TENNANT'S CONSIDERATIONS

As stated, Mr. Tennant was not too concerned about the credit risk of the American Express MMP. He was not sure, however, what a fair rate of return on this new security should be nor whether he wanted to buy it.

To help evaluate the MMP, Mr. Tennant had gathered some rate-of-return information on various investment vehicles available at the time, several of which were already in his firm's portfolio (see Exhibit 8). With his corporation's tax rate at 46%, the MMP's initial yield was attractive. He wondered, however, whether those returns would persist or whether, if the MMP caught on, the yields would plummet.

If Mr. Tennant decided to bid for some MMP securities, he would also have to decide whether to hold on to ARPPS. He was concerned about the long-term viability of all these floating-rate preferred instruments, particularly in light of the increasingly frequent talk in Washington circles about a forthcoming Treasury proposal to reduce allowed depreciation and investment tax credits while reducing corporate tax rates. If such a proposal were to become law, Mr. Tennant wondered, how would the FRPs react?

With all these considerations on his mind, Mr. Tennant sat down at his desk to crunch a few numbers. He would have to call Lehman Brothers in a few hours if he wanted his bid to be included in the auction.

Exhibit 1   Description of J. P. Morgan ARPPS

New Issue   February 24, 1983

2,500,000 Shares

J. P. Morgan & Co. Incorporated

Adjustable Rate Cumulative Preferred Stock, Series A
(Stated Value $100 Per Share)

Dividends on the Adjustable Rate Cumulative Preferred Stock, Series A are cumulative from the date of issue and are payable quarterly on March 31, June 30 and December 31 of each year, except that the initial dividend period will be from the date of issue through June 30, 1983. The dividend rate on the Series A Preferred Stock for the initial dividend period ending June 30, 1983 will be 9.25% per annum. Thereafter, dividends will be at the "Applicable Rate" in effect from time to time. The Applicable Rate for any quarterly dividend period will be (a) 4.875% less than (b) the highest of the "Treasury Bill Rate," the "Ten Year Constant Maturity Rate" and the "Twenty Year Constant Maturity Rate" determined in advance of such dividend period. However, the Applicable Rate for any dividend period will in no event be less than 5.00% per annum or greater than 11.5% per annum.

Price $100 Per Share

(Plus accrued dividends, if any, from date of issue)

Merrill Lynch White Weld Capital Markets Group

Merrill Lynch. Pierce, Fenner & Smith Incorporated

Exhibit 2 Terms of Selected ARPPS Issues, May 1982–March 1984

Issuer[a]	Issue Date	Size of Offering ($millions)	Initial Rate	Adjustable Rate Formula[b]			Credit Rating
				Reset	Floor	Ceiling	
Chemical New York (Ser. A)	5/11/82	$200	14.20%	+.50%	7.50	16.25	Aa2
Chase Manhattan	5/25/82	250	14.10	+.50	7.50	16.25	Aa1/AA
Chemical New York (Ser. B)	8/12/82	100	13.36	-.65	7.50	15.25	Aa2
U.S. Steel	8/25/82	200	13.50	+.35	7.50	15.75	A3/A
First Chicago	10/15/82	125	11.00	-1.00	7.00	15.00	Aa3/A+
BankAmerica (Ser. A)	10/22/82	300	10.25	-2.00	6.50	14.50	Aa2/AA
Norstar Bancorp	2/03/83	75	9.50	-3.00	6.00	13.00	Aa3/A+
BankAmerica (Ser. B)	2/11/83	400	9.25	-4.00	6.00	12.00	Aa2/AA–
Bank of New York	2/15/83	100	9.40	-3.50	6.00	12.00	A2
Citicorp	2/18/83	400	9.75	-4.125	6.00	12.00	Aa1/AA
J.P. Morgan	2/23/83	250	9.25	-4.875	5.00	11.50	Aaa/AAA
Marine Midland Banks	3/02/83	100	10.00	-2.00	6.00	12.00	A2/NR
Continental Illinois	9/07/83	87	11.25	-1.00	7.50	13.50	Caa/A
Houston Light & Power	3/21/84	50	11.00	-1.60	6.00	12.00	A2/A+

a. All ARPPS could be called at 103% of par (its new issue price) after 5 years.
b. In all these ARPPS issues, the adjustable rate was pegged at some spread (reset) over/under a Treasury benchmark rate, which was the highest of the three-month Treasury bill rate, a 10-year Treasury rate, and a 20-year Treasury rate.

Exhibit 3   ARPPS Securities Price Histories, January 1983–July 1984

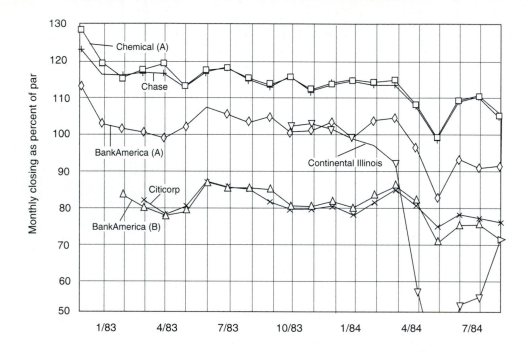

Exhibit 4   Description of Consolidated Foods Company CAPS

PROSPECTUS

1,500,000 Shares

Consolidated Foods Corporation

CONVERTIBLE ADJUSTABLE PREFERRED STOCK

(no par value)

Of the 1,500,000 shares of Convertible Adjustable Stock ("CAPS" or the "Preferred Stock") offered hereby, 456,141 shares are being sold by the Company and 1,043,859 shares are being sold by the Selling Stockholder as set forth under "Selling Stockholder and Exchange Agreement". The Company will not receive any part of the proceeds from the sale of shares sold by the Selling Stockholder.

Dividends on the CAPS are cumulative from the date of issue and are payable quarterly on January 1, April 1, July 1 and October 1 of each year, beginning on January 1, 1984.

Each share of the CAPS may be surrendered for conversion during the period of six business days ending at the close of business on the sixth business day preceding each dividend payment date into shares of Common Stock of the Company having an aggregate "market value" (as defined herein) of $50 on the last business day preceding such payment date, subject to the limitation that a holder of a share of CAPS shall not be entitled to receive more than 2.0 shares of Common Stock for each share of CAPS. Such maximum number of shares of Common Stock is subject to adjustment in the sole discretion of the Company, subject to certain limitations. See "Description of Preferred Stock-Certain Adjustments". In lieu of converting any CAPS surrendered for conversion, the Company may, at its option, elect to purchase for cash any CAPS surrendered for conversion on the terms set forth herein. See "Description of Preferred Stock—Conversion of the Preferred Stock and Right of the Company to Purchase Shares of Preferred Stock Surrendered for Conversion". The last sale price for the Common Stock as reported on the New York Stock Exchange on September 15, 1983 was $45 3/4 per share.

The dividend rate from the date of issue to and including December 31, 1983 will be 8.0% per annum. For each quarterly dividend period thereafter commencing January 1, 1984, dividends on the CAPS will be at the Applicable Rate. The Applicable Rate per annum, for each quarterly dividend period, determined in advance of such period, will be (a) the "Adjustment Percentage" (initially 4.0%) less than (b) the "Benchmark Rate", as defined. The Adjustment Percentage is subject to adjustment in the sole discretion of the Company, subject to certain limitations. See "Description of Preferred Stock-Certain Adjustments". In addition, regardless of any changes in the Adjustment Percentage, the Applicable Rate will not be less than 5.5% per annum or greater than 11.0% per annum. See "Description of Preferred Stock—Adjustable Rate Dividends ".

The CAPS will not be redeemable prior to January 1, 1987. Thereafter, the CAPS will be redeemable, at the option of the Company, in whole or in part, at $50 per share, plus accrued and unpaid dividends.

PRICE $50 A SHARE

MORGAN STANLEY & CO.

Incorporated

September 15, 1983

Exhibit 5 CAPS Securities Terms and Price Histories, September 1983–September 1984

CAPS Terms

Issuer	Issue Date	Size of Offering ($ millions)	Par Value	Initial Rate	Adjustable Rate Formula			Credit Rating	Maximum of shares in conversion	Common share price at issue
					Reset	Floor	Ceiling			
Consolidated Foods	9/15/83	$75	$50.00	8.00%	-4.00%	5.50	11.00	Aa3/AA	2.0	45.75
AMF, Inc.[c]	11/22/83	35	50.00	9.25	-2.80	6.00	12.00	Baa2/BBB	6.15	16.25
GATX	12/21/83	40	50.00	9.50	-2.60	6.00	12.00	Baa3/BBB+	3.17	31.375
GTE	7/2/84	20	50.10	9.88	-4.00	6.00	12.50	Baa2/A-	2.7	37.375
Ohio Edison	7/26/84	45	25.00	13.08	0	7.50	15.50	Baa3/BB	6.15	10.125

CAPS Price Histories, Monthly Closing Prices

	Oct. 1983	Nov. 1983	Dec. 1983	Jan. 1984	Feb. 1984	Mar. 1984	Apr. 1984	May 1984	June 1984	July 1984	Aug. 1984	Sept. 1984
Consolidated Foos[d]	$53	$50 5/8	$53	$54	$51 1/2	$51 1/4	$53	$51	$52	$54	$52	$51 1/4
AMF, Inc.	—	—	—	50 3/8	50 1/2	50 3/8	50 5/8	50 5/8	50 1/2	51	51 1/2	51
Ohio Edison	—	—	—	—	—	—	—	—	—	—	26	26 1/4

a. In all these CAPS issues, the adjustable rate was pegged at some spread (reset) over/under a Treasury benchmark rate, which was the highest of the three-month Treasury bill rate, a 10-year Treasury rate, and a 20-year Treasury rate.

b. This reset spread could be altered at essentially any time, at the issuer's discretion.

c. Within 90 days of initial issue, a major portion of the outstanding AMF CAPS were submitted by their holders to the company for conversion into common stock.

d. It is said that Consolidated Foods at one point considered reducing the yield on its CAPS but ultimately abandoned the idea.

Exhibit 6   Description of Citicorp PARP

NEW ISSUE   February 3, 1984

1,000,000 Shares

Price Adjusted Rate Preferred Stock

(Preferred Stock, Fourth Series)
(without par value)

Dividends are cumulative from the date of issue and are payable quarterly on March 31, June 30, September 30 and December 31 of each year, beginning on March 31, 1984. The dividend rate for the initial dividend period ending March 31, 1984 will be 8% per annum (which is 86.5%, the Applicable Percentage for the initial dividend period, of the bond equivalent of the three-month U. S. Treasury bill secondary market discount rate immediately prior to the offering of the Preferred Stock). The Dividend Rate for each subsequent dividend period, determined in advance of such period, will be the product of (a) the Index Rate times (b) the Applicable Percentage. The Index Rate for any subsequent dividend period will be equal to the arithmetic average of the two most recent three-month U. S. Treasury bill secondary market discount rates (expressed on a bond equivalent basis) as published during the fourteen days prior to the last ten days of the preceding dividend period. The Applicable Percentage for each subsequent dividend period is the Applicable Percentage for the immediately preceding dividend period times the Market Price Adjustment Ratio, which is $100 divided by the Market Price of the Preferred Stock.

Price $100 Per Share

plus accrued dividends from the date of original issue

Copies of the Prospectus may be obtained in any
State in which this announcement is circulated only
from such of the undersigned as may legally offer
these securities in such State.

The First Boston Corporation

Merrill Lynch Capital Markets

Lehman Brothers Kuhn Loeb
Incorporated

Exhibit 7 Description of American Express Company MMP

American Express Company
Money Market Preferred Shares

American Express Company (the "Company") from time to time may issue in one or more series up to 600 shares of its Money Market Preferred™ Shares (the "MMP™"). Each series of MMP will be offered on terms determined at the time of sale. The specific designation, number of shares, redemption terms or other specific terms of the series of MMP in respect of which this Prospectus is being delivered are set forth in the accompanying Prospectus Supplement.

Dividends on the shares of MMP of each series are cumulative from the Date of Original Issue of such series and are payable commencing on the Wednesday that is the 49th day after the Date of Original Issue and on each Wednesday that is the last day of successive 49-day periods thereafter, subject to certain exceptions. The dividend rate on the MMP of each series for the Initial Dividend Period will be as set forth in the Prospectus Supplement relating to such series. For each Dividend Period thereafter, the dividend rate for such series will be the Applicable Rate per annum in effect from time to time. The Applicable Rate for each series for each such Dividend Period will be determined on the basis of Orders placed in an Auction conducted on the Business Day preceding the commencement of such Dividend Period. In each Auction, each Existing Holder will indicate its desire to (i) continue to hold shares of such series without regard to the Applicable Rate that results from the Auction, (ii) continue to hold shares of such series if the Applicable Rate that results from such Auction is equal to or greater than the rate bid by such Existing Holder, and/or (iii) sell shares of such series without regard to the Applicable Rate that results from the Auction. Potential Holders will offer to purchase shares of such series if the Applicable Rate that results from such Auction is equal to or greater than the rate bid by such Potential Holders. The Applicable Rate for any series that results from an Auction for any Dividend Period will not be greater than 110% of the 60 day "AA" Composite Commercial Paper Rate. If the Company fails to deposit funds timely to pay any dividend on or redeem shares of any series of MMP, the Applicable Rate for such series shall be equal to two-month LIBOR plus the additional rate per annum, if any, set forth in the Prospectus Supplement relating to such series.

Prospective purchasers should carefully review the Auction Procedures described in this Prospectus, including its Appendices, and should note that (i) an Order constitutes a commitment to purchase or sell shares of MMP based upon the results of an Auction, (ii) the Auctions will be conducted through telephone communications and (iii) settlement for purchases and sales will be on the Business Day following the Auction.

The shares of MMP of each series are redeemable at any time, as a whole or in part, at the option of the Company, at $515,000 per share if redeemed on or before the first anniversary of the Date of Original Issue of such series and at declining prices thereafter, plus accrued dividends. The shares of MMP of each series are also redeemable at the option of the Company on any Dividend Payment Date, as a whole, at a redemption price of $500,000 per share, plus accrued dividends, if the Applicable Rate for such series for the Dividend Period ending on such Dividend Payment Date is equal to or greater than the 60-day "AA" Composite Commercial Paper Rate on the date of determination of such Applicable Rate.

Shares of MMP may be transferred only pursuant to a Bid or a Sell Order placed in an Auction or to or through a Broker-Dealer or to a person that has delivered a signed Purchaser's Letter to the Trust Company.

Lehman Brothers
Shearson Lehman/American Express Inc.

August 24, 1994

Exhibit 8 Available Rates of Return, August 24 and October 12, 1984

	August 24 Yield	October 12 Yield
Short-term securities		
30-day CDs of large high-quality banks	11.63%	10.15%
90-day CDs of large high-quality banks	11.70	10.49
60-day commercial paper (AA)	11.42	9.89
1-year tax-exempt notes	6.74	5.86
Other capital market rates		
30-day Treasury bills	10.12	9.60
90-day Treasury bills	10.70	9.99
10-year Treasury bonds	12.92	12.19
20-year Treasury bonds	12.87	12.06
10-year AAA non-callable notes	13.23	12.56
30-year callable debentures		
AAA-rated bonds	13.54	12.86
AA-rated bonds	13.67	12.99
A-rated bonds	13.93	13.23
Floating-rate preferred prices (% of par)		
ARPPS Chemical New York Corp.(Ser.A)	108.75%	98.00%
Chase Manhattan Corp.	109.00	102.00
Bank America Corp. (Ser. A)	92.00	88.00
Bank America Corp. (Ser. B)	75.00	69.25
Citicorp	75.25	73.75
Continental Illinois	60.25	74.50
CAPS		
Consolidated Foods Corp.	108.00	103.50
AMF, Inc.	103.00	102.00
Ohio Edison	104.00	109.00

Dart & Kraft, Inc.

Late in 1983, Alan Lacy, assistant treasurer of Dart & Kraft, Inc. (D&K), was putting the final touches on his upcoming presentation to the board of directors. The presentation concerned the redemption of two outstanding debentures, each of which was exchangeable into the common stock of Minnesota Mining and Manufacturing (3M). Unexpectedly, a number of these debentures had started to exchange, and if the trend continued, this would result in a substantial tax liability, given D&K's low tax basis in the underlying 3M stock. As part of a plan to minimize this tax liability, it had been decided to call both issues. Mr. Lacy had been charged with the responsibility for determining D&K's options for funding the proposed redemptions and recommending a course of action.

BACKGROUND

In 1970, Dart Industries, Inc., a consumer products company, sold one of its subsidiaries, Riker Laboratories, to Minnesota Mining and Manufacturing in a nontaxable exchange for 1,483,489 shares of 3M common stock. In July 1972, Dart issued $60 million principal amount of $4\frac{1}{4}$% subordinated debentures due July 15, 1997, which were exchangeable for 3M stock at the rate of 10.75 shares per $1,000 debenture. (See Exhibit 1 for data on the domestic convertible and exchangeable bond markets.) In August 1972, Dart issued, in the Euro-market, $20 million principal amount of $4\frac{3}{4}$% subordinated debentures due August 15, 1987, exchangeable for 3M common stock at the rate of 10.1 shares per $1,000 debenture. (See Exhibit 2 for data on the Euro-convertible and Euro-exchangeable bond markets.) In 1980, Dart merged with Kraft, Inc., one of the world's principal food-processing firms, to create Dart & Kraft, Inc. (Exhibits 3 and 4 present D&K financial statements.)

Although 3M's stock over the past few years had performed well, and the company continued to raise its dividend, Mr. Lacy thought it made no sense for holders of the debentures to exchange now (see Exhibit 5). Nonetheless, over $1 million of debentures had been exchanged already in 1983. Furthermore, an analysis just completed by Mr.

This case was prepared by Scott P. Mason as the basis for class discussion.
Copyright ©1984 by the President and Fellows of Harvard College. Harvard Business School case 284-082.

Lacy's staff indicated a high probability that 3M's stock price and dividend would rise sufficiently by 1986–1987 to cause rational holders to then effect exchanges for the 3M common stock. Given D&K's $6.25 per share tax basis in the 3M stock, these exchanges would produce a tax liability of over $21 million. As part of a plan to minimize this tax liability it had been decided to call both issues before 3M's stock price reached a level above which a call would trigger exchanges by rational holders. (See Exhibits 1 and 2 for the bond prices and call prices on the domestic and Euro issues, respectively.)

It had also been decided that these redemptions should be funded by a Euro-debt offering tied to D&K's 3M common stock holdings. It was believed that tying the new debt offering to the 3M stock made sense because this would result in lower-cost debt financing, and equity-linked securities were currently very popular in the Euro-market. Furthermore, the Euro-market had not recently seen equity-linked securities issued by high-quality companies. The combination of the names Dart & Kraft and Minnesota Mining and Manufacturing would make for a strong issue, given current market conditions.

As a matter of corporate policy, D&K gave $5 million per year to charities. The plan to minimize the tax on the low-basis 3M stock called for D&K to begin using the stock for charitable contributions. Each year the $5 million earmarked for giving was to be used to purchase 3M stock in the market. Then $5 million, market value, of the low-basis 3M stock would be given to charities. The result of this plan, after a number of years, would be to transform the 3M stock backing the proposed equity-linked Euro-debt offering from low basis to high basis. This would result in a lower corporate tax liability upon any future conversions of the Euro-debt offering. (See Exhibit 6 for a description of tax treatment.)

THE PROBLEM

The key issue remaining was the structure of the new equity-linked Euro-bond offering. Mr. Lacy had called one of D&K's investment bankers, Goldman, Sachs & Co., for its opinion. Goldman, Sachs & Co. recommended a Euro-exchangeable bond that, given current market conditions, would carry a 7¾% coupon and be exchangeable into 3M stock at a premium of 15% over the market price at the time of issuance. The bond would have a maturity of 15 years and be immediately callable by D&K.

Mr. Lacy also discussed the structure problem with Morgan Guaranty, Ltd., who proposed a unit consisting of two pieces—a 15-year debenture and a detachable 15-year warrant to purchase 3M stock. The debenture would be noncallable, and the warrant holder would be allowed to use either cash or the debentures as scrip to exercise the warrant. Morgan believed this proposed unit structure had a number of economic advantages, and therefore the debenture coupon would be lower, or the warrant conversion premium higher, than that associated with a standard Euro-exchangeable bond.[1] Goldman, Sachs disagreed with Morgan Guaranty's assessment that terms at least comparable to the exchangeable could be achieved with the debenture with warrants structure because it was common knowledge in the Euro-market that a 15-year warrant had no incremental value over a 5-year warrant; approximately $200 per $1,000 unit. This would require D&K to raise the coupon or lower the conversion premium, on the warrant to achieve par pricing.

Mr. Lacy knew that this was a complex decision. The exchangeable bond was a well-tested security, and the opinion of Goldman, Sachs, an experienced equity-oriented firm, had to be respected. On the other hand, Morgan saw some important advantages to D&K with a unit structure of debt with warrants and believed that a coupon rate and conversion premium at least comparable to the exchangeable could be achieved. Before making his recommendation to the board, Mr. Lacy wanted to review the terms of the two structures carefully. (Exhibit 7 gives a summary of terms of the two structures *assuming* comparable coupon and conversion premiums.)

---

1   Market rates suggested that the 15-year debt portion, if it carried a $7^3/4$% coupon, would be worth approximately $700. With a current 3M stock price of $85 and a conversion premium of 15%, the warrant would have to be worth $300 to result in par pricing for the unit.

Exhibit 1   Domestic Convertible and Exchangeable Bond Data, September 29, 1983

Name of Issuer	Coupon Rate	Maturity date	Shares per 1,000 Bond	Price of Common	Bond Price	Current Return Bond	Current Return Com	Conv Prem	Current Call Price	Note #
ARA Services	4⅝	6/96	9.87	$52.0	$65.0	7.1%	3.9%	27	$101.850	
Allied Stores	4½	9/92	44.94	51.0	224.6	2.0	3.5	-2	102.000	
Allied Stores	9½	11/07	25.00	51.0	132.0	7.1	3.5	4	109.500	a
Ampex	5½	8/94	27.72	35.3	103.0	5.3	2.5	5	101.833	b
Ashland Oil Inc.	4¾	8/93	30.00	30.4	90.5	5.2	5.7	-1	102.950	
AVCO Corp.	5½	11/93	18.52	35.2	75.4	7.2	3.4	16	105.500	
Baxter Travenol Labs	4⅜	11/91	52.63	59.7	317.6	1.3	.9	1	102.500	
Baxter Travenol Labs	4¾	1/01	42.67	59.7	246.7	1.9	.9	-3	104.450	
Becton Dickinson	4⅛	6/88	20.48	40.6	91.1	4.5	2.8	9	101.875	
Becton Dickinson	5	12/89	15.41	40.6	81.0	6.1	2.8	29	103.000	
Boeing Company	8⅞	6/06	23.67	38.7	111.6	7.9	3.6	21	106.510	
Brunswick Corp.	10	8/06	46.58	47.5	186.4	5.3	2.5	-16	108.670	
Burlington Inds. Inc.	5	9/91	25.64	39.6	102.1	4.8	3.8	0	102.250	
Cigna	8	12/07	23.36	39.2	103.4	7.7	1.5	13	107.467	c
Caterpillar Tractor	5½	6/00	19.80	43.6	95.0	5.7	3.4	10	104.950	
Celanese Corp.	4	4/90	10.87	72.7	83.0	4.8	5.4	5	101.000	
Celanese Corp.	9¾	6/06	14.08	72.7	114.3	8.5	5.4	11	108.450	
Chase Manhattan Bank	4⅞	5/93	18.18	47.5	86.0	5.6	7.3	-1	102.680	d
Chase Manhattan Corp.	6½	7/96	17.39	47.5	84.0	7.7	7.3	1	104.550	
Citicorp	5¾	6/00	24.39	35.7	87.4	6.5	5.2	0	103.450	e
Corning Glass Works	8¼	12/07	26.23	37.5	108.4	7.6	3.1	10	107.150	f
Dana Corp.	5⅞	6/06	13.72	41.1	70.0	8.3	3.8	29	100.000	
Dart & Kraft, Inc.	4¼	7/97	10.75	83.3	89.0	4.7	3.9	-1	101.913	g
Deere & Co.	5½	1/01	30.53	40.1	123.4	4.4	2.4	1	104.950	
Deere & Co.	9	3/08	25.00	40.1	116.4	7.7	2.4	16	109.000	h
Eastern Airlines	5	11/92	20.00	5.4	39.0	12.8	0	255	102.500	
Eastern Airlines	4¾	10/93	29.41	5.4	39.0	12.1	0	141	102.500	
Eastern Airlines	11½	6/99	62.50	5.4	57.0	20.1	0	66	108.433	
Eastern Airlines	11¾	11/05	76.92	5.4	65.0	18.0	0	54	110.575	
Eastman Kodak	8¼	12/07	9.78	69.4	93.2	8.8	5.1	37	107.430	i

Exhibit 1 Domestic Convertible and Exchangeable Bond Data, September 29, 1983 (Continued)

Name of Issuer	Coupon Rate	Maturity date	Shares per 1,000 Bond	Price of Common	Bond Price	Current Return Bond	Current Return Com	Conv Prem	Current Call Price	Note #
F M C Corp.	4¼	7/92	24.10	45.4	108.2	3.9	3.9	−1	102.130	
Fedders Corp.	5	5/96	20.00	6.2	48.4	10.3	0	288	103.500	
Fed. Nat'l Mgt. Assn	4⅜	10/96	50.96	26.6	134.4	3.2	.5	−1	101.750	
Ford Motor Credit Co.	4½	11/96	16.00	63.2	102.6	4.3	.4	2	103.080	j
Ford Motor Credit Co.	4⅞	7/98	18.04	63.2	115.0	4.2	.4	1	103.592	j
Fruehauf	5½	4/94	21.62	43.2	98.4	5.5	.9	5	103.000	
GTE Corp.	10½	11/07	21.74	43.7	113.6	9.2	6.8	19	109.500	k
GTE Corp.	4	3/90	22.48	43.7	98.0	4.0	6.8	−1	103.000	l
GTE Corp.	5	12/92	22.98	43.7	100.0	5.0	6.8	−1	102.500	l
GTE Corp.	6¼	9/96	29.74	43.7	127.2	4.9	6.8	−2	104.380	l
Georgia Pacific	5¼	4/96	32.39	25.4	95.0	5.5	2.3	15	103.680	
Grace W.R. & Co.	4¼	3/90	17.45	49.1	85.0	5.0	5.6	−1	101.250	
Grace W.R. & Co.	6½	11/96	33.76	49.1	168.6	3.8	5.6	2	104.400	
Greyhound Corp.	6½	1/90	54.42	22.1	120.0	5.4	5.4	0	103.875	
Hercules Inc.	6½	6/99	28.57	36.5	109.2	5.9	3.9	4	105.525	
Hosp. Corp. of America	8½	3/08	19.28	45.5	106.4	7.9	.8	21	108.500	m
Houston Ltg. & Power Co.	5½	2/85	43.59	22.2	97.5	5.6	10.4	1	103.220	n
Hughes Tool	9½	12/06	21.22	21.6	90.0	10.5	3.8	95	107.770	
International Paper	4¼	11/96	39.48	42.4	167.4	2.5	.9	0	100.00	o
ITT Corp.	8⅝	6/00	39.41	43.4	167.1	5.1	6.3	−3	107.762	p
K Mart Corp.	6	7/99	28.17	36.2	109.2	5.4	2.9	7	105.100	
Kaiser Cement	9	10/05	30.53	21.5	89.0	10.1	2.7	35	107.800	
Litton Inds. Inc.	3½	4/87	22.22	64.4	146.3	2.3	2.7	2	100.000	
Lockheed	4¼	3/92	47.24	41.4	200.4	2.1	0	2	101.060	
Lomas & Nettleton	5½	6/91	51.28	51.0	256.3	2.1	3.9	−2	103.700	
Lomas & Nettleton	9¾	2/08	20.62	51.0	116.0	8.4	3.9	10	106.500	q
MCI Communications	7¾	3/03	38.37	17.2	90.2	8.5	0	36	107.750	
MGM Grand Hotels	9½	9/00	58.82	13.4	93.4	10.1	3.2	18	106.650	
Massmutual Mgt. & Rlt.	6¼	12/91	29.85	17.0	67.0	9.3	10.3	32	103.950	r
Massmutual Mgt. & Rlt.	7	10/00	50.00	17.0	80.5	8.7	10.3	−5	100.000	

Exhibit 1 Domestic Convertible and Exchangeable Bond Data, September 29, 1983 (Continued)

Name of Issuer	Coupon Rate	Maturity date	Shares per 1,000 Bond	Price of Common	Bond Price	Current Return Bond	Current Return Com	Conv Prem	Current Call Price	Note #
Mcgraw Hill Inc.	3⅞	5/92	32.00	50.3	143.0	2.7	2.1	−11	102.625	
Mckesson Corp.	6	6/94	32.62	41.7	141.0	4.2	5.7	3	103.600	s
Mckesson Corp.	9¾	3/06	22.86	41.7	107.2	9.0	5.7	12	108.780	s
Merrill Lynch	8⅞	11/07	31.88	33.6	118.4	7.4	2.3	10	107.211	
Moran Energy	8¾	1/08	50.00	16.0	95.0	9.2	.7	19	108.750	t
Morgan J P & Co. Inc.	4¾	11/98	12.50	69.2	88.0	5.3	5.3	2	103.800	
National Distillers	4½	8/92	39.97	28.3	111.0	4.0	7.7	−2	102.250	
Northwest Airlines	7½	12/07	19.70	37.0	99.4	7.5	2.1	36	106.750	u
Norton Company	9½	11/05	17.86	42.5	101.0	9.4	4.6	33	108.230	
Oak Industries	10½	2/02	29.74	7.6	70.0	15.0	0	204	110.500	
Owen III Inc.	6	11/92	33.90	33.2	113.0	5.3	5.0	0	102.250	v
Paine Webber	8¼	3/08	18.89	39.2	92.0	8.9	1.5	24	107.700	w
Pan American Wold Awys	4½	1/84	103.52	7.2	98.2	4.5	0	31	101.000	
Pan American Wold Awys	4½	8/86	58.96	7.2	74.0	6.0	0	73	101.750	
Pan American Wold Awys	5¼	2/89	60.75	7.2	64.0	8.2	0	45	102.500	
Pan American Wold Awys	15	3/98	36.36	7.2	131.4	11.4	0	399	113.000	x
Pennzoil Co.	5¼	3/96	39.22	36.5	149.0	3.5	6.0	4	103.500	
Pepsico. Inc.	4¾	8/96	47.24	34.6	165.7	2.8	4.6	1	103.340	
Pfizer Inc.	4	2/97	42.11	40.5	167.4	2.3	2.8	−2	103.000	
Pfizer Inc.	8¾	2/06	35.40	40.5	146.0	5.9	2.8	2	107.830	
Piedmont Aviation	11	7/07	37.21	29.0	119.6	9.1	.9	11	108.800	
Piedmont Aviation	6	12/07	28.47	29.0	90.4	6.6	.9	10	106.000	y
Pittson	9.2	7/04	20.00	17.6	78.6	11.6	1.1	122	107.360	
RCA Corp.	4½	8/92	17.84	32.3	72.0	6.2	2.7	25	102.000	
Ramada Inns	5	10/96	58.65	9.7	75.0	6.6	0	29	103.500	
Republic Airlines	10⅛	12/07	100.00	4.1	54.2	18.6	0	32	110.125	
Reynolds Metal Co.	4½	3/91	17.46	38.4	75.4	5.9	2.5	12	101.750	
Rockwell Intl. Corp.	4¼	2/91	86.96	28.1	252.0	1.6	3.1	3	101.920	
SCM Corp.	5½	5/88	22.06	34.3	91.6	5.9	5.8	21	102.800	
St. Regis Corp.	4⅞	4/97	33.04	29.4	96.1	5.0	3.7	−1	103.656	z

Exhibit 1 Domestic Convertible and Exchangeable Bond Data, September 29, 1983 (Continued)

Name of Issuer	Coupon Rate	Maturity date	Shares per 1,000 Bond	Price of Common	Bond Price	Current Return Bond	Current Return Com	Conv Prem	Current Call Price	Note #
Santa Fe Inds. Inc.	6¼	8/98	93.75	29.7	310.0	2.0	3.3	11	101.000	
Sherwin Williams Co.	6¼	3/95	86.96	26.2	230.0	2.7	2.2	1	104.060	
Singer	9	5/08	27.78	24.0	96.0	9.3	.4	44	109.000	aa
Stevens J P & Co. Inc.	4	4/90	42.88	19.4	91.0	4.3	6.1	9	102.000	
Stevens J P & Co. Inc.	9	5/08	33.06	19.4	88.0	10.2	6.1	37	109.000	aa
Sun Company	10¾	4/06	16.67	40.6	98.0	10.9	2.8	44	109.860	bb
Texas Air	8⅜	9/00	58.82	5.1	57.0	14.6	0	89	105.863	
Textron Inc.	7¾	1/05	16.95	57.1	102.7	7.5	4.2	6	105.100	cc
Tiger International	8⅝	7/05	32.26	6.0	69.0	12.5	0	257	106.900	
Trane Co.	4	9/92	27.78	38.6	104.0	3.8	3.5	−3	102.000	
Union Carbide Corp.	10	3/06	15.18	65.6	114.0	8.7	5.1	14	109.000	
Union Pacific Corp.	4¾	4/99	70.00	56.7	417.2	1.1	3.1	5	102.380	
UNIROYAL INC.	5½	2/96	39.41	16.4	79.6	6.8	0	23	103.700	
United Brands Co.	5½	2/94	18.18	17.4	57.2	9.6	0	80	103.500	
United States Steel	5¾	7/01	15.94	28.5	65.0	8.8	3.4	42	105.750	
Wal-Mart Stores	9½	12/06	76.63	40.1	294.0	3.2	.3	−4	107.770	
Walgreen Co.	5½	3/91	124.00	34.7	428.0	1.2	1.7	−1	103.762	
Walter Jim Corp.	5¾	1/91	23.81	35.4	87.4	6.5	3.3	4	103.900	
Walter Jim Corp.	9	12/07	26.85	35.4	108.0	6.3	3.3	13	107.200	dd
Wang Laboratories	10	11/06	49.69	34.2	169.4	5.8	.3	0	108.670	ee
Wang Laboratories	7¾	6/08	19.17	34.2	93.6	8.2	.3	43	107.750	ff
Western Airlines	5¼	2/93	89.45	4.1	55.0	9.5	0	49	102.750	
Western Union	5¼	8/97	15.15	31.5	64.7	8.0	4.4	35	103.750	
Will Ross Inc.	5¼	8/89	22.75	51.6	125.0	4.2	1.0	6	103.250	
Will Ross Inc.	4½	9/92	21.82	51.6	109.0	4.1	1.0	−3	103.250	gg
Xerox Corp.	6	11/95	10.50	42.6	72.4	8.2	7.0	56	103.000	gg
Zurn Industries	5¾	11/94	32.44	27.0	89.1	64	4.8	−6	102.000	

Exhibit 1   Notes to Domestic Convertible and Exchangeable Bond Data (Continued)

a. Not callable until 11/1/85 unless common stock price is 150% of convertible price for 30 successive trading days.

b. Convertible into Signal Companies common stock.

c. Convertible into Paine Webber common stock. Bond is not yet callable. Callable after 12/8/83.

d. New corporate name is Chase Manhattan Corp.

e. Bond is not yet callable. Callable after 6/30/83.

f. Convertible into Owen-Corning Fiberglass common stock. Bond is not yet callable. Callable after 11/30/84.

g. Convertible into Minnesota Mining and Manufacturing common stock. Formerly Dart Industries.

h. Not callable until 3/15/85 unless common stock price is 150% of convertible price for 20 successive trading days.

i. Bond is not yet callable. Callable after 12/14/84.

j. Convertible into Ford Motor Corp. common stock.

k. Not callable until 11/1/84 unless common stock price is 150% of convertible price for 30 successive days.

l. Formerly General Telephone and Electric.

m. Not callable until 3/1/85 unless common stock price is 150% of convertible price for 20 successive trading days.

n. New corporate name is Houston Industries.

o. Convertible into C. R. Bard common stock.

p. Formerly International Telephone & Telegraph.

q. Bond is not yet callable. Callable after 2/14/86.

r. Not callable till 3/15/85 unless common stock price is 140% of convertible price for 30 successive trading days.

s. Formerly Foremost McKesson.

t. Not callable until 1/15/85 unless common stock price is 150% of convertible price for 30 successive trading days.

u. Bond is not yet callable. Callable after 12/14/84.

v. Prior to 5/3/82 the coupon rate was 4.5%.

w. Bond is not yet callable. Callable after 2/29/84.

x. Not callable until 3/1/85 unless common stock price is 140% of convertible price for 30 successive trading days.

y. Not callable until 12/1/84 unless common stock price is $52.69 for 30 successive trading days prior to call date.

z. Formerly St. Regis Paper Company.

aa. Not callable until 5/15/85 unless common stock price is 150% of convertible price for 20 days within 30 successive days.

bb. Convertible into Becton, Dickinson common stock.

cc. Convertible into Allied Chemical stock.

dd. Bond is not yet callable. Callable after 12/15/84.

ee. Convertible into Class B common stock.

ff. Convertible into C1.B common stock. Not callable until 6/1/85 unless common stock price is 140% of convertible price for 30 successive trading days.

gg. Convertible into G. D. Searle common stock.

Exhibit 2 Euro-Convertible and Euro-Exchangeable Bond Data, September 29, 1983

Name of Issuer	Coupon Rate	Maturity Date	Shares per 1,000 Bond	Price of Common	Bond Price	Current Return Bond	Current Return Com	Conv Prem	Current Call Price	Note #
AMF Intl	5	9/87	19.14	$17	$77	6.4%	3.9%	138	$100.000	
Alaska Interstate OS	8¼	12/95	23.53	14	80	10.3	2.9	139	104.000	a
American Can Intl	4¾	5/88	17.09	43	87	5.4	6.6	16	100.000	
American Express O/S	4¼	5/87	33.34	36	139	3.0	3.4	14	100.000	
American Motors Intl	6	4/92	143.47	7	117	5.1	0	5	101.500	
American Tobacco Int.	5¼	8/88	55.56	56	296	1.7	6.4	-5	100.000	
Apache Intl	9½	6/96	43.24	13	86	10.9	2.0	47	104.000	
Beatrice Foods Intl	7¼	11/90	57.14	29	154	4.7	5.4	-9	101.500	
Beatrice Foods Intl	6¼	8/91	43.72	29	122	5.1	5.4	-6	101.500	
Beatrice Foods IntL	4½	9/92	32.72	29	101	4.4	5.4	-4	100.000	
Broadway-hale Oseas	4¾	6/87	24.10	23	82	5.7	5.2	47	100.000	
Carnation Oseas.	4	1/88	19.22	49	100	3.9	4.4	5	100.000	
Chese-Ponds Intl	4¾	12/83	40.82	40	151	3.1	4.6	-8	100.250	
Chese-Ponds Intl	6¼	12/84	37.38	40	138	4.5	4.6	-8	101.000	
Chevron Overseas	5	2/88	64.37	36	226	2.2	6.6	-2	101.000	b
Chrysler Overseas	5	2/88	16.13	29	82	6.0	0	75	100.000	
Chrysler Overseas	4¾	5/88	13.61	29	82	5.7	0	107	100.000	
Continental Tel Intl	5½	3/88	42.18	24	101	5.4	6.6	-2	101.500	
Cummings Intl	5	8/88	27.65	66	185	2.7	3.0	1	100.000	
Cummings Intl	6¼	10/86	18.35	66	128	4.8	3.0	5	101.000	
Damon Intl	5¼	12/87	13.75	26	74	7.0	.7	104	100.500	
Dart & Kraft Intl	4¾	8/87	10.10	83	92	5.1	3.9	10	100.000	c
Eastman Kodak Intl	4½	5/88	10.42	69	91	4.9	5.1	26	100.000	
Fedders Capital Intl	5	5/92	21.16	6	49	10.1	0	274	100.000	
Fedt Dept Stores Intl	4½	12/85	24.39	58	135	3.3	3.7	-5	100.000	
Firestone Tire Oseas	5	5/88	34.04	20	88	5.6	2.8	25	100.000	
Ford Motor Intl	6	3/86	19.81	63	124	4.8	.4	-1	100.460	
Ford Motor Init	5	3/88	17.79	63	112	4.4	.4	0	100.000	
General Electric O/S	4¼	6/87	24.71	52	126	3.3	3.6	-3	100.000	
Gillette Intl	4¾	12/87	14.93	47	87	5.4	4.8	23	100.500	

Exhibit 2   Euro-Convertible and Euro-Exchangeable Bond Data, September 29, 1983 (Continued)

Name of Issuer	Coupon Rate	Maturity Date	Shares per 1,000 Bond	Price of Common	Bond Price	Current Return Bond	Current Return Com	Conv Prem	Current Call Price	Note #
W.R. Grace Overseas	5	4/86	17.45	49	92	5.4	5.6	7	100.000	
Holiday Inns Oseas	8	10/85	28.57	56	147	5.4	1.4	-9	101.000	
Honeywell Overseas	6	11/86	8.33	121	109	5.5	2.9	8	101.000	
ITT Sheraton Intl	6½	7/89	18.55	43	94	6.8	6.3	17	101.000	d
Intl. Std. Elec.-itt	5	2/88	18.70	43	94	5.2	6.3	16	100.750	d
Intl. Std. Elec.-itt	6¼	11/89	16.99	43	89	6.9	6.3	21	101.250	d
Intl. Std. Elec.-itt	5¼	12/88	15.45	43	84	6.2	6.3	26	101.000	d
ITT Corp.	4¾	10/87	17.82	43	90	5.2	6.3	17	0.000	e
Kaiser Aluminum Intl	5	2/88	40.62	20	97	5.1	2.9	16	100.500	
Walter Kidde Oseas	5	2/89	31.88	29	93	5.3	3.7	1	101.250	
Lear Petroleum Intl	6	6/69	42.86	27	120	6.6	.7	3	102.000	
Liv Intl	5	7/88	42.81	16	90	5.5	1.5	27	101.000	
Marine Midland Oseas	5	5/68	25.00	23	83	6.0	5.8	40	100.000	
Massmutual Mtg & Rlty	6¾	7/87	31.01	17	81	8.3	10.3	54	101.000	
Mohasco Intl	5	6/87	20.62	21	74	6.7	.3	66	100.000	
Monsanto Intl.	4½	10/85	11.76	110	129	3.4	3.8	-1	100.000	
Moran Energy Intl	8	11/95	37.61	16	79	10.1	.7	31	104.000	
J. P. Morgan Oseas	4¼	6/87	19.14	69	128	3.3	5.3	-3	100.000	
Nicor Overseas	10¾	5/95	27.40	30	108	9.9	9.9	29	105.000	f
Northwest Intl Fin.	9	7/96	41.24	36	148	6.0	3.8	-7	105.000	g
Owens Illinois Intl	4½	7/87	36.88	33	129	3.4	5.0	5	100.000	
Pan American Oseas	5¼	9/88	62.62	7	77	6.7	0	71	101.250	
J.C. Penny-Europe	6	12/89	18.67	57	103	5.8	3.7	-5	101.000	
J.C. Penny Intl	4½	8/87	12.09	57	87	5.1	3.7	24	100.000	
Pepsico Capital Intl	8	4/96	26.32	34	103	7.7	4.6	13	104.000	
RCA Intl	5	2/88	18.18	32	83	6.0	2.7	41	101.000	
Ramada Capital Oseas	6¼	11/88	64.23	9	93	6.6	0	47	100.750	
Reading & Bates Intl	8	9/95	27.78	16	83	9.5	5.0	88	104.000	
Revlon Intl	4¾	4/87	25.16	30	94	5.0	6.0	23	101.000	

Exhibit 2   Euro-Convertible and Euro-Exchangeable Bond Data, September 29, 1983 (Continued)

Name of Issuer	Coupon Rate	Maturity Date	Shares per 1,000 Bond	Price of Common	Bond Price	Current Return Bond	Current Return Com	Conv Prem	Current Call Price	Note #
Reynolds Metals Intl	5	6/88	22.89	38	95	5.2	2.5	8	100.000	
SCM Overseas	5¼	3/89	22.06	34	91	5.7	5.8	20	100.250	
C.D. Searle Intl	4¾	5/88	54.56	51	284	1.6	1.0	1	100.000	
Southland Corp. Intl	5	7/87	45.19	39	175	2.8	2.1	-3	100.500	
Sperry Corp. Intl	4¼	2/88	19.43	46	99	4.2	4.1	10	100.000	
Squibb Intl	4¼	6/87	17.54	51	98	4.3	2.5	8	100.000	
TRW Intl	5	2/88	19.05	74	128	3.9	3.5	-9	101.000	
Texaco Intl	4½	7/68	22.60	36	94	4.7	8.3	16	100.000	
Texas Air Intl	7½	8/93	68.97	5	67	11.1	0	91	103.500	
Tosco Intl	8	10/95	26.76	10	60	13.3	0	124	104.000	
Transco Energy Intl	8¾	12/95	14.71	38	80	10.8	4.9	42	104.000	h
Viacom Intl	9¼	10/07	29.76	31	115	8.0	1.2	22	107.400	i
Warner Lambert Oseas	4½	4/87	20.83	29	87	5.1	4.8	44	100.000	
Warner Lambert Oseas	4¼	4/88	16.26	29	77	5.5	4.8	63	101.000	
Warner Lambert Oseas	4½	8/88	34.48	29	93	4.8	4.8	-7	100.000	
Xerox Intl	5	12/88	6.76	42	78	6.4	7.0	170	0.000	

Exhibit 2   Notes to Euro-Convertible and Euro-Exchangeable Bond Data (Continued)

a. Effective 6/4/82. New corporate name is Enstar Corporation.
b. Convertible into Standard Oil of California common stock.
c. Convertible into Minnesota Mining and Manufacturing common stock. Formerly Dart Industries.
d. Convertible into ITT common stock.
e. Formerly International Telephone & Telegraph.
f. Convertible into Nicor common stock. Also convertible into Nicor 14¼ nonconvertible. Debentures due 5/1/95 until 5/1/85.
g. Convertible into Northwest Energy common stock. Also convertible into Northwest International 16.5% subordinated debentures until 7/15/88.
h. Formerly Transco Companies International
i. Bond is not yet callable. Callable after 10/14/84.

Exhibit 3   Statements for Years Ending December 31, 1980–1982 (million of dollars except per share data)

	1980	1981	1982
Net sales	$9,411.5	$10,211.0	$9,974.4
Costs and expenses			
Cost of products	7,032.8	7,452.4	7,098.1
Delivery, sales, administrative expenses	1,694.9	1,989.8	2,122.2
Interest expense	72.8	126.6	115.6
Interest income	(49.8)	(40.9)	(63.6)
Other income, net	(33.0)	(68.4)	(46.0)
Total costs and expenses	8,717.7	9,459.5	9,226.3
Income from operations	693.8	751.5	748.1
Nonoperating items	19.3	(107.6)	(90.7)
Income before taxes	713.1	643.9	657.4
Provision for taxes on income	330.0	296.4	307.1
Net income	$383.1	$347.5	$350.3
Net income per common and common equivalent share	$7.03	$6.36	$6.40
No. of common and common equivalent shares (millions)	54.5	54.6	54.8

Source: Dart & Kraft 1982 annual report.

Exhibit 4   Consolidated Balance Sheets at December 31, 1981 and 1982 (millions of dollars)

	1981	1982
Cash and investments	$177.6	$473.0
Trade accounts and other receivables	939.2	951.0
Inventory	1,851.3	1,741.3
Current assets	2,968.1	3,165.3
Investments and long-term receivables	209.9	241.0
Prepaid and deferred items	115.0	91.1
Property, plant, and equipment less accumulated depreciation	1,565.3	1,472.5
Intangibles, less amortization	195.5	163.9
Total assets	$5,053.8	$5,133.8
Current liabilities	1,570.0	$1,486.8
Long-term debt	551.6	616.3
Deferred taxes on income	157.5	129.4
Other liabilities	56.7	127.8
Total liabilities	2,335.8	$2,360.3
Common stock, $2.50 par value, authorized 200 million shares	136.4	137.0
Capital surplus	334.9	344.5
Retained earnings	2,317.3	2,468.6
Cumulative foreign currency adjustments	(70.6)	(176.6)
Shareholders' equity	2,718.0	2,773.5
Total liabilities and shareholders' equity	$5,053.8	$5,133.8

Source: Dart & Kraft 1982 annual report.

Exhibit 5   3M Stock Price and Dividend History

	High	Low	Dividend
1970	$114¾	$71	$1.75
1971	135	75⅛	1.85
1972	87⅛	74¼	1.44
1973	91⅝	70	1.05
1974	80½	44⅝	1.25⅛
1975	68	43	1.35
1976	66⅝	52¼	1.45
1977	57	45	1.70
1978	66	43	2.00
1979	66	48⅛	2.40
1980	62⅛	45⅞	2.80
1981	65	48	3.00
1982	79⅜	48¾	3.20
1983			
First quarter	82½	72⅝	.825
Second quarter	90½	75⅛	.825
Third quarter	85¾	75⅜	.825

Exhibit 6   Summary of Tax Issues

Although similar in structure to exchangeable debt, the exchangeable unit of debt with warrants is significantly different with respect to its tax implications to the issuer. The Internal Revenue Service views the issuance of debt with warrants as equivalent to issuing two separate securities, straight debt and equity warrants, whereas it views the issuance of exchangeable debt as issuing a single security. Two important tax issues exist: (1) the unit debt is deemed to be issued with original issue discount (OID), and (2) the tax implications of exercise or expiration for both the exchangeable debt and exchangeable warrants.

Since the issuer of the exchangeable unit of debt is deemed to be issuing two securities, each must be valued separately. First the warrant value is established and it is then subtracted from the unit value to establish the value of the debt. Because the principal amount of the debt is typically equal to the issue price of the unit, the value of the debt for tax purposes is significantly less than the principal amount, thus creating OID. The issuer must amortize this discount as additional noncash interest expense. For debt issued prior to July 1, 1982, this amortization was on a straight-line basis over the life of the issue. Since July 1, 1982, the amortization of OID is done on an equivalent yield-to-maturity basis.

The portion of the unit issue price attributable to the warrant can create a taxable event, not at issuance date but at the time of exercise or expiration. If the warrant expires unexercised, the issuer recognizes the value of the warrant as ordinary short-term gain. If the warrant is exercised, and is written on another company's stock, then the allocated warrant premium is treated, along with the exercise price, as part of the price paid to the issuer for the third-party stock. The difference between this price and the tax basis in the third-party stock is taxed at long-term rates. If the warrant is written on the issuing company's stock, then exercise of the warrant is a nontaxable event. The expiration of an unexercised exchangeable note is a nontaxable event. If an exchangeable note is exercised, the difference between the exercise price and the tax basis of the third-party stock is taxed at long-term rates. In contrast, no taxable events are associated with a convertible bond because of expiration on exercise.

Exhibit 7   Summary of Terms

Exchangeable Debt		Exchangeable Unit of Debt with Warrant	
Issue Price	$1,000 per bond	Issue Price	$1,000 per unit
Maturity	15 years	**Debenture**	
Coupon	7¾%	Maturity	15 years
Exchangeable for	10.23 shares	Coupon	7¾%
		Mandatory redemption	None
Conversion premium	15%	Optional redemption	None
Mandatory redemption	None	Principal amount	$1,000
		Warrant	
Optional redemption	Callable immediately	Shares per warrant	10.23 shares
		Exercise price per warrant	$1,000
Principal Amount	$1,000	Maturity	15 years
		Payment upon exercise	Either $1,000 cash or principal amount of debenture
		Separability of unit	After 90 days

Note: Assumes current 3M stock price is $85 per share.

WASTE MANAGEMENT, INC

In early 1985, Donald Flynn, chief financial officer and treasurer of Waste Management, Inc., considered his opportunities for refinancing the $350 million in debt the company had taken on to acquire a 60% share of SCA Services, Inc. Waste Management (WMX) did what its name implied: storing, collecting, processing, and disposing of solid and chemical waste. It served commercial, industrial, and municipal customers. Through a subsidiary, the company also handled low-level radioactive waste. With revenues of $1.3 billion in 1984, WMX was the largest waste management company in the United States (see Exhibit 1).

SCA Services was in the same line of business as its new parent. Prior to the acquisition, SCA had been the third-largest waste management company in the United States with facilities in 28 states and 1983 revenues of $390 million. WMX had acquired 60% of the company in the fall of 1984 for $220 million cash and the assumption of $160 million in liabilities. For antitrust reasons, Genstar, a Canadian company, had agreed to purchase the other 40% of SCA. The transaction had been funded primarily by debt, resulting in the increase of WMX's long-term debt to total capitalization to 35.6% at year-end 1984, from 17.9% the year before (see Exhibits 2 and 3).

Donald Flynn was concerned with the level of debt incurred as a result of the acquisition. As WMX had a high degree of operating leverage, the company tended to be financially conservative. Mr. Flynn decided to reduce the company's exposure to variable interest rates and to decrease its leverage by shifting the burden of this financing into equity. WMX had gone public in 1971 and the stock was very well thought of by investors. The price/earning multiple had always been above the market's P/E, and the company's market capitalization had grown dramatically. Although WMX's stock price was relatively high, its price-earning ratio was below historical levels. Therefore, Mr. Flynn was interested in exploring creative ways to issue equity.

Keeping in mind the company's need for a nonvariable cash outflow and an equity-type security, the CFO narrowed the financing options to either convertible debt or Liquid

This case was prepared by Martha D. N. Notaras under the supervision of E. Philip Jones.

Copyright © 1987 by the President and Fellows of Harvard. Harvard Business School case 288-020.

Yield Option Notes (LYONs, a registered service mark of Merrill Lynch and Co., Inc), a new security developed by Merrill Lynch Capital Markets.

BACKGROUND

Waste Management's motto was "Helping the world dispose of its problems." The company achieved this goal through four operating groups, headquartered in Oak Brook, Illinois. Waste Management North America (WMNA), which provided 60% of 1984 revenues and 79% of pre-tax income, focused on waste collection and disposal. The group served 4.7 million households throughout the United States and 326,000 industrial customers. Waste disposal was facilitated through solid waste sanitary landfills. In addition, the group had recently completed a refuse-to-energy converting plant in Florida. This generated energy equivalent to one quarter million barrels of oil annually.

Waste Management International (WMI) provided services similar to WMNA, to communities in Australia, Saudi Arabia, and South America. WMI contributed 10% of 1984 revenues and 6% of pre-tax income. International work involved an understanding of the local economy as well as special challenges of the area. For example, WMI disposed of 17,000 abandoned vehicles from the streets of Jeddah, Saudi Arabia, in the first two years of its contract.

Chemical Waste Management (CWM) dealt primarily with advanced technology to handle hazardous wastes off- and on-site, often in a remedial capacity. The group benefited from the Environmental Protection Agency's establishment of the Superfund, to clean up industrial sites that had been contaminated by their former occupants. CWM contributed 15% of revenues and 8% of income in 1984.

Chem-Nuclear Systems was the leading company offering low-level radioactive waste management, providing this service to over 85% of the nuclear power-generating stations in the United States. This subsidiary accounted for 6% of revenues and 7% of pre-tax income in 1984. New nuclear generating plants going into operation in the coming five years were expected to increase Chem-Nuclear's potential customer base by 40%.

The company's operations were subject to extensive local and federal regulations. One example of this impact was the EPA ruling that waste disposal through ocean incineration should not be made available to the U.S. market, pending additional research and specific regulations. WMX had been prepared to offer this service in May 1984. Regulations increased WMX's operating expenses, legal fees, and regulatory costs. With constantly changing rules in an increasingly stringent environment, WMX expected to be forced to stall other projects (like ocean incineration) and invest substantial capital in maintaining and upgrading its landfills and other facilities.

The fact that the EPA had authority over WMX's operating decisions increased the risk of the company's activities. Once the EPA suspended an activity, WMX could not be sure if or when the company would be able to resume that service. The agency's judgment also reflected the political environment, which WMX could not predict or control. The risks associated with regulation were one of the reasons Flynn preferred to issue equity instead of taking on the burden of debt at this time.

WMX was a highly profitable business, with a before-tax profit margin of 19% in 1984. The business was marked by economies of scale in selling and administrative expense. As the quality of service depended on WMX owning efficient equipment and extensive and well-located landfill property, the level of capital expenditures was high, providing further reason to keep the cash cost of financing low.

The SCA acquisition contributed to WMNA's growth in 1984; in the future, refuse-to-energy was expected to expand, especially in cities. As regulations governing the disposal of hazardous wastes grew, the domestic market for off-site chemical waste management services was expected to nearly triple from $1.2 billion in 1984 to $3.5 billion in 1989. Waste Management believed that its strong position in hazardous and nuclear waste handling positioned the company for growth as these markets expanded. The company planned to grow through internal means, as well as by making strategic acquisitions, as it had in the past.

WMX was accustomed to making small acquisitions. In 1984, WMX bought 71 businesses for $28.5 million cash and half a million shares of common stock. However, the purchase of 60% of SCA Services was considerably larger than most of WMX's acquisitions. WMX expected $260 million in revenues from SCA in 1985. SCA provided WMX with additional customers, as well as more solid and hazardous waste disposal capacity. SCA's facilities were integrated into the operations of WMNA and CWM.

As of December 31, 1984, WMX was paying 8.63% to 9.75% on the debt from the SCA purchase, borrowed under a revolving credit agreement and informal arrangements with several banks. Due to the increased borrowing, WMX's total interest expense had almost doubled, from $25 million in 1983 to $53 million in 1984 (see Exhibit 1). In January 1985, WMX began issuing P1/A1+ rated commercial paper at a cost below bank lending rates (see Exhibit 4). The commercial paper bore interest rates between 8.34% and 9.21%. However, as management noted in the 1984 annual report: "It is anticipated that in 1985 there will be further restructuring of debt and that the amount of variable debt outstanding will be reduced; however, the form of such restructuring has not yet been determined."

In 1982, WMX had issued two million shares of common stock at $48 per share for net proceeds of $95,925,000. At that time, the stock had traded at a price-earnings multiple of more than 19 times. In the first quarter of 1985, the stock's high was $54, less than 16 times projected earnings (see Exhibit 5). While WMX was willing to issue stock, management expected that the price would increase, given the stock's historic levels. Mr. Flynn wanted to capture as much of the potential increase as possible by selling stock at a substantial premium to current market value.

THE CONVERTIBLE DEBENTURE ALTERNATIVE

The terms of a 25-year $200-million convertible debt offering would be an 8% coupon and a 25% premium over the stock price on the issuance date. The issue would count as debt initially, and the cash interest payments would be tax-deductible. If the full issue was converted, the company would have an additional $200 million in equity. After two years, the company could call the debentures, at specified redemption prices, plus accrued interest (see Exhibit 6). The sinking fund requirement starting in ten years effectively shortened the bonds' average life.

The investor could also convert the debentures into stock at any time. The 8% coupon represented a 400–500 basis point savings over straight A2 corporate debt which WMX could otherwise issue.

At a 25% premium to the recent stock price of $54, the conversion price would be $67.50. Mr. Flynn wondered when it would make sense for the investor to convert, and under what circumstances WMX should call the debentures. If WMX's stock price rose to $70, and holders converted, Mr. Flynn knew the company would not have to recognize the $2.50 difference in market value versus conversion price—but would the company have lost money? (See Exhibit 7 for a summary of terms.)

THE LIQUID YIELD OPTION NOTE ALTERNATIVE

LYONs were a new product developed by Lee Cole, vice president of institutional sales and marketing, and Tom Patrick, managing director of investment banking at Merrill Lynch Capital Markets. With a target issuance date of April 22, 1985, Waste Management would be the first issuer, although the investment bank was proposing the product to other clients. LYONs would have a $1,000 face value, but would be issued at a deep discount, initially selling at $250 per bond. As zero coupon bonds, the 9% bond equivalent yield would accrete to increase the principal to 100% of face value by maturity, January 21, 2001. Each LYON would be convertible into 4.36 of Waste Management common shares at any time during the security's life. The LYON would be subordinated debt until put, called, or converted.

Starting June 30, 1988, the company would be obligated to buy back the security on each subsequent June 30th if the investor wanted to sell it, but at a lower effective yield in the early years (see Exhibit 8 for the purchase prices). Starting June 30, 1987, or if the stock traded at 1.65 times the stock price at issuance for 20 days, the company could redeem the LYONs. (Exhibit 9 shows the redemption prices for LYONs. Exhibit 10 gives a summary of terms.)

DONALD FLYNN'S QUESTIONS

Donald Flynn wondered if an investor would perceive a LYON differently if he or she held it for various lengths of time: three years, five years, or until maturity. He was unsure who would invest in the security. In addition, he needed to understand when it would make sense for an investor to convert or put a LYON. When would the company want to call the security or force conversion? Suppose the conversion value was greater than or equal to the call price? If it was in the interest of the LYON holder *not* to convert, would it necessarily be in the interest of WMX to call and force conversion?

Mr. Flynn felt that both a convertible debenture and a LYON issue would fulfill the company's desire to sell equity at a premium. In addition, while the zero coupon feature of the LYON was attractive to WMX, he wondered whether investors would be enthusiastic about it. The zero coupon portion of the LYONs seemed straightforward to put a value on; but how could investors value the put option and the conversion feature they received, and the call option that the company obtained?

Mr. Flynn was inclined to sell equity, and preferred to sell it at a premium, through a LYON or a convertible debenture. He knew that the conversion premium on the convertible debt would be 25%. Mr. Flynn wondered how to evaluate the effective premium commanded by the LYON. Would the effective premium remain constant over time? As the first potential issuer of LYONs, WMX was concerned both about investor acceptance and the impact the issue would have on the investment community's perception of the company. Merrill Lynch had indicated that WMX's stock was well suited to a LYONs issue. Mr. Flynn wondered what characteristics about the stock were attractive, and whether there were many other companies that would be interested in such an issue.

Exhibit 1   Consolidated Income Statement[a] (in thousands of dollars)

	1982	1983	1984
Revenue	$966,548	$1,039,989	$1,314,761
Operating expenses	593,149	657,536	846,364
Selling and administrative costs	158,329	167,973	195,217
Income from operations	215,070	214,480	273,180
Total interest expense	19,676	24,729	53,070
Interest income	9,616	13,564	18,117
Capitalized interest	6,113	7,828	10,445
Sundry, net	15,491	1,828	695
Income before income taxes	195,632	209,315	247,977
Provision for income taxes	89,108	88,868	105,468
Net income	106,524	120,447	142,509
Average primary shares outstanding	44,432	48,237	48,696
Earnings per primary common share	$2.40	$2.50	$2.93

Source: Waste Management annual reports.
a. Includes subsidiaries.

Exhibit 2   Consolidated Balance Sheets (in thousands of dollars)

	1983	1984
Assets		
Cash and short-term investments	$52,030	$8,452
Receivables (net of reserve)	195,106	314,152
Other current assets	139,395	122,503
Total current assets	386,531	445,107
Land and buildings	363,875	474,457
Vehicles and equipment	671,557	874,758
Leasehold improvements	16,625	22,623
Less: Accumulated depreciation and amortization	308,948	377,396
Total net property and equipment	743,109	994,442
Intangibles related to acquired businesses	140,001	424,086
Sundry (including investments)	68,322	102,161
Total assets	$1,337,963	$1,965,796
Liabilities and Stockholders' Equity		
Current maturity of long-term debt	43,623	46,998
Accounts payable	83,491	123,124
Accrued expenses	67,521	139,345
Unearned revenue	38,270	46,751
Total current liabilities	232,905	356,218
Deferred income taxes	81,787	95,921
Deferred investment credit	21,574	26,069
Other	65,892	112,846
Total deferred items	169,253	234,836
Long-term debt	167,940	489,072
Common stock ($1 par value)	47,952	48,734
Additional paid-in-capital	309,711	324,590
Retained earnings	410,202	512,346
Total stockholders' equity	767,865	885,670
Total liabilities and stockholders' equity	$1,337,963	$1,965,796

Source: Waste Management annual reports.

Exhibit 3   Total Cash Flow for the years ended December 31 (in thousands of dollars)

	1982	1983	1984
Net income	$106,524	$120,447	$142,509
Noncash items:			
Depreciation and amortization	76,182	88,964	115,194
Provision for deferred taxes	19,930	16,909	19,534
Amortization of deferred investment credit	(4,684)	(5,128)	(5,697)
Funds from operations	197,952	221,192	271,540
Increase in current assets	(87,531)	(62,770)	(102,154)
Adjusted funds from operations	110,421	158,422	169,386
Increase in current liabilities	6,675	23,179	119,938
Cash generated from the operating cycle	117,096	181,601	289,324
Purchase of property and equipment	(158,856)	(189,453)	(266,424)
Acquisition of property and equipment at market value	(60,989)	(29,473)	(119,178)
(Increase)/Decrease in sundry assets	(43,509)	2,802	(33,839)
(Increase)/Decrease in deferred taxes	(4,219)	1,220	(5,400)
Increase in deferred items	8,215	8,582	46,954
Translation of foreign currency statements	(1,755)	(1,589)	(33,040)
Dividends paid	(21,659)	(30,516)	(37,325)
Cash available before investments and financing	(165,676)	(56,826)	(128,928)
Sale of property and equipment	12,032	15,131	25,077
Deferral of investment credit	7,403	6,059	10,192
Acquisition of treasury stock	(1,270)	(6,453)	(952)
Increase in intangible assets	(76,793)	(27,366)	(290,087)
Cash available before external financing	(224,304)	(69,455)	(384,698)
Increase in long-term debt, net	57,461	13,432	324,507
Net sale of common stock	95,925	0	0
Proceeds from stock options exercised	5,618	9,388	5,778
Tax benefits from stk. options exec.	1,335	6,268	23,350
Common stock issued for employee stock ownership plan	667	773	581
Stock issued in purchases	60,814	5,711	7,904
Change in cash and marketable securities	(2,484)	(33,883)	(43,578)

Source: Information from Waste Management annual reports.

Exhibit 4 Interest Rates, March 1985 (%)

Prime	**10.50**
Commercial Paper:	
30 days	8.80
60 days	8.88
90 days	8.95
Treasury Bonds:	
1 Year	9.83
2 Years	10.50
3 Years	10.95
5 Years	11.40
10 Years	11.75
16 Years	11.87
20 Years	11.86

Recent Corporate Bond Issues

Issuer	Coupon ($)	Maturity	Rating	Yield (%)
Alcoa	7.00	2011	A2	12.70
Sears, Roebuck	6.00	2000	Aa2	12.30
Sears, Roebuck	10.75	2013	Aa2	12.25

Exhibit 5   Waste Management Stock Price Range

1983	High	Low
Quarter 1	61⅞	39½
Quarter 2	57⅛	41⅝
Quarter 3	55⅞	42⅞
Quarter 4	48¼	47½

1984	High	Low
Quarter 1	47⅞	32
Quarter 2	37⅝	27¼
Quarter 3	43½	31⅜
Quarter 4	45¼	40¾

1985	High	Low
Quarter 1	54	43⅜

Note: Estimated volatility of Waste Management stock: 30% per year, based on standard deviation of daily return over 100 most recent trading days.

Exhibit 6   Convertible Debenture Redemption Schedule as Percent of Par

Call Date	%
1985	107.50
1986	106.75
1987	106.00
1988	105.25
1989	104.50
1990	103.75
1991	103.00
1992	102.25
1993	101.50
1994	100.75
Thereafter	100.00

Exhibit 7   Summary of Terms for Proposed Issues of Convertible Subordinated Debentures

Securities Proposed:	$200 million principal amount of 8% Convertible Subordinated Debentures, maturing 25 years after issuance. Under the underwriter's overallotment option, an additional $30 million may be offered. The debentures will be subordinated to all senior debt of the company.
Price to Public:	$1,000 per $1,000 principal value.
Coupon:	8% payable semiannually.
Convertibility:	Convertible into shares of common stock at a 25% premium to the closing stock price on the day of issuance of the debentures.
Sinking Fund Redemption:	Mandatory annual payments sufficient to retire 5% of the debentures per year, starting 10 years after issuance date, calculated to retire 75% of the debentures prior to maturity.
Optional Redemption:	The debentures are not redeemable until June 30, 1987 unless the closing price of the company's stock is at least 140% of the conversion price for at least 20 trading days within the period of 30 consecutive trading days immediately preceding the notice of redemption. In that event, and after June 30, 1987 the debentures are redeemable in whole or in part, at the company's option, at the redemption prices specified, plus accrued interest.
Purchase at the Option of the Holder:	None

Exhibit 8   Liquid Yield Option Note (Purchase Price Payable by Company upon Exercise of Investor's Put Option)

Purchase Date	Purchase Price	Yield to Investor (%)
June 30, 1988	$301.87	6.00
June 30, 1989	333.51	7.00
June 30, 1990	375.58	8.00
June 30, 1991	431.08	9.00
June 30, 1992	470.75	9.00
June 30, 1993	514.07	9.00
June 30, 1994	561.38	9.00
June 30, 1995	613.04	9.00
June 30, 1996	669.45	9.00
June 30, 1997	731.06	9.00
June 30, 1998	798.34	9.00
June 30, 1999	871.80	9.00
June 30, 2000	952.03	9.00

Exhibit 9   Liquid Yield Option Note Redemption Schedule

Call Date	$ Issue Price (A)	% Call Premium (B)	$ Call Premium (A*B=C)	Accrued Discount at 9% (D)	$ Call Price (A+C+D=E)
At Issuance	250	9.0	22.50	0.00	272.50
June 30, 1986	250	8.1	20.25	27.58	297.83
June 30, 1987	250	7.2	18.00	53.14	321.13
June 30, 1988	250	6.3	15.75	81.02	346.77
June 30, 1989	250	5.4	13.50	111.49	374.99
June 30, 1990	250	4.5	11.25	144.75	406.00
June 30, 1991	250	3.6	9.00	181.08	440.08
June 30, 1992	250	2.7	6.75	220.75	477.50
June 30, 1993	250	1.8	4.50	264.07	518.57
June 30, 1994	250	0.9	2.25	311.38	563.63
June 30, 1995	250	0.0	0.00	363.04	613.04
June 30, 1996	250	0.0	0.00	419.45	669.45
June 30, 1997	250	0.0	0.00	481.06	731.06
June 30, 1998	250	0.0	0.00	548.34	798.34
June 30, 1999	250	0.0	0.00	621.80	871.80
June 30, 2000	250	0.0	0.00	702.03	952.03
At Maturity	250	0.0	0.00	750.00	1,000.00

Exhibit 10 Waste Management Summary of Terms for Proposed Issuance of Liquid Yield Option Notes

Securities Proposed:	$750 million principal amount of LYONs due January 21, 2001. There may be an additional $90 million issued under the underwriter's overallotment option. There will be no periodic interest payments on LYONs. The LYONs will be subordinated to existing and future senior debt.
Price to Public:	$250 per $1000 principal amount LYON.
Yield to Maturity:	9.0% per annum computed on semiannual bond equivalent basis.
Convertibility:	Each LYON is convertible into common stock at the rate of 4.36 per LYON, subject to adjustment, until maturity, unless previously redeemed or otherwise purchased.
Sinking Fund Redemption:	None.
Optional Redemption:	The LYONs are not redeemable before June 30, 1987 unless the closing price of the common stock equals or exceeds 165% of the stock price on the issuance date, on any 20 trading days in a period of 30 trading days ending within 5 days before notice of redemption. In that event, and after June 30, 1987 the LYONs are redeemable at the option of the company, in whole or in part, at prices that reflect accrued original issue discount and a declining redemption premium.
Purchase at the Option of the Holder:	The company will purchase any LYON at the option of the holder on any June 30 starting June 30, 1988. The prices will represent a 6% yield to the holder on June 30, 1988; a 7% yield to the holder on June 30, 1989; an 8% yield to the holder on June 30, 1990; and a 9% yield to the holder on June 30, 1991, and on each June 30 thereafter.

PART THREE

ENGINEERING EXPOSURES
WITH DERIVATIVES

MANAGING ISSUERS' EXPOSURES

THE B.F. GOODRICH-RABOBANK
INTEREST RATE SWAP

On Monday, March 7, 1983, B. F. Goodrich and Rabobank simultaneously executed two financings and an interest rate swap, the net effect of which was (1) to provide U.S. investors with an attractive and unique LIBOR-based floating-rate note, (2) to provide Eurobond market investors with an attractive AAA fixed-rate bond, (3) to raise $50 million of floating-rate Eurodollar financing for Rabobank, and (4) to raise $50 million of fixed-rate 8-year financing for Goodrich. It was apparently one of those rare and satisfying financial arrangements where everyone believed he or she had emerged a clear winner.

THE COMPANY

B. F. Goodrich was a diversified manufacturer of tires and related rubber products, chemical and plastics, and a wide variety of industrial products, components, and systems. Among other businesses, it was the fourth largest U.S. producer of tires and the largest U.S. producer of polyvinyl chloride (PVC) resins and compounds.

The steep recession of 1982 had caused significant financial difficulties for Goodrich, as it had for most other companies in comparable businesses. Exhibits 1 and 2 show recent balance sheets and income statements for the company. Goodrich's earnings and cash flow had been adversely affected, its credit rating had been downgraded from BBB to BBB-, and it was about ready to announce the $33 million loss for 1982 shown in Exhibit 2.

THE FINANCING PROBLEM

Early in 1983, Goodrich needed $50 million to fund its ongoing financial needs. In theory, it could have merely borrowed $50 million more from its committed bank lines, with a borrowing cost slightly above the prime rate (plus, of course, compensating balances). But it was reluctant to consume a substantial part of its remaining short-term availability under those lines, or for that matter, to compromise its future flexibility by borrowing in

Jay O. Light prepared this case as the basis for class discussion rather than to illustrate either effective or ineffective handling of an administrative situation.

the short-intermediate-term (2-5 years) range. It wanted to borrow longer term, in either the 8–10-year range, or perhaps in the 30-year range, and it wanted fixed-rate money. The problem was clear, though. With the general level of interest rates quite high and with its lowered credit rating, long-term fixed-rate money would be quite expensive. For example, with 30-year U.S. Treasurys around 10.30% in the current market, it believed it would have to pay about 13% or so for a 30-year corporate debenture.

THE FINANCING OPPORTUNITY

Salomon Brothers, however, had come to Goodrich with another suggestion. As Salomon explained the idea, Goodrich could borrow in the U.S. public debt market with a floating rate debt issue tied to LIBOR (the London interbank offering rate) and then swap interest-payments with a Euromarket bank that had raised funds in the fixed rate Eurobond market. While there had never been a public debt security tied to LIBOR in the U.S. domestic market before, Salomon Brothers was confident it could be done. In fact, Salomon thought that many U.S. thrift institutions would be eager potential buyers of such a security. As Saloman explained, the recent deregulation of deposit markets had allowed deposit institutions (both commercial banks and thrift institutions) to offer new variable-rate MMDA and Super Now Accounts, and this had caused an interesting set of circumstances in the domestic floating-rate markets. Large thrift institutions, and particularly the large mutual savings banks in Eastern cities like New York, had been aggressively pricing their new deposit accounts in early 1983 and successfully recapturing flows of funds from the money market funds, broker-sponsored CMA accounts, and the open-market instruments that had disintermediated them in recent years. These huge new inflows of deposits had to be invested, though, and the dangers of their traditional investments, 30-year fixed-rate residential mortgages, were clear to the savings bankers. Alternatively, they could invest in short-term Treasury bills or in the large CDs of commercial banks (domestic or Euro-CDs), or perhaps the floating-rate notes of major U.S. banks whose yields were tied to Treasury bill notes. Or, alternatively, as Salomon Brothers explained, they might be interested in buying Goodrich floating-rate notes with a yield tied to LIBOR.

THE RABOBANK NEDERLAND

The Rabobank was a major Dutch banking organization, one of the world's 50 largest, with assets exceeding 110 billion Dutch guilders (approximately $42 billion). The organization consisted of more than 1,000 agricultural cooperative banks (Rabobanks) that had a network of 3,100 local offices in the Netherlands. These banks traditionally serviced the agricultural sector and smaller communities, acting as savings banks and lenders to Dutch farmers. They were all connected through a central cooperative bank, the Centrale Rabobank, which operated on behalf of the individual banks in the domestic and international money markets. Not only was Rabobank a dominant factor in the agricultural sector, providing about 90% of all loans to farming and agribusiness, but the organization had also moved into commercial lending and other traditional banking activities in more recent years. It was believed to have relations with one third of all Dutch companies and to hold 40% of all Dutch savings as deposits. Even the central Rabobank, however, was not particularly well known outside the Netherlands. Though it was rated AAA, it had never borrowed in the Eurobond market before. It conducted only a small amount of dollar-based business, and most of the dollar-denominated assets were loans whose rates floated with LIBOR. It was able to fund those assets through inter-bank deposits at LIBOR or prime Eurodollar CDs. Though it has a small branch office in New York City, few American investors had ever heard of Rabobank.

The London branch of a major U.S. bank had approached the central Rabobank and proposed to syndicate a large fixed-rate Eurobond issue with the ultimate intention of swapping interest payments with a U.S. corporation. Rabobank agreed, in principle, to explore the transaction. As its willingness to swap became known, quite a few offers from potential counterparties came pouring in to Rabobank. From these offers, Rabobank and their U.S. bank (the potential syndicater of the Eurobond issue) selected Salomon Brothers' Goodrich proposal.

THE SWAP

While agreed to in principle, the swap was still a difficult piece of financial innovation to effect. Its relative attractiveness was critically dependent upon the fluctuating spreads between interest rates, in particular, the relation between domestic U.S. and Euro-rates. Moreover, two public debt issues had to be sold in completely separate markets as close to simultaneously as possible.

On the first Friday of March, the relation between relative interest rates seemed favorable, and commitments were made over the weekend such that by Monday the overall transaction was ready to be completed. There were, in fact, three separate and virtually simultaneous parts of the swap.

As the first part of the transaction, Salomon Brothers underwrote and sold a B. F. Goodrich 8-year floating-rate note in the U.S. bond market. It was generally believed that most of the note issue was sold to a number of mutual savings banks located in major metropolitan regions. The terms of the note were as follows:

Issuer: B.F. Goodrich
Credit Rating: BBB
Amount: $50 million
Maturity: 8 years (noncallable)
Coupons: The notes will bear interest, payable semiannually, at an annual rate equal to the future prevailing three-month Eurodollar London interbank rate (LIBOR) + .50%.

On the same Monday, the Rabobank-Nederland issued an 8-year fixed rate bond in the Eurobond market. The terms were as follows:

Issuer: Rabobank-Nederland (the central organization)
Credit Rating: AAA
Amount: $50 million U.S. dollars
Maturity: 8 years, noncallable
Coupon: An annual coupon, fixed at 11%

The two issuers then executed a pair of bilateral swap agreements with the Morgan Guaranty Bank as an intermediary guarantor. In particular, one swap agreement included these provisions:

- B. F. Goodrich agreed to pay the Morgan bank $5.5 million once each year for 8 years to cover the 11% fixed annual coupon.
- The Morgan bank agreed to pay to B. F. Goodrich 8 years of semiannual payments, each equal to one-half (because they were semiannual) of $50 million times a floating rate. The floating rate would be set equal to the future prevailing three-month London interbank rate minus a discount (LIBOR − x), where the size of this discount was undisclosed.

And, similarly, the other swap agreement included an identical set of provisions:

- The Morgan bank agreed to pay the Rabobank $5.5 million once each year for 8 years.
- The Rabobank agreed to pay the Morgan bank the 8 years of semiannual payments at LIBOR − x.

As the structure of the provisions suggests, the Morgan Guaranty was merely agreeing to serve as a passive conduit for the swap payments between the two principals, assuming there would be no default. In the event of a default by one party, however, Morgan would continue its agreement with the other party.[1] In effect, by entering into separate bilateral agreements with each party, Morgan was guaranteeing each party's role in the swap to the other. Because of the Morgan's AAA rating and international reputation, this guarantee effectively lowered whatever credit risk might have otherwise been present in the swap agreement to acceptable levels for Rabobank. In exchange for assuming this role, the Morgan Guaranty received from Goodrich a one-time initial fee of $125,000 and an undisclosed annual fee (f) for each of the next 8 years.[2]

Exhibit 3 displays the level of market interest rates on Monday, March 7. Exhibits 4, 5, and 6 display the recent history of various short-term interest rates. At the time other issuers, investment bankers, and commercial bankers were quite intrigued with this entire swap transaction. As one commercial banker put it, "There is no way Goodrich could have gotten that pricing from their banks. It's almost off the market, it's so good."[3]

---

1   Also, if Goodrich defaulted under its bilateral obligation to. pay the fixed-rate stream to Morgan, it could not collect the floating-rate stream from Morgan. The swap was strictly a two-way or no-way transaction. The same was true of the bilateral agreement between Rabobank and Morgan.

2   While the annual fee on this particular deal was undisclosed, it was reasonably well known that during the most recent six months, the going rate for these fees in the swap market had ranged from as low as 8 or 10 to as high as 37.5 basis points times the principal amount. There was, however, some considerable controversy, both among and within financial institutions, as to what really was an appropriate fee for these swap guarantees.

3   *Institutional Investor*, July 1983, p. 39.

Exhibit 1   Balance Sheets at December 31, 1979–1982 (millions of dollars)

	1979	1980	1981	1982
Cash and marketable securities	$67	$40	$212	$45
Accounts receivable	438	515	512	371
Inventory	467	522	464	400
Property, plant, and equipment	851	925	1,333	1,341
Other	258	214	200	214
Total Assets	$2,081	$2,216	$2,721	$2,371
Short-term bank debt	$35	$49	$12	$17
Accounts payable	467	447	487	445
Other	45	35	142	67
Short-term liabilities	547	531	641	529
Long-term debt	376	475	644	503
Capitalized lease obligations	63	58	101	99
Deferred taxes and other accruals	148	163	208	187
Total liabilities	1,134	1,227	1,594	1,318
Net Worth	947	989	1,127	1,053
Total liabilities and net worth	$2,081	$2,216	$2,721	$2,371

Exhibit 2 Income Statements for Years Ending December 31, 1979–1982 (millions of dollars)

	1979	1980	1981	1982
Sales	$2,988	$3,080	$3,185	$3,005
Cost of products sold	2,279	2,367	2,455	2,311
Sales, general, and administrative expenses	548	587	631	643
Operating profit	161	126	99	51
Interest expense	44	56	60	84
	117	70	39	(33)
Income from sale of tax benefits	–	–	73	9
Gain on sale of subsidiary companies				
and disposition of operations	2	8	41	(27)
Equity in earnings of foreign associate companies	5	10	14	(14)
Other income	8	2	(4)	(2)
Income before items below	131	89	162	(68)
Less: Provision for income taxes	45	25	68	(38)
Less: Minority interests	3	3	2	3
Plus: Extraordinary gain	–	–	18	–
Net income	$83	$62	$110	$(33)

Exhibit 3 Market Interest Rates, March 7, 1983

Domestic Markets		Eurodollar Markets	

Federal funds rate: (interbank rate): 8.05%
Prime Rate: 10⅝%

3-Month Maturities

Treasury bills	8.07%	Prime Eurodollar CDs	8.50%
Prime domestic CDs	8.40%	LIBOR	8.75%
Yankee CDs	8.55%		

7–10-Year Fixed Rate Bonds   **7-10-Year Fixed Rate Eurobonds[a] (U.S. dollar obligations)**

Treasurys	10.10%	AAA Eurobonds	10.70%
Federal agencies	10.40%		
AAA industrials	10.50%		
AA industrials	10.70%		
BBB industrials	12-12.50%		

7–10-Year Floating Rate Notes [a,b]

AAA bank holding cos.	T-bills + 1.00%	Foreign govt. guaranteed	LIBOR + ¼
AA bank holding cos.	T-bills + 1.25%	AAA banks	LIBOR + ¼–⅜%

30 Year Fixed Rate Obligation

Long-term bonds	
Treasurys	10.30%
AAA Industrial	11¼–11½%
BBB Industrials	12¾–13%
Residential mortgages	
FHA insured	12½–13%
Conventional	13–13½

a. All these rates are quoted here on a semiannual equivalent yield basis, the conventional yield-to-maturity basis used in the domestic U.S. bond markets. In the Eurobond markets, bonds typically pay interest annually, not semiannually as in the United States An 11% Eurobond (with annual coupons) would have a semiannual equivalent yield to maturity of 10.70%, not 11% $[(I + .1070)^2 = 1.11]$
b. This is a thin market where almost all notes have been issued by high credit quality bank holding companies. It is difficult, therefore, to estimate market rates other than for these AAA and AA bank notes.

Exhibit 4   Short-term (3-month) Yields, January 1980 to February 1983

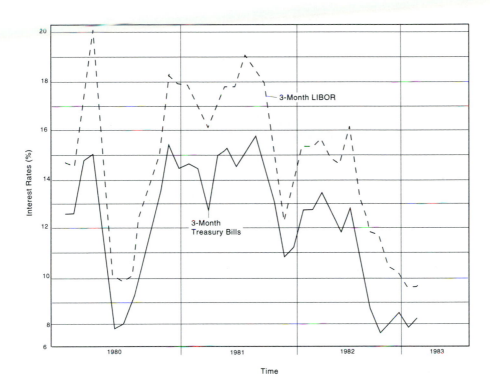

Exhibit 5   Three-month Yield Spreads Relative to U.S. Treasury Bills, January 1980–February 1983

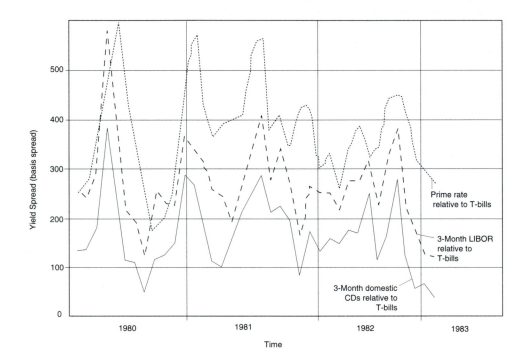

Exhibit 6   Yields and Yield Spreads, 1975–1983

Year	Average 3-Month Treasury Bill Yield	Average Gross Spreads Versus the 3-Month Treasury Bill		
		3-month CDs	Commercial Paper	3-Month LIBOR
1975	5.85%	.76%	.56%	1.36%
1976	5.03	.27	.25	.58
1977	5.17	.37	.27	.75
1978	7.12	.92	.61	1.48
1979	9.84	1.18	.88	1.93
1980	11.25	1.72	1.12	2.81
1981	13.99	1.92	1.17	2.83
1982	10.75	1.66	1.16	2.68
Jan., Feb. 1983[a]	8.00	.59	.30	1.29

Note: Average of 12 monthly observations for each year.
a. Yields and yield spreads averaged over January and February 1983.

LIABILITY MANAGEMENT AT GENERAL MOTORS

Stephane Bello, an analyst in the Capital Markets group at General Motors (GM), oversaw liability portfolio analysis activities for America's largest domestic automaker. In February 1992, GM was planning to raise $400 million through a public offering of a noncallable five-year note, with a fixed interest rate of $7\frac{5}{8}$%. Guided by the firm's stated policy on liability portfolio management, the current structure of its liabilities, and his best reading of likely trends in the bond markets, Mr. Bello had to recommend to senior GM Treasurer's Office managers whether to modify GM's interest rate exposure on the issue and, if so, which transaction to select.

Mr. Bello had been in the Capital Markets group at GM for one year, and during that time was responsible for analyzing the management of GM's interest-rate exposure and making recommendations about how GM could lower its borrowing costs through prudent use of interest-rate derivative products. Before taking this position, Mr. Bello had worked for two years in GM's European Regional Treasury Center, engaged in foreign exchange and corporate financing transactions. Before joining GM, he had worked in a commercial bank for over a year.

Mr. Bello could advise that the firm merely issue fixed-rate debt and not engage in any related transactions. He could also suggest that GM engage in a wide range of derivative activities, which included transacting in interest-rate swaps, caps, Treasury options, or swap options (swaptions). He had solicited competitive bids for each of these instruments from several bankers. His recommendation would hinge on his judgment of the future level of interest rates and volatility, the future shape of the yield curve, and the interest-risk exposure each instrument would create in light of the overall interest-rate management program at GM.

Peter Tufano wrote this case as the basis for class discussion rather than to illustrate either effective or ineffective handling of an administrative situation.

BACKGROUND ON GENERAL MOTORS AND THE AUTO INDUSTRY

In 1991, General Motors was the world's largest automaker and the nation's largest industrial company. It was broadly organized into four major operating segments: Automotive; General Motors Acceptance Corporation (GMAC), which provided a variety of financial services; GM Hughes Electronics, acquired in 1985, which competed in the aerospace, defense electronics, space, and telecommunications industries; and Electronic Data Services (EDS), acquired in 1984, which provided data-processing services to large corporations and institutions. GM's Automotive segment designed, manufactured, assembled, and sold automobiles, trucks, parts, and accessories. Its automotive nameplates included Chevrolet, Pontiac, Oldsmobile, Buick, Cadillac, GMC Truck, and Saturn in the United States, as well as Holdens, OPEL, and Vauxhall in overseas countries.

While GM's nonauto businesses produced profits in 1991, its auto business suffered a second consecutive year of large operating losses. In 1990 the automotive segment reported an operating loss of $3.4 billion, of which $3.3 billion was a special provision for scheduled plant closings and other restructurings. In 1991 the automotive segment reported an even greater loss, $6.2 billion, of which $2.8 billion was a special provision for scheduled plant closings. In 1991 GM cut its annual common stock dividend from $3.00 to $1.60, roughly the level it had been in 1983. In December 1991, GM's chairman and CEO, Robert C. Stempel, announced the newest cutbacks, which were scheduled to close 21 factories, cut 74,000 jobs, and slash capital spending over four years.[1] While analysts generally supported the firm's restructuring efforts, which would ultimately cut costs by $5 billion annually, North American auto operations were not expected to become profitable for at least a few years. Exhibit 2 gives selected financial information on General Motors at a consolidated level, and Exhibit 3 gives the performance of the firm's automotive segment over the past decade. Exhibit 3 also provides information on interest rates and exchange rates during the same period of time.

FINANCIAL POLICIES AT GM

At least two aspects of GM's financial strategy were reviewed in great detail in 1991. In the first of these efforts, Ray Young (who oversaw corporate finance activities in the Treasurer's Office) and his staff carefully analyzed the corporation's current capital structure policy. (See Exhibit 1 for an organization chart of the Treasurer's Office at General Motors at the time of the case.) Ultimately their conclusions regarding the GM balance sheet were reviewed by GM's Treasurer, CFO, and other senior executives. Financial targets examined,

---

1   P. Ingrassia and J. White, "GM Plans to Close 21 More Factories," *Wall Street Journal*, Dec. 19, 1992, p. A3.

which were not announced publicly, included book value debt-to-total capital ratios, interest coverage ratios, and cash flow coverage ratios. The target ranges were set mindful of the rating agencies' guidelines, competitor's debt policies, and Young's estimates of the firm's cost of funds and its likely access to capital under various scenarios. Of utmost concern was the shared belief that declines in the company's debt ratings could make raising funds very difficult and thus lead to unintended shrinkage in the firm's auto activities.

The capital structure recommendation provided policy direction and guidance to the Capital Markets group charged with executing specific transactions. Nevertheless, the Capital Markets group had wide latitude: for example, issuing "debt" implied a set of decisions about which market the instrument would tap (domestic U.S., Euromarkets, or other), the maturity of the instrument, its interest rate (fixed or floating), and other specific terms like callable features, sinking funds, etc.[2] In addition, the capital markets in the 1980s and early 1990s had developed an almost unbounded number of derivative instruments that could dramatically alter the fundamental economics of an offering. For example, a firm could issue a fixed-rate note, and then engage in a swap transaction with a financial institution to pay a floating rate tied to LIBOR and receive a fixed rate. The issuer then effectively transformed the fixed-rate issue into a LIBOR-linked floating-rate note.

GM did not engage in derivative transactions to modify the interest-rate exposure of its debt offerings until 1989, when the manager of the Capital Markets group suggested that the firm experiment with swaps and other interest-rate derivatives to lower GM's borrowing costs. This effort proceeded after receiving ultimate approval from the Finance Committee of the Board of Directors. However, throughout 1989 and 1990, GM's borrowing needs were modest, and thus it engaged in very few interest-rate derivative transactions.

---

2   At the time of the case, GM policy mandated that all borrowings executed by the domestic capital markets group were to be in U.S. dollars or swapped into U.S. dollars. The group was not permitted to borrow in unhedged foreign currencies. In addition, by tradition, the borrowings to support domestic auto operations were over five years in maturity, given that General Motors Acceptance Corporation (GMAC), the automaker's financing arm, typically raised extensive short maturity funds.

The early transactions were structured as relatively low-risk experiments designed to reduce GM's cost of debt. Because the group lacked internal capabilities to price interest-rate derivatives, it was decided that GM would engage in transactions only when they could obtain independent prices from competing financial institutions.[3] Requiring multiple vendors to submit bids may have ruled out some of the most esoteric transactions in the market, but it also gave GM some assurance that it would not be at the mercy of one bank if it wanted to unwind its positions before maturity.

Beginning with its 1990 annual report, GM notified the public of its use of interest rate derivatives to manage its exposure as part of its SFAS 105 disclosure:

> The Corporation primarily utilizes interest-rate-forward contracts or options to manage its interest-rate exposure. Interest-rate-forward contracts are contractual agreements between the Corporation and another party to exchange fixed and floating interest-rate payments periodically over the life of the agreement without the exchange of underlying principal amounts. Interest-rate options generally permit but do not require the purchaser of the option to exchange interest-rate payments in the future. At December 31, 1990, the total notional amount of such agreements with off-balance sheet risk was approximately $7,787 million.[4]

By the end of 1991, this notional principal equaled $7,354 million.[5] The amounts disclosed in GM's annual reports included interest-rate derivatives transactions executed by GMAC. However, the New York Treasurer's Office was not directly involved with GMAC's liability management program, which was handled out of GMAC's Treasury operations in Detroit. The required disclosure contained in the GM financial statements did not reveal the number, complexity, or economic exposure brought about by the firm's recent interest-rate management activities. For example, in its first two years of managing interest-rate

---

3   At first, GM sought price quotations from a large number of banks to ensure that it received fair pricing. In one early instance, it contacted ten banks for quotations on a multi $100-million cap transaction. (The seller of a cap agrees to pay any positive difference between prevailing floating rates and a preset fixed interest rate.) By contacting this large number of institutions for a transaction of this magnitude, GM's intentions became known. Over the course of the day in which it had hoped to enter into the cap transaction, the pricing of the transaction became materially less attractive to GM. GM staff suspected that this movement in prices was due at least in part to certain banks taking positions to be able to profit by taking the other side of the cap transaction. As a result of this experience, GM contacted a smaller number of institutions, but still demanded that all transactions have competitive market quotations. On newer products like swap options (discussed later in this case), GM found relatively large differences among the bids from its group of bankers. On older products like "plain vanilla" interest-rate swaps, bids from competing banks were very similar.

4   1990 Annual Report. Notional principal represents the principal amount upon which a swap or option contract's payoff is based. For example, if you own a call option that gives you the right to buy $100,000 of treasury notes in 60 days for a given price, the notional principal for this contract would be $100,000.

5   In comparison, the firm's off-balance sheet exposure to foreign-exchange forward contracts and exchange options was $16,774 million and $12,301 million, respectively, in 1990 and 1991.

risk actively, GM had entered into seven different transactions, including a single interest swap and a handful of more complicated swap options or swaptions.

In 1991, GM's liability management program became more formalized and increased in scope, for in that year the firm entered into 40 interest-rate derivative transactions. This increase in scale was facilitated by the hiring of a full-time analyst charged with analyzing and recommending potential structures to manage GM's growing liability portfolio. The heightened activity also led to a formal review of GM's liability management policies. This review sought to evaluate the firm's first two years of experience in managing the structure of its debt, as well as to lay out guidelines for future liability management activities. This policy review set broad boundaries within which interest rate management of Central Office debt obligations would take place.[6]

THE 1991 REVIEW OF GM'S LIABILITY MANAGEMENT PROGRAM

The 1991 review established a rationale and a set of policies for managing the debt of GM's auto operations, just as the review of capital structure provided a long-term view of the firm's mix of debt and equity. The report covered the goal of the program, the economic rationale for a "home base" mix of fixed/floating obligations, the role of changing market conditions on the active management of the portfolio, corporate governance concerns, and criteria for counterparty credit exposure. The following excerpts summarize key findings:

Goal: "To actively manage the Central Office liabilities to take advantage of the cyclical nature and volatility of domestic interest rates and shifts in the shape of the yield curve to reduce GM's overall cost of funds.

Home base: "Asset/Liability management can be broadly defined as matching the nature of a company's liabilities to its assets to limit the impact of interest-rate movements on the company's net cash flows and hence corporate value. In general, this is accomplished by adjusting a firm's financial liability portfolio such that any impact on operating cash flow caused by movements in interest rates is largely offset by changes in the value of the firm's liability portfolio.

"(In) industrial companies . . . the impact of changes in interest rates on operating cash flows is hard to quantify . . . In addition, the right-hand side of an industrial company's balance sheet tends to comprise a higher percentage of equity and noninterest-bearing liabilities

---

6   GM's overseas automobile operations, GMAC, GM Hughes, and EDS managed their own liabilities. However, because the Treasurer of the corporation had overall responsibility for the firm's balance sheet, these subsidiaries (other than GMAC) needed Treasurer's Office approval to issue debt beyond certain forecast levels, but the subsidiaries had great latitude in executing details of the transactions. In addition, interest rate and currency exposures were managed directly by the subsidiaries. The "Central Office" debt that the 1991 review addressed was the $7.2 billion in debt specifically associated with domestic auto operations, which was managed by treasury staff in GM's New York office.

(i.e., accounts payable, reserves for warranties, incentives, and deferred taxes) than a financial institution's. This means that, even if the correlation between changes in interest rates and changes in operating cash flows could be perfectly established, the value of financial liabilities would probably have to be hedged to an extreme to obtain the desired results.

"GM's North American automotive revenues and hence operating cash flows are strongly influenced by movements in interest-rates . . . a 1% decrease in auto loan rates results in a 0.2% increase in the dollar volume of cars sold.[7] . . . GM's automotive operations behave more like fixed-rate assets than floating-rate assets . . . Therefore, GM's Central Office liability portfolio should be predominantly fixed-rate in nature to provide the greatest insulation to GM's cash flows from a rising interest-rate/slow automotive market.

"Although a fixed/floating rate mix of 100/0 would completely insulate GM's debt service cash flows from rising interest rates, . . (1) it would ignore the cost benefits to be derived by holding some short-term debt in light of the generally upward sloping shape of the yield curve; and (2) it would force GM to issue fixed-rate debt even when interest rates are at high historical levels.[8]

[The report then summarized GM's interest costs for its Central Office debt portfolio, under various fixed/floating proportions in two scenarios: the fixed-floating spread holds at the historical average level, and the fixed-floating spread widens to early 1980s levels.]

"Given the outlook for weak operating profits in upcoming years, it does not appear appropriate to assume a significant amount of risk with the Central Office debt portfolio. However, neither does it appear appropriate to ignore the savings over time of floating-rate debt. Although not a scientifically determined mix, a fixed/floating split in the neighborhood of 75–80% fixed/25–20% floating appears to be an appropriate balance of these considerations . . . [or a] home base."

Active management around home base: "Essentially, a liability management program is an attempt to take advantage of the cyclical nature of interest rates, the volatility of interest rates, and the changing shape of the yield curve. By adjusting the composition of GM's liability portfolio in step with changes in rates over time, GM should be able to accomplish a meaningful reduction in total debt service costs.

"In general, a fixed/floating mix of less than 75/25 reflects GM's belief that short-term (floating) rates are more attractive than long-term fixed-interest rates, while a fixed/floating mix of greater than 75/25 reflects GM's belief that long-term fixed rates are more attractive than short-term (floating) rates. In addition, option strategies can add flexibility and significantly reduce GM's overall cost of funds. In general, GM would sell options when interest-rate volatility is high or when an abnormally shaped yield curve provides opportunities."

Corporate control concerns: "All swap and swap-option transactions (must) be reviewed with and executed under the approval of the Treasurer . . . Transaction reviews would be conducted with consideration given to historical interest rates, the current interest-rate environment as well as the forecast of our position on the interest-rate cycle and the fit of the transaction within the strategic shift in the Central Office fixed/floating mix. The fixed/floating mix will be maintained within the range of 100/0 and 50/50 which should provide GM with sufficient flexibility to actively manage GM's portfolio while maintaining a minimum conservative level of 50% fixed-rate debt."

---

7   *Caserwriter's note:* Exhibit 3 shows measures of GM's auto division's performance and cash flow as well as various macro-economic variables.

8   *Casewriter's Note:* Exhibit 4 gives selected historical information on interest rates.

Counterparty exposure: The final section of the report described GM's policies regarding swap and option counterparty creditworthiness. Specifically, it detailed the minimum credit ratings required for various types of financial transactions, and the maximum allowable exposure the firm could have to any one financial institution.

THE FEBRUARY 1992 DECISION

In determining what recommendation to make about the interest-rate exposure of the proposed $400-million fixed-rate offering, Stephane Bello had to sort through the mandates of the 1991 policy review, GM's current interest-rate exposure, his best guess of future interest rates, and the specific alternatives from which he could choose. The first two of these were quite clear: the memo set broad restrictions on the liability management activities, especially given the current portfolio of debt obligations and interest-rate derivatives, summarized in Exhibit 5. His recommendation would also be affected by his "rate view" and the instruments at his disposal.

DEVELOPMENT OF THE FEBRUARY 1992 "RATE VIEW"

Predictions of the level of interest rates, the shape of the yield curve, and volatility of interest rates would figure prominently in Mr. Bello's recommendation. The Treasurer, charged with managing the liability management program, relied on his finance staff and the firm's bankers for input. Mr. Bello and other members of the Capital Markets group at GM were in contact with over 20 economists who offered their insights. Exhibit 6 summarizes a few banks' published forecasts as of February 1992. In addition, internal GM data on forecasts of auto sales and other items provided some information about the direction of the economy. Due to the size of GM in the economy and to the magnitude of its banking needs, the staff at GM felt that it had access to more, better, and more timely information than the market as a whole with which it could make more intelligent interest-rate calls. Nevertheless, they acknowledged that arriving at a rate view was an art, not a science, and that their predictions would sometimes be in error.

In February 1992 the rate view shared by the Capital Markets section of the Treasurer's Office was that "rates were likely to decline from their current levels as the market digests the heavy supply of bonds sold by the U.S. Treasury" due to the recent quarterly refunding of Treasury debt, and that the bond market "is likely to rally (i.e., rates will decline) over the next two months as participants focus on fundamentals that point to a continued weak economy during the first half of the year." In addition, they felt that "there is currently a high level of uncertainty in the market with regard to the direction of interest rates over the next few months." Finally, they agreed that the yield curve would flatten as the spread between long and short rates converged. Exhibit 7 shows interest rates and forward rates in February 1992.

STEPHANE BELLO'S ALTERNATIVES

While GM's Treasurer was ultimately responsible for the liability management program, the degree to which the execution of the program was delegated depended on the scope, novelty, and change in rate view implied by the transaction. Transactions of large size or novel structure, or those whose positions reflected fundamental shifts in rate view, were carefully scrutinized by senior Treasury managers. On transactions like the one Mr. Bello was currently contemplating, his recommendation would carry much weight.

The terms of the $400-million five-year 7⅝% coupon note that would be issued were straightforward. GM would make ten semiannual interest payments of $15.25 million and a final principal repayment of $400 million at maturity. Before maturity, GM had no call provisions, nor did the note establish a sinking fund. GM had no right to extend the maturity of the note beyond five years. The notes would be sold to the public for 99.976 per $100 value, for gross proceeds of $399,904,000. GM would pay its underwriters commissions of $1.8 million and expenses of $175,000.

Mr. Bello had an almost unlimited set of alternatives for adjusting GM's interest-rate exposure on this offering. Five generic alternatives were: (1) enter into an interest-rate swap; (2) sell caps; (3) buy or sell an option on an interest-rate swap (known as a swap option or swaption); (4) buy or sell options on a five-year Treasury instrument; or (5) do nothing. The following discussion describes the various choices open to GM, and Exhibit 8 gives representative quotes on these instruments from counterparties meeting GM's credit standards. GM's policy was that any interest-rate derivative position it entered into must be acceptable to the firm if GM was forced to hold it to maturity, or if a counterparty exercised any options against GM. However, GM's expectation, based on its rate view at the time the derivatives were put in place, was that it would be able to unwind its position within six months at a profit.[9] As a result, GM entered into transactions only with multiple bidders, where the firm was likely to be able to unwind its position in the near term with a minimum of transaction costs.

---

9 GM entered into interest-rate derivative contracts only in conjunction with particular financing transactions. While Stephane Bello could unwind a position, say by buying back a swap, he was not free to purchase or sell additional interest-rate derivatives except as related to a debt issuance. This policy was put in place to discourage pure speculation on interest rates. In addition, by attaching its derivative positions to underlying security instruments, GM would receive "hedge treatment" from a tax and financial reporting standards. Under this treatment, gains or losses on hedge positions are not marked to market each year, but rather amortized over the life of the security to which the instrument is attached.

Swaps

To transform the five-year fixed-rate obligation into a floating-rate obligation, GM could enter into an *interest-rate swap*. In an interest-rate swap, two parties in effect agree to exchange their interest rate obligations. For example, GM could agree to pay, over the next five years, a floating rate (based on LIBOR) on $400 million and to receive a fixed interest rate. The counterparty to this transaction would agree to pay a fixed interest rate on the $400 million and receive a floating rate. The $400 million principal amount of the swap (called the notional amount) never changes hands. In practice, the two offsetting interest payments are netted against one another so that only the difference between the payments is exchanged.[10] Typically, no funds change hands at the initiation of a swap. Since 1986 the Treasurer's Office had entered into eight interest-rate swaps, seven of which were done in 1991.[11]

In the early 1980s when first introduced, interest-rate swaps were executed between different borrowers who would come to market simultaneously and also enter into the swap agreement, often with a financial intermediary serving as broker and as guarantor of the differential interest payments. However, financial intermediaries soon began to become dealers in the swap market, taking positions and managing the interest rate and credit risk of their portfolio of swaps on their "swaps book." GM's policies regarding its swap counterparties were thus designed to reduce its exposure were one of its financial intermediary swap counterparties to fail.

A wide variety of interest-rate swap structures could be used: counterparties could agree to virtually any structure of the notional principal (e.g., flat, amortizing over time, stepping up over time) and any set of different interest rates (e.g., fixed for LIBOR, fixed for Treasury bills, LIBOR for Treasury bills). In addition, swaps could be structured for current execution or for future execution (e.g., in a forward, deferred, or delayed-start swap, the counterparties agree to enter into a particular swap whose payments will not begin until some point in the future.) Typically, swap participants were free to buy out their counterparties by paying the market price reflecting the net gain to the other party of canceling the contract.

While the $400-million note had a maturity of five years, GM could enter into a swap for less than that period of time. As many as 20 financial institutions around the world

---

10 Before a market for swaps emerged, firms would occasionally enter into parallel loans, or simultaneous loans, in which they would transfer to one another the equal principal amounts of the loans and make fixed or floating interest payments to one another. The swap arrangements obviate the need to exchange principal and require firms to make only the net interest payments each period.

11 These numbers include only Central Office activities, i.e., financings for GM's domestic auto operations. In the same period, this office entered into nine currency swaps, six of them completed before 1991.

met GM's credit criteria and could offer GM quotes for these plain-vanilla swaps. A swap of under $200 million could be easily and quietly handled by a single large counterparty, but larger deals would more likely involve several institutions and attract attention. Given the commodity nature of the plain-vanilla swaps business, spreads that compensated the market makers were thin, with usually only a few basis points separating bid and ask.

Caps

Firms wishing to change their interest-rate exposure can buy or sell interest-rate caps, floors, or collars. Suppose a corporation has floating-rate debt outstanding whose rate was linked to LIBOR. To limit its maximum interest payments, the corporation can pay a premium and buy a *cap* that pays the difference between LIBOR and the rate cap if LIBOR exceeded the cap rate, or zero otherwise. Entering into this transaction in conjunction with an underlying floating-rate issue gives the corporation a floating-rate obligation whose maximum interest rate is the rate cap.

In conjunction with its issuance of fixed-rate debt, GM would not be a likely buyer of caps, but it could sell them. By selling a cap, GM would be obligated to pay any positive difference between LIBOR and the rate cap. In return for writing this contract, GM would be paid a premium, which would reduce the all-in-cost of the borrowing associated with the cap transaction. Exhibit 8 shows premia GM would receive for selling caps at various rate caps.

Corporations could also purchase *floors*, which place a lower limit on their interest charges. A *collar* is a long position in a cap and a short position in a floor, typically set up so that the premium from writing the floor equals the premium for buying the cap.

GM had never entered into a cap transaction before 1991, but in 1991 and 1992 it entered into 13 transactions, with notional principal of $2.6 billion. Plain-vanilla caps were sold by as wide a group of market makers as plain-vanilla swaps, but more esoteric cap products were offered for sale by only five or six of GM's qualified counterparties.

Swaptions

Stephane Bello could also propose that GM buy or sell a *swaption*, an option to enter into an interest-rate swap with specified terms. For example, GM had in 1991 sold a "2- by 3-year swap put option" in conjunction with a $250-million fixed-rate debt offering. By the terms of that swaption, GM's counterparty had the right, but not the obligation, to enter into a swap with GM in which the counterparty would pay a fixed rate and receive LIBOR for one year, beginning two years from the execution of the contract. In return for writing (selling) this put swaption, GM received a cash premium. A call swaption gives the owner the right to enter into an interest rate swap, in which they receive fixed and pay floating. A put swaption gives the holder the right to pay fixed and receive floating. As in the swap market, a wide variety of forms of swaptions existed.

If GM was to sell a put swaption, its counterparty had the right to force GM to pay floating and receive fixed. The counterparty would exercise this option when interest rates were high. In this case, GM would be left paying high floating rates to honor its swaption terms, offset in part by the premium it would receive for having sold the option. If interest rates were low at the time at which the swaption could be exercised, the counterparty would choose not to exercise. In this case, GM would be left with paying its fixed-rate obligation but would have lowered its all-in-costs of borrowing by the amount of the premium it was paid.

Mr. Bello had received bids from various banks to which GM could sell put swaptions, and he was considering two put-swaption proposals. Both gave the counterparty the right, at the end of a fixed period of time, to force GM to pay LIBOR and receive a fixed rate for the length of the swap. In the "3 by 5" European swaption proposal, at the end of the third year the counterparty had the right to force GM to receive 9% and pay LIBOR for the following two years. In the "2 by 5" proposal, the counterparty had to decide at the end of two years whether to force GM into a three-year swap of 9% for LIBOR. Exhibit 8 gives the premia for these transactions.

GM entered into 25 swaption transactions in 1991, with notional principal involved of $2.6 billion. There were only a handful of qualified banks from which GM received swaption quotations, and it usually solicited bids from two or three institutions.

Treasury bond options

One of its bankers suggested that in light of its current rate view, GM might want to engage in a "bull spread" using five-year Treasury note options, in which GM would buy call options on the five-year Treasury note and simultaneously sell call options on the same amount. These European over-the-counter options gave their holders the right, but not the obligation, to buy the five-year Treasury note on the maturity date at the exercise price.[12] Both options would have the same maturity (60 days) but have different strike prices. The calls GM would buy would have a strike price equal to the current price of the five-year Treasury note (98.095), which was yielding 6.66%. The call options GM would

---

12 The terms of these over-the-counter options differed from the Treasury note derivatives traded on the Chicago Board of Trade. The exchange-listed derivatives are options on Treasury note futures, not on the underlying Treasury notes themselves. In these futures options, the holder of a call has the right, but not the obligation, to acquire a long position in an underlying futures contract for a cash payment equal to the current futures prices minus the exercise price. A futures contract is an agreement in which two parties commit to buy and sell a specific asset at a prespecified time in the future for a prespecified price.

sell would have a strike price of 99.045, to yield 6.46% or 20 basis points below the current yield on five-year Treasury notes.

Do nothing

Finally, Mr. Bello could recommend that GM not enter any additional interest-rate derivative contracts in conjunction with the note offering. However, he recognized that "doing nothing" was as much of a decision as any of the more elaborate choices available.

MR. BELLO'S RECOMMENDATION

Mr. Bello mentally reviewed the factors that would enter into his decision once again: the policy guidelines, GM's current interest-rate exposure, his "rate view," and the instruments at his disposal. Despite his relatively junior status at GM, his recommendations would carry a great deal of weight because he was the only GM employee whose full-time job it was to manage the interest-rate liability of the firm's auto operations. He had collected all the available data by talking to scores of bankers proposing variants of the products described above, and by speaking to many economists whose views of the bond market were quite contradictory. It was his job to make a recommendation, and his managers awaited his advice.

Exhibit 1   Organization of the Treasurer's Office at General Motors, February 1992

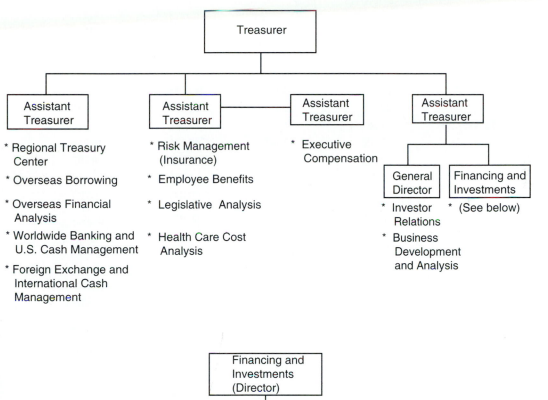

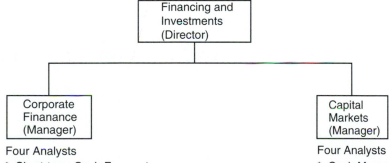

Exhibit 2 Summary Financial Information for General Motors Corporation Consolidated Financial Statements, 1988–1991, $ in millions[a]

	1988	1989	1990	1991
Income Statement				
Sales	123,642	126,932	124,705	123,056
Cost of sales	92,506	93,818	96,156	97,551
Depreciation, depletion, and amortization	7,081	7,168	7,362	7,916
Selling, general & administrative	8,736	9,448	10,031	10,818
Interest expense	7,233	8,757	8,772	8,297
Other deductions	1,351	1,342	1,288	1,547
Special items[b]	0	0	(3,314)	(2,821)
Pretax income	6,735	6,398	(2,217)	(5,892)
Total income taxes	2,103	2,174	(231)	(900)
Income before extraordinary				
Items & discontinued operations	4,632	4,224	(1,986)	(4,992)
Note: Income excluding GMAC	3,409	3,156	(2,755)	(5,306)
Extraordinary items	224	0	0	539
Net income	4,856	4,224	(1,986)	(4,453)
Dividends paid to:				
Preferred shares	26	34	38	70
Common shares	1,632	1,930	1,921	1,100
Cash Flow Statement (summary)				
Operating activities—Net cash flow	14,557	13,006	6,782	5,908
Investing activities—Net cash flow	(9,433)	(15,172)	(8,354)	(4,260)
Financing activities—Net cash flow	(3,011)	1,586	(233)	(997)
Note: Capital expenditures	6,559	9,109	9,744	11,527
If GMAC was not consolidated:				
Operating activities—Net cash flow	11,093	11,553	6,161	3,946
Investing activities—Net cash flow	(6,841)	(8,183)	(5,478)	(4,340)
Financing activities—Net cash flow	(1,986)	(3,443)	(2,517)	(4,340)

Exhibit 2   Summary Financial Information for General Motors Corporation Consolidated Financial Statements, 1988–1991, $ in millions[a] (Continued)

	1988	1989	1990	1991
Selected Balance Sheet Items				
Total assets	164,063	173,297	180,236	184,325
Note: Total assets (GMAC on equity)	90,571	96,765	102,879	104,798
Net plant, property & equipment	36,936	39,126	42,027	45,012
Debt (book value)[c]	88,425	93,686	95,634	94,022
Note: Bond rating (Senior debt)	AA–	AA–	AA–	A
Note: Total debt excluding GMAC	6,174	6,556	7,732	8,523
Note: Long-term debt and leases,				
excluding GMAC	4,536	4,566	4,924	6,699
Stockholders' equity (book value)	35,672	34,983	30,047	27,328
Common equity (market value)				
GM common ($1 2/3 par)[d]	25,553	25,439	20,627	17,781
GM–Class E common stock[e]	2,316	2,767	3,637	6,110
GM–Class H common stock[f]	3,311	2,267	1,552	1,299

Source: GM annual reports, IDC Datasheet.
a. Consolidates GM automotive operations, GM-Hughes, GM-Electronic Data Systems, GMAC, and foreign and domestic subsidiaries more than 50%-owned by GM.
b. Provisions for plant closings and other restructurings.
c. Includes the indebtedness of GMAC.
d. Common shares ($1⅔ par) in General Motors.
e. Common shares whose dividends are linked to the performance of EDS unit.
f. Common shares whose dividends are linked to the performance of Hughes Electronics unit.

Exhibit 3   Interest and Exchange Rates, Car Sales, and GM's Auto Products Segment, 1980—1991

	1980	1981	1982	1983	1984	1985	1986	1987	1988	1989	1990	1991
Macroeconomic Data[a]												
U.S. Treasury Rates:												
6-Mo. T-Bill	13.72	11.95	7.96	9.12	8.20	7.08	5.69	6.17	8.34	7.60	6.42	3.87
5-Yr. T-Note	12.55	13.97	10.09	11.57	11.08	8.49	6.81	8.33	9.14	7.86	7.68	5.93
10- Yr. T-Note	12.39	13.98	10.36	11.82	11.55	9.00	7.23	8.83	9.14	7.93	8.08	6.71
30-Yr. T-Bond	11.98	13.65	10.43	11.87	11.54	9.27	7.49	8.95	9.00	7.98	8.26	7.41
AA Corporate bonds	13.58	15.41	12.40	12.77	12.29	10.42	8.99	10.26	9.85	9.14	9.40	8.44
A Corporate bonds	13.94	16.02	13.57	13.21	12.56	11.05	9.39	10.58	10.14	9.43	9.63	8.63
LIBOR (6-month)	16.25	14.94	9.50	10.19	9.19	8.00	6.31	7.40	9.44	8.31	7.56	4.25
Yen/$	203.00	219.90	235.00	232.20	251.10	200.50	159.10	123.50	125.80	143.50	134.40	125.20
Note: GM Debt Rating	AA+	AA+	AA+	AA+	AA+	AA+	AA	AA–	AA–	AA–	AA–	A
Unit Sales of Vehicles (000s)												
Factory Sales—Worldwide												
General Motors	7,101	6,762	6,244	7,769	8,256	9,305	8,576	7,765	8,108	7,907	7,454	7,015
Retail Unit Sales—U.S.												
All manufacturers	11,692	10,953	10,543	12,383	14,598	15,738	16,336	15,197	15,799	14,855	14,153	12,544
General Motors	5,057	4,644	4,555	5,304	6,036	6,345	6,286	5,273	5,563	5,145	4,973	4,345
Imports	2,882	2,775	2,539	2,878	3,108	3,711	4,243	4,225	4,013	4,071	4,017	3,708

Exhibit 3 Interest and Exchange Rates, Car Sales, and GM's Auto Products Segment, 1980—1991 (Continued)

	1980	1981	1982	1983	1984	1985	1986	1987	1988	1989	1990	1991
General Motors Automotive Products Segment ($ In Millions)[b, c]												
Revenues	$57,729	$62,699	$60,026	$74,582	$83,890	$96,372	$90,864	$89,891	$97,777	$99,441	$97,312	$94,607
Operating profits, excluding special charges	($1,186)	$392	$962	$5,508	$4,700	$4,214	$3,311	$3,380	$5,615	$5,131	($132)	($553)
Special charges[d]	$0	$0	$0	$0	$0	$0	($1,297)	$0	$0	$0	($3,314)	($2,821)
Depreciation & amortization	$4,178	$4,406	$4,551	$5,120	$4,966	$6,209	$5,189	$4,695	$4,051	$4,206	$4,596	$4,671
Assets	$34,581	$38,991	$41,398	$45,695	$52,145	$63,833	$46,708	$60,160	$60,420	$64,598	$69,264	$72,677
Capital expenditures	$7,761	$9,741	$6,212	$4,007	$6,047	$9,174	$10,217	$6,128	$4,525	$6,288	$6,058	$5,784

Source: IDC Datasheet (macroeconomic variables), GM annual reports, *WARD's Automotive Yearbook.*
a. All interest rates are quoted on a bond equivalent basis as of year-end.
b. The automotive segment consists of the design, manufacture, assembly, and sale of automobiles, trucks, and related parts and accessories. It includes operations in North America and overseas. Also included in 1986–1990 are certain operations of GM Hughes and its subsidiary, Delco Electronics.
c. Before 1986, GM operated predominantly in the automotive products industry and, accordingly, did not present industry segment data. Data from 1980–1985 are from GM's financial statements, which do not include GMAC (before 1989, GM accounted for GMAC using the equity method). 1985 data do include EDS, which was acquired in 1984. In 1985, EDS had total assets of $1.595 billion, depreciation and amortization of $79.1 million, and capital expenditures of $633.8 million.
d. Special provisions for plant closings and restructuring of automotive operations.

Exhibit 4 Historical Interest Rates, 1980–1992

Six-Month LIBOR Rates, 1/1/80–2/14/92

Cumulative Distribution of Six-Month LIBOR over Two Periods, 1/1/80–2/14/92 and 1/1/86–2/14/92[a]

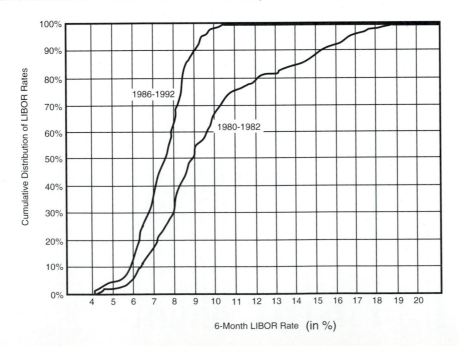

Exhibit 4 Historical Interest Rates, 1980–1992 (Continued)

Difference in Yields between Six-Month and Five-Year Treasuries, January 1980 to February 14, 1992[b]

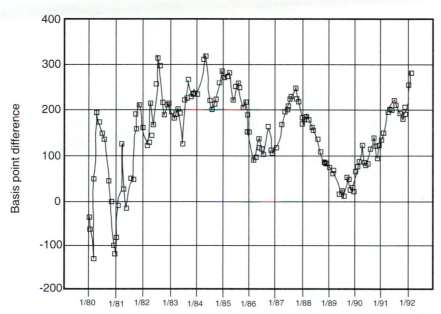

Source: Data from IDC Datasheet.
a. The figure shows the percentage of days in the time period for which LIBOR was less than or equal to the level shown. For example, in the period 1980–1992, six-month LIBOR was less than or equal to 8% for roughly 30% of the daily observations. In 1986–1992, the period of time which the GM finance staff considered, six-month LIBOR was less than or equal to 8% for 60% of the daily observations
b. This chart plots the difference between five-year Treasury note yields and six-month Treasury bill yields. The data represent month-end quotes except for the final point in the series, which reports the difference in yields as of February 14, 1992. As of that date, six-month Treasury bills yielded 3.91% and five-year Treasury notes yielded 6.65%.

Exhibit 5   Central Office Debt and Interest Rate Derivative Position before February 1992

	Distribution of Debt Principal Balances by Interest Rate Exposure in place at end of year							Principal Balance at year end in $ million[e]
	Pure Fixed Rate[a]	Pure Floating Rate[b]	Forward Swap[c]	Floating if LIBOR >9.5%[d]	Floating if LIBOR >9.63%[d]	Floating if LIBOR >10.0%[d]	Fixed if LIBOR >10.5%[d]	
1992	83.3%	10.2%	0.0%	0.0%	0.0%	5.5%	1.0%	7,268
1993	82.9	10.5	0.0	0.0	0.0	5.7	1.0	7,088
1994	84.6	5.7	2.9	0.0	0.0	5.8	1.0	6,902
1995	76.0	6.6	3.4	0.0	5.9	6.8	1.2	5,888
1996	68.3	7.5	3.8	4.8	6.7	7.6	1.3	5,232
1997	65.0	8.2	4.2	5.3	7.4	8.4	1.5	4,743
1998	60.4	9.3	4.8	6.0	8.3	9.5	1.7	4,196
1999	71.5	11.0	5.6	0.0	9.9	0.0	2.0	3,548
2000	87.9	12.1	0.0	0.0	0.0	0.0	0.0	3,232
2001	85.2	14.8	0.0	0.0	0.0	0.0	0.0	2,456
2002	82.4	17.6	0.0	0.0	0.0	0.0	0.0	1,914
2003	81.7	18.3	0.0	0.0	0.0	0.0	0.0	1,847
2004	80.6	19.4	0.0	0.0	0.0	0.0	0.0	1,673
2005	80.7	19.3	0.0	0.0	0.0	0.0	0.0	1,644
2006	80.1	19.9	0.0	0.0	0.0	0.0	0.0	1,390
2007	82.8	17.2	0.0	0.0	0.0	0.0	0.0	1,340
2008	83.4	16.6	0.0	0.0	0.0	0.0	0.0	1,236
2009	90.0	10.0	0.0	0.0	0.0	0.0	0.0	1,070
2010	96.6	3.2	0.0	0.0	0.0	0.0	0.0	965

Source: Internal GM documents.

a. Debt with a fixed-interest rate, or floating rate transformed into fixed-rate debt through an interest-rate swap whose life exactly matches that of the underlying instrument.

b. Debt with a floating-interest rate, typically tied to short-term LIBOR, or fixed-rate debt swapped into floating-rate debt.

c. Fixed-rate debt for which GM has entered into forward swap arrangements such that in the future GM will pay a floating rate.

d. Represent effective interest rate exposure as a result of derivative position in place.

e. Principal balance of existing debt obligations in place as of February 1992, excluding the proposed $400-million five-year note issue. All borrowings by GM's Central Office are denominated in U.S. dollars.

Exhibit 6   Selected Banks' Published Interest Rate Forecasts, as of February 10, 1992

Current forecasts of three-month Treasury rates as of:[a]

	5/92	8/92	11/92	2/93
Barclays	3.5	3.5	4.0	4.5
Chemical	3.7	4.1	4.7	5.0
Commerzbank	4.0	4.0	4.2	4.5
Generale Bank	3.8	4.0	4.3	4.5
Harris Bank	4.3	4.5	4.9	4.9
Industrial Bank of Japan	4.0	4.5	4.8	5.2
Midland Montagu	3.8	3.8	3.9	4.0
Paribas	3.8	3.8	4.0	4.2
Union Bank of Switzerland	4.0	4.5	5.0	5.5
Average	3.9	4.1	4.4	4.2
Forward Rate[b]	4.08	4.32	4.90	5.20

Current forecasts of long-term Treasury rates as of:[c]

	5/92	8/92	11/92	2/93
Barclays	7.5	7.5	7.8	7.8
Chemical	7.9	8.0	7.6	7.8
Commerzbank	7.4	7.7	7.9	8.1
Generale Bank	7.4	7.6	7.7	7.9
Harris Bank	7.4	7.3	7.2	7.2
Industrial Bank of Japan	7.2	7.4	7.8	7.9
Midland Montagu	6.8	6.9	7.2	7.3
Paribas	7.3	7.6	7.7	7.7
Union Bank of Switzerland	8.0	8.2	8.3	8.3
Average	7.4	7.6	7.7	7.8

Source: Compiled from *Risk Magazine,* March 1992.
a. As of February 10, 1992, the three-month rate was 3.8%.
b. Three-month interest rate implied by forward rates.
c. As of February 10, 1992, the benchmark against which these forecasts was compared yielded 7.78%.

Exhibit 7 Current Interest Rates and Forward Rates, February 14, 1992

		Years to Maturity							
		1	2	3	4	5	7	10	20
	Now	4.95	5.75	6.42	6.98	7.33	7.67	8.00	8.45
	1	6.55	7.16	7.66	7.93	7.98	8.15	8.36	8.67
Forward	2	7.77	8.22	8.39	8.34	8.37	8.48	8.56	8.82
Years	3	8.67	8.70	8.54	8.52	8.55	8.68	8.65	8.91
	4	8.74	8.47	8.48	8.52	8.59	8.66	8.66	8.96

Source: GM internal documents.
Note: The row labeled "Now" gives yields to maturity for AA borrowers for instruments with 1 to 20 years to maturity. The other four rows give forward rates. For example, the yield on a one-year instrument to be sold two years hence is quoted as 7.77%. These yields represent midpoints of bid and ask rates.

Exhibit 8   Representative Prices of Various Interest-Rate Derivative Products, February 14, 1992

US$ Interest Rate Swaps:

Quotations represent the fixed rate, quoted on a bond-equivalent basis, that would be exchanged for six-month LIBOR for a swap of the stated maturity.

Maturity (Tenor)	Fixed Rate	Fixed-Rate Spread over comparable Treasuries
2 Years	5.61–5.65%	31–35 basis points
3 Years	6.29–6.33%	49–53 basis points
5 Years	7.13–7.17%	42–46 basis points

Benchmark Caps and Floors:

Quotations represent the premium range for buying and selling caps and floors against six-month LIBOR of various maturities and strike prices. On 2/14/92, six-month LIBOR was about 4.31%.

Type	Maturity	Exercise Price	Premium (in basis points)
Cap	5 years	9%	177–213
Cap	5 years	10%	106–142
Floor	5 years	9%	801–847
Floor	5 years	10%	1108–1154

Over-the-Counter Put Swaption:

Counterparty has the right, at the end of exercise period, to force seller (GM) to pay six-month LIBOR and receive fixed rate for the length of swap.

Exercise Period	Maturity of Swap	Fixed Rate	Premium (in basis points)
2 years (2 by 5)	3 years	9%	89–108
3 years (3 by 5)	2 years	9%	94–111

Over-the-Counter Options on Treasury Notes:

Represent premia for call options on five-year Treasury note. The holder has the right to purchase $100 face value of Treasury notes at the end of 60 days at the strike price indicated. At the time these quotations were made, the five-year Treasury note was selling for 98.095 to yield 6.66%.

Strike Price	Premia
98.095	.625
99.045	.328

Source: GM.
Note: As representative rates, these rates may not reflect the exact terms available to GM.

INTEREST RATE DERIVATIVES

INTRODUCTION

Derivatives are financial instruments whose value depends on the value of other underlying instruments or indices. Interest rate derivatives (IRDs) are financial instruments whose value depends on the price of underlying fixed-income securities or on the level of underlying interest rate indices. Even if one ignores the IRDs embedded in other securities,[1] the market for IRDs is both enormous in absolute terms and rapidly growing. For example, the market for swaps, one type of IRD, has grown from nothing at its inception in 1982 to $3 trillion as of year-end 1993. The purpose of this note is to introduce students to the major IRD products.

WHAT ARE IRDs USED TO DO? BY WHOM?

Through case studies, we will examine how specific entities use IRDs to accomplish a variety of goals. At this point, though, it is useful to note that users of IRDs include not only financial institutions, but also industrial corporations, utilities, investment managers, governments, and households. In general, we will see that these parties all use IRDs as tools to accomplish a set of related objectives that include:

- Managing their exposure to interest rates
- Creating synthetic investments or liabilities
- Minimizing transaction costs
- Exploiting market discrepancies through arbitrage
- Speculation

---

1   For example, a callable corporate bond has an embedded IRD—a call option. This note discusses standalone IRDs and does not treat embedded IRDs.

Jonathan S. Headley prepared this note under the supervision of Peter Tufano as the basis for class discussion rather than to illustrate either effective or ineffective handling of an administrative situation.

A primary motive for the use of IRDs is to manage interest rate exposure. For example, an industrial firm may feel that its need for cash is directly related to interest rates. As interest rates rise, its cash needs rise, possibly because of either a decrease in internally generated cash flows or anticipated increases in strategic investments. This firm might use IRDs to control its payouts to liability holders under certain circumstances so as not to jeopardize its business strategy.

Alternatively, a bank may have fewer floating-rate assets (investments) than floating-rate liabilities (deposits). To better match the two sides of its balance sheet and control the effect of interest rates on its earnings and market values, it could use IRDs to transform some of its fixed-rate investments into floating-rate assets, or alternatively to transform floating-rate liabilities into fixed-rate liabilities. Certain IRDs, such as swaps, can also serve as "synthetic investments," as we shall see below.

Early interest rate swaps appeared to have been created to exploit discrepancies among markets. One firm had relatively cheap access to floating-rate funds but wanted a fixed-rate liability. Another firm could easily raise fixed-rate funds, but preferred to have floating-rate obligations. The natural solution was for each to fund in the market in which it had a comparative advantage, and then exchange interest payments to obtain the desired exposure. The case "The B.F. Goodrich-Rabobank Interest Rate Swap" demonstrates market conditions in the early 1980s that led to the creation of swaps. In the case, B.F. Goodrich had attractive access to floating-rate funds in the U.S. market, while Rabobank had attractive funding in the fixed-rate Eurobond market. By using swaps, the firms (and the financial intermediary assisting them) capitalized on the differences between these markets.[2] It appears, though, as if most of the conspicuous swap-arbitrage opportunities have disappeared over the past decade.

IRD users cite a wide variety of additional reasons for their use of these products over other financial instruments. First, IRDs permit firms to completely customize their interest rate risk profile. Second, relative to other alternatives, they may have lower credit risk and greater liquidity (because derivatives can replicate the interest rate exposure of fixed-income securities without requiring an upfront principal investment). Third, in some instances, IRDs may allow firms to enjoy lower transaction costs. Finally, the accounting treatment of IRDs, as well as their treatment by regulators, can make them attractive. Critics of derivative products protest that the instruments can be used for speculation (as can

---

2   In brief, Goodrich, a BBB-rated issuer, could raise floating-rate funds at LIBOR + 50 bp or fixed-rate funds at 13%. Rabobank, an AAA-rated issuer, could raise floating-rate funds at LIBOR + 25 bp or fixed-rate funds at 10.7%.

every financial instrument), can distort tax and accounting reporting, and could lead to a catastrophic failure of the financial system.

SIX MAJOR INTEREST RATE DERIVATIVES

There are an almost infinite variety of IRDs. Six of the most basic contracts are briefly described below: swaps, forward rate agreements, Eurodollar futures, bond options, caps/floors/collars, and swap options (or "swaptions").

SWAPS

A fixed-floating swap is a contract between two entities ("counterparties") that provides for the regular exchange of payments between the two whereby one counterparty pays a fixed rate of interest and the other pays a floating rate of interest, both of which are calculated based on a fictional principal ("notional") amount. As an example, consider Company A and Company B who have entered into a $100-million interest rate swap in which A commits to pay a fixed rate and B commits to pay a floating rate for the next three years (called the "maturity" or "tenor" of the swap).[3] Assume that A's fixed rate is 5% and B's floating rate (called the "reference rate") is the 6-month London Interbank Offered Rate (6-month LIBOR). Every six months, A pays B the fixed 5% rate (adjusted for semiannual payments) on $100 million (the notional amount), or $2.5 million. At the same time, B pays to A the then-prevailing 6-month LIBOR rate on $100 million.[4] The two opposing payments under the swap are netted so that only the difference between them is paid semiannually. In a standard "par swap," the market value of the swap at the time of inception is zero, so no cash is exchanged when the swap is first arranged. Furthermore, no principal would be exchanged between the counterparties either at the initiation or at the maturity of the swap. The semiannual cash flows of the above swap can be represented by Figure 1:

---

3   By convention, A is called the fixed-rate payer or the buyer of the swap, and B is called the floating-rate payer or the seller of the swap.

4   In a standard swap, the floating rate usually is set, or "pegged," at the beginning of each interest payment period (the "reference date") and then paid at the end of the period (the "settlement date"). The 3-month LIBOR index is the most common floating-rate index for swaps, although many other indices have been used, including Treasury bill rates, commercial paper indices, and short-term municipal bond indices.

Figure 1   Swap Cash Flows

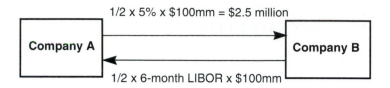

Looking at the above cash flows, it is as if B buys from A a fixed-rate bond, but simultaneously issues to A a floating-rate bond (or finances itself at LIBOR.) In this sense, the swap, from B's perspective, looks like a leveraged bond investment or a synthetic investment. However, unlike a leveraged bond investment, B does not risk losing interest and principal if A defaults, but only the net difference in future interest payments between the two bonds.

Swaps are not traded on exchanges, but are part of the over-the-counter (OTC) market. Financial institutions, including commercial and investment banks and trading firms, act as both brokers and dealers, and quote a bid and an ask rate for buying and selling swaps. The market convention is to quote a fixed rate that the party will pay (receive) in exchange for receiving (paying) LIBOR "flat." The fixed rate is expressed as a "swap spread," or a number of basis points above the Treasury security with the same maturity as the swap. For example, for a 3-year swap, a dealer may quote a swap spread of 100–105 basis points. This means that the dealer will sell swaps (receive fixed) in which it will receive a fixed rate equal to the then-current 3-year Treasury yield plus 105 basis points in exchange for paying LIBOR. The dealer will buy swaps (pay fixed) at a fixed rate of the then-current 3-year Treasury yield plus 100 basis points. The maturity of a swap can range anywhere from one month to ten years or longer (although swaps with maturities greater than ten years are relatively rare).

The swap described above is a "generic" or "plain vanilla" swap. In practice, scores of variants exist. These include the following:

- Non-par swaps: the market value of the swap at initiation is not zero, and therefore one party pays the other at the beginning of the contract.
- Basis swaps: counterparties exchange the difference between two floating rates. For example, a bank might pay 6-month LIBOR and receive the prime rate.

- Forward or deferred swaps: the exchange of net interest payments does not begin until some point in the future.
- Amortizing swaps: the notional principal amount declines over time according to a formula tied to either the passage of time, the level of interest rates, or the amortization of a basket of other securities, typically mortgages.
- Step-up swaps: the notional principal amount increases over time.
- Arrears-reset swaps: the floating rate is *set* and paid at the end of the period.

FORWARD RATE AGREEMENTS (FRAs)

A forward rate agreement ("FRA") is an OTC contract between two counterparties that provides for the exchange of payments between the two over a single future contract period. One counterparty commits to pay a fixed rate of interest (set at inception of the contract) and the other commits to pay a floating rate of interest (set at the start of the contract period) on a predetermined notional amount. An FRA is similar to a swap agreement that covers only one future interest payment period.

For example, assume Company A and Company B have entered into a $100-million "3/9" FRA in which A will pay a fixed rate of 5% and B will pay a floating rate based on 6-month LIBOR.[5] The 3/9 designation refers to the contract period; it will begin 3 months from the date of the agreement and end 9 months from that same date. That is, the contract period of 6 months will start 3 months in the future. If, in 3 months (the reference date), the 6-month LIBOR rate were 4%, then A would pay B the fixed 5% rate (adjusted for semiannual payments) on $100 million for the next 6 months and B would pay A 4% (adjusted for semiannual payments) on $100 million over the same period. In practice, however, just as for swaps, the interest payments are netted so that only one payment is made. Moreover, rather than settling the contract at the end of the contract period (like a swap), FRAs generally require settlement on the reference date. When computing the settlement amount, the net payment otherwise due at the end of the contract period is discounted back to the settlement/reference date using the reference rate (in this example, 6-month LIBOR) as the discount rate. Figure 2 illustrates the gross one-time payments made in 3 months' time under the above FRA:

---

5   Here again, 3-month LIBOR is the most common floating-rate index, but many other indices also have been used. By convention, A is called the fixed-rate payer or the buyer of the FRA, and B is called the floating-rate payer or the seller of the FRA.

Figure 2   FRA Cash Flows

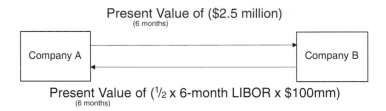

In this example, if at the end of 3 months, 6-month LIBOR were 4%, A would pay B $2.45 million (= $2.5 million discounted over 6 months at 4%), and B would pay A $1.96 million (= ½ × 4% × $100 million, discounted over 6 months at 4%). In practice, the two payments would be netted so that A made one payment to B of $0.49 million ($2.45 million − $1.96 million).

FRAs were first used in 1982, the same year that the first swap transaction took place.[6] They, like swaps, are traded on the OTC market. Bid rates reflect the fixed rate an entity is willing to pay versus receiving LIBOR flat, and ask rates reflect the fixed rate an entity wishes to receive in return for paying LIBOR flat. The maturity of an FRA can be as long as five or more years; however, contracts rarely are written for longer than two years, with 3- and 6-month contract periods being the most common. FRAs in foreign currencies also are traded actively; the sterling and Deutsche mark FRA markets are both very liquid.[7]

FRAs commonly are entered into by commercial banks to lock in a fixed interest-rate expense on variable-rate or anticipated deposits, or to lock in fixed interest rate revenues on variable-rate or anticipated loans. If, for example, a bank had outstanding variable-rate loans that were due to reset in 3 months' time, it could fix its interest revenue on those loans in advance by selling an FRA with a notional amount equal to the outstanding principal on its loans. In return for receiving a fixed interest rate over the future contract period, the bank would pay the then-prevailing floating rate, which would exactly offset the interest revenue it received on its loans once they also reset to the then-prevailing floating-rate index.

6   Clifford W. Smith, Charles W. Smithson, and D. Sykes Wilford, *Managing Financial Risk* (Ballinger Publishing Company, 1990), p. 14.

7   Bernard Manson, *The Practitioner's Guide to Interest Rate Risk Management* (London: Graham & Trotman, 1992), p. 77.

EURODOLLAR FUTURES[8]

A Eurodollar futures contract is similar in many respects to a forward-rate agreement. *Economically*, in fact, the two are almost identical: A Eurodollar future is an exchange-traded contract between two counterparties that replicates the economic effect of an exchange of payments between the two over a single future 3-month contract period. One counterparty commits to pay a fixed rate of interest (set at inception of the contract) and the other commits to pay a floating rate of interest (set at the start of the contract period) based on a predetermined notional amount. The Eurodollar futures contracts traded on the Chicago Mercantile Exchange, for example, can be likened to a $1-million FRA with a contract period of 3 months.[9]

For example, assume that in March Company A sold to Company B a $1-million June Eurodollar futures contract. No payments would be exchanged at the outset, but a price on the contract would be agreed to that would economically set the fixed rate Company A would pay over the 3-month June-to-September contract period. Economically, the floating rate that Company B would pay (3-month LIBOR) would be set on the contract's June expiration date. If interest rates had increased by June, Company A would make money on the contract, and if they had decreased, it would lose money. Note that, because of market convention, the nomenclature of the FRA and Eurodollar futures contracts are exactly opposite. In this example, Company A, the seller of the futures contract, is the fixed-rate payer. Company B, the buyer, pays a floating rate. Thus, buying a Eurodollar future is economically very similar to selling an FRA; in both instances the entity is effectively receiving a fixed interest rate and paying a floating interest rate (i.e., profiting when rates decline).

Eurodollar futures have a few important institutional differences from forward agreements. First, a futures contract's value is recalculated daily by the exchange, with counterparties to the contract settling up with the exchange each day any gains or losses that are incurred on the contract. This process is called marking the futures position to market, and the contracts would be said to be *marked-to-market* each day. Therefore, rather than having a one-time settlement date on the futures contract's expiration date (as in the FRA), the counterparties will make or receive daily payments to or from the

---

8 Eurodollar futures contracts are the oldest of the interest rate derivatives discussed here; they began trading in 1975. For further information, see Manson, pp. 91–107.

9 Four different contracts per year are traded in Chicago; there are March, June, September, and December contracts, each of which has its expiration date (equivalent to an FRA's settlement date) on some specified day in that month and its contract period ending 3 months later. Thus, the June 1995 contract would cover an underlying 3-month contract period starting on June 21, 1995 and ending 3 months later on September 21, 1995. Contracts with expiration dates of up to ten years in the future can be traded, although most activity takes place in contracts with up to five years until expiration.

exchange corresponding to the gain or loss in value of the contract. Futures and forwards differ as well in that forward contracts are customized OTC contracts between counterparties, whereas futures are standardized exchange-traded contracts in which an exchange clearinghouse is the counterparty to all transactions.

In addition, unlike FRAs, Eurodollar futures contracts are quoted in terms of "price" rather than in terms of interest rate. As previously mentioned, the price does not refer to any upfront payment; rather, it is used to calculate the value of the contract for settlement. The price of a contract is always less than 100; by definition, the price of a contract on its expiration date is equal to 100 minus the then-prevailing 3-month LIBOR rate. Thus, if 3-month LIBOR was 4% on the expiration date of the June contract, its settlement price would equal 96.00. The calculated value of a contract (for settlement purposes) can be thought of as the price, in percent, multiplied by the notional contract amount ($1 million). A contract expiring when 3-month LIBOR was 4% therefore would have a calculated value of $960,000.

The net economic gain or loss on a Eurodollar futures contract held to maturity would equal the difference in calculated value between the day the contract was bought or sold and the day it expired (adjusted for its quarterly rate). Thus, the buyer of the contract would gain if interest rates declined during this period. If the buyer purchased the contract at a price of 95.00 and 3-month LIBOR was 4% when the contract settled, it would have realized a net economic gain of $1.00\% \times \frac{3}{12}$ (because the contract period is only 3 months) $\times$ $1 million = $2,500. This is similar to the gain the company would have received if it had instead sold a 5% FRA.[10]

BOND OPTIONS

Swaps, FRAs, and Eurodollar futures contracts entail commitments. Call options on bonds, however, give their holders the right, but not the obligation, to buy fixed-income instruments at predetermined exercise prices. Similarly, put options give their holders the right to sell fixed-income instruments at a preset exercise price. These options are sometimes called "options on physicals," because the underlying instrument is an actual fixed-income security. Some examples of "physicals" underlying these contracts are Treasury bills, Treasury notes, Treasury bonds, municipal bonds, Ginnie Maes (U.S. government agency bonds), and U.K. government bonds (Gilts). In addition, put or call options sometimes are based not on the security itself, but on the security's futures contract. For example, the call option contract on Eurodollars will provide the right to buy the underlying

---

10 This example ignores the time value differences between the two instruments due to the fact that the daily settling-up of the futures contract exposes its holder to intermediate changes in interest rates, but the seller of a forward contract is not affected in the same way.

Eurodollar futures contract rather than an actual Eurodollar deposit.[11] Bond options are traded on exchanges and are also available in the OTC market.

The owner of a 3-month European[12] call option on the 20-year Treasury bond paying 8% coupons has the right to buy the bond in 3 months for a preestablished exercise price. Assume that the exercise price of such an option is $100, or par. If, in 3 months, interest rates are above 8% and therefore the bond is selling for a price below par, the holder of the call option will elect not to buy the bond at par and let the option expire unexercised. However, if interest rates instead have fallen below 8%, the bond will sell for more than par. In this case, the holder of the call will choose to exercise his or her option and buy the bond for $100. Figure 3a shows the payoff to the holder of the call at expiration.

For an option on a physical, we naturally think of the exercise price as being a price, and not a yield. If, however, we were to draw the payoff diagram at exercise to the owner of the call in terms of yields, the result would be Figure 3b. What appears to be a call in Figure 3a seems to be a put in Figure 3b.

Caps/Floors/Collars

A cap is a contract between two counterparties in which one counterparty (the seller, or writer) agrees to pay to the other (the buyer, or purchaser) the greater of zero or the difference between a floating rate (the reference rate) and a predetermined fixed rate (the "strike" rate) on a fixed notional amount over the life of the contract at each settlement date. In return, the buyer pays the seller an upfront premium.

Essentially, a cap can be likened to a series of call options on a floating interest *rate* that entitle the purchaser to the difference between the floating rate and the strike rate. For example, assume Company A purchased from Company B a $100-million 1-year 8% cap. Every 3 months (or whatever other interest payment period was agreed to), if the then-prevailing 3-month LIBOR rate (or other agreed reference rate) exceeded 8%, Company B would owe Company A the difference in rates multiplied by $100 million (adjusted for quarterly payment). If the then-prevailing 3-month LIBOR rate was below the strike rate, B would owe A nothing. Thus, if 3-month LIBOR was 10% on a reference date, Company B would owe Company A a 2% rate on $100 million to be paid at the next settlement date (3 months later). Payments would be calculated in a similar manner over the life of the cap contract (see Figure 4).

---

11 Options on bond futures have surpassed options on physicals in popularity for a variety of reasons. For a discussion, see Frank J. Fabozzi, *Bond Markets, Analysis, and Strategies* (Prentice Hall, 1993), p. 422.

12 Exercisable *only* on the option's expiration date.

Figure 3   Payoffs to holder of bond call options

Panel a

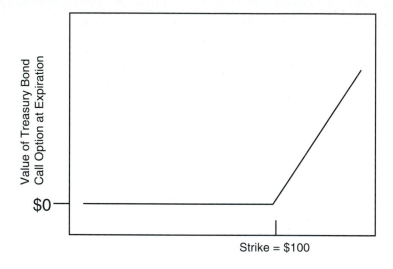

T-Bond Price

Panel b

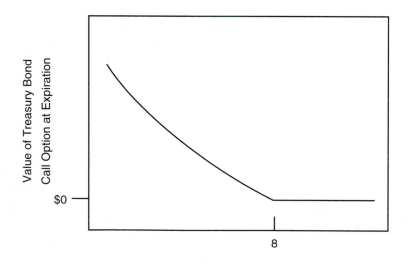

T-Bond Yield (%)

A floor can be thought of as the opposite of a cap. It is a contract between two counterparties in which one counterparty (the seller, or writer) agrees to pay to the other (the buyer, or purchaser) the greater of zero or the difference between a predetermined fixed rate (the "strike" rate) and a floating rate (the reference rate) on a fixed notional amount over the life of the contract at each settlement date. In return, the buyer pays the seller an upfront premium. A floor can be likened to a series of put options on a floating interest rate.

Just as a cap pays whenever the reference rate rises *above* the strike rate, a floor pays whenever the reference rate drops *below* the strike rate. For example, assume Company A purchased from Company B a $100-million 1-year 4% floor. Every 3 months (or whatever other interest payment period was agreed to), if the then-prevailing 3-month LIBOR rate (or other agreed reference rate) fell below 4%, then Company B would owe Company A the difference in rates multiplied by $100 million (adjusted for quarterly payment). If the then-prevailing 3-month LIBOR rate was above the strike rate, B would owe A nothing. Thus, if 3-month LIBOR was 3% on a reference date, Company B would owe Company A a 1% rate on $100 million to be paid at the next settlement date (3 months later). Payments would be calculated in a similar manner over the life of the floor contract (see Figure 5).

A collar merely combines a floor and a cap. From the perspective of a floating-rate note issuer, purchasing a collar is defined as both buying a cap and selling a floor, with the strike rate on the cap set higher than the strike rate on the floor. The premium received for selling the cap offsets the premium paid to purchase the floor. One specialized version of a collar is the *costless collar*, in which the premium paid for the floor exactly equals the premium received for the cap. Thus, no upfront payment is made between counterparties entering into a costless collar.

Figure 4   Payoffs to Cap Buyer

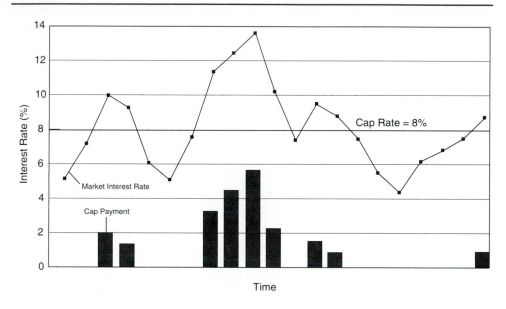

Figure 5   Payoffs to Floor Buyer

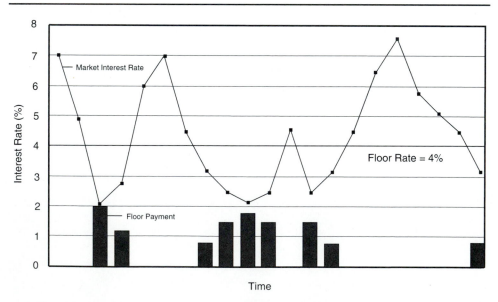

SWAPTIONS

A swaption is an option to enter into a swap; it can be defined as a contract between two counterparties that grants one counterparty (the buyer, or purchaser) the right, but not the obligation, to enter into a specified swap in the future with terms of the swap set at inception of the swaption contract. In return for obtaining this option, the purchaser of a swaption contract pays the seller (or writer) an upfront payment (the "swaption premium").

For example, if Company A purchased from Company B a 3-month swaption on an underlying 9-month $100-million 5% fixed-pay swap, then in 3 months' time, Company A could either exercise its option and enter into the swap or do nothing and let the option expire worthless. Company A would make its decision based on then-prevailing interest rates and predicted future interest rates over the 9-month life of the swap. If A decided to exercise its option, then the swap would perform just like an ordinary swap, with A paying a 5% rate on $100 million every 3 months (if that was the predetermined interest payment period) and B paying the 3-month LIBOR rate (if that was the predetermined reference rate) in exchange. Just as for a regular swap, these two payments would in fact be netted, with the rates determined at the beginning of each interest payment period and the payment paid at the end of each period.

Swaptions are almost always "European-style" options; that is, they are exercisable only at the option expiry date (in the above example, only on the specified exercise date 3 months in the future). Rarely, though, swaptions will be structured as "American-style" options, which are exercisable any time on or before the option expiry date. If a swaption is structured in this way, the underlying swap will begin on the exercise date (in the above example, the 9-month swap would begin on the day that the buyer exercised its option).

FUNCTIONAL SIMILARITY AND INSTITUTIONAL DIFFERENCES

From an institutional perspective, the contracts described above may seem to differ from one another. From a functional perspective, however, many different contracts can deliver similar payoffs. For example, FRAs and Eurodollar futures deliver approximately the same economics to their users. Just as the seller of an FRA will receive a net payment proportional to a drop in interest rates, so will the buyer of a Eurodollar futures contract.

This is not to say that the institutional differences between these contracts are trivial. The standardization and liquidity of the Eurodollar futures market, the operations of a high-credit clearinghouse as a counterparty, and the daily settling-up feature of the futures contract differentiate it from the FRA. Tax and accounting treatment can also differentiate these products. Understanding what functional role each product plays allows users to identify what are the relevant alternatives. A careful consideration of institutional features then will enable a user to choose among functionally similar products.

As another example, there are a number of ways in which a company with a floating-rate liability could transform it into a fixed-rate liability. The simplest method would be to enter into a swap in which it received a floating rate and paid a fixed rate. Alternatively, it could itself purchase a floating-rate note and sell short[13] a fixed-rate bond. The floating-rate income would offset its floating-rate liability and it would be left with fixed interest payments on the short sale. The company would achieve the same interest rate exposure as if it had bought a swap.

A series of FRAs also could be used to transform the floating-rate liability into one with a fixed rate. Intuitively, this should make sense; like the swap, FRAs have payments calculated on a reference date that are determined solely in relation to the then-prevailing floating-rate index. Because Eurodollar futures are much like FRAs, they could be used as well.

Finally, the combination of a cap and a floor could replicate the economic effect of an interest rate swap. Purchasing a cap struck at 5%, say, with the same maturity as the floating-rate note and selling a similar-maturity floor struck at 5% would exactly resemble entering into a pay-fixed 5% swap. When rates are above 5%, the company would receive the floating rate minus 5%, just as if it were paying a fixed 5% and receiving the floating rate. Similarly, when rates moved below 5%, it would pay, under the floor contract, 5% minus the floating rate, just as if it were paying a fixed 5% and receiving the floating rate. As a result, the company would be left with a fixed-rate 5% liability.

CONCLUSION

This note has addressed only the most basic of interest rate derivative instruments; there are many more complex instruments being used in the market today and being developed for use in the future. No matter how complex the derivative, though, all are simply a method of creating or eliminating exposure to future levels of interest rates. As the market continues its rapid development and an increasing number of interest rate derivative instruments become commonplace finance tools (as many have already), it will be imperative for any market participant to understand the fundamentals underlying these and other derivative instruments.

---

13 In selling short a security, an investor borrows the security and sells it to a third party with an agreement to purchase it in the market later in order to return it to the lender. In the interim, the borrower is obligated to pay any interest payments to the lender that he or she otherwise would have received. Thus, in selling short a floating-rate instrument, an investor is obligated to pay the floating-rate interest payments.

EXERCISES

1. Acme Manufacturing wants to raise $100 million of 3-year debt in the Euromarket (where interest is quoted and paid on an annual basis). Its alternatives are either a 3-year fixed-rate note at a spread of 250 basis points over the 3-year U.S. Treasury (currently yielding 4.50%), or a 3-year floating-rate note on which it must pay yearly interest of 1-year LIBOR + 2% (1-year LIBOR currently yields 3.70%; therefore, the floating-rate note's first interest payment of $5.7 million would be paid at the end of year 1). However, Acme wants to have a fixed-rate liability for the entire 3 years. Assuming the following instruments also are available to Acme (with National Trust, an AAA-rated bank, as the counterparty), which strategy will enable Acme to pay the lowest all-in fixed rate of interest (assume all rates are quoted on an annual basis)?

   Swap: 3-year swap has all-in pay-fixed rate of 3-year Treasury + 30 basis points (= 4.50% + 0.30%) versus receiving 1-year LIBOR.

   FRAs:[14]   12/24 FRA has all-in pay-fixed rate of 2-year Treasury + 90 basis points (= 4.10% + 0.90%) versus receiving 1-year LIBOR.

   24/36 FRA has all-in pay-fixed rate of 3-year Treasury + 150 basis points (= 4.50% + 1.50%) versus receiving 1-year LIBOR.

   Caps: Premiums for 3-year caps (with annual pay) on 1-year LIBOR:

Strike Rate	Premium
4.00%	2.23%
4.80%	0.70%
5.00%	0.49%
6.00%	0.08%

   Floors: Premiums for 3-year floors (with annual pay) on 1-year LIBOR:

Strike Rate	Premium
4.00%	0.18%
4.80%	0.70%
5.00%	0.90%
6.00%	3.22%

---

14 FRAs are generally settled at the start of the contract period rather than at the end. However, for the purposes of these exercises, assume that the FRAs listed are settled at the end of the period.

2. Easy Money Trading Company, a Wall Street arbitrageur, has received the same quotes from National Trust for the four instruments listed above. Assuming it only enters into transactions in which it can make a guaranteed profit (while assuming minimal credit risk), what would be its likely course of action?

STATE OF CONNECTICUT
MUNICIPAL SWAP

In May 1990, Benson R. ("Bud") Cohn, Assistant Treasurer-Debt Management for the state of Connecticut, was considering how best to raise $325 million in tax-exempt, 20-year, fixed-rate debt. The funds were needed for the state's capital spending program. On his desk were competing proposals from Merrill Lynch Capital Markets and BT Securities (a wholly-owned subsidiary of Bankers Trust New York Corporation). The proposals each contained a "synthetic" alternative to straight fixed-rate debt that involved pairing a long-term, variable-rate bond issue with an interest rate swap. Depending on the assumptions, it seemed the synthetic approach could save the state 50 basis points or more in financing costs. The market for municipal interest rate swaps was nascent, but growing. If executed, the proposed swap would be the first for the state and the largest to date in the municipal market. Before he could go this route, however, Bud Cohn wanted to satisfy himself not only that the cost savings were real, but also that the transaction was not unduly risky.

FINANCING THE STATE OF CONNECTICUT

Connecticut was first settled in 1633 and was the fifth state to ratify the U.S. Constitution in 1788. In 1990 the state's population exceeded 3.2 million; three metropolitan areas, Hartford, Bridgeport, and New Haven, accounted for 84% of the total. During the 1970s and 1980s, state population growth was slow. The economy was diversified among aerospace/defense (primarily aircraft engines, helicopters, and submarines), services (primarily insurance), and trade. Per-capita income, at $25,000, was 40% higher than for the nation as a whole. The 1990 state general funds budget totaled almost $6.4 billion and the capital budget came to almost $1.7 billion.

Connecticut first issued bonds in the eighteenth century. In recent years, it has ranked among the top 20 issuers of tax-exempt debt (in terms of dollar volume). From 1980 to

Joel Barber and André F. Perold prepared this case as the basis for class discussion rather than to illustrate either effective or ineffective handling of an administrative situation.

mid-1990, the State sold $5.2 billion in fixed-rate, long-term bonds through 39 separate issues.

Interest paid to investors on municipal bonds like those issued by the state of Connecticut was exempt from federal taxation. For Connecticut residents, the interest was also exempt from state taxation. The tax exemption granted municipal issuers enabled them to raise financing at costs substantially below what a taxable entity of comparable credit would have to pay. Exhibit 1 shows prevailing short-term and long-term municipal rates relative to taxable rates.

In the spring of 1990 the state of Connecticut had outstanding approximately $2.8 billion par amount of general obligation (GO) debt, for which the state pledged its "full faith and credit." The standard GO pledge obligated a state or municipality to use its full statutory taxing authority to ensure payment of interest and principal. Because most cities and states held broad taxing powers, GO debt was among the most highly rated in the municipal market. In 1990, all U.S. states had investment grade ratings on their general obligation debts.[1] Connecticut's long-term debt was rated "Aa" by Moody's and "AA" by Standard & Poor's.

In addition to GO debt, Connecticut had outstanding roughly $1.5 billion of "Transportation Infrastructure Purposes" bonds that were secured by a special tax obligation (STO). Certain transportation revenues including motor fuel taxes, motor vehicle receipts, and license, permit, and other fees, were pledged to pay debt service on these bonds. Generally speaking, any (tax-exempt) bond that is not a direct general obligation of a state or municipality is referred to as a revenue bond. Connecticut STO bonds fell into this category.

The state also financed certain activities through various authorities. In 1990 two of the largest in terms of debt outstanding were the Connecticut Housing Finance Authority ($2.6 billion), and the Connecticut Resources Recovery Authority ($600 million).

Like most municipal issuers, Connecticut structured its long-term debt to even out repayments over time. Level payments were less disruptive to the municipal budgeting process. This was accomplished with a serial issue, a sequence of bonds with varying maturities.[2] Typical structures provided for either level principal payments (the first

---

1   The general obligation debt of Massachusetts was rated at the lowest investment grades: "Baa" by Moody's and "BBB" by Standard & Poors. All other states had higher ratings on their GO debts.

2   Often, municipal bond issues employed a combination serial *and* term structure. For example, assuming a typical 20-year maturity, years 3 through 15 might be serial maturities, with term bonds in years 18 and 20. Almost invariably, however, there were mandatory sinking fund payments that, in effect, "serialized" the term bonds. Sinking fund payments were used to immediately retire bonds selected at random within a given term maturity.

maturity coming perhaps one to two years after issuance) or level debt service (principal plus interest), as with home mortgages.[3] The long-term bonds in the series were usually callable at the option of the issuer, following a "call protection" period.

COMMERCIAL PAPER AND VARIABLE-RATE DEBT

For short-term funding, the state of Connecticut relied on commercial paper (CP) programs. In April 1990 the state began a commercial paper program, rated P–1/A1+, with Goldman, Sachs as dealer. It was authorized up to $550 million and was backed by a five-year letter of credit (LOC) from Dai-Ichi Kangyo Bank covering both principal and interest. The LOC assured investors liquidity should the state experience difficulty in "rolling over" the CP when it matured. It cost the state seven basis points on the amount of CP outstanding and three basis points on the remainder (the difference between CP outstanding and $550 million).[4] Connecticut used commercial paper to cover temporary funding shortfalls caused by timing differences between payments coming due and receipt of tax and other revenues. An earlier program started in the late 1970s was discontinued in 1982 during a period of state budget surpluses.

During the 1980s, innovation in the municipal bond markets gave issuers additional short-term debt alternatives. Of particular significance was the development of variable-rate bonds sold under names like "UPDATES" (Unit-Priced Demand-Adjustable Tax-Exempt Securities, a Merrill Lynch product) and, more generically, "VRDOs" or "VRDBs" (variable-rate demand obligations or bonds). By being both puttable by the investor and callable by the issuer, they had many of the features of short-term instruments, yet were nominally long-term securities, affording issuers added financial flexibility. For example, the call feature made refunding easier if conditions changed so that the state could issue debt with less burdensome covenants. It also gave flexibility to issuers who were not certain how long they would need funds, or if they would need funds at all.[5]

---

3   Principal on municipal bonds was paid annually, whereas interest was paid semi-annually. Level debt service, therefore, refers to level *annual* debt service.

4   Dai-Ichi Kangyo Bank was permitted to renegotiate the LOC in the event regulatory authorities substantially increased the bank's required capital ratios.

5   A municipality might be compelled to issue "in advance" of an anticipated requirement for funds if certain authorizations were soon to expire. In addition, municipalities were mindful that federal tax law could change at any time and give less favorable treatment to their debt issues, and there was always the possibility that local laws and procedures pertaining to governmental debt issuance could become more restrictive. However, since new laws were seldom made retroactive, issuers of and investors in any particular bond could be fairly certain that the legal environment at the time of initial issue would be preserved ("grandfathered") in the event of subsequent changes in the law.

The put feature allowed investors to sell the bonds back to the issuer at a price of par; with most bonds, this could be done weekly.[6] In practice, investors never put their bonds to the issuer directly, but rather through the "remarketing agent," an investment bank retained by the issuer.[7] The remarketing agent would use its "best efforts" to remarket (i.e., sell) said bonds to new investors, and, assuming a successful sale, would pay the proceeds over to the investor exercising the put.[8] (Another party, the "paying agent," often acted as intermediary between investors and the remarketing agent and handled all record-keeping and transfers of funds.)

By the terms of the indenture, the remarketing agent could resell the bonds only at par. To make this possible, the remarketing agent, at his or her sole discretion, could reset the coupon. Thus, each reset took into account changes in market conditions and issuer-specific factors. Once the coupon was reset, all the bonds would pay the new coupon. Rates paid on municipal put bonds were usually capped, a typical ceiling being in the range of 12% to 15% per annum.

Should the remarketing agent fail for any reason to resell the bonds put to it, the issuer would be obligated to immediately provide the funds to pay existing bondholders. As it was, few municipal issuers would have the liquidity necessary to immediately redeem even a modest portion of their outstanding debt. Accordingly, they purchased liquidity from a third party, for example, a commercial bank or insurance company, through a letter of credit.

LOC commitments were typically purchased for periods of five to ten years.[9] Draws against the LOC would usually transform automatically into term loans between the bank and the issuer. The decision to draw was left to an independent third party, such as the paying agent who was bound only by the terms of the bond indenture. This distinguished LOCs from lines of credit where the decision to draw was the direct option of the issuer.

Although the LOCs were noncancelable by either the issuer or the provider, the latter often had a limited number of "outs." So-called "liquidity-only" LOCs usually could be canceled by the provider if the issuer was in default on some or all of its debt. In addition, beginning in the late 1980s, LOC contracts increasingly contained language allowing them to be canceled if the regulatory authorities increased the provider's required capital ratios. "Liquidity-*and*-credit" LOCs typically did not carry the above-mentioned default and

---

6   The bonds were also callable at par on the dates that they were puttable.

7   The remarketing agent and the original issue underwriter were, almost invariably, one and the same.

8   For an issue that was reset every seven days (i.e., was in a "seven-day mode"), investors were typically required to give the remarketing agent seven days notice of their intent to put.

9   The issuer was to secure a replacement LOC prior to the expiry of the original and, failing such, was to notify bondholders to allow for redemption prior to LOC expiration.

cross-default provisions, and accordingly, cost issuers more.[10] The majority of LOCs backing municipal put bonds were of the liquidity-only variety.

According to municipal traders, variable-rate debt carried interest rates similar to commercial paper, although it was difficult to draw exact comparisons given that few issuers had both variable-rate bonds and commercial paper outstanding simultaneously. The advent of variable-rate bonds also enabled the development of a municipal interest rate swap market by the mid-1980s. As already noted, long-term, variable-rate bonds and an interest rate swap were the principal features of the synthetic fixed-rate financing proposed for the state of Connecticut. To date, the state had not yet issued variable-rate general obligation or revenue debt.

The variable-rate bond structure described above was also employed in the market for corporate preferred stock. Tax exemption was an important factor to both markets: for corporate investors, dividend income on preferred stock instruments was 70% (earlier 85%) tax-exempt. In both markets, "remarketing" was one of two principal reset mechanisms. The other mechanism—preceding remarketing and pioneered by Lehman Brothers—employed a Dutch auction in which investors would bid for the coupon at which they would be willing to buy the security at par.[11] In 1990 there was approximately $40 billion of such "auction-rate" or "money-market" preferred outstanding, and $120 billion of municipal variable-rate bonds. Both markets were almost entirely institutional; the minimum denomination for a single bond was $100,000. Money-market funds and corporations represented approximately 70% and 20% of the market, respectively, for municipal variable-rate bonds, the remainder being held by bank trust departments and wealthy individuals.

RECENT CREDIT RISK CONCERNS

Because the LOC was central to the credit structure of many municipal put bonds, the credit ratings of the LOC provider were an important determinant of bond credit-worthiness. In the spring of 1990 the credit strength of LOC banks was something of an issue for investors. One Japanese bank alone, Fuji Bank, backed over $8.5 billion in U.S. municipal bonds, most of them variable-rate. As a group, Japanese banks stood behind over half of all variable-rate municipal bonds outstanding. At the time, many of these banks were beset with problems related to the crash earlier that year of the Tokyo equity market and the

---

10 In May 1990 the state of Connecticut could have purchased a liquidity-only LOC for seven to ten basis points, whereas a liquidity-and-credit LOC would have cost perhaps twice as much.

11 These securities were not explicitly puttable. If the auction failed, i.e., if there were insufficient bids below the maximum coupon, holders would receive the maximum, but would be "stuck" with the security.

pressure it put on their capital ratios.[12] To such concerns were added their huge exposures to a softening Japanese real estate market. Already, Moody's was reviewing the ratings of two of the largest Japanese banks, Fuji and Dai-Ichi Kangyo, for possible downgrade. Analysts expected these banks would drop one "notch" (rating category) on their long-term debt ratings, but would maintain the highest short-term ratings.

THE MERRILL LYNCH PROPOSAL

Merrill Lynch quoted the state an all-in cost of 7.060% on a straight 20-year, fixed-rate issue.[13] This included an underwriters' spread of $9.25 per $1,000 par.[14] The issue would be comprised of 20 serial maturities all with the same principal (see Exhibit 1). The final 10 maturities (from 2001 to 2010) would be callable at par after year 10.

To create a synthetic fixed-rate financing, Merrill Lynch proposed a 20-year, variable-rate bond issue, with the same serial structure as above. To underwrite the bonds, Merrill Lynch quoted a spread of $4.25 per $1,000 par. It would also charge a remarketing fee of .125% per annum. Merrill Lynch estimated the state could obtain a liquidity-only LOC for .075% per annum.

In addition, the state would enter into a 10-year interest rate swap with Merrill Lynch & Company. Under the terms of the swap, Merrill Lynch would pay the state a floating rate equal to the J.J. Kenny Index of 30-day, AA-rated municipal put bonds (30-day JJK); in return, the state was to pay Merrill Lynch a fixed rate of 6.905%.[15] Both fixed- and floating-rate payments, and the fees, would be based on the amount of principal then outstanding.[16]

---

12 Japanese regulators allowed the nation's banks to count up to 45% of the unrealized gains on their (substantial) equity portfolios as core capital.

13 The quotations provided by Merrill Lynch and BT Securities were as of May 24, 1990 and reflected market conditions on that day.

14 The gross spread included all fees and commissions for structuring, underwriting, and selling the issue.

15 Thirty-day JJK is computed and made available weekly by Kenny Information Systems, an affiliate of an independent municipal bond brokerage. In 1990 the municipal bond industry recognized the J.J. Kenny Index as "a standard," but not "*the* standard" floating-rate benchmark for municipal swap transactions. Its use was pioneered by Merrill Lynch, an early proponent of municipal swaps. In December 1989, Merrill Lynch claimed it held over 90% of the municipal swap market (*The Bond Buyer*, December 11, 1989). Of the over $20 billion in municipal interest rate swaps outstanding in early 1990, the large majority were based on the 30-day Kenny Index.

16 Standard swap agreements called for payments to be made on a "net" basis; that is, amounts owed by each of the two parties were computed, and the difference between the two figures was paid by the party owing the greater amount to the party owing the lesser.

Regardless of the financing method (or underwriter) selected, Bud Cohn estimated the state would incur $200,000 in out-of-pocket costs, primarily to pay securities lawyers and financial advisers, as well as printing costs for the prospectus.

Merrill Lynch, in its analysis of the proposal, estimated that, on average, the state's bonds would trade at 55 basis points below 30-day JJK:

> ...fifty-five basis points below the J.J. Kenny Index is a reasonable and conservative expectation. This projection is based on an examination of the factors that most greatly influence these short-term interest rate levels including (1) the state's tax rate on interest income, and (2) the availability of purchasers of variable-rate securities issued by Connecticut. Because there have been very few comparable Connecticut financings, it is not possible to look directly at the interest rate experience on past Connecticut issues; however, the interest rate history of financings in states with similar characteristics strongly supports our conclusions.
>
> State tax rates on interest income have the most influence on short-term trading levels; the higher the state's income tax rate, the greater the expected spread vis-à-vis the Kenny Index. At 14%, the state of Connecticut has the highest tax on interest income in the nation. At the short end of the yield curve, the state can anticipate realizing the full benefit of higher state tax levels, because investors are willing to purchase Connecticut securities at a yield that gives them the same yield on an after-tax basis as an out-of-state security. For example, an investor would be willing to accept JJK minus 57 basis points for available rate debt issued by Connecticut if JJK was equal to 5.67% (the index's average level since inception). This 57 basis points is equal to 5.67% × [1 − federal tax rate] × state tax rate, or 5.67% × 72% × 14%.[17]
>
> Our estimate of Connecticut's tax-related trading differential is strongly supported by the experience of issuers in other states with comparable tax characteristics. As Exhibit 2 shows, variable-rate debt issued by New York and California would have trading differentials of 48 and 38 basis points, respectively, based on each state's income tax rates. However, representative issues from New York have shown trading differentials of 47 to 74 basis points. Similarly, a California issue has shown a trading differential of 55 basis points.
>
> In-state demand for variable-rate securities—coming primarily from three sectors: tax-exempt money market funds, corporations, and bank trust departments—also influences short-term rates. It is important to note that two of these sectors—bank trust departments and money market funds—are proxies for individual investors. It is therefore important to have higher-income individuals within the state who are seeking tax-exempt income. As shown in Exhibit 2, Connecticut compares favorably with New York and California in these criteria. Connecticut money market fund assets per-capita are similar to both New York and California. Connecticut per-capita personal income is among the highest in the nation and is considerably higher than both New York and California. In addition, Connecticut is home to a large number of corporations who would also invest in these securities.
>
> While we have only analyzed the trading differential as it relates to specific state tax and demand variables, it is important to note that we would expect Connecticut's securities to trade at yields lower than JJK, even without these factors, if these securities were structured as UPDATES. The J.J. Kenny Index is composed of securities (with a fixed thirty-day maturity). An UPDATES program, however, is structured like tax-exempt commercial paper (TECP).

---

17   State tax is tax-deductible at the federal level.

Historically, TECP and TECP-like variable-rate securities have substantially outperformed (fixed-maturity) instruments.[18]

Three major factors underlie the superior performance of Merrill Lunch's UPDATES product. First, investors are able to use these securities for cash management since they can buy the securities out to the specific maturity (or put) date they request. This ability to fulfill cash management functions is especially important to corporate investors. These investors are willing to accept lower yields to have paper repriced on the dates they select, rather than be restricted to floaters with inflexible put dates. Second, these securities pay interest on the put date and are purchased at par (cash market investors are sensitive to paying accrued interest). Third, and most important, the remarketing agent can actively manage an UPDATES program to avoid the predictable technical spikes and lock in the interest rate troughs that occur regularly in the short-term, tax-exempt market.

Merrill Lynch's ability to manage a program to achieve low cost for issuers has been proven over time, and our experience indicates a trading differential for Connecticut of at least 20 basis points below JJK—even if there was no income tax rate-related trading impact. In fact, for the Port of Seattle in Washington, a state that does not tax interest income, UPDATES have produced average yields 27 basis points below the Kenny Index.

In May 1990, Merrill Lynch's long-term obligations were rated "A2" by Moody's and "A" by Standard & Poor's.

THE BT SECURITIES PROPOSAL

BT Securities quoted an all-in cost of 6.964% on a straight 20-year, fixed-rate issue. Included was a gross spread of $9.25 per $1,000 par. The issue consisted of 14 serial maturities and 2 term bonds (in 2006 and 2010). With sinking funds on the 2 term bonds, principal payments would be equal over the 20 years. After 10 years, remaining maturities would be callable.

The synthetic fixed-rate financing proposed by BT Securities was virtually identical in structure to that proposed by Merrill Lynch. BT Securities offered to underwrite the variable-rate issue for $3.25 per $1,000 par. Its remarketing fee was .100% and its estimate of the LOC fee (payable to the LOC provider, likely a Japanese bank) was .070%. On the swap, BT offered to pay the state a floating rate equal to the TENR index, the rate on the bank's own 7-day, variable-rate program for municipal issuers. In return, the state was to pay BT a fixed rate of 6.67%. The swap term would also be 10 years.

---

18   *Casewriter's note:* With commercial paper, the issuer can alter the maturity of the paper (when it rolls over). For example, the issuer can try to obtain lower rates by lengthening the paper in periods of inverted yield curves or shortening the paper in periods of upward-sloping yield curves. Under the terms of UPDATES, the issuer could achieve the same effect by lengthening or shortening the time between reset (put) dates (with appropriate advance notice).

BT Securities claimed that the state's bonds would trade, on average, at a level 25 basis points below TENR, and supported the contention with an analysis similar to that done by Merrill Lynch.

In May 1990, BT Securities' long-term obligations were rated "Aa" by Moody's and "AA" by Standard & Poor's.

RELATION TO THE LIBOR-BASED INTEREST RATE SWAP MARKET

J.J. Kenny- and TENR-based swaps were unique to the municipal market in that they were tied to short-term, tax-exempt rates (see Exhibit 3). The swap payments were not tax-exempt, however. That is, for Merrill Lynch and BT Securities, inflows or outflows would be fully taxable or tax deductible as interest income or interest expense, respectively. The state itself was exempt from federal taxes.

The amount of these swaps outstanding, estimated around $20 billion in 1990, was small in comparison with the market for the corporate LIBOR-based, fixed-to-floating swaps that exceeded $1 trillion. While 20-year and even 30-year swap quotes were obtainable, the market was most active and liquid for terms of 10 years or less.[19] Activity at the longer terms was dominated by AAA-rated financial companies (see Exhibit 4).

One such company was American International Group, Inc. (AIG), a property-casualty insurer focused on the commercial and industrial sectors. AIG was a large player in the long-term taxable swap markets and had recently entered the municipal swap market. AIG was the primary provider of AAA-rated, long-term (up to 30-year) swaps to municipal issuers. Although AIG quoted both JJK- and LIBOR-based swaps, the firm was able to price more aggressively on the latter given the greater depth of, and facility to hedge in, the LIBOR-based market. In a LIBOR-based swap for municipal clients, AIG would typically "scale" all payments (fixed-rate and floating-rate) by a certain factor—around 70%—that reflected the long-term historic relationship between LIBOR and short-term municipal rates (see Exhibit 5).

BUD COHN'S INITIAL REACTIONS

Bud Cohn found the swap proposals intriguing; interest cost savings of 50 basis points, if achievable, would be worth about $10 million. However, he had concerns:

First was "basis risk," the risk that the differentials between the J.J. Kenny or TENR indices and the rates paid on the state's variable-rate bonds could be narrower than the 55

---

19 Demand for swaps was concentrated on terms of 10 years or less because corporate debt seldom went beyond a 10-year maturity.

and 25 basis points estimated by Merrill Lynch and BT Securities (see Exhibit 6). The estimated savings depended critically on these assumptions.

Second was term mismatch. The variable-rate bonds would be outstanding for 20 years, while Merrill Lynch and BT Securities were not willing to enter interest swap contracts for longer than 10 years. He was not sure how to evaluate this risk. Issuing 10-year debt was not an option since it would require doubling the principal repaid each year. This was impractical given the myriad of other financial commitments of the state.

His third concern was the risk of default on the swap agreement. The state budget, set once a year, might not be able to absorb the unanticipated costs that could arise in a default. This could compel the (publicly elected) treasurer to go back to the legislature and request additional funds. Besides the risk of real economic loss, the political embarrassment from such financial misfortunes would almost certainly be substantial.

Both mismatch and default concerns could be allayed by securing a 20-year, AAA-rated swap; however, a LIBOR-based swap could increase basis risk. Moreover, Mr. Cohn did not have quotes from AIG for the financing at hand as he had only recently become aware of the firm's municipal swap capabilities. Given the advanced stage of the financing, a proposal from a firm the state had not dealt with previously would have to wait until the next time the state ventured into the capital markets.

Finally, the credit-rating agencies had concerns about municipal issuers taking on too much variable-rate debt, including short-term debt. It was possible they would view synthetic fixed-rate debt as being variable-rate. This could impair the state's ability to issue variable-rate debt in the future. Cohn felt capacity to issue variable-rate debt would be essential in the event long-term rates rose to unattractive or even prohibitive levels.

All told, Cohn wondered whether the risks of the synthetic financing were "reasonable" in relation to the potential benefits. He did not want the Office of the Treasurer to be seen as speculating with public funds. Reflecting on everything, Cohn noted matter-of-factly:

> If we (The Office of the Treasurer) did something innovative and saved the state millions of dollars, no one would pay any attention because that's what we're "supposed" to do—but should something go amiss despite our best efforts and intentions, it'd be all over the newspapers. That's the fishbowl we work in every day.

Exhibit 1   Interest Rates on May 24, 1990

Mat.	Treas.[a]	LIBOR[b]	Swap[c]	Muni[d]	ML[e]	BT[e]
1 mo	7.19	8.25	–	–	–	–
3 mo	7.93	8.37	–	–	–	–
6 mo	8.11	8.50	–	–	–	–
1 yr	8.16	–	–	6.05	6.00	5.85
2 yr	8.50	–	43	6.20	6.20	6.00
3 yr	8.54	–	51	6.30	6.30	6.15
4 yr	8.59	–	58	6.40	6.40	6.25
5 yr	8.56	–	63	6.50	6.50	6.35
6 yr	–	–	–	6.60	6.60	6.45
7 yr	8.66	–	66	6.65	6.70	6.55
8 yr	–	–	–	6.70	6.70	6.65
9 yr	–	–	–	6.75	6.75	6.70
10 yr	8.64	–	76	6.80	6.80	6.75
11 yr	–	–	–	6.85	6.85	6.80
12 yr	–	–	–	6.90	6.90	6.85
13 yr	–	–	–	6.95	6.95	6.90
14 yr	–	–	–	7.00	7.00	6.95
15 yr	–	–	–	7.00	7.05	–
16 yr	–	–	–	7.05	7.10	7.00
17 yr	–	–	–	7.05	7.40	–
18 yr	–	–	–	7.10	7.65	–
19 yr	–	–	–	7.10	7.75	–
20 yr	8.74	–	81	7.10	7.875	7.05
30 yr	8.61	–	86	7.25	–	–

a. Bond-equivalent yields on U.S. Government securities.
b. London Inter-Bank Offer Rate.
c. Swap rates for 1- or 3-month LIBOR expressed as a basis point spread (middle of bid-offer) over U.S. Treasury.
d. Delphis-Hanover estimates for a AA-rated municipal issuer. On 5/24/90, 30-d JJK was 6.28%; 7-d TENR was 6.10%.
e. Coupons on individual bonds in the series (paid s.a.). BT Securities priced all maturities at par. Merrill Lynch priced the first 16 maturities at par and the last four at premiums: 102.437, 105.018, 105.646, and 107.096, respectively. In both the ML and BT structures, bonds maturing in years 11 through 20 were callable at par after year 10.

Exhibit 2   Merrill Lynch's Trading Differential Comparison

	New York	California	Connecticut
State interest income rate	11.875%[a]	9.3%	14%
Expected tax rate			
Trading differential (basis points)[b]	48	38	57
Money market assets per capita	$309	$337	$289
Net tax-supported debt per capita[c]	$873	$184	$1,258
Personal income per capita[c]	$19,305	$16,904	$23,059

a. Of this, 3.4% is New York City tax
b. Based on an average 5.67% J.J. Kenny index
c. *Source:* Moody's Municipal Credit Report

Exhibit 3   Short-Term Taxable vs. Tax-Exempt Interest Rates

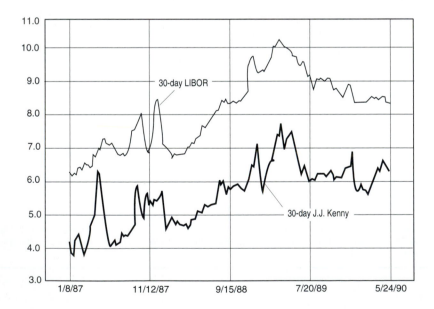

Exhibit 4   Long-Term Taxable vs. Tax-Exempt Interest Rates

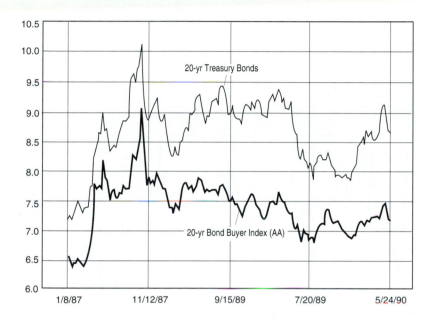

Exhibit 5   Ratio of Tax-Exempt to Taxable Interest Rates

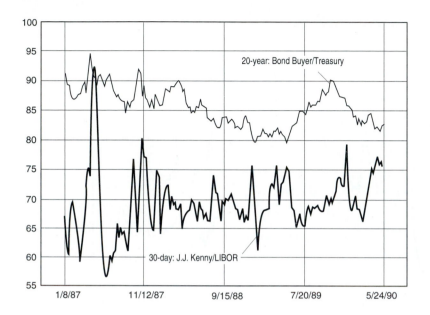

Exhibit 6 Spread of J. J. Kenny (30-Day) Over TENR (7-Day)

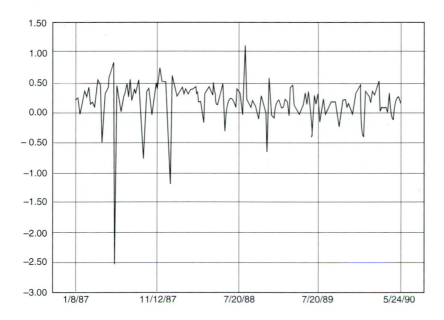

THE WALT DISNEY COMPANY'S YEN FINANCING

Early in July 1985, Rolf Anderson, the director of finance at the Walt Disney Company, was concerned about possible foreign-exchange exposure because of future yen royalty receipts from Tokyo Disneyland. Open for just over two years, Tokyo Disneyland was operated by an unrelated Japanese company and paid royalties on certain revenues to Walt Disney Productions. These yen royalties had notably increased during the last year, and Mr. Anderson foresaw further growth in the years ahead. Given the recent depreciation of the yen against the dollar, he was considering various ways of hedging this exposure.

Mr. Anderson had considered hedging techniques using foreign-exchange options, futures, and forwards. Also, he had thought about swapping out of existing dollar debt into a yen liability. But these choices did not appear particularly attractive, and he had focused on a possible ¥15 billion ten-year term loan with interest of 7.50% paid semi-annually.

However, Goldman, Sachs, who had been working with Disney on this problem, proposed a rather unusual solution. Disney could issue ten-year ECU Eurobonds with a sinking fund that would then be swapped into a yen liability at an attractive all-in yen cost. Although this seemed a rather roundabout way to create yen financing, Mr. Anderson was delighted at the prospects of costs below the yen loan. Furthermore, he wondered what factors in the international capital markets would make a deal like this work.

THE COMPANY

The Walt Disney Company, a diversified international company headquartered in Burbank, California, operated entertainment and recreational complexes, produced motion

William B. Allen, Jr., prepared this case under the supervision of Professor W. Carl Kester. The Walt Disney Company is not responsible for the accuracy of any information contained in the case. The case is not intended as a recommendation or endorsement by the Walt Disney Company of any particular type of financing.
Copyright © 1987 by the President and Fellows of Harvard College. Harvard Business School case 287-058.

picture and television features, developed community real estate projects, and sold consumer products. The company was founded in 1938 as successor to the animated motion picture business established by Walt and Roy Disney in 1923. These early films had immortalized cartoon characters created by the Disney brothers, such as Mickey Mouse and Donald Duck.

The company operated the Disneyland amusement theme park in Anaheim, California, and the Walt Disney World destination resort in Orlando, Florida. The Disneyland park was renowned for its rides and attractions in addition to the seven principal theme areas: Fantasyland, Adventureland, Frontierland, Tomorrowland, New Orleans Square, Main Street, and Bear Country. In each area there were restaurants, refreshment stands, and souvenir shops in keeping with the surrounding theme. The Walt Disney World complex included the Magic Kingdom amusement theme park (similar in concept to the Disneyland park) and Epcot Center (an acronym for Experimental Prototype Community of Tomorrow); three hotels; camping, golfing, and other recreational facilities designed for the whole family; a shopping village; a conference center; and other lodging accommodations.

In addition to the domestic entertainment and recreation revenues from Disneyland and Walt Disney World, the company received royalties, paid in yen, on certain revenues generated by Tokyo Disneyland. Similar in concept to the other Disney centers, this amusement theme park was located just six miles from downtown Tokyo. Owned and operated by an unrelated Japanese corporation, Tokyo Disneyland was opened to the public on April 15, 1983.

Disney produced motion pictures for the theatrical, television, and home video markets for audiences around the world. Although most of Disney's best-known films were fully or partially animated and were targeted at younger audiences, the company also made films designed to appeal to teenagers and young adults. In addition, Disney developed and produced television programs, such as "Disney's Wonderful World" and the Disney Channel, for network, syndicated, and pay television markets.

Through its real estate subsidiary, Arvida Corporation, acquired in 1984, the company planned and developed distinctive resort and home communities, primarily in Florida. Commercial and industrial properties, such as neighborhood shopping centers and office buildings, were also developed within or near the planned communities. In its consumer products segment, Disney licensed its name, its characters, its literary properties, and its songs and music to various manufacturers, retailers, printers, and publishers. The company also produced a variety of educational materials and teaching aids.

Consolidated revenues for the Walt Disney Company and its subsidiaries increased by almost 27% in 1984 to $1.7 billion (Exhibit 1). Total entertainment and recreation revenues, including royalties from Tokyo Disneyland, increased 6% to $1.1 billion in the fiscal year ended September 30, 1984. Although theme park attendance in the United States was down 5% to 31 million in 1984, the increased revenues for 1984 reflected admission price increases, higher per capita spending at the parks, and the inclusion of a full year of royalties from Tokyo Disneyland. Filmed entertainment revenues increased 48% to $245 million in 1984 because of strong domestic theatrical film rentals. Community development and consumer products revenues added another $204 million and $110 million, respectively.

Net income totaled $97.8 million in 1984, an increase of 5% from 1983. This growth was due primarily to the operating profits before corporate expenses contributed by the recently acquired real estate subsidiary and a turnaround in the filmed entertainment segment. Operating profits before corporate expenses for the entertainment and recreation segment actually decreased by 2% in 1984. Corporate expenses increased substantially because of $20 million nonrecurring costs associated with the acquisition of Arvida and increased interest costs on high levels of borrowing. The company also provided for $166 million in unusual charges to write down the values of several motion pictures and various development projects.

Total assets grew 15% to $2.7 billion at the end of fiscal 1984 (Exhibit 2), because of primarily the addition of real estate inventories as part of the acquisition of Arvida. Borrowings more than doubled in 1984 to $862 million because of the $215 million of Arvida debt assumed upon its acquisition and the $328 million expenditure for the repurchase of 4.2 million shares of the company's common stock from Reliance Insurance Company, which had launched a hostile takeover bid for the company. The ratio of debt to total capitalization jumped to 43% at September 30, 1984, from 20% at the end of the previous fiscal year, a level since reduced to 32%. Two thirds of borrowings at the end of 1984 consisted of relatively high interest rate short-term bank loans and commercial paper (Exhibit 3). The company had two separate Eurodollar note issues outstanding, rated single A, totaling $175 million. However, $50 million of the $75 million issue due in 1989 had been swapped into a yen liability at a yen cost of 7.40%. Also, the company had a yen term loan at 8.60% that required semiannual principal and interest payments over the next eight years.

By March 31, 1985, Disney had succeeded in reducing its short-term bank borrowings to $168.7 million. At the same time, commercial paper outstanding had grown to $352.2 million. Also, the 15.75% Eurodollar notes due in 1986 had been called and replaced with two-year Eurodollar notes at a significantly lower coupon.

THE ECU AND THE ECU EUROBOND MARKET

The ECU (European currency unit) was officially accepted in 1978 as the unit of account for the countries that formed the European Monetary System (EMS). It was used as the basis for monitoring exchange-rate divergence among member nations and was an officially sanctioned reserve currency within the EMS. The ECU, a composite currency, was defined as a trade-weighted basket of European currencies. In mid-1985, the ECU consisted of the amounts of currencies shown in Table A. This weighting was scheduled for its next official five-year review in 1989. With the likely admission of Spain and Portugal to the European Economic Community, market participants expected the currencies of these countries to be incorporated within the ECU at that time.

Table A Composition of European Currency Unit (ECU)

Deutsche marks	.719	Belgian francs	3.71
British pounds sterling	.0878	Luxembourg francs	.14
French francs	1.31	Danish kroner	.219
Italian lire	140.00	Irish pounds	.00871
Dutch guilders	.256	Greek drachmas	1.15

The ECU was traded in the foreign-exchange markets like any other currency, with both spot and forward transactions. However, the forward market was relatively thin, and long-dated forwards were not readily available. Banks in most European countries (with the notable exception of West Germany) freely accepted ECU deposits and made ECU loans. Other financial instruments included ECU certificates of deposit, ECU Eurobonds and floating-rate notes, and ECU bonds in the domestic U.S. ("Yankee") bond market. Interest rates in ECU were theoretically the weighted average of the interest rates in the component currencies. However, since it was difficult for nonresidents to access the money markets in some of these countries, and long-term interest rates were often nonexistent, ECU interest rates tended to have a life of their own. ECU interest rates historically exceeded the theoretical rate by 1%–1$\frac{1}{2}$%. Still, ECU interest rates were generally higher than those of the strong component currencies but lower than those of the weak component currencies.

The first ECU Eurobond, ECU 35 million issued by an Italian state agency in April 1981, had a six-year life and a coupon of 13%. Following that issue, the ECU Eurobond market grew impressively and by mid-1985 was the third largest Eurobond market in terms of new issue volume behind dollars and marks. As of mid-1985, there were about 175 fixed-rate ECU Eurobonds totaling over ECU 9.5 billion listed as outstanding by the Association of International Bond Dealers. (In addition, there were seven floating-rate notes totaling ECU 450 million.) ECU Eurobonds had historically averaged ECU 30–ECU 50 million in size, although, more recently, it was not uncommon to see issues of ECU 100 million or more. Three-quarters of ECU Eurobonds were offered with original maturities of 6–10 years, and the majority of the fixed-rate coupons ranged from 9%–11%.

In the early years, ECU Eurobond issuers were primarily European supranationals, banks, and state agencies. The dearth of non-European and nonfinancial corporate borrowers was explained by the scarcity of attractive foreign-currency swaps. However, by mid-1985 nonfinancial corporate borrowers accounted for over one quarter of new issues, while supranationals, sovereigns, and state agencies represented only one third and banks another one third. Although three quarters of the borrowers were still European, U.S. and Canadian borrowers accounted for 10% and Far Eastern borrowers for an additional 7%. Market participants attributed most of the growth of this market and the increasing diversity of issuers to the development of the ECU/dollar swap market.

ECU Eurobonds had been traditionally sold to individuals in France, Belgium, Luxembourg, and Switzerland who had established ECU bank accounts. These Eurobond investors were attracted by the high coupons and relative stability of the ECU to their domestic currencies. Because of this historical concentration of demand, new issues were usually lead-managed by major French or Belgian banks. However, there were signs in mid-1985 of increased institutional demand, not only from European institutions, but also from Japanese and U.S. funds wishing to diversify their portfolios away from dollars.

THE PROBLEM FACING DISNEY

With the opening of Tokyo Disneyland in April 1983 and the inflow of yen royalty receipts, Mr. Anderson was concerned about the possible exposure of Disney to future fluctuations in the yen/dollar spot rate. The current spot rate of 248 yen/dollar represented almost an 8% depreciation in the value of the yen from 229.70 just over a year ago (Exhibit 4). During fiscal 1984, yen royalty receipts had been just over ¥8 billion. However, Mr. Anderson expected these receipts to grow at 10%–20% per year over the next few years as the new theme park attracted the interest of Japanese vacationers and foreign tourists traveling to Tokyo.

Mr. Anderson had considered various ways of hedging a portion of the expected future yen receipts, including foreign-exchange (FX) options, futures, and forwards. One issue that confronted him immediately was how far into the future he should attempt to hedge. Liquid markets for options and futures contracts existed only for maturities of two years or less. A similar problem appeared to exist with bank FX forward contracts, although Disney had obtained an indication of long-dated FX forward rates from its banks

(Exhibit 5). However, the banks would consider the FX forwards as a part of their total exposure to Disney, thus tying up valuable credit lines.

As an alternative, Disney could enter into another foreign-currency swap, as it had done a year earlier, converting more of its existing dollar debt into a yen liability. This type of hedge would also be short-term because Disney's Eurodollar note issues matured in 1–4 years. Mr. Anderson also knew that attractive yen swap rates for maturities less than four years were hard to find. Moreover, this arrangement would not provide any additional cash, and Disney was interested in reducing further its short-term debt. For the moment, Mr. Anderson had ruled out a longer maturity Eurodollar debt issue, which could be more effectively swapped into yen, because of Disney's recent Eurodollar note issue and the company's temporarily high debt ratio. Euroyen bonds were also out of the question. Despite the recent liberalization in the Euroyen bond market, Disney was ineligible to issue Euroyen bonds under the current Japanese Ministry of Finance guidelines.

Thus, should Disney wish to hedge much beyond three or four years, it appeared that its only viable choice was to create a yen liability through a term loan from a Japanese bank at the Japanese long-term prime rate. Disney was considering a ¥15 billion ten-year bullet loan, with principal repaid at final maturity, which required interest of 7.50% paid semiannually and front-end fees of .75%.

However, Goldman, Sachs, which had been working with Disney on this matter, proposed a rather unusual solution. The firm suggested that Disney issue ten-year ECU Eurobonds that would be swapped into a yen liability at a potentially more attractive all-in yen cost than a yen term loan. Specifically, it was prepared to underwrite ECU 80 million ten-year Eurobonds at 100.25% of par, with a coupon of $9\frac{1}{8}\%$, and underwriting fees of 2%. Additional expenses to be paid by Disney were capped at $75,000. The ECU Eurobonds would have an annual sinking fund payment of ECU 16 million beginning in the sixth year and continuing until maturity. (The terms and cash flows for the ECU Eurobond are shown in Exhibit 6.) If the ECU Eurobonds were launched, Disney would be only the second U.S. corporation to access this market. Also, it would be the first ECU bond incorporating an amortization schedule to repay the bond's principal. Thus, Mr. Anderson was concerned about the market reception of such an issue.

Goldman, Sachs could also arrange an ECU/yen swap intermediated by Industrial Bank of Japan (IBJ), a powerful Japanese commercial bank rated AAA. In this arrangement, Disney would exchange its ECU Eurobond net proceeds and IBJ would make future ECU payments to Disney that exactly matched the coupons and principal payments of the Eurobonds (Exhibit 7, column A). At the same time, Disney would receive the yen equivalent of the net ECU proceeds from the Eurobond, converted at the spot rate, and would make future semiannual yen swap payments according to a fixed schedule (Exhibit 7, column B). Disney could then exchange the initial yen proceeds for dollars at the spot rate in order to reduce its short term borrowings. At the time of the proposal, the ECU spot exchange rate was $.7420 per ECU, and the yen/dollar exchange rate was ¥248 per dollar.

THE COUNTERPARTY TO THE SWAP

Goldman, Sachs was aware that a French state-owned utility was interested in swapping some of its yen debt for ECU debt. The utility was a major borrower in the world capital markets because its financing needs were far too large to be supplied by either the domestic French franc debt market or the fledgling Euro-French franc bond market (reopened only in April 1985 after being closed for five years). Rated AAA, it had issued numerous public Eurobonds in dollars, ECU, yen, and Deutsche marks (Exhibit 8) in addition to various domestic borrowings, private placements, and term loans. Like many European state agencies, it preferred ECU liabilities because the ECU most closely matched its natural currency flows. However, European sovereigns and state agencies, including the French utility, were often perceived by the markets as borrowing ECUs too frequently and wearing out their welcome among the retail purchasers of ECU bonds.

At the time of Disney's financing, the French utility wished to swap out of a ten-year yen term loan with sinking fund payments that began in five years. Thus, Goldman, Sachs could arrange for Disney and the utility to enter into a swap, intermediated by IBJ, in which the utility would take on an ECU liability in exchange for future yen receipts, and Disney would take on a yen liability in exchange for future ECU receipts. Specifically, IBJ would pay semiannually to the utility an amount equal to its debt service on the yen term loan. In return, the utility would make ECU payments to IBJ more than sufficient to cover the payments IBJ had to make to Disney (see Exhibit 7, column C). The ECU principal to be "received" by the utility in the swap was strictly notional and would be determined by the size of Disney's financing and the ECU/yen exchange rate; no new funds would actually be received by the utility. Goldman, Sachs believed that the all-in cost of the utility's ECU flows after the swap would be less than that prevailing in the ECU Eurobond market. Moreover, the utility would be able to structure the swap flows to accomplish its objective of perfectly matching future yen payments on this loan and reducing its yen exposure.

As he sat down in his office and began to analyze the proposal, Mr. Anderson could not help but be impressed at the combination of factors in the international capital markets from New York to Europe to Tokyo that made such a deal possible. It had required considerable ingenuity to put the deal together. However, he needed to determine if this arrangement made sense for Disney before giving the go-ahead.

Exhibit 1   Consolidated Income Statements, Walt Disney Company and Subsidiaries, for Years Ending
September 30, 1982–1984 (thousands of dollars except per share data)

	1982	1983	1984
Revenues			
Entertainment and recreation	$ 725,610	$1,031,202	$1,097,359
Filmed entertainment	202,102	165,458	244,552
Community development			204,384
Consumer products	102,538	110,697	109,682
	$1,030,250	$1,307,357	$1,655,977
Costs and Expenses			
Entertainment and recreation	$ 592,965	$ 834,324	$ 904,664
Filmed entertainment	182,463	198,843	242,303
Community development	–	–	162,158
Consumer products	54,706	53,815	55,819
	$ 830,134	$1,086,982	$1,364,944
Income (Loss) before (1)–(4)			
Entertainment and recreation	$ 132,645	$ 196,878	$ 192,695
Filmed entertainment	19,639	(33,385)	2,249
Community development			42,226
Consumer products	47,832	56,882	53,863
	$ 200,116	$ 220,375	$ 291,033
General and admin. expenses	$ 30,957	$ 35,554	$ 59,570
Design projects abandoned	5,147	7,295	7,032
Net interest expense (income)	(14,781)	14,066	41,738
(1) Corporate expenses	$ 21,323	$ 56,915	$ 108,340
(2) Unusual charges	–	–	165,960
(3) Income taxes (benefit)	78,700	70,300	(5,000)
(4) Plus: Accounting change for investment tax credit	–	–	76,111
Net income	$100,093	$93,160	$97,844
EPS before accounting change	$3.01	$2.70	$.61
Cumulative effect of change in accounting	–	–	2.12
EPS	$3.01	$2.70	$2.73
Avg. no. of common and common equivalent shares outstanding	33,225	34,481	35,849

Exhibit 2 Consolidated Balance Sheets, Walt Disney Company and Subsidiaries, for Years Ending September 30, 1983 and 1984 (thousands of dollars)

	1983	1984
Assets		
Cash	$ 18,055	$ 35,346
Net accounts and notes receivable	104,746	172,762
Income taxes refundable	70,000	60,000
Merchandise inventories	77,945	83,467
Film production costs	127,010	102,462
Real estate inventories	–	229,424
Entertainment attractions and other property	2,251,297	2,413,985
Less accumulated depreciation	(504,365)	(600,156)
Construction and design projects in progress	108,190	94,710
Land	16,687	28,807
	$1,871,809	$1,937,346
Other assets	111,630	118,636
Total assets	$2,381,195	$2,739,443
Liabilities and Stockholders' Equity		
Accounts payable, payroll, and other accrued liabilities	$ 182,709	$ 239,992
Income taxes payable	13,982	24,145
Borrowings	352,575	861,909
Unearned deposits and advances	109,556	178,907
Deferred taxes on income	321,845	279,005
Total liabilities	980,667	1,583,958
Common shares, no par, issued and		
outstanding (33,729 and 34,509 shares)	661,934	359,988
Retained earnings	738,594	795,497
Stockholders' equity	1,400,528	1,155,485
Total liabilities and stockholders' equity	$2,381,195	$2,739,443

Exhibit 3   Analysis of Outstanding Borrowings, 1983–1985 (millions of dollars)

	Sept. 30, 1983	Sept. 30, 1984	Mar. 31, 1985
Unsecured borrowings under revolving line of credit and bank term loans	–	$408.0	$168.7
Commercial paper	$118.2	200.2	352.2
15.75% Eurodollar notes, due 9/1/86[a]	100.0	100.0	–
12.50% Eurodollar notes, due 1/10/87	–		150.0
12.50% Eurodollar notes, due 3/15/89[b]	75.0	75.0	75.0
8.60% Yen term loan, due 2/1/93[c]	59.4	53.1	50.0
Other	–	25.6	58.4
	$352.6	$861.9	$854.3

a. Called on October 17, 1984.
b. Of the $75 million outstanding, the company swapped $50 million into yen liabilities of approximately ¥12 billion. This synthetic yen borrowing was due 3/14/89 and had a cost of 7.40% payable annually.
c. Outstanding yen principal at March 31, 1985, was ¥12.5 billion, with semiannual yen principal payments of ¥765 million.

Exhibit 4   Historical Summary of Average Yen/Dollar Exchange Rates and Price Indexes, 1980–1985

	Yen/Dollar	U.S. CPI	Japan CPI
1980	225.70	100.0	100.0
1981	220.10	110.4	104.9
1982	248.30	117.1	107.8
1983	237.40	120.9	109.9
1984:			
1st Qtr	230.80	125.0	111.4
2nd	229.70	125.6	112.3
3rd	243.60	126.6	112.2
4th	246.10	128.3	113.5
Average 1984	237.30	126.1	112.3
1985:			
1st Qtr	257.50	128.6	113.7
2nd	250.80	130.2	114.7

CPI = consumer price index.
Sources:Economic Report of the President and *International Financial Statistics.*

Exhibit 5   Yen Long-Dated Foreign Exchange Forwards

Years	Outright Forward	
	Bid	Offer
Spot	247.95	248.05
1	242.05	242.65
2	235.95	239.05
3	227.95	231.55
4	217.95	222.55
5	208.95	213.55
6	200.95	210.55
7	192.95	204.05
8	185.95	199.05
9	178.95	192.55
10	172.95	189.05

Exhibit 6   Cash Flows of Ten-Year ECU Eurobond with Sinking Fund

Par	ECU 80 million
Price	100.250%
Coupon	9.125%
Fees	2.000%
Expenses	$75,000
Dollar/ECU	0.7420

Year	Cash Flows (million ECU)
0	78.499
1	(7.300)
2	(7.300)
3	(7.300)
4	(7.300)
5	(7.300)
6	(23.300)
7	(21.840)
8	(20.380)
9	(18.920)
10	(17.460)

Exhibit 7   ECU/Yen Swap Flows (millions)

Year	Disney's Swap Flows: Received from/(paid to) IBJ		French Utility's Swap Flows: Received from/(paid to) IBJ	
	ECU (A)	Yen (B)	ECU (C)	Yen (D)
0.0	(78.499)	14,445.153[a]	80.000[b]	(14,445.153)[b]
0.5		(483.226)		483.226
1.0	7.300	(483.226)	(7.350)	483.226
1.5		(483.226)		483.226
2.0	7.300	(483.226)	(7.350)	483.226
2.5		(483.226)		483.226
3.0	7.300	(483.226)	(7.350)	483.226
3.5		(483.226)		483.226
4.0	7.300	(483.226)	(7.350)	483.226
4.5		(483.226)		483.226
5.0	7.300	(1,808.141)	(7.350)	1,808.141
5.5		(1,764.650)		1,764.650
6.0	23.300	(1,721.160)	(23.350)	1,721.160
6.5		(1,677.670)		1,677.670
7.0	21.840	(1,634.179)	(21.880)	1,634.179
7.5		(1,590.689)		1,590.689
8.0	20.380	(1,547.199)	(20.410)	1,547.199
8.5		(1,503.708)		1,503.708
9.0	18.920	(1,460.218)	(18.940)	1,460.218
9.5		(1,416.728)		1,416.728
10.0	17.460	(1,520.450)	(17.470)	1,520.450

Note: These swaps flows exclude fees paid to either Industrial Bank of Japan (IBJ) or Goldman Sachs. Dollar/ECU of $.7420 and yen/dollar exchange rate of ¥248 are assumed.

a. The initial yen principal received by Disney from IBJ is relevant only to the swap transaction and the calculation of an all-in yen financing cost. By exchanging the initial yen for dollars in the spot market, Disney would eventually obtain new dollar financing.

b. The principal amounts for the French utility are strictly notional; no net new funding would be obtained by the utility as a result of the swap.

Exhibit 8   Summary of the French Utility's Outstanding Publicly Traded Eurobonds, Mid-1985

Currency	Amount (millions)	Issue Date	Maturity	Life (Years) Original	Remaining	Coupon	Yield to Maturity
Dollar	20	May 1971	May 1986	15	.8	8.500%	9.32%
Dollar	50	June 1977	June 1987	10	1.9	8.500	9.30
Dollar	100	Aug. 1976	Sept. 1986	10	1.2	8.900	9.08
Dollar	100	Apr. 1979	Apr. 1986	7	0.8	9.625	9.09
Dollar	125	June 1980	July 1988	8	3.0	10.000	10.09
Dollar	225	June 1985	July 1995	10	10.0	10.000	10.80
Dollar	100	Apr. 1983	May 1993	10	7.8	11.125	10.76
Dollar	100	May 1980	May 1990	10	4.9	11.250	10.84
Dollar	150	Oct. 1982	Oct. 1987	5	2.3	12.750	9.57
Dollar	200	Apr. 1982	Apr. 1989	7	3.8	14.375	10.45
Dollar	500	Sept. 1984	Sept. 1994	10	9.2	0.000	11.44
Dollar	300	Mar. 1985	Mar. 1997	12	11.7	LIBOR+¼	9.66
Dollar	400	Feb. 1984	Feb. 1999	15	13.7	LIBOR+⅛	9.70
ECU	75	Feb. 1985	Mar. 1995	10	9.7	9.750	9.37
ECU	60	Dec. 1982	Jan. 1993	10	7.5	12.500	10.00
Yen	20,000	Jan. 1985	Jan. 1995	10	9.6	6.875	6.83
DM	200	Sept. 1983	Oct. 1993	10	8.3	8.375	7.12
DM	100	Sept. 1982	Sept. 1992	10	7.2	8.875	7.38

Source: The Association of International Bond Dealers.
Note: Excludes domestic issues, private placements, and term loans.
LIBOR = London Interbank Offered Rate.

CURRENCY SWAPS

A currency swap, in the simplest sense, is an agreement between two parties to exchange a given amount of one currency for another and to pay back with interest these currencies in the future.[1] Frequently, one counterparty—such as a corporation, bank, sovereign, or supranational—borrows under specific terms and conditions in one currency while the other counterparty borrows under different terms and conditions in a second currency. The two counterparties then exchange the net receipts from the capital markets issues and agree to service each other's debt. For example, a U.S. company that has issued deutsche mark (DM) bonds with an annual all-in DM cost of 8% enters into a foreign currency swap directly with a German company that has issued US$ bonds with an annual all-in US$ cost of 11%. The companies exchange the initial receipts from their respective bonds. At the same time, the U.S. company agrees to pay the interest and principal on the US$ bonds issued by the German company, and the German company agrees to pay the interest and principal on the DM bonds issued by the U.S. company.

From the viewpoint of the U.S. company, such an arrangement is beneficial if the German company has been able to borrow dollars at a lower rate than the rate the U.S. company would have been able to obtain. Likewise, the German company will find the swap attractive if the U.S. company was able to borrow DM at a lower rate than the German company would have been able to obtain. This could happen if (1) there was an overabundance of DM debt issued by the German company compared to the relative "scarcity" of U.S. corporate names in that market, and/or (2) U.S. investors perceived the German company to be a better credit risk than the U.S. company. Thus, in this currency swap, the U.S. company's DM debt service is completely covered and the net cost is represented by

---

1   In addition to the swaps described in this note, there are several other uses of the term "swaps" in international finance. In the foreign exchange markets, a swap is a simultaneous purchase and sale (or sale and purchase) of an amount of currency for settlement at different value dates. Also, the U.S. Federal Reserve has established "swap lines" with other central banks in which it can borrow foreign currencies.

This note was prepared by William B. Allen, Jr., under the supervision of Scott P. Mason.

the US$ flows it must pay to service the German company's US$ debt. From the stand-point of the German company, its US$ debt service is completely covered and the net cost is the DM flows it must pay to service the U.S. company's debt. Both companies, therefore, know precisely their all-in financing cost in the desired currency. The all-in costs of the cash flows associated with the debt issues and the related currency swaps are shown in a typical currency swap diagram in Exhibit 1.

An alternative method for the U.S. company to lock in the dollar cost of servicing its DM debt (or the German company to lock in the DM cost of servicing its US$ debt) would have been to use the bank forward foreign exchange market. However, long-dated forward exchange rates are priced conservatively by banks and the bid-offer spreads tend to be quite wide. Banks are usually not eager to take on the risk of changes in the future level of spot exchange rates, and it is difficult for them to "square" their long-dated for-ward positions with offsetting future cash flows from other natural businesses or other forward trades in the market. In contrast, a currency swap typically results in an immedi-ate matching of two counterparties with opposite hedging needs. The all-in costs of the cash flows in the desired currency using currency swaps arranged directly between two counterparties is usually less than using bank forward exchange contracts because there is no need to build in an extra margin to cover uncertainty from the standpoint of the bank. Nonetheless, for borrowers considering a swap, the forward foreign exchange market and the possibility of a direct swap with another borrowing counterparty represent competi-tive alternatives, each of which may be examined from the standpoint of cost, availability, and counterparty risk and relationships.

One of the first well-publicized currency swaps was in August 1981 between the World Bank and IBM.[2] IBM had outstanding DM and Swiss franc (Sfr) bond issues that it wanted to hedge into a dollar liability given the appreciation of the dollar in the summer of 1981. Essentially, the World Bank agreed to pay each year to IBM the necessary DM and Sfr to cover IBM's debt service on these bonds. In return, IBM paid US$ to cover the World Bank's debt service on a Eurodollar bond. The market for currency swaps grew tre-mendously following this first swap in 1981. It is estimated that $860 billion of notional principal was swapped in currency swaps. Moreover, this huge volume is spread over a wide diversity of currencies as evidenced by Exhibit 2. In recent years, as much as 50% to 70% of the new issue volume in the Eurobond markets has been associated with foreign

---

2   This discussion of the World Bank-IBM swap is adapted from Chapter VIII, Section 3 (pp. 135–140) of *Swap Financing Techniques* published by Euromoney in 1983. Some simplifications have been made for ease of exposition

currency or interest rate swaps. Finding swap counterparties and arranging the deals has become a major source of profits for international investment and merchant banks.

THE MECHANICS OF CURRENCY SWAPS WITH BANK CREDIT INTERMEDIATION

Shortly after its first swap, the World Bank (WB) executed a more typical currency swap that required both counterparties to simultaneously issue two capital markets issues and agree to exchange the initial proceeds and the liabilities for future payments using a bank as an intermediary.[3] In this case, a well-known, BBB-rated U S. company (Company) was seeking fixed-rate dollar financing, but because of its low rating, the coupon on a five-year Eurodollar bond would have been 17%. With front-end fees of $1\frac{7}{8}$%, the annual all-in cost on such an issue would have been 17.59%. The company's target borrowing rate was US$ 16.7% or less. Meanwhile, the World Bank (WB) was able to issue five-year Eurodollar bonds with a coupon of 16% and front-end fees of $1\frac{7}{8}$%, resulting in an annual all-in cost of 16.58%.

In the Swiss market, however, the risk premium for the Company was considerably less than what it faced in the dollar market. Since the Company was well known and its products were considered to be high quality, Swiss investors were willing to accept five-year Sfr bonds with a coupon of 7.35%. Front-end fees of 2.5% resulted in an annual all-in Sfr cost of 7.98%. The WB, however, borrowed heavily in the Sfr markets and most Swiss investment portfolios were well-stocked with WB paper. The WB estimated it would have had to pay a Sfr coupon of 7.75% and fees of 2.5%, resulting in an annual all-in Sfr cost of 8.38%. The WB's target borrowing rate was Sfr 8.10% or less.

One alternative was for both borrowers to launch debt issues in the markets where their respective credits were well received and hedge the future interest and principal payments through the bank forward market into the desired currency. Exhibit 3 shows the Company's Sfr bond flows in column (C) and the fully hedged US$ bond flows in column (E), using the appropriate foreign exchange forwards to convert Sfr to US$. The annual all-in US$ cost (the internal rate of return of the flows) in column (E) was 16.8%. This represented a savings of 79 basis points (bp) compared to directly tapping the US$ market, but was still above the target borrowing rate in US$. The flows from the WB's US$ bond are shown in column (F). In this case, the WB's fully hedged US$ bond resulted in an

---

3   This discussion of the World Bank-U.S. company swap is adapted from pp. 55–56 in *Financial Swaps*, by Carl R. Beidleman, published by Dow Jones Irwin in 1985. Some of the numbers have been slightly disguised, and some simplifications and modifications to the swap structure have been made for ease of exposition.

annual all-in Sfr cost of 8.4% in column (H), or 2 bp more expensive than issuing Sfr bonds directly.

Instead of using the bank forward markets, the two parties issued the bonds and executed foreign currency swaps with a bank intermediary (bank). To demonstrate that the objectives of all the parties can be met, we will assume that the bank offered a swap to the WB such that its annual all-in Sfr cost was 8.10%, and a swap to the Company such that its annual all-in US$ cost was 16.7%. Because of the credit disparity between the WB and the Company, the WB preferred to accept the credit of the bank. Therefore, the bank acted as the direct counterparty to both the WB and the Company, intermediating the swap cash flows between them. In this case, there was substantial arbitrage potential arising from the difference in borrowing costs:

	US$ Rates	Sfr Rates
Available to Company	17.59%	7.98%
Available to WB	16.58%	8.38%
Absolute difference	1.01%	0.40%

These arbitrage profits of 141 bps were split among the three parties—the WB, the Company, and the bank—based upon the target borrowing rates announced by the WB and the Company, the required profits for the bank, and the negotiating strength of each party.

The cash flows from the bond issue and the related swap for the WB are shown in Exhibit 4. Column (A) shows the WB's cash flows from its US$ bond. The US$ swap flows for the WB are shown in column (B). Note that the WB surrendered to the bank the entire net US$ proceeds in exchange for future US$ receipts that exactly matched its debt service requirements. Also, the WB agreed to pay to the bank in years one through five the exact amount of Sfr required to service the Company's Sfr bonds. The WB's initial Sfr receipt of Sfr 97.013 million paid by the bank is the present value of the required future Sfr outflows discounted at 8.10%. Thus, the internal rate of return on the flows in column (C), and, hence, the WB's AIC is 8.10%.

The Company's cash flows from its Sfr bond are shown in Exhibit 5 in column (A). The Sfr swap flows are shown in column (C). The Company surrendered to the bank the entire net Sfr proceeds in exchange for future Sfr receipts which exactly matched its debt service requirements. Also, as shown in column (B), the Company agreed to pay to the bank in years one through five the exact amount of US$ required to service the WB's US$ debt. The initial receipt of US$ 48.872 million paid by the bank is the present value of the required future US$ outflows discounted at 16.70%. Therefore, the internal rate of return on the flows in column (B), and hence, the company's AIC, is 16.70%.

The bank's cash flows are shown in Exhibit 6. Its swap flows with the WB, shown in columns (A) and (B), are equal and opposite to the flows shown in columns (B) and (C) in Exhibit 4. Likewise, the bank's swap flows with the Company shown in columns (C) and (D) in Exhibit 6 are equal and opposite to the flows shown in columns (B) and (C) in Exhibit 5. The net US$ and Sfr cash flows are shown in columns (E) and (F). Note that in years one through five the cash flows are perfectly matched and the bank acts merely as a conduit. However, in the initial exchange, the bank nets US$ 190,000 and Sfr 487,000 (about US$ 243,000) for a total profit of about US$ 433,000. This profit is compensation for brokering the swap, bringing together the counterparties, arranging the deal, and acting as credit intermediary. In currency swaps, the bank faces credit exposure which is a function of both interest rate and foreign exchange risk. If, for example, US$ interest rates fell, and the Company defaulted, the bank would be unlikely to find another counterparty who would pay similar rates, while the bank would remain obligated to make all contractual payments to the WB. Note that if the Company defaulted on its swap payments to the bank, the bank would stop making swap payments in return to the Company (the right of offset). The annual all-in costs associated with the flows from the bond issues and the swaps are shown in Exhibit 7.

It is easy to see from the diagram in Exhibit 7 how the total arbitrage was finally split among the three parties. The following table summarizes these savings:

	US$	Sfr
Savings for WB—Sfr 8.38% direct cost less Sfr 8.1% swap rate		0.28%
Savings for Company—US$ 17.59% direct cost less US$ 16.7% swap rate	0.89%	
Bank profits:		
Sfr 8.1% swap receipts less Sfr 7.98% swap payments		0.12%
US$ 16.7% swap receipts less US$ 16.58% swap payments	0.12%	
Total arbitrage	1.01%	0.40%

Note: The initial flow of $433,000 that the bank recognizes is the present value of the 24 bps of the 141 bps of total arbitrage profits it has appropriated.

THE DEVELOPMENT OF INTEREST RATE AND CURRENCY SWAP MARKETS

With the introduction of interest rate swaps in the spring of 1982, fixed-rate US$ obligations could be converted into floating rate US$ obligations. The development of this market resulted from the needs of major European, Canadian, and Japanese banks to acquire competitively priced longer term floating rate US$ funding for their growing volume of floating-rate US$ assets. They had typically paid slightly higher spreads over LIBOR (London Interbank Offer Rate) for Eurodollar bank borrowings than their U.S. counterparts. However, these banks had not been very active in the fixed-rate Eurodollar bond market and enjoyed, for a while, a "scarcity" value in that market, which resulted in relatively low fixed-rate all-in US$ costs. On the other hand, many large, lower-credit U.S. companies were seeking fixed-rate US$ financing but were forced to use floating-rate loans with rates calculated as spreads over LIBOR because fixed-rate bonds were prohibitively expensive. Some European and Japanese banks began issuing fixed-rate Eurodollar bonds and entering into interest rate swaps whereby they made floating-rate US$ LIBOR swap payments to the U.S. companies. In return, these companies made fixed-rate US$ swap payments to the banks that covered the debt service on their Eurodollar bonds. These arrangements reduced the cost of floating-rate US$ for the banks to LIBOR, and reduced the cost of fixed-rate US$ for the U.S. companies to a level close to the more favorable US$ rates paid by the European and Japanese banks.[4] In late 1982 and 1983, the tremendous volume of foreign-bank, fixed-rate Eurodollar bonds that were swapped into floating-rate dollars put pressure on these markets, and the savings resulting from this strategy were substantially reduced.

As the fixed-rate Eurodollar market became less hospitable to the European, Canadian, and Japanese banks, they sought fixed-rate funding in other currencies, such as DM or Sfr, and swapped these liabilities for fixed-rate dollars. The fixed-rate US$ flows were then swapped into floating-rate dollars. Over time, US$ interest-rate swaps became commodities that were aggressively offered by the banks to their customers. An estimated US $3,851 billion of notional principal amount of interest-rate swaps were arranged in 1992. Major international banks made a market in interest-rate swaps by quoting bid-offer rates for various maturities and holding trading positions. The bid rate was the fixed US$ rate that banks were willing to pay against receiving six-month US$ LIBOR, and the offer rate was the fixed US$ rate that they were willing to receive against paying six-month US$

---

4   In an interest rate swap in which fixed US$ are exchanged for US$ LIBOR, a company's fixed-rate US$ debt cost would be the sum of the fixed rate swap payments made to service a bank's Eurodollar debt plus the spread over LIBOR that it was paying on its loans.

LIBOR.[5] The fixed-rates were typically quoted as spreads over benchmark Treasuries (see Exhibit 8). Thus, borrowers could easily exchange fixed foreign-currency obligations into US$ LIBOR obligations by a combination of fixed-rate currency swaps and US$ interest-rate swaps. The practice of swapping fixed-rate, foreign-currency flows for US$ LIBOR was also attractive for sovereigns and foreign state agencies who wanted fixed-rate, foreign-currency liabilities, but, because of the size of their needs or their lower credit, were forced to issue Eurodollar floating-rate notes (FRNs). These borrowers were natural payers of fixed-rate foreign currency because they often wanted to establish liabilities in these currencies to hedge official reserves or match future foreign-currency trade inflows.

Currency swaps are now frequently quoted as either the annual or semiannual fixed rate on the foreign currency flows against six-month US$ LIBOR. By relating any two quotes to US$ LIBOR, banks can easily determine the fixed swap rate in one currency against the fixed swap rate in another currency. Major international banks now make markets in foreign-currency swaps, and quotes are generally available in several currencies for various maturities (see Exhibit 9).

CURRENCY SWAPS USING MARKET SWAP RATES

In order to illustrate the mechanics of intermediated currency swaps that are structured using quoted market swap rates, we will return to the WB-Company swap described previously in which both parties agreed to make swap payments that exactly covered the required future debt service of the counterparty (see Exhibits 4 through 7). Assume the same basic terms:

	World Bank	Company
Desired financing	Sfr 100 M	US$ 50M
Target rate	Sfr 8.10%	US$ 16.70%
Direct borrowing all-in costs	Sfr 8.38%	US$ 17.59%
Alternative borrowing costs	US$ 16.58%	Sfr 7.98%
Sfr/US$ spot rate	Sfr 1.9995-2.0005	

Now let's assume also that on that date a bank quoted the following annual currency swap rates:

Sfr	7.70–7.80%	against six-month US$ LIBOR
US$	16.25–16.35%	against six-month US$ LIBOR

---

5   Interest rate swaps are also quoted for fixed US$ against one- or three-month LIBOR, commercial paper, T-bill rates, and other benchmarks.

By relating US$ LIBOR, the bank offered to pay to the WB annual US$ 16.25% against receiving annual Sfr 7.8%. In this case, there are market swap rates for both the US$ and Sfr payments. Note, therefore, that the quoted annual US$ 16.25% swap rate that would be paid by the bank to the WB was not the same as the 16.58% annual all-in cost on the bond. As for the cash flows, the bank agreed to pay to the WB in years one through five the exact amount of US$ needed to cover the annual interest and final principal payments on its bond. Also, the WB agreed to pay Sfr equal to the future required debt service on the Company's bond. Therefore, the size of both initial swap exchanges in US$ and Sfr between the WB and the bank were adjusted to achieve the quoted swap rates.

The calculation of the WB's flows from the US$ bond and the swap with the bank are shown in Exhibit 10. Column (A) contains the flows from the US$ bond. In column (B), the WB's US$ swap receipts from the bank in years one through five exactly match its debt service. The amount of the initial US$ payment that the WB must make to the bank is US$ 49.593 million—the present value of the required annual US$ flows from years one through five discounted at the 16.25% quoted US$ swap rate. Similarly, column (C) shows the Sfr swap flows. The size of the WB's initial Sfr receipt is Sfr 98.194 million—the present value of the required annual Sfr swap flows from years one through five discounted at the 7.8% quoted swap rate.

Note that the US$ 49.593 million initial payment by the WB to the bank exceeds the US$ 49.063 million net proceeds from its bond issue. The US$ 0.531 million shortfall, shown in column (D), is purchased by the WB in the spot foreign exchange market out of the initial Sfr proceeds received from the bank. Thus, the Sfr initial swap inflow calculated above is effectively reduced by Sfr 1.062 million—the amount of Sfr necessary to purchase US$ 0.531 million at the spot offer rate. Column (F) shows the WB's effective Sfr cash flows after subtracting the amount of Sfr used to purchase US$ and cover the shortfall. The effective annual all-in Sfr cost to the WB is 8.07%—the internal rate of return of the Sfr flows in column (F). The quoted swap rates for the WB enabled it to reduce its annual all-in Sfr borrowing cost below its target rate of 8.10% by 3 bp.

For the Company, the bank related US$ LIBOR for the market swap rates and offered to pay annual Sfr 7.7% against receiving annual US$ 16.35%. The cash flows between the bank and the Company, calculated similarly to those between the bank and the WB, are shown in Exhibit 11. The cash flows to the bank from the swap, ignoring the foreign exchange transactions, appear in Exhibit 12.

BASIS POINTS CONVERSION

In practice, banks often use another technique to structure the swap flows, although the resulting all-in cost to the counterparty is usually quite close to the one calculated in the method described previously. For the sake of brevity, only the swap between the bank and the WB will be discussed, although the principles described are the same for the swap between the bank and the Company. Since the quoted swap rate paid to the WB was US$ 16.25% compared to the US$ 16.58% annual all-in cost of the bonds, there was a shortfall of US$ 33 bp. The bank converted the swap terms such that the US$ swap rate paid to WB would equal the US$ 16.58% annual all-in cost of the bonds by adding US$ 33 bp. With a higher US$ swap rate paid to the WB, the Sfr swap rate that the bank received also had to be increased. However, US$ 33 bp, paid annually over five years, was not equal to Sfr 33 bp. As the Sfr was at a forward premium to the US$, the amount of equivalent annual Sfr bp was smaller. The calculation of the conversion of US$ 33 bp to Sfr bp using the forward foreign exchange market is shown in Exhibit 13.

The easiest way to think about this computation is to first imagine issuing a hypothetical US$ 100 par bond with annual coupons of US$ 33 bp as shown in column (A). It is evident that the internal rate of return (IRR) on flows in column (A) is US$ 33 bp. Now imagine constructing a similar Sfr bond whose coupon payments will be equal to the Sfr equivalent of the US$ 33 bp converted at forward rates from columns (B) and (C). Since in the actual swap the bank will have to pay these extra US$ 33 bp to the WB, it will buy US$ forward against Sfr.[6] Therefore, we will use the forward offer rates shown in column (D) to calculate the size of the coupons in years one through five on our imaginary Sfr bond. Because the forward rates are not level, the coupons are not equal. For any bond, there is an amount of initial proceeds and the repayment of principal at maturity. In order to scale the size of the imaginary Sfr bond, we will use for convenience Sfr 2 per US$—the average of the spot bid-offer rates. Thus, the initial Sfr inflow on our imaginary par bond issue is Sfr 200 (Sfr 2 x US$ 100) as shown in column (E). In years one through five, there are unequal Sfr coupon payments. In year five, the Sfr 200 principal is repaid at par along with the coupon of Sfr 0.458 for a total disbursement of Sfr 200.458. The internal rate of return of the Sfr flows in column (E) is .27%, which means that US$ 33 bp are equal to Sfr 27 bp.

The effective swap rates, after converting excess US$ bp for Sfr bp, are calculated in Exhibit 14. The quoted US$ swap rate of 16.25% was increased by US$ 33 bp to US$ 16.58%, and the quoted Sfr swap rate of 7.8% was increased by Sfr 27 bp to Sfr 8.07%.

---

6   On the other hand, if the US$ swap rate had exceeded the all-in US$ cost of the bond issue, the bank would sell forward the extra US$ bp against Sfr at the forward bid rate.

These effective rates were used in Exhibit 15 to discount the required flows in years one through five in order to determine the initial swap amounts. In column (B), the required swap receipts of US$ 8 million for interest in years one through four, and the US$ 58 million for interest and principal in year five, were discounted at the effective US$ swap rate of 16.58%, resulting in an initial swap payment of US$ 49.063 million. By converting the quoted swap rate to the effective rate, the initial US$ swap payment exactly matched the net proceeds from the US$ bond because the internal rates of return for the two identical future flows were the same. For the Sfr swap flows shown in column (C), the required Sfr 7.35 million interest payments in years one through four, and the Sfr 107.35 million interest and principal payment in year five, were discounted at the effective Sfr swap rate of 8.07%, resulting in an initial receipt of Sfr 97.132 million. Since there was no shortfall (or excess) of US$ that would reduce (or increase) the Sfr initial swap proceeds, the all-in Sfr cost of the swap was merely 8.07%—the internal rate of return of the Sfr flows in column (C). Note that this is exactly the effective all-in Sfr cost shown in Exhibit 10, where we used the quoted swap rates as discount rates and covered the US$ initial swap payment shortfall with spot purchases from the Sfr initial swap proceeds. This had to be true because, in this case, the forward premium on Sfr was close to the interest rate differentials between US$ and Sfr.[7] Although the all-in costs associated with the cash flows were identical, the actual cash flows were not the same. The actual structure of cash flows is generally negotiable

---

7   The theoretical relationship of the outright forward Sfr rate to the spot rate with interest rate parity is:

$$(S/F) \times (1 + R(Sfr))^N = (1 + R(US\$))^N$$

Where

$$S = \text{spot Sfr rate against US\$}$$
$$F = \text{outright forward Sfr rate for term against US\$}$$
$$R(Sfr) = \text{annual Sfr interest rate for term}$$
$$R(US\$) = \text{annual US\$ interest rate for term}$$
$$N = \text{number of years in term}$$

This can be algebraically simplified to the following expression of the difference in interest rates:

$$[((1 + R(Sfr)/(1 + R(US\$)) -1] = [(F/S)^{1/N} - 1]$$

In this example, by using an average spot rate of Sfr 2.0000, an average forward rate of Sfr 1.3688, an average Sfr interest rate of 7.75%, and an average US$ interest rate of 16.39%, the results are quite close to parity:

$$[((1 + .0775)/(1 + .1630))] - 1 = ((1.3688/2.000)^{.2}) - 1) + \text{error}$$
$$-0.0735 = -0.0731 + \text{error}$$

provided the appropriate all-in costs are achieved. For this reason, most swap diagrams show the all-in costs associated with flows rather than absolute levels of flows or annual coupon rates. The swap diagram, showing the effective swap rates calculated earlier for the WB and those for the Company (not calculated), appears in Exhibit 16.

There is a quicker but less precise method than setting up the forward conversion table using an imaginary bond as shown in Exhibit 13 that bankers often use to roughly calculate the bp conversion rate between two currencies. In this shorthand method, the excess bp in one currency are discounted at the appropriate term interest rate in that currency and then are reannualized using the appropriate term interest rate in the second currency. In the WB example, the following calculations were made:

1. The US$33 bp were discounted for five years at 16.25%, the quoted US$ swap rate received by WB. This resulted in a present value of 107.425.
2. The 107.425 present value calculated in step 1 was then reannualized at 7.80%, the quoted Sfr swap rate that the WB paid. This equaled Sfr 27 bp.

The results from this shorthand calculation will always be close to those obtained using forward foreign exchange rates when the forward premium or discount for the period approximates the difference in interest rates.

COMBINATION CURRENCY AND INTEREST RATE SWAPS

Because of the large number of FRN issuers and borrowers using floating-rate syndicated loans, many swaps are structured where one counterparty receives US$ LIBOR against paying a fixed annual rate on a foreign currency. Often, the other counterparty wants to pay a fixed rate on US$ against receiving a fixed rate on a foreign currency. The bank must adjust the swap flows using both currency and interest rate swaps.

In order to illustrate a combination currency and interest rate swap, let's assume that a U.S. company (Company) wanted to raise US$ 100 million, 7-year, fixed-rate financing and, at the same time, a German bank wanted to raise DM 225.230 million (roughly the equivalent of US$ 100 million), seven-year, fixed-rate financing. Because of substantial US$ borrowings, the Company would have paid a semiannual all-in cost of 70 bp over seven-year U.S. Treasuries. With the Treasuries at 9.03%, the semiannual all-in cost on direct US$ borrowings would have been 9.73% or 9.97% on an annual basis. However, the Company had scarcity value in the Euro DM market and could issue DM bonds at an annual all-in cost of DM 6.50%. The German bank was a frequent borrower in DM and would have been forced to pay an annual all-in DM cost of 7.25%. On the other hand, it could issue a Eurodollar FRN at US$ LIBOR flat. One strategy would have been for each borrower to issue in the market in which it was relatively well received and hedge the debt with bank forwards into the desired currency. The result for the Company's DM bond hedged into US$ was an annual all-in cost of US$ 10.23% (see Exhibit 17), which was higher than the direct US$ borrowing cost. On the other hand, the German bank could have converted its semiannual US$ LIBOR payments into annual fixed US$ at 9.86% with an interest-rate swap (see Exhibit 8) and hedged these flows into an annual all-in cost of DM 6.97% (see Exhibit 18). However, because contracting for the currency forwards would have used up valuable credit lines with other banks, the German bank preferred to explore the costs of a swap.

As an alternative, an American bank offered to intermediate a swap between both the Company and the German bank. The seven-year annual swap rates, shown in Exhibit 9, were quoted as DM 6.7%–7% against US$ LIBOR and US$ 9.7%–9.86% against US$ LIBOR. (The US$ swap quote in Exhibit 9 is the same as shown in Exhibit 8 for US$ interest rate swaps.) The bank then arranged the following transactions:

1. The German bank issued an FRN at US$ LIBOR[8] and entered into a swap agreement with the bank at the quoted swap rates in which it received US$ LIBOR against paying DM 7%.

2. The Company issued a DM bond at an annual all-in cost of DM 6.5%, and the bank agreed to swap terms quoted as annual DM 6.7% against annual US$ 9.86%. However, the bank adjusted the swap terms so that it only paid DM 6.5% to cover the Company's debt service.

3. The bank contracted with a foreign exchange dealer (FX) to sell forward the extra DM 50 bp (the excess of the DM 7% received from the German bank over the DM 6.5% paid to the Company) against US$ bp (see Exhibit 19). The internal rate of return of the US$ flows indicated that annual DM 50 bp was equal to annual US$ 56 bp. The shorthand conversion method confirmed this result.

4. The bank reduced the US$ swap terms for the Company on a pro rata basis. The extra annual DM 20 bp (DM 6.7% quoted swap terms less DM 6.50% actually paid) were equal to annual US$ 22 bp (DM 20 bp/DM 50 bp x US$ 56 bp). Therefore, the Company paid annual US$ 9.64% to the bank (US$ 9.86% quoted swap rate less US$ 0.22%).

---

8 Most bank FRNs would actually have coupons of LIBOR plus some spread. In this case, the investment bank would need to adjust the quoted swap rates by increasing the US$ rate paid to the FRN issuer and increasing the foreign currency rate received. These extra US$ bp are converted into foreign currency bp in the fashion described in the previous section, although a slight adjustment must be made for the semiannual payment of the US$ bp spread over LIBOR.

5. The bank booked an interest-rate swap in which it exchanged annual US$ 9.86% against receiving US$ LIBOR. The US$ 9.86% consisted of annual US$ 9.64% paid by the Company and US$ 0.22 from the US$ 56 bp received from FX. The US$ LIBOR was paid to the German bank as described above in in the first transaction.

In this deal, the bank was left with a profit of annual US$ 34 bp (US$ 56 bp received from FX less US$ 22 bp used to subsidize the Company's US$ swap payment). Note that in this example, we did not even need to discuss actual cash flows to determine the all-in costs to either borrower. The annual all-in costs from the cash flows of the debt issues and the swaps are shown in Exhibit 20.

SUMMARY

Currency swaps can provide an attractive alternative to the use of bank forward foreign exchange contracts for long-dated currency cover. The primary use of currency swaps has been to hedge foreign currency debt. Many US$-based borrowers have issued foreign currency debt to (1) expand their investor base, (2) avoid ratings revisions that are often triggered with new U.S. debt, or (3) exploit arbitrage opportunities where it is less costly to issue debt denominated in foreign currencies and swap back into dollars. These arbitrage opportunities can persist in an age of modern financial markets because of several factors. Markets often become saturated with the paper from one borrower. This is often the case with supranationals, sovereigns, and state agencies seeking to issue debt in low-coupon currencies such as Sfr and DM. In this case, lower all-in costs can be achieved by issuing in the US$ market, finding a surrogate foreign currency borrower—such as a U.S. company—and swapping liabilities. Opportunities are also created when investors in certain countries use different techniques of credit assessment, such as emphasizing name recognition and other qualitative factors. For example, Swiss investors have been attracted to well-known corporate names, especially those that market consumer products, and are willing to pay a premium on bonds from these issuers. In many foreign capital markets, there is much less emphasis on quantitative analysis and credit ratings than in the US$ markets. Also, foreign markets typically demand lower spread differentials for lower credits. In response, many of these companies issued bonds in the yen market, where their debt ratios were well accepted, and swapped into US$ liabilities. Regulations can also make borrowing in one currency more attractive than another. The limitations on purchases by Japanese life insurance companies of foreign-issued bonds, for example, has led to tremendous demand for US$-denominated debt of Japanese resident companies that is excluded from this regulation (Sushi bonds). Because of this demand, Japanese resident borrowers issued US$ debt at lower-than-market rates and swapped back into yen at attractive all-in yen costs.

Currency swaps have also enabled borrowers to indirectly access debt markets that might have otherwise been difficult to tap. For example, the World Bank can indirectly increase its Sfr and DM liabilities by issuing dollars and swapping into these currencies. At this time, such swaps also allow the World Bank to preserve its access to these markets in the future. Other borrowers have used swaps to quickly incur liabilities in currencies where there is a long queue of borrowers waiting to be given permission by the monetary authorities to do capital markets issues.

Currency swaps have proven to be very flexible tools that do not need to be tied to capital markets issues. Companies have used these swaps to quickly transform the currency denomination of existing liabilities. The World Bank pursues a swap program to "fine-tune" its liability structure by actively swapping into and out of different currencies in order to achieve the lowest possible debt costs. Swaps can also be used to hedge anticipated future cash flows. This has led to "asset swaps" used by investors to transform the income on investments into different currencies.

Major international banks are now aggressively offering currency swaps and are often arranging deals before a matching counterparty has been located. Therefore, just as interest-rate swaps became a commodity, so will currency swaps. Banks are often willing to take currency swap positions onto their books until a matching counterparty can be found. While these positions are on their books, banks prefer to hedge their exposure by buying government bonds in the currencies in which they are contracted to pay fixed rates, or shorting government bonds in currencies in which they are contracted to receive fixed rates. It is relatively easy to hedge swaps in US$, Can$, sterling, and DM in this manner. In Sfr, where there are not adequate government bonds that can be used for hedging, banks have occasionally taken on unhedged positions because of the relative stability of Sfr interest rates and currency values. However, even when a counterparty is found, it is rare that the timing or the amount of future swap flows will exactly match. Therefore, the bank usually has future cash flow mismatches that also must be hedged. As these hedging techniques are perfected, one major impediment to continued strong growth of the foreign currency swap market—the ability to find a matching counterparty—will be overcome.

Exhibit 1 Annual All-in Costs of Cash Flows Associated with Currency Swap Between U.S. and German Company

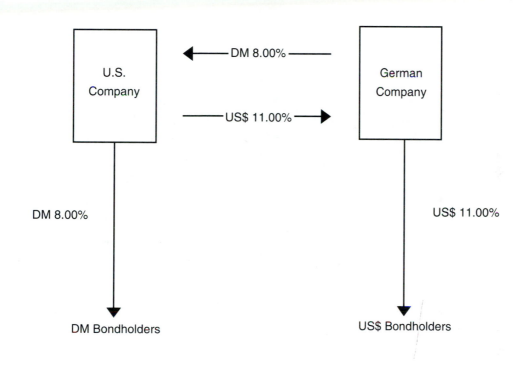

Exhibit 2   Cross-Currency Swaps Outstanding, 1992[a] (US$ billions)

Currency	$ Equivalent	% of Total
U.S. Dollar	619	35.95
Japanese Yen	309	17.94
Swiss Franc	139	8.07
Deutsche mark	107	6.21
Australian Dollar	96	5.57
Canadian Dollar	91	5.28
British Sterling	80	4.65
European Currency Unit	72	4.18
Italian Lira	44	2.56
Spanish Peseta	40	2.32
French Franc	32	1.86
Other Currencies	30	1.74
Swedish Krona	30	1.74
Dutch Guilder	15	.87
Belgium Franc	10	.58
New Zealand Dollar	4	.23
Danish Krone	3	.17
Hong Kong Dollar	1	.06
Total	1,722	

Source: ISDA
a. Counts both sides of swap agreement.

Exhibit 3   Fully Hedged Borrowings for World Bank and U.S. Company

				U.S. Company Sfr Bond Fully Hedged into US$			World Bank US$ Bond Fully Hedged into Sfr		
				Sfr Bond	100.00 M		US$	$50M	
				Fees	2.500%		Fees	1.875%	
				Coupon	7.35%		Coupon	16.00%	
	Sfr/US$ FX Rates		Sfr				US$		
			Bond	Conv.	US$		Bond	Conv.	Sfr
Year	Bid	Offer	Flow	Rate[a]	Flows		Flow	Rate[b]	Flows
	(A)	(B)	(C)	(D)	(E)		(F)	(G)	(H)
0	1.9995	2.0005	97.500	2.0005	48.738		49.063	1.9995	98.100
1	1470	1375	−7.350	1.8525	−3.968		−8.000	1.8630	−14.904
2	2850	2675	−7.350	1.7145	−4.287		−8.000	1.7330	−13.864
3	4150	3900	−7.350	1.5845	−4.639		−8.000	1.6105	−12.884
4	5375	5050	−7.350	1.4620	−5.027		−8.000	1.4955	−11.964
5	6500	6125	−107.350	1.3495	−79.548		−58.000	1.3880	−80.50
All-in costs (AIC):			7.98%		16.80%	16.58%			8.40%

a. Note that the conversion rate for year 0 is the offer rate as the U.S. company is selling Sfr while subsequent years are bid rates as the U.S. company is buying Sfr.
b. Note that the conversion rate for year 0 is the bid rate as the WB is buying Sfr while subsequent years are offer rates as the WB is selling Sfr.

Exhibit 4   Receipts (–Payments) from Bond Issue and Swaps for WB with Bank Intermediation

	World Bank's Receipts (– Payments)		
		Swap Flows with Bank	
	Flows on US$ Bond[a]	US$	Sfr
Year	(A)	(B)	(C)
0	49.063	–49.063	97.013
1	–8.000	8.000	–7.350
2	–8.000	8.000	–7.350
3	–8.000	8.000	–7.350
4	–8.000	8.000	–7.350
5	–58.000	58.000	–107.350
AIC:	16.58%	16.58%	8.10%

a. US$ 50 million, 1.875% fees and 16.00% coupon

Exhibit 5   Receipts (–Payments) from Bond Issue and Swaps with Bank Intermediation

	Company's Receipts (–Payments)		
	Flows on Sfr	Swap Flows with Bank	
	Year Bond[a]	US$	Sfr
Year	(A)	(B)	(C)
0	97.500	48.872	–97.500
1	–7.350	–8.000	7.350
2	–7.350	–8.000	7.350
3	–7.350	–8.000	7.350
4	–7.350	–8.000	7.350
5	–107.350	–58.000	107.350
AIC:	7.98%	16.70%	7.98%

a. Sfr 100 million, 2.500% fees and 7.35% coupon

Exhibit 6   Analysis of Receipts (–Payments) for Bank

| Year | Swap with WB | | Swap with Co. | | Net Cash Flows | |
| | US$ | Sfr | US$ | Sfr | US$ | Sfr |
	(A)	(B)	(C)	(D)	(E)	(F)
0	49.063	–97.013	– 48.872	97.500	0.190	0.487
1	–8.000	7.350	8.000	–7.350	0.000	0.000
2	–8.000	7.350	8.000	–7.350	0.000	0.000
3	–8.000	7.350	8.000	–7.350	0.000	0.000
4	–8.000	7.350	8.000	–7.350	0.000	0.000
5	–58.000	107.350	58.000	–107.350	0.000	0.000

Exhibit 7   Summary Diagram of Swap Between World Bank and Company with Bank Intermediation

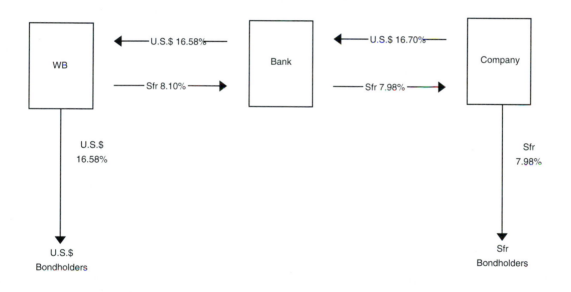

Exhibit 8   Interest-Rate Swap Indications: Fixed US$ Payments Against 6-Month US$ LIBOR

Year	Semiannual Quotations[a] Bid	Offer	Benchmark U.S. Treas. (%)	Semiannual Rates (%) Bid	Offer	Annual Rates (%) Bid[b]	Offer
3	T + 55	T + 73	8.24	8.79	8.97	8.98	9.17
5	T + 55	T + 70	8.66	9.21	9.36	9.42	9.58
7	T + 45	T + 60	9.03	9.48	9.63	9.70	9.86
10	T + 45	T + 60	9.21	9.66	9.81	9.89	10.05

Source: Morgan Guaranty Ltd., London
a. Semiannual basis point spread over benchmark Treasuries.
b. Rates are quoted from the bank's perspective—the bank will pay annual US$ 8.98% against receiving 6-month US$ LIBOR, or the bank will receive annual US$ 9.17% against paying six-month US$ LIBOR.

Exhibit 9   Foreign Currency Swap Indications on December 16: All Rates Are Against 6-Month US$ LIBOR

Currency	3 Years Pay[a] (%)	Receive (%)	5 Years Pay (%)	Receive (%)	7 Years Pay (%)	Receive (%)	10 Years Pay (%)	Receive (%)
Semiannual								
U.S. dollars	8.79	8.97	9.21	9.36	9.48	9.63	9.66	9.81
British sterling	11.18	11.38	11.14	11.34	11.08	11.28	11.20	11.40
Canadian dollars	9.46	9.66	9.81	10.01	9.97	10.17	10.13	10.33
Japanese yen	7.00	7.15	6.90	7.05	7.00	7.15	7.00	7.15
Swiss francs	5.04	5.28	5.28	5.52	5.48	5.72	5.57	5.82
Deutsche marks	5.72	6.01	6.35	6.64	6.59	6.88	6.83	7.07
Annual								
U.S. dollars	8.98	9.17	9.42	9.58	9.70	9.86	9.89	10.05
British sterling	11.49	11.70	11.45	11.66	11.39	11.60	11.51	11.72
Canadian dollars	9.68	9.89	10.05	10.26	10.22	10.43	10.39	10.60
Japanese yen	7.12	7.28	7.02	7.17	7.12	7.28	7.12	7.28
Swiss francs	5.10	5.35	5.35	5.60	5.56	5.80	5.65	5.90
Deutsche marks	5.80	6.10	6.45	6.75	6.70	7.00	6.95	7.19

Source: Morgan Guaranty Ltd., London
a. Rates are quoted from Bank's perspective—the bank will pay semiannual US$ 8.79% against receiving 6-month US$ LIBOR, or the bank will receive semiannual US$ 8.97% against paying 6-month US$ LIBOR.

Exhibit 10 Cash Flows of World Bank Swap Using Quoted Swap Rates World Bank Receipts (−Payments)

Year	From US$ Bond (A)[a]	Swap Flows with Bank US$ (B)[b]	Swap Flows with Bank Sfr (C)[c]	US$ Shortfall (D)[d]	Sfr Equiv. (E)[e]	Effective Sfr Flow for WB (F)[f]
0	49.063	−49.593	98.194	−0.531	−1.062	97.132
1	−8.000	8.000	−7.350			−7.350
2	−8.000	8.000	−7.350			−7.350
3	−8.000	8.000	−7.350			−7.350
4	−8.000	8.000	−7.350			−7.350
5	−58.000	58.000	107.350			−107.350
AIC:	16.58%	16.25%	7.80%			
Quoted swap rates:		16.25%	7.80%			
Effective all-in cost:						8.07%

a. Flows from US$ bond.
b. US$ swap flows with bank. Initial US$ payment is the present value of required debt service discounted at 16.25% quoted swap rate.
c. Sfr swap flows with bank. Initial Sfr receipt is the present value of required annual Sfr debt service of counterparty discounted at 7.8% quoted swap rate.
d. Difference between net US$ proceeds from bond issue in column (A) and initial US$ swap payment in column (B).
e. US$ shortfall in column (D) purchased with Sfr at offered rate of 2.0005 Sfr/US$.
f. Effective Sfr flows for WB after adjusting for FX purchase of initial US$ shortfall.

Exhibit 11   Cash Flows of U.S. Company Swap Using Quoted Swap Rates

U.S. Company Receipts (–Payments)

Year	From Sfr Bond (A)[a]	Swap Flows with Bank US$ (B)[b]	Sfr (C)[c]	Sfr Shortfall (D)[d]	US$ Equiv. (E)[e]	Effective US$ Flow for Company (F)[f]
0	97.500	49.432	–98.591	–1.091	–0.546	48.886
1	–7.350	–8.000	7.350			–8.000
2	–7.350	–8.000	7.350			–8.000
3	–7.350	–8.000	7.350			–8.000
4	–7.350	–8.000	7.350			–8.000
5	–107.350	–58.000	107.350			–58.000
AIC:	7.98%	16.35%	7.70%			
Quoted swap rates:		16.35%	7.70%			
Effective all-in cost:						16.69%

a. Flows from Sfr bond.
b. US$ swap flows with bank. Initial US$ receipt is the present value of required annual Sfr debt service of counterparty discounted at 16.35% quoted swap rate.
c. Sfr swap flows with bank. Initial Sfr payment is the present value of required debt service discounted at 7.7% quoted swap rate.
d. Difference between net Sfr proceeds from bond issue in column (A) and initial Sfr swap payment in column (C).
e. Sfr shortfall in column (D) purchased with US$ at bid rate of 1.9995 Sfr/US$.
f. Effective US$ flows for Company after adjusting for FX purchase of initial Sfr shortfall.

Exhibit 12 Cash Flows to (−from) Intermediary Bank

Year	Swap Flows with WB US$ (A)[a]	Sfr (B)[b]	Swap Flows with Company US$ (C)[c]	Sfr (D)[d]	Net Flows to Bank US$ (E)[e]	Sfr (F)[f]
0	49.593	−98.194	−49.432	98.591	0.161	0.397
1	−8.000	7.350	8.000	−7.350	0.000	0.000
2	−8.000	7.350	8.000	−7.350	0.000	0.000
3	−8.000	7.350	8.000	−7.350	0.000	0.000
4	−8.000	7.350	8.000	−7.350	0.000	0.000
5	−58.000	107.350	58.000	−107.350	0.000	0.000

a. Flows are equal and opposite to those in Exhibit 10, Column (B).
b. Flows are equal and opposite to those in Exhibit 10, Column (C).
c. Flows are equal and opposite to those in Exhibit 11, Column (B).
d. Flows are equal and opposite to those in Exhibit 11, Column (C).
e. Column (A) − Column (C).
f. Column (B) − Column (D).

Exhibit 13 Conversion of US$ 33 Basis Points to Sfr Basis Points

Year	Hypothetical U.S.$ Flows (A)	Sfr/US$ FX Rates Bid (B)	Offer (C)	Conv. Rate (D)	Hypothetical Sfr Flows (E)
0	100.000	1.9995	2.0005	2.0000	200.0000
1	−0.330	1470	1375	1.8630	0.6148
2	−0.330	2850	2675	1.7330	−0.5719
3	−0.330	4150	3900	1.6105	−0.5315
4	−0.330	5375	5050	1.4955	−0.4935
5	−0.330	6500	6125	1.3880	−200.458
	100.000			2.0000[a]	
IRR:	US$ 0.33%				Sfr 0.27%

a. Note that the "principal" repayment in year five is converted at the same Sfr 2.000/US$ as used at time zero. This is because we are trying to calculate the effective internal rate of return of the Sfr "coupons" in years one through five. If the year five forward rate were used to convert the "principal" repayment, the resulting Sfr year five cash flow would seriously distort the IRR for the Sfr "coupons."

Exhibit 14   Calculation of Effective Swap Rates

	US$	Sfr
Quoted Swap Rates	16.25%	7.80%
Add		
Dollar bp	0.33%	
Sfr bp		0.27%
Effective swap rates	16.58%	8.07%

Exhibit 15   Cash Flows of World Bank Swap with U.S. Company Using Effective Swap Rates

	World Bank Receipts (–Payments)		
		Swap Flows	
Year	From US$ Bond (A)	US$ (B)	Sfr (C)
0	49.063	–49.063	97.132
1	–8.000	8.000	–7.350
2	–8.000	8.000	–7.350
3	–8.000	8.000	–7.350
4	–8.000	8.000	–7.350
5	–58.000	58.000	–107.350
AIC:	16.58%	16.58%	8.07%

Exhibit 16 Swap Between World Bank and U.S. Company Using Effective Swap Rates

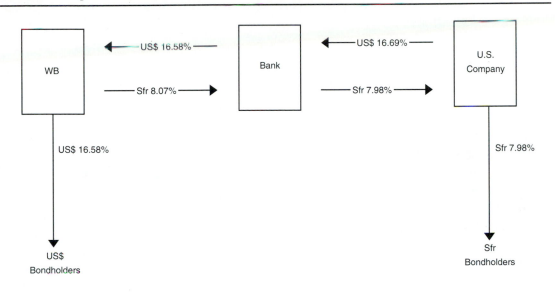

Exhibit 17 Indirect Financing Alternative for U.S. Company[a] on December 16

Year	DM Cash Flow (mil.)	DM FX Rates		Conv. Rate	US$ Cash Flow (mil.)
		Bid	Offer		
0	220.725	2.5225	2.5235	2.5235	87.468
1	−13.795	755	735	2.4470	−5.638
2	−13.795	1672	1472	2.3553	−5.857
3	−13.795	2598	2198	2.2627	−6.097
4	−13.795	3300	2800	2.1925	−6.292
5	−13.795	4000	3400	2.1225	−6.500
6	−13.795	4701	3881	2.0524	−6.722
7	−239.025	5402	4362	1.9823	−120.580
Annual					
All-in costs:	6.50%				10.23%
Semiannual all-in costs:					9.98%

a. Assumes a DM 225.23 million, 7 year issue with an annual coupon of 6.125% and fees of 2.0% fully hedged into US$.

Exhibit 18   Indirect Financing Alternative for German Bank[a] on December 16

Year	US$ Cash Flow (mil)	Interest Rate Swap Rec'd from Bank	Paid to Bank	Fixed Rate US$	DM FX Rates Bid	Offer	Conv. Rate	DM Flows (mil)
0	99.500			99.5	2.5225	2.5235	2.5225	250.989
0.5	–LIBOR	LIBOR						
1	–LIBOR	LIBOR	–9.86	–9.86	755	735	2.4500	–24.157
1.5	–LIBOR	LIBOR						
2	–LIBOR	LIBOR	–9.86	–9.86	1672	1472	2.3763	–23.430
2.5	–LIBOR	LIBOR						
3	–LIBOR	LIBOR	–9.86	–9.86	2598	2198	2.3037	–22.714
3.5	–LIBOR	LIBOR						
4	–LIBOR	LIBOR	–9.86	–9.86	3300	2800	2.2435	–22.121
4.5	–LIBOR	LIBOR						
5	–LIBOR	LIBOR	–9.86	–9.86	4000	3400	2.1835	–21.529
5.5	–LIBOR	LIBOR						
6	–LIBOR	LIBOR	–9.86	–9.86	4701	3881	2.1354	–21.055
6.5	–LIBOR	LIBOR						
7	–LIBOR	LIBOR	–9.86	– 109.86	5402	4362	2.0873	–229.311
	–100							
Annual all-in cost:								6.97%

a. US$ 100.000 million, seven-year FRN, LIBOR coupon, .50% fees swapped into fixed US$ at 9.86% vs. six-month US$ LIBOR and fully hedged into DM.

Exhibit 19 Conversion of DM 50 Basis Points into US$ Basis Points Using Forward Markets

| Year | DM Flows | DM FX Rates | | Conv. Rate | US$ Flows |
		Bid	Offer		
0	−100.000	2.5225	2.5235	2.5230	−39.635
1	0.500	755	735	2.4500	.204
2	0.500	1672	1472	2.3763	.210
3	0.500	2598	2198	2.3037	.217
4	0.500	3300	2800	2.2435	.222
5	0.500	4000	3400	2.1835	.228
6	0.500	4701	3881	2.1354	.234
7	0.500	5402	4362	2.0873	39.875
	100.000			2.5230	
IRR:	DM 0.50%				US$ 0.56%

Using Shorthand Method

1. DM 50 bp discounted for seven years at 7.00% equals 270.
2. 270 reannualized over seven years at 9.90% is approximately US$ 56 bp.

Exhibit 20   Annual All-In Costs on Cash Flows of U.S. Company-German Bank Combination Foreign Currency and Interest-Rate Swaps and Capital Markets Issues

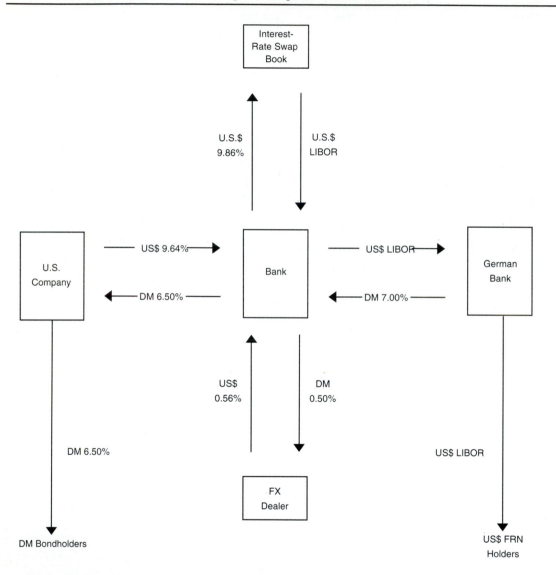

AMERICAN BARRICK RESOURCES CORPORATION: MANAGING GOLD PRICE RISK

During 1992 the financial team of Toronto-based American Barrick Resources Corporation, one of the world's fastest growing and most financially successful gold-mining concerns, met regularly to review strategic and tactical issues related to managing the firm's exposure to gold price risk. Many major gold mines prided themselves on hedging none of the price risk of their output. If unhedged, a gold mine's sole output, and hence its profits, cash flows, and stock price, were tied to gyrations in the price of gold. However, American Barrick had in place a gold-hedging program that was an integral and much publicized part of the firm's corporate strategy. In an environment of falling gold prices, the firm's hedge position had allowed it to profit handsomely and to sell its commodity output at prices well above market rates. For example, in 1992, American Barrick produced and sold over 1,280,000 ounces of gold at an average price of $422 per ounce, while the market price was about $345 per ounce.[1]

American Barrick's gold-hedging program, and indeed all the corporate finance and treasury functions of the $4 billion market capitalization enterprise, were managed by a trio of relatively young but experienced financial executives: Gregory Wilkins (executive vice president and chief financial officer), Robert Wickham (vice president, finance), and Randall Oliphant (treasurer). Messrs. Wickham and Oliphant were responsible for the day-to-day management of American Barrick's highly regarded hedging program, and they reported to and worked closely with Mr. Wilkins. Gregory Wilkins and Robert Wickham had been with the firm since its startup, and Randall Oliphant had joined the firm in 1987.

---

1   All figures in this case are expressed in U.S. dollars unless otherwise noted.

Peter Tufano wrote this case with the assistance of Jon Serbin as the basis of class discussion.

The gold-hedging program was a distinguishing and permanent characteristic of the firm's strategy, and there was no discussion of abandoning the activity. Nevertheless, the implementation of the hedging program raised a number of issues, and American Barrick's latest gold find, the Meikle Mine, naturally brought to the forefront questions of when, how much, and how to hedge its gold production. The recently announced Meikle Mine Development Project required capital investments exceeding $180 million and was projected to yield 400,000 ounces of gold annually for 11 years beginning in 1996.

In addition, the processing of unexpectedly rich ore bodies would increase production to a level much higher than was anticipated. While this development was good news, the firm's output would then be hedged far less than planned. Putting on a new hedge position in an environment of low gold prices and low interest rates challenged the finance team's ingenuity and commitment to its hedging program.

AMERICAN BARRICK RESOURCES CORPORATION

Peter Munk, a successful Canadian entrepreneur and financier, was the chairman, chief executive officer, and founder of American Barrick. Although he had had no prior experience in the gold-mining business, he had created and guided one of the world's premier and fastest growing gold-mining firms. From its entry into the gold-mining business in 1983, American Barrick had grown from an equity market capitalization of $46 million to about $5 billion by the end of 1992, which ranked it as Canada's eighth largest publicly traded company. From 1984 to 1992 its annual production grew from 34,000 ounces to 1.325 million ounces, and its proven and probable reserves increased from 322,000 ounces to nearly 26 million ounces.

American Barrick's growth came in part through almost annual acquisitions, coupled with good fortune in finding gold on its acquired properties. In 1983 the company purchased interests in small Canadian and Alaskan mines. The next year it purchased an interest in the Pinson Mine in Nevada and acquired the Camflo Mine, which would produce more than 30,000 ounces annually. The Camflo acquisition provided American Barrick with a skilled technical and engineering staff, including Robert Smith, American Barrick's president and chief operating officer since 1985. Camflo almost tripled Barrick's reserve base. In 1985, American Barrick made an even larger acquisition, purchasing the Mercur Mine near Salt Lake City, Utah, from Texaco, Inc. In late 1986 and early 1987, it purchased the Goldstrike Mine and surrounding properties in Nevada. At the time it acquired Goldstrike, reserves on the property were estimated to be about 600,000 ounces. Over the following years, Barrick discovered additional reserves on its Goldstrike property, and by 1992 reserves on the property were estimated to be 20.1 million ounces, and its annual production was approximately 1.1 million ounces. American Barrick's growth was expected to continue through the 1990s as the firm began to look overseas for additional mines. Exhibit 1 gives information on the firm's operations since its inception.

American Barrick was not only fast growing but also quite profitable. It generated large operating cash flows, which it continued to invest in its mines (see Exhibit 2). Its rising profitability, despite the drop in gold prices, came from a variety of sources. American Barrick acquired its gold mines for relatively low prices when gold prices were depressed in the mid-1980s, and it later found massive reserves in Goldstrike that enabled it to enjoy scale economies. In its Mercur Mine the company was able to cut expenses and increase production to capacity, thus increasing profits. Finally, the firm's gold price management program enabled it to sell its output at above-market prices and to profit while other firms could not. Exhibit 3 provides comparative financial data on American Barrick and its major North American rivals for 1991.

From the outset, American Barrick's mission was set by Mr. Munk's vision. In the early 1980s, he had sensed a demand by European and North American investors for holding gold stocks without the political risks of holding South African investments. In its first annual report as a publicly owned firm, American Barrick expressed its intention to meet this need: "The corporate strategy is to acquire or develop a diversity of gold-producing interests exclusively in North America."[2] It immediately listed its shares in Toronto, Montreal, and the United States, later adding listings in London, Paris, Zurich, Geneva, and Basel.

A second tenet of the American Barrick strategy was to maintain conservative financial policies by issuing little debt and by moderating the firm's gold price risk. The firm's insistence on bearing low financial risk was attributed to an earlier failed business experience by Mr. Munk and his subsequent distrust of high leverage. It also flowed from his stated belief in the benefits of flexibility: "Our financial strength not only ensures our existing development plans, it will allow us to take advantage of the decade's opportunities." American Barrick's subsequent growth necessitated greater amounts of leverage, but in his 1991 letter to shareholders, Mr. Munk continued to emphasize the importance of having a "strong, liquid balance sheet."

In his original conception, an integral element of financial conservatism was to moderate, although not completely eliminate, American Barrick's exposure to gold price risk. He felt that target investors would be interested in a gold mining firm that lowered the risk of movements in gold prices. American Barrick's appeal would be its positioning as a

---

2   As of 1992, all properties of American Barrick were in North America, although it contemplated looking abroad.

well-run, low-cost commodity producer, willing to sacrifice potential profits from gold price peaks in order to level out potential losses in the troughs. Investors might desire some exposure to gold prices, but they would want this exposure managed prudently.

In general terms, there are three ways to moderate risk: by diversifying it, selling (or hedging) it, or insuring against it.[3] Given its clear focus on being a gold-mining firm, American Barrick could not diversify away its gold price risk. It could, and did, sell (hedge) and insure against its risk. Its earliest efforts to manage price risk involved selling the risk to others; its later efforts used insurance strategies. While American Barrick had a conservative financial orientation with regard to the level of its indebtedness and the price risk it was willing to bear, it was adept at using innovative financing techniques and instruments to finance itself and manage the firm's financial risk.

By 1992 it would appear that Mr. Munk had communicated the unique features of American Barrick to shareholders. The firm's shares were held by European, Canadian, and U.S. investors.[4] Shareholders included many investors who shied away from traditional gold-mining investments:

> Barrick's investor base has now broadened to include institutions that traditionally avoid gold investments. They invest in Barrick because it has an excellent track record, an expectation for future growth, a recognized, proven management team and a strong balance sheet.[5]

Finally, the market seemed to respond positively to American Barrick; its stock outperformed the market and other major gold-mining firms (see Exhibit 4).

---

3   See R.C. Merton, *Operation and Regulation in Financial Intermediaries: A Functional Perspective* (Stockholm: Economic Council, 1993) for additional insights into the general treatment of managing risk. To define these three terms, Merton gives the example of the owner of a ship. To manage the risk of loss, a ship owner can (1) diversify by buying a portfolio of ships to avoid a complete loss if one ship sinks; (2) sell (or hedge) the ship and have no economic exposure to its subsequent outcome; or (3) buy an insurance policy that pays off if the ship sinks, but allows the ship owner to profit if it does not. Merton uses the term *hedging* to mean entering into a position such that the payoff is the same regardless of the outcome, which could be accomplished through selling the ship today or entering into a binding forward contract to sell it at some point in the future. In common usage, as at American Barrick, the term *hedging* often refers to risk management activities broadly defined.

4   An important group of American Barrick shareholders comprised its managers and directors. At the end of 1991, the officers and directors as a group owned directly or indirectly 31.2 million shares, with options to purchase an additional 4.1 million shares. At December 31, 1991, there were 140.9 million shares outstanding. The closing price per share on December 31, 1991, was $27.875. In 1992, there were 141.9 million shares, of which officers and directors owned 29.6 million. The closing price per share on December 31, 1992, was $31.00.

5   "Letter to shareholders," American Barrick Resources Corporation, 1991 annual report, p. 5.

GOLD

While the current primary "uses" of gold were for jewelry (80% of current use) and for industrial and commercial applications such as dentistry and electronics, to understand gold one must appreciate its unique historical role in the international economy as a currency and as a purported hedge against political instability and inflation. Archaeologists have found evidence that gold served as money as early as 2000 B.C., although the use of gold as metallic money is generally traced to its use in Greece in the seventh century B.C. Over the next 3000 years, gold served as a currency and as backing for paper money. In the late nineteenth century, the relation between money and gold was one of great political importance. William McKinley, U.S. presidential candidate and supporter of a gold standard, defeated his opponent, William Jennings Bryan, who insisted that defining currency in terms of gold content would "crucify mankind upon a cross of gold." Debates over the proper role of gold in a macroeconomy, and its impact on real growth, inflation, and deflation have preoccupied politicians, bankers, and economists for centuries.

In 1992, gold no longer played the central role it once did in the world economy, and hence central banks no longer needed to back up their currency with gold reserves. Freed of requirements to hold gold and aware of the profitability of selling or lending gold, central banks had begun to sell gold. From 1968 to 1991 central bank holdings of gold fell from 886 million ounces to 726 million ounces, a drop of nearly 20%.[6] Canada, Belgium, and the Netherlands announced outright sales of their gold, and other governments saw opportunities to earn profits on their gold reserves through gold lending and participating in the swaps and options markets. Many metals analysts predicted that sales by the official sector would depress the real price of gold, even though industrial demand for gold was projected to outstrip the new supply created by mines.

Some analysts and investors viewed gold as an inflation hedge and a store of value. It was argued that in times of economic and political instability, investors demand gold, driving up its price. It was also commonly held that in times of inflation the purchasing power of gold increases while that of money decreases. Unfortunately, academic research failed to bear out this conventional wisdom. Gold appeared to be an ineffective hedge against inflation and political uncertainty in short and medium horizons, but it may have been effective over long horizons and against cataclysmic events.[7]

---

6 See Paul H. Zink, *The North American Gold Industry: A Market in Transition*, J. P. Morgan Securities Inc., Equity Research, July 1, 1992.

7 See E. J. Sherman, *Gold Investment: Theory and Application* (New York: Prentice-Hall, 1986), and Roy W. Jastram, *The Golden Constant: The English and American Experience, 1560-1976* (New York: Wiley, 1977).

Exhibit 5 plots the price of gold in nominal and real terms, along with the inflation rate, from 1980 to 1992. In the two decades prior to 1992, the price of gold fluctuated from a low of $24 per ounce in 1971 to above $850 per ounce in the early 1980s. Prices slid through much of the 1980s, with an upturn around the stock market correction of 1987. Since then, gold prices declined steadily, although daily prices remained quite volatile. Research has shown that gold prices are likely to have more extreme movements, both up and down, than other assets and that positive returns are likely to be followed by subsequent positive returns.[8]

Some analysts predicted that gold would become increasingly commodity-like, enjoying only modest nominal price increases and real price declines. However, large global government deficits might lead countries to monetize their deficits and incite inflationary fears, driving up the demand for gold. Political instability in both South Africa and the former Soviet Union, whose mines produced 35% of world output, could disrupt supplies of gold. Some commentators voiced fears that the massive sales of gold for future delivery by bullion dealers and mines, taken in aggregate, would continue to depress current prices.[9] Finally, it was always possible that a major new gold field would be found, as in the gold rushes of California (1848), Australia (1851), and South Africa (1886).

GOLD PRODUCERS AND PRODUCTION

As producers of commodity products, gold-mining firms had virtually no marketing or distribution costs. There was always a ready market for their product, at market prices, once extracted from the earth and refined. Therefore, a gold mine's profits were a function of the quantity of its production and the difference between the prices at which it sold its output and its costs.

Over the long term, one gold producer can have a competitive advantage over others based on its costs of gold production, driven by the physical features of its gold deposit and the efficiency of the firm's operations. Mines with gold closer to the surface, with ores richer in gold, and with ore in physical forms more amenable to recovery have natural cost advantages over others. Large amounts of ore must be mined, whether in open pits or underground shafts, and then processed to extract small quantities of gold. For example, the ore in American Barrick's Goldstrike Mine contained an estimated .127 ounces of gold for each ton of ore, meaning that to produce a single ounce of gold that might sell for

---

8   See R. Aggarwal and L. Soenen, "The Nature and Efficiency of Gold Markets," *Journal of Portfolio Management* 14(3), Spring 1988, pp. 18-21, and R. Aggarwal and P. S. Sundararaghavan, "The Efficiency of the Silver Futures Market." *Journal of Banking and Finance* 11, March 1987, pp. 1-16.

9   See K. Gooding, "Financial Engineering Tames the Gold Market," *Financial Times*, July 26, 1991, p. 24.

$300-$400, American Barrick would need to mine and process almost 16,000 pounds of rock. Once mined, the ore was treated by a combination of processes that included crushing the ore, heating it, sorting by density, chemically treating it, and finally refining to remove impurities. Both mining and processing were costly activities. For example, at Goldstrike, mining and processing costs were roughly equal in magnitude, and costs of mining and processing varied directly with the amount of ore mined and processed.

In the short term, mining firms have a limited ability to adjust production to changes in the price of gold. They can slightly adjust their rate of mining, or they may be able to choose which ore grade to mine and process. For instance, an open pit mine may be able to stockpile ores, allowing the producer to adjust the grade of ore processed depending on market conditions, and underground mines typically have greater flexibility to select the grade of ore they will mine and process. At the extreme, a mining firm can choose to shut down a mine, but practical concerns (e.g., mine floodings) can make this decision nearly irreversible. American Barrick's policy was to mine and produce as much gold as quickly as possible; thus its production decisions were not affected by the market price of gold.

The differences among the major producers in the natural endowments of their mines and the economic efficiency of their operations combined to make marginal costs of production vary widely in the industry (see Exhibit 3). Gold mines also needed to make large fixed or sunk costs. The geology and economics of gold mining required firms to invest large sums of money to create the infrastructure necessary to dig and process the ore. For example, the Meikle Mine, American Barrick's newest ore deposit, was projected to demand a capital investment of $180 million (in 1992 U.S. dollars) spread out over 4 years. The incremental capital investments of this particular project were relatively low, for the new mine lay only one mile north of the firm's Goldstrike properties and could use the same processing and maintenance facilities, and access roads.

Once at full production, the Meikle Mine was expected to produce 400,000 ounces of gold per year for 11 years. If there were no financial contracts by which American Barrick could lock in, or at least set bounds on, the prices at which it could sell the output of the Meikle Mine, the expected value of the project could fluctuate widely. Fortunately, the gold industry had at its disposal a wide range of contracts to manage risk, ranging from indexed borrowings to esoteric options. According to analysts of gold-mining firms, American Barrick was not only one of the most active users of these opportunities but also one of the most adept.

THE DIVERSITY OF RISK
MANAGEMENT PRACTICES IN THE GOLD INDUSTRY

The level, type, and horizon of risk management activities varied considerably among gold-mining firms. Australian producers were early and heavy users of risk management vehicles, North American firms tended to use fewer risk management contracts, and South African producers managed little of their price risk. For example, according to estimates by one leading gold analyst, by the end of 1991, Australian producers had hedged 17 months of production, North Americans 9.6 months, and South Africans under 4 months.[10]

Among North American producers, there was a wide range of risk management policies and practices. Exhibit 6 gives aggregated information about the risk management activities of the North American producers over time. Exhibit 7 gives survey results showing the risk management activities, as of the end of 1991, of North American producers by level of production. Exhibit 8 gives details on the risk management activities of the top 11 North American firms.

The degree to which firms managed their output price exposure was well tracked, and firms differentiated themselves on the basis of these policies. At one extreme stood large producers like Homestake, which engaged in no risk management activities whatsoever and justified this policy in public statements:

> So that its shareholders might capture the full benefit of increases in the price of gold, Homestake does not hedge its gold production. As a result of this policy, Homestake's earnings are more volatile than those of many other gold producers. The company believes that its shareholders will achieve maximum benefit from such a policy over the long term.[11]

At the other end of the spectrum stood American Barrick, for which managing gold price risk was an integral part of business and one of the firm's four stated business objectives. The value of managing price risk to shareholders was made clear in Peter Munk's letter to shareholders:

> Our unique gold-hedging program gives American Barrick extraordinary financial stability. It protects us from the impact of dips in the gold price, allows us to plan our cash flows with confidence, and, in combination with our rising production, offers investors a predictable, rising earnings profile in the future.[12]

---

10 Ted Reeve, *Global Gold Hedge Survey*, First Boston Equity Research, February 19, 1992.

11 Homestake, 1990 annual report.

12 American Barrick Resources Corporation, 1991 annual report.

Between these two extremes lie a wide variety of firms whose policies evolved over time. For example, in 1990 the management of Battle Mountain Gold announced a major change in policy:

> The company expects to hedge up to 25 percent . . . of its first six months' gold production in 1991. This change in strategy was not taken lightly. We have long held the belief that investors appreciate a gold equity which does not cap upside potential in gold price rallies. However, a recent study of the market indicates that there may now be a share price premium, rather than penalty, for hedging.[13]

Finally, there were hybrid arrangements where investors could choose to buy shares in identical mines, differing mainly in the degree to which they were protected against gold price movement. For instance, investors could buy the stock of Newmont Gold, which engaged in no gold price risk management. Yet Newmont Gold was 90% owned by Newmont Mining, whose shares were also traded publicly and which managed part of its gold price risk.

VEHICLES FOR MANAGING GOLD PRICE RISK

American Barrick's hedging program evolved over the corporation's ten-year history and used a wide range of tools to manage gold price risk. With gold financings, forward sales, options strategies, and spot deferred contracts, American Barrick shed some of its gold price risk while maintaining flexibility to profit from rising gold prices.

GOLD FINANCINGS

Before 1986, most of American Barrick's gold price management activities were incorporated in financings for its mines. In 1983, it funded its purchase of the Renabie Gold Mine in northern Ontario by issuing common shares, but then needed an additional $18 million for capital expenditures to develop the mine. To fund this expansion in February 1984, it raised $17 million through an innovative vehicle, the Barrick-Cullaton Gold Trust. Marketed in Canada and Europe, this trust was the first publicly traded gold royalty trust in Canada. The gold trust paid investors 3% of the mine's output when the price of gold was at or below $399 per ounce, rising to 10% of production when gold was at $1,000 per ounce. In its first annual report, American Barrick explained what it believed to be the win-win nature of this financing:

> The investor benefits not only from increased volumes of gold to the Trust but also from increased gold price. Barrick shareholders benefit from the low cost development funds for mine expansion today and only pay increased royalties in future if there are future gold price increases.

---

13   Battle Mountain, 1990 annual report.

The firm used a related structure to raise $40 million for its Camflo Mine in 1984.[14]

American Barrick's next two large acquisitions used bullion loans and gold-indexed Eurobond offerings to raise capital. To fund the acquisition of the Mercur Mine in 1985, the firm entered into a bullion loan with Toronto Dominion Bank, in which it received 77,000 ounces of gold, which it immediately sold on the market for net proceeds of $25 million. Over the next $4\frac{1}{2}$ years, American Barrick was to repay the loan in monthly installments in ounces of gold at an interest rate of about 2% per year.[15] The bullion loan was collateralized by the assets of the mine, valued at $54.3 million, and a guarantee by American Barrick. In addition, American Barrick was required to make accelerated deliveries to the lender equal to 50% of the cash flow from the mine after deducting approved capital expenditures and mandatory deliveries for the preceding year.[16] As part of its massive capital needs to fund Goldstrike and its other properties' capital needs, American Barrick raised funds through additional bullion loans collateralized by its mines. Its 1,050,000 ounce bullion gold loan used to finance Goldstrike Mine was the largest gold loan in the world at the time. As of the end of 1992, gold loans in place required the firm to deliver the following ounces of gold: in 1993, 33,750 ounces; in 1994, 224,063 ounces; in 1995, 213,125 ounces; and in 1996 through 1997, 315,000 ounces.

American Barrick also raised funds through gold-indexed underwritten offerings. In February 1987, when gold was about $400 per ounce, the firm offered $50 million in 2% gold-indexed notes to Euromarket investors, who were typically European fund managers who purchased the issue either for their own accounts or for their clients. Investors paid $1,308 per note and received annual interest payments of $26.16. In addition, the investors were entitled to redeem the notes at any time between February 26, 1988, and February 26, 1992. If redeemed at the first possible opportunity, the holder could choose to receive an amount of cash or gold bullion whose value equaled 3.2150 ounces of gold. This redemption amount increased over time so that if it were held to maturity, the investor would receive 3.3804 ounces of gold. Unlike bullion loans, this offering was not collateralized by the firm's mines, whose production had been pledged as collateral for its bullion loans.

---

14   In the Camflo transaction, investors got a return of 8% when the gold price was $365 per ounce, and this rate increased or decreased 1% for each $35 change in the price of gold to a maximum of $1,500 per ounce.

15   In 1988, the company retired this gold loan when it entered into a 125,000 ounce revolving gold loan with a term of 7 years. This loan, collateralized by the assets of the Mercur Mine, required payment of interest at .75% over the gold lease rate, and was amortized over 7 years with quarterly payments.

16   In 1986 the mandatory payments on this loan were 9,282 ounces, and the accelerated payments were 7,937 ounces.

FORWARD SALES

In a forward sale of gold, a party commits to deliver a specified quantity of gold, at a specific date, for a price set at the beginning of a contract. Before the termination of the contract, no money changes hands. Forward contracts are private over-the-counter transactions between principals, typically for 10,000 ounces or more, and their terms, such as the maturity of the contract and the size of the transaction, can be tailored by the contracting parties. Most forward contracts do not trade before delivery, although the parties are free to close out their positions through a negotiated settlement. As a practical matter, forward sales are usually for relatively short delivery periods of under a few years.[17]

In most markets, forward sellers receive a premium (commonly called contango) above the current gold price. For example, when gold prices are $350 per ounce, 1 ounce sold for delivery in 1 year might be priced at $367.50, a premium or contango of 5%. In effect, by contracting today to deliver gold in 1 year, the forward seller earns a guaranteed 5% rate of return.

Contango is equal to the difference between the interest rate for lending dollars and the interest rate for lending gold, called the gold lease rate. If the gold lease rate is 2% per year and the current price of gold is $350, someone who lends 1 ounce of gold today will be paid back that ounce plus $7 in cash ($350 × 2%) at the end of the year. If the 1-year dollar lending rate is 7% and the 1-year gold leasing rate is 2%, then the contango or premium for selling gold forward is defined to be 5% per year. In this example, if spot gold prices (for immediate delivery) are $350, and a forward contract is struck for delivery in 1 year, the price for forward delivery at the end of 1 year would be $350 × (1 + .05) = $367.50. If the forward price differed from $367.50, bullion dealers and others could earn arbitrage profits. Exhibit 9 shows the gold lease rate, the dollar interest rate, and contango over time.

A sharp drop in gold prices in 1984 and 1985 led to the first explicit forward sales of gold at American Barrick. As prices fell to levels equal to the firm's estimated break-even, and threatened to fall even further, the company's profitability was jeopardized. In reaction, American Barrick sold forward about 20,000 ounces in 1984 to protect itself against possible continued declines in gold prices. The gold market soon recovered and prices rose. The forward sales proved costly in hindsight, for the firm lost the opportunity to sell at the higher market prices. Nevertheless, this experience sparked new interest in using the

---

17 Futures contracts on gold also exist, although American Barrick and other mining firms did not use them in their hedging programs. These futures contracts trade on exchanges such as COMEX. Unlike forward contracts, futures contracts are "marked to market" on a daily basis, requiring daily transfers of funds among the parties. The longest traded futures contract has a maturity of approximately 4 years, although contracts with delivery dates of more than 2 years traded infrequently.

financial markets to manage gold price risk, and Mr. Wickham (treasurer at that time) began to study ways to protect the firm against adverse price movements using forward sales and option strategies. Exhibit 10 shows the firm's forward sales of gold from 1984 through 1992.

OPTIONS AND WARRANTS

As its forward selling in 1984 and 1985 demonstrated, hedging eliminated American Barrick's downside exposure but also its ability to benefit if prices rose. Beginning in 1987, it began to experiment with insurance strategies that could mitigate the risk of price declines while allowing the firm to retain some of the benefits of rising prices. In 1987 the firm bought and sold options to manage the price risk of its ever-growing production.

In executing a "collar" strategy (also known as a participating min/max program or a bull spread), the firm simultaneously bought put options and sold call options on gold.[18] The calls and puts had the same maturity, but the exercise price of the puts was below that of the calls. The options were purchased in the over-the-counter market from one of American Barrick's 15 trading partners.[19] By using the premiums received from the sale of calls to purchase puts, a collar strategy required no initial cash outlay, which made it more acceptable to the firm's board of directors.

By adjusting the exercise prices and ratios of puts and calls, American Barrick could determine the degree to which it chose to participate in gold price rises. For example, market prices might allow it to buy one put with an exercise price of $420 per ounce and sell one call at $550 per ounce, financing the purchase of the put exactly by the sale of the call, because the two options had the same premium. This pair of market-prices contracts would effectively set a minimum price of $420 from American Barrick's perspective. Between $420 and $550, it would capture all the upside of increases in the price of gold. Above $550, it would enjoy none of the increases in gold prices. Instead of selling one call with an exercise price of $550, the prevailing market prices for gold options might permit it to sell .5 calls with an exercise price of $485 and receive the same premium. Then, it would benefit fully from all price increases between $420 and $485 and would enjoy half of all increases above $485.

---

18 A put option gives the holder the right to sell an asset on a certain date for a prespecified exercise price. A call option gives its holder the right to buy an asset on a certain date for a prespecified exercise price.

19 Alternatively, it could have bought and sold gold options (and options on gold futures) on a number of organized exchanges, including the COMEX (N.Y.), the European Options Exchange (Amsterdam), and the London International Financial Futures Exchange. Exchange-traded gold options have maturities under 1 year.

Exhibit 11 shows American Barrick's option portfolio over time. As the firm became more comfortable with options, its positions grew. But as spot prices declined, it lowered the call strike price and the put/call ratio of its collar positions so as not to allow its floor level to drop. This meant that the firm had to surrender more of the upside potential to protect against drops in gold price. Furthermore, the over-the-counter market in which it transacted with other principals rarely wrote options contracts longer than 5 years, and the market was liquid only for contracts with maturities under 2 years. This horizon was far shorter than the 20 years of expected production currently in reserve. In 1990 the firm stopped adding new options positions, and began to use spot deferred contracts extensively.

SPOT DEFERRED CONTRACTS

A spot deferred contract (SDC) was a type of forward sale of gold. In a standard forward sale, a delivery date is set, and on that date the forward seller delivers gold to the buyer at the prearranged forward price. In an SDC, there are multiple delivery dates, with the final one being 5 or 10 years after the initiation of the contract. The SDC seller chooses on which of these rollover dates it will deliver the gold and has the right to defer the delivery until the end of the contract. Ultimately, the SDC seller must deliver the quantity of gold called for in the contract, but it has a choice when to deliver it.

At the initiation of a spot deferred contract with 1-year delivery or rollover dates, the prices paid for delivery were set only for the first rollover date. Gold that American Barrick delivered at the end of the first year would be paid the 1-year forward price. At that rollover date, American Barrick could deliver on the contract (if the contract price was higher than spot), or it could roll the contract forward to the next period and sell the gold in the spot market. If it chose the latter alternative, no money or gold would change hands between the SDC trading partners at this time, and the price would be set for delivery of gold on the next rollover date. The price set for delivery in the next period would be based on the prior contract price plus the prevailing contango premium on the rollover date. From both American Barrick's and its trading partner's perspectives, the price for the next rollover would be set such that both parties would be indifferent between rolling over the contract for another year and closing out the contract and initiating a new 1-year forward contract.[20]

---

20 If American Barrick were to roll 1-year forward contracts, it would be required to recognize its gains or losses on these contracts at the end of each year for both taxes and financial reporting. The tax and financial reporting treatment of the newer SDCs was unclear, as they had not been tested in the courts. American Barrick's legal counsel believed that because SDCs were long-term contracts for which delivery was not required in the short-term, no gains or losses would be recognized on these trading agreements before the company delivered gold against its SDC commitments.

American Barrick's initial SDC trading agreements called for ultimate delivery within 3 or 4 years, but as a result of its large reserve base and strong financial position, it was able to negotiate subsequent agreements giving the firm 10 years within which to make delivery. SDC contracts were typically written by large producers with bullion dealers, covering no less than 100,000 ounces of gold. An integral feature of spot deferred trading agreements was the covenants that the company's 15 trading partners required it to meet. If American Barrick's finances weakened considerably or if its reserves deteriorated, its ability to continue to roll over its positions could be suspended. Weaker mining firms (with low reserves, high costs, and high leverage) were unable to enter into long-term SDCs or may have been required to deposit funds with their trading partners (or post margins) at each date when the contracts were rolled over.

American Barrick saw spot deferred contracts as a way to profit from increases in the price of gold and yet set a minimum price on its sales of gold. Since 1990, American Barrick's use of SDCs grew rapidly, supplanting its other hedging vehicles, with 1,035,000 ounces pledged to contracts in place at the end of 1990, 2,248,202 ounces at the end of 1991, and 4,341,827 ounces at year-end 1992. As it became more comfortable with SDCs, American Barrick began to experiment with vehicles to manage the inherent contango risk of these contracts by using interest rate forwards and options.

SUMMARY: HEDGING AT AMERICAN BARRICK

Through the 1980s and early 1990s, as American Barrick's reserves and financial strength improved and the market for gold-hedging vehicles matured, the company's risk management activities grew in size and complexity. Moving from gold financings to forwards to options to spot deferred contracts, the firm used virtually every instrument available to manage its gold price risk.

Gold price risk management at American Barrick evolved out of the conservative financing orientation of the firm. However, specific events in the corporation, like the 1984 experience with selling gold forward or the discovery of nearly 18 million unexpected ounces of gold reserves at Goldstrike, accelerated the pace at which hedging activity took place. With Goldstrike, American Barrick's board set a guideline for risk management: The firm would be fully protected against price declines for all production out 3 years, and 20%-25% protected for the following decade. Specific details of the methods and implementation were left to the financial team, who reported the firm's position to the board of directors on a regular basis.

While the program was dedicated to ensuring that American Barrick was protected against falls in the price of gold over the long term, in the short term the financial team strategically managed its positions to capitalize on its expectations of movements in the price of gold. For example, in early January 1991, gold prices were about $386 per ounce. Later that month, as military forces massed near the border of Kuwait, the price of gold began to rise. On the evening of January 17, 1991, while President George Bush made a television address telling of the initiation of Operation Desert Storm, gold prices surged to almost $410. In roughly an hour, the company's finance team sold approximately 1 year of production in the spot market to capitalize on what it perceived was a short-term uptick in prices. The bet proved correct, for gold prices later in the year never approached this level.

Because it lacked the technical training and in-house models to price the various gold derivatives, the financial team made a point of obtaining competitive quotes for its derivative transactions. Given American Barrick's financial strength and reserve base, the finance team felt that it could enter into contracts that many other mines and most gold stock investors could not. Furthermore, the terms of these contracts were more favorable than those other mining firms and investors would receive. Over time, as the finance team became more proficient at using the derivatives, it began to develop customized contracts using financial instruments available from major dealers.

American Barrick's largest positions were established in conjunction with Goldstrike when gold prices were much higher than in late 1992. As a result, as gold prices declined, American Barrick was able to deliver its production against contracts for prices far above market prices and would continue to be able to sell above market prices. Exhibit 12 shows the spot prices of gold and the average price that American Barrick realized on its sales throughout the firm's history.

American Barrick made a point of communicating its risk management program to the investing public. Exhibit 13 is an excerpt of information about the program presented to analysts, including published details of the firm's hedge position. The firm's hedging was prominently mentioned in public reports (including on the cover of the 1990 annual report), and executives gave speeches and wrote articles about the firm's hedging activities. Using publicly available information, analysts attempted to value its futures, options and SDC positions, and while these estimates differed, there was a broad consensus that these financial transaction activities had proven to be wise choices in hindsight.

PLEASANT SURPRISES CHALLENGE THE HEDGING PROGRAM

In 1991 and 1992, American Barrick's good luck in the mine fields put new demands on the firm's hedging program. In September 1989, the firm's geologists began exploring the "Purple Vein," located one mile north of its Goldstrike property. While these early explorations turned up gold in 10 of 17 holes drilled, the amount, the technical feasibility, and the economic attractiveness of the find could not be determined by the end of 1989. The gold lay under the water table at depths where the ground water temperature was over 140oF. In 1990 exploration continued with an additional 31 holes drilled, which indicated that perhaps over 5 million ounces of gold lay in the deposit. But the technical details of mining the gold were daunting, and over the coming year technicians would need to visit deep-shaft South African mines and consult with ventilation and cooling engineers to ensure that the gold could be extracted. During this time, there was substantial technical uncertainty.

Finally, in February 1992, the firm felt confident that the ore could be extracted, and it publicly announced the proven and probable reserves of 4.5 million ounces, renaming the mine the Meikle Mine in honor of the American Barrick executive who was instrumental in acquiring and exploring the Goldstrike property. In its public release announcing the mine, analysts were told, "Given full consideration of the risks inherent in mine development, it has been determined that the economics of the deposit are very attractive even at $350 per ounce gold," although the break-even of the mine was far lower than $350 per ounce. See Exhibit 14 for details of the Meikle Mine project. Construction would not be completed until 1995, and full production would commence in 1996. The finance team had to determine when, during the period in which Meikle was being explored and then constructed, it would begin to manage the price risk of the mine's production and which mix of instruments it would use.

While Meikle promised to boost the firm's production in the long term, good fortune unexpectedly produced a new challenge for the hedging program in the short term. In the fourth quarter of 1992, engineers determined that American Barrick's mined ore was richer in gold than originally anticipated. The firm had planned to produce roughly 1.2 million ounces annually of gold by 1995 and had hedged itself fully at this level for the period 1993-1995. The newer estimates suggested that production would be closer to 2 million ounces annually by 1995; thus the firm suddenly became substantially more exposed to gold price swings as measured against its policy guidelines.

With the price of gold and interest rates at historically low levels, the sudden need to enter into options, forwards, or SDCs became more complicated for American Barrick. While industrial demand for gold was projected to outstrip newly mined supply, and the large bullion sales by the central banks had been absorbed, gold prices were not projected to increase. While some analysts projected a rebound in gold prices with higher U.S. inflation because of President Clinton's economic proposals, others discounted the possibility of inflation. Furthermore, the increase in interest rate, currency, and other financial products, especially derivatives, gave investors alternatives to manage inflation risk more directly and efficiently than gold. Many held that despite upheavals around the world, the fear of global war had declined, and gold would not be bid up in these relatively peaceful times. With the fall in the price of gold, mining firms were reported to be cutting back exploration and development efforts, and analysts estimated that perhaps one in three mines was unprofitable at current prices.

Exhibit 15 shows the price of gold, along with capital market rates, and representative quotes on various gold derivatives available to the American Barrick financial team at the end of 1992. The team needed to decide what to do: whether to stand committed to the guideline of managing all of the price risk of next 3 years' production, and, if so, how to deal with the unexpected 1.7 million ounces of additional production for that period.

Exhibit 1   American Barrick's Operations, 1984–1992

	1984	1985	1986	1987	1988	1989	1990	1991	1992
Gold Production (oz.)									
Renabie Mine, Ontario	8,098	14,858	17,504	19,307	19,408	20,051	21,751	15,187	–
Valdez Creek, Alaska	3,880	5,878	3,108	7,501	10,436	13,975	–	–	–
Camflo, Quebec	18,500	34,637	31,850	29,763	30,888	26,629	24,416	25,001	36,273
Pinson Mine, Nevada	3,600	8,289	22,603	20,116	21,612	19,028	15,966	15,504	13,376
Holt-McDermott Mine, Ontario	–	–	–	–	23,848	63,354	59,164	60,728	43,325
Mercur Mine, Utah	–	52,290	111,007	108,278	115,390	117,536	122,043	127,280	121,239
Goldstrike, Nevada	–	–	–	40,144	119,418	207,264	352,880	546,146	1,108,219
	34,078	115,952	186,072	225,109	341,000	467,837	596,220	789,846	1,322,432
Proven and Probable Gold Reserves (oz.)									
Renabie Mine, Ontario	100,000	85,000	159,100	123,200	98,200	112,000	27,700	–	–
Valdez Creek, Alaska	–	23,000	39,600	28,400	51,300	94,700	–	–	–
Camflo, Quebec	170,000	135,000	102,000	91,200	76,800	62,100	44,800	19,900	–
Pinson Mine, Nevada	52,000	123,000	123,800	115,500	129,500	130,000	105,700	100,500	83,700
Holt-McDermott Mine, Ontario	–	476,000	456,000	308,000	249,000	354,400	387,100	447,300	251,200
Mercur Mine, Utah	–	1,000,000	1,400,000	1,467,000	1,297,100	1,127,700	1,027,100	876,300	739,800
Goldstrike, Nevada	–	–	625,300	8,679,100	15,181,000	17,995,700	17,918,000	18,448,000	20,149,000
Meikle Mine, Nevada	–	–	–	–	–	–	–	4,485,000	4,485,000
	322,000	1,842,000	2,905,800	10,812,400	17,082,900	19,876,600	19,510,400	24,377,000	25,708,700
Cash Cost/Ounce[a]									
Renabie Mine, Ontario	$376	$253	$239	$283	$353	$360	$373	$301	–
Valdez Creek, Alaska	270	237	324	469	451	308	–	295	164
Camflo, Quebe	200	214	219	237	272	294	319	238	260
Pinson Mine, Nevada	175	169	133	169	157	178	215	331	356
Holt-McDermott Mine, Ontario	–	–	–	–	268	284	298	–	–
Mercur Mine, Utah	–	248	199	216	235	253	238	249	259
Goldstrike, Nevada	–	–	–	312	325	352	393	318	199
Weighted average cash cost/oz.	247	217	200	246	280	307	343	305	210

Source: American Barrick Resources Corporation, annual reports.
a. Cash costs include site costs for all mining (including deferred stripping costs), processing, and administration, but do not include royalties, capital costs, exploration costs, resource taxes, depreciation, and financing costs.

Exhibit 2   American Barrick's Financial Performance, 1983–1992 (thousands of dollars except per share data)

	1983	1984ᵃ	1985ᵇ	1986	1987	1988	1989ᶜ	1990	1991	1992
Income Statement Data										
Revenues	$1,286	$4,407	$37,327	$69,106	$92,127	$147,509	$206,069	$251,624	$344,725	$540,437
Operating expenses	(1,180)	(7,635)	(23,315)	(39,482)	(48,090)	(79,545)	(111,010)	(132,356)	(175,357)	(234,205)
Administrative expenses	(1,197)	(2,312)	(2,607)	(4,036)	(5,547)	(6,756)	(8,728)	(10,570)	(11,951)	(14,241)
Income from operations	(1,091)	(5,540)	11,406	25,588	38,490	61,208	86,331	108,698	157,417	291,991
Depreciation, depletion, and amortization	(351)	(3,504)	(8,845)	(11,868)	(17,383)	(25,681)	(35,266)	(42,954)	(49,277)	(68,971)
Exploration and deferred mining costs written off	–	–	(345)	(135)	(3,010)	(501)	(8,299)	(6,925)	(3,465)	(4,310)
Interest and other income	215	3,509	5,315	4,547	10,658	15,369	21,945	31,487	23,961	13,330
Interest expense on long-term obligations	–	(4,343)	(2,935)	(3,844)	(9,985)	(10,671)	(12,770)	(12,787)	(9,427)	(9,296)
Other expenses	–	–	–	–	8,287	–	(9,487)	–	(4,243)	–
Income before taxes	(1,226)	(9,878)	4,595	14,288	27,057	39,724	42,454	77,519	114,966	222,744
Income taxes	–	822	1,500	2,700	6,487	9,229	8,719	19,314	22,526	47,804
Net income	($1,226)	($9,056)	$3,095	$11,588	$20,570	$30,495	$33,735	$58,205	$92,440	$174,940
Net income per share	($.02)	($.12)	$.08	$.28	$.18	$.26	$.28	$.45	$.68	$1.22
Balance Sheet Data										
Cash and short-term investments	$3,093	$1,041	$2,110	$2,215	$167,163	$51,411	$304,673	$311,778	$252,140	$288,023
Note receivable	–	–	–	–	46,161	–	–	–	–	–
Marketable securities	–	1,460	455	99,478	312	–	–	–	–	–
Bullion settlements and other receivables	2,527	5,650	4,044	6,439	9,841	16,786	28,314	32,601	35,193	25,100
Inventories and prepaid expenses	437	1,961	7,547	9,596	15,946	18,760	35,067	46,852	41,114	40,248
Current assets	6,057	10,112	14,155	117,727	239,423	86,957	368,054	391,231	328,447	353,371
Investments	–	33,102	15,332	15,120	120,005	143,144	32,526	–	–	–
Property, plant, and equipment	31,158	122,644	126,760	171,151	289,304	455,776	633,791	716,046	921,701	1,094,402
Other assets	3,207	2,630	9,082	14,885	27,050	14,958	15,698	39,606	56,189	56,520
Total assets	$40,422	$168,489	$165,329	$318,884	$675,785	$700,825	$1,050,069	$1,146,883	$1,306,337	$1,504,293

Exhibit 2   American Barrick's Financial Performance, 1983–1992 (thousands of dollars except per share data) (Continued)

	1983	1984[a]	1985[b]	1986	1987	1988	1989[c]	1990	1991	1992
Accounts payable and accrued liabilities	$4,165	$6,950	$11,627	$16,793	$24,811	$26,209	$42,019	$28,528	$54,532	$58,804
Dividend payable	–	–	–	–	–	–	–	–	3,105	–
Notes and loans payable	1,365	26,323	4,102	53,658	27,807	16,860	46,760	82,973	54,624	79,968
Current part of long-term debt[d] and deferred revenues[e]	–	311	934	24,536	–	–	–	–	–	–
Current liabilities	5,530	33,584	16,663	94,987	52,618	43,069	88,779	111,501	112,261	138,772
Long-term debt[d]	2,783	41,490	9,619	61,942	137,010	91,834	61,271	331,401	262,996	260,098
Deferred revenues and other liabilities[e]	–	5,293	65,894	47,598	142,104	164,300	358,114	31,193	47,989	62,117
Deferred taxes	–	7,070	6,208	5,565	5,612	11,147	16,387	27,912	42,438	50,577
Total liabilities	8,313	87,436	98,384	210,093	337,645	310,350	524,551	502,007	465,684	511,564
Capital stock	37,845	100,175	103,389	98,315	315,850	325,562	427,509	534,707	653,102	664,410
Retained earnings	(5,736)	(19,121)	(36,444)	10,476	24,144	49,799	77,140	92,745	169,766	326,273
Foreign currency translation adjustment	–	–	–	–	(1,557)	15,124	20,869	17,424	17,785	2,046
Shareholder's equity	32,109	81,053	66,945	108,791	338,437	390,485	525,518	644,876	840,653	992,729
Total liabilities and shareholders' equity	40,422	$168,489	$165,329	$318,884	$675,782	$700,835	$1,050,069	$1,146,883	$1,306,337	$1,504,293

Statements of Cash Flow

	1983	1984[a]	1985[b]	1986	1987	1988	1989[c]	1990	1991	1992
Cash from operations		$71	$12,646	$24,466	$37,276	$61,693	$76,801	$94,040	$160,233	$282,782
Cash from investment activities		(99,015)	(20,682)	(95,679)	(192,871)	(195,175)	(114,569)	(160,263)	(303,346)	(272,209)
Cash from financing										
Capital stock		63,392	3,250	31,389	213,190	7,316	102,252	107,198	118,395	11,308
Renabie Gold Trust[f]		5,762	–							
Long-term liabilities		5,505	2,471							
Gold-linked 5.25% notes[g]		–	–	52,903						
Gold Company of America		–	40,778							
Gold loans and long-term liabilities: proceeds		–	26,826		171,004	50,166	218,818			77,000
Gold loans and long-term liabilities: repayments		–	(40,563)	(13,178)	(13,427)	(74,357)	(22,024)	(21,940)	(76,806)	(40,172)
Gold purchase warrants[h]		–	–	4,248						

Exhibit 2   American Barrick's Financial Performance, 1983–1992 (thousands of dollars except per share data) (Continued)

	1983	1894[a]	1985[b]	1986	1987	1988	1989[c]	1990	1991	1992
Note receivable[i]		–	–	–	(46,161)	46,161	–	–	–	–
Dividends		–	–	–	(2,220)	(4,840)	(7,896)	(11,263)	(15,000)	(18,433)
Other[j]		(2,716)	(959)	(1,914)	(1,441)	(2,466)	(796)	(1,019)	1,826	(3,105)
		71,944	31,803	73,446	320,945	21,980	290,354	72,976	28,415	26,598

Source: American Barrick Resources Corporation, annual reports.
Note: Financial data for 1983–1987 were originally reported in Canadian dollars. Subsequent American Barrick financial reports translate these into U.S. dollars at a fixed rate of .77 US$/C$. This convention is used here.
a. Does not include 1984 extraordinary loss of $9,523,000 attributable to divestment of nonmining properties (oil and gas).
b. Does not include 1985 extraordinary loss of $20,305,000 attributable to divestment of nonmining properties (oil and gas).
c. In 1989, Barrick changed the way it accounted for exploration and deferred stripping costs. Financials for previous years have not been restated to reflect this change. Accordingly, there is a mismatch in some accounts when comparing pre-1989 data.
d. Long-term debt includes gold loan obligations at original value.
e. Deferred revenues include gains arising from early repayment of gold loans and adjustments made to value the loan at market prices prevailing at the balance sheet date. In earlier years, deferred revenues included all gold loan obligations as well as long-term obligations to financing trusts and purchase contracts. Other liabilities include reserves for future environmental and land reclamation costs.
f. The Renabie Gold Trust receives a variable percentage of Renabie production, which varies from 3% to 10% based on the price of gold.
g. The Gold Company of America entered into gold purchase agreements to purchase gold from the Camflo mine. The percentage of the contract delivered each year varies with the price of gold. The rate is 8% at $365 gold and increases or decreases by 1% for each $35 change in the price of gold.
h. In September 1986 the company issued 2 million units at $21.5/unit consisting of one common share and two gold purchase warrants. Each warrant entitled the holder to purchase .02 oz. gold at $9.50 until September 1990. At issue, the warrants were valued at $1.50 each.
i. A portion ($46.1 million) of the proceeds from the October 1987 equity issue was used to purchase a note receivable, which was repaid in 1988.
j. Also includes costs incurred in raising capital.

Exhibit 3   Operating and Financial Performance of Major Gold Mining Firms 1991 (millions of dollars except per share and per ounce data)

	American Barrick	Amax Gold	Battle Mountain[f]	Echo Bay	FMC Gold[f]	Homestake Mining	LAC Minerals	Newmont Gold[g]	Newmont Mining[g]	Pegasus Gold	Placer Dome
Operating information											
Production (000 oz.)	789.8	300.2	408.0	733.9	357.0	1,045.2	1,040.0	1,576.9	1,420.9	315.3	1,684.0
Average realized price/oz.[a]	$438	$427	$368	$392	$361	$361	413	$363	$391	$389	$399
Cash costs/oz.[b]	$205	$195	$178	$249	$210	$307	$245	$203	$203	$226	$223
Total costs/oz.[c]	$274	$346	$376	$390	$343	$448	$390	$288	$288	$351	$415
Total reserves (million oz.)	25.3	6.2	7.1	1.3	2.6	13.2	10.6	20.1	18.1	4.0	16.8
Reserve replacement costs/oz.[d]	$13	$17	$19	$23	$66	$29	$33	$9	$9	$54	$104
Risk management activities											
Percent of 1992 production "hedged"[e]	94%	50%	0%	15%	0%	0%	80%	0%	29%	68%	24%
Average price/oz. of "hedged" production[e]	$424	$497	—	$417	—	—	$396	—	$431	$380	$421
Percent of debt gold-linked	100%	6%	0%	100%	0%	0%	26%	—	100%	25%	4%
Percent of revenue from gold sales	100%	100%	95%	91%	92%	94%	85%	100%	89%	79%	70%
Financial information ($ million)											
Cash flow from operations	$160.23	$50.90	$53.84	$97.57	$48.91	$23.80	$122.95	$181.77	$98.33	$32.56	$276.60
Cash flow from investment	($303.35)	($53.70)	($125.92)	($56.34)	($21.19)	($45.23)	($184.48)	($176.46)	($83.68)	($38.33)	($354.00)
Cash flow from financing	$28.42	$12.10	$8.16	($52.32)	($3.67)	($50.16)	$126.42	($5.24)	($126.13)	$60.14	($26.90)
Capital expenditures	$245.50	$60.00	$147.00	$60.00	$19.40	$138.42	$95.15	$97.27	$95.50	$38.70	$226.00
Total assets	$1,306	$198	$525	$875	$275	$927	$1,346	$817	$818	$351	$2,291
Total debt	$336	$26	$128	$234	$127	$52	$348	$0	$224	$71	$310
Stock price information											
Shareholders' equity (book) value	$841	$198	$315	$492	$244	$669	$778	$735	$201	$246	$1,481
No. of shares (millions) (12/31/91)	140.9	60.6	79.8	105.1	73.5	99.5	146.9	104.9	67.8	27.9	236.7
Closing price per share (12/31/91)	$27.88	$11.63	$7.88	$7.50	$5.00	$16.00	$8.13	$39.75	$40.38	$12.37	$11.00
Standard deviation of returns (1988–1992)	.020	.024	.027	.025	.028	.024	.024	.021	.020	.025	.021
% of firm owned by officers and directors	25%	.60%	1.03%	1.14%	.01%	9.08%	2.46%	0%	.56%	1.22%	.52%
Total common stock return in % (1988–1992)	218.7	-46.9	-70.0	-77.0	-60.0	-35.3	-41.0	-9.6	-38.1	37.1	-12.2

Exhibit 3   Operating and Financial Performance of Major Gold Mining Firms, 1991 (millions of dollars except per share and per ounce data) (Continued)

Sources: Company annual reports, 10K's and proxy statements, S&P stock reports, First Boston analysts' reports, J. P. Morgan analysts' reports

a. Average COMEX price of gold in 1991 was $362.

b. Cash costs include site costs for all mining (including deferred stripping costs), processing, and administration but do not royalties, capital costs, exploration costs, resource taxes, depreciation, and financing costs. Data courtesy of Paul Zink, J. P. Morgan. America.. Barrick's definition of cash costs in Exhibit 1 includes its deferred stripping costs, by which the expenses of removing waste rock that lies above ore bodies is amortized over the life of the mine. It treatment of deferred stripping costs differs from that of other firms. The costs in this exhibit have been adjusted so that its costs can be directly compared against other mining firms' cost.

c. Total costs add depreciation, royalties, capital costs, exploration costs, resource taxes, and financing costs to cash costs. Data courtesy of Paul Zink, J. P. Morgan.

d. Reserve replacement costs are the sum of capitalized additions to exploration/development expenditures and exploration expenses divided by the net new ounces added to reserves for 1987–1991. Data courtesy of Paul Zink, J. P. Morgan.

e. At December 31, 199.. Data from Ted Reeve, *North American Hedging Report*, First Boston Corporation, February 1992. See Exhibit 8 for details.

f. FMC Corp. owns 79% of FMC Gold and hedged 88.7% of its share of 1992 production. FMC Gold officers and directors own 943,032 shares of FMC Corp.

g. Newmont Mining owned 90.1% of Newmont Gold and hedged 29% of its share of production as indicated.

Exhibit 4   Return to American Barrick's Common Stock and Common Stocks of Other Major Gold
Mining Firms, 1987–1992

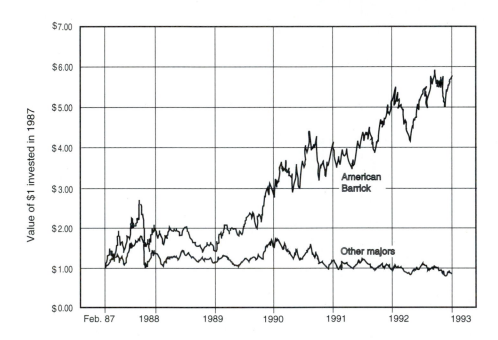

Source: Data from the Center for Research in Security Prices.
Note: This chart shows the value of $1.00 invested in American Barrick on the date of its listing on the New York Stock Exchange (February 25, 1987) and reinvested in the shares of American Barrick as dividends were paid. The line labeled "Other majors" shows the value of $1.00 invested equally in the other major gold mines on the same date, and with dividends reinvested in an equal weighted portfolio of these firms. The "Other majors" include AMAX, Battle Mountain, Echo Bay, FMC Gold, Homestake, International Corona, LAC Minerals, Newmont Gold, Newmont Mining, Pegasus, and Placer Dome.

Exhibit 5   Price of Gold and the Relation Between Inflation Rates and Changes in Gold Prices, 1980-1992

Price of gold per ounce in nominal and real (1980) dollars

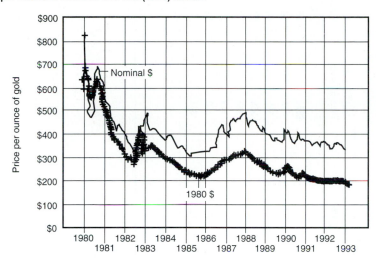

Relation between inflation rates and changes in gold prices

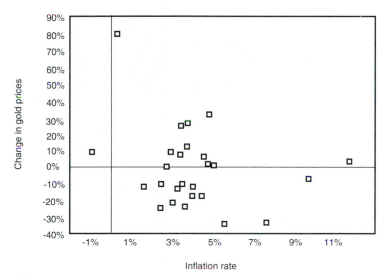

Source: Data from IDC Datasheet.
Note: Annualized inflation rates calculated for each non-overlapping six-month period from January 1980 to December 1992. Annualized changes in nominal gold prices are calculated for same periods.

Exhibit 6   Percent of Production Covered by Price Risk Management Activities by Major North American Gold Producers, 1990–1992

Survey Date	Percent of Production Hedged					Spot Price at Time of Survey	Number of Firms Surveyed
	1991[a]	1992[a]	1993	1994	1995		
June 1990	22.7%	–	–	–	–	$352	35
Sept. 1990	32.8	–	–	–	–	408	38
Dec. 1990	41.8	24.3%	16.1%	–	–	386	40
March 1991	49.0	25.3	16.4	–	–	356	47
June 1991	57.0	30.1	17.4	8.3%	–	368	53
Sept. 1991	53.1	31.1	18.7	14.0	–	349	53
Dec. 1991	–	37.4	21.5	15.3	–	353	52
March 1992	–	42.4	24.3	18.0	7.3%	341	52

Sources: Data from Ted Reeve, *North American Gold Monitor* and *Global Gold Hedge Survey*, First Boston Equity Research. Gold prices from IDC Datasheet.
a. Shows percent covered by price risk management activities as of date shown for the remainder of the year.

Exhibit 7   Percent of Annual Production Covered by Price Risk Management Activities by North American Gold Mines at December 31, 1991

	1992	1993	1994	1995
Seniors	41%	21%	17%	7%
Intermediates	48	16	9	5
Juniors	15	7	4	7
Total	39	18	13	6

Source: Data from Egizio Bianchini, *Gold Producers Based in North America, Hedging Survey*, Vol. II, Nesbitt Research, Spring 1992.
Note: Senior producers are those with estimated 1992 production of more than 400,000 oz. Intermediate producers have estimated 1992 production of 100,000–400,000 oz. Junior producers have estimated 1992 production of under 100,000 ounces.

Exhibit 8   Price Risk Management Activities of Eleven Leading North American Gold Mining Firms at December 31, 1991

	1992			1993			1994		
	Ounces	Price/oz.	Percent of Production	Ounces	Price/oz.	Percent of Production	Ounces	Price/oz.	Percent of Production
American Barrick									
Forward sales	289,273	$415		—	$450		—	$411	
Spot deferred	424,997	439		681,250	419		1,025,937	402	
Gold loans	100,886	455		168,750	419		164,063	402	
Puts	309,844	400		350,000	429		60,000	450	
Total	1,125,000	424	94%	1,200,000	440	96%	1,250,000	412	96%
Calls sold	—	—		140,000	449		18,000	450	
Amax Gold									
Spot deferreds	139,880	507		—	—		—	—	
Puts	12,000	410		42,000	425		42,000	440	
Gold loans	4,000	400		—	—		—	—	
Total	155,880	497	50	42,000	425	12	42,000	440	12
Battle Mountain Gold			0			0			0
Echo Bay									
Forward sales	81,000	412		—			—		
Gold loans	27,670	432		27,670	432		89,670	388	
Total	108,670	417	15	27,670	432	4	89,670	388	12
FMC Gold[a]			0			0			0
Homestake			0			0			0
LAC Minerals									
Forward sales	840,000	395		488,000	399		—		
Gold loans	52,500	414		70,000	414		70,000	414	
Total	892,500	396	80	558,000	401	49	70,000	414	6

Exhibit 8   Price Risk Management Activities of Eleven Leading North American Gold Mining Firms at December 31, 1991 (Continued)

	1992			1993			1994		
	Ounces	Price/oz.	Percent of Production	Ounces	Price/oz.	Percent of Production	Ounces	Price/oz.	Percent of Production
Newmont Gold[b]			0			0			0
Newmont Mining[b]									
Forward sales	8,700	434		–	–				
Gold loans	250,000	449		250,000	449				
Puts	158,500	403		–	–				
Total	417,200	431	29	250,000	449	16			
Calls sold	166,500	455		–	–				
Pegasus Gold									
Forward sales	114,065	420		44,565	494		50,565	492	
Puts	150,000	350		–	–		–	–	
Total	264,065	380	68	44,565	494	10	50,565	492	10
Placer Dome									
Forward sales	372,000	425		231,000	427		231,000	427	
Gold loans	7,000	431		10,000	431		10,000	431	
Puts	34,000	378		–	–		–	–	
Total	413,000	421	24	241,000	427	14	241,000	427	14
Calls sold	31,000	425		–	–		–	–	
Calls purchased	7,000	435		–	–		–	–	

Source: Data from Ted Reeve, *North American Hedging Report,* First Boston Corporation, February 1992.
a. The FMC Corporation owned 78.9% of FMC Gold and hedged its pro rata share of production. As of December 31, 1992, it had hedged 88.7% of its 1992, 79.6% of its 1993, and 0% of its 1994 share of production.
b. Newmont Mining owned 90.1% of Newmont Gold.

Exhibit 9   Gold Lease Rate, LIBOR, Contango, Spot, and Forward Gold Prices,1982–1992

Date	Gold Lease Rate	LIBOR	Contango	Gold Price (per oz.)	Forward Price (per oz.)
Jan. 1982	1.35%	16.83%	15.48%	$384.11	$443.56
June 1982	1.45	15.63	14.18	314.93	359.59
Jan. 1983	0.65	9.45	8.80	479.88	522.11
June 1983	0.85	10.28	9.43	412.82	451.75
Jan. 1984	1.05	10.45	9.40	370.86	405.72
June 1984	1.25	13.40	12.15	377.64	423.53
Jan. 1985	1.35	9.60	8.25	302.77	327.75
June 1985	1.20	8.33	7.13	316.39	338.95
Jan. 1986	1.50	8.31	6.81	344.58	368.06
June 1986	1.50	7.60	6.10	342.77	363.68
Jan. 1987	1.20	6.19	4.99	408.31	428.69
June 1987	0.70	7.86	7.16	449.57	481.76
Jan. 1988	1.30	7.75	6.45	476.57	507.29
June 1988	1.45	8.24	6.79	451.34	481.96
Jan. 1989	1.70	9.77	8.07	403.99	436.60
June 1989	2.25	9.19	6.94	367.59	393.11
Jan. 1990	1.40	8.48	7.08	410.12	439.17
June 1990	1.45	8.54	7.09	352.31	377.28
Jan. 1991	2.40	7.40	5.00	384.47	403.70
June 1991	1.30	6.94	5.64	366.70	387.37
Jan. 1992	1.15	4.52	3.37	354.43	366.38
June 1992	1.10	4.54	3.44	340.80	352.52
Dec. 31 1992	1.80	4.06	2.26	333.33	340.86

Sources: IDC Datasheet, Reuters, Chase Manhattan Bank.
Note: Gold lease rates, LIBOR (London Interbank Offered Rate), contango, and forward prices are quoted for periods of 1 year. Data are averages for each month, except for December 31, 1992.

Exhibit 10 American Barrick's Forward Sales of Gold (Excluding Gold Financings and Spot Deferred Contracts), 1984–1992

	Ounces Sold Forward (000s)	Date of Longest Forward Sale	Average Price at Delivery
1984	0	–	–
1985	79.4	12/86	$336
1986	92.6	12/87	364
1987	37.9	1/89	497
1988	56.6	12/92	486
1989	117.4	12/91	427
1990	0	–	–
1991	0	–	–
1992	0	–	–

Source: American Barrick Resources Corporation, annual reports.

Exhibit 11   American Barrick's Year-End Gold Option Positions, 1983–1992

	Put Positions			Call Positions		
	Ounces (in 000s)	Average Exercise Price/oz.	Longest Maturity	Ounces (in 000s)	Average Exercise Price/oz.	Longest Maturity
1983	–	–	–	–	–	–
1984	–	–	–	–	–	–
1985	–	–	–	–	–	–
1986[a]	–	–	–	–[b]	–[b]	–[b]
1987[c]	549.3	$426	3 years	215.4	$578	3 years
1988[c]	1,084.7	430	4 years	556.4	533	4 years
1989[c]	1,700.0	417	4 years	886.9	461	4 years
1990[c]	1,471.4	418	4 years	723.5	445	4 years
1991[c]	1,009.1	417	3 years	447.3	427	3 years
1992[d]	410.0	432	2 years	–	–	–

Source: American Barrick Resources Corporation, annual reports.

a. In 1986, American Barrick entered into an agreement with a third party to carry out trading in gold options, with profits split equally and losses borne completely by the other party.

b. On September 25, 1986, American Barrick issued 2 million units at $21.50 each, consisting of one share of common stock and two gold purchase warrants. Each warrant allowed the holder to buy .02 oz. of gold at $9.20 (or $460 per ounce) anytime over the following 4 years.

c. In all years, the net premium paid for all new option positions was zero.

d. In this year, American Barrick added no new options contracts to its position.

Exhibit 12 American Barrick's Realized Price for Delivered Gold Versus COMEX Spot Price, 1984–1992

	Average Price for Gold Delivered During Year	Ounces Delivered	Average COMEX Price
1984	$311	34,078	$360
1985	333	115,952	317
1986	348	185,359	368
1987	410	219,776	447
1988	446	330,479	437
1989	436	472,452	393
1990	437	575,656	384
1991	438	787,735	362
1992	422	1,280,320	345

Source: American Barrick Resource Corporation, annual reports.

Exhibit 13   Public Disclosure of American Barrick's Consolidated Gold Price Risk Management Position, at December 31, 1992

| | 1993 | | 1994 | | 1995 | |
	Ounces	Average Price	Ounces	Average Price	Ounces	Average Price
Gold loans[a]	33,750	$515	224,063	$402	213,125	$400
Put options	350,000	429	60,000	450	–	–
Scheduled deliveries	383,750	437	284,063	412	213,125	400
Spot deferred contracts[b]	4,341,827	–	–	–	–	–

Source: American Barrick Resources Corporation.

a. Beyond 1995 the company had delivery obligations under its gold loans of 315,000 oz. at an average price of $400 per ounce through to 1997.

b. Spot deferred contracts have no fixed delivery date and may be rolled forward for up to 10 years under the terms of American Barrick's trading agreements. On each rollover date the value of the contracts increases with the accumulation of the forward premium (contango). Uncommitted gold available from production will be delivered against these contracts when the spot price of gold is less than the price of the contracts. If the spot gold price exceeds the contract price, uncommitted gold available from production will be sold on the spot market and the contracts rolled forward for future delivery at a higher price through the accumulation of additional contango.

Assuming the spot price of gold remains below the contract prices, the company will realize a minimum average price of over $400 per ounce for all its production through to the end of 1994. If the spot price exceeds the contract price, the company's average realized price will be higher as the contracts will be deferred for future delivery and production will be delivered into the higher spot market. From 1995 on, the minimum average price for the unutilized portion of the existing spot deferred contracts will be in excess of $400 per ounce. Ultimately, Barrick's realized price could be significantly higher depending on the timing of deliveries and the forward premiums achieved.

Exhibit 14 Projected Data on Meikle Mine Project

	Amount[a]	Timing of Expenditure
Capital costs prior to production($ millions)[b]		
Surface facilities and mine shafts	$ 55 million	mid-1993–1994
Underground development	31	1994–1995
Refrigeration and ventilation	12	1994–1995
Dewatering	23	1994–1995
Mine equipment	12	1995
Capitalized preproduction	48	mid-1993–1995
Total Capital Costs	$180 million	
Operating costs per ounce of gold[c]	$125/ounce	
Royalties[d]	4% of sales	
Estimated land reclamation costs at termination of project ($ millions)[e]	$2.5	
Effective tax rate[e]	20%	

Source: American Barrick Resources Corporation.
a. In 1992 dollars.
b. Includes contingency of approximately 10%.
c. Planned reserves of 4.5 million oz. were projected to be produced over an 11-year period beginning in full production in 1996. Approximately 400,000 oz. of gold would be produced each year from 1996 to 2006.
d. Royalties paid by American Barrick to the firm that had a royalty interest on the property on which the Meikle Mine was located.
e. The taxation of gold mining firms is quite complex: mines can enjoy both depreciation and depletion tax benefits. The effect of these tax shields was to reduce American Barrick's effective tax rate on its operating profits on the Meikle Mine to approximately 20%.

Exhibit 15 Gold Prices and Other Capital Markets Data, 1990–1992

	Jan 1990	June 1990	Jan 1991	June 1991	Jan 1992	June 1992	Dec 1992
Gold price per ounce	$410	$352	$385	$367	$354	$341	$333
US$ interest rates							
LIBOR: 1 year	8.48%	8.54%	7.40%	6.94%	4.52%	4.54%	4.06%
1-year Treasuries	7.92	8.10%	6.65	6.36	4.15	4.17	3.61
3-year Treasuries	8.13	8.40	7.38	7.39	5.40	5.60	4.93
5-year Treasuries	8.12	8.43	7.70	7.94	6.24	6.48	5.83
Gold lease rates							
1-year	1.40%	1.45%	2.40%	1.30%	1.15%	1.10%	1.80%
3-years	2.90	2.80	3.50	2.60	2.10	1.80	2.25
5-years	4.00	3.75	4.75	3.50	2.90	2.25	2.70
Implied volality of gold[a]	– – – – 18% – – – –		– – – – 12% – – – –		– – – – 9% – – – –		7%

Sources: American Barrick Resources Corporation, IDC Datasheet, Chase Manhattan Bank, and Paul H. Zink, *The North American Gold Industry: A Market in Transition*, J. P. Morgan Report, July 1, 1992.
Note: Data are averages for each month, except for December 31, 1992.
a. Approximate implied volatilities on European options on gold with maturities of 5 years or less. Implied volatilities for gold options had been over 50% in 1980, about 18% in 1987, and 12% in 1988 and 1989. In late January 1991 implied volatilities reached over 20%.

ENRON GAS SERVICES

From his office in Houston, Texas, Jeff Skilling, CEO of Enron Gas Services (EGS), closely reread the May 24, 1993 *Forbes* article "Hidden Risks." The author, Toni Mack, did not directly criticize EGS, a subsidiary of Enron Corporation, as much as she cast doubt on the propriety of the firm's management of its risks. Her article began, "On Wall Street and in the oil patch, Enron Corporation has been a smashing success. Here are some things that could go wrong." Focusing her two-page analysis almost exclusively on EGS, Ms. Mack raised questions about the exposure of the Enron subsidiary to failures of its suppliers, customers, and financial partners; changes in taxes and regulation; and slowdowns in the growth of its business.

At one level, the *Forbes* article had little direct fallout, as Wall Street analysts rallied to Enron's defense by harshly criticizing the piece.[1] Nevertheless, Ms. Mack's innuendoes troubled Mr. Skilling. The enterprise he had founded was a complex hybrid of a natural gas company and a financial institution, which made the task of understanding its business and associated risks extremely difficult for outsiders. However, at the core of this opaque firm that provided producers and users of natural gas innovative ways to manage their risks was a system that allowed EGS to manage its own risks. Toni Mack's article was a disturbing reminder that EGS had not completely communicated the degree to which this internal system had succeeded.

Though Jeff Skilling could dismiss this particular article, he realized that the business environment in which EGS operated was becoming more difficult. Changes in the natural gas business, increased competition, and declining profit margins raised serious questions

---

[1] For example, the Lehman Brothers' analyst covering Enron wrote that the *Forbes* article was "misleading and demonstrates a considerable lack of understanding" in that it overstated the risk borne by EGS. For the two weeks following May 10, 1993 (the date the issue was first available to subscribers), Enron Corporation's common stock fell from \$58 to \$56^5/$_8$, a drop of 2.37%. During this same period, the S&P 500 rose 1.17%. It was not possible to ascertain the effect of the *Forbes* story, because during this two-week period there were no fewer than 79 stories written mentioning Enron, including Enron's dividend announcement on May 12.

Sanjay Bhatnagar and Peter Tufano wrote this case as the basis for class discussion rather than to illustrate either effective or ineffective handling of an administrative situation.

about the firm's direction and future. As an experienced strategist, Mr. Skilling knew that EGS's continued success demanded that it continue to anticipate and move to exploit new opportunities.

THE NATURAL GAS INDUSTRY

In the United States, natural gas, a naturally occurring mixture of energy-rich vapors that produce a relatively clean source of energy, accounted for about one-fourth of energy consumption in the early 1990s.[2] It was used by utilities and commercial firms to produce energy, by industrial firms as a raw material (e.g., to produce fertilizer and synthetic fibers), and directly by households and businesses for heating and cooking.[3]

Historically, the natural gas industry consisted of firms that extracted gas from the earth and processed it (firms like ARCO or Mobil, as well as thousands of independent producers), gas pipeline companies that transported gas molecules across large distances, locally regulated local distribution companies (LDCs) that distributed gas molecules to consumers (e.g., Boston Gas), and end users. Deregulation of the natural gas industry had given rise to gas marketers, who bought and sold gas using the transportation facilities of pipeline companies to deliver gas to LDCs as well as to end users. Exhibit 1 diagrams the supply relationships for natural gas.

For many natural gas consumers, as well as for some producers, having stable and predictable gas prices and supplies could be desirable. Predictable pricing created known cash flows, simplifying firms' investment and pricing decisions. Predictable supplies ensured that activities ranging from large industrial processes to home heating would not be interrupted by shortages. For much of the twentieth century, regulation produced stability in the natural gas industry. Unfortunately, events of the 1970s and 1980s conspired to make gas prices far from stable, leading to major changes in the structure of the industry. Shocks to the prices of other energy sources, dramatic deregulation of the natural gas industry, the effective legal abrogation of a predominant contract form, and erratic shifts in supply and demand led to large swings in the price of gas, as well as increased short-term price volatility. Exhibit 2 shows the prices of natural gas and other fuels from 1974 to 1992, and the volatility of natural gas and oil prices from 1988 to 1993.

---

2   Standard & Poor's Industry Survey, "Utilities," April 29, 1993, p. U82.

3   Of the 19.7 trillion cubic feet of gas consumed in the United States in 1992, roughly 24% was consumed by households directly, 14% by electric utilities to generate power, 45% by industrial users, and 14% by commercial users, largely for heating. (U.S. Government, Energy Information Administration, *Annual Energy Review* 1992, June 1993, p. 183.)

From the passage of the Natural Gas Act of 1938 until 1978, the price of interstate natural gas was regulated. Though the form of regulation varied during this period, prices were set by rulings, not by supply and demand. Responding to the incentives of administered prices, producers in the 1970s cut back on exploration and development, leading to shortages. The reduction in supply was particularly acute relative to the increase in demand created by the Arab oil embargo of 1973 and the Iranian revolution in 1978, which disrupted the supply and increased the price of oil. The severe shortages of natural gas led to regulatory and market-based reactions.

The regulatory response took the form of the 1978 Natural Gas Policy Act (NGPA), which decontrolled the price of newly found gas. The NGPA, administered by the Federal Energy Regulatory Commission (FERC), was intended to spur producers to increase exploration and production of new reserves. It met this objective, as well as a subsidiary objective of encouraging large industrial firms and utilities to reduce their energy consumption.

The market response to the shortages was that pipeline companies and producers entered into long-term natural gas contracts. In these "take-or-pay" contracts, the pipelines committed to pay for a minimum volume of gas in the future at prearranged prices, typically either fixed for the life of the contract or allowed to escalate with inflation. Take-or-pay contracts assured producers of a guaranteed market for their gas and the pipelines with a guaranteed supply at known prices. The pipelines in turn resold the gas to end users such as LDCs, often with contracts with "minimum bill provisions" that mirrored the take-or-pay previsions.

Thus, more gas was supplied at higher, decontrolled prices and was often sold to pipeline companies under long-term take-or-pay contracts. However, the increase in supply, in conjunction with a reduction in demand due to lower oil prices and increased energy conservation, led to a condition of oversupply in the mid-1980s and a sharp drop in the price of gas. However, the take-or-pay contracts left pipelines with commitments to buy gas at the previously set prices, far above the going rate for gas and the prices of alternative energy sources. Minimum bill provisions left LDCs with similar commitments, meaning that they, too, would pay far above going rates.

LDCs and state regulators applied to the FERC for relief from the high-priced minimum bill contracts, and the FERC responded with a series of orders to resolve the conflict between producers, pipelines, LDCs, and consumers. FERC Order 380, issued in 1984, provided relief to the LDCs by voiding the minimum bill provisions of their contract with the pipelines, which consequently were left with asymmetric obligations due to their own take-or-pay contracts with producers. Though the take-or-pay contracts continued to be legally enforceable, as a practical matter, producers could not expect that they could or would be honored.

A flurry of regulation in the late 1980s and early 1990s effectively put into place a market-pricing system for natural gas. Prior to the 1985 FERC Order 436, pipelines needed regulatory approval to transport gas across state lines. The cumbersome approval process made it difficult for gas buyers to take advantage of the emerging spot market for gas because they could not be assured of being able to physically transport the gas they wished to purchase. FERC Order 436 provided a blanket approval for pipelines that chose to become common carriers.[4] The accompanying FERC Order 500 provided incentives for pipelines to become common carriers by assisting them in renegotiating burdensome take-or-pay contracts and granting them permission to serve end users directly, as opposed to selling through LDCs. FERC Orders 436 and 500 introduced more competition and flexibility into the natural gas markets by unbundling, or separating, the selling and transportation components of the transmission business.

FERC Order 451, issued in 1986, essentially deregulated the wellhead (direct from the well) prices of old gas and provided for a process that allowed producers to initiate renegotiation of existing contracts if they included old gas. FERC Order 490, issued in April 1988, authorized producers, pipelines, and others to terminate gas sales or purchases without seeking prior FERC approval. Prior to this order, any abandonment of gas dedicated to the interstate market had to be approved by the FERC. This approval process, combined with the regulation of wellhead prices for interstate gas, had severely affected the ability of interstate pipelines to obtain new gas for interstate transmission and led directly to the shortages that had been experienced in the 1970s.

As a result of these initiatives, by 1990 more than 75% of gas sales were conducted through the spot market. The market was characterized by unprecedented volatility in gas prices. The standard contract provided for interruptible delivery, that is, the supply of gas to the buyer was not guaranteed and could be interrupted for any reason by the supplier without legal penalties. In this regard, the spot market for natural gas differed materially from spot markets in financial instruments in which delivery could be assured.

In a few years, buyers and sellers of natural gas had seen relatively predictable prices (and, to a lesser extent, quantities) suddenly become volatile and unstable. Some buyers

---

4   A common carrier is a transporter obligated by law to provide without discrimination service to all interested parties. If the capacity of a common-carrier pipeline is insufficient to fulfill demand, it has to offer services to all shippers in proportion to the amounts they tender for shipment. A common carrier differs from a private carrier (that owns the commodity it carries) or a contract carrier (that voluntarily provides its service on a contractual basis for other parties). Prior to 1985, gas pipelines were primarily private carriers and secondarily contract carriers.

and sellers might have preferred to mitigate their exposure to this volatility, but as of the late 1980s, this type of arrangement did not exist. Even if a large industrial gas user and a producer could identify one another and agree to a customized delivery contract, they would bear the credit risk of the counterparty and have to arrange for transportation of the gas. The natural gas market appeared ready for innovation.

ENRON GAS SERVICES

In the late 1980s, Enron Corporation was the nation's largest integrated natural gas company. It operated the nation's largest pipeline system, marketed gas globally, was one of the largest independent gas exploration and production companies, and was one of the largest independent producers of electricity in the United States. Enron was involved primarily in the physical side of the business, as a producer, transporter, marketer, and consumer. During the 1980's, Enron had developed a range of new natural gas services, but in 1988 it embarked on a strategy of delivering financial services to the natural gas industry.

Jeff Skilling, a senior partner with McKinsey & Company in the firm's North American Energy and Chemical Practices in Houston, developed the idea that would become Enron Gas Services while working with Enron on a 1988 McKinsey engagement. Mr. Skilling had joined McKinsey in 1979 after graduating from Harvard Business School. He had also worked as a corporate planning officer at a Houston bank and as an associate with a London based investment banking firm. It was Mr. Skilling's experiences in financial services and energy that led him to develop a vision for EGS as a hybrid natural gas and financial services firm.

Mr. Skilling initially conceptualized EGS as a way to build on Enron's strength in the natural gas industry by creating a "gas bank," similar to a commercial bank. The gas bank would intermediate between the buyers and sellers of gas, with the spread between the selling price and the purchase price locked in as profit, much as a bank locks in a spread between deposits and loans. In this banking analogy, gas producers were depositors who put money (gas) into the bank, and consumers were borrowers. Like a bank, the organization would pool deposits (supply commitments) to fund long-term commitments of 15 or more years.

In fashioning the analogy with banking, Mr. Skilling was aware of the banking and thrift crises of the 1980s brought about by the failure of depository institutions to manage their exposure to changes in interest rates. Thrift institutions had assets made up of 30-year fixed-rate loans and liabilities composed of deposits paying short-term interest rates. A dramatic increase in interest rates pushed up the rates paid to depositors without a corresponding increase in inflows from their mortgage portfolios. Were it not for deposit insurance and regulatory forbearance—upon which a gas bank could not rely—the thrifts would have become bankrupt. The banking analogy made clear the need for a gas bank to have a superior asset-liability management program in place.

Initially, natural gas experts were skeptical of the gas bank idea, given their perceptions that end users would not enter into long-term contracts if gas prices were falling and uncertain. To the contrary, Enron's premarketing in March 1989 revealed a large appetite for such contracts; within three weeks, the company had received indications of strong interest in over 600 Bcf of gas in the form of long-term, fixed-price contracts.[5] Fortunately, Enron Oil and Gas, the exploration and production arm of Enron Corporation, agreed to supply the bulk of the long-term gas at fixed prices for these initial contracts.

From the outset, Mr. Skilling recognized the value of complementary physical and financial contracts. In 1989 negotiations broke down with a Louisiana aluminum producer who sought to obtain fixed-price gas from Enron. Enron's costs to physically transport the gas made the transaction unattractive. Just as everyone was getting up from the negotiating table, the negotiating team suggested that the aluminum firm continue to buy its gas locally—at floating prices, but low transportation costs. Enron could then write a financial contract in which the aluminum producer would effectively pay Enron fixed payments while Enron paid the producer's floating prices. The aluminum producer could minimize its costs of physically obtaining gas, while using a financial contract to tailor the form of its payments. Though the Enron team did not realize it at the time, they had executed what in hindsight was one of the first natural gas swaps.

Mr. Skilling took steps to build the financial settlement contract business soon after joining Enron, in 1990, as chairman and CEO of Enron Finance Corporation. From 1990 through 1993, Enron spent $60 million to develop its Financial Trading System, staffed by a mix of gas experts and Wall Street traders, to develop an information and trading system that permitted the organization to function as the trading desk of an investment bank. The potential benefits of integrating the physical and the financial sides of the gas business inspired the vision for Enron Gas Services (EGS), officially established in early 1991 by the merger of the Enron Finance Corporation and Enron's gas marketing organization. EGS was designed to have units specifically targeted toward meeting the needs of gas users (Market Origination Units) and the needs of producers (Supply Origination Units), as well as units that managed intermediation activities for physical and financial contracts

---

5   One Mcf is equal to 1,000 cubic feet of gas, a measure of volume. One MMcf is equal to one million cubic feet of gas and one Bcf equals one billion cubic feet. Often, quantities are expressed in terms of the energy output of gas, expressed in Btus, or British thermal units. A Btu is the energy required to raise the temperature of water from 58.5° to 59.5° F. One MBtu is 1000 Btus, one MMBtu is one million Btus, and one BBtu is a billion Btus. Roughly, one cubic foot of gas contains about 1,000 Btus; thus, 1 Mcf = 1 MMBtu.

(Centralized Logistics and Risk Management). Exhibit 3 shows the organization of EGS as of 1993.

Though EGS offered suppliers and consumers of gas a variety of services, ranging from gas transport, logistics, and back-office systems, its core was a set of relationships among EGS, suppliers, and users that allowed for innovation in contracting, especially concerning long-term, fixed-price gas contracts. According to Enron's analysis, the "modern" natural gas market differed substantially from other developed markets. In natural gas, less than 10% of all sales were on a long-term, fixed-rate basis. In contrast, by EGS staff estimates, two-thirds or more of corporate bonds, mortgages, and gold contracts were long-term, fixed-rate contracts. EGS's leaders believed that the natural gas business ultimately would move to greater reliance on long-term, fixed-rate contracts, and EGS's strategy was clearly laid out in the 1992 Enron *Annual Report:*

> The goal of EGS is to increase the use of long-term, fixed-price contracts, while supporting EGS's position as the high value provider. EGS plans to continue its pursuit of market segmentation and to design specific products for each of its markets.

By many measures, EGS had succeeded in its mission. By 1992 it was the largest non-regulated gas merchant in North America, the largest buyer and seller of natural gas in North America, manager of the largest portfolio of fixed-price gas and natural gas derivative contracts in the world, the largest supplier of gas to the electricity-generating industry in North America, and operator of the largest pipeline system in Texas. EGS became the second-largest contributor to Enron's net income in 1992, reporting an EBIT (earnings before interest and taxes) of $122 million, more than double its 1991 earnings and more than four times its 1990 earnings. See Exhibit 4 for publicly available financial information on Enron and EGS and stock price information on Enron's common stock.

EGS's success had to be judged in light of the risks it bore. The 1992 Enron *Annual Report* quoted above went on to describe the critical issue that the *Forbes* article would later spotlight:

> Perhaps most importantly, EGS will continue to offer products and services that highlight its unique ability to provide reliable gas delivery at predictable prices . . . *all of which will be accomplished with limited commodity risk to Enron.*[6]

To understand the risks EGS took on and managed, one must better understand the contracts the firm entered into with its counterparties and the operations of the EGS unit charged with monitoring and controlling the risks borne by EGS. The next three sections

---

6   1992 Enron Annual Report, page 21. Emphasis was added by casewriter.

describe EGS's contracts with suppliers and consumers of natural gas and the activities of Enron Risk Management Services (ERMS).

CONTRACTING WITH GAS SUPPLIERS: SUPPLY ORIGINATION UNITS

In order to write long-term, fixed-price supply agreements with users of natural gas, EGS had to obtain reliable long-term sources of fixed-price gas. In the late 1980s and early 1990s, financially secure gas producers refused to enter into these supply contracts, because common wisdom held that prices would soon rise. Whereas the strongest producers could wait for an upturn in prices, some of the others were driven into a fragile financial condition by low prices. Faced with ongoing financial commitments and limited external financing, some private producers were forced to sell gas at prices below their average costs.[7] Failure to continue to produce would lead to bankruptcy and loss of control for these independent producers.

Even barring their short-term operating cash flow needs, forward-thinking natural gas producers' strategic plans dictated that they make large capital investments to create new supply to meet the large projected demand.[8] EGS estimated that to bring one Mcf of annual production on-line, investors in the natural gas chain were required to make an investment of more than $23.00, of which roughly half would be used for exploration and production and the other half for distribution and consumption capacity. For instance, Zilkha Energy Company, a medium-sized independent producer, used a three-dimensional seismic exploration of the Gulf of Mexico to locate gas reserves. This effort, along with Zilkha's annual exploration and development needs, demanded annual investments more than twice the size of its annual net revenues, necessitating outside financing.

A wide variety of factors denied producers access to external financing. Most banks were unwilling to advance additional funds to producers, given their existing exposure to wide price fluctuations. The collapse of the Texas banking system in the 1980s was directly related to the volatility of the oil and gas industry. Furthermore, the downturn in the late 1980s meant that those surviving banks could no longer justify the costly engineering activities needed to support collateralized oil and gas lending. Finally, out-of-state banks,

---

7   The marginal costs of production in natural gas were quite low relative to the average costs of production, which included the allocation of fixed and sunk costs involved in creating production and processing infrastructure.

8   Though the market for gas heating was felt to be saturated, analysts projected that greater use of natural gas in power generation, cooling, and innovative vehicles would significantly increase demand. Environmental regulation, along with the economics of natural gas as a fuel source, were held to be important stimuli for these increases in demand.

not steeped in the tradition of reserve lending, were reluctant to lend to high-risk producers, given their disinterest in taking physical ownership of a bankrupt firm's gas fields. Institutional investors failed to provide debt to the industry because they were obligated to deem as speculative any oil and gas investments, against which their charters and regulations mandated they hold large financial reserves for losses.[9] At the current trough of industry performance, equity markets were effectively closed.

By supplying financing to weak producers, EGS could obtain long-term, fixed-rate gas. However, the contract between EGS and its suppliers had to meet EGS's needs as well as those of the suppliers. There was a continuum of contracts used to secure the future supply of gas: some resembling debt and others resembling equity in terms of the legal and economic interest transferred. At the equity end of the continuum, one could buy all of the land and its mineral reserves using fee-simple purchase contracts in which the buyer would have an ownership position and thus be exposed to changes in operating costs, environmental liabilities, and the physical characteristics of the gas field.[10]

At the debt end of the spectrum were gas purchase contracts, first liens, and prepayment contracts. In the gas purchase contract, a producer would agree to sell gas to the buyer for a predetermined price. Timely payments would be made as the buyer received the gas. However, in the event of default, there would be no security and no easily enforceable provision of damages to the buyer. In the event of nonperformance, the buyer could sue the producer in court or settle through arbitration. Sometimes gas purchase contracts specified that the producer was obligated to provide any gas from the field to the buyer before selling it elsewhere. In a traditional secured loan, the lender would receive as security a first lien, or mortgage, on the gas field. In the event of default, the lender would need to foreclose on the property under bankruptcy proceedings before being able to exercise fully its control over the property. A prepayment contract was an advance payment to the producer for a certain amount of gas. The buyer would pay in advance for the gas, with this interest usually secured by the reserves, the producer's balance sheet, or a letter of credit from a third party. In the event of a default, the holder of a prepayment contract could exercise its rights as a secured lender to the firm through the bankruptcy process.

EGS's attorneys and financiers sought to develop an innovative equity contract that would provide long-term gas to EGS with minimal risk of price, quantity, production cost, or credit fluctuations. It would not depend on the process of bankruptcy to enforce its

---

9   An additional complication inhibiting the flow of debt to strapped Texas gas producers was the leniency of Texas bankruptcy judges, perceived to be very forgiving to debtors.

10   One could buy a partial interest in the mineral rights through a working-interest contract.

rights. Finally, it had to be able to be securitized and marketed to investors as a synthetic debt instrument, solving Enron's need to raise funds. The new contract, termed a Volumetric Production Payment (VPP), was based on a structure used in the early twentieth century by oil and coal producers.[11] Modernizing the old contract reportedly took more than 18 months and "millions of dollars" in legal fees to design.

A VPP (also known as a term overriding royalty interest) was an ownership interest in hydrocarbons in place (in the ground) that entitled its owner to a designated share of production for a limited period of time or until a specific amount of hydrocarbons had been delivered. Under the terms of a VPP, EGS would pay for the gas in advance. In return, EGS was entitled to a predetermined volume of produced gas over a certain time period, free from the costs of production. However, unlike a prepayment contract, in the event of bankruptcy, EGS would have a direct legal claim on the reserves. The VPP created an "interest that is distinct from the estate of a producer in an insolvency proceeding." In other words, the reserves would not pass through bankruptcy proceedings; instead, they would belong to EGS, which could produce them to recover its gas commitment.[12]

The first VPP was signed in 1990 between EGS and Forest Oil Corporation, a gas producer struggling to avert bankruptcy. EGS paid $44.8 million, which entitled Enron to approximately 32 billion cubic feet of gas production over a period of five years, or about half of Forest Oil's gas reserves. Under the terms of the VPP, Forest Oil was responsible for all production costs.

EGS's only recourse in its transaction with VPP counterparties was the producers' reserves dedicated to fulfilling the VPP contract. Therefore, a major risk was that the gas reservoir might stop producing before the terms of the VPP were fulfilled. To manage this risk, EGS entered into VPP contracts only against proven, developed, and producing reserves. Furthermore, it employed one of the largest reservoir engineering groups in the industry to determine the life of the reservoir and estimate the possible gas production. Finally, EGS structured its production payments so that its annual gas commitments were only a fraction of the total proven reserves of the gas field.

EGS projected that by the end of 1993, it would have originated more than $1 billion in production payments. VPPs were an effective means of obtaining fixed-price gas, but they required considerable advance payments. To finance these outlays, EGS used the financial technique of securitization. In effect, the gas flows produced a series of cash flows that

11 At the turn of the century, banks were the holders of these equity contracts. With the regulation of the banking industry in the 1930s, banks were restricted in their equity holdings and thus the contracts became virtually extinct.

12 In the one bankruptcy of a gas producer with which EGS had written a VPP, EGS's contractual rights were recognized by the bankruptcy court.

were sold to investors in off-balance sheet limited partnership vehicles, such as EGS's Cactus Funds, which, by mid-1993, had been used to raise $900 million.

To construct the Cactus Funds, EGS contributed to the funds a pool of VPP contracts that would effectively produce a stream of known gas supplies, that could be sold at spot prices. ERMS would enter into a natural gas swap (described in detail below) in which it would exchange floating-rate gas prices for fixed prices for the amount of production committed from the VPP. The net result was that the holder of the VPP-plus-gas swap had a known and fixed cash flow, which, like the fixed payments on a bond, could again be swapped for a cash flow that floated with interest rates (such as LIBOR, the London Interbank Offered Rate). The end result (a VPP and two swaps) was a security paying LIBOR on a principal amount that declined over time (as the reserves were depleted). This security, enhanced with a letter of credit from an AA-rated commercial bank guaranteeing EGS's performance, was a financial instrument marketable to financial institutions comfortable in dealing with amortizing LIBOR-based investments.

VPPs and Cactus Funds were representative of the innovative approach that EGS's Supply Origination Units took to provide financing to gas producers. Their full product line included traditional loans to finance reserves, hedged reserve loans, nonrecourse financing, and acquisition financing. Other innovations included the EnVestor[SM] program, in which Enron pooled suppliers' commitments to provide gas, and partnerships with external equity capital sources to acquire and manage gas reserves.

In a 1991 article, an uncharitable observer labeled Enron's clientele of 35 producers "hard-luck cases."[13] From the producers' perspective, EGS appeared to provide valuable services, not only financing them when other sources were depleted or appeared prohibitively expensive, but also marketing their noncommitted gas production. Furthermore, through financial contracts, suppliers could effectively determine their exposure to fluctuations in natural gas prices, by either selling at market prices, index-linked prices, fixed prices, or prices constrained by contractual lower and upper limits.

CONTRACTING WITH GAS USERS: MARKET ORIGINATION UNITS

EGS's Market Origination Units offered natural gas users products capable of adjusting the certainty of the quantity or price of gas they bought. These products ranged from relatively standard contracts to highly customized gas supply agreements and included contracts leading to physical delivery and financial settlement.

---

13   Thomas C. Hayes, "Bottom Fishing in the Gas Patch," *New York Times*, May 19, 1991, Section 3.

By 1992, EGS had become the largest marketer of natural gas in North America, delivering almost 5.6 billion cubic feet daily to its customers. The firm's gas marketing area was divided into units defined by the customer segment targeted: Enron Gas Marketing sold gas to LDCs; Enron Power Services targeted electric utilities and independent power producers; Enron Hydrocarbon Services supplied natural gas to large industrial and chemical processing firms; Enron Access marketed natural gas to small industrial firms and commercial businesses (essentially in competition with LDCs); and Enron Energy Ventures marketed compressed natural gas for use in vehicles and for commercial applications.

EGS offered gas users more than 100 varieties of contracts for physical delivery or financial settlement. See Exhibit 5 for a breakdown of EGS's contracts from 1989 through early 1993. The contracts that provided for physical delivery could be either for firm delivery (in which EGS guaranteed delivery) or for interruptible delivery (in which EGS did not guarantee delivery).[14] EGS also offered physical contracts with terms giving users the ability to take variable amounts of gas. These quantity options could be used by gas consumers to ensure that they had sufficient natural gas, for example, in the event of a colder-than-anticipated winter.

The fastest growing segment of contracts at EGS was for financial settlement, in which no natural gas molecules were exchanged. For example, in a simple natural gas swap, the user might agree to pay EGS $2.00 per MMBtu for a given quantity for one year, and EGS might agree to pay the user a floating index price for same notional quantity of gas.[15] By combining a swap with an indexed gas supply contract, a user could lock in a fixed cost. EGS financial settlement contracts could also be used to establish caps and floors on gas prices, to index gas prices to other commodities, or to protect users against price differences between alternative gas delivery points.

---

14 In an *interruptible* contract, a supplier could unilaterally refuse to deliver gas for any reason, although suppliers often honored their interruptible contracts to protect their ongoing business relationships. If the supplier in a *firm* delivery contract was unable to make delivery, either because of the unavailability of gas or pipeline capacity to transport it, the buyer would typically be entitled to collect direct damages, which might be specified as the costs of obtaining alternative gas, plus a predetermined penalty. If the contract did not specify damages for nonperformance, the buyer could typically sue under Article 2 of the Uniform Commercial Code. Some firms offered contracts that were for neither interruptible nor firm delivery. For example, the supplier could choose not to deliver for any reason except for changes in natural gas prices.

15 This contract was similar to an interest rate swap, in which one party paid a fixed rate of interest on a notional principal amount and the other party paid a floating rate tied to an index such as LIBOR.

EGS could engineer virtually any type of financial contract its users demanded, and it often bundled physical and financial contracts together for ease in marketing. For example, in marketing gas to LDCs, EGS developed a product line called Enfolio.[16] The Enfolio family of products represented an attempt to create a handful of brand-name, standardized products that would be simple to understand and communicate to users (and their regulators). These products offered users a menu of choices by which they could modify their exposure to quantity or price risk. See Exhibit 6 for a description of the contracts and Exhibit 7 for an example of the advertising supporting the fixed-price-gas campaign.

The five basic Enfolio products could be customized in a variety of ways, varying the quantity of gas delivered, the period of time covered by the contract, the index against which the prices would be set, the level at which prices would be truncated, and other contractual terms. The value of the Enfolio contracts was that they could embed natural gas derivatives into simple standardized structures bearing an Enron promise. Mr. Skilling had said, "Selling natural gas is [finally] getting to be a real business, like selling washing machines. We are taking the simplest commodity there is, a methane molecule, and we're packaging and delivering it under a brand name, as General Electric does."

To electric utilities and independent power producers, EGS offered highly customized long-term gas contracts. Because fuel supply costs were roughly 80% of plant operating costs, contracts mitigating gas price risk were essential in helping independent power producers secure financing for their projects. In many instances, EGS worked with customers to arrange transportation of the gas, secure project financing, or obtain regulatory approvals. An example of this type of contract was the agreement between Enron and Sithe Energies, an independent power producer. The gas supply agreement EGS signed in 1992 with Sithe provided a 20-year supply of natural gas to its 1,000-MW power plant in New York state. The gas EGS supplied to Sithe was sold at a fixed price for five years, then was indexed to power costs. EGS also managed the delivery of gas to Sithe through a massive network of pipelines that spanned the North American continent.

---

16 LDCs and other regulated public utilities faced some regulatory risk by hedging to achieve price stability. With cost-plus pricing, utilities merely passed along their higher costs to customers. If an LDC entered into a hedge, by law, any savings obtained would have to be passed on to consumers. If, however, prices fell and the fixed-price gas it purchased was deemed by regulators to have been "imprudent" after the fact, these costs could be denied. However, in an increasingly deregulated environment in which LDCs had to compete directly with other marketers, risk management could serve as a competitive tool.

CENTRALIZATION AND COORDINATION: ENRON RISK MANAGEMENT SERVICES (ERMS)

Within EGS on any day, the staff of the Supply Origination Units obtained gas from suppliers, and the staff of the Market Origination Units lined up buyers. EGS could offer its diverse range of products to both parties only if it could manage its own risks as an intermediary. As a "gas bank," EGS had to contend with counterparty credit risk and price risk.[17] The counterparty risk arose if a gas buyer or seller defaulted on its contractual obligation. The price risk arose even if the counterparties honored their contracts, but there was a mismatch between the nature of EGS's assets (long-term contracts with buyers) and its liabilities (long-term contracts with producers). To monitor and control EGS's exposure to price and credit risks, to centralize the flow of information within the firm, and to offer a wide array of financial settlement contracts, Enron Risk Management Services (ERMS) stood at the core of EGS. The financial side of ERMS, dominated by a trading floor with more than $60 million in computer systems and 50 staff drawn primarily from Wall Street, safeguarded the firm against bearing undue commodity price risk. The entire operation of ERMS, including back-office and physical (as opposed to financial) traders, included 170 persons in mid- 1993.

No commitment to buy or sell gas could be made, nor could a price be given to a customer, without the explicit guidance of ERMS. All transactions in which EGS was a partner were to be routed through ERMS so that all of the firm's contractual exposures could be monitored. ERMS was not a passive monitor of the firm's exposures but an active creator and manager of these exposures. The ERMS group offered producers, consumers, investors, and lenders in the natural gas business a variety of derivative products, including natural gas swaps, caps, floors, collars, swaptions (swap options), firm forwards, and other structured risk-management products.[18] Finally, ERMS managed EGSs exposures by entering into exchange-listed natural gas futures contracts as well as over-the-counter transactions with Wall Street commodities groups and traders of physical gas, both of which would serve to reduce EGS's net exposures.

In concept, what ERMS did was straightforward. It took the contracts to which the firm was a party and broke them down into five different types or exposures, contained in databases called books. The trader managing each book had a picture of all of the firm's

---

17 As an intermediary with commitments of physical molecules, EGS also had to manage its exposure to the storage and movement of gas. These activities, not discussed extensively in the case, resided in the EGS Physical Delivery units, that specialized in storage, transportation, and logistics.

18 *Risk Magazine* (February 1993) recognized ERMS's activity in this area by naming it the number-one commodity trader in natural gas short-term swaps, long-term swaps, and exotic products/structured transactions, and number two in options trading.

exposures to a particular risk, as well as current market quotations for that risk. The trader therefore was in a position from which he or she could advise Market or Supply Origination Units about the minimum price of particular contracts. In addition, the trader could enter into transactions to permit the book to be matched. With a matched book, EGS's commitments on either side of the market would cancel one another out, leaving the firm with no net exposure.

ERMS was central to EGS's stated mission to offer innovative products and services "with limited commodity risk to Enron."[19] Without ERMS, the firm might unwittingly amass large exposures. Publicized concerns about EGS focused on the risks to which the firm was exposed, and ERMS was charged with managing these exposures. The workings of ERMS would best be understood by dissecting one typical transaction and observing how the system of decomposing contracts into fundamental exposures operated. In the course of a year, ERMS might be party to more than 250 to 300 customer financial transactions, of which the following is representative. In addition, ERMS might engage in three or four times as many financial transactions with noncustomers as part of its trading and hedging activities.

ANATOMY OF A TRANSACTION

Suppose that a marketer from EGS's Gas Marketing Group proposed that ABC, Inc., an AA-rated Arizona-based LDC, enter into an Enfolio GasBank agreement whereby Enron would supply ABC with 15 MMBtus/day of methane over the next three years for firm delivery at the Permian Basin[20] for a fixed price of $2.00/MMBtu. Prior to making this proposal, the marketer would have contacted the ERMS trading desk to obtain the price for which EGS could make the commitment. To provide the price, ERMS traders maintained up-to-date information that established forward curves for gas for the next 15 years. These forward curves were used to provide notional, or indicative, prices for deals on the following day. The actual prices at which contracts were struck depended on the market prices when the deal was executed and incorporated a spread charged by ERMS. Only if the pricing was acceptable to the customer would the marketer ask the ERMS traders to arrange for the transaction.

The ERMS staff did more than quote prices to marketers and measure risk. They entered into offsetting contracts as necessary to reduce the net risk to Enron. What appeared to be a straightforward transaction to a customer (buying gas at a fixed price) could actually involve three of the five books in EGS. These books, which managed different

---

19 1992 Enron Annual Report.

20 The Permian Basin is a gas reservoir in west Texas and southeast New Mexico containing approximately 73 trillion cubic feet of natural gas.

types of exposures, included the price book, the basis book, the index book, the transport book, and the "omicron" book. Exhibit 8 diagrams the decomposition of EGSs exposures as a result of entering into the Enfolio Gas Bank contract with ABC, Inc. The following sections describe the five books.

GAS PRICE BOOK

The gas price book managed the exposure EGS faced as a result of its commitments to buy and sell gas at fixed prices. Specifically, it was a database of commitments calling for Enron to exchange fixed prices for a particular indexed price, that for gas delivered at Henry Hub (the delivery point for the NYMEX futures contract) in central Louisiana. This book was similar to a list of interest-rate swap commitments entered into by a bank, in which the bank had commitments to exchange a fixed interest rate for a given index, such as six-month LIBOR. The gas price book contained information on counterparties with which the deal was made, volumes for each month of the contracts, and the fixed price at which the deal was struck.

If a natural gas user wanted to enter into a swap in which it paid a fixed price and received the floating Henry Hub price, this transaction would pass through the gas price book only. Because ABC, Inc.'s Enfolio Gas Bank contract involved an index other than Henry Hub and because it involved physical delivery, other books would also be involved.

The trader managing the gas price book monitored all of EGS's exposure to buy or sell fixed-price gas in exchange for the floating Henry Hub index price. Exhibit 9 diagrams the gross and net exposures of EGS, and the sources of its long and short exposures. When EGS sold fixed-price gas, it created a short position; contracts with LDCs tended to involve relatively short-term commitments, those with industrial users created commitments of a few years or less, and those with cogeneration plants, such as Sithe Energies, committed EGS to deliver fixed-price gas for many years. When EGS bought fixed-price gas, it created a long position. Volumetric production payments and hedging contracts in which producers accepted fixed prices accounted for most of EGS's long-dated commitments to buy at fixed prices. To obtain short-dated, fixed price commitments for gas delivered within 18 months, the trader managing the gas price book could buy natural gas futures contracts on the New York Mercantile Exchange (NYMEX).[21] This liquid market allowed the price

---

21 The NYMEX natural gas futures contract first traded in June 1990. A buyer of one NYMEX contract committed to purchase 10,000 MMBtus of natural gas for delivery at the Henry Hub location in the month called for by the contract. Futures contracts extended only for maturities of 18 months or less. For example, on June 15, 1993, the December 1993 futures contract closed at $2.59, meaning that on that day, a buyer of the contract committed to purchase 10,000 MMBtus of gas for delivery in December 1993 at a price of $2.59 per MMBtu. As with other futures contracts, NYMEX futures contracts were marked-to-market daily, and gains or losses on the contracts were exchanged between the parties.

book trader to obtain fixed-price gas commitments to offset the firm's short-term commitments to supply fixed-price gas. To obtain additional exposure to fixed gas prices for periods longer than 18 months, the price trader could enter into over-the-counter (OTC), or nonexchange-traded, contracts. The counterparties to these contracts included the trading desks of major oil and gas firms, as well as the commodity groups at major investment banks. By matching the characteristics of its long and short portfolio of commitments, EGS sought to create zero net exposure.[22] As Exhibit 9 shows, its net position hovered close to zero.

BASIS BOOK

The basis book managed the risk that arose as a result of the difference in gas prices between the Henry Hub and other index locations. Because natural gas was not easily transportable and could be moved only through pipelines, prices at different delivery points varied widely, depending on the supply and demand at particular locations. For example, especially cold weather might increase the demand for natural gas at location A, driving up its relative price.

As an example of a firm exposed to basis risk, consider NATGAS, Inc., a producer that in June attempted to lock in the price of gas for delivery in December. NATGAS committed to physically sell its gas at the Permian index location and hedged itself by selling a December NYMEX contract at $2.20. If gas prices at Permian and Henry Hub were initially equal and moved in tandem, then NATGAS would lock in the $2.20 price for the sale of gas.[23] However, if Henry Hub and Permian Prices diverged, NATGAS would no longer be hedged. If NYMEX/Henry Hub rose to $2.70 and Permian prices fell to $2.10, the producer would end up selling gas not at the $2.20 price, but at $1.60.[24] NATGAS would be exposed if the NYMEX/Henry Hub prices and Permian prices did not move in tandem and the producer had not hedged its basis risk (the difference between the two prices). Industry experts estimated that in 1992, 60% of all natural gas swap activity was indexed to locations other than Henry Hub.

---

22 Option contracts, such as caps or floors, were incorporated in the gross position by decomposing them into their exposures. For example, if EGS was to sell a cap on Henry Hub prices, it would effectively write a put on the index price. The put could be expressed as a dynamically adjusted portfolio of long and short positions, in which the delta of the put reflected its economic exposure to the floating price index at any time.

23 In this event, any gains (losses) the producer would make on the physical contract by an increase (decrease) in the gas price would be offset by losses (gains) on the futures contract, which would typically be closed out or settled without any physical delivery of gas.

24 In this event, the producer would receive $2.10 for the sale of gas and would have a $.50 loss on his futures position, leading to a net price of $1.60.

Index prices for the sale of gas at every index location were established once a month during a week called the bid week, and prices were published in several industry magazines. Gas was usually sold at the published index price for the following month. Basis traders tracked current basis differentials and attempted to forecast the basis by collecting information from OTC traders, as well as from producers. Because basis estimation required extremely detailed knowledge of local supply-and-demand characteristics, as well as an intimate understanding of the physical movement of gas through pipelines, basis traders typically had extensive experience in the natural gas business.

The basis book contained the following information for each index or basis location: volume of indexed gas bought and sold at that location, counterparty with which the trade was made, basis price at which the deal was made, and estimated basis for that month for that location. Although the basis trader could speculate on the widening or narrowing of particular index location differentials, her important job was to mitigate EGS's exposure to basis risk by entering into offsetting basis swaps. A basis swap was an exchange of two indices, such that the net difference between the two indices was exchanged by the counterparties. For example, the basis trader could enter into a contract in which she would pay NYMEX/Henry Hub index prices and receive Permian index prices. Basis swaps were over-the-counter transactions. Counterparties for *short-dated* basis swaps were usually commodity traders, whereas counterparties for *long-dated* basis swaps were usually gas producers and users. For particular basis locations, basis swaps could be highly illiquid with large bid-ask spreads.

In the NATGAS, Inc., example given above, the producer could eliminate its remaining basis risk by entering into a basis swap with ERMS in which it paid the Permian index price and received the NYMEX/Henry Hub price. Alternatively, the Supply Origination Units of EGS could have bundled the NYMEX contract and the basis swap and merely offered the producer a financial settlement contract in which the producer would receive $2.20 and pay the Permian index. ERMS would record this transaction on both its price and basis books.

INDEX BOOK

The index book managed the risk that EGS would have enough gas to meet its commitments for delivery at each location. Through its contracts to buy and sell gas at index locations, it bore the risk that the gas would not be physically available at that location at the desired time. The index book contained for each location details of the quantities of gas bought and sold for any given date at that location, and how much gas needed to be sold or bought to balance the book. The index book traders tried to ensure that the book remained balanced at any given location. If the index book was short, the trader could buy gas from gas producers; if it was long, it could sell to users. In addition, EGS had some flexibility in managing the index book because it owned pipelines and several storage locations. Provided that it was possible to transport the gas from a storage location to an index location, it could sell more gas than it bought at that index location.

A transaction in which a customer bought physical gas at an index location at a floating index price would involve only the index book. EGS would deliver the physical molecules to the customer. In turn, EGS would contract to receive the published index price plus $.03 to $.04 per MMBtu. This spread over the indexed price for financial contracts, commonly called the "cost of gas," represented the market price for firm delivery of gas.

THE TRANSPORT AND OMICROM BOOKS

The transport book contained a database of all pipeline capacities available for the transport of gas in any given day or month of the contracts. It enabled EGS to manage the physical risk associated with selling firm gas by ensuring that it could he delivered to the locations required by the contracts. The omicron book was a list of optional quantity commitments made by EGS. For example, an LDC might commit to buy 15 MMBtus from EGS, but also obtain an option to buy as much as 5% more (at floating prices). This option to buy additional quantities at market prices was especially valuable to utilities exposed to the risk of cold or warm weather, both of which increased demand for power and, thus, gas. Enron managed its contingent quantity exposures through its omicron book and might receive a premium of $.05 per MMBtu for bundling a quantity option onto an existing fixed-price contract.

SUMMARY: ABC INC.'S ENFOLIO
GASBANK CONTRACT AND ERMS'S EXPOSURES

The Enfolio GasBank contract between ABC and EGS, in which EGS delivered 15 MMBtus of gas per day to ABC at $2.00 per MMBtu, appeared to be a simple transaction from ABC's perspective. However, as Exhibit 8 shows, this simple transaction entailed at least three of the ERMS books. The *index book* delivered gas at Permian for which it received Permian Index plus the cost of gas ($.01). The index book covered this obligation with contracts with producers. The *basis book* exchanged the Permian index price for the NYMEX/Henry Hub price less $.20, covering itself through other offsetting positions or through basis swaps. The *price book* exchanged the NYMEX/Henry Hub price for a fixed price of $2.17, neutralizing its exposure through NYMEX futures or OTC swaps. The ABC contract was relatively straightforward; other commitments made by EGS could involve much more detailed structures, including caps and floors on prices, links between natural gas and other commodities, and complicated settlement terms.

The system of books allowed EGS to identify and manage price and quantity risks. To manage the risk that its counterparties would default, EGS employed a variety of mechanisms. It transacted primarily with firms with investment-grade credit ratings.[25] ERMS's credit department investigated firms below investment-grade and typically required them to post a letter of credit, or some other type of collateral prior to the initiation of the transaction. Furthermore, the firm's accounting recognized its potential exposure by maintaining reserves against possible losses.

Like some banks, but unlike any other industrial firm, Enron used mark-to-market accounting, in which it recognized as current income a portion of the net present value of hedged transactions at the time the contracts were initiated. Exhibit 10 explains how this accounting choice affected EGS's income statement and balance sheet. The *Forbes* article had questioned whether Enron's use of mark-to-market accounting was appropriate or misleading. Most major dealers of derivatives used mark-to-market accounting at this time, and a financial industry panel called the Group of 30 was rumored to recommend that mark-to-market be adopted by all derivatives dealers.

THE FUTURE OF EGS

By virtually any measure, EGS was a success. The firm had grown to more than 1,000 employees and contributed materially to the growth and profitability of Enron. The unit enjoyed growth in both its volume and per-unit price, leading to an annual doubling in earnings. EGS was touted in the natural gas industry as an innovator in natural gas derivatives. However, as a long-term thinker and strategist, Jeff Skilling could not rest comfortably, given the rapidly changing natural gas industry.

Competitors had quickly followed EGS's lead and came to provide the same or similar products to the natural gas industry. Competition arose from many directions. Producers (such as ARCO and Mobil) as well as gas marketers (such as Clearinghouse and Coastal) could offer many of the firm-delivery contracts that had propelled EGS's growth. "Wall Street Refiners" (such as AIG, Louis Dryfus, Phibro, J. Aron, and Bankers Trust) could provide many of the financial contracts (futures, swaps, options, basis contracts). Commercial banks (such as Chase, Chemical, Morgan Guaranty, and CitiBank) could also provide some of the financial contracts, as well as funding sources for producers. Mr. Skilling believed that no firm but Enron was in the position to offer a full range of physical, financial, and funding transactions. This unique ability to marry these transactions not only

---

25   Of Enron's counterparty credit exposure, 36% was to AA-rated firms, 26% to A-rated firms, and 19% to BBB-rated firms. Another 4% was to firms in which Enron had a production payment interest. The remaining 15% of its transactions was with firms rated BB or lower (7% BB, 5% B, and 3% CCC).

had increased the firm's ability to market integrated solutions to its customers, but also had given EGS valuable access to information flow in all natural gas markets.

Mr. Skilling was concerned that margins would eventually erode in the market for long-term, firm-delivery physical contracts, and for the simplest financial contracts. By analogy, margins in the earliest interest rate swap contracts were more than 50 basis points, but during a decade had fallen to roughly a tenth of this level. In anticipation of the inevitable shrinkage of margins, EGS was already moving toward providing the industry with more customized products such as quantity options, that allowed volume flexibility to customers, as well as cross-fuel hedges and exotic options. Furthermore, the firm sought to continue to identify niches of untapped buyers of fixed-price gas.

Reflecting his background as a strategy consultant, Jeff Skilling drew a diagram reflecting the uncertainty of EGS's immediate future. See Exhibit 11. If the natural gas business became even more competitive, could EGS continue to deliver the projected 20% growth in earnings that Mr. Skilling had announced to analysts? If it flattened, could he maintain the enthusiasm of his staff, many of whom were relative newcomers to the natural gas business? What were the real risks that EGS faced?

Though natural gas marketing was hardly a mature business, Mr. Skilling was already looking at the opportunity to apply EGS's techniques to another emerging commodity: electric power. The highly regulated U.S. electric power industry was beginning to undergo the same type of deregulation that the U.S. natural gas business had seen. In other countries, such as the United Kingdom and Argentina, commodity markets had begun to develop for electricity. In the United States, firms were beginning to position themselves to capitalize on potential opportunities. One independent power producer, AES, had established a power marketing company to sell electric power at market rates, and an EGS subsidiary, Enron Power Marketing, Inc. (EPMI), would soon file with the FERC for the authorization to buy and sell electric power at negotiated rates. In comparing natural gas to electricity, Jeff Skilling noted, "It's deja vu all over again."

Exhibit 1   Industry Participants in the Natural Gas Business

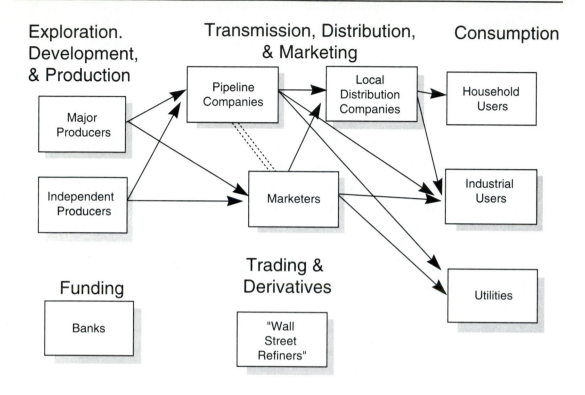

Exhibit 2   Price and Volality of energy sources

Panel A: Price of competing energy sources, 1974 to 1992

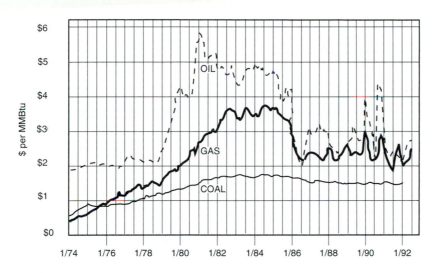

Source: Energy Information Administration, Monthly Energy Review, Jan. 1993.

**Panel B: Annualized volatility of natural gas and crude oil,
calculated on the basis of historical 60-day volatility, 1988–1993.**

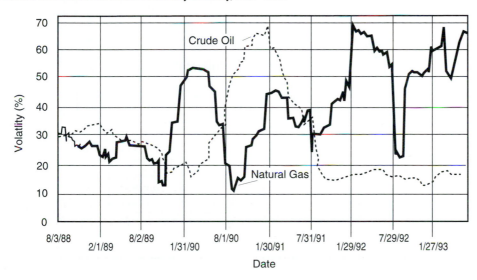

Source: Casewriter's estimate based on West Texas natural gas and intermediate oil prices.

Exhibit 3   Organization of Enron Gas Services, 1992

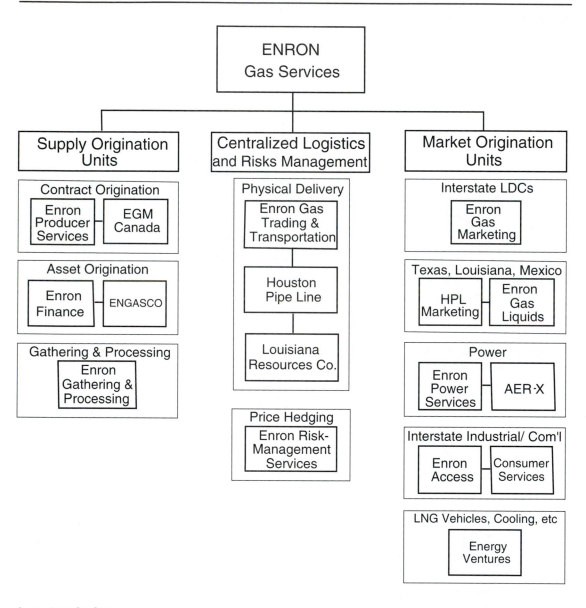

Exhibit 4 Panel A: Financial Information for Enron Corporation and Enron Gas Services,[a] 1990–1992 ($ in millions)

	1989	1990	1991	1992
Selected Income Statement Items				
Sales	$4,512	$5,336	$5,563	$6,325
Earnings before depreciation, interest, and taxes		787	851	981
Depreciation[b]		343	353	361
Operating profit		435	498	620
Interest expense		395	368	327
Non-operating income/expense		163	183	41
Special items		67	28	112
Pretax income		267	341	446
Income from continuing operations[c]	218	209	241	336
Net income	226	202	242	306
Earnings per share[d]	$ 1.93	$ 1.72	$ 2.04	$ 2.42
Dividends per share	1.24	1.24	1.26	1.32
Note: EGS earnings before interest & taxes (EBIT)	15	29	52	122

Exhibit 4 Panel A: Financial Information for Enron Corporation and Enron Gas Services,[a] 1990–1992
($ in millions) (Continued)

	1989	1990	1991	1992
Selected balance sheet items[e]				
Current assets			2,228	2,126
Portion from price risk management activities[f]			147	170
Investments and other assets			1,560	2,064
Portion from price risk management activities[f]			123	361
Net property, plant, and equipment			6,574	6,472
Total assets	8,883	10,138	10,363	10,664
Current liabilities			2,588	2,642
Portion from price risk management activities[f]			23	284
Long-term debt			3,109	2,459
Deferred credits and other liabilities			2,634	2,835
Portion from price risk management activities[f]			151	135
Minority interests			102	181
Shareholders' equity			1,929	2,547
Total liabilities and shareholders' equity	8,883	10,138	10,363	10,664
Note: rating of Enron senior debt	BBB	BBB	BBB	BBB

a. EGS results were not publicly reported prior tp 1989; financial results as given exclude EOTT Energy Corp. which was spun off to Enron shareholders in 1993.
b. Includes depreciation, depletion, and amortization.
c. Does not include extraordinary items or discontinued operations.
d. Fully diluted earnings per share, including extraordinary items and discontinued operations.
e. Enron adopted mark-to-market accounting for its price risk management activities in 1991. Price risk management activities were not material in 1990, and earlier financial statements were not restated to reflect this different treatment.
f. The assets and liabilities arising from Enron's price risk management activities were a product of the firm's mark-to-market accounting, as described in its 1992 annual report:

> Enron accounts for its price risk management activities under the mark-to-market method of accounting. Under this methodology, forward contracts, swaps, options, futures contracts and other financial instruments with third parties are reflected at market value, with resulting unrealized gains and losses recognized currently in the Consolidated Income Statement . . . The assets and liabilities included from price risk management activities in the Consolidated Balance Sheet reflect the market value of the contract portfolio including assets or liabilities which arise as a result of the actual timing of settlements related to these contracts The determination of market value considers factors including closing exchange market quotations, time value and volatility factors underlying the commitments, management's evaluation of future servicing costs and credit risks and the potential impact on market prices of liquidating Enron's position in an orderly manner over a reasonable period of time under present market conditions.

Exhibit 10 works through an example of how a set of transactions would affect EGS's income statement and balance sheet.

Exhibit 4   Panel B: Enron common stock performance, compared to the performance of other natural gas competitors and the S&P 500, 1988-1993 (Continued)

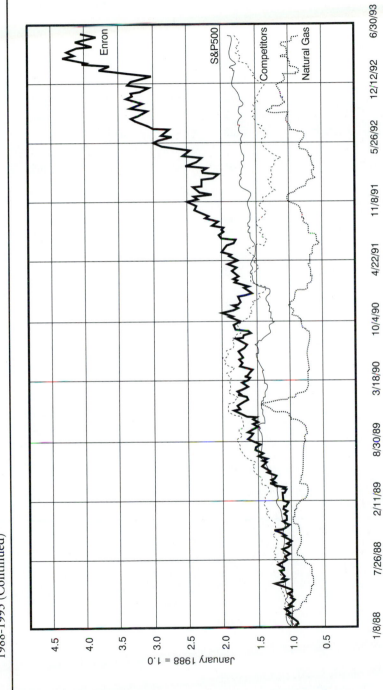

This figure plots the return to investors in Enron common stock as compared to returns to investors in an equally weighted basket of Enron's competitors (Coastal, Panhandle Eastern, Sonat, Tenneco, and Transco). The graph also shows the return to investors in the S&P 500 and the relative price of natural gas over the period.

Exhibit 5   Operating and Financial Information for EGS, 1988–1993

	1989	1990	1991	1992	1993[d]
Physical/notional quantities (BBtu/d)					
Firm[a]	686	1,276	1,539	2,632	4,310
Interruptible[b]	1,837	1,588	1,597	893	828
Total physical	2,523	2,864	3,190	3,525	5,138
Financial settlement[c]	0	69	424	1,536	5,027
Total	2,523	2,933	3,614	5,061	10,165
Fixed-price contracts originated (BcF)	664	410	964	2,165	3,781
Production payments originated ($ million)					
With third parties	46	4	121	189	413
With Enron Oil and Gas				327	
Headcount in "nontraditional" merchant services	95	144	235	548	1,069
Earnings before interest and taxes ($ million)	15	29	52	122	170
Breakdown of gross margin by strategic business unit					
Supply origination			11%	16%	21%
Market origination			14%	21%	28%
Risk management			13%	31%	24%
Physical delivery			62%	32%	27%

Source: Enron Gas Services.
a. Commitments to deliver a specified volume of gas at a fixed or market-responsive price.
b. Deliveries of gas on a best-efforts basis.
c. Notional quantities of swaps, futures, and options settled during the period.
d. 1993 figures represent estimates for full year.

Exhibit 6   Enfolio Gas Resource Agreements

Level[a]	Agreement Name	Volume[b]	Price[c]
	Enfolio GasBank	Firm	Fixed
	Enfolio GasCap	Firm	Truncated
	Enfolio GasBlend	Firm	Dampened
	Enfolio Index	Firm	Floating
	Enfolio 30	30-day firm	Fixed

Source: Enron Gas Services.
a. Graphics show the price paid by the user as a function of indexed gas prices.
b. "Firm" refers to firm delivery for the life of the contract or for the period in question.
c. Description of the price paid relative to the indexed market prices.

Exhibit 7   Enron Advertising Literature

See Spot.

See Spot
having problems
long-term.

See the answer: EnFolio™ Gas Resource Agreements.

Buying only on the spot market makes the cost of natural gas purchased today low. But it definitely raises future risk—especially if Spot starts having "problems." The opportunity: gas customers who begin to build customized natural gas portfolios now can diversify supply commitments and manage the impact of future gas costs.

So Enron Gas Services (part of Enron Corp., America's leading integrated gas company) created the unique EnFolio Gas Resource Agreements, to give local distribution companies and other large natural gas users supply reliability with price predictability over time. We're making significant investments—in dollars, talent and time—to ensure that fuel supply managers benefit from long-term natural gas commitments. That they'll be protected against unpredictable gas pricing. And that they can always count on reliable gas supply and delivery.

EnFolio Gas Resource Agreements are stable, long-term alternatives to short-term gas purchases because we have combined three supporting practices.

First: production financing ensures a reliable reserve of gas to meet Enron customers' long-term needs.

Second: state-of-the-art risk management lets Enron lock in the price of gas long-term, minimizing price volatility for our customers.

And third: comprehensive marketing balances supply and demand nationwide by developing new markets, so that for every provider of gas there's a waiting customer, and vice-versa, at predictable prices.

EnFolio Gas Resource Agreements, one result of this combination of practices, let customers get more flexibility and more reliability in their gas supply programs. With a lot less risk. Why should *you* call 800/742-SPOT (FAX: 713/750-6831) to find out more? Because no one can predict Spot's future health.

ENRON
Gas Services Corp.

A subsidiary of Enron Corp. © 1992, Enron Gas Services Corp.

Source: Enron Gas Services.

Exhibit 8   ERMS Decomposition of EGS's Exposures Due to ABC, Inc., Purchase of Enfolio GasBank Contract

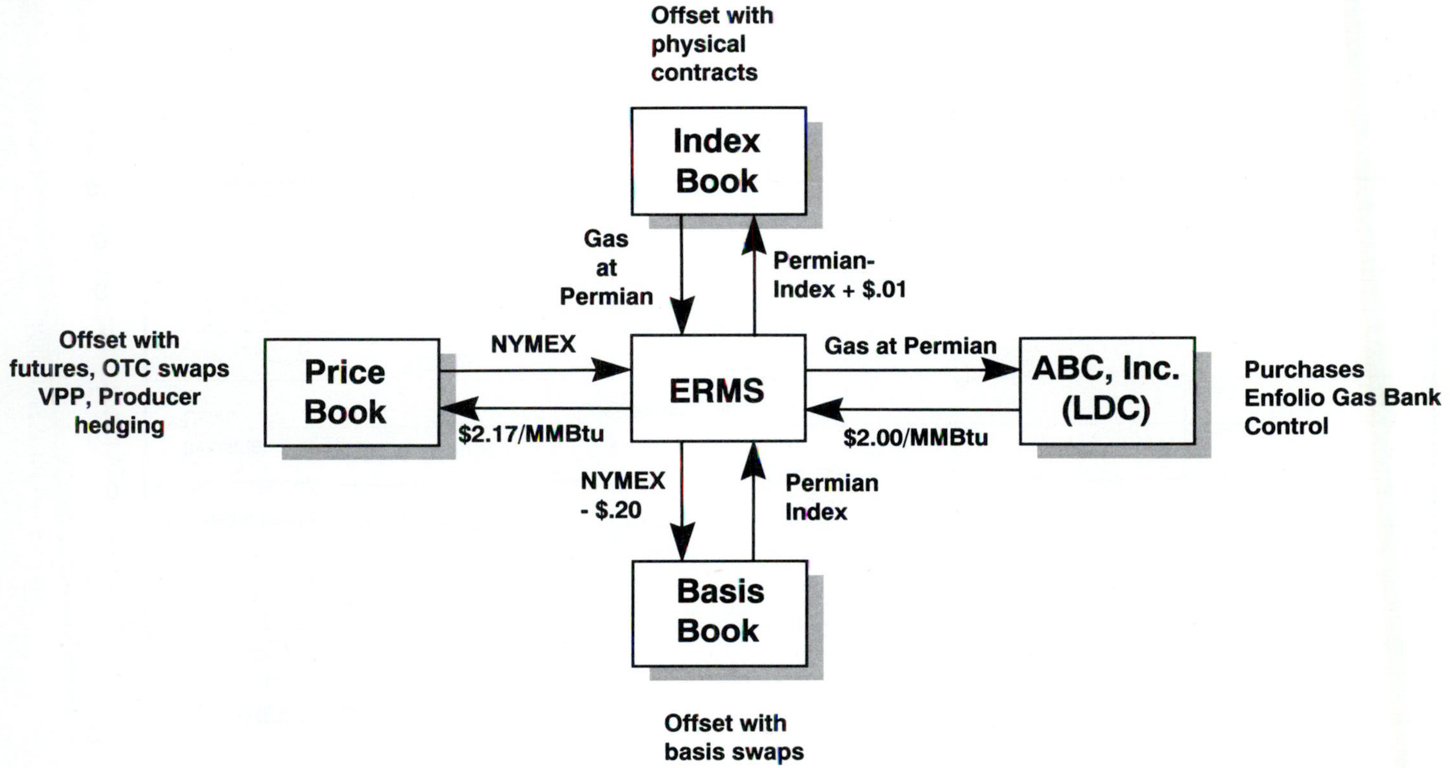

Exhibit 9   ERMS Gross and Net Price Book Exposure, as of June 1993

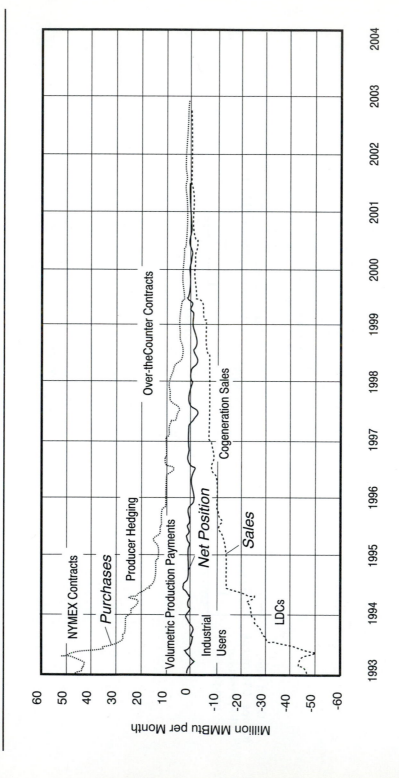

Exhibit 10 An Example of Mark-to-Market Accounting at Enron Gas Systems

Suppose that in November 1993, EGS entered into a five-year sales contract with company ABC to deliver 10,000 MMBtus daily each year from 1994 through 1998, at a fixed price of $1.96/MMBtu. EGS then entered into a matching purchase contract with XYZ to buy the same amount of gas, for $1.84/MMBtu. EGS estimated that transporting the gas from XYZ to ABC would cost $.035/MMBtu. The undiscounted gross margin of this transaction before transportation costs would be $2.19 million = 5 years * 365 days/year * 10,000 MMBtus/day * ($1.96–$1.84)/MMBtu. In this example, EGS would recognize current income of about $720,000 in 1993, even though no physical gas was delivered or cash received. This $720,000 represented the present value of the transactions, after transportation costs and after deducting reserves of $620,000. The reserves, determined by EGS models, were set up to protect against changes in the market value of EGS's position.

The remainder of the margin, less physical delivery costs, would be recorded ratably over the life of the contract, if the contracts were fulfilled and market conditions remained unchanged. Enron's future commitments to buy and sell gas would give rise to assets and liabilities from price risk management activities. (Commitments representing transactions to be made within one year were categorized as current assets and liabilities.) The difference between price risk management assets and liabilities represented the unrealized profits, net of required reserves, that were recognized as income but for which cash would be received in future periods. Income recognized in the periods following the initial period in which the contract was marked-to-market would include the reversal of the credit reserve accretion of the present discount, and changes in the physical cost of performance. Assuming that the portfolio was balanced with identical purchase and sale volume commitments, changes in the price of gas would not have an income statement impact.

The income statement and balance sheet corresponding to the above contracts is shown below:

Income Statement	Year Ending December 31 ($000)						
	1993	1994	1995	1996	1997	1998	Sum
Gas sales revenues[a]	$ 0	$7,154	$7,154	$7,154	$7,154	$7,154	$35,770
Other revenues[b]	720	(111)	(131)	(147)	(159)	(172)	0
Total revenue	720	7,043	7,023	7,007	6,995	6,982	35,770
Cost of gas[c]	0	(6,716)	(6,716)	(6,716)	(6,716)	(6,716)	(33,580)
Physical cost[d]	0	(128)	(128)	(128)	(128)	(128)	(640)
Total costs	0	(6,844)	(6,844)	(6,844)	(6,844)	(6,844)	(34,220)
Net margin	720	199	179	163	151	138	1,550

Exhibit 10 An Example of Mark-to-Market Accounting at Enron Gas Systems (Continued)

	Year Ending December 31 ($000)					
	1993	1994	1995	1996	1997	1998
Balance Sheet						
Assets						
Gross price risk management asset[e]	2,280	1,825	1,369	912	456	0
Credit reserve[f]	(620)	(496)	(372)	(248)	(124)	0
Discount[g]	(310)	(200)	(120)	(60)	(20)	0
Net price risk management asset	1,350	1,129	877	604	312	0
Liabilities						
Gross price risk management liability[h]	(730)	(584)	(438)	(292)	146	0
Discount[i]	100	65	40	20	7	0
Net price risk management liability	(630)	(519)	(398)	(272)	(139)	0
Assets—Liabilities[j]	720	610	479	332	173	0

a. Sales of 10,000 MMBtus/day * 365 days * $1.96/MMBtu.

b. In 1993, mark-to-market income recorded. In subsequent years, initial mark-to-market income reversed as physical delivery was made.

c. Purchases of 10,000 MMBtus/day * 365 days * $1.84/MMBtu.

d. Delivery costs of 10,000 MMBtus/day * 365 days *$.035/MMBtu

e. Equal to the undiscounted market gas revenues less physical costs, assuming the market price of gas was $1.80. In 1993, the asset equaled 10,000 MMBtus/day * 365 days/year * 5 years * (($1.96–$1.80)/MMBtu–$.035/MMBtu).

f. Calculated by EGS model and reduced ratably each year.

g. Difference between the undiscounted and discounted future revenues, assuming a discount rate of 5%.

h. Equal to the undiscounted market costs of the gas purchases, assuming the market price of gas was $1.80 in all subsequent periods. In 1993, the liability equaled 10,000 MMBtus/day * 365 days/year * 5 years * (($1.84–$1.80)/MMBtu).

i. Difference between the undiscounted and discounted future costs, assuming a discount rate of 5%.

j. Difference between net price risk management assets and liabilities equaled amount of recognized, but unrealized, income to date.

Exhibit 11   Future Scenarios for EGS

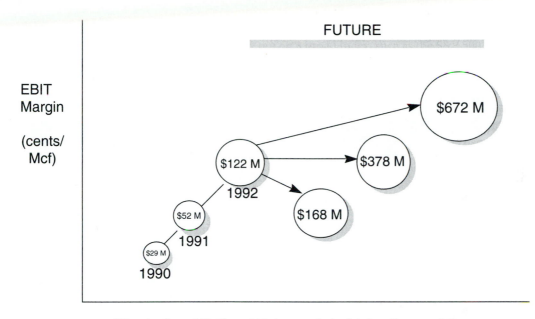

FUTURE

EBIT
Margin

(cents/
Mcf)

$672 M

$122 M

$378 M

1992

$52 M

$168 M

$29 M

1991

1990

Physical and Notional Volumes in bcf / day (log scale)

Source: Enron Gas Services.
Note: The EBIT of EGS is given in the center of each circle.

MANAGING INVESTORS' EXPOSURES

SHEARSON LEHMAN HUTTON, INC. (A) ENTRY INTO THE COVERED WARRANT BUSINESS

On May 1, 1989, William Breck and E. Philip Jones sat in a downtown Manhattan office in the American Express Tower. A wall of glass separated the two men from the equity arbitrage trading area. Twenty trading stations, equipped with banks of telephones, Quotrons, PCs, and workstations, were empty at 7:00 p.m. Mr. Jones was a senior vice president of Shearson Lehman Hutton, Inc., and a former professor of finance at Harvard Business School, and Mr. Breck was executive vice president of SLH and head of the firm's equity arbitrage operations, with over 20 years' experience in the equity arbitrage business. They studied spreadsheets describing all the synthetic covered equity warrants issued to date in the Euromarkets against U.S. blue-chip companies. This product was only weeks old, and SLH had not yet offered any of these securities. The two executives had to determine whether SLH should issue these securities, and, if so, what steps they would need to take to enter the synthetic covered equity warrant business.

SHEARSON LEHMAN HUTTON, INC.

Shearson Lehman Hutton, Inc., the principal subsidiary of Shearson Lehman Hutton Holdings, Inc., was a leading full-line securities firm whose activities included investment banking, merchant banking, capital markets trading, individual and institutional investor services, asset management, and real estate. (See Exhibits 1 and 2 for financial statements of Shearson Lehman Hutton Holdings, Inc.) The firm was created through a series of mergers and acquisitions: American Express, Inc., acquired Shearson Loeb Rhodes in 1981, Lehman Brothers Kuhn Loeb in 1984, and E. F. Hutton Group in January 1988. As of year end 1988, American Express held a majority of Shearson Lehman Hutton Holdings, Inc., common stock, the rest being held by Nippon Life, SLH employees, and the public.

Peter Tufano wrote this case as the basis of class discussion.
Copyright © 1990 by the President and Fellows of Harvard College Harvard Business School case 291-016.

SLH emphasized its creativity and innovativeness in investment banking and capital markets activities. A recruiting brochure addressed to potential SLH employees underscored this point:

> When traditional solutions prove inadequate, [SLH] professionals have been adept at devising new financial instruments or custom-tailoring existing ones, or cultivating special areas of expertise, to meet extraordinary client needs or unusual market conditions. Among our innovations are the first Eurocommercial paper program; the creation of Money Market Preferred Stock,[TM] as well as its more recent offspring Convertible MMP[TM] and FLEXMMP[TM]; the invention of Select Auction Variable Rate Securities[TM] (SAVRS[TM]); the development of Floating Interest Rate Short Tranche Securities (FIRSTS[TM]); and the establishment of Dequity[TM] financing for LDC [less-developed country] debt-equity conversions.

Late in 1988, SLH's newest innovation—Unbundled Stock Units (USUs), a corporate financing vehicle designed by Mr. Jones and his colleagues—was unveiled to the public. After working for nearly 11 months to develop this corporate financing vehicle, SLH announced in December that four firms were prepared to issue the security. In the weeks following this announcement, the product received widespread publicity and attention. *Business Week* wrote that USU's "could become the financial craze of the '90s."[1]

USUs were proposed as an exchange offer in which firms would give shareholders the right to swap shares of common stock for a bundle of securities consisting of a bond, a preferred stock whose dividends were tied to changes in the common stock dividend, and an equity appreciation certificate. The third piece of the bundle was essentially a warrant, which gave holders the right to purchase common stock any time over the next 30 years by surrendering their preferred stock plus a fixed cash payment.

In one part of the USU project, Messrs. Breck and Jones spent over ten weeks calling on potential institutional USU investors in the United States and Europe, meeting with more than 300 pension plan sponsors, money managers, and major institutional investors. While SLH had lined up four blue-chip corporations that publicly announced their willingness to issue $5.6 billion in USUs (American Express, Dow Chemical, Pfizer, and Sara Lee), and even though the firm had apparently identified willing investors, the transactions were never consummated. In March 1989 the firm announced that it had advised its four would-be issuers against proceeding, because of an unfavorable ruling by the Securities and Exchange Commission.[2]

---

1 "Shearson may have a hot new way to sell stocks," *Business Week*, December 19, 1988, p. 84.

2 The SEC's formal objection to the plan seemed to relate to the method by which USU issuers would be required to report earnings per share. The SEC apparently insisted that firms issuing USUs calculate earnings per share on the basis of the number of common shares plus USUs outstanding, rather than on the basis of simply the number of shares outstanding.

The USU project solidified SLH's relationship with the Union Bank of Switzerland, one of the three largest Swiss banks. In addition, their market canvassing had convinced Messrs. Jones and Breck that European investors would buy warrants on blue-chip U.S. firms.

On Friday, April 28, Nick Ricciardi, an SLH analyst, bounded into Mr. Jones's office. He had noticed a group of recent deals in the Euromarkets that looked intriguing from SLH's equity arbitrage perspective. These "synthetic covered equity warrants" sold European investors long-term call options on high-quality U.S. firms. Mr. Ricciardi had taken the initiative to lay out the particulars of the transactions and to collect information on the prices of traded options on the firms on which the covered warrants were written.

OPTIONS AND COVERED EUROWARRANTS

Call options are contracts that give holders the right to purchase stock at a prespecified price (the strike or exercise price) on or before a prespecified date (the expiration date).[3] In the United States call options were traded on the Chicago Board Options Exchange as well as on the American, Philadelphia, Pacific, and New York Stock Exchanges. Exchange-traded options are typically American-style options, with expiration dates not exceeding nine months, and the contracts are bought and sold (or written) by investors, not issued by the companies upon whose stock the option is written. In the United States the term *warrant* usually referred to a long-maturity call option written by the firm into whose stock the option can be exercised.[4] If their call warrants were exercised, firms issued new shares, thus diluting the equity ownership of existing equity holders by selling shares at the below-market exercise price. A package of debt plus warrants closely resembles convertible debt.

Warrants were much more frequently issued in the Euromarkets than in the U.S. capital markets. Exhibit 2 shows that bonds plus warrants accounted for a negligible fraction of total debt issuances in the United States but 16.5% of all Eurobond issues. Virtually all the debt-plus-warrant packages in the Euromarkets were issued by Japanese firms. Market observers claimed that the growth of the Japanese warrant market was driven by the investors' preference to make highly levered bets on Japanese firms. At the same time, Japanese firms apparently felt that debt-plus-warrant packages offered lower-cost funding than alternative sources of financing.

---

3   A European-style option permits exercise only on the expiration date. An American-style option permits exercise on or before the expiration date.

4   Put warrants also exist. A put allows its holder to sell a given stock at a prespecified exercise price on (or before) the expiration date.

A typical debt-plus-warrant offering by a Japanese issuer included a 5-year fixed-rate bond with a low coupon (3%–6%) attached to a warrant with a 4-year life. The warrant's exercise price typically was 2.5% above current share price (in yen). The package was most frequently denominated in U.S. dollars, i.e., an investor paid dollars to buy the bond-plus-warrant package. The warrants and bonds could be separated and thus traded independently of one another.

By 1989 the Euromarket for Japanese equity warrants was considered by some to be mature. Twelve full-fledged market-makers regularly traded 200–320 of the largest issues, and turnover was around $2 billion per day. Japanese regulators took notice of this large, offshore, and unregulated market in Japanese securities. Japan's postal funds had recently been given permission to invest in warrants, and trust banks were allowed to invest up to 5% of their funds in these foreign-currency-denominated securities. At the same time, Japan's Ministry of Finance was rumored to be studying proposals that would bring issuance and trading of the warrants back to Japan, and hence under regulatory supervision. As much as 70% of the warrants issued in the Euromarkets were ultimately bought by Japanese investors.

The success of the Euromarket in Japanese warrants spawned new products. Beginning in 1985 investment banks and merchant banks began to issue covered warrants. Unlike the Japanese equity warrants or those issued in the United States, Euromarket covered warrants were call options issued by financial intermediaries, not by the firm into whose securities they were exercisable. They were covered, or collateralized, because the writer of the option held some security that could be used to satisfy the claim if the call was exercised. Under law, these warrants were considered securities, not options, and therefore investors otherwise prohibited from investing in "speculative derivatives" like options could purchase the warrants.

In the few years since their appearance, three types of covered warrants had emerged. The first of these was back-to-back warrants, first issued by Citicorp in Zurich in late 1985. According to published reports of the early deals, banks bought at-the-money warrants issued by Japanese companies, which traded in large lot sizes and which were bought and sold with U.S. dollars. The banks then sold retail investors out-of-the-money options against the underlying warrants in smaller lot sizes, with the warrants bought and sold with Swiss francs. These warrants were sold to Swiss retail investors, described by one banker as "the dustman and his wife," with option premiums 2%–4% higher than on the underlying warrants.[5]

---

5   "The Giddy World of the Spin-Off," *Euromoney*, September 1989, p. 4.

The second product was *stillhalter*, or warrants on Swiss shares. This 1986 innovation was attributed to Martin Ebner, founder and chief executive of BZ Bank. BZ Bank, a small Swiss bank, paid holders of companies' shares a fee, in exchange for which the shareholders deposited their shares into blocked safe-custody accounts. The bank then wrote long-term call options against these shares. The bank profited on the difference between the fee it paid to the shareholders and the revenues it earned from the sale of the options. The shareholders became covered-call-writers. If the share price rose above the exercise price, warrant holders exercised their options and called the shares. If the shares fell in value, the calls expired worthless and the shareholders kept their shares. In either event, the covered call writer kept the call premium.

Swiss common stocks were typically divided into bearer shares, registered shares, and participating certificates. Registered shares could not be held by non-Swiss investors and traded at up to 50% discounts to bearer shares (which were available to non-Swiss citizens). Warrants were written against the registered shares. While non-Swiss investors could not take delivery of the registered shares, they could enjoy their appreciation because the warrants had cash settlement terms, i.e. at exercise, the holder was paid the difference between the registered share value and the stillhalter at the exercise price.

The stillhalter concept was broadened to include options on baskets of companies, such as banks and pharmaceutical firms. The market for stillhalter was called by some "a wild success": in 2 years, 2.1 billion Swiss francs ($1.5 billion) of stillhalter warrants were issued.[6] Another measure of the success of these issues was the fact that 7.5% of the total capitalization of registered shares were held in stillhalter, and for ten major Swiss stocks, including Ciba-Geigy, Sandoz, and the Union Bank of Switzerland, over one tenth of their market capitalization was in shares held to cover stillhalter issues.[7] BZ Bank was reported to have had a virtual monopoly issuing early stillhalter.

The next and most recent development—"synthetic covered warrants"—differed fundamentally from the two prior versions of covered warrant products. The first two types of warrants were covered, or collateralized, by underlying warrants or shares held by the bank issuing the covered warrant. Issuers of synthetic warrants were not obligated to hold stock, and thus the security was an obligation of the issuer, which customarily was an off-shore subsidiary of an investment or merchant bank. A standard prospectus for a synthetic read as follows:

6 "See the Warrant Officer," *Economist*, July 29, 1989, p. 63.
7 "Success and Skepticism Greet Covered Warrants," *Financial Times*, October 10, 1989, p. 40.

The issuer does not hold shares of XYZ, Inc., to secure the warrants. The issuer will, however, depending on the market situation, hedge its obligations as it considers appropriate to deliver shares under the warrants.

On April 6, 1989, Bankers Trust issued the first synthetic covered equity warrant in the Euromarkets, exercisable into shares of Merck. In the 20 days since the launch of the Merck offering, ten synthetic covered equity warrants on U.S. firms were issued. Exhibit 4 lists the synthetic deals launched prior to April 28 and the public statements made by the underwriters regarding the market reception of each issue. Exhibit 5 gives the terms of each of the offerings. Exhibit 6 presents prices of call options traded in the United States on the stock of the ten firms. Exhibits 7 and 8 provide additional information the SLH team could use to evaluate the early synthetic covered warrant offerings.

"WHAT SHOULD WE DO NOW?"

In the final weeks of the USU project, which wound up in early April, Messrs. Breck and Jones met with potential European investors. They developed strong working relationships with the Union Bank of Switzerland and with the SLH sales staff in Geneva, Lucerne, Lugano, and Milan. If SLH went ahead with a synthetic warrant product, these relationships would prove valuable in structuring and marketing the warrants to Europeans.

In contrast to the product development of the USU, a new and revolutionary security, SLH's entry into the covered equity warrant business would be relatively easy. With ten deals already done, the standard product structure was now well known by investors. Messrs. Breck and Jones felt that the legal, tax, and regulatory obstacles would be minimal, as other issuers would have gone the same route.

Because the issuer of the security would be a subsidiary of SLH, there would be no legal requirement to obtain the approval of the company upon whose stock the warrant would be written. However, given SLH's strong client relationships, the two executives needed to consider whether it would be wise to get the blessing of the company whose stock would be used in the transaction. In addition, they needed to determine against which firms' common stock the warrants should be written.

If SLH issued covered warrants, it would have to determine how it would limit the risk to which it might be exposed by writing calls against the stocks. At one extreme, it could follow a naked call-writing policy, i.e., hold no shares or options to offset its obligation to warrant-holders. In this case, SLH would face unlimited down-side losses if the stock price rose at the maturity of the contract. If SLH bought and held enough stock to cover all of its potential obligations under the warrant program, it would risk large losses if stock price fell dramatically. Between these two buy-and-hold extremes, the firm could pursue a dynamic hedging strategy, continually adjusting its positions in the stock, riskless investments, and traded short-term options.

If this product was to go forward, Messrs. Breck and Jones would need the approval of Herbert Freiman, vice chairman of the firm and chairman of the capital markets group. Issuing synthetic covered equity warrants would put the firm's capital at risk, and Mr. Freiman would want to know answers to the following questions: What does SLH stand to gain? To how much risk will this proposal expose the firm? How else could Swiss investors make this type of investment? How would they limit the risk they would face? Why does this market exist?

Exhibit 1 Consolidated Income Statements for Shearson Lehman Hutton Holdings, Inc., and Subsidiaries for Years Ending December 31, 1986–1988 (millions of dollars except per share data)

	1986	1987	1988
Commissions	$938	$1,151	$1,515
Investment banking	888	793	1,433
Market making and principal transactions	983	818	1,129
Interest and dividends	3,344	3,349	5,635
Investment advisory fees	310	417	536
Mortgage banking	71	93	95
Other	214	128	186
Total revenues	6,748	6,749	10,529
Compensation and benefits	1,919	2,045	2,972
Interest	3,187	3,159	5,376
Communications	277	334	539
Occupancy and equipment	236	330	534
Advertising and market development	139	155	212
Professional services	112	153	181
Brokerage, commissions, and clearance fees	50	68	87
Other	348	352	344
Nonrecurring merger-related	–	–	165
Total expenses	6,268	6,596	10,410
Income before taxes	480	153	119
Provision for income taxes	139	52	23
Net income	$341	$101	$96
Net income per common share	$4.34	$1.00	$.81
Weighted average number of common and common equivalent shares outstanding used in the computation (000s)	78,500	83,400	88,000
Cash dividends declared per common share, subsequent to initial public offering	–	$.5625	$.75

Source: Shearson Lehman Hutton Holdings, annual reports.

Exhibit 2   Consolidated Balance Sheets for Shearson Lehman Hutton Holdings, Inc., and Subsidiaries
at December 31, 1987 and 1988

	1987	1988
Cash and time deposits	$2,188	$2,583
Cash and securities segregated under federal and other regulations	908	2,109
Receivables	14,158	16,430
Securities purchased under agreements to resell	19,160	23,489
Securities and commodities owned	22,395	28,161
Mortgage and construction loans	5,257	7,049
Net buildings, furnishings, equipment, and leasehold improvements, at cost	1,122	1,559
Other	1,411	3,460
Total assets	$66,599	$84,840
Commercial paper and short-term debt	$11,532	$13,257
Payables	8,420	8,901
Accrued liabilities and other payables	2,202	3,865
Deposit liabilities, principally demand deposits, time deposits, and money market funds	11,527	16,733
Securities sold under agreements to repurchase	21,485	26,611
Securities and commodities sold but not yet purchased	5,949	7,316
Term notes	1,844	3,258
Subordinated indebtedness	1,897	3,153
Total liabilities	64,856	83,094
Total shareholders' equity	1,743	1,746
Total liabilities and shareholders' equity	$66,599	$84,840

Source: Shearson Lehman Hutton Holdings, annual reports.

Exhibit 3   Debt and Debt-with-Warrants Issues in the U.S. and Eurobond Markets (millions of dollars), 1988–1989

	U.S. Market		Eurobond Market		
	All Debt Issues	Debt with Warrants	All Debt Issues	Debt with Warrants	Japanese Debt with Warrants
Jan. 1988	$10,952	–	$18,791	$2,190	$2,190
Feb.	8,074	–	19,779	1,916	1,916
Mar.	10,188	–	18,681	1,304	1,232
Apr.	10,401	–	18,836	2,656	2,656
May.	10,857	–	18,458	2,759	2,759
June	16,187	–	25,699	5,390	5,227
July	6,209	–	18,806	4,226	4,045
Aug.	8,967	$ 16	13,706	3,066	3,048
Sept.	11,383	244	18,420	2,267	1,981
Oct.	10,073	–	19,484	1,669	1,561
Nov.	14,054	385	16,797	1,307	1,280
Dec.	6,122	–	8,867	500	500
Jan. 1989	7,741	–	39,567	9,216	9,089
Feb.	12,941	195	17,793	3,360	3,295
Mar.	17,890	–	25,306	8,250	8,103

Source: Securities Data Corporation.
Note: "All Debt Issues" represents all public debt offerings except mortgage-backed and asset-backed securities. The volumes represent proceeds from the issues. Debt-plus warrant packages are valued by the proceeds of the package, not on the basis of the warrant portion alone.

Exhibit 4   Early Swiss Franc–Denominated Synthetic Covered Equity Warrant Issues, April 1989

Warrant on	Bond Rating[a]	Launch Date	Issuer[b]	Stated Market Reaction[c]
Merck	None[d]	April 6[e]	BTI	"The deal was quickly placed, mainly with institutional investors, and it is estimated that more such deals could emerge soon."
Coca-Cola	AA	April 10	BTI	"The deals have been welcomed as diversification opportunities, but have not met with the same general approval as Japanese warrants. Some market participants consider the premium too high and the exercise period too short."
Amoco	AAA	April 13[f]	MSC	
Du Pont	AA	April 14	MSC	
Philip Morris	A	April 18	BTI	"A hot favorite with many investors"
MMM	AAA	April 19	MSC	"'Exceedingly successful,' comments Morgan Stanley on this deal, and the issuer's opinion is shared by all participants."
Procter & Gamble	AA	April 20	BTI	"A very good transaction."
Eastman Kodak	A	April 20	MSC	"The lead manager is pleased with the transaction, which was somewhat affected by the share performance of Kodak's stock."
Bristol-Myers	AAA	April 25	GSW	"A success partly due to perfect timing."
Squibb	None[d]	April 26	SI	"Very well received."

a. Rating of senior bonds of company into which warrants are exercisable.
b. BTI = Bankers Trust International, Ltd.; GSW = Goldman, Sachs Warrants, Ltd.; MSC = Morgan Stanley Capital (Jersey), Ltd.; SI = Salomon International.
c. As reported in *International Financing Review*.
d. Firm had no rated public debt.
e. Announced 60,000 warrants; increased to 75,000.
f. Announced 80,000 warrants; increased to 125,000.

Exhibit 5   Swiss Franc–Denominated Synthetic Covered Equity Warrants on North American Companies as of April 28, 1989

	Merck	Coca-Cola	Amoco	Du Pont	Philip Morris	MMM	Procter & Gamble	Eastman Kodak	Bristol-Myers	Squibb
Ticker	MRK	KO	AN	DD	MO	MMM	PG	EK	BMY	SQB
Issue date	4/6/89	4/10/89	4/13/89	4/14/89	4/18/89	4/19/89	4/20/89	4/20/89	4/25/89	4/26/89
Maturity[a]	1/5/91	1/17/91	1/25/91	1/25/91	1/30/91	2/1/91	1/15/91	2/1/91	2/15/91	4/26/91
No. of warrants[b]	75,000	80,000	125,000	150,000	40,000	100,000	50,000	150,000	80,000	80,000
No. of shares/warrant	5	5	5	2	5	5	5	5	5	5
Stock price(US$)[c]	65.875	52.875	42.5	106.75	122.375	70	93.25	47.375	47.625	75.25
Exercise price (US$)[d]	60.5	49.375	38	97.125	110	59	81.75	41	41.20	70
Warrant price										
Per warrant (SwF)[e]	127	110	90	84	238	157	199	105	105	162
Per share (US$)[f]	15.58	13.23	10.76	25.61	29.23	19.23	24.38	12.82	12.76	19.58
Bid/ask prices (SwF)[g]	126/129	101/105	90/92	84/86	239/244	154/156	193/197	100/103	103/106	161/165
Premium[h]	15.5	18.4	14.74	14.98	13.77	11.75	13.81	13.61	18.94	19.04
Gearing[i]	4.23	3.98	3.95	4.17	4.19	3.64	3.82	3.70	3.75	3.84

Source: Shearson Lehman Hutton, Inc.
a. All warrants are American-style and may be exercised on or before the maturity dates shown.
b. All warrants are options on multiple shares, e.g., one warrant gives holder right to purchase five shares.
c. Stock price at time of issue, as reported by SLH to casewriter.
d. Exercise price per share. All warrants have exercise prices set in U.S. dollars.
e. Warrants are bought and sold in Swiss francs.
f. Per share prices represent price paid per option on one share. Calculated in US dollars using the exchange rate as of the launch date.
g. Prices at which warrants were bought and sold in the "when issued" or "grey" market.
h. Defined as (warrant price + exercise price - stock price) divided by stock price.
I. Defined as stock price divided by warrant price.

Exhibit 6   Prices of Exchange-Traded Call Options April-September 1989

Warrant on:	Date and Closing Stock Price	Exercise Price	Call Prices in $ Expiration Date: April 22	May 20	June 17	July 22	Aug. 19	Sept. 16
Merck	April 6	$50	15.7500	–	–	–	–	–
	$65.8750	55	11.1250	–	–	12.0000	–	–
		60	6.0000	–	–	7.5000	–	–
		65	1.6875	2.7500	–	4.0000	–	–
		70	.1875	.3750	–	1.6250	–	–
Coca-Cola	April 10	45	–	8.5000	–	–	–	–
	$52.875	50	3.0000	3.8750	–	–	6.0000	–
		55	.2500	.7500	–	–	2.5000	–
Amoco	April 13	37.5	–	5.0000	–	–	–	–
	$42.375	40	2.5000	2.7500	–	–	3.7500	–
		42.5	–	.8750	–	–	–	–
		45	–	.2500	–	–	–	–
Du Pont	April 14	80	23.7500	–	–	–	–	–
	$106.75	85	21.8750	–	–	22.6250	–	–
		90	16.8750	–	–	17.3750	–	–
		95	11.5000	–	–	13.6250	–	–
		100	6.7500	7.5000	–	9.5000	–	–
		105	2.1875	3.6250	–	6.1250	–	–
		110	.2500	1.5000	–	3.7500	–	–
		115	–	.5000	–	2.0000	–	–
Philip Morris	April 18	100	–	–	23.7500	–	–	–
	$122.375	110	12.5000	13.0000	13.5000	–	–	–
		115	7.2500	8.7500	9.2500	–	–	–
		120	2.4375	4.6250	5.6250	–	–	–
		125	.2500	2.0000	3.0000	–	–	–
		130	–	.6875	1.2500	–	–	–
MMM	April 19	60	11.0000	–	–	–	–	–
	$70.75	65	6.1250	6.0000	–	6.6250	–	–
		70	.8750	2.2500	–	3.2500	–	–
		75	.0625	.5000	–	1.2500	–	–

Exhibit 6   Prices of Exchange-Traded Call Options on Dates When Synthetic Covered Equity Warrants on These Companies Were Issued, April-September 1989 (Continued)

Warrant on:	Date and Closing Stock Price	Exercise Price	Call Prices Expiration Date:					
			April 22	May 20	June 17	July 22	Aug. 19	Sept. 16
Procter	April 20	85	–	–	–	10.0000	–	–
& Gamble	$93.25	90	3.3750	4.2500	–	6.2500	–	–
		95	.0625	1.1875	–	3.1250	–	–
Eastman	April 20	40	6.8750	7.0000	–	7.5000	–	–
Kodak	$47.00	45	1.9375	2.4375	–	3.1250	–	–
		50	.0625	.3125	–	1.0000	–	–
Bristol-Myers	April 25	45	–	3.2500	3.7500	–	–	4.6250
	$47.625	50	–	.2500	.6250	–	–	1.6250
Squibb	April 26	70	–	–	–	7.5000	–	–
	$76.00	75	–	1.7500	2.7500	–	–	–
		80	–	.5000	1.0000	1.7500	–	–

Source: The Wall Street Journal.

Exhibit 7 Ex-Dividend Dates and Cash Dividends Paid, 1988 and 1989

	1988 Dividends						1989 Dividends	
	Date	Amount	Date	Amount	Date	Amount	Date	Amount
Merck	6/3	$.32	8/29	$.37	11/29	$.37	3/2	$.41
Coca-Cola	6/9	.30	9/9	.30	11/25	.30	3/9	.34
Amoco	6/27	.44	8/4	.44	11/3	.44	2/2	.48
Du Pont	5/9	.95	8/9	.95	11/8	.95	2/9	1.05
Philip Morris	6/9	.90	9/9	1.125	12/9	1.125	3/9	1.125
MMM	5/16	.53	8/15	.53	11/18	.53	2/17	.65
P & G[a]	4/18	.70	10/17	.71	1/13	.80	1/13	.80
Eastman Kodak	5/25	.45	8/26	.50	11/25	.50	2/23	.50
Bristol-Myers	6/27	.42	10/3	.42	12/30	.50	4/3	.50
Squibb	5/16	.40	8/15	.40	11/14	.40	2/13	.50

Source: Compiled from the Center for Research in Securities Prices.
Note: Shareholders owning the stock prior to the ex-dividend date are entitled to the next dividend payment. Shareholders who buy the stock on or after the ex-dividend date are not entitled to the next dividend payment.
a. Procter & Gamble's stock went ex-dividend on 4/17/89, with a dividend of $.80.

Exhibit 8 Treasury Bill and Note Yields in April 1989

	Bill/Note Maturing in:			
Date	1 month	3 months	6 months	15 months
April 6	8.45%	8.83%	8.74%	9.58%
April 10	8.61	8.81	8.76	9.64
April 13	8.76	8.69	8.78	9.69
April 14	8.68	8.77	8.83	9.45
April 18	8.31	8.43	8.42	9.31
April 19	8.48	8.43	8.40	9.28
April 20	8.31	8.65	8.49	9.45
April 25	8.49	8.66	8.72	9.38
April 26	8.33	8.61	8.65	9.38

Source: Compiled from IDC Datasheet. All yields are quoted on a bond-equivalent-yield basis.

GOLDMAN, SACHS & CO.:
NIKKEI PUT WARRANTS—1989

Bankers at Goldman, Sachs & Co. were busy in November and December 1989 as they moved closer toward announcing a new product that would allow American retail investors to bet against the nearly unstoppable rise in the Japanese stock market. The Goldman Sachs team had been working since spring 1988 to design and bring to market a product they thought would be of great interest to American investors—exchange-traded put warrants on Japan's Nikkei 225 Stock Average. By December 1989 the product design was ready, but the team had to set the price at which the Nikkei put warrants (NPWs) would be offered to the public. The ultimate success of the product launch would depend on the market's reaction to the offering, which in turn would depend on the price that was set.

PRELUDE TO NIKKEI PUT WARRANTS

Put options give their holders the right, but not the obligation, to sell an underlying asset by a certain date for a predetermined price. In the case of the NPWs, the underlying asset that investors could sell was the Nikkei 225 Stock Average. Comparable to the Dow Jones Industrial Index in the United States, the Nikkei 225 Stock Average was a broad-based, price-weighted index of the 225 largest stocks trading on the Tokyo Stock Exchange.[1] NPWs would enable investors to profit from a decline in the Nikkei index while exposing them to limited risk from rises in the index. If brought to market, the NPWs would be the first securities listed on a U.S. exchange and available to retail investors explicitly permitting investors to speculate on or hedge against falls in the Nikkei index.

Goldman Sachs first sensed U.S investors' demands for Nikkei put warrants in mid-1987. On June 10 of that year, Bear Stearns had underwritten a public offering of currency

---

1   In a price-weighted index like the Dow Jones Industrial Index or the Nikkei 225 Stock Average, each stock contributes to the index based on its per share price. In contrast, in a value-weighted index like the Standard & Poor's 500 Index, each stock contributes to the index based on its total market capitalization.

warrants issued by General Electric Credit Corporation and listed on the American Stock Exchange. These warrants entitled the investor to sell yen to the issuer at any time within 2 years at a fixed exchange rate. The currency warrants appealed to retail investors who had few other opportunities to purchase long-dated currency options. The initial offering was apparently heavily subscribed. The deal was carefully scrutinized by rival investment banks, and Morgan Stanley offered a similar product within days. By June 22, Goldman Sachs became the third investment bank to launch an offering of currency warrants, as an underwriter for Citicorp. In the Citicorp transition, as in the other deals, the issuer simultaneously offered the warrants to the public and entered into an exactly offsetting option contract with the investment bank involved. Thus, the corporate issuers of the currency warrants were completely insulated from exchange rate risk and, in effect, earned a fee for facilitating the transaction.

The experience of selling exchange-listed currency warrants made three important impressions on the Goldman Sachs team. First, sales force reports made clear that while investors were interested in puts on the yen, puts on the Nikkei would be much more widely demanded. Second, the product concept seemed to show that there were profits to be made from buying options (called "sourcing volatility") in institutional markets and reselling them to retail customers who were unable to buy the large lot-sized institutional deals. Third, their experience with currency warrants persuaded the team that new markets could quickly become satiated. The Citicorp currency warrants deal, although it was only the fourth to come to market, was difficult to place. In addition, the prices of the currency warrants fell quickly from the initial deal levels. Exhibit 1 shows the implied volatilities of the first currency warrants brought to market.[2]

In 1987 selling exchange-listed put warrants on the Nikkei 225 Stock Average seemed a remote possibility. The Japanese Ministry of Finance did not support this idea and through a variety of direct and indirect channels could effectively veto any proposal to sell puts on the Nikkei. Perhaps more important, Goldman Sachs had no readily available liquid source of puts they could use to hedge or produce the put contracts.

In spring 1988 the Goldman Sachs capital markets group in Tokyo began to hear rumors that someone was willing to sell put options on the Nikkei. Soon thereafter, *International Financing Review*, a trade publication that tracked world financial markets, reported the first of a series of recent Eurobonds whose redemption values at maturity were tied to the level of the Nikkei 225 Stock Average. These Euro-yen bonds became a source of puts that

---

2   Implied volatilities, which can be backed out of option prices given a model such as the Black-Scholes model, reflect the market's estimate of the dispersion of future outcomes, in this case of future exchange rates.

could be sold to institutional and retail accounts. Exhibit 2 provides data on two representative Nikkei-linked Euro-yen offerings issued in mid-December 1989.

The typical issuers of Nikkei-linked bonds were non-Japanese financial institutions. Exhibit 3 shows the related contracts into which a hypothetical Nikkei-linked bond issuer might enter. It sold a bond that promised to make annual interest payments in yen at a fixed interest rate. However, through a set of swaps, the issuer transformed its annual fixed-rate yen payments into dollar-denominated LIBOR-based payments.[3]

At maturity, the issuer would redeem the bonds from the investor at a price tied to the Nikkei. If the Nikkei fell since the bonds were issued, the issuer would pay less than par to redeem the bonds. Thus, it would be as if the issuer sold bonds with final principal payments at par but also bought a put option on the Nikkei maturing in the same year as the bond. If the Nikkei fell, the put would rise in value, benefiting the issuer.

Usually, the issuer had no interest in holding this embedded Nikkei put. However, it could, and often did, resell the embedded put options to financial intermediaries like Goldman Sachs by promising to deliver, at maturity, the difference between the bond's par value and its Nikkei-linked redemption price. In the Skopbank example in Exhibit 2, if the Nikkei fell to 23,000 in 1 year, Skopbank would not be required to make any principal payments to the holders of its notes. However, if it had sold the embedded put to a financial institution, it would be required to deliver the difference between par and its required payment to its bondholders (in this case, ¥ 6.7 billion) to the buyer of the put at the end of 1 year. In exchange for promising to make this payment, which equaled the intrinsic value of the embedded put, the bond issuer would be paid an up-front put premium.[4]

Japanese financial institutions bought the Nikkei-linked Eurobonds. Based on administrative guidelines set by the Ministry of Finance, Japanese life insurers were permitted to pay dividends out of interest income but not from capital gains. Payment of dividends was perceived to be an important competitive action in the insurance industry in Japan, and the high-coupon, yen-denominated bonds gave life insurers enhanced interest income to support dividend payments. In exchange for receiving enhanced interest income, the institutions were willing to risk capital losses on their principal value if the Nikkei fell.

Investment banks, such as Goldman Sachs, that executed Euro-yen Nikkei-linked transactions had a ready source of Nikkei puts bought from the issuers of the bonds. These

---

3 LIBOR is the London Interbank Offered Rate, which often served as the benchmark in the Euromarkets for floating-rate note issues.

4 In practice, the bond issuer would pay the put premium to its swap counterparty to compensate it for making an attractive sub-LIBOR swap. In other words, the up-front put premium has the effect of reducing the annual floating coupon the issuer would pay on its bond-plus-swap package.

put contracts could be held by the firm in inventory. Alternatively, they could be resold to institutional investors in the form of over-the-counter (OTC) put warrants by writing offsetting contracts against the puts purchased from Euro-yen bond issuers. OTC puts thus often had the exact features of the puts the banks had purchased; hence, they were typically unlisted, European-style options, paid off in yen, and sold in large denominations. As of early December 1989, Goldman Sachs' trading and arbitrage division, a unit of the equity securities area, could buy 3-year, yen-denominated put options on the Nikkei from bond issuers and resell them to institutions at implied volatilities of about 13.6%.

The firm did not sell all its Nikkei puts in the form of OTC puts to institutional customers. As of December 1989, Goldman Sachs had a significant inventory of European-style puts on the Nikkei, and the proposed NPW transaction could use as much as half of that inventory. The firm mitigated most, but not all, of its risk in holding these puts by taking offsetting futures positions in the Nikkei futures contracts offered by the Singapore, Osaka, and Tokyo stock exchanges. As a policy matter, Goldman Sachs chose to hold a small amount of the puts without direct offsetting positions in order to hedge the firm's overall exposure to the Japanese securities business and to the global securities business that was related to the performance of the Japanese stock market.

Given the sales force feedback from its 1987 currency warrant experience, and the new supply of Nikkei puts, the capital markets group, a unit of the investment banking area at Goldman Sachs, began to consider the possibility of selling exchange-listed NPWs. To bring exchange-listed Nikkei put warrants to market, many different activities within and outside Goldman Sachs needed to be coordinated. The NPW team needed to design the contract, produce the analysis to demonstrate the product's feasibility, and assemble marketing documents. They needed to test the concept internally with sales, research, and capital markets staff. Regulators in both the United States and Japan needed to approve the plan, because it would involve selling a Nikkei-linked, U.S. exchange-listed security. Goldman Sachs needed to work with the exchange where the puts would be listed, in this case, the American Stock Exchange. The trading and arbitrage division had to be able and willing to sell the puts and to construct any currency hedge that might be needed. Senior management had to approve the plan.

DESIGN OF NPWs

In their simplest form, NPWs would merely allow investors to profit from declines in the Nikkei index while limiting their risk from increases in the index. However, in bringing the product to market, a number of specific design issues needed to be resolved, with concern both for investor preferences and for Goldman Sachs' ability to produce the warrants. Key contract features that needed to be set included the following:

1. *American- vs. European-style option.* With an American-style option, the holder can exercise the option on or before the expiration date, but with a European-style option the holder can exercise the option only on the expiration date. The raw material from which the puts were constructed tended to be European-style options. However, the sales staff noted that U.S. investors were more comfortable with American-style options, and therefore the design team decided that the NPWs would be American-style.

2. *Length of contract (expiration date).* In theory, the expiration date of the warrants could be set at any date. The American Stock Exchange had expressed a preference that the warrants have lives as long as possible, but in any event not less than 1 year long, in contrast with the shorter-term options typically offered by the Chicago exchanges. Goldman Sachs' trading and arbitrage division had puts in inventory with maturities typically under 4 years. The final decision was to set a 3-year life.

3. *Treatment of exchange-rate risk.* The Nikkei is denominated in yen, and Nikkei-linked Eurobonds and the OTC puts all pay off at exercise in yen. The retail NPW product could be written so that the strike price, and thus the payoff, would be calculated in yen and the payoff converted to dollars at exchange rate at the exercise or maturity date. However, this arrangement would force U.S. investors to directly bear movements in the exchange rate. A second alternative would be to fix the exchange rate at the outset of the contract and to use that fixed exchange rate to translate yen payoffs into dollars at exercise or maturity. A third alternative would be to set the exercise price in dollars and calculate the payoff as the difference between this fixed-dollar exercise price and the level of the Nikkei translated into dollars at the exchange rate at the time of exercise or maturity. The sales staff felt that U.S. investors would prefer the second of these alternatives.

4. *Treatment of contract rights in the case of extraordinary events.* The Nikkei-linked bonds and OTC puts contained provisions for settlement in the event that the Tokyo Stock Exchange closed, or if war or natural disaster materially and adversely affected the Japanese economy. The NPW contract needed to specify how investors' claims would be settled in these instances.

5. *Size of offering and per warrant size.* Because the NPWs were designed for individual investors, it was important that they be sold in relatively small lot sizes, in contrast to OTC puts, which required minimum investments of $250.00. At the same time, the Goldman Sachs team sought to keep the per warrant price above

$5.00 because below this level the contracts would not be eligible for short sales on the American Stock Exchange. To accomplish these objectives, the proposed NPW contract gave holders one-fifth of an option on the value of the Nikkei. The team expected to offer 9.5 million warrant contracts in the first one or two offerings.

Throughout the fall of 1989, Goldman Sachs had been working with officials at the American Stock Exchange to bring the Nikkei put warrant offering to market. A key roadblock to actually issuing the warrants was the Japanese Ministry of Finance, which had not yet approved the put warrants. The American and Tokyo stock exchanges had an information-sharing or "mutual surveillance" agreement. Under the terms of this agreement, the Tokyo Stock Exchange effectively was given the right to veto the American exchange listing of Nikkei-linked instruments. On Friday, December 15, 1989, officials at the American Stock Exchange finally received approval to list the Nikkei warrants.

In addition, Goldman Sachs would need to find an issuer for the warrants. As a private partnership and a non-SEC registrant the firm could not issue the warrants publicly without making material public disclosures. Therefore, it was imperative that it be able to work with an issuer registered with the SEC. Specifically, as in the currency warrant transactions, the issuer would sell the warrants to the public but simultaneously enter into a private contract with Goldman Sachs that exactly offset the obligation under the warrant contract. In return, the issuer effectively would receive a fee from Goldman Sachs but economically would have no Nikkei exposure. For accounting purposes, U.S. corporate issuers would be exposed to adverse reporting implications because they would not be allowed to cancel out the warrant transactions for financial reporting.[5] Therefore, the team felt that the most likely issuers were highly creditworthy, non-U.S. sovereign entities with broad name recognition among U.S. retail investors. Goldman Sachs had entered into a tentative agreement with the Kingdom of Denmark to issue the NPWs and to buy an exactly offsetting contract from Goldman Sachs. The Kingdom of Denmark would net approximately $1.3 million for executing these transactions.

To sell the amount of warrants it hoped to offer, Goldman Sachs, felt that it was appropriate to increase its retail distribution capacity by collaborating with other Wall Street firms. They selected Paine Webber and Dean Witter Reynolds to co-manage the offering because of their strong retail clienteles and because these organizations were not considered to be competitors on the investment banking side of the business. Having co-managers on

---

5   The warrants would give rise to a liability (the obligation to buy the Nikkei from the investors) and a simultaneous asset (the put purchased from Goldman Sachs). While economically these offsetting obligations would leave the issuer with a perfectly hedged position, for accounting purposes the set of transactions would appear to show an increase in leverage for the firm.

the deal would also provide additional assurances that the pricing decision would be carefully scrutinized.

PRICING QUESTIONS

One key question that needed to be resolved was how to price the NPWs. The Goldman Sachs team spent many hours collecting the information they would need and discussing how to set the right price for the product. The higher the price they set—assuming that the market bought the product at that price—the larger the profits to Goldman Sachs. However, if the price was too high, the firm could find itself with an unsold inventory of NPWs. In addition, competitors could copy the NPW structure, price their warrants lower, and have a more successful launch. More important, if the first deal was priced too high and the NPWs traded down in the secondary market, both investors and the issuer (the Kingdom of Denmark) would be displeased with the outcome. Goldman Sachs' reputation, which was highly valued at the firm, could be tarnished by a well-publicized poor showing for this new product.

The sales staff had been instrumental in guiding the product team by conveying their perceptions of the market's preferences for the features of the NPW. However, the sales staff was less informative about the price the market would bear. Thus, the product team had to arrive at a price by thorough analysis and a well-informed guess.

COSTS

One factor the group needed to consider was the lower boundary of pricing—Goldman Sachs' break even. For an offering of the size planned, direct costs, other than the fee to the issuer, included legal and listing fees projected to be about $350,000. Selling concessions (commissions) would total about $3 million, much of which would leave Goldman Sachs because its co-managers, Paine Webber and Dean Witter Reynolds, were expected to sell much of the deal. As noted earlier, the Kingdom of Denmark would also be paid a fee of $1.3 million. The team discussed how they should think about the costs of R & D time and effort, which consumed nearly 2 calendar-years and 10 person-years.

The largest cost components were clearly the costs of hedging, or producing the NPWs. The firm planned to buy American-style at-the-money 3-year yen-denominated puts from Goldman Sachs' trading and arbitrage area. Currently they could buy those puts with an implied volatility of about 13.6% per year. Having purchased them, the firm would still need to hedge its currency risk, which would not be a trivial task.

The proposed NPWs would pay investors dollars, with the exchange rate to be used at the time of exercise set at the time of the offering. The puts that the trading and abitrage division would provide paid off in yen. If this yen payoff at maturity were known with certainty, the firm could buy a forward contract on dollars to ensure that it could meet its obligation to the holders. However, neither the size nor timing of the firm's need for dollars was known. Early exercise or extraordinary events could lead to immediate needs to settle the contracts and deliver dollars. More important, drops in the Nikkei along with the appreciation of the dollar would require the firm to deliver more dollars and expose the firm, if unhedged, to losses on the transaction. In the 1980s, the Nikkei and the yen/dollar exchange rate tended to move in opposite directions. Decreases in the Nikkei tended to be associated with slight increases in the yen/dollar exchange rate, or with an appreciation of the dollar.[6]

The J. Aron currency and commodity division of Goldman Sachs offered a product called QUANTOS™ to its customers to solve the type of dynamic currency hedging problem the firm would face. If Goldman Sachs wanted to hedge out all of the currency risk from its issue of the warrants, it estimated that its hedge would cost approximately $1.00 per warrant to set up. If the company wanted to offset approximately 80% of the exchange rate risk it might bear, it might cost approximately 50 cents per warrant. The imperfect hedge would still leave Goldman Sachs subject to some exchange-rate risk. These estimates of the cost of the hedge were subject to revision, because the actual hedge would be adjusted based on movements in the Nikkei and exchange rates.

OTHER PRICING BOUNDARIES

No other product provided U.S. retail investors with the package of features available in the proposed NPWs: U.S. exchange listing and liquidity, small denomination, and no currency risk. U.S. citizens could buy futures on the Nikkei trading on Singapore International Monetary Exchange, but these contracts settled in yen and provided no limit to downside risk. The Chicago Mercantile Exchange was gearing up to trade options on Nikkei futures, and the Chicago Board of Trade was planning to trade futures on TOPIX, a

---

6   Formally, we observe that the covariance of the daily return on the Nikkei average and the daily return to buying yen with dollars has been negative for much of the decade. This covariance is defined as

$$\text{cov}(N_i, Y_i) = \frac{1}{n} \sum (N_i - \overline{N})(Y_i - \overline{Y}) \quad \text{where}$$

N_i = log(Nikkei$_{today}$/Nikkei$_{yesterday}$)

$\overline{N}$ = mean of N_i

Y_i = log[(yen/dollar)$_{today}$/(yen/dollar)$_{yesterday}$]

$\overline{Y}$ = mean of Y_i

n = number of observations

For the period January, 1980 through December 18, 1989, the cov(N_i, Y_i) was -.0000020. For the period January 1989 through December 18, 1989, the cov(N_i, Y_i) was -.0000065.

broad market capitalization-weighted Japanese stock index, but as of December neither product was traded.

As of December 1989, the closest substitutes for the proposed NPWs were a pair of Nikkei put warrants first offered earlier in 1989 and listed on the Toronto Stock Exchange. The two warrants could be purchased by U. S. citizens 90 days after they were first offered for sale in Canada; therefore by December both could be owned by Americans. Unlike the proposed NPWs, the Canadian warrants paid off in Canadian dollars, not U. S. dollars, and their treatment of exchange rates differed from that proposed by Goldman Sachs. The terms of the Canadian warrants are shown in Exhibit 5.

The product team also collected data on the Nikkei, exchange rates, and other relevant capital market data (see Exhibits 6–9) and met late in December 1989 to price the proposed transaction.

Exhibit 1   Daily Implied Volatilities of Exchange-Listed Yen Currency Warrants

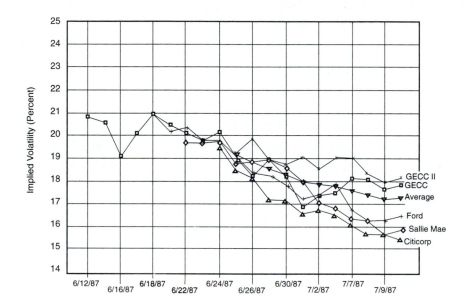

Source: Goldman Sachs & Co.

Note: Implied volatilities represent the market's estimate of the variability in exchange rates inferred from the prices at which the warrants trade. For each warrant, the chart shows the implied volatilities for each of the contracts from the first trading day for that contract.

Exhibit 2   Representative Nikkei-Linked Euro-Yen Offerings, December 1989

Issuer:	Skopbank
Size of Offering:	¥ 6.7 billion
Coupon:	7%
Maturity:	1 Year
Issue Price:	101⅛
Call Options	None
Denomination:	¥ 100 million
Commissions:	1 ⅛%
Redemption:	Redemption is linked to the Nikkei 225 Stock Average (*N*) at maturity by the following formula: If, at maturity, $N \geq 31{,}870.04$, then redemption at par; if $N \leq 23.902.53$, then redemption zero; if in between, then redemption

$$\text{¥ 100 million} \times \left[\left(1 - \frac{(31{,}870.04 - N) \times 4)}{31{,}870.04} \right) \right]$$

Nikkei Level at Issue:	Approximately 38,200

Issuer:	State Bank of South Australia
Size of Offering:	¥ 3.5 billion
Coupon:	1.916667% payable 4/12/90; 5.5833333% payable 1/10/91; 7.5% payable 1/10/92
Maturity:	2 Years (1/10/92)
Issue Price:	101⅛
Call Options:	None
Denomination:	¥ 100 million
Commissions:	1⅛%
Redemption:	If at any time during the life of the contract, the Nikkei equals or exceeds 40,930, then redemption at par. Otherwise, redemption is linked to the Nikkei 225 Stock Average (*N*) at ten days prior to maturity by the following formula: If, at maturity, $N \geq 37{,}724$, then redemption at par; if $N \leq 25{,}149$, then redemption zero; if in between, then redemption =

$$\text{¥ 100 million} \times \left[\left(1 + \frac{(N - 37{,}724) \times 3)}{37{,}724} \right) \right]$$

Nikkei Level at Issue:	37,724.

Source: Compiled from *International Financing Review* December 16, 1989.
Note: *International Financing Review* reported that seasoned Euro-yen bonds yielded 6.10% (1-year maturity), 5.94% (5-year maturity), and 5.58%(10-year maturity) in December 1989. For other capital markets data, see Exhibit 6.

Exhibit 3   Hypothetical Nikkei-Linked Euro-Yen Transactions

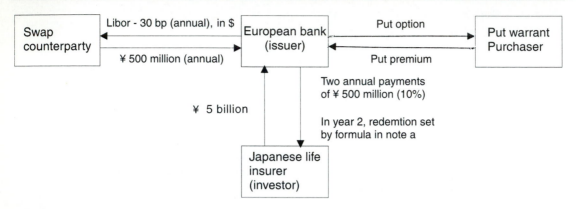

Note: bp= basis point, $\frac{1}{100}$ of 1%.

a. At maturity, the bond's redemption value is equal to the following: If Nikkei > 38,000, redemption=100%; if Nikkei < 25,333, redemption-zero;

$$\text{otherwise, redemption-100\%} \times \left[\left(1- \frac{(38,000 - N) \times 3)}{38,000}\right) \right]$$

where N = level of Nikkei at maturity.

b. At maturity, the issuer delivers to the put purchaser a payment equal to par less the redemption value of the bond.

c. The bond issuer typically pays the put premium to the swap counterparty in order to compensate them for making a sub-LIBOR swap.

d. For the investor, non-Nikkei-linked fixed-rate yen investments would typically yield 7%. One alternative for the issuer would be to issue 2-year, U.S.-dollar-denominated, floating-rate notes at LIBOR (with no Nikkei-linked feature).

Exhibit 4   Terms of Proposed Kingdom of Denmark Nikkei Put Warrants

Issuer:	Kingdom of Denmark.
Date:	January 1990.
Amount:	9.5 million warrants.
Expiration:	Any date within 36 months of issue.

Cash Settlement Value

The cash settlement value shall be an amount in U.S. dollars of the excess, if any, of (1) the exercise price over (2) the expiration value. The exercise price will equal $N/(5Y)$, where $N =$ closing Nikkei average on the day prior to the issuance of the NPWs, and $Y =$ ¥/$ exchange rate on the day prior to the issuance of the NPWs. The expiration value is one fifth of the dollar amount obtained by converting the closing value of the Nikkei average on the exercise date into U.S. dollars at a fixed exchange rate equal to Y.

For example, if the deal had been issued on 12/19/89, it would use the prior day's Nikkei level and exchange rate to set the exercise price. On 12/18/89 the Nikkei was 38,586.18 and the exchange rate was 144.28 ¥/$; thus the exercise price would be set at $N/(5Y) = (38,586.18)/(5 \times 144.28) = \$53.49$. If an investor later wanted to exercise her option when the Nikkei was 30,000 and the current exchange rate was 115 ¥/$, the expiration value would be 30,000/(5 × 144.28) = \$41.59; and the cash settlement value would be \$53.49-41.59=\$11.90. It is important to note that the calculation of the expiration value uses the exchange rate in effect on the date when the issue was sold, not the rate in effect when the warrants were exercised.

Because of the time difference between New York and Tokyo, warrants exercised in New York by 3 p.m. will receive a cash settlement value calculated with the Nikkei 225 Stock Average on the close of business on the Tokyo Stock Exchange on the next succeeding business day.

Conditional Exercise

Any warrant holder may elect to make the exercise of its warrants contingent on the closing value of the Nikkei average on the exercise date not being more than 500 points above the closing value of the Nikkei average on the relevant notice date.

Limitation Event

All exercises of warrants (other than on the expiration date or the delisting date) are subject, at the Kingdom's option, to the limitation that not more than 2 million warrants in total may be exercised on any exercise date and not more than 500,000 warrants may be exercised by or on behalf of any person or entity, either individually or in concert with any other person or entity, on any exercise date.

Extraordinary Events

Defined as suspension of trading on the Tokyo Stock Exchange, government action that would make the warrants unlawful, or outbreaks of "hostilities or other national or international calamity or crisis...which has or will have a material adverse effect on the ability of the Kingdom to perform its obligations under the warrants or to modify the hedge of its position with respect to the Nikkei average."

If the Kingdom determines that an extraordinary event has occurred and is continuing on an exercise date, then the cash settlement value of any warrants that would otherwise be calculated on such day shall be calculated on the next succeeding business day on which there is no extraordinary event, provided that if the cash settlement value of such warrants is not calculated on or prior to the expiration date or the delisting date, then the cash settlement value shall be calculated as if such warrants had been exercised on the expiration date or the delisting date, as the case may be.

Exhibit 5   Terms of Put Warrants Listed on the Toronto Stock Exchange, 1989

Warrant:	NKP.WT.
Issuer:	BT Bank of Canada.
Date:	February 17, 1989.
Amount:	C$20 million, increased to C$32 million.
Expiry Date:	February 17, 1992.
Type:	American put.
Price at Issue:	C$3.55.

Cash Settlement Value in C$: $100 \text{ NKP.WT} = 11.68 \times \left[\dfrac{(32{,}174 - \text{Nikkei at exercise})}{\text{¥/C\$ at exercise}} \right]$

Calculation of Value when Exercised

If exercised by 3 p.m., Toronto time, the contract cash settlement value shall be determined as of close of the following business day in Tokyo.

Limit Option

Any holder has the right to make the exercise of such holder's warrants contingent on the value of the closing quotation for the Nikkei index on the valuation date being not more than 500 Nikkei index points higher than the closing quotation on the relevant notice date. If such contingency is not met, such holder's warrants will be deemed not to have been exercised.

Maximum Exercise of Warrants

In the event that BT Bank determines, on the business day following any notice date, other than the expiration date, that more than 1 million warrants are being exercised by a single holder or a group of holders acting in concert, then BT Bank may deem the valuation date for the first 1 million of the warrants exercised by such holder or group of holders to be the business day next following such notice date and the valuation date for each additional tranche of 1 million of the warrants (or part thereof, in the case of the last tranche) exercised by such holder or group of holders to be each succeeding business day thereafter until all warrants exercised on such notice date by such holder or group of holders have been valued.

Extraordinary Events:

Defined as "any event, circumstance or cause (whether or not reasonably foreseeable) beyond the reasonable control of BT Bank...which has or will have a material adverse effect on the ability of BT Bank to perform its obligations or hedge its position with respect to the warrants." These include suspension of trading or limitations of prices on the Tokyo Stock Exchange, suspension of trading on the Nikkei 225 Futures Contracts on SIMEX or Osaka, government action that would "affect payment of amounts due under the warrants," government action that has "material adverse effect on the financial markets of Japan," or "any outbreak or escalation of hostilities or other national or international calamity or crisis." If BT Bank determines that on a valuation date an extraordinary event has occurred and is continuing, then the net cash settlement value shall be calculated on the basis that the valuation date shall be the next business day in which there is no extraordinary event.

Exhibit 5 Terms of Put Warrants Listed on the Toronto Stock Exchange, 1989 (Continued)

Warrant:	NKP.WT.A.
Issuer:	BT Bank of Canada.
Date:	June 15, 1989.
Amount:	C$32.8 million.
Expiry Date:	June 15, 1992.
Type:	American put
Price at Issue:	C$2.65.

Cash Settlement Value in C$: 100 NKP.WT.A $= 10.31 \times \left[270.54 - \dfrac{\text{Nikkei at exercise}}{\text{yen/C\$ at exercise}} \right]$

Other Terms: Materially the same as NKP.WT.

Note: A third Nikkei put warrant was announced by the Bank of Nova Scotia on May 22, 1989. The product was to be a 3-year, at-the-money Nikkei put warrant. On June 13, 1989, the *Financial Post* reported the following brief news item:

There is some justifiable jubilation at BT Bank of Canada these days. Last Friday, an issue of Nikkei put warrants—to be brought to the market by Bank of Nova Scotia—was yanked after the underwriters failed to reach the minimum target of $15 million. The Scotiabank product was in competition with an issue being bought to market by BT Bank. The Scotiabank product had the support of the cream of Canada's investment dealers. By contrast, Walwyn Stodgell Cochran Murray, Ltd., was the lead and sole underwriter for the BT product, which was considered more attractive by many. The BT deal closes tomorrow, and the word is that lots of buyers have snapped it up.

Exhibit 6   Capital Markets Data as of December 18, 1989

Closing value of the Nikkei Index: ¥ 38,586.18
Dividend yield on the stocks included in the Nikkei Index: .49% per year.
Exchange rates: US $1= ¥144.28 = C$1.16.

Interest rates (Treasury or equivalent government rates):	U.S. ($)	Canada (C$)	Japan(¥)
1 year	7.62%	11.72%	6.375%
2 years	7.75	10.48	5.85
3 years	7.69	10.22	5.85

NPWs traded on the Toronto Stock Exchange	NKP. WT	NKP. WT. A.
Price (C$)	$2.60	$1.90
Average daily volume (000)	105	171

Sources: Interactive Data Corporation, Toronto Stock Exchange, Goldman Sachs.

Exhibit 7 Relative Performances of Nikkei 225 Stock Average and Standard & Poor's Index, January 1980–December 18, 1989

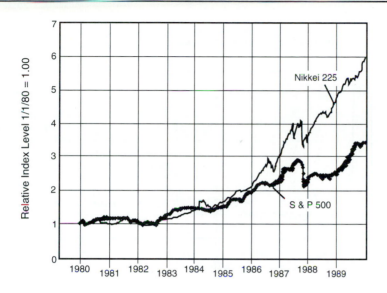

Exhibit 8 ¥/$ Exchange Rate, January 1980–December 18, 1989

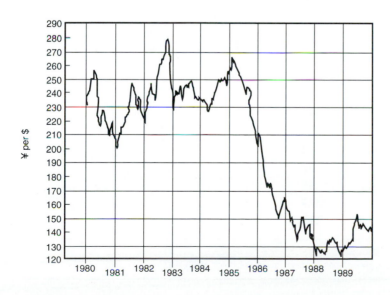

Exhibit 9   Annualized Volatility of the Nikkei 225 Stock Average

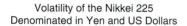

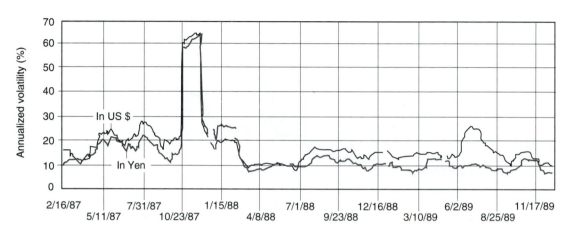

Note: Volatility calculated by the caeswriter on the basis of past three months' returns, and annualized using a 250-day trading year. Volatility is shown for the Nikkei returns denominated in Yen and for the returns to a Nikkei investment translated into US$ using the spot exchange rate each day. As of mid-December 1989, the most recent volatility was approximately 6% (in yen) or 9% (in dollars). The volatility for the Nikkei denominated in Canadian dollars is very similar to the volatility of the Nikkei in U.S. dollars. A longer history of the volatility of the Nikkei index (denominated in yen) is shown below:

Period	Annualized Volatility
1949–53	20.0%
1954–58	9.7
1959–63	13.4
1962–68	11.1
1969–73	14.4
1974–78	9.8
1979–83	8.5
1984–88	12.7
Average	12.5

Source: William T. Ziemba and Sandra L. Schwartz, *Invest Japan* (Chicago: Probus Publishing, 1992), p.97.

AN INVESTMENT LINKED TO COMMODITY FUTURES

In November 1991, the Swedish Export Credit Corporation, an AAA credit, issued a 3-year zero coupon note whose prospective returns were linked to the returns from commodity futures. The total size of the issue was $100 million, and the notes matured in November 1994. Institutional investors participated in the issue, buying the notes for par in denominations of $100,000 and $50,000 (Exhibit 1).

Unlike typical zero coupon notes, the Swedish Export issue had no fixed interest rate. Instead, the prospective return on the notes was tied exclusively to the future value of the Goldman Sachs Commodity Index (GSCI). The GSCI was computed on the basis of the cumulative total returns from a fully collateralized investment in an index of commodity futures. At maturity, investors would redeem the notes according to the following formula:

Par × .9557 × GSCI End/GSCI Begin

GSCI Begin represented the value of the commodity index—2590.81—on the note's issuance date, November 7, 1991. GSCI End represented the unknown future value of the commodity index on the note's maturity date of November 7, 1994. According to the redemption formula, an index level of 2710.90 on the ending date would retire the notes at 100% of par value (Exhibit 2).

The commodity-linked notes could not be called by the issuer nor could they be redeemed by the investor prior to the maturity date. The notes, however, did trade in the secondary market. Since their issuance, they had been trading at prices ranging between 80% and 100% of par value.

GOLDMAN SACHS AND THE COMMODITY BUSINESS

Goldman Sachs, founded in 1869, was a leading investment banking and securities firm with offices in the United States, Europe, and Asia. Goldman performed a full range of

A. Nancy Donohue, Kenneth A. Froot, and Jay O. Light prepared this case as the basis of class discussion.

activities in the equity and fixed-income markets for institutions and individuals. Goldman also managed operations in corporate finance, municipal finance, merchant banking, and real estate.

The creation of the Goldman Sachs Commodity Index was an extension of Goldman's expertise in commodities. Through its J. Aron Currency and Commodities Division, Goldman acted as a major dealer in the commodity futures market. J. Aron, which Goldman acquired in the early 1980s, also had a significant presence in the spot commodity market. Aron purchased crude oil and petroleum from major oil producers to supply refiners and industrial users worldwide. It sourced metals from mines around the world, arranged for their refining, and supplied them to industry. Aron advised over 50 central banks in the management of gold reserves, was one of the world's largest coffee merchants, and was a merchant in grains and oil-seed products.

DESIGN OF THE GOLDMAN SACHS COMMODITY INDEX

Goldman Sachs introduced the GSCI in 1991 with the objective of opening the commodities market to greater institutional investor participation. The proprietary index measured the total return from investing in a basket of collateralized commodity futures in the energy, livestock, agricultural, industrial metal, and precious metal sectors (Exhibit 3).

Goldman believed that the weights incorporated in its commodity futures index reflected the relative impact each commodity had on the worldwide economy. The design of the GSCI was analogous to that of a capitalization-weighted stock market index that reflects the relative impact each individual stock has on the overall market. Specifically, commodity futures in the GSCI were weighted (arithmetically) according to the dollar value of their physical quantity of worldwide production. This gave heavy representation to energy futures, which in 1992 composed almost 48% of the index's value. Livestock futures, meanwhile, represented 23% of the index, and agricultural futures represented 21%. The remaining sectors, industrial and precious metals, composed 6% and 2% of the index, respectively.

Each commodity future in the index had to pass strict tests for liquidity. Only commodities with active futures contracts denominated in U.S. dollars and traded on exchanges in major industrialized countries were included. The composition of the index became broader over time because fewer futures had been traded in the past. Between 1970 and 1980 the index was over 80% weighted in livestock and agricultural futures. During the 1980s, as new futures contracts were introduced and trading activity in metals and energy futures increased, the index became more diversified.

The GSCI was calculated from the total returns of futures contracts rather than from the spot prices for each commodity. Unlike spot prices (or common stocks), there were a number of alternative futures contracts for every commodity, each representing a different futures maturity date. The index computation therefore required a set of decision rules for selecting futures contracts in individual commodities. In general, the decision rule was to hold the most active (the nearest) contract month until the contract had one month until expiration. At that time, the contract was rolled over into the next nearest contract. The rolling process entailed selling the future with only one month remaining and purchasing the next nearest futures contract. The most actively traded commodity futures (crude oil, unleaded gasoline, heating oil, aluminum, and zinc) had contracts maturing each month and therefore were rolled every month. Other commodity futures had bimonthly maturities and were thus rolled approximately six times per year. Futures with only four maturities per year (sugar, cotton, and platinum) were usually rolled only four times a year. To avoid delivery of the commodity, positions in any contract scheduled for delivery in the next month were rolled forward in the month prior to maturity.

Goldman Sachs normalized the GSCI index to a value of 100 on January 2, 1970. On the last day of trading in 1991 the index stood at a level of 2291.90. (Over this same time, a comparably weighted index of spot prices, called the Goldman Sachs Spot Index, rose from 100 to 176.92.) Cumulative returns for the period 1970–1990 are plotted on a logarithmic scale in Exhibit 4. The returns on the S&P 500 and U.S. Treasury bonds are plotted for comparison. Over the period, the returns from the GSCI collateralized futures portfolio were clearly attractive.

MEASURING THE RETURNS ON THE GSCI

The returns on the GSCI were generated so as to replicate the returns that would have been earned on a fully collateralized portfolio of commodities futures. In particular, the returns assumed that an investor posted collateral consisting of U.S. Treasury bills equal to the value of the commodity futures prices.[1]

The total returns on this portfolio consisted of two components, the yield from the collateral Treasury bills and the return from the futures. The return from the futures could be broken into two components: the spot return and the roll yield. The spot return came from the changes in the commodities' spot prices. The roll yield represented the additional gain or loss captured when rolling forward the commodity futures in a portfolio as

---

1   This collateralized futures index portfolio is completely analogous to a fully collateralized synthetic S&P 500 index fund where the investor takes a long position in an S&P 500 future and collateralizes it fully with U.S. Treasury bills.

described previously. As each futures contract approached maturity, its price approached the spot price. It was this movement in price that allowed an investor to earn a return from the roll yield. When a commodity's price structure was contango (futures prices greater than spot prices), the roll yield was negative because the futures' price decreased toward the spot price as the future matured. When a commodity's price structure was in backwardation (futures prices below spot prices), the roll yield was positive because the futures' price increased toward the spot price as the future matured. In general, then, the total return on the GSCI had three components:

GSCI total return = Spot return + T-bill yield + Roll yield

Exhibit 5 shows the year-by-year total return on the GSCI from 1970 to 1991. Note that the contribution of the spot return was relatively small on average (about 2%) and extremely variable. The contribution of the T-bill yield was substantial and relatively less volatile. The contribution of the roll yield was positive though somewhat volatile.

The annualized average returns and standard deviations of return for the three components of the GSCI are shown in Table A for two different periods: the inflationary 1972 – 1980 period and the disinflationary 1981 – 1990 period. An important contribution to the total return in the 1981 – 1990 period came from the roll yield. Since the mid-1980s the GSCI had held substantial weightings in energy futures (particularly oil) and livestock futures. In both of these types of commodity futures, the price structure was often in backwardation, which produced a positive roll yield. Some experts estimated that since crude oil futures first opened for trading in 1983 on the New York Mercantile Exchange their prices had been in backwardation 80% – 85% of the time. The crude oil future had been included in the GSCI since 1984.

Table A   Historical GSCI Returns and Standard Deviations

	Spot Return	Roll Yield	T-bill Yield	Total Return
1972 – 1980				
Annualized return	12.6%	1.8%	7.3%	21.6%
Standard deviation	24.0	6.1	.8	23.2
1981 – 1990				
Annualized return	−.9%	5.0%	8.7%	12.8%
Standard deviation	15.2	4.4	.8	15.4

COMMODITIES AND INFLATION

An attractive feature of the GSCI, or any investment tied to commodity prices, was its ability to act as a hedge against inflation (Exhibit 6). Both the Goldman Sachs Spot Index[2] and the Goldman Sachs Commodity Index had a strong positive correlation with the two most widely used measures of inflation: the Consumer Price Index (CPI) and the Producer Price Index (PPI).

Commodities had long been used by investors to hedge portfolios with large amounts of inflation risk. Gold, most notably, was a safe haven because it retained value in times of economic and political instability. To preserve wealth, many European investors held gold after the world wars, when confidence in currencies decreased and hyperinflation sometimes prevailed.

The use of commodities as an inflation hedge worked especially well for two reasons. First, dramatic increases in commodity prices often triggered inflationary surges in an economy. The oil shocks of 1973 – 1974 and 1978 – 1979 reverberated throughout the worldwide economy. The supply shock increased not only gasoline and home heating oil prices for consumers but also raised raw material prices for industry. This in turn pushed consumer prices and ultimately wages into an inflationary spiral.

The second reason that commodity investments worked well as a hedge against inflation was that commodity prices could react quickly to perceived monetary policy changes. For example, the Federal Reserve (or other central banks around the world) could pursue an expansionary monetary policy by lowering interest rates. The necessary increase in money supply, many believed, would raise inflation—actual and expected—as more paper currency would soon be chasing after the same number of goods. These expectations would then be incorporated more or less instantaneously into spot and futures commodity prices around the world. Indeed, because of their extreme responsiveness, commodity prices were a good leading indicator of inflation. Economists often used the behavior of commodity prices to forecast future inflation rates.

ASSET ALLOCATION AND AN INVESTMENT IN COMMODITIES

A fully collateralized portfolio of commodity futures, such as that represented by the GSCI, would have been an interesting investment in its own right in the 1970 – 1991 period as these average returns and standard deviations shown in Table B suggest. More important, though, an investment in the GSCI had the potential to decrease the risk of the portfolio as well. Using the GSCI to decrease the risk of an investment portfolio worked

---

2   The Goldman Sachs Spot Index differed from the GSCI in that it measured the spot prices of the commodities in the GSCI.

well because returns on the GSCI were negatively correlated with returns on stocks and bonds.

Table B   Comparative Returns and Standard Deviations, 1970–1991

	GSCI	S&P 500	Long-Term U.S. Treasury Bonds
Annualized return:	14.2%	11.0%	8.9%
Standard deviation:	18.6	16.3	6.4

Over the 1970 – 1990 period, Goldman Sachs estimated that the correlation of quarterly GSCI returns with the S&P 500 was −.32, and the correlation of quarterly GSCI returns with U.S. Treasury bonds was −.19. In contrast, the correlation of the S&P 500 with U.S. Treasury bonds was +.39. Because the calculated returns on the GSCI were high and the correlation of the GSCI with stocks and bonds was negative, an addition of GSCI to an investment portfolio would not only have increased overall return but also would have decreased risk. For example, by reallocating just 5% of a 60/40 stock/bond portfolio to an investment in the GSCI, the average returns over the 1970 – 1990 period would have increased from 9.6% to 9.8%, and the standard deviation of returns would have decreased from 12.1% to 11.5%. Exhibit 7 shows how the expected returns and standard deviations of a portfolio composed of the S&P 500 and the GSCI would vary for different sets of future return assumptions.

A look at portfolio theory, a quantitative optimization tool for determining how alternative asset classes might interact with each other in a portfolio, shows how an investment in the GSCI might be perceived. Standard computer-based portfolio optimization techniques tend to select for investment in assets whose returns are assumed to be large and whose correlations are negative (or slightly positive). Obviously, if the GSCI were offered as a possible investment with its 1970 – 1990 returns, standard deviations, and correlations, any portfolio optimizer would have found it an extremely attractive asset class and would have recommended a very large position. Indeed, as long as the negative correlation of returns was assumed to continue into the future, a portfolio optimizer would include the GSCI as an attractive investment, even if the future returns were assumed to be very low (Exhibit 7).

AN ALTERNATIVE: MANAGED FUTURES FUNDS

There were, of course, other ways to participate in the commodity futures markets. Managed futures funds had grown in popularity with retail investors during the 1980s as futures markets around the world expanded and as investors gained sophistication in using derivative instruments. A few pioneering institutional investors had begun to participate in these funds in recent years. Organized as limited partnerships, the managed funds invested in commodity as well as financial futures. The funds also took both long and short positions in the futures markets. Most fund managers used technical analysis (charting) to follow and attempt to ride the trend in any given market. Other fund managers had creative approaches based on weather forecasting, for instance, or used complicated computer modeling systems. In general, the portfolio positions of those funds changed dramatically from period to period. They were really more like trading pools that happened to use commodity futures as their main vehicle rather than an indexed investment in commodities.

In any given time period, performance for a handful of these managed funds seemed very impressive; for example, some firms had generated 1991 returns of 30% or higher. Underlying these figures, however, was a maze of fees and charges amounting to over 15% of capital invested in some cases. Other complications included separating the good futures managers from the bad. There were literally hundreds of firms competing in the business, some registering 1991 performance records of worse than negative 60% return.

There were very few careful studies of the past performance of these funds. However, one well-regarded study (which examined a sample of these funds from 1980 to 1988) found that the average fund returned 2.36%. This could be compared with the GSCI's return of 7.66% over the same period (Exhibit 8).

ALTERNATIVES LINKED TO THE GSCI

In addition to the zero coupon notes described in this case, Goldman Sachs offered a number of other products related to the index. For investors in the European market Goldman designed and issued a very similar product, a $100 million 3-year zero coupon note issued by the Finnish Export Credit Corporation.

For investors interested in a more leveraged transaction (which would free up more of their principal), Goldman designed swap transactions against LIBOR (Exhibit 9). In these deals, investors would pay Goldman LIBOR. In exchange, Goldman would pay investors the return on the GSCI minus 150 basis points (bp). The 150 basis points covered transaction costs and tracking error in managing investments in the GSCI's commodity futures. Goldman conducted swap transactions on principal amounts of $5 million and more.

As of the spring of 1992, Goldman Sachs was continuing to innovate in the commodities market. It had begun to design and trade options on the GSCI and was also seeking to list GSCI-based futures and options on a U.S. exchange.

AN ALTERNATIVE LINKED TO THE CRB INDEX

The Commodity Research Bureau (CRB) maintained an index called the CRB Futures Index. The New York Futures Exchange (NYFE) designed and offered futures and options contracts based on the value of this index. The index itself was an equal-weighted combination of the performance of 21 commodities futures, with relatively heavy representation from agricultural commodities, particularly grains.

Investing with this index was difficult, however, because the NYFE contracts had proved unpopular and illiquid. Also, the returns from this index had been substantially less in recent years than those from the GSCI. Because of its relatively heavy representation of grains (rather than energy futures), the roll yields in this index had often been quite negative. Exhibit 10 shows the 1984 – 1990 comparisons. While, in principle, some firms might design various collateralized commodity securities replicating the performance of the CRB Index (just as Goldman Sachs had done for the GSCI), there were no known efforts under way to do this.

Exhibit 1   Prospectus for the Zero Coupon Notes

Filed Pursuant to Rule 424(b)(3)
Registration No. 33-42537

PRICING SUPPLEMENT NO. 3 , Dated October 24, 1991
(To Prospectus Dated September 16, 1991 and
Prospectus Supplement Dated September 30, 1991)

AB SVENSK EXPORTKREDIT

(Swedish Export Credit Corporation)
(Incorporated in the Kingdom of Sweden with limited liability)
$1,500,000,000

Medium-Term Notes, Series A
Due not less than Nine Months from Date of Issue
Zero-Coupon GSCI Indexed Notes due November 7, 1994

For a discussion of certain risks associated with the Zero-Coupon
GSCI Indexed Notes due November 7, 1994 offered hereby (the
"Offered Notes"), see "Risk Factors Related to the GSCI" herin.

Indexed Principal Amount:	The Face Amount as adjusted in accordance with the procedures set forth under "Description of Offered Notes" below
Face Amount:	$100,000,000
Issue Price:	100.00% of the Face Amount
Issue Date:	November 7, 1991
Maturity Date:	November 7, 1994
Settlement Date:	The later of the Maturity Date or the second Business Day after the Validation Date
Interest Rate:	None
Form:	(X) Book Entry
	( ) Certificate
Specified Currency:	U.S. dollars
Authorized Denominations:	$100,000 and integral multiples of $50,000 in excess thereof
Commodity Index:	The Goldman Sachs Commodity Index (the "GSCI")
Determination Agent:	Goldman, Sachs & Co. ("Goldman Sachs")
Redemption (Other Than For Tax Reasons:	(X) The Offered Notes cannot be redeemed prior to maturity.
	( ) The Offered Notes may be redeemed prior to maturity.
Discount Notes:	( ) Yes (X) No
Agent's Commission:	.350% (equal to $350,000)
Net Proceeds To Company:	$99,650,000

Goldman, Sachs & Co.

Exhibit 2   GSCI Zero Coupon Note Redemption Values

| GSCI Begin | GSCI End | Redemption | | Rate of Return |
		% of Par ($100,000)	Value	
2590.81	1200	44.27%	$44,270	−23.79%
2590.81	1400	51.64	51,640	−19.77
2590.81	1600	59.02	59,020	−16.12
2590.81	1800	66.40	66,400	−12.76
2590.81	2000	73.78	73,780	−9.64
2590.81	2200	81.15	81,150	−6.72
2590.81	2400	88.53	88,530	−3.98
2590.81	2600	95.91	95,910	−1.38
2590.81	2800	103.29	103,290	1.08
2590.81	3000	110.66	110,660	3.44
2590.81	3200	118.04	118,040	5.68
2590.81	3400	125.42	125,420	7.84
2590.81	3600	132.80	132,800	9.92
2590.81	3800	140.17	140,170	11.92
2590.81	4000	147.55	147,550	13.85
2590.81	4200	154.93	154,930	15.71
2590.81	4400	162.31	162,310	17.52
2590.81	4600	169.69	169,690	19.27
2590.81	4800	177.06	177,060	20.98
2590.81	5000	184.44	184,440	22.64

Exhibit 3 Components of GSCI Index

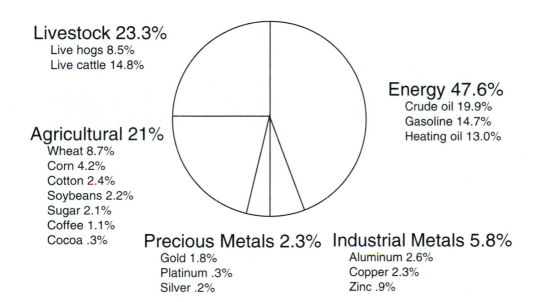

January 1992

Livestock 23.3%
Live hogs 8.5%
Live cattle 14.8%

Energy 47.6%
Crude oil 19.9%
Gasoline 14.7%
Heating oil 13.0%

Agricultural 21%
Wheat 8.7%
Corn 4.2%
Cotton 2.4%
Soybeans 2.2%
Sugar 2.1%
Coffee 1.1%
Cocoa .3%

Precious Metals 2.3%
Gold 1.8%
Platinum .3%
Silver .2%

Industrial Metals 5.8%
Aluminum 2.6%
Copper 2.3%
Zinc .9%

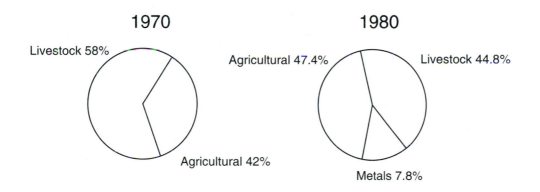

1970

Livestock 58%

Agricultural 42%

1980

Agricultural 47.4%

Livestock 44.8%

Metals 7.8%

Exhibit 4 Cumulative Total Returns, 1970 – 1990

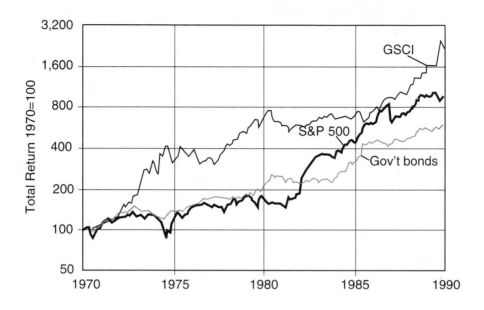

Exhibit 5   Returns on the GSCI, 1970 – 1991

	Spot Return	T-Bill Yield	Roll Yield	Total Return
1970	4.80%	6.53%	2.73%	14.06%
1971	6.47	4.44	8.22	19.14
1972	27.35	4.13	3.88	35.36
1973	39.64	7.22	9.07	55.94
1974	18.82	8.07	6.41	33.30
1975	−36.41	5.96	11.55	−18.90
1976	−14.88	5.11	−2.92	−12.68
1977	.78	5.35	3.73	9.86
1978	19.21	7.34	.92	27.46
1979	20.84	10.37	−2.09	29.13
1980	12.21	11.90	−13.60	10.51
1981	−28.70	14.53	−11.98	−26.15
1982	−.09	11.02	.01	10.94
1983	7.03	8.82	−.79	15.06
1984	−10.02	9.88	1.18	1.04
1985	.26	7.66	1.62	9.54
1986	−20.78	6.10	16.70	2.02
1987	3.13	5.95	12.25	21.33
1988	11.52	6.81	6.30	24.63
1989	11.68	8.29	12.44	32.41
1990	5.96	7.73	11.84	25.53
1991	−21.78	5.53	9.92	-6.33
Compound annual returns	2.59	7.67	3.97	14.24

Exhibit 6   GSCI Correlation with Inflation

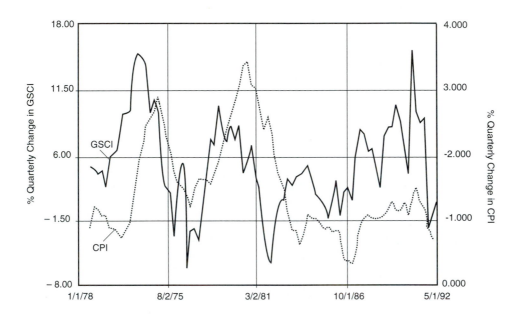

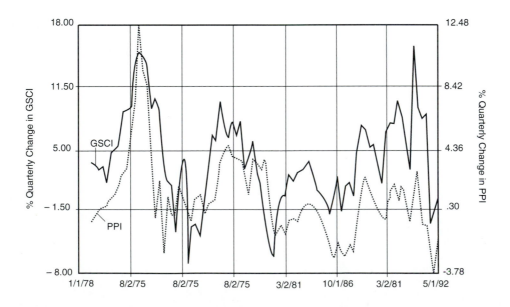

Exhibit 7   Risk-Return Scenarios—Portfolio of Stocks (S&P 500) and Commodity Futures (GSCI)

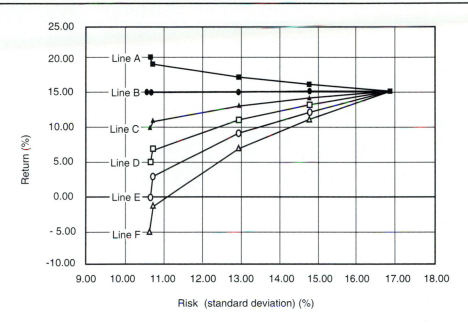

Lines A, B, C, D, E, and F measure risk-return trade-offs for portfolios of stocks and commodity futures at different levels of expected return.

	Return on Stocks	Return on Commodity Futures
Line A	15%	25%
Line B	15	15
Line C	15	5
Line D	15	−5
Line E	15	−15
Line F	15	−25

The Five Points on Each Line represent different weightings of stocks and commodity futures in the portfolio. From right to left the weightings are as follows.

Exhibit 7 Risk-Return Scenarios—Portfolio of Stocks (S&P 500) and Commodity Futures (GSCI) (Continued)

	Stock	Commodity Futures
First Point	100%	0%
Second Point	90	10
Third Point	80	20
Fourth Point	60	40
Fifth Point	50	50

The following historical figures were used in the above calculations:

Standard deviation, S&P 500, 1970 – 1990	16.34%
Standard deviation, GSCI, 1970 – 1990	18.34%
Correlation of returns, S&P 500 versus GSCI	−.32

Exhibit 8 Comparison of GSCI and Managed Futures Funds

	GSCI Total Return	Managed Futures Funds Return
1980	10.51%	2.07%
1981	−26.15	4.07
1982	10.94	−.09
1983	15.06	−15.08
1984	1.04	7.67
1985	9.54	10.88
1986	2.02	−17.16
1987	21.33	28.32
1988	24.63	.56
Compound annual return	7.66	2.36

Source: E.J. Elton and M.J. Gruber, "The Performance of Publicly Offered Commodity Funds," *Financial Analysts Journal*, July-August 1990.

Exhibit 9   Swap Transaction Designed by Goldman Sachs

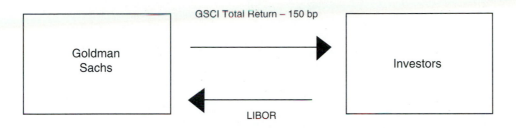

Exhibit 10   Comparison of GSCI and CRB Futures Index

	GSCI Total Return	Comparable CRB Futures Index Return[a]
1980	10.51%	22.26%
1981	−26.15	−2.98
1982	10.94	2.82
1983	15.06	27.45
1984	1.04	−2.15
1985	9.54	1.52
1986	2.02	−2.67
1987	21.33	17.14
1988	24.63	15.11
1989	32.41	−.41
1990	25.52	4.55
Compound annual return	11.50	5.42

a. Return on a fully collateralized investment in CRB futures (return on the futures index plus return on collateral investment in T-bills).

FIDELITY INVESTMENTS:
SPARTAN FLORIDA MUNICIPAL FUND

On August 5, 1993, Anne Punzak, portfolio manager of Fidelity Investments Spartan Florida Municipal Fund, found herself facing an investment decision regarding some municipal zero-coupon bonds she had purchased a month earlier. The zeroes, of a Florida water and sewer tax-exempt issuer, had been attractively priced to yield 6.05%, 45 basis points above insured zero-coupon bonds. Ms. Punzak had purchased these bonds with the intention of making a short term capital gain, by reselling them within a month. However, she had just been informed by a trader that the bonds had now dropped in price and were currently yielding 6.10%. Anne Punzak had to decide whether this was an opportune time to:

- Sell the zeroes and cut her losses. However, being uninsured, the bonds would not be very liquid, and selling them might be difficult.
- Add to her investments by buying more zeroes and wait for the market to correct its perception of the issuer credit.
- Buy secondary market insurance for the zeroes from a municipal bond insurance company and resell the bonds as insured bonds, which would be more liquid.

THE MUNICIPAL BOND MARKET

Municipal bonds were debt instruments issued by state and local governments. Interest paid on most municipal bonds was exempt from federal income taxation and in the issuing state also free from state and local taxation. Munis were subject to capital gains taxes, however, assessed when the bonds matured or when they were sold by the investor for more than the purchase price. The largest holders of munis were, in order: retail investors

Sanjay Bhatnagar and André F. Perold prepared this case as the basis for class discussion rather than to illustrate either effective or ineffective handling of an administrative situation.

(either directly or indirectly through mutual funds), commercial banks, and property and casualty insurance companies.

There were two principal types of municipal bonds: General Obligation (GO) bonds, which were backed by the full faith and the credit (that is, the taxing power and further borrowing ability) of the issuer; and Revenue bonds, which were backed by the revenues from particular projects or by the municipal agencies operating the projects. Revenue bonds were typically issued by airports, hospitals, and turnpike and port authorities. At the end of 1992, total municipal debt outstanding exceeded $1 trillion. Newly issued debt that year amounted to $233 billion, of which 37% was in the form of GOs.

MUNICIPAL BOND INSURANCE

Municipal bond insurance was a guarantee that in the event of a default by the issuer (failure to pay interest or principal), a third-party insurer would pay the coupon and principal on the bond when due. The bond insurer was typically not required to accelerate payments in the event of default. Bond insurance was available for new as well as seasoned issues.

In return for assuming the risk of default, the insurer charged the bond issuer an up-front fee or "premium," usually a fraction of total insured cash flows (undiscounted sum of coupons plus principal). Typical premia for new issue bonds were around 45 basis points of total cash flow for GOs and 55 basis points for Revenue bonds, figures that had changed little over the last 5 years. (Exhibit 1).

Demand for insured municipal bonds had grown rapidly, with 34% of newly issued debt being insured in 1992, up from 15% in 1983 (Exhibit 2). An industry observer explained this increase in demand: "After the turbulent 1980s which saw a number of defaults especially in real estate, investors became increasingly concerned with the credit quality of their investments. Retail investors who continue to dominate municipal bond purchases lack the resources to analyze the credit quality of bonds and thus seek the security of insurance. In return, these investors are willing to accept a lower yield. Also, rating downgrades of municipalities in recent years have made the insurance more cost effective for certain issuers."

Others pointed to the rising incidence of default and ratings downgrades in the municipal bond market as a possible reason (Exhibit 3.) They pointed out that insured bonds were also more liquid and the lower yield received by the investor was actually a liquidity premium paid by the investor. Yet others believed that municipal bond insurers were providing a means for portfolio diversification to the retail investor who was limited to investing in his or her home state in order to avoid state and local taxes.

The primary municipal bond insurers were MBIA, AMBAC, FGIC and FSA, with market shares of 35%, 28%, 22%, and 6%, respectively. All were rated AAA. These insurers in turn ceded a portion of their business (about 20% in 1992) to reinsurers like Capital Reinsurance and Enhance Reinsurance. The net outstanding exposure of the bond insurance industry was $604 billion as of December 1992 (insured principal plus interest); the risk leverage ratio was 135:1.[1] Exhibit 4 shows the growth of the industry exposure during the last decade. Exhibit 6 analyzes the exposure of MBIA, the largest insurer, and Exhibit 7 presents MBIA's summary financial statements.

The principal sources of revenue for an insurer were investment income and earned premiums. Although most of the premium was collected up front, only a small portion of it was earned in each year. The remainder was recognized as an unearned premium reserve. When a bond was advance refunded[2] or retired early by the issuer, the insurer was able to immediately earn the entire unearned premium less any credit given by the insurer to the issuer toward the premium due on the newly issued bond. In recent years, falling interest rates had led to a large number of refinancings, giving rise to a dramatic increase in the earnings of the major insurers.

Insured bonds historically traded at higher yields than uninsured AAA bonds. See Exhibits 5 and 8 for municipal and treasury bond pricing on August 5, 1993, and Exhibit 9 for Standard & Poors ratings definitions. The market priced insured bonds differently depending primarily on the credit rating of the bond issuer and the relative strength of the insurance company guaranteeing the performance of the bond. The percentage of municipal bonds with "natural" AAA ratings was quite low. Natural AAAs were primarily GO and tax-backed securities. Currently, natural AAAs represented only about 6% of all outstanding municipal bonds. This low percentage of natural versus the relatively large amount of outstanding insured municipal bonds was cited as a possible explanation for the higher yield on insured AAAs over natural AAAs.

FIDELITY INVESTMENTS

Fidelity Investments was the largest competitor in the mutual fund industry, managing over $221 billion in fixed-income and equity mutual funds. Fidelity's 208 mutual funds offered investors a broad range of investment choices, including a variety of state tax-free investment vehicles. Fidelity employed over 13,000 people including 300 investment professionals.

---

1   Insured cash flows/statutory capital.

2   See footnote 6 for an explanation of "advance refunding."

At Fidelity, tax-exempt funds were managed by a group consisting of 8 portfolio managers, 15 analysts, and 3 traders (Exhibit 10.) Anne Punzak described the fund management process at Fidelity: "It is a team effort with the portfolio managers working closely with the bond analysts and traders. I view the portfolio manager as a coordinator of resources, and the decisions he or she makes are based on the market information provided by the traders and the credit information provided by the analysts."

Since Fidelity employed its own traders, the portfolio managers were freed from monitoring the execution of the trade and were able to manage more than one fund. Anne Punzak managed three tax-exempt bond funds: the Fidelity Aggressive Tax Free Fund, the Fidelity Insured Tax Free Fund, and the Fidelity Spartan Florida Municipal Fund.

The Spartan[3] Florida Municipal Fund was designed for investors seeking income exempt from both federal income taxes and the Florida intangibles tax. Florida levied a .2% (20 basis points) intangibles tax on interest and dividend income, and did not tax earned income. Despite such favorable tax treatment, Florida residents tended to be extremely tax-conscious, as many relocated there in order to avoid high state estate taxes. The fund's prospectus required it to be invested primarily in bonds that were investment grade although up to one third was permitted to be in bonds rated noninvestment grade (below BBB). In addition, the fund was required to be invested in long-term bonds, generally maintaining a dollar-weighted average maturity of 15 years or longer.

The portfolio managers gave close consideration to a number of factors when evaluating an investment opportunity. These included attempting to anticipate possible changes in interest rates and positioning the duration of the portfolio at a level consistent with this outlook but also in accordance with fund objectives. In addition, the portfolio managers would pay close attention to their in-house credit analysis rather than be dependent simply on credit ratings. Ms. Punzak explained: "The credit agencies for the most part lag the market. The market may start to price a particular bond higher if it feels that there is a change in the underlying credit or a change in the environment that will benefit the bond issuer. Rating agencies, however, are slow to revise their ratings due to the large number of issuers in the market and the difficulties associated with following all of them minutely. Our analysts try to stay ahead of the rating agencies and alert us to the possibility of any such changes so that we may benefit from them."

---

3   Fidelity's Spartan funds were created "for the cost-conscious investor that is looking for higher yields through lower costs." Investors were required to make higher initial investments and to pay for sales and redemptions of fund shares. In return, the Spartan funds had lower expenses than other Fidelity funds. They were designed for long-term investors who would not transact very often.

The portfolio managers also had to make trade-offs between choosing a bond for its high current income or buying a bond that was selling at a discount for its capital gain opportunity. This trade-off was important since capital gains were not tax exempt. The situation was more complicated with zero-coupon bonds that had an implied coupon based on the discount at which the bond was sold at the time of issue (also called OID or original issue discount). For example, a 5-year zero-coupon bond with a face value of $100 had a notional annual interest of 4.56% if it was issued at $80, that is, at an original issue discount of $20. If the bond was then sold for $90 after 1 year, the seller would record a capital gain of $6.35 and interest income of $3.65. Internally, Fidelity evaluated the performance of its portfolio managers on the basis of pre-tax total return, measured against other funds with similar objectives.

Finally, the portfolio managers had to remain cognizant of the need to be diversified not only to control portfolio risk, but also to preserve liquidity so that the fund could move out of its investments fairly quickly if necessary. Liquidity was especially needed in environments where portfolio managers feared large fund redemptions by investors which, in turn, could force them to sell in a declining market With higher-rated insured bonds generally being more liquid than lower-rated bonds, portfolio managers frequently confronted the dilemma of trading off the purchase of an uninsured bond offering a higher yield against buying an insured bond with a lower yield.

HILLSBOROUGH FLORIDA WATER AND SEWER BONDS

Hillsborough Water and Sewer (HW&S) was a municipality that supplied water and sewer facilities to residents in southern Florida. HW&S derived revenues from two sources: connection fees charged to new subscribers, and usage fees charged to all subscribers depending on their monthly water usage.

In 1991, HW&S had proposed a debt offering consisting of a mixture of current income and zero-coupon bonds[4]. In their proposed offering, HW&S had projected an optimistic revenue growth rate of 7–8% per annum with about 40% of the debt repayment being dependent on connection fees to be collected from new customers. When S&P was approached to rate the new issue, it expressed concerns about the ability of the

---

4 Zero-coupon bonds were typically more expensive to issue in an environment in which the market desired current income. However, HW&S had insufficient revenues to pay interest on current income bonds. The issuer believed that with a rising customer base and rising water rates, it would have little difficulty redeeming the zero-coupon bonds at maturity.

utility to meet the debt repayment schedule principally because it was so dependent on acquiring new customers. Further, S&P pointed out that because the utility already had the highest water rates in the state—it had recently modernized its equipment—there was little possibility that it could increase its revenues through further rate increases. As a result the new issue was only able to get a rating of BBB+. Prior to the offering, HW&S had been rated A– by S&P and Baa by Moodys. Moodys continued to rate HW&S as Baa.

The lower rating by S&P had a number of unfavorable consequences. Municipal bond insurers were reluctant to insure the bonds and Florida retail investors (mostly "old rich folk") were reluctant to buy the uninsured bonds. Due to the subsequent lack in demand, the bonds sold at a substantial discount when issued in 1991.

On July 7th, 1993 the zero-coupon bonds of HW&S were brought to Anne Punzak's attention by Wayne Fitzgerald, a bond trader at Fidelity. The zeroes, which were noncall-able and matured in 2007, were trading at a yield of 6.05%, 45 basis points higher than typical insured zero-coupon bonds. Ms. Punzak liked zero-coupon bonds since her experience showed that zeroes typically traded cheaper than their theoretical value. This was especially true in a retail market such as Florida where investors desired current income and were thus reluctant to invest in zero-coupon bonds. However, this also meant that the HW&S zeroes were not very liquid. Further, their duration of 14 years was much longer than her fund's present duration of 9 years which already exceeded the Shearson Lehman Bond Index duration of 7 years.[5] Although Ms. Punzak thought the higher yield more than compensated for the lack of liquidity and higher duration, she was unwilling to hold the zeroes for the long term. Municipal bonds had lagged the tremendous run up in the stock and taxable bond markets, mainly due to municipal issuers taking advantage of low interest rates and refinancing their debt, and the uncertainty about President Clinton's plan to raise taxes. She was, however, willing to purchase the bonds for their short-term capital gain potential.

Before deciding, Ms. Punzak had consulted Greg Markel, the Fidelity credit analyst following Hillsborough Water & Sewer. He described current market opinion as viewing HW&S as a BBB credit with little room for improvement. However, he felt that the credit had actually improved in light of a number of changes. HW&S no longer had the highest water rates in Florida as a number of other water and sewer facilities had raised their rates after being forced to update their equipment to ensure compliance with the safe drinking water act. In addition, HW&S now was able to meet 100% of its debt service requirements through usage fees due to an impressive growth in its customer base. Ms. Punzak also learned that HW&S was planning to advance refund the coupon bonds issued in 1991 by

---

5   Exhibit 11 shows the relationship between duration, maturity, coupon, and yield-to-maturity.

August 15th.[6] She wondered what affect this may have on the price of the zero-coupon bonds. Traditionally, advance refundings had a positive effect on the prices of the tax exempt bonds being refunded. However, she was concerned that the additional supply of bonds from HW&S might further reduce the liquidity of the zeroes. On the positive side, she could hope for the credit improvement that Greg was confident would occur and resell the zeroes at a profit, although Greg had cautioned that it might be as long as 3 years before the credit improvement was recognized by the rating agencies. Anne Punzak decided to invest $9.25 million in the HW&S zeroes on July 7th for the account of the Spartan Florida Municipal Fund.

It was now August 5th and the zeroes had declined in price to yield 6.10%. Punzak tried to evaluate her options. She could sell the bonds now and cut her losses, or she could hold the bonds and wait for the market to recognize the credit improvement in HW&S. However, if the bill to raise taxes currently before Congress was defeated, municipal bonds could fall further.

A third alternative involved the purchase of insurance for the zero-coupon bonds. The fundamentals of HW&S had improved to the point where municipal bond insurers had become willing to insure the bonds that would be issued in the upcoming refunding. This also opened up insurance for the existing HW&S debt trading in the secondary market. Anne Punzak learned that insurance for the HW&S zeroes was available at 95 basis points or $9.50 per $1,000 face value due in 2007. She could purchase this insurance, and then sell the insured bonds in the market or hold them for the long term. Trader Wayne Fitzgerald remarked that he saw no reason why these insured zeroes would not trade at yields similar to other insured zero-coupon municipal bonds.

---

6   After August 15, new restrictions would apply to the "arbitrage profits" a municipal issuer could realize through advance refunding. These profits derived from the spread between taxable and tax-exempt interest rates. For example, say a municipality issued debt maturing in 2013 and callable in 1998. To advance refund these bonds in 1993, the issuer would typically issue enough new debt to be able to purchase 5-year treasury bonds. The principal on these treasury bonds would be used, in 1998, to retire the original issue; in the meantime, the coupon on the treasury bonds would more than offset the coupon payments owed on the newly issued debt. The announcement of the refunding typically increased the value of the original bonds since they were now backed by treasurys.

Exhibit 1   The Pricing of Municipal Bond Insurance (aggregate industry totals; up-front fee expressed as basis points on total principal and interest)

Year	GO	Revenue Bonds
1988	45	55
1989	42	57
1990	47	57
1991	45	54
1992	49	54

Exhibit 2   New Issue Volume in the Municipal Market

Year	Total New Issue ($billions)	Insured ($billions)	Insured (%)
1983	83	13	15
1984	102	16	16
1985	207	43	21
1986	151	22	14
1987	105	19	18
1988	118	25	21
1989	125	29	23
1990	128	34	26
1991	173	52	30
1992	233	80	34

Source: *Bond Insurers' New Horizons*, Fitch Investors Service, Inc.

Exhibit 3 Municipal Bond Defaults[a]

Year	No. Issues	Volume ($millions)
1983	25	2,300
1984	47	498
1985	56	374
1986	150	1,287
1987	175	1,683
1988	139	899
1989	105	1,091
1990	162	1,964
1991	252	4,919
1992	174	2,081

Municipal Ratings Changes by Standard & Poors Corp.

	1990	1991	1992	1993 (through 9/93)
Upgrades	140	145	396	127
Downgrades	465	607	478	157
Upgrades/downgrades	30%	24%	83%	81%

Source: Bond Investors Association and Fidelity Investments
a. "Default" includes bond issues in which technical abrogations of covenants have occurred but principal and interest payments remain on schedule. Some of these defaults need not result in any losses to investors.

Exhibit 4   Exposure of Municipal Insurers[a] ($ billions except leverage)

Year	Total insured (Par)	Muni new issues (Par)	Secondary market (Par)	Non-municipal (Par)	Total net exposure (Par+Coupons)	Leverage[b]
1988	39.6	28.0	5.6	6.0	305	115:1
1989	45.4	32.2	5.3	7.9	356	125:1
1990	51.9	34.8	6.2	10.9	421	133:1
1991	71.4	52.6	7.8	11.0	503	135:1
1992	99.3	81.9	5.2	12.2	604	135:1

Source: Bond Insurers' New Horizons, Fitch Investors Service, Inc.
a. Monoline primaries and reinsurers.
b. Net exposure/qualified statutory capital.

Exhibit 5   Pricing of Treasury Securities on August 5, 1993 (Bond-equivalent semiannual yields-to-maturity)

Maturity (years)	Coupon bonds	Strips
1	3.51	3.60
2	3.97	4.04
5	5.20	5.28
10	5.84	6.14
30	6.52	6.70

Source: The Wall Street Journal, August 6, 1993

Exhibit 6   Composition of MBIA's Insured Portfolio

By credit rating

	Insured during 1992	Total outstanding as of 12/31/92
AAA	.1%	.3%
AA	3.7	5.9
A	68.7	64.9
BBB	27.3	28.3
Below BBB	.2	.6
Total	100.0	100.0

By issuer type

	Insured during 1992	Total outstanding as of 12/31/92
GO	21.5%	22.4%
Utility	19.1	17.4
Health care	14.3	18.2
Asset-backed	11.4	10.1
Higher education	4.6	4.6
Corporate	6.8	4.4
Special tax	7.9	7.4
COP/LR	7.1	8.9
Other	7.3	6.5
Total	100.0	100.0

Source: Bond Insurers' New Horizons, Fitch Investors Service, Inc.

Exhibit 7   MBIA Summary Financials (GAAP; $ millions unless otherwise specified)

	1992	1991	1990	1989	1988	1987
Summary Income Statement						
Net premiums written	336	223	181	137	145	152
Premiums earned	163	132	107	91	82	81
Net investment income	150	132	115	80	67	54
Net income after tax	189	145	127	102	92	74
Summary Balance Sheet						
Investments	2,529	1,961	1,724	1,501	1,104	979
Total assets	2,885	2,278	2,024	1,786	1,283	1,159
Unearned premiums	1,032	859	768	693	494	432
Loss and LAE reserves	26	21	5	0	0	0
Long-term debt	299	199	200	195	0	0
Shareholders' equity	1,382	1,063	932	777	705	620
Per Common Share						
Net income	4.62	3.74	3.33	2.74	2.45	1.98
Dividends paid	.72	.59	.44	.31	.19	.12
Book value	33.00	27.58	24.35	21.08	18.80	16.54
Stock Price (December 31)	63.5	48.25	28.25	32.25	19.75	12.875
GAAP Financial Ratios						
Loss ratio	3.4%	13.0%	4.7%	0.0%	0.0%	0.0%
Underwriting expense ratio	33.2%	31.5%	33.7%	38.5%	39.6%	35.2%
Combined ratio	36.6%	44.5%	38.4%	38.5%	39.6%	35.2%
Exposure						
Insured total debt service ($bil)	$233	$185	$158	$137	$ 90	$ 73
Insured par amount ($bil)	$112	$ 90	$ 76	$ 65	$ 43	$ 34

Source: MBIA annual report

Exhibit 8 Pricing of Municipal Bonds on August 5, 1993 (bond-equivalent semiannual yields-to-maturity)

Maturity (years)	Uninsured Coupon Bonds (callable)			Insured Bonds	
	AAA	A	BBB	Coupon (callable)	Zero-coupon (noncallable)
1	2.50				
2	3.20	3.65	3.97	3.60	
3	3.60	4.00	4.41	3.95	
4	3.90	4.20	4.74	4.10	
5	4.10	4.40	4.97	4.30	4.75
6	4.30	4.60	5.14	4.50	4.90
7	4.45	4.80	5.28	4.65	5.00
8	4.55	4.90	5.39	4.75	5.10
9	4.65	5.00	5.50	4.85	5.25
10	4.75	5.10	5.61	4.95	5.30
11	4.85	5.20	5.71	5.05	5.35
12	4.95	5.30	5.81	5.15	5.45
13	5.05	5.40	5.90	5.25	5.55
14	5.15	5.50	5.98	5.35	5.65
15	5.20	5.55	6.05	5.40	5.75
20	5.40	5.60	6.24	5.55	5.95
25	5.45	5.80	6.31	5.65	6.00
30	5.50	5.90	6.36	5.70	6.05

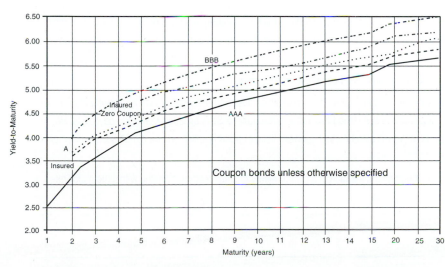

Source: Fidelity Investments

Exhibit 9   Description of Standard & Poors Corporation Municipal Bond Ratings

AAA—Debt rated AAA has the highest rating assigned by Standard & Poors to a debt obligation. Capacity to pay interest and repay principal is extremely strong.

AA—Debt rated AA has a very strong capacity to pay interest and repay principal and differs from the highest-rated debt and issues only in small degree.

A—Debt rated A has a strong capacity to pay interest and repay principal. Whereas it normally exhibits adequate protection parameters, adverse economic conditions or changing circumstances are more likely to lead to a weakened capacity to pay interest and repay principal for debt in this category than in higher-rated categories.

BBB—Debt rated BBB is regarded as having an adequate capacity to pay interest and repay principal. Whereas it normally exhibits adequate protection parameters, adverse economic conditions or changing circumstances are more likely to lead to a weakened capacity to pay interest and repay principal for debt in this category than in higher-rated categories.

BB—Debt rated BB has less near-term vulnerability to default than other speculative issues. However, it faces major ongoing uncertainties or exposure to adverse business, financial, or economic conditions which could lead to inadequate capacity to meet timely interest and principal payments.

B—Debt rate B has a greater vulnerability to default but currently has the capacity to meet interest payments and principal repayments. Adverse business, financial, or economic conditions will likely impair capacity or willingness to pay interest and repay principal. The B rating category is also used for debt subordinated to senior debt that is assigned an actual or implied BB or BB- rating.

CCC—Debt rated CCC has a currently identifiable vulnerability to default, and is dependent upon favorable business, financial, and economic conditions to meet timely payment of interest and repayment of principal. In the event of adverse business, financial, or economic conditions, it is not likely to have the capacity to pay interest and repay principal.

CC—Debt rated CC is typically applied to debt subordinated to senior debt which is assigned an actual or implied CCC debt rating.

C—The rating C is typically applied to debt subordinated to senior debt which is assigned an actual or implied CCC debt rating. The C rating may be used to cover a situation where a bankruptcy petition has been filed but debt service payments are continued.

CI—The rating CI is reserved for income bonds on which no interest is being paid.

D—Debt rated D is in payment default. The D rating category is used when interest payments or principal payments are not made on the date due even if the applicable grace period has not expired, unless S&P believes that such payments will be made during such grace period. The D rating will also be used upon the filing of a bankruptcy petition if debt service payments are jeopardized.

The ratings from AA to CCC may be modified by the addition of a plus or minus to show relative standing within the major rating categories.

Source: Standard & Poors Corp.

Exhibit 10 Fidelity Tax-Exempt Fixed Income Resources

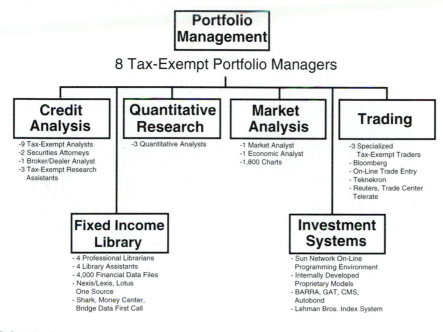

Exhibit 11 Relationship Between Duration, Maturity, Coupon and Yield-to-Maturity (calculated assuming semiannual coupon payments)

Yield-to-maturity	Coupon	Duration (years) Maturity (Years)				
		5	10	15	20	30
	0%	5.0	10.0	15.0	20.0	30.0
3%	3%	4.7	8.7	12.2	15.2	20.0
	5%	4.5	8.2	11.2	13.8	18.0
	7%	4.4	7.8	10.6	13.0	16.9
5%	3%	4.7	8.6	11.8	14.3	17.7
	5%	4.5	8.0	10.7	12.9	15.8
	7%	4.3	7.6	10.1	12.0	14.9
7%	3%	4.6	8.4	11.3	13.3	15.4
	5%	4.5	7.8	10.2	11.9	13.7
	7%	4.3	7.4	9.5	11.1	12.9

Note: The duration of a bond is the weighted average time to receipt of its coupons and principal. The duration of fixed-rate debt is also an approximate measure of sensitivity of price to changes in yield-to-maturity. Specifically, the percentage change in price is approximately equal to the negative of the duration of the bond multiplied by the change in yield-to-maturity.

BEA ASSOCIATES
ENHANCED EQUITY INDEX FUNDS

On the afternoon of July 13, 1992, Messrs. Jeffrey Geller and David DeRosa, derivatives portfolio managers at BEA Associates, were considering alternative ways of investing the assets of a new $100 million enhanced equity index account. They wanted to find the most attractive combination of derivative and cash market positions to achieve the client's objective, which was to outperform the S&P 500 stock index by 50 basis points in a low-risk manner. The alternatives included the use of over-the-counter equity swaps, a relatively new financial instrument that had proliferated in recent years.

BACKGROUND

BEA Associates was an investment advisory firm founded as Basic Economic Appraisals in 1934. As of March 31, 1992, the firm managed $15.4 billion representing over 164 institutional clients. Its separate accounts clients were principally corporate, public, and multi-employer pension funds, and foundations and endowments. BEA also managed several mutual and commingled funds, and a number of closed-end country funds. The firm employed 33 investment professionals—most of whom had 10 years or more of experience—and 76 support staff.

BEA offered a variety of specialized investment management services grouped under equities ($3.4 billion), fixed-income ($5.6 billion), derivative-based strategies ($5 billion), and international equities ($1.6 billion) (see Exhibit 1). The firm boasted strong performance records in each of these product areas. BEA also offered clients investment consulting services in the areas of hedging and asset/liability management, pension funding and asset allocation, and transactions cost measurement, all fields in which the firm considered itself to be an innovator and industry leader.

This case was prepared by André F. Perold as the basis of class discussion.

DERIVATIVES MANAGEMENT

BEA's investment philosophy was to emphasize return enhancement as well as risk control, the objective being to seek maximum return per unit of risk, or minimum risk per unit of return. The firm also aimed to offer clients a high degree of product customization. In pursuit of these aims, BEA made extensive use of derivative instruments such as options, futures, and swaps.

In its more traditional equity and fixed-income portfolios, where outperformance was sought principally by investing in attractively valued stocks, bonds, and other physical securities, derivatives were used mainly as a low-cost way of controlling market risk and currency risk. In its derivatives-based portfolios, derivative instruments were used much more extensively both to manage desired portfolio risk exposures and, through various arbitrage-like strategies, to generate incremental returns. Derivatives-based products consisted primarily of *enhanced equity index funds* ($1.6 billion), and *portfolio hedging* ($3.2 billion). Portfolio hedging involved overlaying on top of an already existing portfolio a series of derivative hedge positions designed to tailor the portfolio's exposure to broad market risks such as currency risk, interest rate risk, or equity market risk. A typical hedge program would be aimed at limiting the portfolio's downside exposure while retaining much of the upside exposure to the risk in question.

BEA's derivatives group was formed in 1982. Currently, the group consisted of three portfolio managers, two traders, and two portfolio assistants. The portfolio managers were Jeffrey Geller, managing director and founder of the group, David DeRosa, and Vincent Bailey; the traders were Mark Barres and Mario Montoya. Each member of the group had a particular area of specialization and a strong background in the area of derivatives.[1] Investment decisions were made by each portfolio manager individually, but only after discussion with the traders and other portfolio managers. No "new" kinds of trades could be implemented without Jeffrey Geller's approval. The complexity and ongoing maintenance requirements of derivative strategies made such group consultation a critical part of quality and risk control.

ENHANCED EQUITY INDEX FUNDS

David DeRosa explained the basis of BEA's approach to enhanced equity index fund management:

---

1   Messrs. Geller and DeRosa, for example, each had 14 years of experience investing with derivatives, and had authored books (in the case of Mr. DeRosa) and articles on the use of derivatives. Both had graduated from the University of Chicago Graduate School of Business, Mr. Geller with an MBA, Mr. DeRosa with a Ph.D.

Compare investing in an S&P 500 index fund with the synthetic alternative of investing in money market securities and buying S&P 500 futures. In the case of the index fund, your cash goes to purchase the stocks in the index, and your return comes in the form of dividend income plus capital gains or losses on the stocks. You forgo interest on the cash.

In the synthetic alternative, you do not pay anything for your futures position, and you earn capital gains or losses on the futures contract that will closely mirror the gains or losses in the index. You forgo the dividends on the stocks, but you earn interest on the cash.

If the futures are correctly priced,[2] these two strategies should produce virtually identical results—regardless of the subsequent direction taken by the market. The two methods will thus be economically equivalent.

The futures approach has several actual and potential advantages. First, index futures have much lower transaction costs than stocks (roughly a 15:1 advantage) and much lower custodial and administrative costs. Second, implicit in the futures price is an interest rate, usually above the Treasury bill rate and slightly below LIBOR (applicable to the term of the contract). If you can earn returns on your cash in excess of this "implied repo" rate, say by 40 basis points, the futures strategy will outperform the index fund strategy by the 40 basis point spread. Third, futures contracts need to be rolled over on or before their maturity date. This "calendar roll" can be accomplished at a profit whenever the further out contract is attractively priced.

The principal disadvantages of the derivatives approach stem from the loss of potential stock loan fees (quite small in the case of the S&P 500) and from the risk that the far contract will be unfavorably priced at the time of a rollover.

To date, BEA had been highly successful in implementing the synthetic approach (see Exhibit 2), consistently earning returns in excess of the index averaging 80 basis points per annum. This outperformance stemmed mainly from historically favorable mispricing of the futures calendar roll—from which the firm had devised ways to profit by as much as 30 basis points per annum—and also from various arbitrage techniques that the firm employed to obtain enhanced cash returns.

The enhanced cash strategies involved buying certain securities and selling short related securities. BEA had done arbitrage trades involving a broad range of fixed-income securities, convertible bonds, stock index baskets, stock index options, currency options, and other derivative instruments. The riskiness of these strategies varied from almost no risk to moderate risk, and the returns tended to vary commensurately. Accounts were categorized by degree of risk tolerance, and matched with enhanced cash strategies of appropriate riskiness.

Recently, the bulk of BEA's cash enhancement trades involved positions designed to take advantage of the mean-reverting pattern in the volatility of markets. In these trades, BEA would usually be a "buyer of cheap volatility," but occasionally a "seller of expensive volatility" after a large informational shock to a market as in October 1987. For example,

---

2　That is, according to the cost-of-carry model in which the futures price equals the price of the underlying stocks plus the interest that can be earned on the cash minus the dividends forgone by not owning the stocks.

the actual volatility of U.S. stocks and the $/DM and $/Yen exchange rates currently appeared far higher than the volatility assumptions implicit in the prices of options on the S&P 500, the $/DM and the $/Yen. BEA was considering trying to benefit from this discrepancy by purchasing "straddles" (combinations of puts and calls) on these markets and dynamically hedging out the exposure of the position to directional moves in the markets. BEA was also contemplating doing the exact opposite—*selling* puts and calls—in the Japanese stock market, which after its recent tumultuous plunge appeared far less volatile than what was implied by the prices of Japanese stock index options.

OVER-THE-COUNTER DERIVATIVES

Gaining exposure to the S&P 500 through index futures was but one way to obtain the index return synthetically. Over-the-counter derivative securities like index-linked swaps represented another alternative. (The exact mechanics of some of these securities is described later in the case.) Unlike derivatives traded on organized exchanges, over-the-counter derivatives involved bilateral negotiations between parties (usually between dealers and their customers). Standardization of terms was less important in this market, permitting a greater degree of customization. There was also no central clearing house to monitor collateral and enforce the performance of counterparty obligations. Accordingly, participation in this market required close attention to the management of counterparty risk.

Over-the-counter derivative contracts have existed at least since the seventeenth century.[3] However, the volume in over-the-counter derivatives only began to mushroom in the mid 1980s, first with the proliferation of interest rate swaps, caps and floors, then foreign currency swaps and options, and quite recently, equity-linked swaps and related securities. The notional amount of all swap contracts outstanding in 1992 was estimated at in excess of $3 trillion.

While the interest rate swap market initially grew out the needs of debt issuers, the equity-linked swap and related derivatives market was primarily investor-driven. Financial institutions would write these contracts to create custom products for investors. Examples of some of the more esoteric contracts included currency-hedged equity index swaps, which would allow the investor to contractually receive the return on a foreign stock market hedged into dollars without the investor having to own any foreign stocks or engage someone to perform the currency hedging; and asset allocation swaps, which, for example,

---

3 A 1688 treatise by Joseph de la Vega reveals that options and other derivative contracts were actively traded on the Amsterdam stock exchange at that time. In *Capital Ideas* (Free Press, 1992), Peter Bernstein reports that in Book I of *Politics*, Aristotle tells an anecdote about Thales that makes mention of a financial option.

could allow the investor to maintain a constant 60/40 stock/bond allocation without having to rebalance as market movements drove the existing allocation away from its target ratio. Any of these swaps could be tailored to have additional features such as a minimum downside risk or early termination under certain market conditions, for example, after a market index had appreciated 20%.

Variants of these swap contracts came in the form of over-the-counter index-linked notes. These were medium-term notes whose final redemption value floated with the return on the index of choice (for example, the currency-hedged return on a foreign stock market; or the return on the S&P 500 with downside protection).

Index-linked notes and swaps were not always accorded the same tax treatment. For example, until recently, swaps had not been granted safe harbor from the unrelated business income tax (UBIT) that could be assessed on U.S. tax-exempt investors like pension funds. On the other hand, index-linked notes were exempt from UBIT because they qualified as debt securities. Index-linked notes had increasingly been issued to meet demand from U.S. tax-exempt investors. A long-awaited July 1992 ruling from the Internal Revenue Service that U.S. tax-exempt institutions could not be taxed on income earned on swap contracts was expected to give a strong boost to the over-the-counter derivatives market.

THE CLIENT

BEA's new enhanced index client was a Luxembourg subsidiary of a Japanese life insurance company. The $100 million was part of the insurer's global equity portfolio and was to be invested with the goal of outperforming the S&P 500 by 50 basis points per annum without taking substantial risk.[4] The insurer had approached BEA after hearing a presentation from a Wall Street firm on index-linked notes. The firm had offered to issue the insurer a 3-year note with a 2.65% coupon paid semiannually, and final principal equal to par value multiplied by the ratio of the S&P 500 index level at the end of year 3 to the level of the S&P 500 currently. The all-in price of the note was par, here equal to $100 million. The issuer's publicly traded medium-term notes were A-rated. The insurer had invited a comparison of BEA's enhanced equity product with this note offering and had decided to invest instead with BEA.

Under the terms of the investment advisory agreeement, the client permitted BEA to create the portfolio's S&P 500 exposure with the use of futures, options, swaps, or index-linked notes, and to seek enhanced cash returns by taking offsetting positions in cash market and derivative securities. Counterparties had to have A1/P1 commercial paper ratings

---

4   Performance would be measured in U.S. dollars.

and be rated A or better for longer-term debt. Swap agreements had to conform to the standards set by the International Swap Dealers Association (ISDA).

The client had also asked BEA to be cognizant of withholding taxes in performing its calculations. Most countries imposed substantial withholding taxes on dividends declared by publicly held corporations, of which about half usually could be recovered under tax treaties, if applicable. Ironically, investors domiciled in countries normally regarded as "tax havens," like Luxembourg, usually were unable to recover withholding taxes. Exhibit 3 contains information on withholding taxes for specific countries.

THE DECISION

In deciding how to invest the money, Messrs. Geller and DeRosa first wanted to evaluate how to best create the portfolio's exposure to the S&P 500. They started by evaluating the current pricing of the S&P 500 index futures contracts. Trader Mark Barres had supplied them with pricing and other information pertinent to the September and December contracts (see Exhibit 4.) With the S&P 500 index futures market being one of the most liquid in the world, transaction costs would be small. Commissions were $20 per contract on a round-trip basis (about one basis point per dollar of exposure), and the bid-ask spread for $100 million of exposure was currently .10 "S&P points" or 2.4 basis points. The position would require initial margin of $10,000 per contract (4.8%), which BEA would post in the form of U.S. Treasury bills maturing within six months. Mr. Barres opined that the futures contracts seemed better priced than in recent days, as did the calendar roll.

Instead of using index futures to obtain its stock market exposure, BEA could enter into an S&P 500 index swap. In conversations with various dealers earlier in the day, the best Mr. DeRosa could find in the required size was a 3-year swap at LIBOR minus 10 basis points. That is, BEA would make quarterly payments to the dealer of 3 month LIBOR minus 10 basis points, and the dealer would make quarterly payments to BEA of the total quarterly return on the S&P 500,[5] both payments based on a notional amount that would begin at $100 million and be increased or decreased at the end of each quarter in proportion to the total return on the S&P 500. Payments would be netted so that only the difference between the index return and LIBOR minus 10 basis points would be paid to BEA if the difference was positive, or paid by BEA to the dealer if the difference was negative. The dealer was a prominent A and A1/P1-rated New York investment bank.

---

5   The index level was calculated by Standard & Poor's Corporation; dividend payments were to be calculated by the dealer and approved by BEA.

ENHANCED CASH ALTERNATIVES

Mr. Geller and Mr. DeRosa currently were considering two enhanced cash alternatives. The first involved purchasing the basket of stocks in the Morgan Stanley Europe Australia Far East (EAFE) index and entering into a swap agreement much like the S&P 500 swap described, except that BEA would pay the EAFE return on the basket and receive LIBOR plus or minus a spread. EAFE swaps were being done fairly regularly, reflecting increased investing abroad by U.S. institutions. Summary information on the EAFE index is provided in Exhibit 5.

During the morning, Mr. DeRosa had tried to negotiate favorable terms on a 3-year swap with a AAA-rated bank. As in the previously mentioned swap, payments would be netted and made quarterly; the notional amount would begin at $100 million and be increased or decreased at the end of each quarter in proportion to the total return on the EAFE index. The index return—calculated by Morgan Stanley—assumed withholding taxes on dividends from the perspective of a Luxembourg investor. Initially, the bank had offered to pay Mr. DeRosa 3-month LIBOR minus 80 basis points in return for receiving the total return on the EAFE index. After considerable haggling, the bank had agreed to do it for LIBOR even. Mr. DeRosa felt he could probably do still better (perhaps by 5 basis points or so) if he bided his time and waited for a special opportunity.

There were a variety of factors to be taken into account in analyzing this alternative. First, BEA's traders had estimated that the round-trip transaction cost to purchase, and eventually sell, the EAFE stocks would be about 200 basis points inclusive of all transfer taxes, commissions, and bid-ask spreads. (See Exhibit 6 for further information on the costs of trading and holding index baskets.)

Second, he thought the client could negotiate a custody fee of 7 basis points per annum, a little higher than the custody costs for a typical S&P 500 basket.[6]

Third, there would be potentially large stock loan fees that could be earned on the portfolio of stocks. In many countries, especially Japan and Germany (which constituted a large fraction of the EAFE index) large amounts of shares were held by institutions that, for reasons of relations with the underlying companies or for regulatory reasons, were unwilling lenders of stock. Short sellers thus found it difficult to borrow shares of stock and had to pay premium loan fees. How these fees were to be divided between custodian and client had to be negotiated. The custodian's willingness to share the fees generally

---

6   Custody fees usually had a fixed per annum charge plus a "per ticket" amount (i.e., per company in the portfolio). Typical charges for an S&P 500 basket were 3 basis points per annum plus $18 per ticket, or $36 on a round-trip basis. On $100 million, the round-trip ticket charges would amount to 500 × $36 $100 million = 1.8 basis points. Total charges would thus be around 5 basis points for a 1-year holding period.

depended on the account size, the portfolio turnover, and the ongoing nature of the client relationship.

Based on previous experience, Mr. DeRosa estimated that an EAFE portfolio would, on average, generate about 40 basis points per annum in lending fees, occasionally going as high as 1% on an overnight basis. In contrast, lending fees that could be earned on stocks in the S&P 500 could range as high as 30 basis points per annum on an overnight basis, averaging more like 10 basis points per annum. Negotiations on lending fees were usually a "long and arduous affair." Mr. DeRosa thought the client could probably get its custodian to agree to a 50/50 share of these fees.

The second enhanced cash alternative was an inventory financing trade. BEA had been approached by a major U.S. financial institution wanting to move part of its inventory of Japanese stocks off balance sheet. The institution would sell BEA a $50 million portfolio of these stocks and, for an additional $50 million, a European put option to sell the identical basket of stocks back to it in 1 year at a price of $100 million plus 1-year LIBOR plus 40 basis points (calculated on $100 million). The portfolio contained about 200 names and closely resembled the portfolio composing the Nikkei stock average. The transaction would be directly between the institution and BEA (acting on the client's behalf) and would involve no additional transactions costs (including savings of Japanese stamp tax of 30 basis points), both at the outset or at the time of exercise of the put option. Mr. DeRosa had received indications that the custody fees for this portfolio would be 10 basis points per annum plus "ticket" costs of $40 each way, and that stock loan fees averaging 60 basis points per annum could be earned, with the split between client and custodian again to be negotiated.

The institution in question had an A rating. However, the put option would be written by one of its off-shore subsidiaries created expressly for the purpose of this kind of transaction. The subsidiary had no operations other than a balance sheet of financial assets and liabilities. Having no publicly traded debt outstanding, it was unrated. However, the subsidiary was capitalized and managed in such a way so as to be "about AAA." BEA would be able to inspect its balance sheet and hedging operations on a confidential basis prior to entering into the transaction.

Exhibit 1 BEA Product Line

Equity Management

    U.S. equity management

    Convertible security management

    Futures and options integrated equity

    Balanced portfolio

    Global equity management

    Portfolio hedging

Fixed-Income Management

    Structured active bond portfolios

    Investment grade bond management

    Enhanced bond indexing

    Immunization/dedication

    Intermediate bond management

    Fixed-income hedging

    High-yield bond management

    Cash management

    Municipal bond management

Derivatives Management

    Portfolio hedging

    Enhanced index funds

    Market neutral arbitrage

    Currency hedging

    Portfolio liquidation/pension plan restructuring

    Immunization/structured fixed income

    Futures and options integrated asset management

International Equity Management

    International equity

    Global equity

    Emerging markets equity

Exhibit 2   BEA Enhanced Equity Index Composite, Annualized
Returns for Periods Ending March 31, 1992

Year	BEA	S&P 500
1	11.5%	11.1%
2	13.1	12.7
3	15.3	14.8
4	16.4	15.6
5	11.2	10.4

Note: Returns are before management fees and custodial costs.

Exhibit 3   Dividend Taxation

Shareholder's Domicile	Company's Domicile								
	France	Germany	Hong Kong	Italy	Japan	Luxembourg	Switzerland	U.K	U.S.
France	–	15	0	15	15	15	5	15	15
Germany	0	–	0	32.4	15	15	15	0	15
Hong Kong	25	26.9	–	32.4	20	15	35	0	30
Italy	15	26.9	0	–	15	15	15	15	15
Japan	15	15	0	15	–	15	15	15	15
Luxembourg	25	26.9	0	32.4	20	–	35	0	30
Switzerland	15	15	0	15	15	15	–	15	15
U.K.	15	15	0	15	15	15	15	–	15
U.S.	15	10	0	15	15	7.5	15	15	–

Source: Morgan Stanley & Co.
Note: Effective rate of dividend withholding tax (%) after deductions and tax credits under tax treaties.

Exhibit 4 Miscellaneous Pricing Information, July 13, 1992

S&P 500 Index Futures Contracts

Expiration	Price	Days until Expiration	Dividends[a]	LIBOR[b]
September 1992	$414.65	66	$2.43	3.49%
December 1992	$415.15	160	$5.52	3.56%

Level of S&P 500 Index: $414.87

Interest Rates

LIBOR[c]

1-month	$3\frac{3}{8}$%
2-month	$3\frac{7}{16}$
3-month	$3\frac{1}{2}$
6-month	$3\frac{5}{8}$
9-month	$3\frac{3}{4}$
12-month	$3\frac{7}{8}$

Yields on U.S. Treasury Notes and the spread of corporates over Treasuries

1-year	3.51%[d]	AAA	10 basis points
		AA	15
		A	20
2-year	4.28	AAA	20
		AA	35
		A	45
3-year	4.77	AAA	20
		AA	35
		A	45

a. Estimated dividends to be received on one unit of the S&P 500.
b. Applicable LIBOR rate for the term of the contract (expressed as a 365-day bond-equivalent yield).
c. 360-day money market yield.
d. Bond-equivalent yield to maturity.

Exhibit 5   Morgan Stanley EAFE Index (June 30, 1992)

Country	Capitalization Weight as a Percentage of Index	Dividend Yield
Austria	.6%	1.8%
Belgium	1.3	5.2
Denmark	.8	1.8
Finland	.3	2.1
France	7.0	3.4
Germany	7.8	3.5
Italy	2.3	3.3
Netherlands	3.4	4.3
Norway	.5	1.9
Spain	2.5	5.1
Sweden	1.7	3.2
Switzerland	4.1	2.2
United Kingdom	21.2	5.1
Europe	53.6%	4.1%
Australia	3.0	3.7
Hong Kong	3.1	3.4
Japan	38.5	1.1
New Zealand	.4	5.6
Singapore/Malaysia	1.4	1.8
Pacific	46.4%	1.5%
Total EAFE	100.0%	2.9%

Source: Morgan Stanley & Co.

Exhibit 6 Estimated Costs Associated with Direct Equity Ownership

	Stamp taxes Commissions	Dealer Spread	Portfolio Rebalancing[a]	Custody[b]
Australia—All-Ordinaries	1.60%	1.60%	.32%	.15%
France—CAC-40	.90	1.50	.23	.15
Germany—DAX	.50	1.40	.19	.15
U. K.—FTSE-100	.90	1.20	.21	.15
Japan—TOPIX	.80	.90	.17	.15
Netherlands—EOE	.75	1.50	.23	.15
Switzerland—SMI	.80	1.50	.23	.15
U.S. —S&P 500	.25	.70	.10	.05

Source: J. A. Allen and J. L. Showers, "Equity-Index-Linked Derivatives—An Investor's Guide," Salomon Brothers, April 1991.
a. Assumes 10% portfolio turnover.
b. Estimates of annual safekeeping, dividend collection, reporting, and other miscellaneous expenses.

LELAND O'BRIEN RUBINSTEIN ASSOCIATES INCORPORATED: PORTFOLIO INSURANCE

The months following the market crash of October 19, 1987 were marked by uncertainty in the U.S. financial community. Both the S&P 500 Index and the Dow Jones Industrial Average had declined by almost one-third during a six-day period, representing a loss of approximately $1 trillion in the value of all outstanding United States stocks.[1] Many securities firms and portfolio managers were coping with losses and reevaluating their investment strategies. The mood was distinctively sober at the firm of Leland O'Brien Rubinstein Associates Incorporated (LOR), whose three principals were reassessing their firm's continued survival in the postcrash world. LOR's principal product, portfolio insurance, which accounted for more than 95% of its revenues and had brought the firm not only economic success but also notoriety, had not performed up to investors' expectations during the crash. Even more devastating, portfolio insurance had been vilified as a contributor to the crash, by both the press and the Presidential Task Force appointed to study the events of mid-October 1987. Some observers were so harsh in their criticism that they blamed "the mad scientists at LOR for blowing up the market."[2]

Portfolio insurance is a trading strategy that uses dynamic hedging technology from option-pricing theory to produce investment returns that allow investors to protect their portfolios against declines in the equity market.[3] LOR's success in the early and mid-1980s was inextricably linked to this trading strategy, whose use LOR had pioneered in 1981. Throughout the decade, LOR developed and promoted the strategy and, by October 1987,

---

1   See Exhibit 1 for a graph of the return and volatility of the S&P 500 Index from 1973 to 1987.

2   Hal Lux, "LOR's Big Gamble on SuperShares," *Investment Dealers' Digest*, November 30, 1992, p. 14.

3   LOR prefers the phrase "dynamic hedging," or more formally Dynamic Asset Allocation[SM], to distinguish the trading strategy from a traditional insurance policy in which an insurer acts as a principal.

Barbara Kyrillos prepared this case under the supervision of Peter Tufano as the basis for class discussion rather than to illustrate either effective or ineffective handling of an administrative situation.

either directly or indirectly managed portfolio insurance for $50 billion worth of assets. Portfolio insurance generated an estimated $8 million in fees for LOR in 1987 alone and fostered the firm's growth from just 3 employees in 1981 to 35 by September 1987. (See Exhibit 2 for a description of LOR's size, the assets under its management, and the fees generated by its portfolio insurance business). This $50 billion business evaporated to $10 billion soon after the crash and looked as though it would continue to decline further. In late 1987, the three principals faced the choices of folding up shop, trying to defend portfolio insurance against its detractors and resurrect the product, or developing a new product to sustain the firm into the 1990s and beyond. They did not want to close the firm's doors, but, given the public outcry, portfolio insurance could not easily be resurrected. They hoped their experience gained from providing portfolio insurance to investment managers, as well as the technical skills that had enabled them to succeed in creating and marketing a complicated financial product, would be valuable in helping them develop new investment vehicles to meet these investors' ongoing demands.

LELAND O'BRIEN RUBINSTEIN ASSOCIATES INCORPORATED[4]

The firm of Leland O'Brien Rubinstein Associates Incorporated was formed in February 1981 by Hayne Leland, John O'Brien, and Mark Rubinstein, for the purpose of using the latest financial technologies to deliver new investment vehicles to institutional investors. LOR differed from most money management firms in that it did not offer products intended to outperform the market; its products permitted investors to adjust the risk/return characteristics of their portfolios. Leland and Rubinstein, professors at the University of California at Berkeley, were prominent academics well versed in the relatively new technology of option pricing. The two academics had joined forces earlier in 1976 to form Leland-Rubinstein Associates, a venture intended to capitalize on this new technology and augment their academic salaries.

The inspiration for this commercial venture came from a chance conversation between Leland and his brother, a San Francisco investment counselor who was ruminating on the 1974 equity market doldrums, which had scared some investors out of the market. He lamented that "It's too bad there is no way to buy insurance on your portfolio. Then people wouldn't have to sell out at the very worst time and have no way to participate in the subsequent market rally."[5] Leland recognized that the fledgling option-pricing theory, developed by Myron Scholes, Fischer Black, and Robert C. Merton in 1973, could provide

---

4   For a lengthy and colorful description of the origins of LOR, see Peter L. Bernstein, *Capital Ideas: The Improbable Origins of Modern Wall Street* (New York: The Free Press, 1992), Chapter 14.

5   See Ibid., p. 270.

a solution to his brother's problem as well as to many other problems faced by institutional investors.

Leland and Rubinstein agreed to collaborate on the project and, over the next few years, worked out the details of a product they would call "dynamic asset allocation," but which was more popularly called "portfolio insurance." In 1979, Leland began a marketing campaign to sell the product, holding seminars with portfolio managers around the country. While all seemed very interested, none were convinced by the complicated strategy promoted by the pair of professors. Leland and Rubinstein recognized their need to bring in a full-time professional marketer, but they knew few practitioners.

At one of his presentations, Leland had been impressed by the questions asked by John O'Brien, whom he sensed had a feel for the concept they were trying to market. O'Brien had worked on Wall Street since the early 1970s and founded a well-known pension advisory firm, which he sold in 1975. In 1981, O'Brien was a successful vice president at the pension division of A.G. Becker, but because of a reorganization of the firm, was interested in finding a new entrepreneurial venture. The new and exciting ideas proposed by Leland and Rubinstein immediately appealed to him, and he agreed to join the two men to form LOR. John O'Brien's marketing skills complemented Hayne Leland and Mark Rubinstein's technical skills:

> O'Brien tosses around academic theory like his professorial partners, but he is also a born salesman. He is especially effective as an up-front man for a hard-sell, hard-to-understand product. . . . Some people have said that he is the ultimate salesman, but he is really a patient teacher. He is willing to go and spend literally hours to describe all of the details in plain English to get to the root of what is being innovated without using complex math.[6]

O'Brien refocused LOR's marketing efforts away from money managers, hired to select securities, and toward pension administrators, entrusted as fiduciaries to oversee the assets of employees' retirement plans. The pension administrators seemed more concerned with controlling their portfolios' risks than were the fund managers. This adjustment in the firm's marketing plan, along with the addition of a full-time professional marketer, began the commercialization of the ideas Leland and Rubinstein had been developing for the past five years.

---

6   Hal Lux, "LOR's Big Gamble on SuperShares," *Investment Dealers' Digest* (November 30, 1992), p. 14.

MARKETING AND MANUFACTURING PORTFOLIO INSURANCE IN THEORY

What united the principals of LOR was their belief that financial technology could be used to create any return pattern sought by investors, especially by pension plan investors. Because fund managers were unfamiliar with the possibilities of using new technologies to produce customized returns, LOR focused its marketing efforts on educating potential investors on the diverse investment returns they could construct. An early seminar, titled "Sculpting Investment Returns," demonstrated the various exposures that managers could manufacture. Of the various returns, managers were most interested in products that would control the risk of their equity portfolios.

During the late 1970s and early 1980s, the pension fund community could measure the risk of their portfolios, but, consistent with Leland's brother's lament, apparently could do little to alleviate it. Fund managers would often select and hold a stock and bond mix whose worst-case projected return was tolerable. Of course, the managers could systematically adjust the composition of the portfolios in response to the relative prices of various investments, but regular rebalancing was not the norm.[7] Investors seemed to demand a payoff with limited risk of declines in value while maintaining most of the portfolio's upside potential. LOR's discussions with practitioners confirmed their belief that there was a large unsatisfied demand for this type of insurance on their portfolios. In 1981, there were $266 billion worth of pension assets invested in equities. An investment product that protected managers from declines in their equity portfolios might attract a sizable fraction of these assets.

An investor seeking to manage the risk of holding an asset has three fundamental alternatives: diversification, hedging, or insurance. By holding a diversified portfolio, the investor can minimize risks attributable to only one asset. For example, by holding a broad portfolio of equities, such as the S&P 500 Index, an investor can reduce her exposure to idiosyncratic or nonsystematic risk. However, the investor with a diversified portfolio still has to cope with fluctuations in value common to all assets, in this instance, exposure to the equity market in general. One solution would be to completely eliminate this exposure through hedging, either by selling the portfolio immediately or selling it for future delivery, using either forward or futures contracts. Hedging eliminates the investor's exposure to downward and *upward* subsequent moves. Unfortunately, in 1981, neither index futures nor forward contracts on the S&P 500 were available.[8]

---

7   The systematic adjustment of a portfolio's composition in response to relative prices of assets is sometimes called tactical asset allocation.

8   In April 1982, the Chicago Mercantile Exchange started trading S&P 500 index futures.

Investors seeking to maintain exposure to upward moves, but also to shed exposure to downward moves, would be attracted to *insurance* strategies. The functional product—insurance—could be delivered in a variety of forms. Firms could serve as principals, selling an "insurance" policy contract to portfolio managers and guaranteeing a floor value of the portfolio in exchange for the advance payment of some insurance premiums. An important insight to understanding portfolio insurance is the recognition that these contracts could be structured as put options. By combining an underlying portfolio, such as the S&P 500, with a put on the portfolio in a "protective put strategy," the investor could establish a floor on the value of the portfolio's position. This method would work well—if the investor could find a counterparty willing to sell the precise put he sought (in terms of index, exercise price, maturity, and style) at a reasonable price, without the investor's bearing significant credit risk to the put writer. In 1981, the market for puts on the S&P 500 was virtually nonexistent.

In 1980, Leland wrote an academic article demonstrating which classes of investors would benefit from using portfolio insurance.[9] He identified two classes of investors who should buy portfolio insurance:[10]

> "1. Investors who have average expectations, but whose risk tolerance increases with wealth more rapidly than average, will wish to obtain portfolio insurance.
>
> 2. Investors who have average risk tolerance, but whose expectations of returns are more optimistic than average, will wish to obtain portfolio insurance.
>
> Institutional investors falling into class (1) might include pension or endowment funds which at all costs must exceed a minimum value, but thereafter can accept reasonable risks. "Safety first" investors would find portfolio insurance attractive on this basis.
>
> Institutional investors falling in class (2) would include well-diversified funds that their managers believe to have positive "α's"—that is, funds that are expected on average to achieve excess returns by virtue of superior stock selection. To exploit

9   Hayne Leland, "Who Should Buy Portfolio Insurance," *Journal of Finance* 35 (1980): pp. 581–594.

10 *Casewriter's note:* The term "average expectations" is used to imply that the investor has the same expectations of future returns as the average investor, or has no anticipation that she can outperform a risk-adjusted benchmark. A portfolio's alpha (α) is a quantitative measure—derived from an asset-pricing model such as the Capital Asset-Pricing Model—of the degree to which a portfolio earns a return larger than that of a risk-adjusted benchmark. "Risk tolerance" is a measure of an investor's unwillingness to pay in order to reduce the variability of a future outcome. The more a person can tolerate risk, the less he is willing to pay to eliminate it.

these excess returns to equities, but at the same time keep risk within tolerable levels, insured-type strategies are optimal."

Given the large holdings of equities by pension plans, charged and regulated as fiduciaries to invest prudently to meet the needs of retirees, portfolio insurance would seem an easy product to sell. Furthermore, continuing appreciation of their equity portfolios would likely drive fund managers to seek to protect themselves against unanticipated declines of their positions. With the peace of mind afforded by portfolio insurance, investors could hold a greater share of their portfolios in equities than they would without insurance.

Even with the large latent demand for portfolio insurance, to profit from selling it, LOR would have to devise a way to produce the insurance. "Insurance" is normally associated with policies to compensate individuals and firms for losses due to death, ill health, fire, accidents, and other calamities. Most "insurers" produce their product through risk sharing and diversification among a large pool of policyholders whose exposures are unrelated to one another. By writing a large number of policies against uncorrelated risks, the insurer can statistically ensure that it can satisfy the demands of its policyholders.

However, sellers of portfolio insurance could not depend on the law of large numbers and diversification to produce their brand of insurance. The insurance policy investors sought protected them from marketwide movements, systematic risks common to all investors that could not be diversified away. However, new financial technologies, specifically option-pricing technology, initially developed in the academic work of Fischer Black, Myron Scholes, and Robert Merton in the first half of the 1970s, provided the key to manufacturing the insurance policies. Mr. Leland and Mr. Rubinstein, as academics studying option pricing, were poised to refine these technologies to meet their perceived demand for portfolio insurance.

Hayne Leland recognized that the insurance that investors demanded was merely a put, and that option-pricing technology had developed a set of instructions whereby puts—as well as calls—could be manufactured. The insight that led to option-pricing models was that an option could be reproduced with a constantly adjusted portfolio of primitive assets (a risk-free asset and the risky underlying asset upon which the option is written.) The models provided a recipe by which a "replicating portfolio" could be created through the continuous adjustment of the portfolio, called "dynamic hedging." Anyone who understood the relatively new science of option pricing could follow an investment strategy that could reproduce the payoff to the puts demanded by investors, although the practical issues involved in constructing portfolio insurance were more complicated, as the climate of the late 1980s would demonstrate. The Appendix discusses a simple example of how options could be created by combining stock and Treasury bill investments.

MARKETING AND MANUFACTURING PORTFOLIO INSURANCE IN PRACTICE

Despite its elegant rationale, portfolio insurance was difficult for John O'Brien to sell in the early 1980s. LOR's portfolio insurance product allowed its clients to pay to determine the level of risk they would bear. LOR's risk-return engineering differed sharply from traditional investment management products, which tried to outperform the market without a commensurate increase in risk. All the LOR principals, in particular John O'Brien, spent an enormous amount of time between 1981 and 1984 educating pension fund managers. LOR faced hurdles selling its product even to those investors with an interest in averting a drop in their portfolio's value. Some potential buyers were skeptical of the complex mathematics underlying the concept and feared that the dynamic trading strategy just would not work. Others claimed that portfolio insurance was too expensive and, in its initial form, cumbersome for fund managers because of the need to frequently rebalance stocks. Still others were skeptical of making a major nontraditional investment with a new untested firm.

"Perfect" replication of an option demands continuous adjustment of a portfolio in response to changes in stock price and the remaining time of the option, among other variables. Practically, however, continuous adjustment and the infinite number of buy and sell transactions entailed made *perfect* replication prohibitively expensive because of transaction costs. Managing these transaction costs created a situation in which the skill or computer algorithms regarding the timing of rebalancing became critical. LOR monitored the parameters of its clients' portfolio to determine risk and weighed the costs associated with the necessary adjustments against the value of having the portfolio continuously match the characteristics of the clients' desired option.

Even with imperfect replication, dynamic hedging required frequent rebalancing. In its initial implementation, LOR's portfolio insurance programs involved buying and selling shares as described in part (3) of the Appendix. For example, a fall in stock prices would trigger LOR's program to call for the portfolio to sell shares. LOR would transmit this information to its client, who would then be required to buy or sell a fraction of his or her portfolio in order to continue to produce the desired put. These adjustments were a practical nuisance and costly (because of bid-ask spreads and other transaction costs) to potential clients of LOR. LOR could not execute the transactions to create the put itself because it was impractical to maintain a massive short position, called for by its models, in a basket of 500 stocks.

The business took off slowly because of the complications in producing and marketing LOR's portfolio insurance product. In early 1984, the firm was running pilot programs that provided portfolio insurance against approximately $350 million in equity assets.

A significant turning point in LOR's business came in 1984, when two events dramatically altered the manufacturing and marketing of portfolio insurance. First, a forward-thinking vice president at Kidder Peabody, R. Steven Wunsch, urged Hayne Leland and Mark Rubinstein to use futures for their dynamic hedging techniques. Index futures had started trading on the Chicago Mercantile Exchange in April 1982 and investors were still learning their potential applications.[11] Both Leland and Rubinstein knew that, in theory, futures could be used as part of the dynamic replication strategy, but they were hesitant to market portfolio insurance as a product dependent on the relatively new index futures products. Index futures could be used in dynamic hedging to substantially reduce the transaction costs associated with adjusting exposures. It was believed that the cost of using futures to adjust a portfolio was considerably less than the cost of buying and selling stocks.[12] In addition, the use of index futures would allow LOR to control clients' equity exposure in a noninvasive overlay fashion, without having to ask the client to buy or sell stocks.[13] The client would deliver to LOR cash equivalent to a fraction, say 4%, of the insured portfolio's value. LOR could then use this pool of funds to dynamically create puts by adjusting its portfolio of index futures. This implementation of portfolio insurance

---

11 A futures contract is similar to a forward contract in that it is an agreement to buy or sell an asset for a specified price on a specified date. Trading takes place on organized exchanges. A futures contract is different from a forward contract in that parties to a futures contract must deposit an initial margin or deposit margin as soon as the contract is executed. The contract is then marked to market each day, and a variation margin is calculated. This variation margin is paid to the exchange's clearinghouse by the party showing a loss and credited to the party showing a gain. Index futures are futures contracts based on the performance of an underlying stock index, such as the S&P 500 Stock Index. The S&P 500 Index futures contracts are priced at 500 times the value of the S&P 500 Index and are settled in cash, not by the delivery of the underlying asset.

12 LOR estimated that bid/ask spreads on S&P 500 Index futures were 1 to 2 ticks (5–10 cents on an underlying value of $250, or 2–4 basis points), in contrast to spreads of about $.25 on an average $40 stock (60 basis points). Commissions were about 3–5 cents per share for stocks (10 basis points) and $20 to $30 round trip (2 basis points) for a futures contract.

13 Buying a portfolio of stocks that is comparable to the index and simultaneously selling an index futures contract creates a hedged portfolio because the futures contract fixes the selling price. When setting up a synthetically hedged portfolio using short futures, the portfolio manager holds the entire amount of the portfolio in the index and then sells index futures to replicate the desired portfolio of Treasury bills and the index. When the index rises, the investor reduces his synthetic bill position by buying futures contracts. When the index falls, the investor increases his synthetic bill position by selling futures contracts.

implied a subtle change in the LOR product: it would now almost exclusively insure against moves in major indices such as the S&P 500 and not write puts against clients' particular baskets of stocks.

The second significant event in 1984 occurred when the Manville Corporation requested that LOR set up a portfolio insurance program for its pension fund. Until this date, LOR had implemented only small pilot programs for clients. The Manville Corporation was involved in bankruptcy proceedings in 1984 related to its asbestos liabilities.[14] It had a talented group of portfolio managers who had successfully built up a surplus of assets in its pension fund. The Creditor's Committee for the bankruptcy proceedings wanted to lock in this surplus by selling the stock and investing the entire pension fund in Treasury securities. The creditors were concerned that if the pension fund was kept in equities, the surplus could be lost through a potential market decline. Manville's management, however, did not want to dismantle their successful portfolio management system. They asked LOR if they could use a portfolio insurance strategy on the fund as a whole to protect the surplus against drops in the broad market, yet still afford them the ability to actively manage the fund for positive appreciation. LOR implemented a program for the entire $350 million portfolio, using S&P 500 Index futures. This program doubled the value of assets under LOR management from $350 million to $700 million.

When Manville's management announced to their bankers that they had hired LOR to implement a portfolio insurance program on the entire pension fund, the response was lukewarm. Manville's lead banker, J.P. Morgan, was particularly displeased that Manville, a long-standing client (since the early 1900s), would hire a relatively unknown firm to provide this new investment service. Despite their displeasure, J.P. Morgan was sufficiently impressed with the concept of portfolio insurance that it sought and received a mandate to supply 20% of Manville's portfolio insurance needs.

The LOR principals could do little to prevent rivals from producing similar portfolio insurance products. The basic ideas underlying the product were well described in the academic literature and could not be patented.[15] Furthermore, because potential customers were hesitant to entrust their assets to an unknown trading strategy, LOR's marketing

---

14 Until the mid-1980s, Manville mined and sold asbestos for use in insulation, building, aerospace, and other industries. Throughout the 1980s, Manville was enmeshed in substantial litigation brought by asbestos workers with claims on the effects of working with the material. This litigation as well as poor operating performance led the company to file for protection under Chapter 11 of the U.S. Bankruptcy Code on August 26, 1982.

15 For the most part, the intellectual property underlying new financial products can not be patented. For a discussion of protecting intellectual property in the financial services sector, see C. Petruzzi et al., "Patent and Copyright Protection for Innovations in Finance," *Financial Management* 17 (1989), pp. 66–71.

presentations included a great deal of detailed information on their trading strategies. Hayne Leland recalled in one instance, watching in dismay as a competing firm used slides and a precise example virtually identical to those used in LOR's presentation.[16]

Nevertheless, the entry of prominent firms into the portfolio insurance business lent credibility to the concept and permitted LOR to enjoy a share of the rapidly growing business. LOR would benefit not only from the entry of large firms into the portfolio insurance business but from their exit as well. One large financial institution made a strategic decision to stop selling portfolio insurance and to concentrate on other businesses instead, referring many of its portfolio insurance customers to LOR.

From 1984 to 1987, as the equity market essentially doubled, portfolio insurance grew explosively, reaching an estimated $75 billion to $100 billion in insured assets in pre-crash 1987 (see Exhibit 3). It was one of the hottest money management products of the mid-1980s. An investment program manager at one company said, "You can't help but be familiar with it if you answer your phone."[17] Although it did receive some criticism for being too expensive a strategy, the argument for portfolio insurance was that with dynamic hedging, a portfolio can hold riskier securities and therefore reap higher returns than before. One fund manager explained that, "Since you're protecting yourself from severe market losses, you can take on additional risk with respect to asset allocation, increase your equity exposure, increase your beta."[18]

As the competition accelerated and firms like Morgan Stanley, Bankers Trust, Chase Investors Management, and Kidder Peabody entered the business, LOR's principals knew that their small firm did not have the distribution power to fully benefit from the product they had commercialized. Consequently, in 1985, they decided to license their portfolio management systems to other financial services firms and found two willing licensees: Aetna Life Insurance Co. and Wells Fargo Investment Advisors, among others. LOR provided software, substantial employee training, and assistance in the preparation of marketing presentations. Aetna used this information to market its own branded version of portfolio insurance, Guaranteed Equity Management (GEMs), and Wells Fargo referred to its product as its Hedged Core Strategy. LOR received advance fees as well as fees based on the size of its licensees' assets under portfolio insurance. Licensing grew in importance for LOR until, by 1987, $45 billion worth of assets was covered under portfolio insurance

---

16   See Bernstein (1992), pp. 283–284.

17   Barbara Donnelly, "Is Portfolio Insurance All It's Cracked Up To Be?," *Institutional Investor*, November 1986, p. 125.

18   Trudy Ring, "Cash, Futures Methods Used: Hedging Growth 'Dynamic'." *Pensions & Investment Age*, November 25, 1985, p. 22.

through these arrangements, as compared with $5 billion in assets covered directly by LOR programs.

Initially, the standard portfolio insurance contract provided its purchasers with protection over a fixed period (typically, three years). LOR would set up a trading strategy to produce a three-year at-the-money put on a broad index, such as the S&P 500 Index. LOR estimated the total cost of hedging to be 3% to 4% of the client's portfolio for a three-year period. They would not request the full amount up front, but rather a line of credit for the total cost that could be used as needed. This cost was akin to the premium on a traditional insurance policy or equal to the premium on a put. The funds would be used either to invest in Treasuries or to cover margin requirements on futures positions. In addition, the client would pay LOR an annual fee based upon a declining scale related to asset size for managing the portfolio insurance trading strategy portfolio.[19]

Over time, LOR developed a variety of alternative portfolio insurance products. Although three years was the standard fixed-term product, they sold insurance for other terms. Clients would sometimes choose an out-of-the-money exercise price for their insurance protection levels, in effect having a "deductible" on their insurance policies in order to reduce the premiums they would need to pay. Furthermore, clients would often ask LOR to adjust the insurance level, or strike price, of their protection as the market moved. For example, if a portfolio insurance contract was written at-the-money, but, later in the year, the equity market rose by 20%, the holder of the contract would have no protection against the drop in the market from the existing level to the previously set protection level. Therefore, as the equity market rose, as it did through most of the 1980s, clients routinely asked LOR to change the protection level. This new level of protection would typically require a larger deposit by the clients (a higher premium), but the LOR management fee normally would not change.

Perhaps the most important innovation was the creation of perpetual portfolio insurance. In a fixed-term portfolio insurance contract, the buyer has full protection for the life of the contract and then no protection afterward. For most pension fund sponsors, which face very long-lived liabilities consisting of future payments to pensioners, fixed-term insurance is less attractive than policies that promise perpetual protection. Leland and Rubinstein devised a perpetual policy to meet the needs of these equity investors and, by 1987, perpetual policies accounted for approximately half of the firm's portfolio insurance business.

---

19 For example, the annual fee schedule for a $100-million account would be $150,000 (15 basis points), whereas for a $200-million account the schedule would be $250,000 (12.5 basis points). The average LOR account prior to 1987 was approximately $275 million and the average annual management fee was about $225,000 (8.2 basis points).

In addition, LOR offered portfolio insurance customers an optional product called "jump protection," which in effect protected the investor against large sudden shifts in the index's value. This additional insurance typically gave LOR's customers protection against 3% to 5% jumps in the S&P 500, which would have reflected relatively large daily jumps—before 1987.

THE MARKET CRASH OF OCTOBER 1987

Although portfolio insurance enabled fund managers to manufacture a customized insurance product, the manufacturing process was not flawless, as Mr. Rubinstein's and Mr. Leland's own academic writings recognized. If there were very large jumps in stock prices, discontinuous adjustment became a significant concern because the replicating portfolio would fail to mimic a protective put. In the extreme, the dynamic replication process would break down altogether if the fund manager did not have access to an active and orderly market. Furthermore, it was critical that the futures market and the stock market move systematically together, because the futures contracts were traded as a substitute for buying and selling stocks.

Many of these problems became critical on October 19, 1987, "Black Monday," when the Dow Jones Industrial Average plunged a record 508 points, or 22%, and the S&P 500 dropped 57.6 points, or 20.5%. On this chaotic market day, portfolio insurers could not execute all of the necessary trades called for by their computer models. LOR, on October 19, was able to execute perhaps a third of its program's instructions. Furthermore, it discovered at the end of the trading day that its execution was only a fraction of the planned levels. As a result, the replicating positions deviated from those of the puts it had sought to create. The users of portfolio insurance therefore had only partial protection against the crash. LOR estimated that its clients were protected against 80% of the drop, but because of imperfect dynamic replication, they were forced to bear 20% of the decline in the market.[20]

---

20 Hayne Leland recounted that the rapid rebound of the markets on Tuesday and Wednesday was as trying for portfolio insurance accounts as the drops in the equity market. In particular, as the index rose on Wednesday, the large short futures positions in their clients' portfolio insurance accounts, which LOR was finally able to place on Tuesday, demanded that the clients post additional margin. To raise funds to post these margins within one day (the standard settlement in futures markets), fully invested clients would need to sell shares to raise funds. Because equity transactions settle in five days, immediate sales of equity would not generate cash soon enough to meet the timing of needs generated by the futures program. Investors were forced either to find other sources of cash or to settle on special terms and receive lower prices for their equity sales.

Portfolio insurance was implicated in the crash by a wide circle of critics, ranging from members of the press to the Presidential Task Force on Market Mechanisms, which produced the Brady Report. Hayne Leland was called before the Brady Commission to testify. Almost instantly, LOR and portfolio insurance—the darlings of the 1980s' investment community—became scorned. The press carried overwhelmingly negative reports, including comments such as: "I suppose portfolio insurance is O.K., if you put a sign on it saying, 'Beware: causes cancer'" and "Portfolio insurance has replaced [index arbitrage] as everyone's favorite scapegoat [for the crash]."[21]

The Brady Report claimed that during October 14 to 16, the Dow fell by over 250 points because of news regarding foreign trade and proposed tax legislation, yet it maintained that the market's decline was accelerated by portfolio insurers and others that were selling in reaction to the price-insensitive mechanical dictates of their models.[22] In addition to the pressure directly created by portfolio insurers, a small number of aggressive trading-oriented institutions such as hedge funds and investment banking houses created downward pressure by profiting from the portfolio insurers' situation. The aggressive trading institutions understood that the portfolio insurers and mutual funds were falling behind in their selling programs, thus presenting an opportunity for the traders to sell in anticipation of the forced selling by portfolio insurers and mutual funds, with the prospects of repurchasing at lower prices. The Brady Report claimed that when the market opened on Monday, October 19, these forces combined to create massive selling pressure.

Like LOR, most portfolio insurers adjusted their stock-cash ratios by trading index futures. In fact, several portfolio insurers were authorized to trade only futures and had no access to their clients' stock portfolios. The Brady Report found that throughout the morning of October 19, index arbitrage had succeeded in transmitting the heavy futures selling by portfolio insurers and others back to the stock market. In the early afternoon, however, index arbitrage slowed because of concerns about delays in the DOT (Designated Order Turnaround) System (the New York Stock Exchange's automated transaction system used by index arbitrageurs to link the stock and the futures markets) and the consequent ineffective execution of basket sales. The result of this reduction in index arbitrage was that enormous discounts of futures relative to stocks were free to develop as the futures market plummeted, disconnected from the stock market (See Exhibit 3 for the prices of

---

21   Evan Sminoff, "If You Have to Point a Finger, Aim It At Portfolio Insurance," *Investment Dealers Digest*, March 7, 1988.

22   The typical portfolio insurance model called for stock sales in excess of 20% of a portfolio in response to a 10% decline in the market. With the market already down 10%, portfolio insurance models dictated that, at a minimum, $12 billion (20% of the estimated minimum of $60 billion in assets covered by portfolio insurance) in equities should already have been sold. Less than $4 billion in aggregate had in fact been sold.

the S&P 500 Index and Index futures contracts on October 19, 1987, and the purchases and sales by portfolio insurers). The appearance of this dysfunctionally large discount inhibited buyers in the stock market. With these stock buyers gone, the Dow sank almost 300 points in the last 75 minutes of trading, to close down 508 points. Portfolio insurance futures selling continued, even after stocks closed.

In conclusion, the Brady Report claimed that reactive selling by institutions, which followed portfolio insurance strategies and sought to liquidate large fractions of their stock holdings regardless of price, played a prominent role in the market break. It further claimed that the formulas used by portfolio insurers dictated the sales of $20 billion to $30 billion in equities throughout the week.

Mark Rubinstein responded in print to the criticism of portfolio insurance.[23] After establishing that the crash undermined the preconditions of low transactions costs and price continuity, Rubinstein argued that the dependency of portfolio insurance strategies on these preconditions should have been well known to both those marketing the strategy and those using the strategy on their own portfolios. He added that users of portfolio insurance lost less than those without insurance and rebutted claims that portfolio insurance caused or exaggerated the decline.

Despite Rubinstein's defense, the harsh criticism that portfolio insurance received wrought severe damage to LOR's business and to the careers of some of its clients. Because portfolio insurance was generally thought to be destabilizing to the market, few firms wanted to be associated with it. Within a few months, LOR's assets under management and through licensing arrangements shrank from approximately $50 billion to $10 billion. Immediately after the crash, litigation seemed imminent, and John O'Brien recalled that "We felt a little like the witches of Salem." The thought of just "folding up shop" even crossed the minds of the principals at LOR.[24]

LOR'S NEXT CHAPTER

While LOR was considering its alternatives after the crash, it quickly focused on three observations: (1) pension fund managers were trading entire portfolios more frequently than individual stocks (see Exhibit 4 for the growth in pension funds and investment index funds); (2) investors had serious credit concerns regarding using the futures markets (during the crash, a number of people were frightened when the index futures market disconnected from the stock market and futures discounts of up to 20 index points developed); and (3) the crash may have actually increased institutional *desire* for insurance, but

---

23   Mark Rubinstein, "Portfolio Insurance and the Market Crash," *Financial Analyst's Journal*, 1988.

24   Hal Lux, "LOR's Big Gamble on SuperShares." *Investment Dealers' Digest*, November 30,1992, p 12.

reduced its appetite for the manufacturing of this insurance through a dynamic trading strategy.

Based on these observations, LOR was confident that the postcrash investment community would buy two products. The first was an index security that an investor could use to trade an entire investment portfolio at once without making hundreds of separate trades and without using the futures markets. Reinforcing LOR's observed demand for an index product was the Brady Report's challenge to exchanges to develop a basket security that would allow trading without engaging in the futures markets. Second, the continued demand for the functional product of insurance would likely be satisfied by another type of manufacturing process. It was clear that this new product could not involve futures or dynamic trading and it could not depend on the creditworthiness of a particular financial intermediary, whose future appeared tenuous at times in October 1987. Instead, the product would best be delivered in the form of a collateralized put option, that is, a put option backed by a buy-and-hold portfolio, which could ensure its ability to pay off if the market fell.

The principals at LOR believed that if they could create a system whereby an investor could trade an index security and *also* trade collateralized puts on the market, investors would flock to it and the firm would once again flourish. When attempting to design a set of securities to satisfy the perceived needs of institutional investors, two related equity-index security designs attracted their attention. In both, a pool of assets was assembled against which a variety of securities were carved out, much as if pools of mortgages were bundled together and then broken apart to form collateralized mortgage obligations.

The first idea was suggested by a Berkeley colleague, Professor Nils Hakansson. In a 1976 article in the *Financial Analysts Journal*, Hakansson proposed a new type of financial intermediary, a purchasing power fund, which offered a "novel, simple, apparently feasible and above all flexible means for smaller investors especially to own the kind of slice of their nation's real assets that they perhaps always wanted to have—but were afraid to ask for."[25] The assets of this purchasing power fund, the superfund, would consist of a portfolio of basic securities (e.g., S&P 500 stocks), against which the superfund would issue "supershares." Mark Rubinstein describes Hakansson's elegant supershare design as follows:

---

25   Nils H. Hakansson, "The Purchasing Power Fund: A New Kind of Financial Intermediary," *Financial Analysts Journal*, (November–December 1976): pp. 49–59.

A supershare is a security, which on its expiration date entitles its owner to a given dollar value proportion of the assets of the superfund, provided the value of those assets on that date lies between a lower and an upper value. Otherwise, the supershare expires worthless.[26]

With a supershare, an investor could buy a security that would pay off approximately $1.00 if the S&P 500 was in a narrow band, say 400 and 410, and nothing if the S&P was outside of this band. By combining various patterns of supershares, an investor could create virtually any payoff desired, including default-free bonds, a stock market index, a short position in an index, calls, and puts. Mark Rubinstein and co-author John Cox wrote about the superfund concept in glowing terms:

> The superfund is an exciting financial concept. Its successful introduction might dramatically alter and streamline existing financial markets. We would be delivered from the chaos of existing securities to their natural building blocks. Hakansson has compared the investment positions in supershares to chemical formulas relating molecules to their constituent elements.[27]

The superfund was an elegant, but untested, financial product. A more mundane but successful financial set of securities that bore some resemblance to the supershares were "Primes" and "Scores," which were issued in the 1980s. The Americus Trust program deposited shares of common stock of firms into trusts that would be terminated at a pre-specified date, with each trust holding only the shares of one firm. Against each of these trusts, Americus Trust issued two separate claims. Holders of "Primes" received all of the dividends over the life of the trust, plus a payoff at the termination of the trust equal to the lesser of a prespecified termination claim and the market value of the stock as of the termination date. For example, Primes on Merck common stock were scheduled to receive the dividends paid on Merck common stock through the expiration of the Trust. On April 14, 1992 (the termination date) the holder of the Prime would receive the lesser of $200 (the termination claim) or a share of Merck common stock. The holder of "Scores" received no payment until the termination date, at which time the Score-holder received the excess of the stock price over the termination claim of the Prime, if any. Primes and Scores were traded on the American Stock Exchange.

By 1987 an unfavorable tax ruling had shut down any attempts to create new Americus Trusts, because the dividends paid to the Trusts were deemed taxable both to the Trust and to the Prime-holders. Nonetheless, the popularity of the existing grandfathered Score and Prime securities—in effect, collateralized calls and covered calls—provided inspiration to the LOR principals. Where Hakansson's superfund concept was elegant, it was

---

26   Mark Rubinstein and John C. Cox, *Options Markets* (Englewood Cliffs, New Jersey: Prentice-Hall, Inc., 1985) pp. 461–468.

27   Ibid. pp. 561–468.

likely to be impractical to execute. The Americus Trust example could be implemented, but did not quite deliver the full set of securities that the principals felt the market demanded.

As they ruminated about the design of the product that would, they hoped, reestablish LOR as the preeminent vendor of sophisticated investment management products, the three men recounted the change in competition in the six years they had worked together. In 1987, index futures and index options were traded on major exchanges. Equity-derivative desks of major investment banks were eager to create customized products for their clients. The financial technology that had formed the base for LOR's success was now widely disseminated throughout Wall Street. Investors had become increasingly sophisticated and insisted that costs not be excessive. Nevertheless, with the technical skills of Hayne Leland and Mark Rubinstein, the marketing savvy of John O'Brien, and the contacts they had made in the six years of doing business—if combined with a good idea and no major obstacles—the principals were optimistic that they could get LOR back on track. The task at hand was to brainstorm about what products to offer and how LOR could create them.

Exhibit 1   Return and Volatility of the S&P 500 Index (1973–1987)

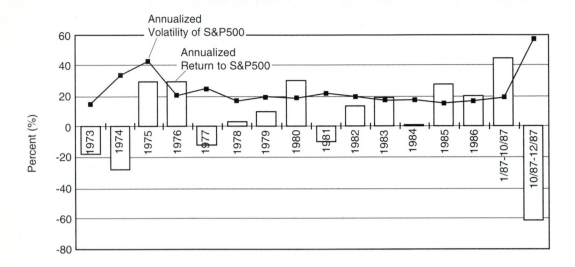

Source: Annualized return on S&P calculated by casewriter. The negative 63% return for 10/1/87–12/31/87 period is an annualized return; the actual decline in the Index for the 3-month period was approximately 16%. Volatility is taken from *Report of the Presidential Task Force on Market Mechanisms*, January 1988, p. II-6. Volatility represents an average of 60-day annualized volatilities.

Exhibit 2   LOR Portfolio Insurance Programs

Year End	1981	1982	1983	1984	1985	1986	1987 through September
Total LOR employees	3	5	5	9	15	25	35
Assets protected directly by LOR portfolio insurance programs (millions of dollars)	30	250	350	850	1,500	3,000	5,000
Assets protected by LOR-licensed portfolio insurance programs (millions of dollars)	0	0	0	0	13,500	27,000	45,000
LOR fees generated from direct portfolio insurance programs[a] (thousands of dollars)	24	247	629	983	1,300	2,600	4,000
LOR fees generated from licensing programs[b] (thousands of dollars)	0	0	0	0	250	2,000	4,000

a. The approximate formula used to calculate fees for direct programs was based on a percentage of the market value of the portfolio's assets. The annual fees were .2% of a $0- to $50-million portfolio, .1% of a $50-million to a $250-million portfolio, .05% of a $250-million to a $500-million portfolio, and .025% of portfolios greater than $500 million.
b. License rates were essentially half the schedule for direct accounts.

Exhibit 3   Panel A: S&P Index and Futures Contract Spread: Monday, October 19, 1987[a]

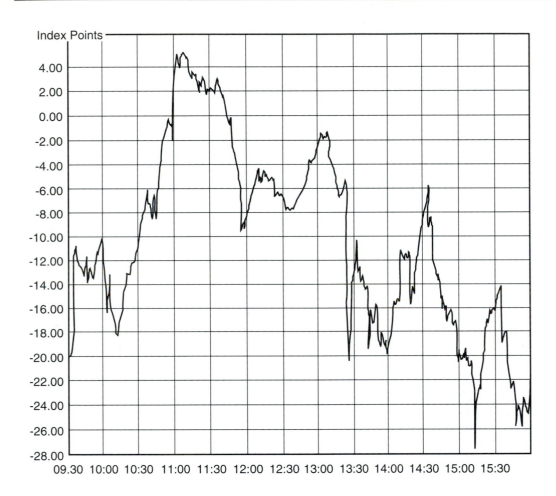

Source: Report of The Presidential Task Force on Market Mechanisms, January 1988.
a. The above chart depicts the index point spread between the S&P 500 futures contract and the S&P 500 cash index (futures contract less the cash index) throughout the day of Monday, October 19, 1987. Normally, the price of a futures contract exceeds the price of the underlying portfolio by an amount reflecting the "cost of carry," which relates to the difference between the Treasury bill rate and the dividend yield on the portfolio. The initial drop of the futures contract beneath the S&P Index was largely due to many large stocks that opened late on Monday and whose prices therefore were quoted as the previous day's closing price. Once stocks opened, the futures market tracked the Index relatively closely until about 1:30 p.m., at which point the tremendous delays in the DOT system led to a continuous and "real" discount of the futures versus the S&P 500 Index.

Exhibit 3   Panel B: S&P Index and Futures Contract Price Levels and Portfolio Insurance Sales and Purchases as a Percent of Public Futures Volume: Monday, October 19, 1987[b]

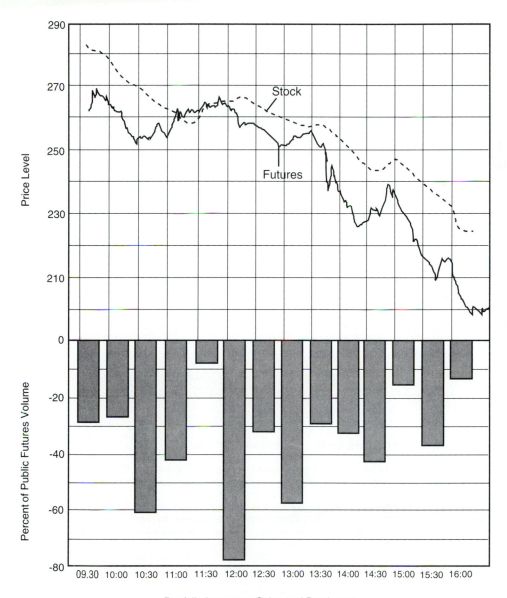

Portfolio Insurance Sales and Purchases

b. The above chart depicts the divergence of the S&P 500 Index from the S&P 500 Futures throughout October 19, 1987. Additionally, it emphasizes the magnitude of portfolio insurance sales and purchases of S&P 500 Index futures as a percentage of total S&P 500 Index futures volume. The Brady Report maintained that the market's decline was accelerated by portfolio insurers selling in reaction to the price-insensitive mechanical dictates of their models.

Exhibit 4   Selected U.S. Equity Markets (1981–1987)

Years	1981	1982	1983	1984	1985	1986	1987
Estimated corporate equities directly held by pension funds (billions of $)[a]	266.3	366.9	458.3	462.0	582.7	703.9	744.0
Estimated value of pension fund equities invested in index funds (billions of $)[b]	6.0	9.9	25.3	26.2	46.6	76.4	92.9
Estimated value of total assets covered by portfolio insurance strategies[c] (billions of $)	.03	.25	.35	1.0	20.0	50.0	100.0
Yearly average open interest in S&P 500 index futures contracts (number of contracts)[d]	–	6,899	25,238	36,312	62,176	100,535	120,632
Yearly average open interest in S&P 500 Index options (number of contracts)[e]	–	–	2,230	743	521	86,019	343,642
Yearly average open interest in options on S&P 500 index futures contracts (number of contracts)[f]	–	–	10,829	27,850	38,374	51,220	62,729

a. Federal Reserve, Flow of Funds.
b. *The Money Market Directory of Pension Funds and Their Investment Managers*, McGraw Hill, 1982–1988.
c. LOR estimates.
d. IDC Datasheet. Each futures contract represents 500 times the S&P 500 Index. Index futures started trading on 4/21/82. Open interest equals the amount that investors with short positions are currently obligated to deliver. It also equals the amount that investors with long positions are currently obligated to receive.
e. Chicago Board Options Exchange. Each contract settles on 100 times the S&P 500 Index. Index options started trading on 7/1/83.
f. Chicago Mercantile Exchange. Each contract settles on one futures contract. Options on Index futures started trading on 1/28/83.

APPENDIX—INSURING PORTFOLIOS

Suppose an institutional investor held a $100-million portfolio consisting of the S&P 500 stocks, in the same proportion as the index. If this investor wanted to guarantee that at the end of three years the value of the portfolio would be no lower than $100 million but would enjoy rises in the equity market, she could pursue any number of strategies:

1. *Buy a put:* The most straightforward solution would be to buy a three-year at-the-money put on the S&P 500 index for a notional amount of $100 million. Unfortunately, the first exchange-traded S&P 500 options with maturities of three years were not listed until January 1991. An investor could seek to obtain a quote for an over-the-counter put from a financial institution, such as the equity derivatives trading desk of a major investment bank.

2. *Sell the stocks, and buy Treasury notes and calls:* Put-call parity suggests that the combination of a long investment in stocks plus a European put has the same payoff as an investment in riskless assets plus a call on the S&P 500. To execute this strategy, the investor would have to find a counterparty willing to sell long-dated calls.

3. *Manufacture the put, using stock and Treasury bills:* The Black-Scholes model provides instructions for manufacturing options using the underlying instrument (in this example, the S&P 500 stocks) and investments in risk-free assets (such as Treasury bills). A trader can manufacture the put called for by the first strategy[28] by adding to its existing long stock position an incremental short position in stocks and an incremental long position in risk-free assets, and by adjusting this position continuously (in a process called dynamic replication) to ensure that the replicating portfolio has the same change in value in response to changes in small movements in stock price (defined as a position's delta) as does the put being manufactured.[29] As the stock price rises (the put becomes increasingly out of the money), the replicating portfolio contains a smaller short stock position. In effect, the replicating portfolio, like a put, has no equity exposure if stock prices are very high relative to the strike price. However, as the stock price falls (the put becomes increasingly in the money), the replicating portfolio contains a larger short stock position and has greater equity exposure.

---

28 This financial technology would also allow the investor to create the call option integral to the second strategy.

29 In the extreme, the entire portfolio of stocks would be sold; however, the investor would never have a net short position in stock.

Suppose a client wanted a three-year European-style put, on $100 million of the S&P 500 with an exercise price struck at the existing S&P level. Option-pricing models suggest that this put would cost $3.42 million and could be constructed by setting up an initial short position of $15.9 million worth of stock, with $19.3 million invested in Treasury bills, for an initial net investment of $3.42 million in the put position. In the next instant, suppose stock prices were to move either up or down 1%.[30] The put value would change, as shown in Exhibit A-1. The new replicating portfolios and the change in the replicating portfolio are also shown on the diagram. Changes in the value of the stock—as well as changes in the life of the option and the risk-free rate—necessitate continuous adjustment of the replicating portfolio.[31] By "delta hedging," the replicating portfolio would be maintained so that at all times it has the same delta as does the put to be manufactured.[32]

To create the put, an investor who did *not* hold the index would sell short $15.9 million of the portfolio's value and invest $19.3 million in Treasuries. As the index falls, and the put becomes more in the money and more valuable, the total investment in the replicating portfolio increases. To maintain the delta of the replicating portfolio equivalent to that of the put, the manufacturer would need a larger short position and an even larger long investment in Treasuries.

An investor with a *preexisting long position* in the S&P would not need to short shares, but could merely sell part of the existing portfolio and invest it in Treasuries (along with additional funds). Market conditions would dictate that, over time, other shares would need to be bought or sold, with the risk-free investment correspondingly adjusted. As a practical matter, portfolios are rebalanced infrequently, with the size of transaction costs influencing rebalancing.[33]

4. *Manufacture the put using stocks and index futures:* The manufacturing process outlined above requires that stocks be bought and sold, necessitating high transaction costs (commissions, bid-ask spreads, and market impact costs.) Furthermore, it

---

30   This simplified example ignores dividends paid on the S&P 500 and assumes risk-free rates of 10% per annum and volatility of 20% per annum.

31   For a more thorough description, see Mark E. Rubinstein and Hayne E. Leland, "Replicating Options with Positions in Stock and Cash," *Financial Analysts Journal*, 1981.

32   Other hedging schemes attempt to adjust other exposures. Gamma is the rate of change of the portfolio's delta with respect to the stock price; vega is the rate of change of the portfolio's value with respect to the asset's volatility. By making a porfolio's gamma equal to zero, an investor can reduce the sensitivity of the portfolio delta to fairly large changes in the stock price. By making its vega equal to zero, an investor can reduce the sensitivity of the portfolio to changes in the underlying asset's volatility.

33   For a discussion, see Hayne Leland, "Option Pricing and Replication with Transaction Costs," *Journal of Finance* 40 (1985), pp. 1283–1301.

requires coordination between the investment manager overseeing the stock portfolio and the advisor running the manufacturing process.

An alternative to manufacturing puts by using short positions in stock and long positions in risk-free securities would be to maintain the entire portfolio in stocks and short index futures. Selling index futures against a long stock position produces a long position in riskless assets called for by the manufacturing strategy given in (3). Using futures, which have transaction costs considerably less than stocks, lowers the manufacturing costs and allows the insurance to be manufactured with less coordination between the stock portfolio manager and the insurance program. The insurance program can serve as a transparent overlay to the stock portfolio.

To use futures to manufacture the put, an initial amount of index futures is sold against the entire portfolio. This amount is equal to the delta of the put to be manufactured times a factor equal to exposure of the futures contract for small changes in the change in the stock contract. As the stock index falls (rises), the investor would sell (buy) additional index futures contracts.

Exhibit A-1: Stylized Replication of a Put Option Using Stock and Treasury Bills.

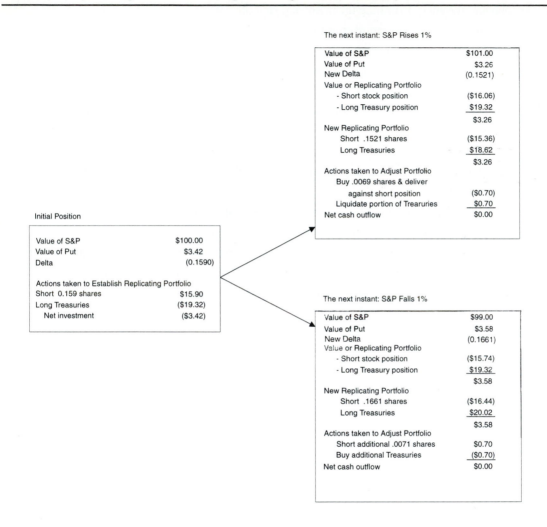

The next instant: S&P Rises 1%

Value of S&P	$101.00
Value of Put	$3.26
New Delta	(0.1521)
Value or Replicating Portfolio	
- Short stock position	($16.06)
- Long Treasury position	$19.32
	$3.26
New Replicating Portfolio	
Short .1521 shares	($15.36)
Long Treasuries	$18.62
	$3.26
Actions taken to Adjust Portfolio	
Buy .0069 shares & deliver	
against short position	($0.70)
Liquidate portion of Trearuries	$0.70
Net cash outflow	$0.00

Initial Position

Value of S&P	$100.00
Value of Put	$3.42
Delta	(0.1590)
Actions taken to Establish Replicating Portfolio	
Short 0.159 shares	$15.90
Long Treasuries	($19.32)
Net investment	($3.42)

The next instant: S&P Falls 1%

Value of S&P	$99.00
Value of Put	$3.58
New Delta	(0.1661)
Value or Replicating Portfolio	
- Short stock position	($15.74)
- Long Treasury position	$19.32
	$3.58
New Replicating Portfolio	
Short .1661 shares	($16.44)
Long Treasuries	$20.02
	$3.58
Actions taken to Adjust Portfolio	
Short additional .0071 shares	$0.70
Buy additional Treasuries	($0.70)
Net cash outflow	$0.00

LELAND O'BRIEN RUBINSTEIN ASSOCIATES, INC.: SUPERTRUST™

In May 1991 the principals at the securities firm of Leland O'Brien Rubinstein, Associates Incorporated (LOR) encountered yet another roadblock in a nearly four-year effort to launch their newest product: SuperTrust. The selling syndicate of top Wall Street firms they had assembled for the initial public offering of their new SuperTrust series of securities had fallen apart. Although Morgan Stanley, Salomon Brothers, Goldman Sachs, First Boston, Kidder Peabody, PaineWebber, and Smith Barney, among others, had expressed interest in being in the syndicate, one by one each had dropped out throughout Super-Trust's four-year development period. Salomon Brothers, which had intended to act as lead soliciting dealer, and Morgan Stanley were the last to depart, in March and May 1991, respectively. LOR had been able to attract only two small securities firms, Parallax Group and The Chicago Corporation, and one other regional firm, Alex Brown & Sons, Inc., to help them sell $2 billion worth of SuperTrust securities. If the SuperTrust was to move forward, LOR had to decide whether to proceed with the offering as planned with their small selling group, try to assemble a larger selling syndicate of regional firms, or change the product or fee structure to entice the large Wall Street firms to join the syndicate. This latest setback led them to question privately whether SuperTrust was a viable product, given the developments in the markets since late 1987.

The SuperTrust product, born of the market crash of October 1987, was a family of securities: two mutual funds, two SuperUnits, and four SuperShares.[1] One mutual fund would hold S&P 500 Index stocks and the other would hold short-term U.S Treasury securities. Shares in each fund could be exchanged for a corresponding SuperUnit, basket securities that would trade on the American Stock Exchange. The two SuperUnits could each

---

Barbara Kyrillos prepared this case under the supervision of Peter Tufano as the basis for class discussion rather than to illustrate either effective or ineffective handling of an administrative situation.

be separated into two other securities, SuperShares. SuperShares resembled equity options and allowed their holders to customize their exposure to the equity market.

The regulatory approval process for LOR's new securities had been long and arduous. To date, the legal bills alone were well over $4 million. In May 1991, LOR still had a few more regulatory issues to be resolved, but it was fairly confident of receiving approval from the Securities and Exchange Commission (SEC) to launch the SuperTrust. A regulatory victory would be useless, however, if it could not assemble an adequate distribution network to sell the SuperTrust securities.

BACKGROUND TO THE SUPERTRUST PROJECT[2]

The SuperTrust was a critical project for LOR. Throughout the pre-Crash 1980s, LOR had been a profitable and innovative financial services vendor that capitalized on the talents of the three principals for whom the firm was named. Hayne Leland and Mark Rubinstein were prominent academics at the University of California at Berkeley and specialists in the fields of options and financial engineering. Since 1976, Mr. Leland and Mr. Rubinstein had worked together to apply the modern concepts of option theory to solve vexing problems facing investment managers. John O'Brien was a savvy marketer of complex financial products who had joined with Leland and Rubinstein in 1981 to commercialize the ideas the two researchers had developed.

The combination of intellectual and marketing acumen possessed by the three, along with the good fortune to be one of the first to market option theory to the investment management community, had brought their firm notoriety and financial success. From 1982 to 1987, pensions' holdings of equities doubled, and the rising market both increased pension funds' desire to hold equities and their fear of losses in the volatile asset class. Sold to ambivalent investors, LOR's first product—portfolio insurance—was a wild success. Portfolio insurance was a computer-directed trading strategy that permitted pension plans to manufacture puts on the equity market. By combining their investments in equities with synthetic puts on the market, pension plan sponsors could protect their portfolios against drops in the index. At the height of its popularity, it is estimated that portfolio insurance was written against as much as 16% of all pension equity assets. LOR and licensees accounted for well over half of all portfolio insurance written, and this product accounted for virtually all of LOR's revenues and profits. The trading scheme used the concept of dynamic replication, which underlies option pricing theory, to manufacture the put options that delivered the "insurance" LOR's clients sought.

---

2   For further information, see "Leland O'Brien Rubinstein Associates, Inc. : Portfolio Insurance," HBS Case No. 294-061.

Unfortunately, the erratic market conditions of October 1987, when the stock market lost 20% in a single day, highlighted the known flaws in the manufacturing process of dynamic replication. (See Exhibit 1 for the return and volatility of the S&P 500 Index in 1973–1987). When portfolio insurance proved to offer less coverage than its users had anticipated, most of LOR's clients stopped using it. Even worse, both the press and the Presidential Commission charged with studying the events of October 1987 pointed a finger at portfolio insurance—and LOR, its leading vendor—as a contributor to the crash. LOR's portfolio insurance business nearly evaporated, its reputation was damaged, and the firm's future was quite uncertain. It was in this environment that the firm's principals met to decide LOR's next steps. Rather than disband, or attempt to resurrect portfolio insurance, they chose to draw upon their experiences manufacturing and selling portfolio insurance to design a new product.

UNSATISFIED INVESTOR DEMANDS: THE PRODUCT CONCEPT

Throughout late 1987, the LOR principals contemplated what they had learned from selling portfolio insurance. In meetings and long telephone conversations[3], they identified three salient market trends: (1) pension funds were increasingly choosing to purchase and trade portfolios or indices rather than individual stocks (see Exhibit 3 for information regarding the increase in indexed portfolios); (2) the crash may have increased institutions' demands for the functional product of insurance, while it destroyed virtually all demand for the delivery of this product through a dynamic trading strategy; and (3) institutional investors would have reservations about any product based on futures trading or any product dependent on the creditworthiness of any single financial institution. Based on these observations, they concluded that there was unsatisfied investor demand for an exchange-traded basket as well as for a superior form of portfolio insurance.

Were institutions content to merely buy and hold broad indices or to trade them in a leisurely fashion, an exchange-traded basket security might not be commercially viable. During the 1980s, households, small institutional investors, and the largest pension plans could purchase buy-and-hold index portfolios that offered varying degrees of liquidity. For households and small institutional investors, mutual fund complexes like The Vanguard Group offered funds that held the stocks constituting the S&P 500 and whose returns very closely tracked the index. Although these funds levied low annual expense ratios (e.g., 20 basis points for Vanguard's Index Trust 500 Portfolio), they were inadequate for investors who wished the maximum trading flexibility. An investor could redeem fund

---

3   Mr. Leland and Mr. Rubinstein spent much of their time in Berkeley, whereas Mr. O'Brien, LOR President Larry Edwards, and the rest of the LOR staff were headquartered in Los Angeles.

shares only at the end of each day, at the fund's closing net asset value.[4] Funds did not permit intraday purchases or sales and discouraged extensive trading by their clients. Exchange-traded basket securities would provide traders substantially more flexibility than mutual funds. An investor could buy or sell an exchange-traded basket security throughout the trading day, margin up to 50% of her position, sell the index short, or place limits or stop-loss orders on her investment.

Larger institutions that sought to invest in large portfolios could either hold the stocks underlying the index directly or invest in commingled indexed portfolio accounts offered by firms like Wells Fargo or State Street Bank. For the direct investor, trading an S&P 500 portfolio would usually entail the simultaneous purchase and sale of hundreds of securities, typically executed by the program trading desk of a large investment bank and routed through the exchange's DOT system.[5] The transaction costs of trading hundreds of individual stocks were high. The equity basket security that LOR hoped to trade would have estimated transaction costs of less than 25% of the costs associated with trading individual stocks. Institutions holding the indexed portfolio through an intermediary like Wells Fargo or State Street Bank could increase or decrease their positions, but could not generally execute such trades immediately. It might take hours, days, or weeks to buy or sell a large block; trades could not be executed to take advantage of temporary pricing discrepancies, nor could rapid portfolio adjustments be made without large transaction costs. Institutions (and individuals) could easily trade in and out of large exposures to broad indices using index futures, which had considerably lower transactions costs than trading stocks. However, the LOR principals felt that investors would prefer to avoid the futures market, given that the crash had raised the question of whether the futures-stock link was as tight as academics suggested it should be, and that many investors had qualms about the soundness of the futures clearing system.[6]

If institutions sought to trade even a tenth of their approximately $100 billion in investments in indexed portfolios in 1987, a large market would exist for a basket security

---

4   Net asset value is the value of the investments, less liabilities, held by a mutual fund divided by the number of that fund's shares outstanding.

5   The Designated Order Turnaround (DOT) System was the New York Stock Exchange's automated execution system. Index arbitrage activity, which links the futures and the stock index market, was usually carried out through this system. During the 1987 market crash, the DOT was unable to immediately execute the enormous volume of orders, resulting in substantial delays. These delays encouraged many index arbitragers to significantly reduce their activity, which arguably allowed the stock index and the futures market to disconnect.

6   Futures contracts are settled through a clearinghouse, a division of the exchange that verifies trades, guarantees trades against default risks, and transfers margin amounts. Legally, a market participant makes a futures transaction with the clearinghouse.

backed by the stocks in the index, but which could be bought or sold on an exchange in a single transaction. In their words, the LOR principals believed that an exchange-traded basket would satisfy the requirements of "large investors who need to trade entire portfolios of stocks for hedging and for arbitrage." The Report of the Presidential Task Force on Market Mechanisms (the Brady Report) echoed this view: It called upon exchanges to develop traded baskets to lessen the trading burden that institutions were placing upon exchanges. The LOR principals resolved that their development of an exchange-traded basket security would put their firm back on track.

Just as they reached the conclusion that the markets did not adequately satisfy investors' needs for a tradeable index security, the LOR principals realized that the market did not satisfy the market's needs for portfolio insurance. Before the crash, this business had grown to cover an estimated $70 billion to $100 billion in assets. However, the variant of portfolio insurance that *manufactured* puts through dynamic replication and frequent trading of stock or futures had been discredited by the crash.

Though investors could purchase long-dated index puts on the CBOE (Chicago Board Options Exchange) since October 1987, these instruments had maturities of less than two years, and they were thinly traded.[7] Investors could use short-term options to construct long-term exposure, by rolling over shorter put positions, but the LOR team felt this strategy was both expensive and risky. If volatility increased dramatically, rolling over to a new contract could significantly increase the put's cost. Also, exchange-traded options depended on a clearinghouse to recognize each transaction and to make cash settlements and, if the clearing function failed, option contracts might not be honored.[8]

The equity derivative desks of major investment banks sold clients customized OTC indexed puts, but the volume of this business was small in early 1988. Buyers of OTC puts had to accept the credit of their writers, financial institutions whose soundness had been tested in 1987.[9] The LOR principals judged the market had a latent demand for index puts,

---

7   In late 1987 and early 1988, when the LOR principals were designing their product, the open interest of all long-dated index puts was approximately 55 contracts, each representing 100 times the S&P 500 Index.

8   Mark Rubinstein and his co-author John Cox had written about the potential problems of the Options Clearing Corporation, the entity that clears options trades: "The (OCC) system makes it highly improbable that any properly negotiated option contract will not be honored. Indeed it would appear that the collapse of the entire listed options market would be required. The only event that could conceivably create this debacle would be a very sudden and strong movement in stock prices, one considerably more extreme than any on record." John C. Cox and Mark Rubinstein, *Options Market* (Englewood Cliffs, New Jersey: Prentice-Hall, Inc., 1985, p. 71).

9   The securities industry was shaken by the events of 1987; security industry profits were $1.2 billion in 1987, down almost 80% from $5.5 billion in 1986. (*Securities Industry Yearbook*, Securities Industry Association, 1988.)

backed by easy-to-value collateral, rather than by a trading strategy nor by the creditwor-thiness of securities dealers.

Its reflection on the market suggested that LOR's future lay with a set of exchange-traded products including, but not limited to, a basket security and a collateralized put.

PRECURSORS TO THE SUPERTRUST

Two sets of bundled equity securities served different role models for the product that would become the SuperTrust. Both carved out collateralized, distinct claims from a pool of assets, just as collateralized mortgage obligations split apart the cash flows of mortgage pools. The two precedents differed in the variety of types of exposures they created as well as in the details of their implementation.

The first role model was an elegant plan proposed by Nils Hakansson, a colleague of Leland and Rubinstein at Berkeley. In a 1976 article in the *Financial Analysts Journal*, Hakansson proposed a new financial intermediary, a purchasing power fund, that would hold a portfolio of stocks like the S&P 500.[10] Against this traded basket security, the "superfund" would issue "supershares." With Mr. Hakansson's supershare, an investor could buy a security that would pay off approximately $1.00 if the S&P 500 were in a nar-row band, say 400 and 410, and nothing if the S&P was outside of this band. By buying and selling bundles of supershares, an investor could create virtually any payoff desired, including default-free bonds, a stock market index, a short position in an index, calls, and puts. Mr. Rubinstein and co-author John Cox reviewed the superfund concept in glowing terms:

> The superfund is an exciting financial concept. Its successful introduction might dramatically alter and streamline existing financial markets. We would be delivered from the chaos of exist-ing securities to their natural building blocks. Hakansson has compared the investment posi-tions in supershares to chemical formulas relating molecules to their constituent elements.[11]

Nils Hakansson's supershares were a theoretical device by which investors could trade the underlying bundle (the purchasing power fund) as well as create the collateralized puts sought by the market. However, bringing supershares to market would involve a host of practical implementation questions, as Mr. Rubinstein and Mr. Cox's discussion elaborates:

---

10 Nils H. Hakansson, "The Purchasing Power Fund: A New Kind of Financial Intermediary," *Financial Analysts Journal.* (November–December 1976): pp. 49–59.

11 John C. Cox and Mark Rubinstein, *Options Markets* (Englewood Cliffs, New Jersey: Prentice-Hall, Inc., 1985), p. 466.

The hard questions of eventual implementation fall into three categories: (1) operation, (2) regulation, and (3) liquidity. What institutions would first experiment with the concept? How would newly issued supershares initially be sold? How would the secondary market be organized? What would be the exercise procedure? Would the concept be approved by the Securities and Exchange Commission? What special regulation of superfunds would be required to prevent fraud? And, most important, how high would and could transaction costs be to maintain the market? How would the viability of other sectors of the securities industry be affected?[12]

The second role model that guided the LOR principals was a more mundane but practically successful set of products called Americus Trust "Primes" and "Scores." The Americus Trust program deposited shares of common stock of each of 26 firms into 26 separate unit investment trusts. Against each of these trusts, Americus Trust issued two separate claims: Holders of Primes received all of the dividends over the life of the trust, plus a payoff at the termination of the trust equal to the lesser of a prespecified termination claim and the market value of the stock as of the termination date. For example, holders of Primes on Merck common stock received the dividends paid on Merck common stock, and on April 14, 1992 (the termination date), they were entitled to receive the lesser of $200 (the termination claim) or a share of Merck common stock. Holders of Scores received no payment until the termination date, at which time they received the excess of the stock price over the termination claim of the Prime, if any. Primes and Scores were traded on the American Stock Exchange.

By 1987 an unfavorable tax ruling killed any attempts to create new Americus Trusts, because the dividends paid were deemed taxable both to the trust and to the Prime holders. Nonetheless, the popularity of the existing grandfathered Score and Prime securities—in effect, collateralized calls and covered calls—provided inspiration to the LOR principals. If LOR could deposit not a single stock, but a basket of stocks such as the S&P 500, into a trust, it could allow investors to buy Primes and Scores on the market, as well as trade the basket security. Mr. Hakannsen's plan gave the LOR team a conceptual framework and inspiration, and Americus Trust gave them hope that a practical solution to their design problems existed.

DESIGN SPECIFICS: THE TRADED BASKET AND RELATED SECURITIES

It is conceptually simple to construct a basket security that could (1) exactly produce the return of the S&P 500 stocks, (2) trade on an exchange with one transaction, and (3) accommodate continual sales and redemptions. In theory, LOR could have created

---

12 Ibid.

an open-end mutual fund and then requested that a major exchange list it.[13] The only complication was that U.S. law, in the form of the Investment Company Act of 1940 (the 1940 Act), prohibited securities dealers from acting as principals in holding shares of an open-end mutual fund. This restriction on dealer ownership essentially destroyed the possibility of an exchange-traded open-end mutual fund because the specialist for the security could not hold any inventory.[14] Furthermore, it was inconceivable that the SEC would approve as sweeping a change as to permit the exchange listing of an open-end fund.

However, LOR's counsel believed that the firm could rely on the SEC to permit it to exchange list a unit investment trust,[15] similar to the trusts set up by Americus Trust. However, the lawyers thought that the trust would have to hold *a single security*, not 500 different stocks that had to be regularly traded in response to changes in the index, payments of dividends, and other events.[16] Therefore, LOR would set up an open-end mutual fund, which would hold the S&P 500 stocks (Capital Market Fund/Index Portfolio). It would also set up a listed unit investment trust, the SuperTrust, whose subtrust (Index Trust SuperUnits) would hold only shares of the Indexed mutual fund (see Exhibit 2 for SuperTrust Structure). On payment of a deposit-fee, the mutual fund shares could be exchanged for the exchange-traded Index Trust SuperUnits. At the end of three years, the Index trust would terminate, and the holders of the Index Trust SuperUnits would receive shares in the fund. Initially, the Index SuperUnits would have a price of $100 per unit and

---

13 An open-end mutual fund is an investment company registered under the Investment Company Act of 1940 that offers and redeems shares continually, at net asset value, in response to market demands.

14 A specialist works on the New York Stock Exchange acting as a *dealer* in certain stocks. The NYSE requires the specialist to maintain a "fair and orderly market" in those stocks in which he is registered as a specialist, necessitating that the dealer buy and sell shares from his own account when there is an order imbalance. The 1940 Act would effectively prohibit the specialist from holding and thus making a market on an open-end mutual fund. LOR could have structured its basket product as a closed-end fund. A closed-end fund is a management investment company that cannot create new shares, but can be listed on an exchange. Structuring the product as a closed-end mutual fund would mean that LOR could not create new shares of the basket at will. Furthermore, closed-end fund shares tend to trade at a discount to their net asset value, an anomaly puzzling to investors and financial economists. To the extent that the basket security traded at a value not exactly equal to that of the underlying shares it contained, it would not serve as an effective substitute for the shares in the index.

15 A unit investment trust (UIT) is an investment company, registered under the 1940 Act, that owns a specified set of securities for the life of the company. It is not actively managed. To form a UIT, a sponsor typically purchases a specific set of securities, deposits them with a trustee, and then sells units of beneficial interest that represent a proportional interest in the securities.

16   In retrospect, this decision may have been overly conservative in that a registrant in 1991 obtained a listing for a trust containing the securities underlying an indexed basket.

would therefore represent a fraction of one unit of the S&P.[17] Although most investors were not used to thinking of S&P 500 Index products trading as low as $100, LOR chose to price the Index SuperUnit at the arbitrary $100 level rather than the actual price of the S&P 500, so that investors could quickly calculate the percentage changes in the performance of the security.

The success of Americus Trust suggested that the SuperTrust could be separated into components similar to Primes and Scores so as to create long-dated call and covered call positions. Furthermore, the Americus Trust precedent suggested that this type of splitting of the cash flows would be acceptable to the SEC. By paying a separation fee, the holder of an Index Trust SuperUnit could receive two SuperShares, a Priority SuperShare, and an Appreciation SuperShare. The Priority SuperShare, similar to a Prime, would provide investors the dividends paid by the stocks in the index fund plus all of the net asset value in the fund at the end of its three-year life, up to a maximum of $125. At the end of the three years, the Appreciation SuperShare would provide its holder the net asset value of the Index SuperUnit above $125, if any.[18] For example, if the SuperUnit had a net asset value of $140 at the end of three years, the Priority SuperShare would be entitled to $125 and the Appreciation SuperShare $15. A holder of both a Priority SuperShare and an Appreciation SuperShare could combine them to reconstitute an Index Trust SuperUnit, with no incremental fees. The ability to move between SuperShares and the SuperUnit, and between the SuperUnit and the underlying mutual fund would ensure that the net asset values and secondary market prices of the parts remained in close relationship with one another. With all of the parts traded, were pricing discrepancies to appear, arbitrageurs would likely act quickly to eliminate them.

DESIGN SPECIFICS: COLLATERALIZED PUTS AND RELATED SECURITIES

The second step of the design process was the creation of collateralized puts on the S&P 500 index. The LOR principals could not use the Index SuperUnit as collateral for a put on the index, because the put would need to pay off precisely when the Index had declined. Therefore, they would need to create a pool of assets whose value was not tied to the value of the Index and from which a put could be carved. They chose to use a series of the open-end mutual fund that would hold Treasury bills (Capital Market Fund/U.S.

---

17 In early 1988, the S&P 500 Index level was about 250.

18 The decision to set the strike price of the Appreciation SuperShare at 25% above the initial price of the Index SuperUnit was determined by two considerations. First, in casual conversations with option traders, the LOR team had tried to identify options which would be most popular with investors. Second, Mr. Leland and Mr. Rubinstein's simulations of replicating options with transaction costs suggested that these out-of-the-money options would be the costliest for investors to manufacture using a dynamic trading strategy.

Treasury Money Market Portfolio). Like the Index Series, shares in the Money Market Series could be converted into exchange-tradeable units, Money Market SuperUnits, which were initially priced at $50.[19]

LOR would use these SuperUnits to carve out collateralized index puts called Protection SuperShares. In concept, a Protection SuperShare would pay its holder nothing if the S&P 500 rose above its initial level. However, if the Index fell and therefore the Index Trust SuperUnit fell below $100 at the end of the three-year Trust, the Protection SuperShare holder would receive a payment at that time. The Protection SuperShare's three-year maturity would be the same as the most common life for the fixed-term portfolio insurance LOR had sold pre-1987 and one year longer than the put options traded on the CBOE since October 1987. Unlike the portfolio insurance it would replace, the Protection SuperShare would be a security and not a trading strategy. It would depend on U.S. Treasuries and not on the credit of a single firm to guarantee its payments if the market fell.[20] One derivatives expert described the evolution of the LOR products this way: "Dynamic portfolio insurance said if the fire takes place at your house you could buy the insurance fast enough to cover the damage. But in 1987 every house was on fire; with collateralized options, you're buying insurance up front."[21]

The most critical design issue surrounding the Protection SuperShare was to determine *how much* protection it would offer and how this protection would be structured. From their experience selling portfolio insurance, the LOR team knew that investors often were willing to buy *capped* insurance in order to lower its costs. A capped put would pay off more as the Index fell to a point, leaving the holder of the put with a maximum fixed-dollar upside.[22]

The idea of capping the payoff to the Protection SuperShare was attractive for a second reason. Carving a Protection SuperShare from a Money Market SuperUnit would leave a second SuperShare—dubbed the Income and Residual SuperShare (I&R)—that would have to be sold. The I&R SuperShares would pay investors all cash distributions on the U.S. Treasury Money Market SuperUnit during its three-year life, and a final payment

19 Shares of the Money Market Series and the Money Market SuperUnit were likely to have stable net asset values, based on the short duration and high creditworthiness of the underlying portfolio of Treasury bills. While its value at the termination of the three-year trust could not be guaranteed to be $50, investors would expect that the Money Market SuperUnit would be very close to $50 at termination.

20 LOR believed that investors would value the collateralized Protection SuperShare enough to pay a premium price for it over other put options.

21 Hal Lux and Aaron Pressman, "Can We Prevent the Next Crash?," *Investment Dealers' Digest, Inc.*, October 19, 1992.

22 LOR's customers sometimes structured their portfolio insurance as out-of-the-money puts, which in effect produced a "deductible" to the insurance policies.

equal to the final net asset value of the U.S. Treasury Money Market SuperUnit, less the value paid to the Protection SuperShare (if any). To maximize the marketability of both the Protection SuperShare and the Income and Residual SuperShare, LOR decided to limit the index put protection to 30%. If at the end of three years, the net asset value of the Index SuperUnit was greater than its initial value of $100, the Protection SuperShare would receive nothing and the I&R SuperShare would receive the full net asset value of the Money Market SuperUnit, expected to be $50. If the Index SuperUnit had a net asset value of between $70 and $100 at termination, the Protection SuperShare would receive $1 for each $1 below $100 in the final net asset value of the Index SuperUnit, and the holder of the I&R SuperShare would receive between $20 and $50. If the net asset value of the Index SuperUnit was below $70 at termination, the holder of a Protection SuperShare would receive $30, and the I&R SuperShare would receive a minimum payment of $20 at the termination of the trust.

With the Money Market Shares, the Money Market SuperUnit, the Protection Super-Share, and the I&R SuperShare, the full product line consisted of eight products. Though not affording flexibility as complete as Hakanssen's original conception, the family of products was thought to give investors a convenient way to design virtually any investment position they sought. Furthermore, the exchange listing of the securities would provide for ease in trading and up-to-date pricing information. Finally, the contractual ability to shift between SuperUnits and the associated SuperShares would ensure that the prices of each of the pieces would stay in the appropriate relationship to one another.

PHASE I: NOVEMBER 1987–DECEMBER 1988

From December 1987 through early 1988, confident of the strong potential demand for the SuperUnits and SuperShares and cognizant of the temporary void of competing products, the principals at LOR began to tackle the two most pressing practical issues: distribution and regulation.

The small LOR office, which in late 1987 consisted of about 15 professionals including 2 marketers, would need help to sell the SuperTrust.[23] Just as LOR had needed to enlist licensees to sell the firm's portfolio insurance product, it would need a large and effective distribution network or selling syndicate to ensure a smooth execution of the potentially large IPO.[24] It approached the senior bankers at many of Wall Street's top-tier investment banks, spending hours explaining the SuperTrust concept. The effort seemed to pay off:

---

23 SuperTrust™ was the brand name LOR gave to the entire family of products.

24 At the height of selling portfolio insurance, the LOR staff sold insurance that covered about $5 billion, whereas various worldwide licensees sold nine times as much.

Salomon Brothers, Goldman Sachs, Morgan Stanley, Kidder Peabody, First Boston, Smith Barney, and Paine Webber all expressed serious interest in joining the selling syndicate. Additionally, when LOR began its search for an exchange to list the SuperTrust securities, both the New York and the American Stock Exchanges appeared eager to list the entire system of securities. The American Stock Exchange's (AMEX) promise to provide promotional support convinced the firm to list its products on the AMEX.

The only existing roadblock to the SuperTrust launch appeared to be the regulatory approval process. In early 1988, LOR's legal counsel, the New York law firm of Donovan Leisure Newton & Irvine (Donovan Leisure), estimated that the SuperTrust would require six months and $600,000 in legal fees to come to market. LOR would pay Donovan Leisure's fees with cash raised through the security offering.

The regulatory approval process for SuperShares was multifaceted, including the need to: (1) ensure compliance with existing securities regulations or obtain the appropriate exemptions, (2) obtain SEC approval to offer the securities, and (3) obtain exchange approval to list the securities. Given the SuperTrust's design, exemptions from the 1940 Act would ultimately be necessary.[25] In 1988, Donovan Leisure advised LOR to tackle the exemptions process by filing a "No-Action" memorandum with the SEC stating that LOR intended to use the existence of the Americus Trust as a precedent to avoid the exemptions request. In other words, they argued that the SuperTrust required only the same exemptions as the related Americus Trust, which the SEC had approved in the early 1980s. The No-Action memorandum was filed on December 15, 1988.

With the exemptions process under way, LOR went on to organize SuperShares Services Corporation (SSC) to serve as adviser to the mutual fund and sponsor of the unit investment trust, and to file the registration statements necessary to raise $2 billion during an initial subscription period. The SEC had required LOR to specify a minimum which LOR believed would assure its ability to operate the mutual fund and unit investment trust for at least three years. The principals felt that $2 billion, though large, would be manageable. They believed it would satisfy the SEC's requirement and would create a "critical mass" necessary to encourage large commitments by investors.[26] By imposing a $2 billion minimum subscription, investors could commit to a substantial investment and still be confident that they were only a small fraction of the total offering. LOR lined up Wells

---

25 The 1940 Act, together with the Securities Act of 1933 and the Securities and Exchange Act of 1934, was designed to instill investor confidence in investment companies after the Great Depression. These acts require that continual and full disclosures be made to present and potential investors in mutual funds. They also regulate appointments of boards of directors, and management and underwriting contracts that effect fund operations and fund sales.

26 There was only one other $2 billion IPO sold during the five years before 1991.

Fargo Nikko Investment Advisors to serve as the manager of the index securities portfolio and Western Asset Management Company, a smaller California-based investment advisor, to manage the money market securities portfolio.

PHASE II: JANUARY 1989–JANUARY 1991

REGULATORY ROADBLOCKS

During the first quarter of 1989, several months after LOR had filed its No-Action letter, LOR and Donovan Leisure received shocking news: the SEC staff rejected the Americus Trust precedent and required that LOR file a full application for exemptions. This decision would not only slow the SuperTrust launch by at least another six months, but would also cost LOR another projected $600,000.

Through April 1989, LOR and Donovan Leisure prepared the application for exemption.[27] If the SuperTrust was to proceed, the SEC would have to approve exemptions from two specific provisions of the 1940 Act: Sections 4(2) and 22(d). Section 4(2) stated that a Unit Investment Trust may issue only *redeemable securities* that represent an *undivided interest* in a unit of specified securities. However, the SuperShares were not separately redeemable and created divided interests. Section 22(d) prohibited dealers from buying or selling units at prices other than those offered by the fund itself. However, the Index Series of the open-end mutual fund would transact only at closing net asset value, but the *intraday* trading of the Index SuperUnits would require trading at other prices.

In its April 1989 application, LOR sought exemptive relief under section 6(c) of the 1940 Act, in which Congress gave broad powers to the SEC to exempt any person or security from any provision of the Act "if and to the extent that such exemption is necessary or appropriate in the public interest and consistent with the protection of investors and the purposes fairly intended by the policy and provision of . . . [the Act]." A critical aspect of LOR's legal argument, therefore, was its proof that the SuperTrust was in the public interest. They argued that the SuperTrust securities would benefit the public because they would enable investors to trade a standardized U.S. equity market basket at low costs and to shape their expected market risks and returns. LOR's costs to bring the SuperTrust to market were mounting steadily and, by April 1989, had reached $1.5 million.

---

27 LOR could have tried to appeal to the SEC Commissioners the decision by the SEC staff to reject its No-Action memorandum, but felt that the application route had a higher likelihood of leading to a successful SuperTrust launch. The SEC staff had privately told LOR that it was "sympathetic" to the SuperTrust proposal.

In September 1989 the SEC demanded *further* justification for the exemptions it would grant. Over the next few weeks, Hayne Leland and Mark Rubinstein prepared a 25-page response that described the conceptual and historical background that led to the demand for market baskets and investment products to control risks and returns in the equity markets.[28] LOR's filing was greeted by further SEC queries. LOR went on to file a total of five amendments to its application before it finally received the necessary exemptions from the 1940 Act in the fourth quarter of 1990, two years after it filed its No-Action Memorandum.

The complexity of the regulatory process amazed the LOR team. Like peeling a noxious onion, cutting through one layer of regulation revealed only another layer. They wondered whether the SuperTrust approval process was so complicated because the product was radically different or because LOR was involved. Surely, the SuperTrust approval would create a precedent for other securities hoping to use a similar structure, demanding careful SEC scrutiny. Yet, was LOR, inventor of much-maligned portfolio insurance, subject to even closer scrutiny than others might be?

Once the SEC approved the SuperTrust exemptions, the product registration had to be approved. In the exemptive process, the SEC had imposed conditions on the marketing and distribution of SuperTrust, which LOR was forced to accept to gain the exemptions. Among the more onerous of these conditions was a requirement that LOR disclose in all advertising materials the differences between the Fund shares, SuperUnits, and Super-Shares and the different fees, expenses, and sales loads applicable to these securities. All

---

28 The 25-page response included a discussion of: (1) the academic development of modern portfolio theory, which concludes that investors should divide their wealth between a single standardized market portfolio and a risk-free interest-bearing asset; (2) academic studies demonstrating informational efficiency of well-developed securities markets, thus showing that indexing is a rational approach when it is impossible to identify who in the market has superior information; (3) the development of exchange-traded index options and futures; (4) the popularity of dynamic hedging and market-timing strategies; and (5) the Brady Report, which called for smooth links between stock index futures and equity markets and indicated that basket securities would reduce market volatility. The brief argued that SuperTrust securities would provide significant public benefits to both investors and the market in general. Investors would benefit because (1) large and small investors could own a market basket that provided intraday trading; (2) unlike closed-end funds, SuperUnits would be redeemable; (3) SuperUnits and SuperShares enable investors to obtain return patterns uniquely suited to their risk and return objectives, including *long-term* portfolio objectives. The markets would benefit from SuperTrust because (1) during a market crisis, even large outstanding positions in SuperUnits or SuperShares would not deepen the crisis through worries about the integrity of the market or clearing mechanisms because the underlying Fund holds full title, without leverage, to the relevant market securities; (2) SuperTrust permits portfolio insurance strategies that do not require trading during periods of market unrest and, unlike options or futures, do not involve creation of short positions; (3) Index Trust SuperUnits would allow arbitragers to complete their hedges with one cash market transaction.

advertisements also had to provide disclosure of the risks attendant upon investment in SuperShares, making it difficult for LOR to publish concise, effective marketing information. (See Exhibit 4 for selected LOR promotional material.)

In addition, though the holder of a SuperUnit might never hold a SuperShare, the SEC demanded that all holders of the SuperUnits be "suitable" investors in the option-like SuperShares. Brokers selling any of the products had to be sure that a customer had "knowledge and experience in financial matters, that he may be reasonably expected to be capable of evaluating the risks and the special characteristics of the recommended transaction, and is financially able to bear the risks of SuperUnits and SuperShares." As a practical matter, this meant that prospective buyers would have to be "option-qualified." Option-qualification was generally interpreted by brokerage firms to mean that a customer had a high level of income, liquid assets, and experience with investing, as demonstrated through existing holdings and trading of other securities. Documenting option qualifications increased the level of paperwork required by brokers, as well as requiring the brokerage firms to make additional disclosures.

By the time LOR had finally worked its way through the exemption labyrinth, it received additional questions from the SEC regarding its registration statement. Like the exemption process, the approval process quickly became a complicated tangle of issues and questions from the SEC. The SEC staff was particularly concerned that the SuperTrust might be construed as having a futures component. The SEC also paid close attention in the prospectus to the description of the risks—and even to the actual names of the securities, worrying that they might be misleading.[29] Other SEC questions related to the redemption procedures, particularly how to value the securities when they came up for redemption. No questions were particularly grave, but collectively they required a tremendous amount of response time.

Time was expensive for LOR at this point; legal bills continued to mount at approximately $100,000 per month as the firm generated thousands of pages of legal documents. As the regulatory approval process slowed down, the costs to launch the SuperTrust escalated so that by early 1991, total costs were approaching $4 million, mostly unpaid bills from Donovan Leisure for legal services.

COMPETITIVE PRESSURES

As the lengthy regulatory approval process progressed, the LOR principals had to watch competitors introduce products aimed at the same investors LOR hoped to entice with its

---

29 Originally, LOR had planned to call the four SuperShares Upside Appreciation, Index Income, Downside Protection, and Money Market Income SuperShares. They also contemplated calling the I&R a High Yield SuperShare.

SuperUnits and SuperShares. The competing products came from investment banks and exchanges, and they ranged from equity derivatives to basket securities.

Throughout the period from 1987 to 1991, the equity derivatives desks of major firms had grown in size and sophistication, becoming increasingly willing and able to execute large program trades for their customers and to arrange for equity swaps. In an equity swap, one party might pay the return on the S&P 500 while the counterparty paid six-month LIBOR, with the net payments exchanged between the parties. The equity derivative activities of major firms sometimes leaked onto public exchanges. For example, in January 1990, Goldman Sachs orchestrated the issuance of the first long-dated put option written on the Nikkei 225 stock index and listed on the AMEX. The trade press covered scores of Euromarket deals each month in which large indexed puts and calls were sold. The equity derivatives activity even found its way into corporate financing transactions, with firms issuing notes whose returns were linked to the performance of major stock market indices.

Furthermore, investment banks made special efforts to address the credit concerns of their customers. In 1991, Merrill Lynch created Merrill Lynch Derivative Products, Inc. (MLDP), a special-purpose company designed to serve as a counterparty for derivative products. MLDP was funded by $300 million in common equity issued to Merrill Lynch and $50 million in preferred stock. This AAA-rated company would mitigate some of the credit risk associated with OTC derivative products and provide Merrill with a valuable marketing advantage. Other firms were known to be considering similar approaches.

Exchanges themselves provided new products to challenge the SuperUnits and Super-Shares. On May 12, 1989, the Philadelphia Exchange's Cash Index Participations (CIPs) and AMEX's Equity Index Participations (EIPs) both started trading under SEC registration. CIPs were a basket security designed to give small investors an easy way to trade a portfolio of stocks. EIPs were similar in concept to a short sale of a portfolio of S&P 500 stocks. As soon as CIPs and EIPs started trading, the Chicago Mercantile Exchange and the CBOE sued, claiming that these products were inherently futures contracts as a result of their "future delivery" feature and, therefore, should fall under CFTC, rather than SEC, jurisdiction. On August 18, 1989, the U.S. Court of Appeals of the Seventh Circuit ruled that the newly listed IPs indeed fell under CFTC, not SEC, jurisdiction, and all investors were forced to close their positions.

Although these first-traded index participation securities did not survive, the LOR principals believed it was only a matter of time before exchanges succeeded in launching basket products. By early 1991 they had heard rumors of a new exchange-traded S&P 500 basket security that the AMEX itself was developing. Exchange-traded equity derivatives became more prominent during the period leading up to 1991. On January 21, 1991, the CBOE started trading LEAPs, S&P 500 options with maturities of up to three years. The CBOE also launched Index CAPS in November 1991. Its put CAPS offered a payout that resembled that of the Protection SuperShare.[30]

LISTING PROBLEMS

A new problem developed during the first quarter of 1990. The CBOE approached LOR to say that they were impressed with the SuperTrust system, but that the exchange had an exclusive license to list "option-like" products based on the S&P 500. Furthermore, the CBOE threatened to sue S&P if it granted LOR the right to list the SuperTrust on another exchange.

The LOR principals had no knowledge of this potential problem and had already promised to list the entire SuperTrust system on the AMEX. After extended negotiations, they ultimately resolved the conflict by allowing the CBOE to list the SuperShares and the AMEX to list the SuperUnits. Although this resolution was satisfactory to the exchanges, the LOR team was concerned that the split listing might confuse potential investors.

Additionally, the exchanges informed LOR that they required at least 400 separate investors in each series to list the SuperTrust securities. Though the SuperTrust was primarily aimed at institutional investors, to have at least 400 investors, LOR realized that it would need the help of securities firms with a large retail brokerage units.[31] This requirement shed a new light on the importance of their distribution network.

The distribution network was the one bright spot in the long struggle to launch the SuperTrust. Interest among the top Wall Street firms remained high, and LOR's inquiry for a lead soliciting dealer was met with enthusiastic proposals from Salomon Brothers, Kidder Peabody and First Boston. In September 1988, Leland, Rubinstein, and O'Brien ultimately chose Salomon Brothers to be the lead soliciting dealer. During the late summer and fourth quarter of 1990, negotiations with Salomon Brothers were "intense, difficult, and costly" for LOR. Nevertheless, Salomon Brothers professed continuing commitment to getting the job done, although it did suggest that LOR rethink the product design.[32]

---

30 One major distinction between CAPS and Protection SuperShares is the CAPS's automatic exercise feature. Once the price of the index fell below the floor of the Put CAPS, they were automatically exercised and the positions closed out.

31 At the height of the portfolio insurance business, LOR estimated that it and its licensees served approximately 95 accounts.

32 At one point in 1990, Salomon Brothers suggested that LOR abandon the SuperShares and market only the SuperUnits. This strategy would lower regulatory hurdles and speed the SuperUnit to market, before more competition arose. The LOR principals rejected the advice, which would jettison an integral part of the product they had designed.

LOR's bill from Donovan Leisure for the fourth quarter of 1990 alone was nearly $750,000, predominantly attributable to these negotiations with Salomon Brothers.[33]

SUPERTRUST: NEXT STEPS?

On January 7, 1991, LOR's contacts at Salomon Brothers informed LOR that it would suspend its efforts in order to "review" the level of retail interest for the product with the retail-oriented wirehouses (e.g., Paine Webber and Smith Barney). If these latter firms were to drop out, the SuperTrust might fail to attain the 400-investor minimum imposed by the exchanges. After Salomon's announcement, LOR immediately began efforts to enhance its retail coverage. It approached Alex Brown & Sons, The Chicago Corporation, Shearson Lehman, A.G. Edwards, Oppenheimer, Dean Witter, and Charles Schwab. Only The Chicago Corporation and Alex Brown were interested.

Later in the first quarter of 1991, one of LOR's greatest fears came true: Salomon Brothers, PaineWebber, and Smith Barney officially dropped out of the selling syndicate. LOR scrambled to interest other distributors and encouraged Morgan Stanley, the last remaining large Wall Street firm in the syndicate, to assume the role of lead soliciting dealer. By this time LOR had been successful in attracting Alex Brown & Sons and The Chicago Corporation, a pair of regional securities firms with a total of approximately 450 brokers, and Parallax Group, a five-person Connecticut derivatives firm founded in 1991, to join the syndicate. In May 1991, Morgan Stanley decided to bow out of the selling effort.

The burdens of the changing competitive landscape, legal bills far in excess of expectations, a seemingly endless regulatory approval process, and an implosion of their distribution network collectively caused the LOR principals to question their ability to launch the SuperTrust. Despite LOR's experience and success with marketing an innovative financial trading strategy in the early 1980s, none of the partners were prepared for the complexity of the regulatory process for an exchange-listed security, or for the fast pace at which the financial markets were now evolving. The three men struggled to determine how best to proceed with the SuperTrust project.

---

33 Donovan Leisure's bills continued to mount, but were not paid in cash, as they were to be paid from the proceeds of the SuperTrust offering.

Exhibit 1   Return and Volatility of S&P 500 Index (1973-1987)

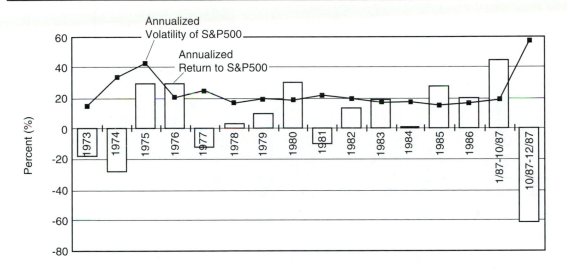

Source: Annualized return on S&P calculated by casewriter. The negative 63% return for 10/1/87–12/31/87 period is an annualized return; the actual decline in the Index for the three-month period was approximately 16%. Volatility taken from Report of the Presidential Task Force on Market Mechanisms, January 1988, p. II-6. Volatility represents average of 60-day annualized volatilities.

Exhibit 2   SuperTrust Structure and Function.

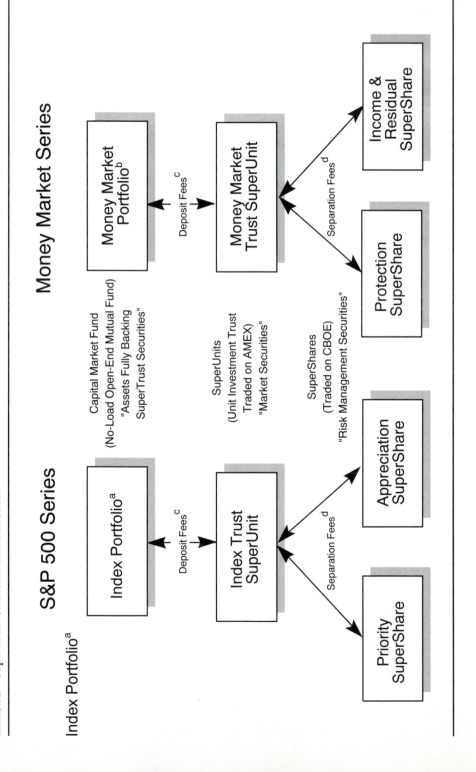

Exhibit 2 SuperTrust Structure and Function (Continued).

a. *Index Series Expenses*—An investor can purchase Index Series shares with either an in-kind payment of common stocks or a cash payment plus a purchase transaction fee of .125% of their investment. Similarly, with a redemption, an investor can pay a redemption transaction fee of .125% of their investment and receive up to $3 million in cash. Above this amount, there is no fee and investors receive an in-kind payment of common stocks. The cash purchase and redemption fees are paid to the fund, not to LOR, and are used to offset brokerage costs. An annual series operating expense of about .25% is also charged to the fund. Operating expenses include management fees and other expenses. Management fees are based on a sliding scale ranging from .13% to .04% of the average net assets of the series. SuperShares Services Corporation (SSC), a subsidiary of LOR received .03% of the first $1 billion of assets, and .02% of assets in excess of $1 billion, but SSC had agreed to waive all management fees for the early life of the Trust.

b. *Treasury Money Market Series Expenses*—An annual series operating expense of .495% is charged to the fund. This fee is for management and other expenses. Management fees are based on a sliding scale ranging from .155% to .04% of the average net assets of the series. SSC's portion was .03% of the first $1 billion, and .02% of assets in excess of $1 billion, but SSC had agreed to waive all management fees for the early life of the Trust.

c. *Deposit Fees*—Fees based on a sliding scale are charged in connection with the exchange of fund shares for SuperUnits. These fees range from 1.11% of net asset value of shares exchanged for amounts less than $500,000, to .015% of net asset value of shares exchanged for amounts in excess of $500 million. Approximately 55% of these deposit fees were to be paid to a unit of LOR.

d. *Separation Fees*—Fees based on a sliding scale are charged in connection with separating SuperUnits into SuperShares. These fees range initially from 1.5% of net asset value of SuperUnits submitted for separation for amounts less than $500,000 to .15% of net asset value of SuperUnits submitted for separation for amounts in excess of $500 million. Approximately 50% of these fees were to be paid to a unit of LOR.

Exhibit 3 Selected U.S. Equity Markets Data (1982–1991)

Years	1982	1983	1984	1985	1986	1987	1988	1989	1990	1991
Estimated corporate equities directly held by pension funds (billions of $)[a]	367	458	462	583	704	744	853	1,084	1,002	1,334
Estimated value of pension fund equities invested in index funds (billions of $)[b]	10	25	26	47	76	93	120	126	165	183
Estimated value of total assets covered by portfolio insurance strategies (millions of $)[c]	250	350	1,000	20,000	50,000	100,000	NA	NA	NA	NA
Yearly average open interest in S&P 500 Index futures contracts (000s of contracts)[d]	7	25	36	62	101	121	120	128	133	151
Yearly average open interest in S&P 500 Index options (000s of contracts)[e]	—	2	.7	.5	86	344	397	484	763	876
Yearly average open interest in options on S&P 500 Index futures contracts (000s of contracts)[f]	—	11	28	38	51	63	29	54	71	85

a. Federal Reserve Flow of Funds Data.
b. *The Money Market Directory of Pension Funds and Their Investment Managers*, McGraw Hill.
c. LOR Estimates.
d. IDC Data Sheet. Each futures contract represents 500 times the S&P 500 Index.
e. CBOE. Contracts settle on 100 times the S&P 500 Index. Index options started trading on 7/1/83.
f. CME. Contract settles on one futures contract. Options on Index futures started trading on 1/28/83.

Exhibit 4   LOR Promotional Material.

WHAT THE SUPERTRUST™ IS

SSC Distribution Services, Inc.

An Affiliate of Leland O'Brien Rubinstein Associates Incorporated

 *SuperTrust*™

A BASKET TRADING VEHICLE:

INDEX SUPERUNITS™

To change market exposure currently, large investors typically buy or sell hundreds of individual stocks, with the consequent cost and effort associated with each transaction.

By trading the Index SuperUnit, investors can trade an entire "basket" of stocks (representing an S&P 500 Index portfolio) as a single stock exchange transaction. No program trades, derivatives, or swaps are needed to complete the transaction. And the underlying stocks can be reclaimed by redeeming Index SuperUnits (in an amount greater than about $3 million).

Arbitrage between stocks, index futures, and Index SuperUnits should provide important additional liquidity and depth to the market. With a $\frac{1}{32}$ tick size on a $100 SuperUnit, spreads may be as low as 3 basis points.

BENEFITS TO INVESTORS:

- A single trade rather than hundreds of separate trades;
- Low trading costs due to concentration of trading in a single asset and small tick size. Small initial round lot size ($1,000) will provide equal access and advantages to individual investors;
- Simultaneous execution of entire basket, vs. trades which may not be executed at the same time;
- Ability to use limit, stop-loss, or other types of orders if desired;
- No specialized investment bank services needed to execute trades;
- No special closure of trading facilities (as in SuperDot) when markets are volatile;
- Close tracking of underlying asset value because of availability of daily redemption;
- Right to reclaim the actual portfolio of stocks if desired (SuperUnits are fully backed by actual securities portfolios); and
- Subject to taxes and regulations of ordinary securities*.

A RISK CONTROL VEHICLE:

SUPERSHARES™

SuperShares represent different claims to performance of the Index SuperUnit as of the end of a three-year period.

- The Appreciation SuperShare gives the owner the right to any net asset value the Index SuperUnit may have in excess of 25% above its initial level. It is a low-cost, highly speculative security.
- The Priority SuperShare gives the owner rights to all Index SuperUnit value up to a maximum gain of 25%, plus all dividends less expenses. A more conservative vehicle, its returns will exceed that of the Index SuperUnit except when the S&P 500 Index increases strongly.
- The Protection SuperShare pays off when the final Index SuperUnit level is less than its initial level. It will provide protection (up to 30%) against losses in the value of the Index SuperUnit as of the end of the three-year period.
- The Income and Residual SuperShare receives the dividends payable on a Money Market SuperUnit, plus the remainder of the value of such SuperUnit not paid to the Protection SuperShare. It bears downside risk if, after three years, the market has suffered a considerable decline.

Mixtures of SuperShares and SuperUnits can be used to implement various investment strategies, such as portfolio protection, without further trading required. Payoffs are fully backed by securities. It is anticipated that SuperShares will be treated as ordinary exchange-traded securities for tax and regulatory purposes.* They are not subject to position limits, and thus are suitable for use by large investors.

Exhibit 4   LOR Promotional Material. (Continued)

MORE ABOUT THE SUPERTRUST

The "SuperTrust" structure combines two registered investment companies. The Capital Market Fund, Inc. (the "Fund") is a no-load management investment company organized in series. The two initial series are the Index Series and the U.S. Treasury Money Market Series ("Money Market Share"). Shares issued by the Fund may be exchanged, upon payment of the applicable Deposit Fee (sales charge), for units of beneficial interest ("SuperUnits") in The SuperTrust Trust for Capital Market Fund, Inc. Shares (the "SuperTrust"), an "open-end" unit investment trust with two initial sub-trusts, the Index Trust and the U.S. Treasury Money Market Trust. **There can be no assurance that the Money Market Series will be able to maintain a stable net asset value of $1.00 per share. An investment in the Money Market Series or in Money Market Trust SuperUnits is neither insured nor guaranteed by the U.S. Government.**

SuperUnits are listed and traded on the American Stock Exchange, and may be separated, upon payment of the applicable separation fee, into component interests with different investment characteristics ("SuperShares"). An Index Super-Unit may be separated into an Appreciation Super-Share and a Priority SuperShare. A Money Market SuperUnit may be separated into a Protection SuperShare and an Income and Residual Super-Share. SuperShares may not be separately redeemed, but complementary SuperShares (those created by separating that respective SuperUnit) may be recombined and redeemed. Purchase of complementary SuperShares, if not already held by an investor, will involve brokerage costs. Super-Shares are listed and traded on the Chicago Board Options Exchange, and involve substantial risks not associated with shares of index funds or money market funds generally. In particular, an Appreciation SuperShare or a Protection Super-Share may be without any value upon termination of the relevant sub-trust of the SuperTrust.

For more complete information about The SuperTrust for Capital Market Fund, Inc. Shares and the Capital Market Fund, Inc. including charges and expenses, please obtain their prospectuses from SSC Distribution Services, Inc. P.O. Box 1078, Framingham, MA 01701-1078, or by telephone 1-800-328-7408. Read the prospectuses carefully before you invest or forward funds.

S&P® and S&P 500® are service marks of Standard & Poor's Corporation and have been licensed for use by SuperShare Services Corporation ("SSC"). Capital Market Fund, Inc. (the "Fund"), The SuperTrust Trust for Capital Market Fund, Inc. Shares (the "SuperTrust"), and SSC Distribution Services, Inc. ("SSCD") are authorized sublicensees of SSC.

SuperTrust™, SuperUnits™, and SuperShares™ are trademarks of Leland O'Brien Rubinstein Associates Incorporated and have been licensed for use by SSC. The Fund, the SuperTrust, and SSCD are sublicensees of SSC.

* A private letter ruling from the Internal Revenue Service as to certain tax issues affecting the SuperTrust has been requested but has not yet been received.

Exhibit 5   Selected Capital Markets Data

Date	S&P 500 Index	Dividend Yield on S&P 500 in Prior Year	Yield on Three-Year Treasury Notes[a]	Yield on Three-Year Treasury STRIPS[a]	Historical Volatility of S&P for 90 Prior Days[b]	Implied Volatility of S&P from Traded Options[c]
12/31/87	247.08	3.08%	8.02%	8.22%	53%	29%
12/31/88	277.72	3.64%	9.16%	9.32%	13%	19%
12/31/89	353.40	3.45%	7.87%	8.00%	16%	15%
12/31/90	330.22	3.61%	7.36%	7.39%	19%	20%
5/1/91	380.29	3.41%	7.08%	7.23%	16%	14%

Sources: Data compiled from *Bloomberg Financial Markets Database, Standard & Poor's Security Price Index Record, Salomon Brothers Bond Market Roundup, The Center for Research in Securities Prices*, and *The Wall Street Journal.* Calculations were made by the casewriter.
a. Expressed on a bond-equivalent-yield basis.
b. Represents annualized volatility of S&P 500 over the prior 90 days.
c. Annualized implied volatility based on longest-dated index options.